JEWELS FROM GOD'S WORD

GEMS
of truth

A BIBLE STUDENT'S DEVOTIONAL

and

A BIBLE TEACHER'S
RESOURCE HANDBOOK

DR. JOHN MANNION

Ambassador International
Greenville, South Carolina & Belfast, Northern Ireland
www.ambassador-international.com

GEMS OF TRUTH
JEWELS FROM GOD'S WORD
A Bible Student's Devotional and A Bible Teacher's Resource Handbook
©2024 by Dr. John Mannion
All rights reserved

ISBN: 978-1-64960-715-7 hardcover
ISBN: 978-1-64960-410-1, paperback
eISBN: 978-1-64960-458-3

No part of this publication may be reproduced, distributed, or transmitted in any form or by any means, including photocopying, recording, or other electronic or mechanical methods, without the prior written permission of the publisher, except in the case of brief quotations embodied in critical reviews and certain other noncommercial uses permitted by copyright law. For permission requests, contact the publisher using the information below.

Unless otherwise marked, Scripture quotations taken from the New American Standard Bible (NASB) Copyright © 1960, 1962, 1963, 1968, 1971, 1972, 1973, 1975, 1977, 1995 by The Lockman Foundation.

Scripture marked TLB taken from The Living Bible copyright © 1971 by Tyndale House Foundation. Used by permission of Tyndale House Publishers Inc., Carol Stream, Illinois 60188. All rights reserved.

Scripture marked KJV taken from the King James Version. Public Domain.

Edited by Katie Cruice Smith, Kate Marlett, and Sydney Witbeck
eBook edition by Anna Riebe Raats

Ambassador International titles may be purchased in bulk for education, business, fundraising, or sales promotional use. For information, please email sales@emeraldhouse.com.

AMBASSADOR INTERNATIONAL
Emerald House
411 University Ridge, Suite B14
Greenville, SC 29601, USA
www.ambassador-international.com

AMBASSADOR BOOKS
The Mount
2 Woodstock Link
Belfast, BT6 8DD, Northern Ireland, UK
www.ambassadormedia.co.uk

The colophon is a trademark of Ambassador, a Christian publishing company.

In Memory of
Dr. J. Rodman Williams, who taught me what is in the Bible,
and Dr. Charles Holman, who taught me how to study the Bible

"I want those already wise to become the wiser and become leaders by exploring the depths of meaning in these nuggets of truth" (Proverbs 1:5-6, TLB).

Contents

JANUARY	8
FEBRUARY	44
MARCH	80
APRIL	118
MAY	156
JUNE	194
JULY	232
AUGUST	272
SEPTEMBER	314
OCTOBER	352
NOVEMBER	392
DECEMBER	430

INTRODUCTION

Gems of Truth is the second devotional in the *Nuggets of Truth* devotional trilogy. In *Gems of Truth*, inspirational writing meets Bible commentary as it continues where *Nuggets of Truth* left off. These are different kinds of devotionals. They are, perhaps, more in keeping with Oswald Chamber's *My Utmost for His Highest* in that they are meant to teach more than they are to simply inspire. Not that each nugget does not inspire. On the contrary, they stand as very inspirational books, even as the Scriptures themselves never fail to inspire. Indeed, the content of each daily devotional is full of Scripture. Each one is designed to provide the reader with a short Bible study. Hence, the reader is more of a student than simply a reader. The considerable content of each day's study digs deeply enough with a pointed focus that the student effectively goes through a mini Bible college program once having gone through the entire year.

Each excerpt should be read and studied. The reader/student should have both the devotional and the Bible open at the same time. Many of the Scriptures are included word for word within the context of the study. These Scriptures can still be looked up to take in a little bit more of the passage's context. Some Scriptures are simply referenced. In these cases, it is, perhaps, more important and helpful to look up the passages in one's Bible. As students are studying the Scriptures, they will find it useful to take some notes and document some thoughts and insights.

The sub-title of *Gems of Truth*—*A Bible Student's Devotional and A Bible Teacher's Resource Handbook*—reveals the two-fold purpose and use of this book. It is meant to be a devotional for Bible students *and* for Bible teachers/preachers. In keeping with this second purpose, the devotional is exhaustively indexed. The indexes include a more general Systematic Theology Index that serves as a Table of Contents (organized according to the major doctrinal studies of systematic theology, including Anthropology, Christology, Ecclesiology, Epistemology, Eschatology, Missiology, Pneumatology, Practical Theology, Soteriology, and Theology Proper), as well as a much more detailed Scripture Index and Word/Subject Index. The idea with these indexes is that the devotional can be used by Bible teachers and preachers as a resource for their teaching and preaching ministries. Lessons and messages can be developed as teachers and preachers find, via the indexes, pertinent material to use in building their lessons and messages.

And so it is hoped that *Gems of Truth* will be a blessing for Bible students and Bible teachers/preachers. It is for those who want to study the Scriptures daily and grow in wisdom. It is for those who want to preach and teach the Scriptures and grow in leadership. May Proverbs 1:5-6 become the voice of *Gems of Truth*: "I want those already wise to become the wiser and become leaders by exploring the depths of meaning in these nuggets of truth" (TLB).

January

JANUARY 1

IT'S TIME TO WORK OUT

"Work out your salvation."

Philippians 2:12

When you go to the gym, you are hoping to have a good workout. It's true. If you want to stay in top shape, you must workout. As much as it is true of your physical body, it is just as true of your spiritual self. In fact, the Scripture commands you to "work out your salvation with fear and trembling; for it is God who is at work in you, both to will and to work for *His* good pleasure" (Phil. 2:12-13). Yes, *work out!* Of course, you cannot work out unless you first work in.

You are lying on the "bench press of life"; the heavy weight is staring you in the face, and you must "work out your salvation with fear and trembling." Why does "working out your salvation" come along with "fear and trembling?" It is because "God is at work in you." You work out because God works in. He works Himself in you as He anoints you; He works in you both a desire to do His will and an ability to do His will ("at work in you both to will and to work for His good pleasure"). No wonder you are lying there "with fear and trembling!" When the Creator of the universe and the One Who has no beginning is actually dwelling in you and working His will in you, there is no other response but awe and wonder, fear, and trembling.

You are not saved by your own works. You do not push up the weight of life in your own strength. No, you can only work out because He is working in. You can only walk out the life of faith because the faithful One is miraculously walking in and through you. This is "Christ in you, the hope of glory" (Colossians 1:27). This is the life of the Christian: "I have been crucified with Christ; it is no longer I who live, but Christ lives in me; the *life* which I now live in the flesh I live by faith in the Son of God, who loved me and gave Himself up for me. I do not nullify the grace of God, for if righteousness *comes* through the Law, then Christ died needlessly" (Gal. 2:20-21).

So, who is actually working out, then? Is God sovereign, or does man have a free will? This paradox must be understood as an "and" thing. It is not one *or* the other; it is one *and* the other. God is sovereign, *and* man has a free will. God works in, *and* man works out. When His will (work in) becomes your will (work out), He is sovereign; and you have a free will. In other words, His choice becomes your choice. Awesome! Fear and trembling!

So, what is it that man actually does in his free will? He receives, since he is a receivera creation. He does not source, since he is not the Source—the Creator. His reception comes in the form of faith.

A crowd of people approached Jesus. They were looking for the bottom line of life. What works do we have to do to be godly? Give us the bottom line. "'What shall we do, so that we may work the works of God?' Jesus answered and said to them, 'This is the work of God, that you believe in Him whom He has sent'" (John 6:28-29). Wow! They wanted to know how much weight they would have to lift to be deemed successful. They may have thought, "If I max three hundred pounds and work out with 240 pounds, then I will be saved." Jesus says, "You will *work out* with 240 pounds, but you will only be able to do it if I first *work in* you. So, believe in Me, have faith in Me, *work in* with Me."

How do you work in with Jesus so you can work out? It is impossible to work out or please God without faith because what pleases God, and therefore what working out is, has to do with seeking

Him: "And without faith it is impossible to please *Him*, for he who comes to God must believe that He is and *that* He is a rewarder of those who seek Him" (Hebrews 11:6). That is how you work in to work out. You seek Him; you walk with Him; you know Him.

When you "Set your mind on the things above, not on the things that are on earth" (Col. 3:2), you lay on the bench eager to go about your business of working out as God goes about His business of working in. There is a major difference, however, in this "spiritual gym." There is no boasting or showing off. How can you be full of yourself when the only way to be your successful self is to be full of Him? "For who regards you as superior? What do you have that you did not receive? And if you did receive it, why do you boast as if you had not received it?" (1 Cor. 4:7).

Hey, potential boasters who might max three hundred pounds. Your heavy lifting (working out) with your free will is consistent with who you are and not with who you are not. You are not the Source; you are a receiver. To understand this is to understand that it is nonsensical to boast; it makes no sense to try to save yourself by your own workout.

"For by grace you have been saved through faith; and that not of yourselves, *it is* the gift of God; not as a result of works, so that no one may boast. For we are His workmanship, created in Christ Jesus for good works, which God prepared beforehand so that we would walk in them" (Eph. 2:8-10).

So, where is the power on the bench? It is in your free will faith, which God sovereignly sourced. It is not a result of your own work out, so there is no need to boast. In fact, we work out because we are His workmanship. God has already done His work, and now we can walk in it. We can get on the bench! So, have the reps already been created? Where are they? They are *in* Christ Jesus. They are in seeking and knowing Him. No wonder the Scripture exhorts us to "trust in the LORD with all your heart And do not lean on your own understanding. In all your ways acknowledge Him, And He will make your paths straight" (Prov. 3:5-6). He will work in the reps for you to work out. So, get on the bench of life and have a great workout!

JANUARY 2

THE GREATEST FLIP-FLOP

"Whoever then humbles himself as this child, he is the greatest in the kingdom of heaven."
Matthew 18:4

"But the greatest among you shall be your servant."
Matthew 23:11

The kingdom of God is very different than the kingdoms of this world. A worldly attitude regarding service says that to not serve is "neutral." It is your choice. To serve is worthy of rewards. A kingdom attitude regarding service says that to not serve—sins of neglect—is equivalent to disobedience. It is not neutral; it is God's command. To serve is neutral. It is an assumed obligation. It earns no reward. Is there no reward, then? Reward is the result of the grace of God.

People who do acts of service hold onto what they perceive they have earned, what they deserve. Those who are servants or "slaves of Christ" (Eph. 6:6), let go of their rights; they do not insist on "getting something out of it." A servant is a server, whereas a server is not necessarily a servant. What is the difference? A server only serves under certain conditions—who to serve; what to do; and where, why, when, and how to serve. If the conditions are violated, the service ends.

A servant of Christ serves Him unconditionally. The service does not end when conditions are violated because there are no conditions to violate. Someone who serves does acts of service. Something you *do* comes to an end. Someone who *is* a servant does acts of service because he is a servant. Something you *are* does not come to an end. The difference is in the existence of a self-agenda versus a lack of a self-agenda. The challenging question is, "Would I serve God even if I got nothing out of it?"

What enables someone to be a servant instead of just being someone who does acts of service? The opposite of selfishness is selflessness or humility. Humility is the Christian character trait that opens the door for many others. It is that which lets in the One Who *is* the fullness of godly character. To die to self is to live to Christ; to "die to sin and live to righteousness" (1 Peter 2:24). For Christ to live in you, you must first empty yourself; so "it is no longer I who live, but Christ lives in me" (Gal. 2:20). It is no longer I doing acts of service but Christ the Servant Who lives in me.

Jesus' first public sermon, the Sermon on the Mount, highlighted many important character traits of those living in the kingdom of God. It is not by chance that the first character quality concerns humility: "Blessed are the poor in spirit, for theirs is the kingdom of heaven" (Matt. 5:3). Those who are humble can serve because they empty themselves and make room for the Servant to come in. He increases when we decrease (John 3:30). He can only produce fruit in our lives if we first die (John 12:24). The essence of humility is death to self; it is getting rid of self so Another can live in you.

Humility does not result in decrease. It results in increase. It is not marked by weakness but ends in strength. You die to that which is weak (yourself), but you live to what is strong (Christ). Humility is about Who Christ is and what Christ does, not about who you are not and what you cannot do. Humility moves us from "I can do nothing" to "I can do all things."

In John 15:5, Jesus says, "I am the vine, you are the branches; he who abides in Me and I in him, he bears much fruit, for apart from Me you can do nothing" (John 15:5). And Philippians 4:13 encourages us to remember, "I can do all things through Him who strengthens me" (Phil. 4:13).

Humility and service are marks of those who live in the flip-flopped kingdom of God. The poor become rich, and "those who do not see may see" (John 9:39). Those who die may live, and those who are emptied are filled. The humble "will obtain honor" (Prov. 29:23), and the servant will be the leader (Luke 22:26). Those who are humble and those who are servants become the *greatest* (Matt. 18:4; 23:11). So, take off your shoes and put on your flip-flops! Walk with God in His kingdom.

JANUARY 3

STOP HIDING AND START LEADING

> *"And the man and his wife hid themselves from the presence of the LORD God."*
> Genesis 3:8
>
> *"But Jonah got up to flee to Tarshish from the presence of the LORD."*
> Jonah 1:3
>
> *"Where can I go from Your Spirit? Or where can I flee from Your presence?"*
> Psalm 139:7

The essence of Christian leadership is leading others to Christ. The degree to which this is true is the degree to which Christian leaders must know Christ. If you do not know Christ, then how can you lead others to Him? A leader's devotion and zeal for the Lord should motivate and influence others to draw closer to God. Nehemiah was a godly leader who knew God and His promises. Because of his relationship with God, he was able to lead his people to God in prayer.

> Remember, please, the word which You commanded Your servant Moses, saying, "*If* you are unfaithful, I will scatter you among the peoples; but *if* you return to Me and keep My commandments and do them, though those of you who have been scattered were in the most remote part of the heavens, I will gather them from there and bring them to the place where I have chosen to have My name dwell." They are Your servants and Your people whom You redeemed by Your great power and by Your strong hand (Neh. 1:8-10).

It is the quarterback that the other players look to for direction since he, better than any other player on the field, knows and understands the signals from the coach on the sideline. Knowing God forms and shapes godly leaders. Godly leaders know the Leader enabling them to lead others to Him. The quarterback knows the ways of the coach and how he thinks. He follows his directions. The godly leader must know God's voice and obey what He says.

Abraham became a worldwide leader because he knew God's voice and obeyed it. God said to Abraham, "And in your seed all the nations of the earth shall be blessed, because you have obeyed My voice" (Gen. 22:18). The godly leader fears God. It is the fear of God that will enable the leader to be a servant leader and not become a tyrant leader.

Nehemiah served those he was leading because he feared God. "But the previous governors who were before me laid burdens on the people and took from them bread and wine besides forty shekels of silver; even their servants domineered the people. But I did not do so because of *my* fear of God" (Neh. 5:15). The rejection of tradition can be motivated by rebellion against authority, bitterness, or a desire to gain a following. Nehemiah was not motivated by any of these things; he was motivated by his fear of God. He only wanted to please God. He was not concerned with pleasing himself or pleasing others.

Nehemiah's "radical" actions became normal relative to the will of God. "And do not be conformed to this world, but be transformed by the renewing of your mind, so that you may prove what the will of God is, that which is good and acceptable and perfect" (Rom. 12:2). Relative normality is where a leader must live lest God inquires, "Do you not know that friendship with the world is hostility toward God? Therefore whoever wants to be a friend of the world makes himself an enemy of God" (James 4:4). Godly leaders must fear God and not man. To fear God—as opposed to being afraid of God and wanting to avoid Him—is to want to draw closer to Him. "The fear of the LORD is the beginning of knowledge" (Prov. 1:7).

Leaders must fear God and not be afraid of Him so as to hide from Him like Adam and Eve: "Now they heard the sound of the LORD God walking in the garden in the cool of the day, and the man and his wife hid themselves from the presence of the LORD God among the trees of the garden" (Gen. 3:8). Leaders must draw near to Him and not flee from Him like Jonah did. "But Jonah got up to flee to Tarshish from the presence of the LORD" (Jonah 1:3). To hide from God and still be able to lead others to Him is an oxymoronic idea. Ultimately, you will not be able to hide from God anyway; this is His mercy and loving kindness:

Psalm 139:7-10 reminds us that we cannot run from God: "Where can I go from Your Spirit? Or where can I flee from Your presence? If I ascend to heaven, You are there; If I make my bed in Sheol, behold, You are there. *If* I take the wings of the dawn, *If* I dwell in the remotest part of the sea, Even there Your hand will lead me, And Your right hand will take hold of me."

So stop hiding and start seeking. Start seeking and start knowing. Start knowing and start fearing. Start fearing and start leading!

JANUARY 4

STOCK UP ON THESE SECURITIES

*"For you were called to freedom, brethren; only do not **turn** your freedom into an opportunity for the flesh, but through love serve one another."*

Galatians 5:13

Servants are secure people. Secure people know *who* they are, *what* they have, and *why* they are here. Insecure people are not able to serve because they have to serve their own *who, what,* and *why.* Instead of serving others, they have to serve themselves. They have to spend their time, energy, and resources proving *who* they are, gaining *what* they do not think they have, and validating *why* they are here. All of this serves to slow down their service. Servants must be secure!

God calls you to serve others. The Scripture says, "Through love serve one another" (Gal. 5:13). The fallen world and our fallen nature oppose such suggestions. To serve others, we must stop insisting on serving ourselves. Self must yield to selflessness, so serving others may take the place of serving self. This is not easy. There are always challenges that try to impede your service. One of these challenges is the inevitability of having to fight temptation. Temptation needs to be jumped over on the way to serving others.

Jesus hurdled this barrier. Before He began His ministry, He had to fight temptation. Three temptations came His way to try to keep Him from service. First, "The tempter came and said to Him, 'If You are the Son of God, command that these stones become bread.' But He answered and said, 'It is written, MAN SHALL NOT LIVE ON BREAD ALONE, BUT ON EVERY WORD THAT PROCEEDS OUT OF THE MOUTH OF GOD'" (Matt. 4:3-4). To begin to serve, you have to know *why* you are here. Jesus knew He was not here for earthly things; He was here for heavenly things. He was secure.

The second temptation challenged Jesus' identity:

> Then the devil . . . said to Him, "If You are the Son of God, throw Yourself down; for it is written, 'HE WILL COMMAND HIS ANGELS CONCERNING YOU;' and 'ON *their* HANDS THEY WILL BEAR YOU UP, SO THAT YOU WILL NOT STRIKE YOUR FOOT AGAINST A STONE.' Jesus said to him, "On the other hand, it is written, 'YOU SHALL NOT PUT THE LORD YOUR GOD TO THE TEST'" (Matt. 4:5-7).

To begin to serve, you have to know *who* you are. Jesus knew He was the Son of God, so He did not need to prove anything. He was secure.

With the third temptation, the devil "said to Him, 'All these things I will give You, if You fall down and worship me.' Then Jesus said to him, 'Go, Satan! For it is written, *YOU SHALL WORSHIP THE LORD YOUR GOD, AND SERVE HIM ONLY*'" (Matt. 4:9-10). To begin to serve, you have to know *what* you have. Jesus knew He owned everything (Psalm 50:10), so He did not need to grab for anything. He was secure. Security turns back temptation and moves forward ministry. "From that time Jesus began to preach" (Matt. 4:17).

Servants are secure in *who* they are, *what* they have, and *why* they are here. This enables them to begin serving, continue serving, and multiply serving. Invest in your ability to serve. Stock up on these securities!

JANUARY 5

GOD HAS A PLAN. ARE YOU PART OF IT?

"God be gracious to us and bless us, And cause His face to shine upon us."
—Selah.

That Your way may be known on the earth, Your salvation among all nations."
Psalm 67:1-2

God has a plan. He has always had a plan. He did not just start planning last year or even just two thousand years ago. He is a missionary God and has always been a missionary God. Thus, we see His plan proclaimed the minute that it is needed—salvation for man via the provision of the blood of God shed on a cross. "And I will put enmity Between you and the woman, And between your seed and her seed; He shall bruise you on the head, And you shall bruise him on the heel" (Gen. 3:15).

God has loved the world from the beginning of time. He has had a plan of redemption for all people from the beginning. Thus, for example, He chose Israel to be a missionary nation (Gen. 12:1-3). God reveals Himself through His people. That has been, is, and will be His missionary plan.

Jesus is Salvation, and Jesus did not just start showing up after His incarnation. God revealing Himself in Christ has been the highlight of all of history. His Good News for man, the Gospel message, has been proclaimed since the beginning of sin. The problem has always had a solution; the need has always had a provision. Jehovah is always *Jireh* (He sees and provides); Jehovah is always *Shammah* (He is there).

According to Jesus, there were three things that were planned by God long before He said the Great Commission words of Matthew 28:19-20:

> Now He said to them, "These are My words which I spoke to you while I was still with you, that all things which are written about Me in the Law of Moses and the Prophets and the Psalms must be fulfilled." Then He opened their minds to understand the Scriptures, and He said to them, "Thus it is written, that the Christ would suffer and rise again from the dead the third day, and that repentance for forgiveness of sins would be proclaimed in His name to all the nations, beginning from Jerusalem. You are witnesses of these things. And behold, I am sending forth the promise of My Father upon you; but you are to stay in the city until you are clothed with power from on high (Luke 24:44-49).

First, Jesus must die and rise from the dead. Second, the Spirit must be sent. Third, His Spirit-filled people (witnesses) must spread the message of salvation to all nations. And so, Jesus died, rose from the dead, and was exalted so that the Spirit would be sent to enable God's people to be witnesses to the nations (John 16:7; Acts 1:8).

The proclamation of Good News went forth long ago at the very beginning of man's existence, and it goes forth now and will go forth until the end. "Jesus Christ **is** the same yesterday and today and forever" (Heb. 13:8). Jesus, the Content of the Gospel, is the Alpha and the Omega (Rev. 1:8), even as the proclamation of that Gospel is from the beginning to the end: "This gospel of the kingdom shall be preached in the whole world as a testimony to all the nations, and then the end will come" (Matt. 24:14).

Do our evangelistic efforts actually affect the return of Jesus? Amazingly, in the context of the idea that God wants all people to be saved, we are told to be "looking for and hastening the coming of the day of God" (2 Peter 3:12). How can we *hasten* the return of Christ? What is the requirement for

Christ's return? "This gospel of the kingdom shall be preached in the whole world as a testimony to all the nations, and then the end will come" (Matt. 24:14).

Logically, then, to *hasten* Christ's return is to *hasten* our missionary activity. This might be done by going directly to an unreached people group, or it may be done by being people who live in "holy conduct and godliness" (2 Peter 3:11). As it was in the Old Testament with Israel, so it is in the New Testament that a form of witness and method of evangelism is to live our lives before others in holiness and obedience to God (Phil. 1:27, 2:15-16; 1 Peter 2:12, 3:1-2; 1 Thess. 1:6-8).

Do you want to see Jesus return? Do you want to hasten His coming? Then remember that God says to you, "I will save you that you may become a blessing" (Zech. 8:13). How can you be a blessing to the nations? Do not bury your blessing in the ground. Do something with it, so someday, your Master will say to you, "Well done, good and faithful slave" (Matthew 25:21).

God be gracious to us and bless us, *And* cause His face to shine upon us—*Selah*. That Your way may be known on the earth, Your salvation among all nations. Let the peoples praise You, O God; Let all the peoples praise You. Let the nations be glad and sing for joy; For You will judge the peoples with uprightness and guide the nations on the earth. *Selah*. Let the peoples praise You, O God; Let all the peoples praise You. The earth has yielded its produce; God, our God, blesses us. God blesses us, That all the ends of the earth may fear Him (Psalm 67).

JANUARY 6

MAKE SURE YOU DON'T MISS *THE* TURN

"Then Samuel spoke to all the house of Israel, saying, 'If you return to the LORD with all your heart, remove the foreign gods and the Ashtaroth from among you and direct your hearts to the LORD and serve Him alone; and He will deliver you from the hand of the Philistines.'"

1 Samuel 7:3

The opposite of staying away from Jesus is returning to Him. This is the act of repentance. Without repentance, we will remain in our sin and thus, remain unspiritual (Rom. 14:23). Why can't we break some of the cycles of sin in our lives? Why do we find ourselves going back to the same sin over and over again? We sin. We are convicted. We confess. The key dynamic comes at that point of confession and which way we will then turn. Once we confess, we either turn (repent) to our own abilities; or we turn (repent) to God's abilities.

Repentance is much more than saying "I will not do this thing again" or "I will turn from this way." The focus is not on a thing or a way. It is on a Person. The focus is not on *me*, it is on Jesus. Repentance is the point of coming to the end of yourself and turning to God's ability. It does not have so much to do with what you will or will not do—which are results of repentance, not so much the actions of it—but with what *only* God is able to do.

We sin. We are convicted. We confess. Then we must repent and believe. In order to break the cycle of sin, we must turn to God's abilities and put our trust in Him. The key to breaking the sin cycle is to more fully understand what it means to truly *repent*. It is to turn and go to God: "And all who lived at Lydda and Sharon saw him, and they turned to the LORD" (Acts 9:35). It is to turn your heart toward Him: "Then Samuel spoke to all the house of Israel, saying, 'If you return to the LORD with all your heart'" (1 Sam. 7:3).

The turning is not simply toward an action or the ridding oneself of an action. It is specifically and wholeheartedly toward God. And so, Paul was "solemnly testifying to both Jews and Greeks of repentance toward God" (Acts 20:21). God calls us to repentance. He calls us to come back to Him, and then He will come back to us. "Return to Me, and I will return to you" (Mal. 3:7).

In Hosea 5:15-6:3, we read:

> I will go away *and* return to My place Until they acknowledge their guilt and seek My face; In their affliction they will earnestly seek Me. "Come, let us return to the LORD. For He has torn us, but He will heal us; he has wounded *us*, but He will bandage us. "He will revive us after two days; He will raise us up on the third day, That we may live before Him. "So let us know, let us press on to know the LORD. His going forth is as certain as the dawn; And He will come to us like the rain, Like the spring rain watering the earth" (Hosea 5:15-6:3).

What does it mean to truly repent? It means to turn to a Person. It is not simply turning to *a* way but turning to *the Way*. Jesus Christ is "the way, and the truth, and the life" (John 14:6). To repent is to turn to the abilities of Jesus Christ. It is not so much the process of declaring your actions as it is the process of asking to be acted upon.

JANUARY 7

WILL YOU BE A 40 OR 100 WATT LIGHTBULB?

*"Now he who plants and he who waters are one; but each will receive his own reward according to his own labor. For we are God's fellow workers; you are God's field, God's building. According to the grace of God which was given to me, like a wise master builder I laid a foundation, and another is building on it. But each man must be careful how he builds on it. For no man can lay a foundation other than the one which is laid, which is Jesus Christ. Now if any man builds on the foundation with gold, silver, precious stones, wood, hay, straw, each man's work will become evident; for the day will show it because it is **to be** revealed with fire, and the fire itself will test the quality of each man's work. If any man's work which he has built on it remains, he will receive a reward. If any man's work is burned up, he will suffer loss; but he himself will be saved, yet so as through fire."*

1 Corinthians 3:8-15

Who does not like to be rewarded? The possibility of getting a reward can be a great motivator. Just ask any dog trainer! There exists a biblical doctrine of rewards. It is not wrong that such offers should motivate us. Rewards should inspire us to "go for what counts." There is a difference between the doctrine of salvation for the lost and the doctrine of rewards for the saved. Rewards are only gained in the context of living out a Christian life. Salvation is not a reward for one's works, but rewards for those who are saved are based on works. Salvation is free and in no way linked to works, but rewards are determined by the works of the believer. "For the Son of Man is going to come in the glory of His Father with His angels, and WILL THEN REPAY EVERY MAN ACCORDING TO HIS DEEDS" (Matthew 16:27).

In a class lecture, Dr. J. Rodman Williams once explained the difference between salvation and rewards with a metaphor: "Those who are saved and go to Heaven will be like light bulbs. Although all are light bulbs, some will be forty-watt, some sixty-watt, others seventy-five-watt, and still others one-hundred-watt." It is not that some will be more saved than others; it is that some will have more rewards than others. Another way to say this is "if any man's work which he has built on it remains, he will receive a reward. If any man's work is burned up, he will suffer loss; but he himself will be saved, yet so as through fire" (1 Cor. 3:14-15).

The Scriptures reference five "crowns" as though they are potential rewards for believers: the "crown of life" (James 1:12), the incorruptible crown or "imperishable wreath" (1 Cor. 9:25), the "crown of righteousness" (2 Tim. 4:8), the "crown of glory" (1 Peter 5:4), and the "crown of exultation" (1 Thess. 2:19). Paul explains, "Now he who plants and he who waters are one; but each will receive his own reward according to his own labor" (1 Cor. 3:8). Jesus promises, "Behold, I am coming quickly, and My reward *is* with Me, to render to every man according to what he has done" (Rev. 22:12).

There seem to be two general categories of potential rewards. First, there are rewards for one's ministry. The crown of exultation, the crown of righteousness, and the crown of glory all are presented as possibilities based on ministry. Second, there are rewards for one's personal life. Both the crown of life and the incorruptible crown are presented as possibilities based on a believer's personal relationship with God.

What crowns might you receive? A minister stood by the bed of a dying Christian man. The man was distraught. The minister tried to encourage the man in his salvation. The man responded, "I am not afraid to die. I know that I am saved in Christ. I am not afraid. I am ashamed. I have lived much of my Christian life in selfishness and must now meet my Savior empty-handed." Go for what counts. It is worth your while. You can be a brighter lightbulb!

JANUARY 8

WHAT KIND OF KINGDOM ARE YOU LOOKING FOR?

"My kingdom is not of this world."

John 18:36

The transition from the Old Testament to the New Testament is an interesting one. The missiological plan of God as seen in the Old Testament will continue in the New Testament. The final book of the Old Testament is Malachi. The prophet Malachi emphasizes God's missionary plan and, at the same time, denounces Israel's failure to be an effective witness to the nations:

Oh that there were one among you who would shut the gates, that you might not uselessly kindle *fire* on My altar! I am not pleased with you," says the LORD of hosts, "nor will I accept an offering from you. For from the rising of the sun even to its setting, My name *will be* great among the nations, and in every place incense is going to be offered to My name, and a grain offering *that is* pure; for My name *will be* great among the nations," says the LORD of hosts. But you are profaning it (Mal. 1:10-12).

Malachi also promotes the anticipation of the coming Messiah, Who is, of course, both the ultimate Deliverer and contents of God's missionary plan. "Behold, I am going to send My messenger, and he will clear the way before Me. And the Lord, whom you seek, will suddenly come to His temple; and the messenger of the covenant, in whom you delight, behold, He is coming" (Mal. 3:1).

Just as Israel, for the most part, did not understand their missionary obligation prior to the coming of the Messiah, so, too, they did not understand the nature of the coming kingdom. They were waiting for a political change. They were anticipating a physical dominion. Christ brought a spiritual dominion. They were confused with Jesus' statements, such as "Repent, for the kingdom of heaven is at hand" (Matt. 4:17) and "Truly, truly, I say to you, unless one is born again he cannot see the kingdom of God" (John 3:3). They could only make sense out of these statements within the context of two assumptions: first, that they were referring to judgment upon the nations and second, that they were informed by the coming of a political Messiah Who was going to defeat Israel's enemies and establish her as a mighty geo-political nation.

This misunderstanding resulted in the crucifixion of Jesus because He did not fulfill the Jews' model of a Messiah. They called Him a blasphemer (Matt. 9:3). Their understanding of the Messiah could only fit with their nationalistic desires. They were blinded. They could not see the true plan and purpose of the Messiah. They could not get beyond seeing the kingdom of God as a place—a prosperous city with a great wall around it for protection. They could only see the kingdom as a relatively favored people, who would dominate other peoples and thrive at their expense.

The Jews, for the most part, misunderstood the kingdom of God to the point that they missed the kingdom of God. For them, the kingdom was a mystery. It was hidden (Mark 4:11). Nevertheless, the mystery was revealed to those who had ears to hear. The kingdom is already and not yet. It is "already" because it attacks Satanic rule. It is "not yet" because it has not yet destroyed human rule.

Instead of political and external changes, the kingdom produces spiritual and internal changes. Instead of being here with destruction, it is here with persuasion. It is not yet here for judgment, but it is here for salvation "For God did not send the Son into the world to judge the world, but that the world might be saved through Him" (John 3:17). It is here with power but not a power that will judge and destroy world empires yet. Right now, it is a power that will convict and redeem people. "For the Son of Man did not come to destroy men's lives, but to save them" (Luke 9:56).

To view the kingdom of God, primarily, through physical and worldly spectacles remains the mistake of those who prefer "things" over "hearts." This is not, however, the nature of the kingdom of God; for as Jesus said, "My kingdom is not of this world. If My kingdom were of this world, then My servants would be fighting so that I would not be handed over to the Jews; but as it is, My kingdom is not of this realm" (John 18:36).

We can still make this mistake today. When understanding God's blessing solely in terms of living in prosperity, a hyper-prosperity theology can move us dangerously close to building such a desire for material things that a physical kingdom can begin to replace the spiritual kingdom. This, of course, is not accurate "for the kingdom of God is not eating and drinking, but righteousness and peace and joy in the Holy Spirit" (Rom. 14:17). We might call this erroneous way of looking at the kingdom the "Esau Syndrome" (Gen. 25:34). Do not despise your salvation. Do not miss the kingdom and the King of that kingdom just so you can have a bowl of soup!

JANUARY 9

MANAGE. ORGANIZE. LEAD!

*"Then Eliashib the high priest arose with his brothers the priests and built the Sheep Gate . . . Next to him the men of Jericho built, and next to them Zaccur the son of Imri built. Now the sons of Hassenaah built the Fish Gate . . . Next to them Meremoth the son of Uriah the son of Hakkoz made repairs. And next to him Meshullam the son of Berechiah the son of Meshezabel made repairs. And next to him Zadok the son of Baana **also** made repairs. Moreover, next to him the Tekoites made repairs."*

Nehemiah 3:1-5

Good leaders understand principles of management and organization. A basic principle of good management is to determine what the situation is before making a plan so as to build a strategy based on the needs at hand. Nehemiah acted on this principle in the Jerusalem wall building project when he asked questions that focused on people: "I asked them concerning the Jews who had escaped and had survived the captivity, and about Jerusalem" (Neh. 1:2). Nehemiah was trying to ascertain the need so that he could formulate a plan. A coach does not decide on a strategy without first considering the strengths and weaknesses of his players. He first evaluates his players' abilities and then forms a strategy around them.

A basic principle of organization is to organize people according to already existing social networks or structures. In chapter three, Nehemiah followed this principle and organized his workers according to family units (vv. 1, 3), towns (vv. 2, 13), crafts (v. 8), callings (vv. 1, 28), tribes (v. 17), and leadership positions (vv. 9, 12, 15-17). Nehemiah was obviously a skillful organizer. At least thirty-nine different groups of workers were involved in his building program.

A critical part of good management is the delegation of authority. A leader who does not delegate is really no leader at all. He will stymie those he is leading and eventually destroy his own leadership. Effective leaders delegate authority and responsibility because they are willing to trust others. They are secure in their positions, power, and authority. Insecure leaders cannot delegate because they cannot let go of authority and responsibility. The problem with this is the ironic truth that what you do not let go of, you eventually lose (Matt. 16:25). Some indicators of true leadership are made evident in the selection, training, and promotion of others. The long list of workers Nehemiah recruited, trained, and delegated authority and responsibility to revealed Nehemiah's strong managerial skills.

An effective manager avoids an imbalance between authority and responsibility. A worker who is given more authority than responsibility will be frustrated and bored. A worker who is given more responsibility than authority will be overwhelmed and ineffective. If your assigned task is to defend a trash can in a park and you are given tanks and nuclear weapons to do so, you will most certainly be bored. If your assigned task is to defend New York City and you are given three pencils and two erasers, you will soon become overwhelmed. Nehemiah avoided this imbalance. He assigned each builder a specific area of the wall that he was responsible to build. He was given authority over the work in that area. "Then all of us returned to the wall, each one to his work" (Neh. 4:15). The result was that the builders were more motivated and effective because they knew exactly what was expected from them.

Good leaders are good managers and good organizers. Nehemiah was a good manager. He was a good organizer. He was a good leader!

JANUARY 10

PUT SUFFERING IN ITS PLACE

"This sickness is not to end in death, but for the glory of God, so that the Son of God may be glorified by it."

John 11:4

Of course, we do not like to think about suffering; nevertheless, it is true. Suffering *is* part of the fall of man and has become a reality of man's experience. Jesus became a Man so He could engage in man's reality. Jesus had to suffer because of the Fall. He suffered physically. They whipped Him, drove a crown of thorns into His head, beat Him, and nailed spikes into His hands and feet (Matt. 27:26-31). Jesus also suffered mentally. In the Garden of Gethsemane, He crucified His will, saying, "Let this cup pass from Me; yet not as I will, but as You *will*" (Matt. 26:39). He suffered emotionally. Anticipating the cross, He cried out, "My soul is deeply grieved, to the point of death" (Matt. 26:38) and "being in agony, He was praying very fervently; and His sweat became like drops of blood, falling down upon the ground" (Luke 22:44).

Jesus even suffered spiritually. On the cross, He cried out, "'MY GOD, MY GOD, WHY HAVE YOU FORSAKEN ME?'" (Matt. 27:46). Jesus, Who is God and is One with God (John 1:1), paradoxically, through suffering on our behalf, became separated from God. Yes, "the wages of sin is death" (Rom. 6:23), and "He made Him who knew no sin to *be* sin on our behalf" (2 Cor. 5:21). In becoming sin, He took on the wages of sin, which is death or separation from God. In an unexplainable way, God became separated from Himself, yielding the greatest suffering of all and resulting in the final and loudest *suffering shout* ever heard in this earth.

In general, it might be said most foundationally that the source of all pain and suffering is the fall of man. Pain goes back to the Garden of Eden and is built into our very nature. Its manifestation is sometimes traced back to the fallen individual. Suffering is often linked directly to personal sin. The Israelites suffered in the wilderness due to unfaithfulness (Heb. 3:8-11) and suffered at the hands of their oppressors due to disobedience (Judges 2:11-23). Herod was eaten by worms "because he did not give God the glory" (Acts 12:23).

Suffering can also be traced back to the fallen world. Suffering is often linked directly to "collective sin." It does not so much come from a particular sin of a particular individual but from the effects of sin in the world.

> Now on the same occasion there were some present who reported to Him about the Galileans whose blood Pilate had mixed with their sacrifices. And Jesus said to them, "Do you suppose that these Galileans were *greater* sinners than all other Galileans because they suffered this *fate*? I tell you, no, but unless you repent, you will all likewise perish. Or do you suppose that those eighteen on whom the tower in Siloam fell and killed them were *worse* culprits than all the men who live in Jerusalem? I tell you, no, but unless you repent, you will all likewise perish" (Luke 13:1-5).

Most important to understand is that God is sovereign over all, even over suffering. And so, He uses suffering for His purposes. "As He passed by, He saw a man blind from birth. And His disciples asked Him, 'Rabbi, who sinned, this man or his parents, that he would be born blind?' Jesus answered, '*It was* neither *that* this man sinned, nor his parents; but *it* was so that the works of God might be displayed in him'" (John 9:1-3).

When Jesus heard that Lazarus was sick, He said, "This sickness is not to end in death, but for the glory of God, so that the Son of God may be glorified by it" (John 11:4). Epaphroditus became deathly sick while he was ministering for the Lord. Paul described the situation to the Philippians and said, "Receive him then in the Lord with all joy, and hold men like him in high regard; because he came close to death for the work of Christ" (Phil. 2:29-30).

Whether it be "for the work of Christ" or "for the glory of God," or "that the works of God might be displayed," the actuality of suffering is always associated with two truths:

- God is never wrong. It is never God's fault. Suffering is a result of sin, both individual and corporate.
- God is never out of control. It is never God's inability. Suffering is under God's sovereignty.

This does not make suffering good or enjoyable. It does not make the fallen nature and the fallen world palatable. However, it does make suffering more understandable, and it does put suffering in its place. Suffering has a master, and that Master is the Lord Jesus Christ!

JANUARY 11

ARE YOU A STRATEGIST?

*"Immediately the one who had received the five talents went and traded with them, and gained five more talents. In the same manner the one who **had received** the two **talents** gained two more. But he who received the one **talent** went away, and dug **a hole** in the ground and hid his master's money."*

Matthew 25:16-18

History is the account of how God has worked to redeem a people and to reestablish His rule upon the earth. He has chosen to do this through the very people whom He has redeemed. Unfortunately, these people have not always cooperated with God's strategy. Sometimes, He has had to complete His purposes—as with His "creative" use of a big fish for Jonah—via exile, persecution, dispersion, and invasion. At times, the people of God have responded to the call of God to take part in His missionary strategy. They have established structures and movements that are designed to spread the Gospel to the nations. God has blessed these movements.

Movements require the power of the Holy Spirit as well as strategies to foster and channel that power. Wait a minute! Does strategy negate the leading of the Holy Spirit or can strategy and the activity of the Holy Spirit live together? Yes, if the strategy is a Spirit-led strategy. Of course, if a strategy is merely a human attempt to complete a task, then it will not mesh with the Spirit and will only lead to futility. Psalm 127:1 tells us, "Unless the LORD builds the house, They labor in vain who build it; Unless the LORD guards the city, The watchman keeps awake in vain."

Nonetheless, the use of a strategy can be consistent with the leading of the Holy Spirit. We are called by God to use our intelligence. We must use what we have learned in the past and form strategies that will work. Not only can strategy be a godly thing, it can also be required by God. Remember the lesson from the parable of the talents (Matt. 25:14-30). Two stewards formed strategies with respect to how to handle their talents. One steward did not. He was severely reprimanded for not forming a strategy.

Strategy is important in the work of ministry. What is strategy? It is the method that will be used to fulfill an objective. You want to get somewhere—strategy does not exist outside of a clearly defined direction—so you determine what the best way is to get there. Strategy answers the question, "How?" Whether we know it or not, we have strategies that we use to achieve our goals. The question is not whether we will use a strategy. The question is, "Will we use a good strategy?"

What determines whether a strategy is good or not? First, is the strategy consistent with biblical principles? You need money, so you rob a bank. This strategy is not effective in God's eyes because it is not consistent with His truth. It is a false strategy.

Second, is the strategy efficient? A good strategy will define the needs and the resources. It will then match them together in an efficient way (1 Cor. 12:14-21; Rom. 12:4-8; Eph. 4:11-13). One way to do nothing is to try to do everything. Efficient strategies are not afraid to make choices and determine priorities.

Third, is the strategy effective? Good strategies tend to work. They bear fruit. It may be necessary to consider the idea of relevance. A strategy must be appropriate for the specific situation and time. A strategy that worked in one situation twenty-five years ago may not work in another situation now. The contents of the Gospel do not change, but the method of presenting the Gospel does change.

A strategy is not concerned with details. It is a general idea, method, or manner of doing something. Within the general strategy, the daily details will change; but the overall strategy remains the same. Paul's strategy was to go to the big cities, preach in the synagogues, and continue from there, depending upon what happened in the synagogue:

> Now when they had traveled through Amphipolis and Apollonia, they came to Thessalonica, where there was a synagogue of the Jews. And according to Paul's custom, he went to them, and for three Sabbaths reasoned with them from the Scriptures ... But the Jews, becoming jealous and taking along some wicked men from the market place, formed a mob and set the city in an uproar; and attacking the house of Jason, they were seeking to bring them out to the people ... The brethren immediately sent Paul and Silas away by night to Berea, and when they arrived, they went into the synagogue of the Jews (Acts 17:1-2, 5, 10).

Consider a goal that you have in your life right now. What strategy are you using to achieve that goal? Is it a good strategy? Is it consistent with biblical principles, efficient, and effective? Are you a strategist?

JANUARY 12

THE TENSION IN PRAYER

"Pray, then, in this way: 'Our Father who is in heaven, Hallowed be Your name. 'Your kingdom come. Your will be done, On earth as it is in heaven. 'Give us this day our daily bread. 'And forgive us our debts, as we also have forgiven our debtors. 'And do not lead us into temptation, but deliver us from evil. [For Yours is the kingdom and the power and the glory forever. Amen.'"

Matthew 6:9-13

With respect to prayer, we sometimes feel the tension between prayer as a task (with the focus on effectual results or answers to prayer) and prayer as relationship (with the focus on simply spending time with God and being transformed through it). It should be understood that these two aspects of prayer are not mutually exclusive. One cannot be done without the other.

The tension between task and relationship in prayer is the "tension" between cause (relationship) and effect (task). It is when we get closer to God (cause) that things get done (effect). The effect of intimacy is that it changes the one who prays—making that person more useful to God—and it moves God's hand. Prayer is intimate *and* effectual.

Our sense of dependence in prayer must be understood in terms of dependence upon a Person, not a certain result. It is not so much the "what" of prayer but the "Who" of prayer that matters. It is not so much arriving at the solution of a problem as it is coming to the One Who is the solution to the problem. When the result becomes the object of our faith, we are not far from having faith in ourselves and, thus, practicing idolatry. We must be determined to not focus so much on the "answer" as on the "Answer-Man." To pray is to gaze upon God!

With respect to our prayer lives, we should remember that there are many types of prayer and many biblical methods that can assist us. Fasting, combined with prayer, is a powerful "means of grace" that can be employed to intensify prayer and make it more effectual. It is an important Christian discipline that naturally is connected to improving one's prayer life. The use of God's name in prayer can also enhance it. The biblical names of God (i.e., "God Almighty" or "I Am") can be employed to focus in on an aspect of God's character as we pray.

In order to describe God, the Bible relies heavily on His names. It also relies heavily on metaphors. Metaphors like "rock" and "fortress" are used to describe the nature and functions of God. They can effectively be used in prayer to focus on various aspects of God's character. Metaphors make us think, imagine, and have emotion. When we pray to God our "Rock," for example, we must think about the dynamics of a rock that are descriptive of Who God is. We begin to imagine or picture situations in which rocks exist and functions that they serve. We might see, for example, waves crashing against the rocks and the rocks not moving. When we pray to God our "Rock," we are led into feeling the emotions consistent with that object—the emotions of deep peace and relief as we sense the emotional responses to the reality of the stability of God in our lives.

Prayer is the cornerstone of the Christian's life. We talk to God because He is there. We talk to God because He is able.

JANUARY 13

MULTIPLICATION VS. ADDITION— NO CONTEST!

"The things which you have heard from me in the presence of many witnesses, entrust these to faithful men who will be able to teach others also."

2 Timothy 2:2

The Great Commission is *the* mandate. And Jesus came up and spoke to them, saying, 'All authority has been given to Me in heaven and on earth. Go therefore and make disciples of all the nations, baptizing them in the name of the Father and the Son and the Holy Spirit, teaching them to observe all that I commanded you; and lo, I am with you always, even to the end of the age'" (Matt. 28:18-20).

The return of Christ is *the* motivation. "This gospel of the kingdom shall be preached in the whole world as a testimony to all the nations, and then the end will come" (Matt. 24:14).

Multiplication is *the* strategy. "'The things which you have heard from me in the presence of many witnesses, entrust these to faithful men who will be able to teach others also'" (2 Tim. 2:2).

The mandate—and thus, the goal—is to "make disciples of all the nations." This mandate goes back to the commissioning of Abraham when he was also told to go and use his blessings to be a blessing to all the nations (Gen. 12:1-3). The motivation to engage in this activity is nothing less than to arrive at the end of the book—the return of Christ. We want to see Him come, so we go. How are we going to get this done? Multiplication must be our strategy!

The essence of multiplication is entrusting or equipping others. It is true that if you give a man a fish, you feed him for a day. It is also true that if you teach a man to fish, you feed him for a lifetime. More significantly, it is true that if you teach a man to fish and equip him with boats and nets and fishing poles, then you prepare him to feed others. Multiplication as a strategy seeks to reproduce. It is not enough for the teacher to teach. The teacher must teach so that others will also teach. It is not enough for the missionary to go. The missionary must go so that others will also go. It is not enough for ministry to be done. Ministry must be multiplied.

What does this look like on the mission field? It should look like Paul's methods in Acts 13-28. Paul and his team were able to facilitate a rapid expansion of the Gospel because they multiplied their work. They taught others, who would be able to teach others also. They reproduced themselves. In order to do this successfully, they could not insist on a paternalistic approach. They could not minister simply to develop their own ministry. They had to work themselves out of a job. They had to implement a go, give, leave strategy. (The longest Paul stayed in any one location was the three years he spent in Ephesus).

This is the hardest part of being a multiplier. You have to hold on only to let go. It is the way of the multiplier. Nothing is reproduced until it is doing what the reproducer did, which cannot be done if the reproducer is still doing it. Multiplication implies release. A "three self" strategy was used by Paul in order to promote and realize this "release." Churches were developed that would be self-governing, self-supporting, and self-propagating. Instead of addition, there was multiplication.

Ultimately, if we use a multiplication strategy, we should see missions producing more missions. This principle is true in all areas of life. Who or what are you reproducing? Find some faithful ones who you can entrust with your blessings so they can then entrust and equip others also. Multiply!

JANUARY 14

SHOULD YOU DESIRE SPIRITUAL GIFTS?

> *"Pursue love, yet desire earnestly spiritual **gifts**, but especially that you may prophesy."*
> 1 Corinthians 14:1

As we get older, Christmases and birthdays might begin to be a bit awkward. Oddly, you may feel somewhat uncomfortable telling someone what present you want. Aha, there is the tricky phrase, "I want." To some degree, it feels just a little bit presumptuous to tell someone else what you want them to get you. Maybe it is this same kind of feeling that makes us, to some degree, feel like we are not supposed to desire the spiritual gifts that God may have for us. We certainly should not ask for them. Should we?

The Scripture answers this question with a resounding "Yes!" We are told to not only desire the gifts but to "desire *earnestly* spiritual gifts" (1 Cor. 14:1). We are even told to pray for them (1 Cor. 14:13). Pray for them and earnestly desire them. From the Greek word *zeloo*—that is translated as "desire"—we get our word "zealous." It means to seek after or to be zealous for something.

Having a desire for spiritual gifts is not in conflict with the sovereignty of the Spirit in distributing those gifts. The idea of the Spirit "distributing to each one individually just as He wills" (1 Cor. 12:11) is not opposed to the idea of desiring and praying for the gifts. The gift of the Holy Spirit is given to those who ask for, desire, and seek Him:

> So I say to you, ask, and it will be given to you; seek, and you will find; knock, and it will be opened to you. For everyone who asks, receives; and he who seeks, finds; and to him who knocks, it will be opened. Now suppose one of you fathers is asked by his son for a fish; he will not give him a snake instead of a fish, will he? Or *if* he is asked for an egg, he will not give him a scorpion, will he? If you then, being evil, know how to give good gifts to your children, how much more will *your* heavenly Father give the Holy Spirit to those who ask Him? (Luke 11:9-13).

It is not wrong to desire to have something that is good. God delights to "give what is good to those who ask Him" (Matt. 7:11). The Christian community should be zealous for all of the gifts so as to edify the church (1 Cor. 14:12). What can be wrong are the person's motives in wanting to have spiritual gifts? The purpose of the gifts is other-oriented. Thus, the desire cannot be a self-centered desire.

Are some gifts more important or more desirable than others? Paul encourages the Corinthians to "earnestly desire the greater gifts" (1 Cor. 12:31). So, what are the greater gifts? First of all, it cannot simply be stated that the answer to this question has to do with the order in which the gifts are listed in 1 Corinthians 12:8-10. This would make prophecy the third least important gift, yet Paul indicates that prophecy is a greater gift: "Pursue love, yet desire earnestly spiritual *gifts*, but especially that you may prophesy" (1 Cor. 14:1). He repeats this idea in 1 Corinthians 14:39. It is not that love is the greater gift either. Love is not a gift. It is a fruit (Gal. 5:22). Certainly, one of the greater gifts seems to be prophecy, since "greater is one who prophesies . . . so that the church may receive edifying" (1 Cor. 14:5).

Should you desire and ask for spiritual gifts? Why not? God actually instructs you to desire and ask for them. Stay humble. Seek to be selfless. Focus on helping others. This is why you should be zealous for spiritual gifts.

JANUARY 15

HELPING OTHERS TO SEE THEIR ROOT PROBLEMS

"If you forgive others for their transgressions, your heavenly Father will also forgive you. But if you do not forgive others, your Father will not forgive your transgressions."
Matthew 6:14-15

Of all the potential root problems that may be causing other problems in a person's life, one seems to stand out. Bitterness is built up over time when a lack of forgiveness continues to be the response to a perceived wrong. The consequences of holding on to bitterness are far reaching and very damaging. The dangers are easily seen in that "if you forgive others for their transgressions, your heavenly Father will also forgive you. But if you do not forgive others, your Father will not forgive your transgressions" (Matt. 6:14-15). The bigger issue than not forgiving someone else's sins is that your sins are not forgiven. That is what causes problems. This is why the lack of forgiveness toward others is often the root of many other problems.

Many times, the symptoms of a problem may be easy to see, while the root of the problem is hidden. A common root is a lack of forgiveness, which leads to bitterness. Bitterness leads to anger, hostility, and even hatred. That can lead to rebellion. Ultimately, rebellion can result in indifference and apathy.

Take, for example, a husband who is having marital problems and comes into a counselor's office. They begin to talk. The husband may actually be willing to share the more obvious problem with the counselor since he feels like it is more acceptable, less embarrassing, or simply more matter-of-fact. He might say, "I just don't care anymore. Whatever." The husband, however, did not start out as apathetic. There is a root somewhere earlier in the road. Apathy began with a lack of forgiveness.

Before he had reached the point of apathy, his wife had consistently rejected his attempts at displaying affection and rarely was willing to engage in sexual relations. He felt like she had sinned against him, since "the husband must fulfill his duty to his wife, and likewise also the wife to her husband. The wife does not have authority over her own body, but the husband *does*; and likewise also the husband does not have authority over his own body, but the wife *does*. Stop depriving one another" (1 Cor. 7:3-5). Because he felt sinned against, he refused to forgive her. Eventually, this led to bitterness.

He began to resent his wife, even though the Scriptures admonished, "Husbands, love your wives and do not be embittered against them" (Col. 3:19). This bitterness led to feelings of anger, hostility, and even hatred. Many nights, he went to bed angry about the sexual inactivity in his marriage, even though the Scripture warned him, "Do not let the sun go down on your anger" (Eph. 4:26). So many "suns going down" finally led to outright rebellion. The husband began to act on his bitterness and anger and drifted into a habitual use of pornography. This manifestation of rebellion made the husband more vulnerable to even more advanced forms of porn, like going to strip clubs, as his rebellion turned into apathy.

Inasmuch as apathy is the opposite of love and love is "the greatest of these" (1 Cor. 13:13), love is a critical component of healthy relationships and healthy lives. Without love, nothing else matters (1 Cor. 13:3). Love is powerful. Its opposite, apathy, is impotent and destructive.

This is when the husband sat down in the chair in the counselor's office and defiantly said, "Whatever!" Now, the counselor has the difficult job of working the husband backward—apathy to rebellion to anger to bitterness to lack of forgiveness—so that the root can be dug up. Ultimately, in order to help the husband, the counselor will have to skillfully move the husband step by step until he is able to challenge the husband to forgive. Until this root is dug up, many and various problems will remain in the husband's life, not the least of which would include apathy, rebellion, anger, and bitterness toward his wife.

Roots serve as foundations. They are "feeders." They either feed you with good "food," or they contaminate you with bad "food." The root of a lack of forgiveness feeds your life with bitterness, anger, rebellion, and apathy. The root of forgiveness, however, feeds you with sweetness, joy, obedience, and love. And "the greatest of these" is . . . Choose forgiveness

---

JANUARY 16

MERCY ME!

"Since we have gifts that differ according to the grace given to us, each of us is to exercise them accordingly: . . . he who shows mercy, with cheerfulness."

Romans 12:6, 8

God equips His people with gifts for ministry. There exist various lists of gifts in the New Testament. One such list is found in Romans 12:6-8: "Since we have gifts that differ according to the grace given to us, *each of us is to exercise them accordingly*: if prophecy, according to the proportion of his faith; if service, in his serving; or he who teaches, in his teaching; or he who exhorts, in his exhortation; he who gives, with liberality; he who leads, with diligence; he who shows mercy, with cheerfulness."

The Giver of these gifts is God the Father (Rom. 12:3). The gifts are called *charismata* (grace gifts). They are compared to body parts that "function" in different ways (Rom. 12:4) and that are "effects" enacted by "God who works all things in *all persons*" (1 Cor. 12:6). The Romans 12 gifts are gifts that direct how a person functions; they determine the effects of a person's personality or tendencies. They are not so much gifts that a person is temporarily and situationally used in (as in the 1 Corinthians 12:8-10 gifts) or gifts that dictate a person's actual ministry (as in the Ephesians 4:11 gifts) as they are gifts that reside inside of a person and shape what that person is like. They are what are often called "motivational gifts."

What if you are not "motivated" in any particular way? What if you do not have the gift of service or exhortation or showing mercy? Are you excused, then, from serving others, or encouraging them, or showing mercy? Of course not! All Christians are called to serve. All believers should look to encourage others. All members of the body of Christ can show mercy to others. The difference is simply that those with that particular gift have more of an impetus or natural drive to do those particular actions. The gifts produce certain tendencies in some people, not absolution in other people. To not be gifted in showing mercy does not mean that you cannot, should not, or will not show mercy. It just means that someone else might be more *inclined* to show mercy than you.

How can the Romans 12 gift of showing mercy be understood? People who have the gift of showing mercy are more inclined to feel and understand the pain of others. People with this gift desire to defend those who are oppressed. Like the "Good Samaritan," they easily feel compassion for others in need and then are inclined to tend to their needs. "But a Samaritan, who was on a journey, came upon him; and when he saw him, he felt compassion, and came to him and bandaged up his wounds, pouring oil and wine on *them*; and he put him on his own beast, and brought him to an inn and took care of him" (Luke 10:33-34). In terms of personality traits, a person who has the gift of showing mercy tends to be a bit more "low key" and one who generally avoids confrontation and does not like to argue.

Just like any strength that has its correlated weaknesses, the gift of showing mercy has its vulnerabilities or carnal tendencies that need to be avoided. If someone with this gift is not careful, he or she may become overly emotional to the point that being able to make sensible decisions might become difficult. In an odd sort of way, those with the gift of showing mercy need to be careful not to become excessively partial; they may begin to act like the only people worthy of attention are people who are in pain. A person with this gift may also need to be careful that they do not avoid confrontation to such an extent that important matters are not addressed. These, of course, are vulnerabilities. It does not mean that they have to be done. They just need to be watched out for.

Here is the Romans 12 gift of showing mercy. Life is seen through the lens of sharing pain with others. The orientation is toward having compassion on people. More than anything else, people with this gift view themselves as those who want to and are able to show concern and caring for other people. They especially want to comfort people who are in pain. They would say of themselves, "If someone is hurting, I want to hurt with them!" Are you this person? Do you have the Romans 12 gift of showing mercy?

January 17

IS IT REALLY WORTH IT?

"Blessed are the gentle, for they shall inherit the earth."

Matthew 5:5

To be meek is to be submissive. It is to be gentle with others through the exercise of self-control. It means you are able to be spit on without having to spit back. It is a submissive strength that is characterized by a freedom from vengeance. This ability comes from a true perspective of yourself. You embrace the understanding that you have no rights to grasp or hold onto.

The least meek people are those who vehemently demand their rights. Assertiveness tends to be the enemy of submissiveness. It is not easy to lay down your rights. This is especially true in the United States where the very foundation of the country—the Bill of Rights—screams out in the public square, "Stand up for your rights!" It does not even seem *right* to lay down your rights. Jesus' words may not seem right to us either: "'You have heard that it was said, AN EYE FOR AN EYE, AND A TOOTH FOR A TOOTH. But I say to you, do not resist an evil person; but whoever slaps you on your right cheek, turn the other to him also. If anyone wants to sue you and take your shirt, let him have your coat also. Whoever forces you to go one mile, go with him two'" (Matt. 5:38-41).

Those who are gentle or meek give of themselves and inherit the earth via putting self-worth or self-esteem on the cross, and thus, bearing the fruit of gentleness. "Blessed are the gentle, for they shall inherit the earth" (Matt. 5:5).

Blessings are free. Like salvation, you cannot earn them (Eph. 2:8-10). That does not mean, however, that they are not costly because we try to hang onto that which is not our own (1 Cor. 6:19-20). The beatitude (blessing) includes a challenge or an obligation, a cost. It is quite a challenge to give up your rights. How can you enter into this beatitude? You have to have the right *attitude*.

Jesus is our Example on how to live this out: "Have this attitude in yourselves which was also in Christ Jesus, who, although He existed in the form of God, did not regard equality with God a thing to be grasped, but emptied Himself, taking the form of a bond-servant, *and* being made in the likeness of men. Being found in appearance as a man, He humbled Himself by becoming obedient to the point of death, even death on a cross" (Phil. 2:5-8).

Jesus "emptied Himself." He laid aside His privileges. He gave up His rights. It is not that He did not have those rights. He just did not demand them. He "humbled Himself." He laid His rights "on a cross." The path to meekness goes through the cross. It nails self-worth or worthiness to the cross. A person is equipped to do this by not thinking "more highly of himself than he ought to think" (Rom. 12:3). The attitude of entitlement—the opposite of "this attitude . . . which was also in Christ Jesus"—suffocates meekness.

Those who are gentle inherit the earth. They prosper in God's kingdom. Their impotent *self*-worth is converted into a powerful *Jesus*-worth. People do not need more *self*-esteem; they need more *Jesus*-esteem. Those who are gentle are worth a lot. They are the recipients of a huge inheritance. The fruit of the spirit that corresponds to this beatitude is gentleness (Gal. 5:23). More gentleness, more inheritance!

The nature of the kingdom of God—relative to the kingdoms of this world—is backward; it is "flip-flopped." Each beatitude in the Sermon on the Mount, therefore, is cloaked in irony. "Blessed are the gentle, for they shall inherit the earth" (Matt. 5:5). We must not perceive ourselves as worthy; then we will be worth a lot in Christ.

JANUARY 18

IT'S NOT NECESSARILY WHAT IT APPEARS TO BE

"Beware of practicing your righteousness before men to be noticed by them; otherwise you have no reward with your Father who is in heaven."

Matthew 6:1

Perhaps the greatest danger for those who live in the kingdom of God is to fall into the trap of only *appearing* to live in the kingdom. The greatest enemy of Christianity is outward religion. The greatest enemy of that which is real is that which is false. The greatest enemy of the eternal can often be the temporal. The greatest enemy of that which is profound is that which is superficial. Those who live in the kingdom of God must constantly beware of falling into hypocrisy.

There is nothing wrong with "forms" in and of themselves. The problem comes when there is form without substance or when form goes ahead of substance. Since God "looks at the heart" and not simply at the outward appearance (1 Sam. 16:7), form is not enough. Jesus aggressively came against form without substance. He clearly opposed the Pharisees. To say that He was not a fan of the emptiness of hypocrisy would be a severe understatement:

> Woe to you, scribes and Pharisees, hypocrites! For you are like whitewashed tombs which on the outside appear beautiful, but inside they are full of dead men's bones and all uncleanness. So you, too, outwardly appear righteous to men, but inwardly you are full of hypocrisy and lawlessness. Woe to you, scribes and Pharisees, hypocrites! For you build the tombs of the prophets and adorn the monuments of the righteous, and say, "If we had been *living* in the days of our fathers, we would not have been partners with them in *shedding* the blood of the prophets." So you testify against yourselves, that you are sons of those who murdered the prophets. Fill up, then, the measure *of the guilt* of your fathers. You serpents, you brood of vipers, how will you escape the sentence of hell? (Matt. 23:27-33).

There is a clear distinction between your testimony of God and ministry for Him) and your relationship with God and righteousness before Him (Matt. 6:1). In the first case, you are commanded to "let your light shine before men in such a way that they may see" your good works (Matt. 5:16). In the second case, you are warned not to practice your "'righteousness before men to be noticed by them'" (Matt. 6:1). Is this a contradiction? Show off but do not show off? Be a hypocrite but do not be a hypocrite?

This is not a contradiction. We must realize two things. First, when we let our light shine, we are not drawing attention to ourselves. We are testifying to the world about Jesus by letting Him shine through us. Jesus is the Light (John 1:7; John 8:12). There is a difference between ministry for God and private relationship with God. Our ministry for God should be seen by men for a witness. This is the very purpose of ministry. Our relationship with God, although it will sometimes have a public aspect, should not be on display. It should not be used to demonstrate our righteousness to others lest it be just that—*our* righteousness. When our light shines before men, it is God's righteousness that is being displayed. When our relationship with God shines before men, it is our righteousness that is being displayed.

The subtle difference is motivation. Why are you doing something? "But seek first His kingdom and His righteousness, and all these things will be added to you" (Matt. 6:33). Remember "forms" are not necessarily bad. Even ministry for God is, in a sense, a form. It is not bad. It just cannot come first. Why do you minister? Why do you desire a position in which to do ministry? Neither of those things are wrong desires. The question is, "What comes first?" The desire to do ministry must come out of the desire to please God—the desire to seek Him *first*. Then all these other desires will be added unto you.

So, how do you make sure your Christianity is not simply what it appears to be; not false but real? It is a matter of the heart. It is a matter of motives. Who is your Lord? Who comes first? "Whatever you do, do your work heartily, as for the Lord rather than for men" (Col. 3:23).

> Hear, O Israel! The LORD is our God, the LORD is one! You shall love the LORD your God with all your heart and with all your soul and with all your might. These words, which I am commanding you today, shall be on your heart. You shall teach them diligently to your sons and shall talk of them when you sit in your house and when you walk by the way and

when you lie down and when you rise up. You shall bind them as a sign on your hand and they shall be as frontals on your forehead. You shall write them on the doorposts of your house and on your gates (Deut. 6:4-9).

JANUARY 19

HISTORY IS HIS STORY

"And Jesus came up and spoke to them, saying, 'All authority has been given to Me in heaven and on earth. Go therefore and make disciples of all the nations."
Matthew 28:18-19

Who does God love? How does John 3:16 read? Is it, "For God so loved the Jews?" Or is it, "For God so loved Americans?" Or is it, "For God so loved me, my family, and my denomination?" None of these "translations" are correct. John 3:16 reads, "For God so loved the *world*" (emphasis mine). God's plan of salvation is vast and inclusive. The purpose and plan of God is for all of mankind to know Him through Jesus Christ.

What do you study in school? Is it "Man's story"? Or is it, "Nature's story"? Or is it simply, "Its story"? None of these made-up course names are correct. The course is actually called "*His story*." What is His story? It is the entire history of God's mission to glorify Himself through the redemption of man. The Bible is the textbook for this ultimate "course." It is the story of the mission of God. The Bible is His story. Without a mission, there is no reason for the Bible. Without the Bible, there are no instructions for the mission. The mission of God is world evangelization. Thus, the Bible is the story of all that goes into making God known.

It goes something like this: God created the world. Then He made man. He wanted a relationship with man; but then sin entered the world through man's choice. It separated man from God. Because of sin, death became inevitable for everyone. Everyone sins, so all will die in their sins without God's help. God gave His Son. He became a Man. He knew no sin. He bore our sin. He suffered for us. He was crucified. He was buried. He was raised from the dead. He ascended to Heaven. Jesus provides eternal life. He has all authority. Jesus will judge all people. Repent. Believe. Salvation is by faith. "'Go into all the world and preach the gospel to all creation'" (Mark 16:15).

The Bible gives us the mandate for world evangelization. From "you shall be a blessing . . . And in you all the families of the earth will be blessed" (Gen. 12:2-3) to "Go therefore and make disciples of all the nations" (Matt. 28:19), we are commanded to be God's witnesses. Why do we go to all the nations? We go because God commanded it in the Bible.

How serious is this command? How authoritative is the Bible? The importance of missions has changed over the course of Church history. When the Church put much emphasis on the authority of the Bible, it also put much emphasis on missions. When the church put little emphasis on the authority of the Bible, it also put little emphasis on missions. It makes sense that, historically, there has been a direct correlation between the perceived authority of the Bible and obedience to the mandate of the Bible. Following a command is only as pressing as the authority behind that command.

Participation in God's mission and the authority behind that mission live together necessarily. Why did you obey your parents? When you were a young child, it was enough for your parent to simply say, "Because I told you to!" It was an issue of perceived authority. There was authority behind the command. Matthew 28:18-19 discusses Christ's authority to us: "And Jesus came up and spoke to them, saying, 'All authority has been given to Me in heaven and on earth. Go therefore and make disciples of all the nations'" (Matt. 28:18-19).

God loves you, and He loves the person He is going to love through you. What is His story? It is the story of His love for all people as He uses His people to love and reach all people. Dr. Martin Luther King, Jr. said, "We are not makers of history. We are made by history." This statement could be tweaked just a bit to confirm God's use of us in His plan: "Because we are made by history, we then become makers of history." Indeed, "We love, because He first loved us" (1 John 4:19). History is the story of His love for all people as He uses His people to love and reach all people. Be a history maker!

JANUARY 20

TRIVIAL PURSUIT OR *STRATEGO?*

"Where there is no vision, the people are unrestrained."
Proverbs 29:18

Stratego is a strategy board game in which two players control forty military officers with the objective of capturing the opponent's flag or capturing enough enemy pieces to force surrender. The key to the game, of course, is strategy. This may include calculating sequences of moves, lying in wait, guessing, concealment, and bluffing. Why does it feel so different to play *Trivial Pursuit* than it does to play *Stratego*? *Trivial Pursuit* is . . . trivial. *Stratego* takes strategy. It takes much more effort to play *Stratego* because it requires the formulation of strategy and its implementation. This is hard work, but it is worth it. The player who has the best strategy usually wins the game.

To play *Stratego* without a strategy is like walking through a maze with a blindfold on. This is also the situation in the game of life. Lives that are lived with no strategies to achieve goals tend to be very trivial lives. Strategies help us to live rich lives.

First, strategies require prayerful dependence upon God. Strategies for living, working, and ministering should be borne out of the study of God's Word, godly counsel, prayer, and experiences with God. So, strategies help us grow closer to God. Second, strategies require us to put our faith into practice. Faith is future-oriented as it "is the assurance of *things* hoped for, the conviction of things not seen" (Heb. 11:1). Strategies are also future-oriented. We do not have faith in our strategies. Rather, we execute our strategies by faith. So, strategies help us grow in faith. Third, strategies serve to provide us with a way to communicate God's vision to others. So, strategies help us to grow as co-laborers in God's community.

One way to never hit a target is to not have one. Strategy commits us to move in a certain direction. It helps us to be people of vision *and* purposeful action. A particular strategy necessarily excludes other strategies. This is important. Focus breeds success. A person with a vision for everything is actually a person with no vision at all. They do not accomplish anything, although they get involved in everything. "Where there is no vision, the people are unrestrained" (Prov. 29:18).

What are some different categories of strategies? There is the "standard solution" strategy. This type of strategy decides on a specific way to do something. It then uses the same strategy for every situation. There is the "step by step" strategy. This strategy appears to lack a strategy. There are no plans for the future. The assumption is that God will lead you to the next step when the time comes. There is the "foundations" strategy. This strategy makes plans to start something. God will complete the task. It focuses on beginnings instead of results. There is the "unique solution strategy." This strategy assumes that every situation is different. There must be a special strategy for each situation.

No assumptions are made. Strategy is received instead of simply being imposed. Prayer is especially critical with this type of strategy. Being proactive in prayer must be followed by being proactive in actions and decision-making. It might be said, "We must pray as if we could not plan, and plan as if we could not pray."

So, if you are going to play *Stratego,* make sure that you are being strategic. Remember, the person with the best strategy usually wins!

JANUARY 21

YOU CAN BE VICTORIOUS!

"And upon this rock I will build My church; and the gates of Hades will not overpower it."
Matthew 16:18

The surest way for an army to lose a battle is for it to be divided against itself. "If a house is divided against itself, that house will not be able to stand. If Satan has risen up against himself and is divided, he cannot stand, but he is finished!" (Mark 3:25-26). In unity, there is strength.

> Two are better than one because they have a good return for their labor. For if either of them falls, the one will lift up his companion. But woe to the one who falls when there is not another to lift him up. Furthermore, if two lie down together they keep warm, but how can one be warm *alone*? And if one can overpower him who is alone, two can resist him. A cord of three *strands* is not quickly torn apart (Eccl. 4:9-12).

An effective strategy in war is to divide the enemy to separate allies from each other. Sometimes, the church allows the enemy to divide it when the presence of that common enemy should actually be unifying it. The United States and the Soviet Union were allies during World War I and World War II. Entities that would normally be divided find unity in a common enemy.

The Pharisees and the Herodians were enemies. The existence of their common enemy (Jesus) had as its result that "the Pharisees went out and immediately *began* conspiring with the Herodians against Him, *as to* how they might destroy Him" (Mark 3:6). If "politics makes strange bedfellows," how much more should the reality of spiritual warfare against a common enemy (Satan) unify the Church?

Conflict among Christians is, to some extent, the result of a lack of recognition of the reality of spiritual warfare. Where the war is more obvious, Christians tend to find it much easier to be unified. Denominational divisions tend to break down on the mission field. Christians are more unified. They have no choice. The war is very near. They can more easily see how much they need each other. This same result seems to manifest itself in the midst of persecuted Christians. They usually do not have a problem with being unified.

In a war, there is a demand for unity; and unity demands that there be a clear recognition of the war. Who is your enemy? Do you see bigger churches as your "competition"? Do you see churches with different doctrinal beliefs as your enemy? What would happen if we put away our differences and united to stand against Satan's efforts? What would happen if we recognized the reality of the spiritual war that was right in front of us? As the spiritual bombs are exploding all around us, do you think we would care anymore how many were in attendance at our church last Sunday relative to how many attended the church down the street or how much emphasis the church down the street puts on the sovereignty of God relative to our emphasis on the free will of man? All of those things quickly fade away in the midst of a war.

If in the war, there is a demand for unity, how much more is there a demand for obedience? A leader of an army cannot be successful unless his soldiers follow orders. Satan understands this principle. He tries to steer those in the Lord's army down a path of disobedience. Christ is victorious. If His followers walk in His victorious footsteps, then there is nothing Satan can do to stop them.

The Church is on the offensive. Satan is on the defensive. His defensive gates cannot hold off the advance of the Church. "I also say to you that you are Peter, and upon this rock I will build My church; and the gates of Hades will not overpower it" (Matt. 16:18). Being on the defensive, Satan's only strategy is to deceive disciples of Christ into defeating themselves. He does this in three primary ways. First, he tries to make Christians unaware of the reality of the spiritual war that is going on around them. Second, he tries to promote disunity within the army of God. Third, he tries to promote disobedience to the General of that army.

What happens to soldiers who fail to recognize the presence of the enemy? What happens to soldiers in a war who get separated from each other? What happens to a platoon when it refuses to obey the orders of its commanding officer? Defeat! Instead, Christians need to be aware, stay unified, and practice obedience. Victory!

JANUARY 22

HUMBLE YOURSELF IN THE SIGHT OF THE LORD

"And all of you, clothe yourselves with humility toward one another,
for GOD IS OPPOSED TO THE PROUD, BUT GIVES GRACE TO THE HUMBLE.
Therefore humble yourselves under the mighty hand of God,
that He may exalt you at the proper time."

1 Peter 5:5-6

A Christian leader who is full of himself cannot lead because there is no room for *the Leader* to lead through him. Emptiness is a prerequisite for fullness. Humility is an indispensable attribute of a Christian leader. Moses was a superlative leader because his was a superlative humility. We read in Numbers 12:3, "Now the man Moses was very humble, more than any man who was on the face of the earth." Leaders must be humble.

Christian leaders must look at themselves in a humble way. They cannot have a haughty or arrogant attitude that keeps them separated from their people. Instead, their humility will result in their ability to work side by side with people. Nehemiah's humility allowed him to say to those he was leading, "You see the bad situation we are in, that Jerusalem is desolate and its gates burned by fire. Come, let us rebuild the wall of Jerusalem so that we will no longer be a reproach" (Neh. 2:17). Humility speaks with a "we" and not with a "you." Nehemiah did not say, "This is *your* problem. This is what *you* must do." He said, "This is *our* problem. This is what *we* must do."

Nehemiah put his words into practice. "So neither I, my brothers, my servants, nor the men of the guard who followed me, none of us removed our clothes, each *took* his weapon *even* to the water" (Neh. 4:23). Nehemiah worked with his people. He stood by their side and got his hands dirty along with them. He was not too proud to work hard. He was humble enough to take part in the common work as he led the common people.

A Christian leader must identify himself with Jesus, Who identified Himself with the cross. Only in this way does the victory of the resurrection come to pass in a leader's life and ministry. "Truly, truly, I say to you, unless a grain of wheat falls into the earth and dies, it remains alone; but if it dies, it bears much fruit" (John 12:24). This aspect of leadership, more than in any other way, is formed through a strong and intimate relationship with God. We might say that a good leader may be able to perform well when he is in the spotlight. However, a great leader is able to perform well when he is all alone. Great leaders are made during their time spent in the "secluded" place with God (Mark 1:35).

A Christian leader must have an excellent attendance record at the "School of the Cross." His prayer must be, "Teach me the way of the cross that I might be empty of self and full of you." The answer to this prayer is that the leader would have Christ leading through him, which is "the hope of glory."

> Of *this church* I was made a minister according to the stewardship from God bestowed on me for your benefit, so that I might fully carry out the *preaching of* the word of God, *that is*, the mystery which has been hidden from the *past* ages and generations, but has now been manifested to His saints, to whom God willed to make known what is the riches of the glory of this mystery among the Gentiles, which is Christ in you, the hope of glory (Col. 1:25-27).

JANUARY 23

HOW LOW ARE YOU WILLING TO GO?

*"Then He **poured** water into the basin, and began to wash the disciples' feet and to wipe them with the towel with which He was girded."*

John 13:5

Are you willing to do the most menial acts of service? Jesus was! Jesus set the standard for Christian service when He washed His disciples' feet. Foot-washing was a common practice in the Middle East that went all the way back to the time of Abraham (Gen. 18:4; 19:2). The dry climate of that region made the dirt roads very dusty. People wore open sandals on their feet when they traveled. Foot-washing was a practical service, not a ceremony. It was also the lowest form of service in the Hebrew culture. The Hebrews would not even allow their Hebrew workers to do the service. They made their lowest Gentile slave wash the feet of guests. The only exception to this was when a disciple would wash the feet of a teacher as a demonstration of loyalty to him.

When Jesus washed His disciples' feet He set the standard for Christian service at the lowest point possible. God lowered Himself to become a man. Now through foot-washing, Jesus symbolically depicts that menial act of service in the context of His cultural surroundings as a man. If Jesus, Who was the Teacher, washed the feet of His disciples, how much more should those disciples be willing to wash the feet of others? The message is clear: "He said to them, 'Do you know what I have done to you? You call Me Teacher and Lord; and you are right, for so I am. If I then, the Lord and the Teacher, washed your feet, you also ought to wash one another's feet. For I gave you an example that you also should do as I did to you" (John 13:12-15).

In a very real sense, the follower of Christ's motivation to serve should be nothing less than the service of Christ Himself. Christians should be willing to serve others because the One Who is greater was willing to make His whole life a service for them. Jesus would say, "Since I set the bar of service at its lowest level, there should be no act of service too menial for you." If you answer, "I am above certain acts of service," then you, in effect, practice idolatry. You become your own idol, placing yourself above Jesus!

Pride and selfishness can keep us from serving. At the end of a church meeting, many people began to assist with putting away the chairs. The pastor was asked by a visitor why he was not helping.

The pastor responded, "I do not put away chairs. I went to a Bible college!"

The visitor replied, "With all due respect, Pastor Mark, that is all the more reason for you to put away chairs."

It is a good thing that is not Jesus' attitude. Can you imagine Jesus saying, "I do not have to become a Man, die on the cross, or wash your feet because I am the President of the College of Creation"? Instead of having an *attitude* of selfishness and pride that would keep Him from serving, Jesus' ultimate service was rooted in another attitude:

> Do nothing from selfishness or empty conceit, but with humility of mind regard one another as more important than yourselves; do not *merely* look out for your own personal interests, but also for the interests of others. Have this attitude in yourselves which was also in Christ Jesus, who, although He existed in the form of God, did not regard equality with God a thing to be grasped, but emptied Himself, taking the form of a bond-servant, *and* being made in the likeness of men (Phil. 2:3-7).

The worldly mentality says, "I have more, so I have earned the right to give less." The heavenly mentality says, "I have more, so I have inherited the responsibility to give more"; for "from everyone who has been given much, much will be required; and to whom they entrusted much, of him they will ask all the more" (Luke 12:48). The enemy of a servant is "to think more highly of himself than he ought to think" (Rom. 12:3) because that promotes the deception that he has earned, gained, or deserved something. This mentality is corrected in 1 Corinthians 4:7: "For who regards you as superior? What do you have that you did not receive? And if you did receive it, why do you boast as if you had not received it?"

Insecurity may keep us from serving. Like Zacchaeus, we perceive ourselves to be *little* so we try to make ourselves *bigger*. In so doing, we remove ourselves from the arena of service. We climb up trees to see Jesus, only to put Jesus' lowly standard for service below us while He says, "'Hurry and come down'" (Luke 19:5). Like Christ "humbled Himself" (Phil. 2:8), we must lower ourselves if we want to engage in transformative service. Get down from that tree of insecurity, selfishness, and pride. Serve!

JANUARY 24

DISOWN YOURSELF TO FIND YOUR REAL OWNER

"Blessed are the pure in heart, for they shall see God."

Matthew 5:8

Pure water is defined as water from which all impurities have been removed. Pure gold has no other metals mixed in. A pure heart is a heart that is not mixed with falsehood or deceit—deceiving others or yourself. Deceit is a mixing of actions—doing one thing while showing to others another thing or thinking one thing while telling yourself another thing. Psalm 24:4 defines a pure person as "he who has clean hands and a pure heart, Who has not lifted up his soul to falsehood And has not sworn deceitfully." James 4:8 describes impurity of heart and commands us to deal with our sin:

"Draw near to God and He will draw near to you. Cleanse your hands, you sinners; and purify your hearts, you double-minded."

To be pure in heart includes an inward moral purity and sincerity. It also includes an outward commitment or separation (holiness) as exemplified in the lives of Samuel and Samson, who were "dedicated to the LORD" (1 Sam. 1:28; Judges 13:5). It implies an acceptance that your body and life are not your own. The beatitude in the Sermon on the Mount says, "Blessed are the pure in heart, for they shall see God" (Matt. 5:8). Those who are pure in heart give of themselves and, in so doing, see God as they put self-ownership on the cross and bear the fruit of goodness.

Blessings are free. Like salvation, you cannot earn them (Eph. 2:8-10). That does not mean, however, that they are not costly. We try to hang onto that which is not our own. The beatitude (blessing) includes the cost of a challenge or an obligation. It is quite a challenge to forfeit ownership of yourself.

First Corinthians 6:18-20 commands, "Flee immorality. Every *other* sin that a man commits is outside the body, but the immoral man sins against his own body. Or do you not know that your body is a temple of the Holy Spirit who is in you, whom you have from God, and that you are not your own? For you have been bought with a price: therefore glorify God in your body."

Jesus is the ultimate Example of One Who laid down His life and renounced self-ownership. "I am the good shepherd; the good shepherd lays down His life for the sheep" (John 10:11). Like Jesus, those who live in the kingdom of God must nail self-ownership to the cross. The freedom to do whatever you want to do must be relinquished.

The provision or blessing of being pure in heart is seeing God. To see God is to see your Creator. Only God is good (Luke 18:19). So, to see God is to see goodness, which is the fruit of the Spirit that corresponds to this beatitude (Gal. 5:22).

The nature of the kingdom of God—relative to the kingdoms of this world—is backwards; it is "flip flopped." Each beatitude in the Sermon on the Mount, therefore, is cloaked in irony. "Blessed are the pure in heart, for they shall see God" (Matthew 5:8) = We must renounce seeing ourselves as our own owners; then we will see our real owner.

JANUARY 25

GRIN AND BEAR IT

"Bear one another's burdens."

Galatians 6:2

Someone might say, "Bear someone else's burdens? I have enough burdens of my own." The implication is that the existence of your burdens somehow *exempts* you from bearing someone else's when in actuality, you are *more* qualified. In order to carry the load of another, you must first carry your own load.

> Brethren, even if anyone is caught in any trespass, you who are spiritual, restore such a one in a spirit of gentleness; *each one* looking to yourself, so that you too will not be tempted. Bear one another's burdens, and thereby fulfill the law of Christ. For if anyone thinks he is something when he is nothing, he deceives himself. But each one must examine his own work, and then he will have *reason for* boasting in regard to himself alone, and not in regard to another. For each one will bear his own load (Gal. 6:1-5).

An interpretive translation of this passage might be:

Brethren, even if anyone is caught in any trespass, you who are spiritual, restore such a one in a spirit of gentleness [a non-judgmental spirit which is what being spiritual means since gentleness is a fruit of the spirit]; each one looking to yourself [and your own tendency to sin], so that you too will not be tempted to sin since in looking to yourself you will understand that you certainly could sin, and therefore, you will be more likely not to sin in the area of judging another). Bear one another's burdens [show mercy and offer grace], and thereby fulfill the law of Christ ["For sin shall not be master over you, for you are not under law but under grace" (Rom. 6:14)]. For if anyone thinks he is something [not looking to yourself and your own sin] when he is nothing [looking to yourself and your own sin], he deceives himself [he thinks that he is "all that" and therefore is judgmental toward others]. But each one must examine his own work [his own tendency to sin], and then he will have reason for boasting in regard to himself alone [in other words, he will not boast since he sees his own sin], and not in regard to another [boasting comes when you compare yourself with another having given yourself the comparative benefit of the doubt]. For each one will bear *his own* load [when you understand that you are responsible for yourself first and foremost, then you will take out the log in your own eye and then be able to take out the speck in someone else's eye; first experience, understand and admit that you have your own "load" and then you can better experience, understand and bear someone else's "load"].

To bear someone else's burdens is to have compassion on that person. The word "compassion" comes from two Latin words—*con* (with) and *pati* (suffer). To have compassion on someone is "to suffer with." This explains why people who have suffered much in life are also people who are able to bear other's burdens. Sufferers are more likely to look at others relative to themselves en route to helping others.

Do not judge so that you will not be judged. For in the way you judge, you will be judged; and by your standard of measure, it will be measured to you. Why do you look at the speck that is in your brother's eye, but do not notice the log that is in your own eye? Or how can you say to your brother, "Let me take the speck out of your eye," and behold, the log is in your own eye? You hypocrite, first take the log out of your own eye, and then you will see clearly to take the speck out of your brother's eye (Matt. 7:1-5).

In order to carry the load of another, you must first carry your own load. In order to take the speck out of someone else's eye, you must first take the log out of your own eye. In order to help someone who is suffering, you must "suffer with" that person. Bear one another's burdens and fulfill the law of Christ!

JANUARY 26

AN OPEN DOOR TO THE POOR

"Seeing the people, He felt compassion for them,
because they were distressed and dispirited like sheep without a shepherd."

Matthew 9:36

If we want to minister to the poor, then we need to try to see life through their eyes and embody attitudes that will motivate us to effectively help them. People living in extreme poverty live very difficult lives. Their plight may be much of their own doing; or they may be victims, for the most part. Often, it is some level of a combination of the two. In any case, the person was probably born into some degree of poverty and has been conditioned to live that way. In many cases, a poor person has never seen or felt hope. Ministry to the poor, more than anything else, must focus on the hope that is offered by the Gospel. Jesus offers a hope to the needy that can free them from their chains.

Living in poverty for an extended period of time can develop in a person a "poverty culture" or a "poverty mentality." This mentality is detrimental to any attempt to escape their circumstances. It feeds poverty by insisting that it is necessary. Actions are based on the idea that "what I do does not matter because nothing will ever change." This must be addressed via a renewing of the mind. The poor person must be encouraged not to accept their chains. In order to change, a person must be taught and encouraged to define attainable goals. Casting vision and offering motivation are necessary activities in helping someone who is bound up in a poverty mentality.

The most important words to describe an effective attitude for ministering to the poor are "empathy" and "compassion." To help the needy, there must be a sincere interest in and concern for the needy. To have compassion on someone is to suffer with that person. The poor person needs to feel that you sincerely care about him. He needs to see that you understand him and his problems and are willing to "step into his shoes" and see life through his eyes. Of course, the expression, "But for the grace of God, there go I" is helpful to keep in mind. On the way to developing and keeping an empathetic attitude, remind yourself that you could have been born into a family of poverty. It is compassion that often moved Jesus to reach out to the needy (Matt. 9:36; Matt. 15:32). It was the compassionate Good Samaritan—not the compassionless priest or Levite—who helped the needy man on the road to Jericho:

> But a Samaritan, who was on a journey, came upon him; and when he saw him, he felt compassion, and came to him and bandaged up his wounds, pouring oil and wine on *them*; and he put him on his own beast, and brought him to an inn and took care of him. On the next day he took out two denarii and gave them to the innkeeper and said, "Take care of him; and whatever more you spend, when I return I will repay you" (Luke 10:33-35).

What can I do to help a person in extreme need? First, build a strong relationship with him or her. Then, you can more authoritatively confront and challenge him in an appropriate way. However, do not speak with an attitude of superiority. A poor person will perceive this type of negative attitude, and he will resent it and reject you. Showing respect can open the door. Poor people are not used to being shown respect, so that sentiment is highly valued. A poor person is a human being just like you. Treat him or her the same as you would any other human being.

Jesus provides a rationale for showing respect to the needy. He says, "But when you give a reception, invite *the* poor, *the* crippled, *the* lame, *the* blind, and you will be blessed, since they do not have *the means* to repay you; for you will be repaid at the resurrection of the righteous" (Luke 14:13-14).

An attitude of commitment is critical in ministry to the poor. Promises must be kept. The poor person probably needs to learn how to have this attitude in his own life. He needs to have a model of commitment by which he can eventually live. This offer of commitment will also produce a sense of trust that will enable the one who is helping the poor person to lead and motivate him. A poor person will have received many empty promises for help in the past. It may be difficult for him to have confidence in other people. He may have many reasons to be skeptical. With an attitude of commitment, sincerity, and compassion, the one who seeks to help the poor builds trust and destroys the sense of skepticism that would close off that help.

If we want to minister to the poor, then we need to try to see life through their eyes and embody attitudes that will motivate us to effectively help them. Compassion, empathy, relationship-building, and commitment all stand as attitudes that can open doors in reaching out to those in need. Will you walk through the doors?

JANUARY 27

IF PRAYER DOES NOT CHANGE GOD

"God is not a man ... that He should repent."

Numbers 23:19

Can prayer change God? Can I pray things into existence and make God change His mind? If not, then is prayer useless? In order to answer these questions, we must first answer three other questions.

First, who is man? Man is not a creator, he is a receiver. He is not *the grace*; he is the means of grace. He is a conduit for the flow, the vessel for the contents, and the pot for the potter. Second, what is the free will of man? Man's free will is not the free will to create; it is the free will to receive. "But as many as received Him, to them He gave the right to become children of God, even to those who believe in His name, who were born, not of blood nor of the will of the flesh nor of the will of man, but of God" (John 1:12-13). Third, what is prayer? Prayer is not creating or changing God's will; it is receiving or agreeing with God's will.

How does man's free will operate within God's sovereignty? Man chooses God's choice (Matt. 22:1-14). Man's free will comes alongside God's sovereignty and, thus, is involved with it. Man either freely agrees with and, therefore, becomes a carrier or conduit of God's sovereignty; or he freely disagrees with and, therefore, does not become a carrier or conduit of God's sovereignty. In both cases, man's free will is exercised and is involved with God's sovereignty, while at the same time it does not become sovereign itself by creating, changing, or thwarting God's will.

Does our choice change God's mind? God's mind cannot "change," since God exists outside of time and change is a "within time" concept. His choice is neither before, during, or after our choice. As it is both never and always, it is sovereign with respect to our choice. It is "outside" and "above" the realm of our choice.

If prayer does not change God, then what is changed? Does prayer matter? Change, by definition, is a time-bound concept. Thus, change, as it relates to prayer, cannot occur with a timeless Being, Who does not change (Mal, 3:6). Change can only occur with a time-bound being (man). Prayer does not change God; it changes man.

So, the point of prayer is to be involved in what God is doing. It is not doing it ourselves or changing it; it is being involved in it. Prayer is very significant, powerful, and worthwhile. God uses prayer as an avenue or channel through which His will is done. It is not creating or changing His will; it is delivering it. It is not the letter in the mailbox; it is the mailman who delivers it.

To be a deliverer of God's will is an incredibly impacting activity, an incredibly significant pursuit, and an incredibly rewarding endeavor. This "mystery of the kingdom of God" (Mark 4:11) in which He uses us to accomplish His will does not diminish His sovereignty; it actually magnifies it, since He is sovereign over both the ends and the means. Neither does the mystery diminish our free will; it actually magnifies it because we get to be involved.

The answer to all the previous questions can rightly be summed up this way. God is God, and man is not. Man is man, and God is not. You are only useless if you try to be who you are not. Praying as if you were the Creator is useless. Praying as if you were the creation can accomplish much. So, go on. Get in your prayer closet—or your mail truck—and deliver the mail!

JANUARY 28

SO WHAT IS THE GOSPEL, ANYWAY?

"For I am not ashamed of the gospel, for it is the power of God for salvation to everyone who believes."

Romans 1:16

What do you think of when you hear the word "gospel"? Perhaps you think of the Gospel of Matthew. Maybe you think of a sort of exclamation, "That's gospel!" Perhaps you think of a "gospel choir" or "gospel music." What does the word itself actually mean, and where did it come from?

The word *gospel* means "good news." Most specifically, it refers to the Good News of salvation that is found through knowing Jesus Christ. The New Testament term is derived from an Old Testament word—*basar*. It was originally used as a military term, meaning "to report the good news of a victory in battle" (2 Sam. 4:10). A messenger would be sent after a successful battle to tell the people back home about the results. The "good news" of victory in battle was directly associated with being saved (Isa. 52:7) from total destruction or being delivered (Psalm 40:10) from death at the hands of the enemy. The messenger would run from village to village announcing this good news. Also, he would announce that the victorious king would soon arrive to celebrate with the people that the enemy had been defeated. Naturally, the Christian community adopted this understanding and applied it to the saving work of Jesus Christ. A messenger of the Gospel became understood as being anyone who announced the Good News of salvation in Christ.

The basic Gospel message includes a flow of thought or a list of facts that build the Good News idea. First, God created man and desired fellowship with him (Gen. 1:27); however, man became separated from God by sin (Rom. 3:23). Sin leads to eternal death (Rom. 6:23). God has a plan of redemption, however, that allows Him to buy man back. This plan centers on the incredible act of God's only Son, Jesus Christ, Who becomes a man and lives a sinless life (John 1:14). Jesus died sacrificially on a cross on behalf of all people to restore them to relationship with God (2 Cor. 5:14-21; 1 John 4:9-10). God then raised Jesus from the dead and, thus, defeated sin (1 Cor. 15:4). Therefore, those who repent (turn away from their sin and turn to God) and believe in Christ are restored to God by His grace (Eph. 2:8-9).

The term *gospel* assumes a gospel messenger. It is not just the existence of good news, but it is also the proclamation of this good news. The one who would run all the way back from the battlefield with the good news would not be satisfied to just wait outside the gates of the city and keep the gospel to himself. Someone who has good news has a hard time keeping it to himself. Gospel content assumes Gospel-sharing (Rom. 1:16). When proclaiming the Gospel, the messenger should focus on the work of the cross. Paul exclaimed, "For I determined to know nothing among you except Jesus Christ, and Him crucified" (1 Cor. 2:2). Emphasize that Jesus, although sinless Himself, willingly bore our sin. Stress the idea that Jesus died a sacrificial death—that is, that He died instead of us. Highlight God's resurrection power to raise Christ from the dead and the victory that His resurrection assures for us.

Summarize the good news by explaining that we had an insurmountable problem that, otherwise, could not be fixed; but God provided the miraculous solution. Now that surely *is* Good News!

JANUARY 29

SKILLS OF GOOD COUNSELORS

"All Scripture is inspired by God and profitable for teaching, for reproof, for correction."
2 Timothy 3:16

Perhaps, most specifically, wisdom is the single most important thing to be able to offer someone who needs counsel or help. So, it is no wonder that it is Proverbs—the book of wisdom—that serves as the counselor's handbook. People who are able to help others are helped themselves by having certain "wisdom skills."

Just as having certain traits are typical of effective counselors, so, too, are having certain skills essential for those who want to help others. The skill of asking questions is one of those critical skills. Effective question-asking allows a counselor to draw out both information and therapeutic thinking from the one he is helping. This sort of Socratic method of counseling provides an opportunity for self-exploration.

Some of the more basic questions might be understood as information-gathering questions. "What did you do then?" A bit more involved are clarifying questions. "How did that happen?" Even more facilitating are reflective questions. "You knew you were wrong, but you saw no way to avoid it?" Similar to reflective questions are connecting questions. "You were happy until . . ."

Perhaps the questions that might produce the most fruit are "confronting" questions. "Do you ever hug your son? When was the last time you hugged your son?" The counselor must not shy away from these more uncomfortable questions. When engaging in confrontation, the counselor can ease the feeling of awkwardness by beginning with a statement of assurance that tells the person, "I understand. I am aware of all of the circumstances. I have considered the whole situation."

Scripture should be used when confronting someone. "All Scripture is inspired by God and profitable for teaching, for reproof, for correction" (2 Tim. 3:16). Be firm. Be specific. Be direct. When the time comes to confront the person, it does not help to be general or vague. Be careful to not only allow a response but to also encourage a response.

We all need help at some time or another. When someone needs a listening ear and a voice of wisdom, it is a great blessing that there be someone who is able to use their traits and skills to offer effective biblical counseling. Are you ready to help?

JANUARY 30

PEACE, CHILD

"Blessed are the peacemakers, for they shall be called sons of God."
Matthew 5:9

The hardest thing about being a peacemaker is that peacemakers do not insist on holding onto their rights; they are willing to relinquish their rights for the sake of preventing strife. Take Abram for example:

> Now Lot, who went with Abram, also had flocks and herds and tents. And the land could not sustain them while dwelling together, for their possessions were so great that they were not able to remain together. And there was strife between the herdsmen of Abram's

livestock and the herdsmen of Lot's livestock. Now the Canaanite and the Perizzite were dwelling then in the land. So Abram said to Lot, "Please let there be no strife between you and me, nor between my herdsmen and your herdsmen, for we are brothers. Is not the whole land before you? Please separate from me; if *to* the left, then I will go to the right; or if *to* the right, then I will go to the left" (Gen. 13:5-9).

Abram had the right to get his first choice as to where to go. He was Lot's uncle and his elder. For the sake of harmony, he allowed Lot to have his preference. He laid down his rights for the sake of peace. "Blessed are the peacemakers, for they shall be called sons of God" (Matt. 5:9). Peacemakers promote harmony between men and between man and God. They give of themselves and are sons of God via putting self-rights on the cross and, thus, bearing the fruit of kindness.

Blessings are free. Like salvation, you cannot earn them (Eph. 2:8-10). That does not mean, however, that they are not costly because we try to hang onto that which is not our own (1 Cor. 6:19-20). The beatitude (blessing) includes the cost of a challenge or an obligation. It is quite a challenge to "give in" so as to "peace out."

Jesus is our Example. He had the attitude of a peacemaker. "Have this attitude in yourselves which was also in Christ Jesus, who, although He existed in the form of God, did not regard equality with God a thing to be grasped, but emptied Himself, taking the form of a bond-servant" (Phil. 2:5-7). In order to make peace between God and men, Jesus was willing to empty Himself by laying aside His privileges and His rights.

The provision or blessing of being a peacemaker is that you are called a son of God; you acquire the rights of a son. The fruit of the Spirit that corresponds to this beatitude is "kindness" (Gal. 5:22). Peacemakers are kind-hearted people. They are like their Father!

The nature of the kingdom of God—relative to the kingdoms of this world—is backwards. Each beatitude in the Sermon on the Mount, therefore, is cloaked in irony. "Blessed are the peacemakers, for they shall be called sons of God" (Matt. 5:9). We must lay down our rights; then we will be given the rights of a son.

JANUARY 31

THE PURPOSE OF MONEY AND POSSESSIONS

*"The land of a rich man was very productive. And he began reasoning to himself, saying, 'What shall I do, since I have no place to store my crops?' Then he said, 'This is what I will do: I will tear down my barns and build larger ones, and there I will store all my grain and my goods. And I will say to my soul, 'Soul, you have many goods laid up for many years to **come**; take your ease, eat, drink **and** be merry.' But God said to him, 'You fool!'"*

Luke 12:16-20

Money and possessions are a big part of our lives. But a wrong and selfish understanding of the purpose of money and possessions is that they only exist in order to provide a comfortable and luxurious life for mankind here on earth. This perspective is not consistent with the type of life that Jesus lived. Jesus did not live for Himself. "For even the Son of Man did not come to be served, but to serve, and to give His life a ransom for many" (Mark 10:45). He did not view money and possessions as being vehicles for His own comfort. He did not just die on the cross; He lived the life of the cross and directed His followers to live that life also. "If anyone wishes to come after Me, he must deny himself, and take up his cross and follow Me" (Matt. 16:24).

God *can* bless us with money and possessions, but He wants us to consider the idea of *stewardship*. God's blessings are not simply meant to make our lives *enjoyable* but to also make us more *employable*. To begin to have any chance to take on this view and apply it to your life, you must submit to a "God" point of view instead of a "self" point of view. This is very difficult to do, especially when your culture—everyone and everything around you—is screaming the opposite.

Even church culture often champions a "self" point of view when it comes to money and possessions "You deserve it. God wants to bless you. You are a King's kid. You are on top, looking down—the head, not the tail. Living in luxury is living in the kingdom." There is a little bit of a biblical problem with this kind of "kingdom logic." For Jesus, the living in the "kingdom" and being "a King's kid" is more associated with *giving* than *consuming* for your own pleasure.

Luke 12:31-34 encourages, "But seek His kingdom, and these things will be added to you. Do not be afraid, little flock, for your Father has chosen gladly to give you the kingdom. Sell your possessions and give to charity; make yourselves money belts which do not wear out, an unfailing treasure in heaven, where no thief comes near nor moth destroys. For where your treasure is, there your heart will be also (Luke 12:31-34).

The purpose of any blessing—including money and possessions—is to glorify the name of Jesus. Does that mean that we cannot enjoy God's blessings? No, it only means that enjoyment is not the **purpose** of the blessing. It is an *effect* of using the blessing correctly. When we begin to understand this difference, we begin to be balanced with respect to the question of purpose. We do not seek after the blessing for ourselves. We seek after it to bless others and to glorify God. More specifically, we seek after it to glorify God by blessing others. Followers of Christ are givers who are motivated by love for God and love for others. They are followers of the One Who loved and, therefore, gave. "For God so loved the world, that He gave His only begotten Son, that whoever believes in Him shall not perish, but have eternal life" (John 3:16). Stewardship is a "pass it on" concept. It seeks to use the blessing and multiply it.

At the same time, we do not need to refuse to enjoy the natural side effects that are included with blessings. A lack of a balanced understanding of material blessings results in either legalism or uncontrolled license. It results in Christians who cannot enjoy life or in Christians who are selfish, superficial, and carnal.

Stewards do not bury their blessings in the ground to hide them (Matt. 25:24-28), nor do they pile them up in barns to store them away (Luke 12:16-21). They do not view money and possessions as simply being that which establishes and sustains their own comfort. "And I will say to my soul, 'Soul, you have many goods laid up for many years to come; take your ease, eat, drink and be merry.' But God said to him, 'You fool!'" (Luke 12:19-20).

What is the purpose of money and possessions? Whatever you understand that answer to be, you want to make sure you eventually hear the words, "Well done, good and faithful slave. You were faithful with a few things, I will put you in charge of many things; enter into the joy of your master'" (Matt. 25:21). You do not want to hear the words, "You fool! This *very* night your soul is required of you; and *now* who will own what you have prepared? So is the man who stores up treasure for himself, and is not rich toward God" (Luke 12:20-21).

Make it a matter of prayer. "God, how should I look at my money and possessions? What do you want me to do with them? Teach me how to be blessed by them by being a blessing with them."

February

FEBRUARY 1

HOW ARE YOU? . . . I AM BLESSED!

*"And I will make you a great nation, And I will bless you, And make your name great;
And so you shall be a blessing."*

Genesis 12:2

In what are often referred to as prehistoric times, the Bible describes Creation, the Fall of man, the progressive wickedness of man leading to the Flood, and finally, the scattering of the nations at the tower of Babel (Gen. 1-11). Then comes Genesis 12 and God's choosing of an individual through whom He could work. What happened? Did God suddenly decide to forsake the human race? Maybe He was frustrated. Did He choose a favorite person in order to appease Himself? No, nothing had changed from Genesis 3:14-15 and the initial hint that God had a grand plan for the salvation of man. God simply used a new approach. He began to work His plan *through* chosen instruments. We might call this "vessel theology." Since the nations were now spread out, He chose a missionary nation through which He could reach all nations—Abraham and the nation of Israel.

God selected Israel to be a missionary nation. His missionary plan did not begin in Matthew 28 with the Great Commission. It began in the book of beginnings, Genesis. After the tower of Babel, God scattered the people of the earth into nations and languages (today, there are over five thousand different languages). Then God began to work His plan nation by nation and family by family. The rest of the Bible tells this great missionary story.

Israel was selected as a missionary nation. Israel was not selected in order to exclude others. Rather, Israel was selected in order to *include* others. Israel is not God's "teacher's pet" while all the other students in "the class" are not preferred. Israel's choosing is simply a result of the nature of God's plan. If God is going to work through a vessel to reach others, then, of course, He has to initially choose someone to work through. And so, we can understand the Old Testament better when we study it from three different viewpoints: Israel's opportunity,; Israel's obligation, and Israel's response.

The Abrahamic covenant is a missionary covenant. Through it, Israel is promised the resources and ability to be a blessing to all the families of the earth (Gen. 12:3). Accordingly, Israel received great authority and opportunity, but it came with great responsibility or obligation. "Now the LORD said to Abram, 'Go forth from your country, And from your relatives And from your father's house, To the land which I will show you; And I will make you a great nation, And I will bless you, And make your name great; And so you shall be a blessing'" (Gen. 12:1-2). Just as there are three separate statements of being a blessing There are three separate statements of being blessed: "make you a great nation," "bless you," and "make your name great."

God does not expect us to do what He does not equip us to do (Matt. 25:15; 1 Cor. 10:13). God did not expect Israel to be able to bless the nations unless He first blessed them. In other words, God provided the opportunity to keep the obligation. For example, He provided the opportunities to attract others. Certainly, the temple attracted many people to Israel (1 Kings 8:43). Remember that God said that He would make their name great. Why? Was it just so that they could feel like they were awesome? No! It was so that all the peoples of the earth may know His name. "'Also concerning the foreigner who is not of Your people Israel, when he comes from a far country for Your name's sake (for they will hear of Your great name and Your mighty hand, and of Your outstretched arm) . . . in order that all the peoples of the earth may know Your name, to fear You, as *do* Your people Israel'" (1 Kings 8:41-43). In this and many other ways, Israel was given the opportunity to keep their obligation.

Of course, the application question for us is: what are we doing with the blessings that we have been given? Especially with respect to spreading the gospel all over the world, what are we doing with the resources and abilities that God has given us? God says to us, just like He said to Abraham, "I will bless you *so that* you can be a blessing. Maybe you need to recharge your SO THAT!

FEBRUARY 2

LET'S BUILD A BRIDGE

"But you are A CHOSEN RACE, A royal PRIESTHOOD, A HOLY NATION, A PEOPLE FOR
God's *OWN POSSESSION, so that you may proclaim the excellencies of*
Him who has called you out of darkness into His marvelous light."

1 Peter 2:9

Jesus presented the Gospel in a particular way to Nicodemus, who was a Jew (John 3). He then presented the Gospel in another way to the woman at the well, who was a Samaritan (John 4:7-26). The contents of the Gospel do not change. The method to present the Gospel does change. These different methods are often rooted in the building of relevant "bridges" that are designed to reach someone where they live. Bridges are structures that join together things that, otherwise, are separated.

Christians can use bridge-building to reach Muslims. A Muslim knows that he has not reached God's standards. He prays repeatedly for forgiveness. In Islam, however, there is no assurance of forgiveness, no way to know if you are good enough. A Muslim can only hope. A Christian can use this desire as a bridge to offer the definite forgiveness of God in Christ. Muslims are not pagans or atheists. Islam is a monotheistic religion that emphasizes the reality of one God, the need to submit to that God, and the requirement to revere Him. This can be a bridge to the Gospel. Avoid condemning Islam or speaking negatively of Muhammad. Focus more on speaking positively of Jesus. Speak truth and let *it* do the condemning (John 3:18).

Islamic culture is different than postmodern Western culture in which it is generally not acceptable, as the saying goes, to talk about politics and religion "at the dinner table." Muslims are inclined to speak about the things of God and to converse about religion. This creates a very useful bridge—the *interest* bridge. Muslims view Jesus as a prophet. A Christian can use the interest bridge to connect a Muslim to discussions about Jesus.

Islamic belief about Jesus includes many bridges that can help connect a Muslim to Christianity. The virgin birth is mentioned in the Koran. A Christian can use this as a bridge to establish Jesus as a unique Person, Who is the only way to God. The Koran does not deny the supernatural ministry of Jesus. It affirms that Jesus cast out demons, healed lepers, gave sight to the blind, made the deaf to hear, and raised people from the dead. Muslims are very curious about the miracles of Jesus. This curiosity is a bridge to establish Jesus' deity.

The Koran also affirms Jesus' sinless life. This can be used as a bridge to lead the Muslim to recognize the perfect substitutionary death of Jesus. The Koran affirms the second coming of Christ. According to the Koran, Jesus (not Muhammad) will return to earth to reign for forty years. This can be used as a bridge to lead the Muslim to accept Jesus as the Judge.

Muslims accept the Gospels as holy books. They must be challenged with the question, "If you believe Jesus' teachings, then why do you not obey His commands?" Their own hypocrisy can be used as a bridge. The Koran refers to Jesus as the "Word of God." This can be a bridge that can be used to ask the Muslim to consider more closely the identity of Jesus Christ. What is the Word of God? Who is Jesus?

Bridges connect things. The wise presenter of the Gospel can use bridges to connect Muslims to Jesus. This is the work of a *priest*. He connects people to God. Paul said, "Because of the grace that was given me from God, to be a minister of Christ Jesus to the Gentiles, ministering as a priest the gospel of God" (Rom. 15:15-16). Christians are bridge-builders. They are the royal priesthood that proclaim the Gospel and serve to connect people to God. Put on your priestly garments. Build bridges!

FEBRUARY 3

TO BE READY FOR THE END IS TO BE A GOOD STEWARD

"For this reason you also must be ready."

Matthew 24:44

The question is not so much "When will the end come?" as it is "Are you ready?" If that is true, then the most important question is "How can you be ready?" Jesus answers these questions initially in Matthew 24 and then more fully in Matthew 25. Jesus' disciples asked Him, "'When will these things happen, and what *will be* the sign of Your coming, and of the end of the age?'" (Matt. 24:3). Jesus proceeds to describe what will happen before He returns and the end comes (Matt. 24:4-29). He then says, "Then the sign of the Son of Man will appear in the sky . . . they will see the SON OF MAN COMING ON THE CLOUDS OF THE SKY with power and great glory" (Matt. 24:30).

Jesus tells us what will happen and how it will happen, but He does not tell us when it will happen. Since we do not know when it will happen, we have to make sure we are ready at all times. "'Therefore be on the alert, for you do not know which day your Lord is coming'" (Matt. 24:42). The answer to knowing *when* is the answer to knowing *how* to be ready. Jesus proceeds to tell His disciples three parables to explain how to be ready.

First, in the parable of the ten virgins, He emphasizes the importance of being ready. "And while they were going away to make the purchase, the bridegroom came, and those who were ready went in with him to the wedding feast; and the door was shut" (Matt. 25:10). Some were ready; some were not. Some were allowed in; some were shut out.

Before He offers His disciples a specific description of how to be ready for the end, Jesus paints a more general picture using the parable of the talents. "For *it is* just like a man *about* to go on a journey, who called his own slaves and entrusted his possessions to them'" (Matt. 25:14). A master gives resources to his servants. They are expected to be good stewards of what they have received; they are expected to use the resources and multiply them. Two of them are ready when the master returns because they multiplied his possessions. The master applauds them and deems them "good" and "faithful" stewards (Matt. 25:21, 23). The third servant is not ready for the master's return, since he "dug a *hole* in the ground and hid his master's money" (Matt. 25:18). He does not use it. He does not multiply it. He does not give it. Instead, He keeps it. The master reprimands him and deems him "wicked," "lazy," and "worthless" (Matt. 25:26, 30).

In general, being "ready for the end" has to do with being faithful now, using what you have received in order to multiply God's blessings by giving them away and not simply keeping them for yourself. Jesus uses His last parable to specify such actions. *"I was hungry, and you gave Me something to* eat; I was thirsty, and you gave Me **something** to drink; I was a stranger, and you invited Me in; naked, and you clothed Me; I was sick, and you visited Me; I was in prison, and you came to Me" (Matt. 25:35-36). Those who are needy are in need of help. The hungry, the thirsty, the stranger, the naked, the sick, and those in prison all have one thing in common—they need resources (money, possessions, hospitality, concern, time).

In any case, blessings need to be used. They need to be multiplied by giving them away instead of keeping them or hiding them. Giving resources to those in need multiplies those resources; it is good stewardship. "One who is gracious to a poor man lends to the LORD, And He will repay him for his good deed" (Prov. 19:17). When you give a dinner for the needy, it multiplies resources; it is good stewardship and depicts "being ready" for the end. "'But when you give a reception, invite *the* poor, *the* crippled, *the* lame, *the* blind, and you will be blessed, since they do not have *the means* to repay you; for you will be repaid at the resurrection of the righteous'" (Luke 14:13-14).

Bad stewardship includes keeping what we are given, not using it, not multiplying it, and not helping others with it. Good stewardship is marked by giving. Good stewards are ready for the end to come. In that sense, answer the question, "When will the end come?" The point of Matthew 24-25 is that the end *will* come. Either you will be ready, or you will not be ready. The results are also two-fold. "Then there will be two men in the field; one will be taken and one will be left" (Matt. 24:40).

> For this reason you also must be ready . . . "Who then is the faithful and sensible slave whom his master put in charge of his household to give them their food at the proper time? Blessed is that slave . . . But if that evil slave says in his heart, 'My master is not coming for a long time,' and begins to beat his fellow slaves and eat and drink with drunkards; the master . . . will cut him in pieces and assign him a place with the hypocrites; in that place there will be weeping and gnashing of teeth" (Matt. 24:44-51).

The question, "Are you ready?" is very sobering. Which option will you choose? "'These will go away into eternal punishment, but the righteous into eternal life'" (Matt. 25:46). Choose life!

FEBRUARY 4

WHO OR WHAT IS YOUR "WHO SAYS?"

> *"'By what authority are You doing these things.'"*
>
> Matthew 21:23

What is worldview? It is the lens through which you view the world, authoritative spectacles that fashion what you believe to be true. A worldview is a collection of presuppositions or assumptions that are applied to one's life based on what is perceived to be real or authoritative. It is the underlying authority structure that determines how a person thinks and acts.

Someone who has a "biblical worldview" is a person who holds the Bible as his or her final authority. Why do you believe that Jesus loves you? "The Bible tells me so!" Who or what is your boss? The answer to that question dictates your worldview. Young children have a "Mommy and Daddy" worldview. Mommy and Daddy are their bosses, their authorities. They represent to the child what is real. If Mommy and Daddy say it, then it must be so! Everybody has a worldview. Everybody has a "Who says?"

Worldviews create cultures. The most obvious and outward level of culture is behavior. What do people do? How do they act? What patterns can be observed with respect to how they do things? The next level of culture is represented by the values of people. What do they think is good or beneficial?

What do they think *should* be done? The next level of culture is represented by the beliefs of people. What is true? The most profound level of culture is worldview. What is real? What is authoritative? What someone thinks is real or authoritative will lead to what someone believes to be true. What someone thinks is true will form what someone values. What someone values will result in what someone does. People do not just do things "out of thin air." They do what they think is beneficial to do. They think it is beneficial because they think it is right. They think it is right because some authority told them so. That is their worldview.

Actions ultimately come from worldview. A person whose worldview includes the belief that there is no life after death will believe that there is no judgment by a God after death. This can open the door to hedonistic values in which pleasure is understood to be the most important experience. Hedonistic values lead to hedonistic actions. A promiscuous lifestyle may be traced back to the belief that there is no life after death.

Utilitarianism is a worldview that says that truth is determined by the usefulness of results; the end justifies the means. Someone robs a bank, and you wonder why he would do such a thing. It is not simply because "it was there." It goes back to what that person perceives as being real or authoritative. Hedonism is a worldview that says that truth is based on pleasure and the avoidance of discomfort. Someone becomes a heroin addict, and you wonder why she would do such a thing. It is not simply because there was nothing else to do. It can be traced back to what that person perceives as being real or authoritative. Postmodernism is a worldview that says that truth is created by the individual; it is true because you say it is true. A girl insists that she is a boy, and you wonder why she feels like she could say such a thing. It may go back to a postmodern worldview that encourages her to be whatever gender she wants to be, since people make their own reality.

Worldviews play a central and defining role in our lives. They shape what we believe, how we interpret our experiences, how we behave in response to those experiences, and how we relate to others. Our thoughts and our actions are conditioned by our worldviews. The connection between authority and actions was expressed by the chief priests when they said to Jesus, "'By what authority are You doing these things'" (Matt. 21:23). You can only have one boss. You cannot have two final authorities, two worldviews. Jesus makes this point with regard to materialism when He says, "'You cannot serve God and wealth'" (Matt. 6:24).

So, what is your worldview? Who is your boss? Who is your "Who says?" Make the Word of God your final authority and reap the benefits of a godly life.

FEBRUARY 5

ARE THE GIFTS OF THE SPIRIT FOR TODAY?

*"Now concerning spiritual **gifts**, brethren, I do not want you to be unaware."*
1 Corinthians 12:1

Are the gifts of the Spirit for today, or did they cease to exist? One way to answer this question is with another question. What is "today"? Is it 50 A.D. or is it 140 or maybe 200 or perhaps 397? Maybe it's none of those "todays," and it is actually 1647 or 1865. Or maybe, just maybe, it is actually 2020. If it is 2020 or even 397, then how did it work? At what time of the "today" did the Holy Spirit stop manifesting Himself through the distinguishing of spirits or the word of wisdom? Was it 11:00 a.m. or was it 7:38 p.m.? Did the Spirit manifest Himself through a word of wisdom at 10:59 a.m. but then cut Himself off when the clock struck eleven?

Another way to approach this question is, again, with another question. Why would the gifts not be for today? Does the Scripture present them, in any way, as being temporary? No, in fact, the Scripture puts significant emphasis on them with regard to the ministry of the church (1 Cor. 12-14). There are even commandments given to "desire earnestly" and "not forbid" the gifts of the Spirit (1 Cor. 14:39).

Perhaps, the most serious question to ask is "What other aspects of ministry or activities of God have ceased to exist?" If the gifts stopped operating at some point in Church history, did preaching, teaching, counseling, hospitality, evangelism, or serving also stop operating? If God stopped manifesting Himself in certain biblical ways, did He also stop exhibiting His mercy, faithfulness, or provision at some point in time? Nothing in Scripture would make us think that any of these things ceased. So, too, there is nothing in Scripture that would make us think that the gifts that are presented in Scripture as being normative and ongoing in the Church ceased from being manifested.

The cessationist position that says the gifts have ceased tends to be built on a faulty hermeneutic of 1 Corinthians 13:10, which says, "But when the perfect comes, the partial will be done away." Somehow, this verse is interpreted as meaning when the canon is closed, then the gifts will cease. There is nothing, however, in the context and content of this passage that would lend itself toward this interpretation.

> Love never fails; but *if there are gifts of* prophecy, they will be done away; if *there are* tongues, they will cease; if *there is* knowledge, it will be done away. For we know in part and we prophesy in part; but when the perfect comes, the partial will be done away. When I was a child, I used to speak like a child, think like a child, reason like a child; when I became a man, I did away with childish things. For now we see in a mirror dimly, but then face to face; now I know in part, but then I will know fully just as I also have been fully known (1 Cor. 13:8-12).

There is a very clearly repeated structure in this passage. In this age, knowledge and prophecy are imperfect, "but *when* the perfect comes," the imperfect will pass away (vv. 9-10, emphasis mine). Similarly, I used to speak, think, and reason like a child, but "*when* I became a man, I did away with childish things" (v. 11). Also, now I see "dimly," and I only "know in part"; but *then* I see "face to face" and "will know fully just as I have been fully known" (v. 12).

Two conclusions can easily be made here. First, something is definitely going to cease, and it is the gifts (v. 8). These gifts are referred to as that which will be "done away" and that which "will cease." They are "childish things" that are "in part" and only "partial." They are tantamount to seeing "in a mirror dimly" and only knowing "in part." The second obvious conclusion is that something is going to "come" at some time— that will supersede the gifts and, therefore, do away with them. That "something" that is to "come" is said to be that which is "perfect." It is described, relative to "childish things," as becoming "a man." It will happen when I see "face to face" and "know fully just as I also have been fully known."

In conclusion, the passage declares that the gifts will cease when the perfect comes. Whatever the "'perfect'" is, we do know that it is going to "come" and will include us seeing it "face to face." As a result, we will "know fully." The perfect is not the closing of the canon. The Perfect is Jesus Himself. It is the return of Christ. Many passages in Scripture refer to the return of Christ as His coming (Matt. 24; 1 Thess. 2-5; 2 Thess. 2; Heb. 10:37; James 5:7-8; Rev. 22:20). When the "perfect comes," the gifts will no longer be needed Why? It is because we will then know Him fully just as we have been fully known. When and how does this transformation happen? The Scripture tells us that "it has not appeared as yet what we will be. We know that when He appears, we will be like Him, because we will see Him just as He is" (1 John 3:2-3).

Perfect revelation results in perfect transformation. When Christ comes—that is, when the perfect comes—we shall all be changed because we will see Him face to face. In 1 Corinthians 13, we see that we do not have full knowledge and that the gifts will be done away *when* the perfect comes and we see "face to face." In 1 John 3, we see that *when* He appears, we will be changed and have full knowledge because we see Him "just as He is." The gifts will cease when Jesus returns. But until then, the gifts are still being manifested. And there is no reason to think otherwise (1 Cor. 1:4-7).

Prior to the "love chapter" (1 Cor. 13), we are commanded to desire the gifts (1 Cor. 12:31). We are certainly not instructed to negate or forbid them (1 Cor. 14:39). We are shown how to use them in "a still more excellent way" (1 Cor. 12:31). The point of emphasizing "love" in the middle of the long discourse on spiritual gifts is in no way to suggest the disuse of the gifts but to encourage a better use of the gifts—to use the gifts in love. The gifts of the Spirit have not ceased. The Spirit continues to manifest Himself!

FEBRUARY 6

WAR HAS BEEN DECLARED

"For though we walk in the flesh, we do not war according to the flesh, for the weapons of our warfare are not of the flesh, but divinely powerful for the destruction of fortresses."

2 Corinthians 10:3-4

The devil hates the spread of the Gospel more than anything else. It is the thing that both converts men (whom he hates) and wins back the kingdom to God (Whom he hates even more). Thus, spiritual warfare and evangelism naturally go together. Gospel messengers who do not engage in spiritual warfare leave themselves exposed to the wiles of the enemy. The existence of a war requires that soldiers fight in order to gain victory.

The following is a letter from a missionary who worked in the jungles of New Guinea. He wrote these words to friends at home:

> Man, it is great to be in the thick of the fight, to draw the old devil's heaviest guns, to have him at you with depression and discouragement, slander, disease. He does not waste time on a lukewarm bunch. He hits good and hard when a fellow is hitting him. You can always measure the weight of your blow by the one you get back. When you are on your back with fever and at your last ounce of strength, when some of your converts backslide, when you learn that your most promising inquirers are only fooling, when your mail gets held up, and some do not bother to answer your letters, is that the time to put on mourning? No, sir! That is the time to pull out the stops and shout Hallelujah! The old fellow's getting it in the neck and getting it back. Heaven is leaning over the battlements and watching. Will he stick with it? And as they see who is with us, as they see the unlimited reserves, the boundless resources, as they see the impossibility of failure, how disgusted and sad they must be when we run away. Glory to God! We are not going to run away.[1]

Engaging in spiritual warfare is an essential activity for all Christians because all Christians, in one way or another, are witnesses for Christ and propagators of the kingdom of God. Spiritual warfare is not optional for anyone who is willing to enter enemy territory by spreading the Gospel.

Often, missionaries experience more spiritual warfare than others for two main reasons. First, they are on the frontlines of battle and get attacked more often. Second, on many mission fields in more remote and primitive settings, the forces of Satan are much more obvious. Witchcraft and pagan worship make the war much more visible than it is in Western cultures. This in no way means that spiritual warfare does not exist in Western cultures. It is just not as visible and obvious. In some ways, this makes the war that *is* going on in these places more difficult.

Although those living out a more "comfortable" type of Christianity may not recognize it, there is a spiritual war taking place. This war is real and constant. Christians are to "suffer hardship with *me* as a good soldier of Christ Jesus" (2 Tim. 2:3). It is possible for a Christian to avoid this war. If he does not bother the enemy, then he may—for a time—be able to live as though the war is not going on. However, the enemy will have an easier time gaining a foothold because the inactive soldier is not prepared.

Each believer must make a conscious decision to participate in the spiritual war. The primary motive must be to please the Commander. "No soldier in active service entangles himself in the affairs of everyday life, so that he may please the one who enlisted him as a soldier" (2 Tim. 2:4).

There are two primary ways that the devil deceives people. He either tries to convince them that he is unbeatable, or he tries to convince them that he does not exist. The devil is real, and the spiritual war against him is real. What if you lived in a town where a battle was being fought? Battalions of soldiers with machine guns, tanks, and fighter jets are everywhere. Would you ignore them and live as though they were not there? No, of course not! You are already beaten if you fail to recognize the war. Spiritual warfare is real!

FEBRUARY 7

IMPROVE YOUR MINISTRY OF THE WORD

"How can a young man keep his way pure? By keeping it according to Your word. With all my heart I have sought You; do not let me wander from Your commandments. Your word I have treasured in my heart, that I may not sin against You."

Psalm 119:9-11

Are you living your best life? There cannot be a better life than eternal life. Can you live eternal life now? Yes! "This is eternal life, that they may know You, the only true God, and Jesus Christ whom You have sent" (John 17:3). And so, the ultimate question is whether you are walking with God and growing in your relationship with Him? To live your best life is to know God. To know God is to know His Word. How can you improve your "ministry of the Word"?

You can take advantage of the information that is already at hand. Interaction with other believers, past and present, can improve your ministry of the Word. Much understanding and explanation of the Bible can be gleaned from godly theologians, scholars, and practitioners. The reading of quality commentaries, for example, can provide much help for the student of the Bible.

You can improve your ability to study the Bible by engaging in different aspects of hermeneutics (Bible interpretation). Historical analysis is the process that encourages the student of the Word to look at the Bible as though trying to look through a window. Increased exposure to references that explain the culture and historical setting behind biblical content can be of great value to your understanding of the Scriptures. Basic "Bible book survey" types of summaries can serve to refresh your awareness of author, audience, date, setting, and occasion for writing and major topics. All of this will be helpful in preparing to study the Word as though "looking through a window."

Even as historical analysis in hermeneutics allows the student of the Word to view the Bible as a window, literary analysis allows you to view it as a picture. There is the tendency to get lost in the details of Bible study. A literary analysis perspective encourages the student of the Word to allow the more expanded context to inform his or her understanding of the details. You will see things when you look at the forest that you will not see when you only look at the individual trees. Bible students need to practice looking for the wider flow of a passage in the Bible. One way to do this is to think of a passage in terms of scene division. Study can be done from the perspective of looking at the text as a play. The "scenes" could then be separated, organized, and presented as such. In preaching and teaching, one will then be more apt to use the pace of the text, more inclined to not neglect allusions to the senses offered by the text, and more equipped to utilize body language and other communication techniques to convey those allusions in the presentation of the Word.

As helpful as engaging in various aspects of hermeneutics can be, more impacting is gleaning information from others in a context of personal interaction. As part of a small group that meets regularly, for example, you can study the Word with other believers. Each member can glean insights and information from the others in the group that will add to their own ministry of the Word. In an inspiring model of this dynamic, John Wesley, the founder of the Methodist movement, was a member of a small group called the "Holy Club." For two hours every morning, those in the club would read, study, and discuss the Word together. This sort of thing can really fuel one's life in the Word and flavor the proclamation of it.

To live your best life is to know God. To know God is to know His Word. It is to live eternal life now. "This is eternal life, that they may know you, the only true God, and Jesus Christ whom you have sent" (John 17:3). The more you improve your ministry of the Word, the more you live eternal life since eternal life is to know God. Declare to God, "I will not forget Your word" (Psalm 119:16). Read the Bible. Study the Word of God. Live your best life!

FEBRUARY 8

WALKING IN FLIP FLOPS BACKWARD

"It is more blessed to give than to receive."

Acts 20:35

It is not as difficult to receive as it is to give. All people want eternal life, but not everyone wants to repent and believe. Salvation is free, *and* it is costly. It is not costly in the sense that we must give something in order to earn salvation. God is the only One Who has enough what is needed to pay for your salvation. "You have been bought with a price" (1 Cor. 6:20). It is costly in the sense that we must give of ourselves in order to surrender to God what is rightfully and already His (1 Cor. 6:19). Salvation is free because it has to be; we have nothing by which to pay for it. It is costly because we try to hang onto that which is not our own.

Giving is the action of love. God loved the world, so He gave (John 3:16). Giving must be our focus. "*It is more blessed to give than to receive*" (Acts 20:35). Giving is more important than receiving because giving precedes and leads to receiving: "'Give, and it will be given to you'" (Luke 6:38). Blessed are the givers. Blessed are those who give of themselves by dying to themselves. "'Blessed are the poor in spirit, for theirs is the kingdom of heaven'" (Matt. 5:3). The character of those who live in the kingdom of God is described by the word "give." Love leads to giving, and giving leads to life. "For God so loved the world, that He gave His only begotten Son, that whoever believes in Him shall not perish, but have eternal life" (John 3:16).

The Dead Sea is the salt-filled sea in Palestine. It is so stagnant that nothing can live in it (that is how dead the Dead Sea is!). The Dead Sea is not dead because it does not receive any water. It is forty-eight miles long and ten miles wide. Each day, 6.5 million tons of water flow into the Dead Sea. There is much water (potential for life), but nothing can live there. The Dead Sea is dead because it does not give. Nothing flows out of the Dead Sea. It does not give, and so it does not live.

This is the message of the Sermon on the Mount and its beatitudes. To give of yourself (die to yourself) is to receive life (to live in the kingdom of God). Jesus repeats this idea many times and in many ways: "Then Jesus said to His disciples, 'If anyone wishes to come after Me, he must deny himself, and take up his cross and follow Me. For whoever wishes to save his life will lose it; but whoever loses his life for My sake will find it" (Matt. 16:24-25). The kingdom of God relative to the kingdoms of this world is a "flip-flop" kingdom. To be blind is to see; to be last is to be first; to lose is to find; and to die is to live. "Truly, truly, I say to you, unless a grain of wheat falls into the earth and dies, it remains alone; but if it dies, it bears much fruit" (John 12:24).

Each of the eight beatitudes (Matt. 5:3-11) centers on giving and receiving via putting something of self on the cross and, thus, bearing fruit (Gal. 5:22-23). Those who are poor in spirit give of themselves and receive the kingdom of God via putting self-reliance on the cross, bearing the fruit of faithfulness. Those who mourn give of themselves and are comforted via putting self-comfort on the cross, bearing the fruit of peace. Those who are meek give of themselves and inherit the earth via putting self-worth/esteem on the cross, bearing the fruit of gentleness. Those who hunger and thirst for righteousness give of themselves and are satisfied via putting self-fulfillment on the cross, bearing the fruit of self-control. Those who are merciful give of themselves and receive mercy via putting self-righteousness on the cross, bearing the fruit of patience. Those who are pure in heart give of themselves and see God via putting self-ownership on the cross, bearing the fruit of goodness. Those who are peacemakers give of themselves and are sons of God via putting self-rights on the cross, bearing the fruit of kindness. Those who are persecuted, mocked, and slandered give of themselves and receive the kingdom of heaven and its rewards via putting self-reputation on the cross, bearing the fruit of joy.

God is a good Manager of resources. He distributes blessings for a purpose. Like Abraham, you are blessed so that you can be a blessing (Gen. 12:2-3). If you stop being a blessing and stop producing fruit, then you will stop being blessed. That is the deal! That is the covenant. "Therefore I say to you, the kingdom of God will be taken away from you and given to a people, producing the fruit of it" (Matt. 21:43). Receiving beatitudes requires being beatitudes. "From everyone who has been given much, much will be required; and to whom they entrusted much, of him they will ask all the more" (Luke 12:48). Jesus is the greatest Blessing and Giver ever. He died to Himself completely and gave all of Himself to those He loved. He had the right be-*attitude!* "Have this attitude in yourselves which was also in Christ Jesus, who, although He existed in the form of God, did not regard equality with God a thing to be grasped, but emptied Himself" (Phil. 2:5-7). Jesus was a walking demonstration of the beatitudes.

Blessed are the givers, and fruitful are the cross bearers. Those who live in the kingdoms of this world think that to have that mentality is absurd nonsense that is totally backward. Well, the truth of the matter is, you *do* need to be a bit backward to live in the kingdom of God!

FEBRUARY 9

DON'T GET SNARED. BE DISCIPLINED WITH WORDS!

"If you have been snared with the words of your mouth, have been caught with the words of your mouth."

Proverbs 6:2

Sometimes, we disappoint ourselves with regard to how we speak to others. We might respond, "That was a really *dumb* thing to say!" We try to be wise with our words, but sometimes we are "dum." Three unwise styles of speech make up this *dum* style: "d" is the destructive style; "u" is the *u*ndisciplined style; "m" is the manipulative style. Although each one of us may be more prone to one of these styles than the other two, we all need to avoid all three and replace them with a wise style of speech.

The undisciplined style is the way that does not count words. The undisciplined talker babbles endlessly. He conducts empty conversations and is not in control of what he says; he is not disciplined. The undisciplined speaker makes promises that he later regrets. "If you have been snared with the words of your mouth, have been caught with the words of your mouth," then your lack of discipline may result in regret (Prov. 6:2). You might say, "I wish I could get those words back!" Those words, however, are like excess toothpaste squeezed out of the tube. It is very difficult to get it back in once it is squeezed out. It is just wasted.

Undisciplined speech can lead to your downfall. "The wise of heart will receive commands, but a babbling fool will be ruined" (Prov. 10:8). More is not necessarily better. "When there are many words, transgression is unavoidable, but he who restrains his lips is wise" (Prov. 10:19). Wisdom is associated with discipline or restraint, not the lack of it. Undisciplined and unguarded speech can lead to disaster. "The one who guards his mouth preserves his life; the one who opens wide his lips comes to ruin" (Prov. 13:3).

Sometimes, silence is golden because silence can be wise. The undisciplined speaker's lack of control can result in foolishness. "A prudent man conceals knowledge, but the heart of fools proclaims folly" (Prov. 12:23). There needs to be a discipline of waiting. "He who gives an answer before he hears, it is folly and shame to him" (Prov. 18:13).

The wise way is the opposite of the undisciplined way. The undisciplined speaker speaks without thinking. The wise speaker thinks before he speaks. "The heart of the righteous ponders how to answer" (Prov. 15:28) and "the heart of the wise instructs his mouth and adds persuasiveness to his lips" (Prov. 16:23). Words are counted and weighed. Wisdom knows when to be silent. "He who goes about as a talebearer reveals secrets, but he who is trustworthy conceals a matter" (Prov. 11:13).

The undisciplined speaker cannot control himself. The wise man exercises restraint with his words. He does not feel compelled to add his views to every part of a discussion. And so, his words carry more weight when he does speak. The undisciplined speaker babbles. He does not consider when to speak. The wise speaker understands the importance of timing. "A man has joy in an apt answer, and how delightful is a timely word!" (Prov. 15:23). The words of the wise are pertinent and relevant. "*Like* apples of gold in settings of silver is a word spoken in right circumstances" (Prov. 25:11). The wise speaker is not only concerned with the "what" and the "how" of speech, but with the "when."

A meaningful message said in an effective way may make no impression at all unless it is spoken on the right occasion and at the right time.

Based on personality, experience, and relational orientation, you might be prone to using more of an undisciplined style of speech than a destructive style or a manipulative style. Being aware of this is half the battle. You must try to be more attentive to your words. You must make it a habit to ask yourself some challenging questions: Do I talk too much? Do I complain too much? Do I often fall to the temptation of speaking poorly of another person? Do I add meaningful content to conversations when I do talk? Am I being wise with my words? When all is said and done, we want to avoid being *dum* and make sure we are being wise!

FEBRUARY 10

IMPROVE YOUR PRAYER LIFE

"With all prayer and petition pray at all times in the Spirit, and with this in view, be on the alert with all perseverance and petition for all the saints."

Ephesians 6:18

How can you improve your prayer life? You may find that when you have a prayer time early in the morning, you tend to fall asleep or have a difficult time staying focused. We all have weaknesses in our prayer life and want to improve it. One of the secrets of a consistent prayer life is using a variety of types of prayer.

You can use a "prayer list" strategy in which you pray through a list of requests and needs. You can use different types of prayer to change things up. Sometimes, you might focus on thanksgiving. Other times, you might focus on supplication and lift up requests on your own behalf. You may also focus on intercession and offer requests on behalf of others.

Along with different types of prayer, you may use different methods. You may engage in expository praying, in which you allow the Bible to dictate the content, flow, and direction of your prayers. You read a portion of Scripture, and it prompts you to pray according to what has been read. You read the Bible and pray—a double winner. Regardless of which type or method of prayer you use, the use of different prayer strategies can be helpful. If "variety is the spice of life," how much more can variety be the spice of your prayer life!

You can improve your prayer life by improving your life of holiness. It is true that sin pushes you away from Christ. It hinders your relationship. You must be committed to focusing on avoiding sin. One of the added blessings of this commitment is that as holiness can facilitate more of an intimacy with God (Matt. 5:8), so, too, can intimacy with God make us more holy (1 John 3:2).

Sometimes, a proper theological understanding of Who God is and who man is can improve our prayer life. In a somewhat paradoxical way, God is Sovereign; and man has a free will. God's decrees cannot be changed. At the same time, prayer can "change" things. We might employ what could be called a "vessel theology" in bridging the gap between this seeming contradiction. God's decrees cannot change, but our involvement in them can. As vessels (receptors) we cannot cause (first cause) nor create anything by ourselves; only God can do that (God's decrees do not change). However, we do have a free will. We can decide—with the help of the Holy Spirit—to be involved or not be involved in God's unchangeable decrees. We cannot make things happen, but we can be vessels through which God makes things happen. In this way, prayer is effectual. To understand this is to be motivated to pray.

The practical response to such a "vessel theology" is to focus more than we might have on the means of grace—that is, to focus more on doing the things, like prayer, that facilitate God working in and through us. This increases our desire to see Him work through us and directs our goals in life more toward being instead of doing, surrendering instead of accomplishing, and facilitating instead of creating. The result of all this should be more of a focus on prayer and contentment in prayer.

The motivation to pray is not simply to be involved but to be involved with what God is doing. It is to desire to have God act and intervene in this world. It is the understanding that "I have been crucified with Christ; and it is no longer I who live, but Christ lives in me" (Gal. 2:20). This is the most significant way to improve your prayer life. Increase your desire to pray. This is theology made practical. When we more clearly understand Who God is (Creator, Causer, Controller) and who we are relative to Him (vessel, receiver, steward), we are more motivated to seek God. We improve our prayer lives!

FEBRUARY 11

COUNSELING AS A PRIEST

"When Jesus went ashore, He saw a large crowd, and He felt compassion for them because they were like sheep without a shepherd; and He began to teach them many things."

Mark 6:34

Sometimes, people need help. They need wisdom and advice. They need a helper or a counselor. When helping someone who needs counsel, there is a flow from a sort of priestly emphasis to what might be called a more prophetic style and, finally, to a more kingly type of approach. In general, this might be described as the movement from a more downward or relational phase, where the main goal is to build a bond, to a more upward or outward phase, where the main goal is to promote action. This general paradigm, along with its particular principles and actions, can be used in a more formal counseling situation as well as in a more informal setting. It can be used in the counselor's office with a "client" over the period of several months, and it can be used at the coffee shop with a friend over a cup of coffee.

The goal of the priestly helper is to promote self-exploration and self-understanding in the one being helped. This is done by imparting a sense of belonging, mutual trust, and rapport. The word "compassion" is derived from two words—"suffer" and "with." The priestly counselor can "suffer with" in order to relate to the person being counseled. He can show compassion in order to build a bond. "When Jesus went ashore, He saw a large crowd, and He felt compassion for them because they were like sheep without a shepherd; and He began to teach them many things" (Mark 6:34). Sometimes, the main thing people need is to know the care and concern that God has for them. The counselor can model this, since after all "[a]re not two sparrows sold for a cent? And *yet* not one of them will fall to the ground apart from your Father. But the very hairs of your head are all numbered" (Matt. 10:29-30).

Similarly, rapport can be established by expressing acceptance just as "Jesus said to her, 'Woman, where are they? Did no one condemn you?' She said, 'No one, Lord.' And Jesus said, 'I do not condemn you, either'" (John 8:10-11). The counselor should look to identify with the problem in the same way Jesus did with those whom He counseled who were in need: "For we do not have a high priest who cannot sympathize with our weaknesses, but One who has been tempted in all things as *we are*, yet without sin. Therefore let us draw near with confidence to the throne of grace, so that we may receive mercy and find grace to help in time of need" (Heb. 4:15-16).

And so, the priestly helper looks to establish trust. In one way or another, he is asking, "Where are you? What do you want? What do you need?" He is saying, "Go ahead. You can talk to me." Jesus said it this way: "'What do you want Me to do for you?'" (Mark 10:51). Helping someone starts here, in the arena of building trust. In this way, the priestly counselor can be thought of as a facilitator.

FEBRUARY 12

FREED UP TO SERVE

"Jesus knowing that His hour had come that He would depart out of this world to the Father, having loved His own who were in the world, He loved them to the end."

John 13:1

A Christian is a disciple of Jesus Christ. He or she is a follower of the One Who "did not come to be served, but to serve" (Mark 10:45). A Christian follows the Servant and is, therefore, a servant. Disciples follow a way of life modeled for them by their master. Followers of the infamous murderer, Charles Manson, became murderers themselves. Followers of the highly respected advocate of nonviolent protest, Martin Luther King, Jr., became practitioners of nonviolent protest themselves. Followers of the champion of evolutionary theory, Charles Darwin, became proponents of evolution themselves. Followers of the Servant, Jesus Christ, become servants themselves.

Jesus did not simply provide the ultimate act of service. He became the ultimate Servant. His followers must not simply do acts of service; they must be servants. Someone who does acts of service may hold onto a hidden agenda. Motives for service may not be pure. The service may only be done in order to receive something in return. Instead of selfless service that is done by someone who *is* a servant, "hidden agenda acts of service" represent self-filled service.

Selfishness is the opposite of love. Real service that is done by a servant is the result of real love. Service without love is nothing. "And if I give all my possessions to feed *the poor*, and if I surrender my body to be burned, but do not have love, it profits me nothing" (1 Cor. 13:3). Real service requires real love.

Symbolically, Jesus did the greatest act of service when He got down on His knees and "[t]hen He poured water into the basin, and began to wash the disciples' feet and to wipe them with the towel with which He was girded" (John 13:5). What enabled Him to do this most menial act of service? He was motivated by love and security.

> Now before the Feast of the Passover, Jesus knowing that His hour had come that He would depart out of this world to the Father, having loved His own who were in the world, He loved them to the end . . . *Jesus*, knowing that the Father had given all things into His hands, and that He had come forth from God and was going back to God, got up from supper, and laid aside His garments; and taking a towel, He girded Himself (John 13:1, 3-4).

It is love that produces service. Jesus loved His disciples so He served them; "for God so loved the world that He gave His only begotten Son" (John 3:16).

This love-based service is fueled by security. Insecure people cannot serve others because they have to serve themselves. Jesus was secure in where He was going. He *knew* "He would depart out of this world to the Father." He was secure in what He had. He *knew* "that the Father had given all things into His hands." He was secure in where He had come from and Who He was. He *knew* "that He had come forth from God and was going back to God." He knew all these things. He was secure. He was free to serve.

The enemy of service is insecurity. When you do not know, then you have to give your energy to try to find out. When you know where you are going, what you have, where you have come from, and who you are, then you are freed up to serve others instead of serving yourself. Our prayer should be, "Oh God, fill us with love and security that we might be like You—servants!"

FEBRUARY 13

MESSAGE OR MESSENGER— THAT IS THE QUESTION

"You are our letter, written in our hearts, known and read by all men."
2 Corinthians 3:2

Which is more important? Is it the message or the messenger? How do these two variables, both essential in the ministry of preaching and teaching the Word of God, affect each other? Like Jeremiah the prophet, one might say that preaching and teaching starts from deep down inside a person. "But if I say, 'I will not remember Him or speak anymore in His name,' then in my heart it becomes like a burning fire shut up in my bones; and I am weary of holding *it* in, and I cannot endure *it*" (Jer. 20:9). The sermon or the teaching must be a message that was born and that lives in the messenger. It has been said that there are only two kinds of speakers—those who have something to say and those who *have* to say something. Preachers and teachers of the Word of God must have something to say. In that sense, they must be walking epistles Paul would address, saying, "You are our letter, written in our hearts, known and read by all men; being manifested that you are a letter of Christ, cared for by us, written not with ink but with the Spirit of the living God, not on tablets of stone but on tablets of human hearts" (2 Cor. 3:2-3).

The messenger, perhaps more than anything else, must be a person full of love people and love for the Word of God. A preacher or teacher must love the one to whom he or she speaks. A messenger who does not love people is like a shepherd who is allergic to sheep. He is like someone who wants to have a family but hates children. This kind of contradiction has no place in the ministry of the Word.

Similarly, a messenger who does not love the Word of God is like a shepherd who is not willing to search for a grassy field for her sheep. She is like someone who wants to have a family but is not willing to give birth. Ultimately, a preacher or a teacher must be a person full of love for people and love for the Word of God. If not, the messenger most certainly will experience burnout. Burnout in ministry can happen due to a variety of things—being out of your gifting, giving out substantially more than taking in, having wrong motives, lacking variety, not moving on when God has a new calling for you—yet the most definite issue leading to burnout is a lack of love.

It is hard work to prepare a good sermon or teaching. You must seek God and search for revelation in the Bible. It is a process. You must give birth to the message. So what is more important? Are you more important, or is revelation from the Bible more important? Is it the contents or the container, the ingredients or the chef, the substance or the method, the center or the point guard, the mission or the missionary, the evangel or the evangelist, the coffee or the cup the coffee is poured into?

What is more important—the message or the messenger? The most common answer to this question is probably the message. After all, is it not true that though the messenger might change, the message always stays the same? Whether the messenger was Balaam the prophet (Num. 23:7) or a donkey (Num. 22:28), God's message went forth. God says that His message will not fail:

"So will My word be which goes forth from My mouth; it will not return to Me empty, without accomplishing what I desire, and without succeeding *in the matter* for which I sent it" (Isa. 55:11). It is the message that we should be proud of since that is where the power comes from: "For I am not ashamed of the gospel, for it is the power of God for salvation to everyone who believes, to the Jew first and also to the Greek" (Rom. 1:16). The very credibility of the messenger depends on the credibility of the message making the messenger subordinate to the message (Deut. 18:22). Ultimately, "faith *comes* from hearing, and hearing by the word of Christ" (Rom. 10:17). What is more important? What is it that outlasts the other? "The grass withers, the flower fades, but the word of our God stands forever" (Isa. 40:8).

What is more important—the message or the messenger? That is still the question! Not as common of an answer but equally as plausible is "the messenger." While it is true that "faith *comes* from hearing, and hearing by the word of Christ" (Rom. 10:17), it must also be asked, "How will they hear without a preacher?" (Rom. 10:14). It is the messenger who is lauded: "How lovely on the mountains are the feet of him who brings good news" (Isa. 52:7). God searches for these messengers, saying, "Whom shall I send, and who will go for Us?" (Isa. 6:8). Ultimately, inasmuch as we represent Jesus the messenger on this earth, the messenger is at least equal in importance to the message since the messenger is the message.

So, what is more important? Well, I do like my coffee, but I also have my favorite mug to put it in. For the preacher and teacher of God's Word, the message is critical; but so is the messenger who delivers that message. So, let's look to have a pure message (1 Peter 2:2) and a pure messenger (2 Tim. 2:21). What's more important? They need each other! Coffee without my mug is messy, and my mug without my coffee is useless. The Gospel without a preacher does not go very far, and a preacher without a message is mute.

FEBRUARY 14

MERCY IS A TWO-WAY STREET

"Blessed are the merciful, for they shall receive mercy."

Matthew 5:7

Mercy is one of those kinds of things. Everybody wants it to be shown to them, but few tend to show it to others. To be merciful is to be able to forgive others and to have compassion for the suffering and the needy. It assumes a lack of self-righteousness that would inhibit someone from showing mercy. When you are full of self-righteousness, you are not able to show mercy to those who have wronged you. You tend to say, "I could understand if this is what happened or if that is why you did it or if you did it while you were . . . *but* I would never have . . ." This is just another way of saying, "I am better than you." In declaring your own righteousness, you end up rejecting mercy.

This same kind of thing can happen with the way you view the needy. "I could understand if you never had this opportunity or if you had this happen to you or if there were extenuating circumstances . . . But I would never have . . . ." There it is again. "I am better than you." Mercy rejected! "Blessed are the merciful, for they shall receive mercy" (Matt. 5:7). Those who are merciful give of themselves and receive mercy via putting self-righteousness on the cross and, thus, bearing the fruit of patience.

Blessings are free. Like salvation, you cannot earn them (Eph. 2:8-10). That does not mean, however, that they are not costly. They are costly because we try to hang onto that which is not our own (1 Cor. 6:19-20). The beatitude includes a challenge or an obligation—a cost. It is quite a challenge to not give yourself the benefit of the doubt to such a degree that you discard mercy. It is very difficult to show sympathy to someone who you think you are better than. How can we be more merciful? Jesus is our Example. "For we do not have a high priest who cannot sympathize with our weaknesses, but One who has been tempted in all things as *we are, yet* without sin. Therefore let us draw near with confidence to the throne of grace, so that we may receive mercy and find grace to help in time of need" (Heb. 4:15-16). The fact that a perfectly holy God shows mercy to perfectly unholy people should trigger in us a sense of mercy for others. "Be merciful, just as your Father is merciful" (Luke 6:36).

We must die to self by giving away or letting go of self-righteousness. The judging of and disgust toward others that is produced by self-righteousness must be rejected. We must have the same attitude that Paul had: "For I am the least of the apostles, and not fit to be called an apostle, because I persecuted the church of God. But by the grace of God I am what I am, and His grace toward me did not prove vain" (1 Cor. 15:9-10). When you understand yourself as grace-produced and not self-produced, you are more likely to show mercy.

Mercy results in being given another chance. Who does not want another chance? The merciful are blessed. They are blessed "for they shall receive mercy"; they shall receive another chance and then another chance and then another chance and then . . . "The LORD'S lovingkindnesses indeed never cease, for His compassions never fail. *They* are new every morning; great is Your faithfulness" (Lam. 3:22-23).

The fruit of the Spirit that corresponds to this beatitude is patience (Gal. 5:22). Self-righteous people are not patient people. When self-righteousness is put on the cross, the happy (blessed) result is patience. Instead of being short with and belittling others because you are so much better than them and they are so far below you, people who have crucified their self-righteous, pompous attitudes are freed up to show mercy.

The nature of the kingdom of God—relative to the kingdoms of this world—is backward. Each beatitude in the Sermon on the Mount, therefore, is cloaked in irony. "Blessed are the merciful, for they shall receive mercy" (Matt. 5:7). We must give others another chance; then God will give us another chance. This same ironic principle is true with respect to forgiveness: "For if you forgive others for their transgressions, your heavenly Father will also forgive you. But if you do not forgive others, then your Father will not forgive your transgressions" (Matt. 6:14-15). It is the Golden Rule to "treat people the same way you want them to treat you" (Matt. 7:12). Do unto others! Mercy is, indeed, a two-way street.

FEBRUARY 15

SEWN INTO THE GOSPEL

"Truly I say to you, wherever the gospel is preached in the whole world, what this woman has done will also be spoken of in memory of her."

Mark 14:9

Can you imagine being sewn right into the Gospel? Your actions are spoken of in memory of you wherever the Gospel is preached all over the world. Sometimes, people are honored with a brick laid in a walkway that has their name on it. At Grauman's Chinese Theater in Hollywood, California, even Herbie the Love Bug was honored with leaving an impression of its tires in the famous walk of fame. Herbie was sewn into Hollywood fame! As amazing as that is, it pales in comparison to being sewn into the Gospel.

> While He was in Bethany at the home of Simon the leper, and reclining *at the table*, there came a woman with an alabaster vial of very costly perfume of pure nard; *and* she broke the vial and poured it over His head. But some were indignantly remarking to one another, "Why has this perfume been wasted? For this perfume might have been sold for over three hundred denarii, and *the money* given to the poor." And they were scolding her. But Jesus said, "Let her alone; why do you bother her? She has done a good deed to Me. For you always have the poor with you, and whenever you wish you can do good to them; but you do not always have Me. She has done what she could; she has anointed My body beforehand for the burial. Truly I say to you, wherever the gospel is preached in the whole world, what this woman has done will also be spoken of in memory of her (Mark 14:3-9).

Giving is the action of the Gospel—"For God so loved the world, that He gave" (John 3:16)—and so it is remembered with the Gospel. Whether it was Mary the sister of Lazarus or Mary Magdalene, the act of giving to Jesus sewed *her* into the Gospel. She was written into it in perpetuity. Others in that same room were not written into the Gospel, perhaps due to their insistence on engaging in overanalysis.

Blind faith includes no analysis, but blinded faith comes from overanalysis. Faith is not opposed to questions, but it can be snuffed out by excessive questions. Mary did not overanalyze her giving to Jesus. Others were indignant with her as they overanalyzed the management of the money. To be sewn or not to be sewn in—that is the question!

There are many ways in which people are not sewn into the Gospel due to overanalysis. Should I tithe? Can I trust the church to use my money wisely? Do they even need the money? This overanalysis evaporates in the hearing of "bring the whole tithe into the storehouse" (Mal. 3:10). No need to overanalyze and not be sewn in. Just tithe!

Should I accept Christ as my Savior? Did Jesus even exist? Do I really need a Savior? Why can I not just save myself? Is there really anything after this life, anyway? Then the Scripture speaks: "If you confess with your mouth Jesus as Lord, and believe in your heart that God raised Him from the dead, you will be saved" (Rom. 10:9). No need to overanalyze and not be sewn in. Just believe!

Is the Bible the Word of God? How do they know it was not fabricated by imposters? What about all the inconsistencies? How could it have been preserved for thousands of years? Why should I not believe in the Koran or the Hindu Vedas instead? The Bible says of itself, "All Scripture is inspired by God" (2 Tim. 3:16). Stop already with the overanalysis through which you may not be sewn in. Trust in the Bible!

Does prayer really work? Am I just speaking into the air? Why would God be interested in what I have to say, anyway? Isn't God too busy to listen to me? Then all of that overanalysis is washed away with the biblical encouragement that "in everything by prayer and supplication with thanksgiving let your requests be made known to God" (Phil. 4:6). Let it be sewn in!

Mary did not overanalyze the situation. She just walked in simple faith. The result was anything but simple. She was sewn into the Gospel forevermore. Do not allow your fleshly tendency to overanalyze things keep you from partaking in the heavenly sewing machine. Be sewn in!

FEBRUARY 16

ARE YOU TELLING THE STORY?

"But sanctify Christ as Lord in your hearts, always being ready to make a defense to everyone who asks you to give an account for the hope that is in you, yet with gentleness and reverence."

1 Peter 3:15

Evangelism is one of the foundations of the Church. It is the builder of the Church and should naturally be connected to the Church. Certainly, the church should be the place where the cries of newborn babes in Christ are constantly being heard. Of course, evangelistic crusades and evangelistic preaching from the pulpit are respected as concrete forms of evangelism. However, most Christians do not evangelize others from these platforms. Moreover, most people do not hear the Gospel in these venues. Research suggests that as much as 80 percent to 90 percent of people who come to Christ do so in more of a one-to-one "venue" in which friends or relatives share the Gospel with them. As important and effective as mass evangelism may be, personal evangelism yields more fruit. The initial setting for most evangelism will occur outside of a church environment in the typical places where lost people live, work, and socialize.

Most Christians are not called to be evangelists in the Ephesians 4:11 sense. An evangelist has a unique gifting and anointing to lead people to receive Christ, to equip other Christians for more effective evangelism, and generally, to encourage the Christian body as a whole (Eph. 4:11-12). However, *all* Christians are called to be messengers for Christ as we are charged to "preach the word; be ready in season *and* out of season" (2 Tim. 4:2). We are all commanded to be witnesses and to testify about the lordship of Jesus in our lives. As messengers, we should be compelled to share the Gospel message with people who are lost without Christ. You are not expected to be a super evangelist, but you are expected to be unashamed of the Gospel and willing to testify as a messenger for the Lord. Of course, this includes your words; however, with or without words, your life communicates a message. And so, you must seek to be living as a Gospel messenger in order to most effectively share the Gospel message.

Having said this, do not get caught in the trap of thinking that you are not worthy of sharing the Gospel with others. Sometimes, Christians are reluctant to evangelize because they misunderstand what is actually happening in such a situation. They might think that they are not an actual evangelist or pastor and, therefore, do not have the authority to evangelize. This is what might be called the "I am not sanctioned" roadblock. In addition, they might think that they need to be perfect to share the Gospel. This is what might be called the "I am inferior" roadblock. These are lies that simply keep us from doing that which we are mandated to do.

We need to gain a new perspective. Martin Luther, the initiator of the Protestant Reformation, described evangelism as "one beggar telling another beggar where to find food." We need to see ourselves as beggars and Jesus Christ as the Food. This image reminds us not only of our need for humility when we are involved in evangelism but also for our need to look at ourselves in the right way so as to more readily launch ourselves into evangelism. "He must increase, but I must decrease" (John 3:30). When I am humble, I lift Him up before other people.

We all desperately need Jesus. God's love for people is universal and impartial "for God so loved the *world*" (John 3:16, emphasis mine). Let us allow this perspective to jump-start our evangelistic batteries so that we reach out to those who are without Christ. "But sanctify Christ as Lord in your

FEBRUARY 17

THE CHURCH IS . . .

*"And He gave some **as** apostles, and some **as** prophets, and some **as** evangelists, and some **as** pastors and teachers, for the equipping of the saints for the work of service, to the building up of the body of Christ; until we all attain to the unity of the faith, and of the knowledge of the Son of God, to a mature man, to the measure of the stature which belongs to the fullness of Christ. As a result, we are no longer to be children, tossed here and there by waves and carried about by every wind of doctrine, by the trickery of men, by craftiness in deceitful scheming; but speaking the truth in love, we are to grow up in all **aspects** into Him who is the head, **even** Christ, from whom the whole body, being fitted and held together by what every joint supplies, according to the proper working of each individual part, causes the growth of the body for the building up of itself in love."*

Ephesians 4:11-16

Of course, the goal of an evangelist is to make converts. A single convert, however, cannot be the ultimate goal, since a single convert cannot live out the Christian life. Christian living takes place in the church. In terms that a missionary might use, there must be a local church planted so that the missionary work will remain.

What is the Church? The biblical analogies that are used to describe the Church—the *body of Christ* and the *household of God*—emphasize a real, alive, and loving relationship between Jesus and His Church. In a cosmic sense, the Church is the body that is given to Christ. It continues His work, which is the work of the kingdom of God. In a historical sense, the Church consists of the people of God through whom Jesus has continued to do His work throughout the history of redemption.

The Church is dynamic and "charismatic" in the sense that it exists by the grace of God. It is built by the gifts of grace—*charismata* in the Greek—and is structured like a human body in that there are many different parts with different abilities who all work together toward common goals (Eph. 4:11-16). It is more of a community than it is a hierarchy. It is more of an organism than it is an organization or an institution. "For just as we have many members in one body and all the members do not have the same function, so we, who are many, are one body in Christ, and individually members one of another. Since we have gifts that differ according to the grace given to us, *each of us is to exercise them accordingly*" (Rom. 12:4-6).

The Church is the community of God's people. It is the people of God in fellowship with one another. They are called out of the world—the *eklesia* or "called out ones"—so as to come together. At the end of the day, the Church is people. It is not an institutional structure, although it does have structure and order. These people are not an isolated people. They are a people in community, people who fellowship with one another.

The people of the Church are called out of the world to assemble together under the message of the Gospel *and* to then take that message back to the world. The church is made up of God's people, who proclaim His greatness to others. "But you are A CHOSEN RACE, A royal PRIESTHOOD, A HOLY NATION, A PEOPLE FOR *God's* OWN POSSESSION, so that you may proclaim the excellencies of Him who has called you out of darkness into His marvelous light" (1 Peter 2:9). The church gathers together *and* scatters (Matt. 21:44).

The Church has been entrusted with the Gospel. It is the proclaimer of the greatness of God and the explainer of His gracious provision. The Church is a light in a dark world. It is the voice of God that speaks His Word to all the nations. It is a missionary community!

FEBRUARY 18

LET HUMILITY HIDE YOU

"Seek humility. Perhaps you will be hidden in the day of the LORD'S anger."
Zephaniah 2:3

Since there is right, there can be wrong. Since there is truth, there can be lies. To understand humility, it can be helpful to understand false humility. Moses "was very humble, more than any man who was on the face of the earth" (Num. 12:3). Some commentators view Moses' humility as a false humility—which is a ridiculous viewpoint, since God says he is number one in the entire world in humility. Some people believe Moses' humility was a reaction to his sudden fame and importance. They say that Moses purposely tried to portray himself as humble in order to protect himself from becoming too proud. Moses' humility was a reaction to men instead of a response to God. It was something that he tried to create. That depiction is a description of false humility. It has nothing to do with the humility that we see in the life of Moses. False humility is often couched in the legalistic showmanship of religiosity. It seems powerful, but it is impotent.

> Therefore no one is to act as your judge in regard to food or drink or in respect to a festival or a new moon or a Sabbath day—things which are a *mere* shadow of what is to come; but the substance belongs to Christ. Let no one keep defrauding you of your prize by delighting in self-abasement and the worship of the angels, taking his stand on *visions* he has seen, inflated without cause by his fleshly mind, and not holding fast to the head, from whom the entire body, being supplied and held together by the joints and ligaments, grows with a growth which is from God. If you have died with Christ to the elementary principles of the world, why, as if you were living in the world, do you submit yourself to decrees, such as, "Do not handle, do not taste, do not touch!" (which all *refer to* things destined to perish with use)—in accordance with the commandments and teachings of men? These are matters which have, to be sure, the appearance of wisdom in self-made religion and self-abasement and severe treatment of the body, but are of no value against fleshly indulgence (Col. 2:16-23).

Humility is a response to God. Humility that is a reaction to men is false humility. When "I cannot do it" stops at "I," then it is said in the fear of man and can be identified as false humility. True humility says, "I cannot do it, but God can" and is said in the fear of God. When "I am nobody" stops at "I," then it is said in order to get glory from man and can be identified as false humility. True humility says, "I am nobody, so God can stand out as the only Somebody" and is said in order to give glory to God.

Being humble does not mean that you are necessarily unimportant or unimpressive. It does not have to mean that other people do not look up to you. Moses was certainly respected by the Israelites. He was understood by them to be a very important and impressive person. Yet he was the humblest man "on the face of the earth." It is not that a humble person cannot be a great person; it is what that person's humility does with that greatness. Humility does not seek after greatness; it seeks after God. Humility points a person away from himself in the midst of greatness. True humility results in being almost unconscious of your importance. It is not about you; it is about God. If your humility is about you, then it is false humility. True humility always seeks and points to God and forgets about self.

Humility is connected to obedience and righteousness. Ultimately, it is connected to hiddenness. Our only hope is that God does not see us. We must be hidden so that in the end, when God looks at us, He only sees Christ. "Seek the LORD, all you humble of the earth who have carried out His ordinances; seek righteousness, seek humility. Perhaps you will be hidden in the day of the LORD'S anger" (Zeph. 2:3).

FEBRUARY 19

THE WAY NOT TO SEAT YOURSELF

"When you are invited by someone to a wedding feast, do not take the place of honor, for someone more distinguished than you may have been invited by him, and he who invited you both will come and say to you, 'Give your place to this man,' and then in disgrace you proceed to occupy the last place. But when you are invited, go and recline at the last place, so that when the one who has invited you comes, he may say to you, 'Friend, move up higher'; then you will have honor in the sight of all who are at the table with you. For everyone who exalts himself will be humbled, and he who humbles himself will be exalted."

Luke 14:8-11

There can be great embarrassment in presumption. By way of deception, misunderstanding, assumption, or presumption, you can try to take a place that is not actually there for the taking. Forcing yourself into these kinds of situations can result in very awkward experiences; they can lead to disgrace and shame. It is important to know how to seat yourself. The most important tip that will help you get better at this skill is to never seat yourself in front of God.

Jesus tells a parable about a man who was invited to a wedding feast. His advice for how he should conduct himself is, "Do not take the place of honor" (Luke 14:8). Jesus then describes how the problem with taking the place of honor is that "someone more distinguished than you" may come, and then you will have to give up your seat in disgrace (Luke 14:8-9). When it is God Who is the "more distinguished" one and we are those who try to seat ourselves in front of Him, it is not only awkward but also idolatrous.

Some theological persuasions are prone to a superficial, man-centered perspective. When our theology assumes that it is all about us—when, in fact, it is all about God—we end up seating ourselves up front, expecting God to tag along in the back. To a large extent, this has occurred because we have spurned a theology that has the cross as its focus. A cross-centered theology has been replaced by a consumer theology built on a perception of God as a sort of "Santa Clause."

How does this play out in the Church? It can produce a church-hopping mentality. You can begin to assess the desirability of a church from the me-centered perspective of what is available to meet *my* needs instead of the Him-centered perspective of what is available to glorify God. The "what can I get" mentality replacing the "what can I give" mentality has resulted in church-hoppers who leave God in the dust. He is asked to sit in the back because, after all, it is all about me, isn't it?

Seating yourself up front is often prompted by convenient rationalizations. "After all, doesn't God want me to be elevated? Doesn't He say, 'You are the head and not the tail, on top looking down, a King's kid'? The problem is not found in the actuality of sitting up front. It is found in the problem of *seating* yourself up front.

Only God can elevate you. You cannot be elevated rightly by elevating yourself and, in so doing, telling God that you are seated in front of Him. "So, seat yourself behind the one who is seated up front, and then He can pull you up. "For everyone who exalts himself will be humbled, and he who humbles himself will be exalted" (Luke 14:11).

FEBRUARY 20

CHANGE IS HARD, AND IT CAN BE DANGEROUS!

"From that time on, Jesus began to preach and say, 'Repent, for the kingdom of heaven is at hand.'"
Matthew 4:17

We do not like change. Change stirs the pot. It is just so much easier to leave the pot alone; it is less likely that stuff will spill out. Change brings friction, and the friction that comes from change often impedes that change. Herein lies the tension between change and effort. We avoid change because we are inclined to seek the comfort of the lesser challenge. Yet change in our lives is essential. In fact, it is mandated. Jesus commands us to "repent" (Matt. 3:2). The Greek word *metanoia* means to "turn" or "change direction." Change is good. Moreover, it is critical since "unless you repent, you will all likewise perish" (Luke 13:3).

Change sometimes requires destruction. It is not always just a *refurbishing* of the house or ministry or program or lifestyle. It can sometimes require a tearing down of the house or a closing down of a ministry or a "putting to bed" of a program or a letting go completely of a certain aspect of your lifestyle. This type of change is especially difficult. Nobody wants to go to those metaphorical funerals. It is hard to die, and it is even harder to "kill." Nevertheless, we are called to put some things to death. "So then, brethren, we are under obligation, not to the flesh, to live according to the flesh—for if you are living according to the flesh, you must die; but if by the Spirit you are putting to death the deeds of the body, you will live" (Rom. 8:12-13). Sometimes, we need to bury that which is already dead. Yes, the death that marks that inappropriate relationship that you may be engaging in, for example, needs to be put in a "casket" and placed in the ground.

How can I be motivated to change? Jesus said, "Repent, for the kingdom of heaven is at hand" (Matt. 4:17). Change (repentance) does not tend to come by being your own mirror. Revelation is a relative issue, and you cannot be relative to yourself. That is why "repent" (turn/change) is due to the kingdom (rule) of God being at hand (literally, "near you" or "in your midst or presence"). When you come into the presence of God, it changes you because relative to Him, you lack and need to change. When God reveals Himself to you, you can change; "the kindness of God leads you to repentance" (Rom. 2:4). Our ultimate change will happen when we see Him perfectly. "We know that when He appears, we will be like Him, because we will see Him just as He is" (1 John 3:2). In revelation, there is life; there is change.

Change can also be dangerous if it is empty. Change (or any method, form, or structure) must always be driven by content, lest the method alone becomes the content; and, hence, there is no actual change at all, only the appearance of change. Appearance is not change because appearance by itself is empty—that is, absent of substance. So, the key is to define "content or substance" rightly and to realize that change must be birthed, not just fabricated. Another way to say this is that form must follow substance. It cannot go in front of substance, lest it become the substance itself. The change must be substantive; and then appropriate methods, structures, or routines can be placed around it.

Change and routine are *both* needed. Contents and methods are not antagonistic or exclusive entities. When it comes to substance and structure, it is a "both/and" issue. Routine seeks to keep things the same, while creativity seeks to change things. The boredom of routine—from a lack of creativity and a lack of "not being used to"—leads you to creativity. The pressure of creativity—from a lack of routine and a lack of "being used to"—leads you back to routine. This is a healthy cycle. Stability is seasoned by shake-up, and shake-up is preserved by stability. When you see God more clearly and conviction stirs you to change the way you spend your time, for example, you need structure to assure discipline. You want to spend more time with God, so you establish a routine early in the morning in which you read one chapter of the Bible and pray for twenty minutes. Form follows function. They live together in their proper order.

Change is hard, and it is dangerous. It is also necessary and inevitable. People who live in Boston say, "If you don't like the weather, wait five minutes." Whether you like it or not, change is coming. The anthem of the civil rights movement, Sam Cooke's, "A Change is Gonna Come," provided an emotional expression of that truth. Change will happen. What will you do with it?

FEBRUARY 21

THE BASICS OF PREACHING AND TEACHING

"Be diligent to present yourself approved to God as a workman who does not need to be ashamed, accurately handling the word of truth."

2 Timothy 2:15

One way to understand what preaching and teaching are is to understand the differences between them. These are general differences that are tendencies as opposed to hard and fast rules; that is to say, they are relative differences, not absolute differences. In general, for example, regarding its nature, a sermon tends to be more practical, while a teaching tends to be more theoretical. Regarding its purpose, a sermon tends to put more emphasis on persuasion and encouragement, while a teaching tends to put more emphasis on instruction and information.

Regarding their methods of application, preachers often use more stories and descriptions of the events of everyday life, while teachers might use more analogies and Scripture illustrations. Regarding the method of communication, preachers tend to be more inclined to act things out; whereas, teachers tend to use more visual aids, charts, diagrams, and lists. Regarding its focus, a sermon might stress one point or one specific challenge, while a teaching might have more of a focus on one theme or on one specific section of Scripture. Regarding its form, a sermon tends be more of a monologue; whereas, a teaching might use class participation to promote more of a dialogue. Regarding its direction and contents, preachers tend to appeal more to the emotions and the will using more communication about everyday life; whereas, teachers tend to appeal more to the intellect using more communication about ideas and concepts. Regarding the response, sermons tend to encourage listeners to stare, while teachings encourage listeners to take notes. Regarding their results, preachers tend to encourage their listeners to proclaim, act, or change, while teachers tend to encourage their listeners to possess. Sermons often leave people inspired or convicted, and teachings often leave people informed. It might be said that a preacher puts gas in your vehicle, while a teacher makes sure you know how to change a spare tire. The sermon tends to answer the question, "Why?" whereas the teaching tends to answer the questions, "What?" and "How?"

How does one go about developing a sermon or a teaching? Think of the development of a sermon or a teaching as a process that has several steps. First, pray. Ask God what He wants to share with that particular group of people at that particular time. Second, search the Bible and write down specific Scripture references. Next, meditate; engage in a reflective focus. This may include many days of keeping the topic in your mind. God may add revelation through events that happen in your life. He may show you something more in the Bible. Current events, news, or circumstances might suggest more information that relates to the topic and can be used to apply a certain point of your message to everyday life.

Now it is time to begin to organize. Organize your thoughts into categories. Number the categories in a logical and useful way. Try to form a logical flow from one category to the next. Write out a basic outline. This is done by writing out your most important thoughts and placing them in the order that is best fit for your audience to understand and follow. Fill in the specific parts of the outline. Here, such tools as Bible commentaries and dictionaries can be helpful. Fill in details under the key points of the basic outline. Next, it is helpful to read over the outline five or six times before the presentation. Consider how and when to build momentum with your voice. Consider when to use pauses and how to use body communication. Finally, of course, deliver the sermon or teaching after praying for God's anointing and for the presence and ministry of the Holy Spirit.

Remember that a sermon or a teaching must be born in you before it can be presented effectively. There is a process that is analogous to giving birth. There is much hard work before the beautiful new baby is presented to the public. Similarly, the preacher or teacher must first engage in intimacy with God and His Word. Then there is conception. There is a waiting period in which the messenger "carries" the message. After a long time of carrying the message, there is a shorter time of delivering the message. This is hard work. You might say it includes "labor pains." A handler of the Word of God is called to be a diligent workman: "Be diligent to present yourself approved to God as a workman who does not need to be ashamed, accurately handling the word of truth" (2 Tim. 2:15).

Once the laboring over the message is completed, it is time to give birth to it. This is when it all comes together and is finalized. Now, all that is left is to present your baby to the public; the actual preaching or teaching of the message.

FEBRUARY 22

HOW DO YOU TEND TO FUNCTION?

"Since we have gifts that differ according to the grace given to us,
each of us is to exercise them accordingly: *if prophecy, according to the proportion of his faith;*
if service, in his serving; or he who teaches, in his teaching; or he who exhorts, in his exhortation;
he who gives, with liberality; he who leads, with diligence; he who shows mercy, with cheerfulness."
Romans 12:6-8

The New Testament talks about gifts in a variety of places and in a variety of ways. There are three completely different lists of gifts that are mentioned—one list in Ephesians 4:7-11 that is specifically linked to God the Son, another list in 1 Corinthians 12:8-10 that is particularly associated with God the Holy Spirit, and a third list in Romans 12:6-8 that is expressly connected to God the Father. Paul seems to be referring to these distinctions when he writes, "Now there are varieties of gifts, but the same Spirit. And there are varieties of ministries, and the same Lord. There are varieties of effects, but the same God who works all things in all *persons*" (1 Cor. 12:4-6). Each set of gifts has its own distinct nature and purpose that defines it and sets it apart from the other lists. The list of seven gifts found in Romans 12:6-8 include prophecy, serving, teaching, exhorting, giving, leading, showing mercy. The Giver of these gifts is God the Father (Rom. 12:3). The gifts are called *charismata* (grace gifts). They are described as being "functional gifts" (Rom. 12:4) that are "effects" enacted by "God who works all things in all *persons*" (1 Cor. 12:6).

The Romans 12 gifts are gifts that direct how a person functions; they determine the effects of a person's personality or tendencies. They are not so much gifts that a person is temporarily and situationally used in (as in the 1 Corinthians 12 gifts) or gifts that dictate a person's actual ministry (as in the Ephesians 4 gifts) as they are gifts that reside inside of a person and shape what that person is like. There is, then, for example, a "prophetic action" derived from the 1 Corinthians 12 list of gifts (an occasional use of a word of prophecy for a specific purpose), a "prophetic authority" derived from the Ephesians 4 list of gifts (more than a style of ministry, it is an actual ministry; it is more what a person is than what a person is like), and a "prophetic being" derived from the Romans 12 list of gifts (a prophetic style, tendency, emphasis, or personality), And so, since there are different lists of gifts, there are different kinds of gifts that function in different ways.

The Romans 12 gifts are "allotted" (Rom. 12:3) to each one in such a way that causes them to "function" (Rom. 12:4) in life somewhat differently than others; the gifts paint a picture of who they are in terms of their tendencies, unction, emphases, inclinations, and personalities. Thus, the presentation of the gifts in Romans 12 includes wording like "if service, in his serving . . . or he who exhorts, in his exhortation" (Rom. 12:7-8). In other words, if your gift is "service," then your tendency or inclination will be to serve. If your gift is exhortation, then your very personality will be that of an exhorter. These gifts energize, strengthen, and enable a person to fulfill certain functions. Because of this, they are often referred to as "motivational gifts." They establish a default mode in terms of how someone, almost automatically, thinks and then tends to act. They even could be said to be undercurrents that shape a person's personality and what they are like in their interactions with others. People who know that person well might say, "Audrey is just such a servant," or "Fred is such an encourager."

Each member of the body of Christ has at least one gift. The natural tendency is to function in corresponding types of ministries. For example, people with the gift of teaching might gravitate toward the Sunday school ministry in a church, while those with the gift of leadership might be more inclined to lead a home group. The person will have a natural passion for that ministry that will help him or her to "work out your salvation with fear and trembling; for it is God who is at work in you, both to will and to work for His good pleasure" (Phil. 2:12-13). The gift anoints a person for ministry; it moves that person "to will and to work" or to want to do ministry and to be able to do it. This is an awe-inspiring thing that when considered might cause "fear and trembling." To think that God saved you and is now working out that salvation via the way in which He has actually made you, even in your mother's womb (Gal. 1:15; Isaiah 49:1, 5), so that He might fulfill His plan for your life, is amazing!

The Romans 12 gifts seem to be permanent gifts that reside inside a person and make up that person's very identity and character. You are such a character! The man who puts letters in your mailbox is called a "mailman" because that title describes his function or identity. Who are you? Are you a prophet, a server, a teacher, an encourager, a giver, a leader, or one who gives mercy? This is an amazing thing because it is not simply mail that is being delivered but God's activity that is going forth!

FEBRUARY 23

MARRIAGE CAN BE OFFENSIVE, BUT LOVE CAN . . .

"Love never fails."

1 Corinthians 13:8

Approximately 50 percent of all marriages in the United States end in divorce. This, of course, is devastating for a culture; since the most foundational building block of society is the family, and the most foundational relationship in the family is the marriage. A society will only be as strong as its marriages. A strong society needs strong marriages, not broken ones.

The destruction of a marriage occurs when two people become divided. Disunity is the result of many unhealthy aspects of a relationship. Offense is often present—giving offense and being offended. It is self that gets offended; and when we are full of self, we will be full of offense.

So, the answer is to get rid of self. Healthy marriages are selfless marriages. That is easier said than done. But you get rid of self when you get full of something or someone else. "I have been crucified with Christ; and it is no longer I who live, but Christ lives in me" (Gal. 2:20). We are rid of self ("crucified") and full of Christ ("Christ lives in me"). Here is the secret to strong Christian marriages that do not fall victim to the 50 percent divorce rate. When it is not about you and, instead, is about Jesus, then your potential to be offended is greatly reduced. People who do not tend to get offended do not tend to get divided. Marriages are not destroyed. Societies are strengthened.

The "mechanism" for this solution is the power of love. To be full of God instead of self is to be full of love. God is love (1 John 4:8). Love is other-oriented. It is selfless, not selfish. "Love is patient, love is kind *and* is not jealous; love does not brag *and* is not arrogant, does not act unbecomingly; it does not seek its own, is not provoked, does not take into account a wrong *suffered,* does not rejoice in unrighteousness, but rejoices with the truth; bears all things, believes all things, hopes all things, endures all things. Love never fails" (1 Cor. 13:4-8a).

I am impatient with you because you are hindering *my* schedule. Impatience can offend. Love is patient. Love does not offend and is not offended. "I am angry with you because you did not do what I wanted." Anger can cause someone to offend and to be offended. Love is kind. Jealousy can cause someone to offend and be offended. Love, however, causes someone to not be jealous.

Bragging and arrogance are fuels for offense. "Do you not know who *I* am, and that it is all about *me*? Love does not brag. It is not arrogant. Love does not cause someone to offend or to be offended. It does not seek its own. It is not provoked. It does not take into account a wrong suffered.

Self keeps detailed accounts. "You always do this to *me.* I am offended." Love does not keep those accounts. "Love . . . bears all things, believes all things, hopes all things, endures all things.: Without love—without being full of Jesus but being full of self (Gal. 2:20)—self is king; and since the king comes first, if you do not satisfy the king's desires, then he is offended. Offense leads to disunity, and division means the marriage is broken. It fails.

We all have a sin nature. Our marriages are polluted by those sin natures. Sin always fails. Each partner's sin nature fights against the other. "I" is championed with the result that there is no room for "you." When "you" insists that it is really about its own "I," then offense is inevitable. Offense then becomes a fence. The only thing that breaks down the fence of offense is the cross. Love "never fails" (1 Cor. 13:8).

FEBRUARY 24

CHECK MOTIVES AT THE CIRCUMSTANTIAL DOOR

"Not that I speak from want, for I have learned to be content in whatever circumstances I am. I know how to get along with humble means, and I also know how to live in prosperity; in any and every circumstance I have learned the secret of being filled and going hungry, both of having abundance and suffering need. I can do all things through Him who strengthens me."
Philippians 4:11-13

That which resides in your heart constitutes the hidden things of your being. Motives, for example, are internal dynamics that cannot be seen. They are hidden in the sense that only you can really know them. They are crafty in the sense that even you sometimes, seemingly, do not see them clearly; you are not always willing to be honest with yourself with regard to what your motives really are. And so, you may need to check your motives at the *circumstantial* door!

We walk through a variety of doors every day—relational doors, ambition doors, task doors. "Why?" is the question that points to our motives. Why am I engaging in this relationship in this way? Why do I want to accomplish this goal? Why am I involved in this activity? Only you know the answers to these questions. There is always an agenda behind an action. You can only have one agenda, one focus, or one motive. Jesus put it this way: "No servant can serve two masters; for either he will hate the one and love the other, or else he will be devoted to one and despise the other. You cannot serve God and wealth" (Luke 16:13). He then said, "But seek first His kingdom and His righteousness, and all these things will be added to you" (Matt. 6:33).

The complicated thing about consistently walking in honorable motives is that it is difficult to remain focused. It is easier to walk through doors with other agendas. Idolatry—allowing a competing agenda to take the place of a God-agenda—creeps into our lives in a much easier way than we care to admit. And so, we may need to check our motives at the *circumstantial* door!

Paul met this challenge head on at the jailhouse door. Paul was a minister of the Gospel. His agenda was to spread the Word of God. Was this really his agenda? Other agendas and hidden motives get exposed in the midst of circumstances. When the going gets tough, the stated agenda might "get going." Do you want the Gospel to be preached or not? Is your motive that Christ is proclaimed, or is it that Christ is proclaimed only if it is building up your own ministry? Under what circumstances, do you want the Gospel to go forth? It is in the midst of circumstances that hidden things come to light. If the "proof is in the pudding," then the pudding is circumstances.

> Now I want you to know, brethren, that my circumstances have turned out for the greater progress of the gospel, so that my imprisonment in *the cause* of Christ has become well known throughout the whole praetorian guard and to everyone else, and that most of the brethren, trusting in the Lord because of my imprisonment, have far more courage to speak the word of God without fear. Some, to be sure, are preaching Christ even from envy and strife, but some also from good will; the latter *do it* out of love, knowing that I am appointed for the defense of the gospel; the former proclaim Christ out of selfish ambition rather than from pure motives, thinking to cause me distress in my imprisonment. What then? Only that in every way, whether in pretense or in truth, Christ is proclaimed; and in this I rejoice. Yes, and I will rejoice (Phil. 1:12-18).

The challenge for Paul at the prison door is clear. It is one thing to want Christ proclaimed by your own preaching outside of prison in such a way that is consistent with your own acceptable methods. It is another thing for that to happen without your involvement, and even more annoying, by the preaching of others who are getting credit for it instead of you. Here is the test! What are you in it for, Paul? Are you in it for Paul or for Christ?

Paul answers that question when he says, "What then?" or "Who cares?" or "What's the difference?" He says, in effect, "I don't care how it happens or who gets the credit as long as Christ is proclaimed." Paul is able to say this because that is truly his motive. His agenda is not to build his own ministry or to get credit for it. It is not to be comfortable. None of those things are wrong in and of themselves, but they are not what he is in it for.

The same challenge awaits each one of us at the various circumstantial doors of our lives. Why are you doing that nice thing for your wife, teacher, or boss? Is it for them, or is it for you? You will know the answer when your circumstances result in not getting what you want for yourself. Suddenly, you do not do those things for your wife, teacher, or boss anymore. You may need to check your motives at the circumstantial door!

FEBRUARY 25

CONTENTS STAY THE SAME— METHODS CHANGE

*"And according to Paul's custom, he went to them, and for three Sabbaths reasoned with them from the Scriptures, explaining and giving evidence that the Christ had to suffer and rise again from the dead, and **saying**, 'This Jesus whom I am proclaiming to you is the Christ.' And some of them were persuaded."*

Acts 17:2-4

The Gospel includes the message and the messenger—the content and the methods of delivering that content. Contents stay the same, but methods can change. The Gospel message is the Gospel message. It has always been the Gospel message, and it will always be the Gospel message. It does not change. Methods of presenting those contents can be different. They do change.

The contents of the Gospel can be summarized in five concepts: God's view of us, our problem, the consequences, God's provision, and our response. First, God loves people (John 3:16). Second, all people have sinned and are, therefore, separate from God (Rom. 3:23). Third, the payment for that sin is separation from God (Rom. 6:23). Fourth, "God demonstrates His own love toward us, in that while we were yet sinners, Christ died for us. Much more then, having now been justified by His blood, we shall be saved from the wrath of God through Him" (Rom. 5:8-9). Fifth, "repent and return, so that your sins may be wiped away, in order that times of refreshing may come from the presence of the Lord" (Acts 3:19). It is a story of redemption. We were initially deemed as those who walked with God and enjoyed His presence (Gen. 3:8). That got broken. And so, we were re-*deemed* as those who would again walk with God and enjoy "the presence of the Lord" (Acts 3:19).

The methods of communicating the Gospel include a variety of styles of presentation and personalities of presenters. Some messengers use an invitational style of evangelism in which they invite others to come and hear about Jesus. After the Samarian woman at the well came to faith in Jesus, she returned to her city and said, "'Come, see a man who told me all the things that

I *have* done; this is not the Christ, is it?' They went out of the city, and were coming to Him" (John 4:29-30). Other messengers use an endorsement style of evangelism in which they highlight the validity of Christ's ministry by testifying how He has changed their lives. After the man born blind was healed, he testified of Jesus to the doubting Pharisees, "'One thing I do know, that though I was blind, now I see'" (John 9:25).

Other sharers of the Gospel do so in a more thought-provoking way as they appeal to them like Paul did with the Thessalonians when he "reasoned with them from the Scriptures, explaining and giving evidence that the Christ had to suffer and rise again from the dead, and *saying*, 'This Jesus whom I am proclaiming to you is the Christ'" (Acts 17:2-3). Some messengers use a more direct style in which they confront people with the Gospel. Peter certainly did this with the Jews when he declared, "'Therefore let all the house of Israel know for certain that God has made Him both Lord and Christ—this Jesus whom you crucified'" (Acts 2:36). Some disciples of Christ, like Dorcas, use a giving style of evangelism by helping those who are in need (Acts 9:36). Still others use an affiliation style in which they share the Gospel with people they have relatively strong relationships with, which is what Jesus encouraged the formerly demon-possessed man to do when He told him, "'Go home to your people and report to them what great things the Lord has done for you, and *how* He had mercy on you'" (Mark 5:19).

There are different platforms from which to jump into the pools of evangelism, but the contents of the water are always the same. Water has always consisted of hydrogen and oxygen and will always consist of hydrogen and oxygen. Like the contents of the Gospel, it does not change. On the other hand, like the methods of presenting the Gospel, the platforms from which to jump into a pool do change. The question is not so much, "From which platforms do you like to jump?" The question is, "Are you jumping?"

FEBRUARY 26

THIS MYSTERY IS GREAT

"This mystery is great."

Ephesians 5:32

Bible-believing people are called to a high view of marriage. Marriage is established by God as the most foundational institution of human society. As soon as God created man, He declared, "'It is not good for the man to be alone; I will make him a helper suitable for him'" (Gen. 2:18). The word "helper" is often translated as "helpmeet" as it comes from two separate Hebrew words—one meaning "help" and the other meaning "other side, hence, an "other side helper." The descriptive definition of the combination of these terms is "one part comes together with its counterpart to form a complete whole." And so, God makes a completion of the man in response to His declaration that "it is not good for the man to be alone." A clear implication of this is that the man without the woman was incomplete.

This foundational act of creation that included the first surgery— God put the man to sleep, took a rib out of his side, and then sowed his flesh back together (Gen. 2:21)—resulted in what is sometimes called man's "better half." God declared that it was not *good*, so He made it *better*. Perhaps, this is why she is called "whoa-man"! Adam woke up and saw her and said, "Whoa! I am now complete!" Now, the man had the woman as his companion. His response to this is interesting. He says, "This is now bone of my bones, and flesh of my flesh; she shall be called Woman, because she was taken out of Man" (Gen. 2:23). He recognizes that they are two ("woman" and "man"), but he also recognizes that they are one ("bone of my bones and flesh of my flesh"). They are a singular plurality.

Out of this understanding—a singular (one) plurality (two) understanding—comes the singular plurality institution of marriage. The reason for such a thing is because that is the way God created it. And so, immediately after Adam's singular plurality declaration in Genesis 2:23, we see the establishment of marriage: "For this reason a man shall leave his father and his mother, and be joined to his wife; and they shall become one flesh" (Gen. 2:24). A paraphrase might be: "Since God created them as a singular plurality and commanded them to multiply (Gen. 1:28), the man shall leave family in order to multiply family by joining to her who completes him, and the two shall become one; the plural shall become singular."

Why is the marriage a singular plurality? It is derived from the nature of God that is stamped into the nature of mankind. Thus, Bible-believers should have a "high view" of marriage and a high view of humanity; human life is highly valued, and marriage and the family is highly valued. God, Who is a singular plurality—in the Trinity, He is Three-in-one—created man in His image.

Genesis 1:26-27 says, "Then God said, 'Let Us make man in Our image, according to Our likeness; and let them rule over the fish of the sea and over the birds of the sky and over the cattle and over all the earth, and over every creeping thing that creeps on the earth.'" God created man in His own image, in the image of God He created him; male and female He created them."

And so, the singular-plural God creates man in the image of a singular plurality in the sense that an individual "male" and an "individual "female" are a "them." The high view of the institution of marriage is being inaugurated. It is a high view because God Himself is high. This is why to take a low view of marriage is so offensive to God. This is why God "hates divorce" (Mal. 2:16). This is why Jesus said to the Pharisees: "Have you not read that He who created *them* from the beginning MADE THEM MALE AND FEMALE, and said, 'FOR THIS REASON A MAN SHALL LEAVE HIS FATHER AND MOTHER AND BE JOINED TO HIS WIFE, AND THE TWO SHALL BECOME ONE FLESH'? So they are no longer two, but one flesh. What therefore God has joined together, let no man separate" (Matt. 19:4-6).

Marriage means that two are one. There is distinction yet unity. There is equality without being the same. Out of this comes discussions with regard to the nature of marriage roles—simply because husband and wife are equal does not mean they are the same, and simply because they are not the same does not mean they are not equal—and discussions with regard to the nature of the Church. To have a high view of humanity and marriage is to have a high view of the Church. It is a mystery. Speaking about marriage, Paul says "This mystery is great; but I am speaking with reference to Christ and the church" (Eph. 5:32). It is the mystery of the singular plurality.

The Divine singular plurality makes man and marriage in His image, and then the Church also reflects that image as it is the body of Christ—the body of a singular plurality. And so, we see this picture painted in depictions of the Church, which is described as "we, who are many, are one" (Rom. 12:5) and "is one and yet has many members" (1 Cor. 12:12) and "the whole body, being fitted and held together by what every joint supplies, according to the proper working of each individual part" (Eph. 4:16). The Church is a singular plurality called to unity in diversity. This mystery is great! And so, we take a high view of humanity, marriage, and the Church. These are the foundational institutions of society, and Bible-believers are called to value them highly.

FEBRUARY 27

HAVING A KINGDOM PERSPECTIVE

"But seek first His kingdom and His righteousness, and all these things will be added to you. So do not worry about tomorrow."

Matthew 6:33-34

The kingdom life is a radical life. It is in no way a "nominal" or non-committed life. Halfway or "lukewarm" is not an option (Rev. 3:16). You cannot serve God and something else. To have a kingdom perspective is to have a 100 percent commitment to God. Less than 100 percent is really no commitment at all. It is all or nothing.

Since the kingdom dweller is sold out to God, he or she trusts God completely. "No one can serve two masters . . . for this reason I say to you, do not be worried about your life" (Matt. 6:24-25). A complete trust in God is rooted in a complete dedication to God. When there is nothing else to be dedicated to, there is nothing else to trust in.

God calls kingdom-dwellers to "seek first His kingdom" (Matt. 6:33). This is not a call to a chronological sequence of events: "Do this first; then do this second; and then do that third." It is not even a call to a hierarchical sequence of events: "This is most important; then this is of secondary importance; and then that is of third importance." It is more a call to a singular sequence of events. It is to constantly seek His kingdom in all things. His kingdom is not just number one. It is number two and three and four and five. We seek His kingdom "only" in the sense that we seek His kingdom in all things.

To make the kingdom of God your only desire—to consider no other options—is to put that kingdom and its King "first." It is to line Him up with nobody else in the line. This does not mean that the person who lives in the kingdom must reject all other things. Instead, "all these things will be added to you" (Matt. 6:33), and you will dedicate them to God; you will put them under the rule of God. This is how "other" lives with "only." The idea is that the perspective of the kingdom-dweller is one of complete and total trust in and dedication to God.

It is important to see how in the context of this kingdom-teaching, Jesus is very focused on encouraging His listeners not to be anxious:

> For this reason I say to you, do not be worried about your life, *as to* what you will eat or what you will drink; nor for your body, *as to* what you will put on. Is not life more than food, and the body more than clothing? Look at the birds of the air, that they do not sow, nor reap nor gather into barns, and *yet* your heavenly Father feeds them. Are you not worth much more than they? And who of you by being worried can add a *single* hour to his life? And why are you worried about clothing? Observe how the lilies of the field grow; they do not toil nor do they spin, yet I say to you that not even Solomon in all his glory clothed himself like one of these. But if God so clothes the grass of the field, which is *alive* today and tomorrow is thrown into the furnace, *will He* not much more *clothe* you? You of little faith! Do not worry then, saying, "What will we eat?" or "What will we drink?" or "What will we wear for clothing?" For the Gentiles eagerly seek all these things; for your heavenly Father knows that you need all these things. But seek first His kingdom and His righteousness, and all these things will be added to you. So do not worry about tomorrow; for tomorrow will care for itself. Each day has enough trouble of its own (Matt. 6:25-34).

This is the perspective of the person who lives in the kingdom of God. It is the perspective of a radical commitment that leads to a profound trust that leads to a pervasive peace. Kingdom people are people who do not worry because they have their eyes fixed on the King and not on everything else.

Maybe the most practical question for the kingdom-dweller is, "What are you worried about?" or "What are your eyes fixed on?" Worry about seeking His kingdom in all things. Let us concern ourselves with "fixing our eyes on Jesus" (Heb. 12:2). This is the kingdom perspective!

FEBRUARY 28

PURE AND UNDEFILED RELIGION

"Pure and undefiled religion in the sight of our God and Father is this."

James 1:27

The English word "religion" is derived from the Latin term religio, meaning "to tie back." The word "religion" or "religiosity" often connotes negative associations because it is linked to hypocrisy. Hypocrisy is empty and produces nothing of value. In referencing this sort of emptiness in a person, the Scripture states, "This man's religion is worthless" (James 1:26). When form takes the place of function and appearance outweighs content, then there is "no value": "These are matters which have, to be sure, the appearance of wisdom in self-made religion and self-abasement and severe treatment of the body, *but are* of no value against fleshly indulgence" (Col. 2:23).

Pure religion is to "tie back" to God's heart; it is to tie back to reality and not simply a show or the appearance of reality. "Pure and undefiled religion in the sight of our God and Father is this: to visit orphans and widows in their distress" (James 1:27). Why is this "pure and undefiled religion"? It is unblemished because it "ties back" to the heart of God. God's heart is for the needy because He is their Provider. When we minister to those in need, we reflect God's heart. It is not so much our actions of giving to the needy that represent undefiled religion as it is what lies underneath those actions. Out of compassion, mercy, and justice flow actions of compassion, mercy, and justice. It is the heart of God that "ties back" to God.

Since religion is associated with ministry to the needy, if I give to the poor, does that automatically make me a practitioner of "pure and undefiled religion"? Not necessarily. Jesus rebuked the hypocritical Pharisees in the midst of their giving to the poor. They brought their tithe of mint, dill, and cumin to the temple. This "spice offering" was used as a contribution to the poor. For these Pharisees, however, it was just a show—a way for the religious man to show off his religiosity. There may have even been trumpets sounding while the Pharisee placed his donation into the container, so to alert people of his momentous act. "Hey, look at me! I am so righteous and religious. Everyone should respect me."

Jesus does not sanction such "religion." In fact, He says, "'Woe to you, scribes and Pharisees, hypocrites! For you tithe mint and dill and cumin, and have neglected the weightier provisions of the law: justice and mercy and faithfulness; but these are the things you should have done without neglecting the others'" (Matt. 23:23).

There is nothing wrong with giving to the poor. It is a good thing. It should not be neglected. However, it must come along with and flow out of justice and mercy and kindness. When the actions are empty, it is just a show. The actions of the law must be preceded by "the weightier provisions of the law." That which is surface must be driven by that which is profound. Method without contents is hypocrisy.

Since there seems to be such a vulnerability to fall into hypocrisy when giving to the needy, maybe we should just avoid that sort of ministry. May it never be! The heart of the law is to "'LOVE YOUR NEIGHBOR AS YOURSELF'" (Gal. 5:14). Who is your neighbor?

> And a lawyer stood up and put Him to the test, saying, "Teacher, what shall I do to inherit eternal life?" And He said to him, "What is written in the Law? How does it read to you?" And he answered, "YOU SHALL LOVE THE LORD YOUR GOD WITH ALL YOUR HEART, AND WITH ALL YOUR SOUL, AND WITH ALL YOUR STRENGTH, AND WITH ALL YOUR MIND; AND YOUR NEIGHBOR AS YOURSELF." And He said to him, "You have answered correctly; DO THIS AND YOU WILL LIVE." But wishing to justify himself, he said to Jesus, "And who is my neighbor?" Jesus replied and said, "A man was going down from Jerusalem to Jericho, and fell among robbers, and they stripped him and beat him, and went away leaving him half dead. And by chance a priest was going down on that road, and when he saw him, he passed by on the other side. Likewise a Levite also, when he came to the place and saw him, passed by on the other side. But a Samaritan, who was on a journey, came upon him; and when he saw him, he felt compassion, and came to him and bandaged up his wounds, pouring oil and wine on *them*; and he put him on his own beast, and brought him to an inn and took care of him. On the next day he took out two denarii and gave them to the innkeeper and said, 'Take care of him; and whatever more you spend, when I return I will repay you.' Which of these three do you think proved to be a neighbor to the man who fell into the robbers' *hands*?" And he said, "The one who showed mercy toward him." Then Jesus said to him, "Go and do the same" (Luke 10:25-37).

Anyone in need is your neighbor. You are a neighbor when you show mercy. This is the heart of the law. This is God's heart. This is "pure and undefiled religion" (James 1:27) and "blessed are the pure in heart, for they shall see God" (Matt. 5:8). They shall tie back!

NOTES

March

MARCH 1

THE PARADOX OF THE FRUIT OF THE DESERT

"Remember all the way which the LORD your God has led you in the wilderness."
Deuteronomy 8:2

Wandering through the wilderness or in the desert is no fun. Difficult seasons of life are not what we look forward to. Nevertheless, God can use them. He uses them for His own glory as He reminds us of our desperate need for Him and of His unmeasurable love for us. The desert makes it especially clear to us that we desperately need water. The oasis in the desert shouts, "Come, take of my provision." It is the oasis that makes the desert palatable, and it is the desert that gives meaning to the oasis.

God may lead you into the wilderness: "Then Jesus was led up by the Spirit into the wilderness" (Matt. 4:1). He may use the wilderness experience to test you—not for the purpose of failing you but for the purpose of preparing you. "You shall remember all the way which the LORD your God has led you in the wilderness these forty years, that He might humble you, testing you, to know what was in your heart, whether you would keep His commandments or not" (Deut. 8:2).

In the wilderness, God provides for you and is always with you. "Even though I walk through the valley of the shadow of death, I fear no evil, for You are with me; Your rod and Your staff, they comfort me" (Psalm 23:4). The rod and staff are preparatory in that they are used by the shepherd to guide, protect, and discipline his sheep. God uses wilderness experiences this way. In referencing their forty years of wandering in the wilderness, God explains to the Israelites, "Thus you are to know in your heart that the LORD your God was disciplining you just as a man disciplines his son. Therefore, you shall keep the commandments of the LORD your God, to walk in His ways and to fear Him" (Deut. 8:5-6). Just as nobody enjoys discipline, nobody desires a wilderness experience either. Nevertheless, everyone wants the fruit that can come from it.

> And you have forgotten the exhortation which is addressed to you as sons, "MY SON, DO NOT REGARD LIGHTLY THE DISCIPLINE OF THE LORD, NOR FAINT WHEN YOU ARE REPROVED BY HIM; FOR THOSE WHOM THE LORD LOVES HE DISCIPLINES, AND HE SCOURGES EVERY SON WHOM HE RECEIVES." It is for discipline that you endure; God deals with you as with sons; for what son is there whom *his* father does not discipline? But if you are without discipline, of which all have become partakers, then you are illegitimate children and not sons. Furthermore, we had earthly fathers to discipline us, and we respected them; shall we not much rather be subject to the Father of spirits, and live? For they disciplined us for a short time as seemed best to them, but He *disciplines us* for *our* good, so that we may share His holiness. All discipline for the moment seems not to be joyful, but sorrowful; yet to those who have been trained by it, afterwards it yields the peaceful fruit of righteousness (Heb. 12:5-11).

God uses the "hidden dynamic" of wilderness experiences in our lives in preparatory ways. We see that, for example, in Moses' forty years in the wilderness of Midian (Acts 7:29-30) where God turns a shepherd into a king, and in Joseph's fourteen years spent in the wilderness of prison (Gen. 37:2, 41:46), in which God turns one who was thrown into a pit into one who was put on the throne. David fled from Saul for many years before becoming king, and Paul "went away to Arabia" (Gal. 1:17) for years before entering into his apostolic ministry.

God uses the wilderness (Deut. 8:2-6) to test you in order that you might receive more from Him and be used more by Him. He humbles you. He promotes less of you, so there can be more of Him. He promotes a trust and dependence on Him, which will enable Him to lead you since being led by God necessitates being dependent upon God and trusting in Him. He promotes obedience through discipline. All of these promotions can more easily take place in the wilderness. "All discipline for the moment seems not to be joyful, but sorrowful; yet to those who have been trained by it, afterwards it yields the peaceful fruit of righteousness" (Heb. 12:11).

God wants to use the barren wilderness to grow His crops. This is the paradoxical "fruit of the desert." The result of a wilderness experience can be that you enter a promised land—the reception of provision and satisfaction that comes from a greater enablement to obey and follow God and to remember Him!

> You shall remember all the way which the LORD your God has led you in the wilderness these forty years, that He might humble you... and let you be hungry... that He might make you understand that man does not live by bread alone, but man lives by everything that proceeds out of the mouth of the LORD... therefore, you shall keep the commandments of the LORD your God, to walk in His ways and to fear Him. For the LORD your God is bringing you into a good land, a land of brooks of water... where you will eat food without scarcity, in which you will not lack anything... when you have eaten and are satisfied, you shall bless the LORD your God for the good land which He has given you... He led you through the great and terrible wilderness, with its fiery serpents and scorpions and thirsty ground where there was no water; He brought water for you out of the rock of flint... you shall remember the LORD your God... (Deut. 8:2-18).

MARCH 2

LOVE AND LAW ARE MARRIED, NOT DIVORCED

> *"By this we know that we love the children of God, when we love God and observe His commandments. For this is the love of God, that we keep His commandments; and His commandments are not burdensome."*
>
> 1 John 5:2-3

Ethics is defined as the moral principles or definitions that govern behavior. Law is defined as a system of rules or definitions that are recognized by an individual or community of individuals to regulate and account for their actions. Ethics and law are almost synonymous terms. Ethics build laws, and laws express ethics. Some theologians feel more comfortable to describe the ethics of the New Testament in terms of love and grace and would prefer to somehow avoid the idea of law. This, of course, is impossible since the definitions of ethics and law are inseparable and since "love" represents for Jesus the summing up of the Law and the Prophets.

"Teacher, which is the great commandment in the Law?" And He said to him, "'YOU SHALL LOVE THE LORD YOUR GOD WITH ALL YOUR HEART, AND WITH ALL YOUR SOUL, AND WITH ALL YOUR MIND.' This is the great and foremost commandment. The second is like it, 'YOU SHALL LOVE YOUR NEIGHBOR AS YOURSELF.' On these two commandments depend the whole Law and the Prophets (Matt. 22:36-40).

Just as the New Covenant is a better or clearer revelation of the same God and not a different covenant than the Old Covenant, so, too, it is redundant to speak of a "New Testament ethic" and an "Old Testament ethic." Nevertheless, some theological positions promote the perception of a mutually exclusive relationship between law and grace and, therefore, do not recognize the law as being the hub of "Christian ethics."

It may be most consistent with biblical theology to talk about a love ethic or a love law. Certainly, loving relationships must have some form and structure. Neutral love or undefined love is actually an oxymoron. A love ethic must have rules. Jesus promotes His "love law" when He challenges His disciples, "If you love Me, you will keep my commandments" (John 14:15). Love and grace are not separate from ethics and laws. Love and grace do not exempt us from the law; rather, they enable us to obey the law.

This relationship between love and law is established in both the New and Old Testaments. The New Testament's "for this is the love of God, that we keep His commandments" (1 John 5:3) is wed to the Old Testament's "but showing lovingkindness to thousands, to those who love Me and keep My commandments" (Exod. 20:6). The New Testament's "He who has My commandments and keeps them is the one who loves Me" (John 14:21); and "if we keep His commandments . . . whoever keeps His word, in him the love of God has truly been perfected" (1 John 2:3, 5) is no different than the Old Testament's "keep all His statutes and His commandments . . . you shall love the LORD your God" (Deuteronomy 6:2, 5). Love and law stand together. It is not the God of love and grace in the New Testament and the God of law and holiness in the Old Testament as if there are two different Gods. No, "the LORD is our God, the LORD is one!" (Deut. 6:4). We cannot understand love without law, and we cannot understand law without love.

Ethics build laws, and laws express ethics. The nature of love is not that of neutrality. It has definition. A person oxymoronically says, "I love people, so I am not a person of belief or conviction. My refusal to define truth is my act of love." But they are, in fact, defining truth and expressing it with a degree of belief and conviction. You cannot love and parent your children by simply "letting them go and letting them grow" as if you can guide them by not guiding them. To love them, you must define, guide, enforce, and restore. The idea that you can do these things without definitions or laws is not only senseless, but it is also lazy and hypocritical (Matt. 23:28).

Lawlessness is the opposite of love. "Because lawlessness is increased, most people's love will grow cold" (Matt. 24:12). This is a dangerous game. Anarchy is the opposite of order. It is a dangerous dynamic for any society. Safety and security come with the marriage of love and law. An ethical society is a loving society, and a loving society is not a lawless society. Love and law exist together. Celebrate the wedding and not the divorce!

MARCH 3

THE SHEPHERD COUNSELOR AND HIS SHEEP

"And the sheep hear his voice, and he calls his own sheep by name and leads them out. When he puts forth all his own, he goes ahead of them, and the sheep follow him because they know his voice. A stranger they simply will not follow, but will flee from him, because they do not know the voice of strangers."

John 10:3-5

Jesus, the Good Shepherd, calls His sheep by name. The sheep follow Him because they know His voice. The sheep will not follow a stranger. How can we best be available to help people? How can we most effectively counsel others in their time of need? We have to be "people persons." Highly relational people tend to be the best counselors. Those who really know others and allow others to know them, by definition, are most likely to be able to help others because "the sheep follow him because they know his voice" (John 10:4).

Having established this—the importance of relationship-building in order to be effective in counseling—it must also be said that the person who regularly uses his or her wisdom to help people must understand, with respect to the one he is helping, that there is a difference between motivation and responsibility. The counselor can offer advice and motivation. However, the person being counseled is ultimately responsible for his or her own life (Gal. 6:5). It must be remembered that it is the person who is being counseled who must be willing to change. Accepting and applying this principle will help counselors avoid burnout and help them to stay away from the error of taking the place of God in people's lives.

This point in no way implies that the counselor cannot have compassion on the counselee. The word "compassion" is derived from two words—"suffer" and "with." The counselor can "suffer with" in order to relate to the person being counseled. He can show compassion in order to build a bond. To "suffer with" someone is to put yourself in their place or to "walk in their shoes." Having compassion on someone yields the desire to shepherd that person—the desire to help or to counsel him or her. And so, "When Jesus went ashore, He saw a large crowd, and He felt compassion for them because they were like sheep without a shepherd; and He began to teach them many things" (Mark 6:34).

MARCH 4

IT'S NOT SOPHIE'S CHOICE; IT'S GOD'S CHOICE

"God has chosen you ... because the LORD loved you and kept the oath which He swore to your forefathers."

Deuteronomy 7:6, 8

One of the most riveting movies I ever remember watching was the 1982 film, *Sophie's Choice*. In an incredibly emotional scene, Sophie, who is imprisoned in Auschwitz along with her two young children during World War II, is forced to choose which one of her children will live and which one will die. She chooses her son, Jan; and he is sent off to a work camp, while her daughter, Eva, is sent to the gas chambers. The idea of being chosen, by its very nature, seems to warrant a discussion about fairness and justice. "Chosen" seems to imply "not chosen." Is that fair? Is it just to choose one and not the other?

Those questions actually assume something that may not be true. What if Sophie's choice was a different kind of choice? What if in choosing her son, it did not send him off to a work camp but, instead, put him in charge of the prisoners at Auschwitz? What if not choosing her daughter did not automatically send her to the gas chambers but, instead, placed her under the authority of the person in charge of the prisoners in the death camp? The story then plays out that Jan releases Eva, and both survive. Jan, then, was not chosen to exclude Eva but, rather, to include her. One was chosen so that another could be chosen as well. Now, that is a totally different scene in the movie!

There is also a totally different scene in the movie called, God's Choice: His Plan of Redemption for Mankind. God chooses a people so that other people can be chosen as well. He first chooses Israel. Why did God choose Israel? One of the most well-known verses in the Bible, John 3:16, makes sure that we understand what kind of choice it is: "For God so loved Israel . . . " Is that what it says? No. Of course, God does love Israel but that in no way means He does not love others. Why does He enact His plan of redemption? It is "for God so loved *the world* . . ."

So, why did God choose Israel? Was it a "teacher's pet" type of situation? That is how I remember my fourth grade teacher making Sharon Pembrook the obvious favorite. She was the —*est*—the smart*est*, the cut*est*, the overall b*est*. That must be why God chose Israel, right?

"For you are a holy people to the LORD your God; the LORD your God has chosen you to be a people for His own possession out of all the peoples who are on the face of the earth. The LORD did not set His love on you nor choose you because you were more in number than any of the peoples, for you were the fewest of all peoples, but *because the Lord loved you and kept the oath which He swore to your forefathers*" (Deut. 7:6-8, emphasis mine).

No, God did not choose Israel as the teacher's pet. Israel was definitely not the —est. They were not the biggest. If anything, they were smaller than those around them. God is very clear He chose Israel for two reasons, both of which revolve around one idea found in John 3:16—that is, God is love. First of all, God chose Israel because God loves Israel. He says straight up that they were chosen *"because the Lord loved you."* Second, God chose Israel because He loves all people; He chose them so as to keep *"the oath which He swore to your forefathers."* When we understand that this oath—the Abrahamic covenant—was a missionary covenant, then we understand more fully why God chose Israel.

God chose Israel because it would *include* others, not *exclude* them. The Abrahamic covenant is a missionary covenant made with Israel in the Old Testament just like the Great Commission is a missionary covenant made with the Church in the New Testament. Of course, God charges His missionary people in the New Testament to "Go" (Matt. 28:19). He also charges His missionary people in the Old Testament to "Go" (Gen. 12:1). Even as the church is to "Go into all the world" (Mark 16:15), so, too, is Israel to "spread out to the west and to the east and to the north and to the south" (Gen. 28:14).

This missionary outreach is inclusive. The New Testament missionaries are to "make disciples of all the nations" (Matt. 28:19). The Old Testament missionaries are to "be fruitful and multiply, and fill the earth" (Gen. 1:28) for "in you all the families of the earth will be blessed" (Gen. 12:3). God's missionaries in the New Testament will accomplish their mission because they are commissioned under God's authority and with His presence. God says to the Church, "All authority has been given to Me in heaven and on earth. Go therefore" (Matt. 28:18-19). He then says, "And lo, I am with you always, even to" (Matt. 28:20). In the same way, God's missionaries in the Old Testament would accomplish their mission because they were commissioned under God's authority and with His presence. In reference to His missiological charge, God said to Israel, "And behold, the Lord stood above it and said, 'I am the Lord'" (Gen. 28:13). He then said, "Behold, I am with you and will keep you wherever you go, and will bring you back to this land; for I will not leave you until I have done what I promised you" (Gen. 28:15).

God is a missionary God. He is an Entrepreneur. He has created man in His own image; thus, man is entrepreneurial and apostolic. He is the "Sent One." He is a Missionary. Israel and the Church were chosen so that all people could be chosen as well.

MARCH 5

I'LL SCRATCH YOUR BACK IF YOU SCRATCH MINE

*"If you love those who love you, what credit is **that** to you?*
For even sinners love those who love them. If you do good to those who do good to you,
*what credit is **that** to you? For even sinners do the same.*
*If you lend to those from whom you expect to receive, what credit is **that** to you?*
*Even sinners lend to sinners in order to receive back the same **amount**.*
But love your enemies, and do good, and lend, expecting nothing in return."
Luke 6:32-35

The guarantee of an unhealthy marriage is the use of "50/50" love. Each partner gives only 50 percent. This is a worldly or fleshly kind of "love." Each person gives with the expectation that the other person will give an equal share. The problem with this is that each partner is waiting for the other partner to contribute. Husband and wife are both saying at the same time, "I will love and serve you when you love and serve me; you scratch my back, and I will scratch yours." It is a damaging waiting game in which neither person tends to ever come out of the waiting room.

This danger must be avoided in any relationship in which love and service should prosper. Love is selfless. "Love is patient, love is kind . . . it does not seek its own" (1 Cor. 13:4-5). Divine "agape" love is unconditional love or "100/100" love. Each person in the relationship is willing to help the other person, regardless of what he or she may get in return. Any type of "50/50" service is a selfish and fake service. Pure service is unconditional service.

To be a servant and not just be somebody who does acts of service, you must forget your own desires and remember the desires of others. You must also remember your own responsibilities and forget the responsibilities of others. This requires death to self. In order to *live* to someone else, you must *die* to yourself. "For through the Law I died to the Law, so that I might live to God. I have been crucified with Christ; and it is no longer I who live, but Christ lives in me" (Gal. 2:19-20).

In many ways, the ability to love and the ability to serve come down to expectations. "But love . . . and do good . . . expecting nothing in return" (Luke 6:35). Absolute love and service requires that you have absolutely no expectations. You put no demands on the other person. Your service is not conditional. Any other way is of the flesh and no different than the ways of sinners. Luke 6:32-34 tells us, "If you love those who love you, what credit is *that* to you? For even sinners love those who love them. If you do good to those who do good to you, what credit is *that* to you? For even sinners do the same. If you lend to those from whom you expect to receive, what credit is *that* to you? Even sinners lend to sinners in order to receive back the same *amount*."

Service cannot be a payback. It must be a gift. To love and serve conditionally is human, while to love and serve unconditionally is Divine. Service that waits for the other guy to scratch your back before you will scratch his back is really no service at all. Everybody just waits around, and nobody can stop itching!

MARCH 6

SPEAKERS MUST START AND END SOMEWHERE

"Preach the word; be ready in season and out of season."
2 Timothy 4:2

A memorable way to concisely describe the sections of a sermon or teaching is with the rhyme, "hook, look, took." About 10 percent of a message should be the introduction (hook). About 80 percent of the message should be the body (look). The final 10 percent should be the conclusion (took). In the introduction, you *tell* your audience what they can expect from you. In the conclusion, you *tell* them what you expect from them. In the body, you *tell* them what you want to tell them by using explanations, so they can understand your point; illustrations, so they can see the picture you are painting; and applications, so they can feel it in their own lives.

Preachers and teachers of the Word of God have to start somewhere. Where is that somewhere? It is in the introduction of a message. Introductions are very important. What will I say? An introduction should tell people what you will be speaking about. This can be done in creative ways that not only prepare listeners for the message but also spark their interest. An introduction should clearly tell your listeners what you are going to tell them. At the end of the introduction, a brief outline can be offered that will identify the various parts or purposes of your message. An example of an outline given at the end of an introduction might be, "And so we will consider some common causes of discouragement, some effective solutions for discouragement, and some ways to avoid discouragement." Introductions should also give your audience a reason to listen. It must arouse interest. There was a man who wanted to train his mule. So he hit the mule between the ears with a big stick. The mule almost fell down. Someone asked the man, "Why did you do that?" The man answered, "To teach a mule you must first get his attention." This, of course, is very true with people also. Interest must be awakened before learning can occur.

There are various ways to try to promote interest. One way is that you might try to challenge people. For example, when preaching a message concerning the efficacy of prayer, you might ask rhetorically, "Do you know how to pray effectively? Do you get results when you pray?" Another way to promote interest is to promise your listeners that you will give them something. You might say, "Today I will show you how you can get more results from your prayers." You may also explain how your topic is important and relevant to their lives: "Prayer changes things. Your prayers can make the difference." Similarly, you might propose a problem and promise a solution or make a proposition. For example, you could propose, "Much time is wasted in ineffective prayer. Today we want to learn how to pray effectively so that every one of our prayers will count."

An introduction should be like an alarm clock. It should wake up people. It should get them interested in what you are going to preach or teach. Humor is a useful tool. Often times, the naked truth about real-life personal situations provides for an effective platform from which to put forth, perhaps, a sort of self-deprecating "elephant-in-the-room" type of humor. An introductory story might be, "Yesterday I prayed for one hour. The only problem was that I was distracted the whole time; I was thinking about all that I had to do that day. At the end of the hour, I had a very well-organized plan in my mind of how to schedule my day, but I did not pray that much. What a fruitful hour. The rest of the day was terrible. I did not get anything done. Well, at least I was organized while I got nothing done. Maybe I should try to pray more effectively."

Humor is a very powerful communication tool. It creates a good "listening climate" and lowers defenses, which people tend to put up when they think someone is trying to persuade them to do something. Humor arouses interest. Most importantly, a person who laughs at something is better prepared to think seriously about that thing. When he stops laughing, he must consider the more profound message that is associated with the humor.

Sometimes, the use of somewhat surprising statistics can capture attention. For example, the speaker who is speaking on the importance of prayer might report that "50 percent of all marriages end in divorce; however, less than 1 percent of the married couples who pray together get divorced." An especially memorable or impacting point that is made in the introduction can then dramatically be revisited in the conclusion of a message. This "wrap-around" technique tends to tie the message together as the end goes back to the beginning after the beginning had already effectively prepared the listener for the end. The speaker may end with: "So married couples, today you must decide. Do you want to be in that 50 percent group, or are you going to make sure you are one of the 1 percent? Choose the 1 percent. Pray together!"

In building a sermon or a teaching, the preacher or teacher should take time to craft an appropriate conclusion. The conclusion should answer the question, "What did I say?" It should include a brief summary of the message. A conclusion should also answer the question, "What are the implications for you?" It should include a strong challenge that is specific and compels the listener to make a decision while still offering encouragement and casting vision. The conclusion should not be long. Avoid turning it into another sermon by repeating, "In conclusion . . ." It is important to know when and how to end. Someone once gave the following advice to a young preacher: "A sermon is like a good meal. You should end it just before we have had enough."

Preachers must preach, and teachers must teach. Both need to effectively package their messages by using effective introductions and conclusions. And so, "preach the word; be ready in season *and* out of season" (2 Tim. 4:2).

MARCH 7

WALKING ON THE WORD OF GOD

"And He said, 'Come!' And Peter . . . walked on the water and came toward Jesus."
Matthew 14:29

Faith must be based on obedience to the Word of God, lest it be presumption. "Peter said to Him, 'Lord, if it is You, command me to come to You on the water.' And He said, 'Come!' And Peter got out of the boat, and walked on the water and came toward Jesus" (Matt. 14:28-29). Peter did not so much walk on the water as he walked on the Word of God. Jesus said, "Come"; and so, Peter "came." Peter *heard* the Word and acted on it in faith: "So faith *comes* from hearing, and hearing by the word of Christ" (Rom. 10:17).

Faith is different than presumption. Faith is based on your own personal revelation from God that results in your obedience. Presumption is based on the example or experience of someone else and results in your attempt to copy that person. Presumptuous faith is a "cheating faith." We should not say, "Now I will walk on water. I will have the faith of Peter." We must receive our own revelation from God. Nobody can walk in the faith of another person. Our faith must be connected directly to our personal relationship with God. Do not, for example, become a "conference speaker chaser" living on the faith of others at the expense of your own seeking of God. Presumptuous faith is a "vulture faith." The tragedy of presumption is that it bypasses relationship. Faith in God equals relationship with God (Heb. 11:6). Presumptuous faith is a "distant faith."

Faith must be launched by the Word of God. It must also continue in the Word of God, lest it turn into doubt: "Peter . . . walked on the water . . . . But seeing the wind, he became frightened, and beginning to sink, he cried out, 'Lord, save me!' Immediately Jesus stretched out His hand and took hold of him, and said to him, 'You of little faith, why did you doubt?'" (Matt. 14:29-31).

When we lose sight of Jesus and start focusing on other things—like the strong winds and the big waves in our lives—we begin to sink. Doubt leads to fear, and fear leads to a lack of faith. We must keep our eyes on Jesus. "Let us also lay aside every encumbrance and the sin which so easily entangles us, and let us run with endurance the race that is set before us, fixing our eyes on Jesus, the author and perfecter of faith" (Heb. 12:1-2).

If we have a lack of faith, then we need to call upon Jesus. Peter "became frightened, and beginning to sink, he cried out, 'Lord, save me!' . . . they got into the boat" (Matt. 14:30-32). With Jesus, there is always another chance to walk in faith. Peter walked on the water and went *away* from the boat, and then he began to sink. Jesus pulled him up, and they went *back* to the boat. The implication of this rendition of the story is that Peter walked on the water again when he went back to the boat with Jesus. Jesus keeps pulling us up to faith!

The conclusion is that faith begins with your relationship with God. Within that relationship, God speaks His Word to you. He reveals Himself. He guides you and directs you. By faith, you must obey that direction. You can build your faith through prayer and fasting (Matt. 17:20-21; Jude 20) and through hearing and reading the Bible (Rom. 10:17). Your faith can be made stronger when you study, understand, accept, and believe in the sovereignty of God and His promises. You must believe that God is able to do it (His sovereignty) and that He wants to do it (His promises). God is "all in all" (Eph. 1:23) as He is the Source, Contents, and Object of your faith. Faith looks to God!

MARCH 8

THE FRUIT OF HUMILITY

"And all of you, clothe yourselves with humility toward one another, for GOD IS OPPOSED TO THE PROUD, BUT GIVES GRACE TO THE HUMBLE."

1 Peter 5:5

God is a multiplier. That is the way He grows His kingdom. He does not divide, nor does He subtract, nor does He simply add. He multiplies (Matt. 25:14-30). Multipliers give away; they are willing to let go of what they have. "The things which you have heard from me in the presence of many witnesses, entrust these to faithful men who will be able to teach others also" (2 Tim. 2:2). Humility is the fuel of the multiplier. Pride cannot give away and multiply ministry. The humility of Moses allowed him to give away ministry without trying to hold it back (Deut. 31:7; Num. 27:16-23). Let it go and let it grow; do not be the one who "dug a hole in the ground and hid his master's money" (Matt. 25:18).

The humility of Moses (Num. 12:3) enabled him to respect others. Moses and his father-in-law Jethro had an agreement (Exod. 2:21), and Moses was humble enough to respect that (Exod. 4:18) at a time when he could have easily ignored it. Moses had just received Divine direction from God Himself (Exod. 4:1-17). Yet he did not regard himself as being so special that he did not have to show respect to his elder. Obedience to God and respect for others can go together. The glue is humility.

Moses was the leader of a miraculous Exodus. He was famous throughout the land, a big shot. Nevertheless, he was still able to receive council from Jethro (Exod. 18:17-27). His humility enabled him to respect Jethro enough to be able to benefit from his council. Humility makes you teachable.

A lack of humility often leads to a life of complaining. Moses was not one to complain, although he had many opportunities to do so. Humility includes an acceptance of the fact that you have no rights to hold onto. It understands that you do not deserve anything. God gives and takes away as He pleases because He is God. A humble person accepts that and, therefore, does not complain. Pride yields an attitude of entitlement. Eventually, that results in a lot of complaining.

Moses did not even complain when God would not allow him to enter the Promised Land. If any man ever had a "right" to claim something before God, it was Moses. He had given his whole life to lead the Israelites into the Promised Land. Moses did not complain. His humility enabled him to accept his judgment without questioning God. He did not rebel. He did not try to "claim" his rights. Instead, he praised God (Deut. 33:2-3).

Humility is a critical part of Christian character. It opens the door to many godly attributes. It helps us to be multipliers. It enables us to respect others. It makes us teachable. It helps us to not be complainers. The humble live in the "kingdom of heaven" and "inherit the earth" (Matt. 5:3, 5). So, "humble yourselves in the presence of the Lord, and He will exalt you" (James 4:10). "He has told you, O man, what is good; and what does the LORD require of you but to do justice, to love kindness, and to walk humbly with your God?" (Micah 6:8).

MARCH 9

YOU'RE GOING TO BE A FOOL TO SOMEBODY

> *"When Jesus saw the crowds, He went up on the mountain; and after He sat down, His disciples came to Him. He opened His mouth and **began** to teach them."*
>
> Matthew 5:1-2

To some degree, the importance of any topic can be measured by the number of books that have been written about it. There have been more books written about the Sermon on the Mount than any other portion of the teachings of Jesus. It is Jesus' first recorded sermon that could very well be understood as His quintessential sermon. In three brief chapters, the sermon says what the wisdom of man could not say in thousands of books. Its importance to the Christian is obvious. In his book, *A Few Buttons Missing: The Case Book of a Psychiatrist,* James Fisher describes the importance of the sermon in the following way:

> If you were to take the sum total of all the authoritative articles ever written by the most qualified of psychologists and psychiatrists on the subject of mental hygiene—if you were to combine them and refine them and cleave out the excess verbiage—if you were to have these unadulterated bits of pure scientific knowledge concisely expressed by the most capable of living poets, you would have an awkward and incomplete summation of the Sermon on the Mount.[2]

In many ways, the sermon is a commentary on John 18:36: "My kingdom is not of this world. If My kingdom were of this world, then My servants would be fighting so that I would not be handed over to the Jews; but as it is, My kingdom is not of this realm." The sermon is a practical teaching on how the kingdom of God is not of this world. It is not a political kingdom, and it is not a religious kingdom. (This explains why the political and religious people of the day tended to butt heads with Jesus).

The kingdom of God represents a "counter-culture." This is not like the counter-revolution of the drug-using, flower children hippies of the 1960s and 1970s. It is not so much an "against culture" issue as it is an "opposite culture" issue. It is not one sinful culture against another sinful culture. It is "counter" in the sense of being opposite of a fallen culture, even as righteousness is opposite of sinfulness; thus, Peter's statement, "We must obey God rather than men" (Acts 5:29), counters with a sharp contrast without wielding a sharp sword (Matt. 26:51-52).

The kingdom of God is not simply a different *form* of worldliness. It is *not* the secular superficiality of the world that is best described as a farce: "The kings of the Gentiles lord it over them; and those who have authority over them are called 'Benefactors.' But it is not this way with you, but the one who is the greatest among you must become like the youngest, and the leader like the servant" (Luke 22:25-26). It is *not* the spiritual superficiality of religiosity that is best described as phony: "Woe to you, scribes and Pharisees, hypocrites! For you are like whitewashed tombs which on the outside appear beautiful, but inside they are full of dead men's bones and all uncleanness. So you, too, outwardly appear righteous to men, but inwardly you are full of hypocrisy and lawlessness" (Matt. 23:27-28).

The kingdom of God is not just a different *form* of worldliness; it is entirely different *from* worldliness. It is the opposite of the superficial political and religious worlds. It is a God-ruled reality that breeds fanatics—people who are "sold-out" for the coming of His kingdom: "Our Father who is in heaven, hallowed be Your name. Your kingdom come. Your will be done, on earth as it is in heaven" (Matt. 6:9-10).

Relative to the world, those who respond to the Sermon on the Mount and live in the kingdom of God are fanatics. They are those who say, "We have become a spectacle to the world, both to angels and to men. We are fools for Christ's sake" (1 Cor. 4:9-10). Which world do you want to live in? You are going to be a fool to somebody. Why not be a fool for Christ?

MARCH 10

FROM WHERE SHALL MY HELP COME?

"I will lift up my eyes to the mountains; from where shall my help come? My help comes from the LORD."
Psalm 121:1-2

Dying to self is how we move toward spirituality because the life of spirituality assumes the death of the flesh. In order to sustain spirituality, we must continually go through the process of coming to the end of ourselves. To one degree or another, we are all like the children of Israel as they are depicted in the book of Judges. We forget about God when we perceive that we have everything under control and, therefore, do not need Him. Then, something goes wrong. We lose control. Something happens that reveals our desperate need for God, and therefore, we seek Him again. God responds and makes things right. Eventually, we begin to take him for granted all over again. We forget about God until the next thing happens that prompts us to recall our need for Him. There it is—the book of Judges!

And so the cycle goes! Times of testing can lead us back to God. Self-imposed "wilderness experiences" can be God's platform used to draw us to Himself. In a very real sense, in order to be comforted, you first must be uncomfortable (Matt. 5:4). This does not make discomfort, in and of itself, desirable or good; but it does make it useful to a sovereign God, for He "is our refuge and strength, a very present help in trouble" (Psalm 46:1).

When a consumer critic runs a public test on a car, it is with the goal of exposing the negative aspects of the vehicle. Oppositely, when the company that makes the car runs public tests, it is to highlight the positive aspects of the car. Satan, the critic, tries to use times of testing in your life for negative purposes. God, the Creator, uses times of testing for positive purposes. Perhaps you are in a time or season of testing right now in your life. Where do you get relief? The burden seems too heavy to handle. – What do you do? The answer to the "what question" is found in the answer to the "where question":

> I will lift up my eyes to the mountains; from where shall my help come? My help *comes* from the LORD, who made heaven and earth. He will not allow your foot to slip; He who keeps you will not slumber. Behold, He who keeps Israel will neither slumber nor sleep. The LORD is your keeper; the LORD is your shade on your right hand. The sun will not smite you by day, nor the moon by night. The LORD will protect you from all evil; He will keep your soul. The LORD will guard your going out and your coming in from this time forth and forever (Psalm 121).

Your wilderness experiences are used by God for your good and His glory. God does not allow times of testing so you can get an "F." The purpose of wilderness experiences is to bring you into a fuller realization that you must depend completely on God and not on yourself. "You shall remember all the way which the LORD your God has led you in the wilderness these forty years, that He might humble you, testing you . . . that He might make you understand that man does not live by bread alone, but man lives by everything that proceeds out of the mouth of the Lord" (Deut. 8:2-3).

The result of wilderness experiences is an expansion of your spiritual life through a contraction of your fleshly life. As more of you leaves, more of God is able to come in. "In the wilderness He fed you manna . . . that He might humble you and that He might test you, to do good for you in the end. Otherwise, you may say in your heart, 'My power and the strength of my hand made me this wealth.' But you shall remember the LORD your God, for it is He who is giving you power" (Deut. 8:16-18).

Wandering through the wilderness is no fun. Difficult seasons of life are not what we look forward to. Nevertheless, God can use them. He uses them for His own glory as He draws us to Himself. My help comes from God!

MARCH 11

SOME HELP FOR HELPERS

> *"Therefore you have no excuse, everyone of you who passes judgment, for in that which you judge another, you condemn yourself; for you who judge practice the same things. And we know that the judgment of God rightly falls upon those who practice such things. But do you suppose this, O man, when you pass judgment on those who practice such things and do the same **yourself**, that you will escape the judgment of God?"*
>
> Romans 2:1-3

We all have opportunities to help people from time to time because at one point or another, we all need someone to guide, direct, challenge, or just listen to us. There is never a shortage of people who need help, so there is never a shortage of opportunities to be a helper. And like anything else, there are ways in which we can be more effective helpers or counselors.

For example, a counselor should avoid counseling when the person being helped is emotionally disturbed or distraught. This is the time to simply listen and comfort. "*Like* one who takes off a garment on a cold day, or *like* vinegar on soda, is he who sings songs to a troubled heart" (Prov. 25:20). Once a person is ready to receive help, the counselor should ask for a summary—one or two sentences—of the problem. In this way, a multitude of details or excuses that tend to accompany an attempt to rationalize or deny problems can be avoided. "Every man's way is right in his own eyes" (Prov. 21:2).

Effective counselors get into the habit of looking for evidence of three root problems: bitterness, greed, and moral impurity. These three problems line up with the three original sins of man: boastful pride of life, lust of the eyes, and lust of the flesh. "See to it that no one comes short of the grace of God; that no root of bitterness springing up causes trouble, and by it many be defiled; that *there be* no immoral or godless person like Esau, who sold his own birthright for a single meal" (Heb. 12:15-17). There are, of course, many other root problems that lurk below the more surface issues. Counselors must seek to uproot these source issues.

Counselors should look for two levels of a problem. The more surface problem will often be the more "respectable or understandable" issue, while the root problem will be a bit more hidden. So while a man may be willing to talk about his shame that comes from his financial difficulties, he may not be so quick to open up about his laziness and lack of discipline. "Poverty and shame *will come* to him who neglects discipline" (Prov. 13:18). He might admit his battle with jealousy but not be willing to admit his lack of security. Effective counselors are willing and able to take their shovels and dig up the roots of, for example, laziness and lack of security. The person being helped begins his journey to healing when he is able to admit, "I feel like I will lose something," or "My lack of discipline makes me feel like a failure."

This issue of finding the root shows forth the importance for a helper to build a relationship with the one being helped. The root is typically the more serious and more embarrassing problem. The counselee will evaluate the counselor's response to the revealing of the surface problem. If he is comfortable with the counselor's response and feels a sense of trust and rapport with him, then he might allow the counselor to see the root problem. The experienced counselor will listen patiently and then at the opportune time ask, "In addition to that, do you have any other problems?" Counselors who dig up the unhealthy root are then able to plant something healthy.

Let's end with a few more "helps" for helpers. First, it is often—except when it is time to confront—more effective to ask questions than it is to make assertions. Ask, "Were you lying?" as opposed to saying, "You were lying." Second, assume that the person who comes with the problem is usually the key to the solution (Rom. 2:1-3; Luke 12:13-15). Third, be patient as to allow time for self-resolution or for the process of drawing things out: "A plan in the heart of a man is *like* deep water, but a man of understanding draws it out" (Prov. 20:5). Finally, be very careful when two Christians have a potentially legal conflict with each other. Every measure must be taken to discourage lawsuits between Christians since "actually, then, it is already a defeat for you, that you have lawsuits with one another" (1 Cor. 6:7). Wisdom within the faith should be available for such situations (1 Cor. 6:1-8).

There is never a shortage of people who need help, so there is never a shortage of opportunities to be a helper. Applying these methods and skills will make for more effective helpers or counselors.

MARCH 12

A DIFFERENT KIND OF BOXING MATCH

"The LORD has established His throne in the heavens, and His sovereignty rules over all."
Psalm 103:19

What in the world is God doing? Exactly! God is at work *in the world*. "Now all *these* things are from God, who reconciled us to Himself through Christ and gave us the ministry of reconciliation, namely, that God was in Christ reconciling the world to Himself" (2 Cor. 5:18-19). God is in the business of "winning back." He is reuniting us to Himself and then using us to reunite others to Him. So, this is "what in the world" God is doing. Now we must ask, "Why in the world is He doing it?"

God is *the* eternal King (1 Tim. 1:17; Psalm 10:16), Who has *the* eternal kingdom (2 Peter 1:11). He is *the* Sovereign (1 Tim. 6:15), Who rules *the* world (Psalm 103:19). There was, however, a primeval rebellion. This was the rebellion of one named Lucifer (Isa. 14:1-23; Ezek. 28:1-19) along with a following of one-third of the angels (Rev. 12:4-7). They formed a counterfeit kingdom of darkness, which appears as a kingdom of light, in order to deceive (Isa. 14:14; 2 Cor. 11:14-15).

The question remains, "If God is sovereign, then why did He not destroy this kingdom of darkness immediately?" The more popular version of this question is, "Why do bad things happen to good people?" or "If God is good, then why is there still evil in the world?" The answer lies in understanding the nature and extent of God's sovereignty. God is not simply more powerful than Satan. He is sovereign over him! God actually uses Satan to achieve His own purposes. Thus, the sovereignty of God is magnified, and God is glorified. The sovereignty of God is so profound that He is able to make the wrath of men to praise Him and his enemies to serve Him (Psalm 76:10). Incredible! God uses the wrath of men against Him to be His praises. He makes it so that His enemies end up being His servants. God could have destroyed Satan in the beginning. However, this would actually have understated the sovereignty of God. It would have shown the strength of God but not necessarily the sovereignty of God.

To understand this, let's imagine a special sort of boxing match that includes special rules. Each man is allowed to throw one punch at a time. You throw the first punch. You knock out your opponent. This means you are strong. Imagine that in the next competition, you allow your opponent to throw the first punch. His punch does not knock you out. Then, you throw your punch. You knock out your opponent. This means you are stronger. Imagine that in the final competition, you allow your opponent to throw the first punch. This time, through superior wisdom and creativity, you avoid the punch in such a way that the punch returns to your opponent, and it knocks him out. This means you are sovereign over your opponent.

This portrays what happened to Satan. Satan tried to kill Jesus. On Friday, the day of His crucifixion, it appeared as though Satan threw a knockout punch. Surely, there was a ticker tape parade down in Hell for the newly crowned champion of the world. However, on Sunday, the day of Christ's resurrection, it was clear that it was Satan who had been knocked out. He was knocked out by his own punch!

God is not only stronger than Satan; He is also sovereign over Him. There is only room for one world champion. And that champion is Jesus Christ of Nazareth. "The LORD has established His throne in the heavens, and His sovereignty rules over all" (Psalm 103:19).

MARCH 13

THERE IS NO VICTORY WITHOUT A FIGHT

"Beloved, do not be surprised at the fiery ordeal among you, which comes upon you for your testing, as though some strange thing were happening to you; but to the degree that you share the sufferings of Christ, keep on rejoicing, so that also at the revelation of His glory you may rejoice with exultation."
1 Peter 4:12-13

How can you win unless you beat something? There is no victory without a fight. Since victories necessitate contests, advancement includes conflict. No pain, no gain. Another way to say this is, "Be careful what you pray for!"

When you pray, "Teach me patience," you should not be surprised to be surrounded by annoying people. How are you going to gain patience outside of the arena of impatience? The "patience fight" can only be won by fighting against its enemy. The draw toward impatience must be overcome. The only way to overcome it is to fight it.

When you pray, "Make me more like Jesus," you should not be surprised to be thrown into the Refiner's fire. "For He is like a refiner's fire and like fullers' soap. He will sit as a smelter and purifier of silver, and He will purify the sons of Levi and refine them like gold and silver, so that they may present to the LORD offerings in righteousness" (Mal. 3:2-3). In answer to your prayer, God will burn away anything that does not look like Jesus. It hurts to die to self. The cross is painful. The victory necessitates the cross. Sunday does not come without Friday. There is no resurrection without the cross.

When you pray, "Give me more faith," you should understand that there will be a fight. There is no other way for your faith to grow than for it to be tested. When you pray, "Give me victory over sin and temptation," you should be ready to enter into temptation. You cannot beat it if it is not there!

This principle of "no victory without a fight" or "no advancement without conflict" is even true within the life and ministry of the God-Man, Jesus Christ. The first three chapters of the Gospel of Luke survey Jesus' life prior to the launch of His ministry. Then, His ministry begins in Galilee: "And Jesus returned to Galilee in the power of the Spirit, and news about Him spread through all the surrounding district. And He *began* teaching in their synagogues and was praised by all" (Luke 4:14-15). Prior to this "launch," Jesus wins a necessary and preparatory victory as the Spirit leads Him into the wilderness and He is tempted by the devil (Luke 4:1-13). Jesus was really tempted. There really was a fight, and there really was a victory. There could not be the one without the other.

The fight is necessary because of the nature of "taking ground" and advancing. It must be taken from something or somebody. That something or somebody may be yourself or your own flesh. If you want to advance with Jesus (follow Him), you will need to take up your cross and die to yourself (Luke 9:23). That hurts! That is not easy. That is a fight. The ground taken may be from the evil powers of this world—a spiritual war! As 2 Corinthians 10:3-5 says, "For though we walk in the flesh, we do not war according to the flesh, for the weapons of our warfare are not of the flesh, but divinely powerful for the destruction of fortresses. We are destroying speculations and every lofty thing raised up against the knowledge of God, and we are taking every thought captive to the obedience of Christ. (2 Cor. 10:3-5)

To take ground from the devil, there must be a fight. Just as with your own flesh, he is not going to just give it up. Victory and advancement, by definition, necessitate a fight. The fight is necessary and it is preparatory. The fight does something to you. The process of the conflict produces something in you. The very taking of the ground equips you to then take the ground! And so, Jesus fights the devil and takes the ground in the spiritual realm and then returns to Galilee "in the power of the

Spirit" (Luke 4:14). It is in this "power" that Jesus enacts His ministry for the next three years. The necessary nature of the fight allowed Jesus to take the ground, and the preparatory nature of the fight equipped Him to keep taking the ground.

If you want to take the ground of pride in your life, there will be a necessary fight. You will be "led around by the Spirit in the wilderness" (Luke 4:1)—the wilderness of humbling situations. People may throw false accusations your way or speak negatively about you. It is only in that cage match against your flesh that you have an opportunity for victory. It is out of that "cage match victory" that you are equipped to continue in that victory.

It is shocking that it was the Spirit Who led Jesus into the wilderness to be tempted. It was also the Spirit Who led Him out in victory. The battle was necessary—and so, Jesus was led into it— and the battle was preparatory; and so, Jesus was led out of it. The common denominator is the battle. Jesus did not shy away from it. He fought it—and won! In that same Spirit's power, you can do the same. So do not shy away from the battle. Fight it—for you "can do all things through Him who strengthens [you]" (Phil. 4:13).

MARCH 14

REPENT FAST AND FAST

"If you return to the LORD with all your heart, remove the foreign gods and the Ashtaroth from among you and direct your hearts to the LORD and serve Him alone; and He will deliver you from the hand of the Philistines ... they gathered to Mizpah, and drew water and poured it out before the LORD, and fasted on that day and said there, 'We have sinned against the Lord.'"

1 Samuel 7:3, 6

The biblical affirmation of fasting as a Christian discipline is clearly established by Jesus' own assumption that His followers would fast (Matt. 6:17). A Christian fast must have as its focus nothing less than Christ Himself. Like the Prophetess Anna, we need to be worshipping with fasting (Luke 2:37). Every other purpose must be secondary, for the motive of fasting must ultimately stem from a desire for a deeper communion with Christ, which can then lead to certain benefits: a more effective prayer life, discipline and strength to overcome temptation, an expression and prompting of sincere repentance, a clearer mind and increase in spiritual discernment and guidance, an increased sense of peace and spiritual confidence, increased awareness and sensitivity to others' needs, and an increase in bodily health and energy.

Fasting naturally aligns itself with humility and, thus, repentance, which might be called the attitude of fasting. It is not surprising that a national day of humbling or fasting was observed on the Day of Atonement (Lev. 16:29-31)—surely, a day of repentance. Similarly, God called Israel to repent of their idolatry, and so they expressed their repentance with fasting (1 Sam. 7:6). As with Ahab, fasting may facilitate an expression of a proper position before God, humbling yourself before Him (1 Kings 21:27-29). As a means of grace, fasting can be an expression of repentance that may simultaneously prompt you toward an even deeper sense of repentance.

Four hundred years after Ahab, the returning Jewish exiles to Jerusalem fasted as an expression of their repentance toward God. This resulted in ongoing penitence as "they confessed and worshiped the Lord their God" (Neh. 9:3). Fasting became a facilitator for the expression of an inward attitude. Fasting, without an attitude of repentance, is like feasting without an attitude of joy and thanksgiving.

It must be an expression of a *sincere* attitude. "Yet even now... return to Me with all your heart, and with fasting, weeping and mourning" (Joel 2:12).

It is the inward attitude that moves God, not simply the outward action. "Rend your heart and not your garments. Now return to the LORD your God, for He is gracious and compassionate, slow to anger, abounding in lovingkindness and relenting of evil. Who knows whether He will *not* turn and relent and leave a blessing behind Him" (Joel 2:13-14). Even the newly converted pagans in Nineveh somehow understood the connection between fasting and repentance and God's grace:

> Then the people of Nineveh believed in God; and they called a fast and put on sackcloth from the greatest to the least of them. When the word reached the king of Nineveh... He issued a proclamation and it said, "In Nineveh by the decree of the king and his nobles: Do not let man, beast, herd, or flock taste a thing. Do not let them eat or drink water. But both man and beast must be covered with sackcloth; and let men call on God earnestly that each may turn from his wicked way and from the violence which is in his hands. Who knows, God may turn and relent and withdraw His burning anger so that we will not perish" (Jonah 3:5-9).

It must be remembered, as with all spiritual disciplines, that fasting is not a self-righteous act but an admittance of a lack of righteousness. It should be done in repentance from unrighteousness, not in an attempt to *earn* righteousness. Fasting is an expression of reliance upon God, not a task to gain trust in self. It is not Pharisaical!

> And He also told this parable to some people who trusted in themselves that they were righteous, and viewed others with contempt: "Two men went up into the temple to pray, one a Pharisee and the other a tax collector. The Pharisee stood and was praying this to himself: 'God, I thank You that I am not like other people: swindlers, unjust, adulterers, or even like this tax collector. I fast twice a week; I pay tithes of all that I get.' But the tax collector, standing some distance away, was even unwilling to lift up his eyes to heaven, but was beating his breast, saying, 'God, be merciful to me, the sinner!' I tell you, this man went to his house justified rather than the other; for everyone who exalts himself will be humbled, but he who humbles himself will be exalted" (Luke 18:9-14).

So, go ahead. Hurry up! Repent fast... *and* fast!

MARCH 15

THE ROMANS 12 GIFT OF TEACHING

"Since we have gifts that differ according to the grace given to us,
each of us is to exercise them *accordingly:... he who teaches, in his teaching."*

Romans 12:6-7

God equips His people with gifts for ministry. There exist various lists of gifts in the New Testament. One such list is found in Romans 12:6-8: "Since we have gifts that differ according to the grace given to us, each of us is to exercise them accordingly: if prophecy, according to the proportion of his faith; if service, in his serving; or he who teaches, in his teaching; or he who exhorts, in his exhortation; he who gives, with liberality; he who leads, with diligence; he who shows mercy, with cheerfulness."

The Giver of these gifts is God the Father (Rom. 12:3). The gifts are called *charismata* (grace gifts). They are described as being "functional gifts" (Rom. 12:4) that are "effects" enacted by "God who works all things in all *persons*" (1 Cor. 12:6). The Romans 12 gifts are gifts that direct how a person functions; they determine the effects of a person's personality or tendencies. They are not so much gifts that a person is temporarily and situationally used in (as in the 1 Corinthians 12:8-10 gifts), or gifts that dictate a person's actual ministry (as in the Ephesians 4:11 gifts), as they are gifts that reside inside of a person and shape what that person is like and result in their default perception of life. They are what are often called "motivational gifts."

How can the Romans 12 gift of teaching be understood? People who have the gift of teaching are likely to have a love for research and discovering truth. Moreover, they have a passion for explaining that truth to others (Acts 18:24-28). Teachers are fueled by a desire to define truth in a systematic way (Luke 1:1-4). They put an emphasis on details and the importance of words (Acts 18:24-28). They also have a tendency to evaluate others' teaching. Luke, for example, was motivated by helping Theophilus to "know the exact truth about the things you have been taught" (Luke 1:4). Similarly, when Priscilla and Aquila heard Apollos, "they took him aside and explained to him the way of God more accurately" (Acts 18:26). The teaching gift, in general, results in more of a bent toward the objective and theoretical than the subjective and practical. In terms of emphases, the teaching gift drives a person to be more of a thinker—who uses his or her mind—than a doer who uses his or her body.

Just like any strength that has its correlated weaknesses, the gift of teaching has its vulnerabilities or carnal tendencies that need to be avoided. If someone with this gift is not careful, he or she may become proud and critical of others who are perceived to be inferior in their ability to think well. People with the gift of teaching must avoid becoming overly wordy, dogmatic, and impractical in their teaching.

Herein is the Romans 12 gift of teaching. Life is seen as a collection of information. The orientation is toward details and the accuracy of the truth. More than anything else, people with this gift view themselves as those who explain truth to others. They would say of themselves, "We are learners who love to see others learn as well!" Are you this person? Do you have the Romans 12 gift of teaching?

MARCH 16

KNOWING WHAT PEOPLE KNOW CAN HELP YOU HELP THEM

"His eternal power and divine nature, have been clearly seen."

Romans 1:20

Apologetics, put simply, is a field of Christian theology used to defend God's word—that is, "to make a defense to everyone who asks you to give an account for the hope that is in you" (1 Peter 3:15). What should you know about these people who ask you "to give an account for the hope that is in you"? You should know what it is that they know. All people know two things. First, they know that God exists, and therefore, they know that they are not God. Second, they know that they have made mistakes, that they are not perfect, and that they have problems.

These two tracks of "common knowledge" are by no means mutually exclusive issues. They are inextricably wed together. Because they know that they are not God—and therefore, that God exists—they know that the perfect exists and, therefore, that the imperfect exists. They know that God is God (perfect), and they are not God (imperfect). "For since the creation of the world His invisible attributes, His eternal power and divine nature, have been clearly seen, being understood through what has been made, so that they are without excuse. For even though they knew God, they did not honor Him as God or give thanks, but they became futile in their speculations, and their foolish heart was darkened" (Rom. 1:20-21).

This reality results in another epistemological dichotomy—even more useful for the apologist-evangelist—which defenders and proclaimers of the faith should be aware of—that is, "what people know" and "what people need." People know God exists. They are aware of the eternal because that is how God made them. It is part of their very nature since "He has also set eternity in their heart" (Eccl. 3:11). And so, in this sense, they are "without excuse." It is here that we arrive at what people need. They need to be forgiven. They need to be justified. All people know that God exists because all people are made with eternity in their hearts. The existence of God is built into human nature. It is equally true, then, that all people know that they are not God, are not perfect, and have made mistakes. All people feel their need to be forgiven because all people have sinned in Adam (Rom. 5:12). The need for a solution to the human problem is implicit in the human fallen nature just as the need and desire to know God is built into the human pre-fallen nature.

Although clouded now by the fallen nature, the fact that we are made "in the image of God" (Gen. 1:27) still lingers deep inside of us as it cries out for redemption. Paul describes this dynamic when He writes in Galatians 3:24, "Therefore the Law has become our tutor *to lead us* to Christ, so that we may be justified by faith." God is Love, and God is Sovereign. So, He uses the fallen to lead us to the risen. He uses our knowledge of the perfect (the law) to tutor us toward the knowledge that we are not perfect (cannot do the law). It is very useful for the apologist-evangelist to know that people know these things. People know that they are not God and that they are not perfect. People need God, and they need forgiveness. Jesus loves them, and they need Jesus!

As an apologist-evangelist, you know that people do not see this clearly, but you also know that they have an "inkling." They are not animals which are not made in the image of God, but they are severely polluted eternity-minded creations (Eccl. 3:11), who "grope" (Acts 17:27-28) for God, albeit in an almost "impossible" way—except that we know that "with God all things are possible" (Matt. 19:26). The apologist-evangelist must expect, anticipate and look for these "gropings"—both ones produced by man's two combatant natures and ones that cannot be awakened by general revelation but can be ignited by special revelation. And so, the apologist-evangelist speaks the Word, knowing what he knows his listener knows!

The Gospel can be presented to people in such a way as to take advantage of these "known things." Knowing that people, somewhere deep inside their very being, want to know God should lead the sharer of the Gospel to focus on its offer of relationship with God. "Do you want to know God? He came all the way here to earth and became a man so that you can know Him. Why don't you knock on His door? He will open it and invite you in!" Similarly, knowing that people, somewhere deep inside their very being, know they need God and want to be forgiven should lead the sharer of the Gospel to focus on its offer of salvation. "Do you want to be forgiven? He died on the cross to pay for your sins so that you would not have to. Why don't you ask for His receipt that's stamped, 'Paid in full'? He will give it to you!"

The apologist-evangelist understands he has knowledge because he knows God. He also understands when someone does not know God, so he knows how to invite them into that knowledge. If it all seems like it is an issue of "knowing," then we are on the right track, since God did, indeed, put eternity in our hearts and since "this is eternal life, that they may know You, the only true God . . . " (John 17:3).

These are matters of eternity. This is ultimately what the apologist is "defending." This is particularly what the evangelist is proclaiming.

MARCH 17

GOD IS A GREAT BUSINESSMAN

"And I will make you a great nation, and I will bless you, and make your name great; and so you shall be a blessing; and I will bless those who bless you, and the one who curses you I will curse. And in you all the families of the earth will be blessed."

Genesis 12:2-3

God is in the business of saving people. He employs people He has already saved to be the salesmen for His soteriological product. This is His business of missions.

God is a missionary God. Thus, He chooses a missionary people to bless (choose) so that they can be a blessing (choose others). There are two equal halves of the Abrahamic covenant (Gen. 12:2-3). The first half includes three ways to express the same thing: God blesses His people. He will make them a great nation; He will bless them; and He will make their name great. The second half also includes three ways to express the same thing: God's people will be a blessing. Through them, others will be blessed or cursed; and in them, all people will be blessed.

God gives His missionary people—whom He tells to "go" (Gen. 12:1; Matt. 28:19)—privilege, authority and blessing and matches it with obligation, responsibility, and being a blessing. God is a very good Businessman. He makes sure His workers are provided with a similar amount of authority and responsibility. God says three times, "I will supply you with what you need to do the job." He then says three times, "I will expect you to use that supply to enact My mission."

He manages His "employees" in such a way that will not, on the one hand, get them frustrated because they are bored or, on the other hand, get them frustrated because they are overwhelmed. When workers have too much authority and not enough responsibility, they actually become unproductive due to boredom. Oppositely, when workers have too much responsibility and not enough authority, they become equally unproductive due to being overwhelmed. The missionary, entrepreneurial God knows how to run His business.

Israel was blessed so that she could bless others. Israel was enabled to know God so that she could make Him known. Israel was given blessings and authorities so that she could fulfill specific responsibilities. God blessed Israel so that He could bless others. God chose Israel because "God so loved the world" (John 3:16). God chose Israel because it would include others, not exclude them. The Abrahamic covenant is a missionary covenant that God makes with Israel in the Old Testament just like the Great Commission is a missionary covenant that God makes with the church in the New Testament.

God is an Entrepreneur. He has created man in His own image; thus, man is entrepreneurial and apostolic. He is a "sent one." He is a missionary. Israel and the Church were chosen so that all people could be chosen as well. God is in the business of saving people. He employs people He has already saved to be His salesforce who will "sell" His salvation product. This is the business of missions. "For God so loved the world, that He gave His only begotten Son, that whoever believes in Him shall not perish, but have eternal life. For God did not send the Son into the world to judge the world, but that the world might be saved through Him" (John 3:16-17).

MARCH 18

INVESTING IN OPTIONS

*"Your abundance **being a supply** for their need."*

2 Corinthians 8:14

The debate over how much money people should use to give to meet others' needs versus how much money people should use to take care of their own needs should be discussed with respect to lifestyle; specifically, it is an issue of options. I might be motivated to spend less on my own wants so that I can have more to give to others' needs. Options!

The opposite of living in luxury is living according to what one actually needs. The Bible seems to advocate the latter for two reasons: to avoid the temptations of riches and to be able to give more to others who are in need. Giving to those in need is not for the purpose of being in need yourself—there is nothing holy about being poor—but for the purpose of using your excess for someone else's want. "And all those who had believed were together and had all things in common; and they *began* selling their property and possessions and were sharing them with all, as anyone might have need" (Acts 2:44-45).

This is not a picture of communism. Giving is not mandatory, nor is it automatically enforced by the ruling system. It is an option. It is based on using excess to supply lack. It is not based on supplying others' lack with the result that the supplier now has his or her own lack.

> For if the readiness is present, it is acceptable according to what *a person* has, not according to what he does not have. For *this* is not for the ease of others *and* for your affliction, but by way of equality—at this present time your abundance *being a supply* for their need, so that their abundance also may become *a supply* for your need, that there may be equality; as it is written, "HE WHO *gathered* MUCH DID NOT HAVE TOO MUCH, AND HE WHO *gathered* LITTLE HAD NO LACK" (2 Corinthians 8:12-15).

The consideration of living a simpler lifestyle for the purpose of having more to give to others' needs should include a balanced perspective. "Keep deception and lies far from me, give me neither poverty nor riches; feed me with the food that is my portion, that I not be full and deny *You* and say, 'Who is the LORD?' Or that I not be in want and steal and profane the name of my God" (Prov. 30:8-9).

Walter Pilgrim describes the "options" mentality and its balanced approach: "What he (Luke) seeks to create is a radically new evaluation of possessions and their proper use by Christians. His purpose is not to advocate some form of Christian asceticism on the one hand, or some kind of Christian communism on the other. Rather, Luke attempts to define and encourage a discipleship of one's material gifts in the service of love."[3]

Why should I live with less? Is it so I can come off as a more holy person? Is it because I believe there is something inherently evil about money and possessions? No, it might be because I want to avoid the potential temptations that can come with excess. More importantly, it should be because I want to help others with my excess. Ultimately, it is a matter of investing in the options market.

MARCH 19
CULTURE SHOCK! THIS IS SO FRUSTRATING!

*"Work out your salvation with fear and trembling; for it is God who is at work in you, both to will and to work for **His** good pleasure."*

Philippians 2:12-13

Missionary work usually includes the difficulties of communicating across cultures. How can cultural differences affect the work of a missionary? How can missionaries adjust to cultural differences? How can cultural misunderstandings be avoided? A North American missionary is told that a meeting is at 9:00 a.m. He arrives at 9:00 a.m. The Argentinean leaders who organized the meeting arrive at 10:00 a.m. They do not apologize for being "late" because in their culture, they are not late. As this sort of thing happens multiple times, the missionary begins to experience "culture shock."

Culture shock might better be called "culture frustration." Culture shock occurs when a person realizes that their cultural background is not relevant in their new setting. The missionary begins to feel like a child who must learn the most basic things—language, proper etiquette, customs, signs of respect. The daily stress of being a stranger and the frustration of everything being unfamiliar affects the missionary negatively after the first months of living in the new land. He realizes that he must relearn many aspects of his lifestyle and that he must live in this "different way" for a long period of time.

Tourists do not experience culture shock for two reasons. First, there is excitement and adventure in experiencing new things, people, and places. Initially, the changes are positively perceived as they are processed through the romantic lens that searches for a genuine experience. Second, there is always the understanding that they are only visiting. They do not need to adjust to the lifestyle of the culture. In this sense, short-term missionaries must be careful. They can easily get a false perception of what it is like to be a missionary. If they return to the mission field as long-term missionaries, they might become disillusioned.

Is there a cure for culture shock? Avoiding the culture is not the correct solution. It would be ineffective to hide and create your own cultural bubble to live in. Although it is beneficial, wise, and unavoidable to retain a remnant of his own culture, the missionary must not avoid the host culture. Instead, he must challenge himself to experience the culture and embrace it. This especially requires flexibility and humility. Flexibility is necessary to be able to successfully live in the culture. Humility is necessary to be willing to live in the culture. For a missionary, praying through Philippians 2:13 is very helpful: "God, please help me to be humble and flexible in response to this culture. Anoint me to be willing to work within this culture and to be able to live in it. I trust You for this because You are at work in me 'both to will and to work for (Your) good pleasure.'"

Culture shock or culture frustration is an unavoidable reality for cross-cultural missionaries. It is both a blessing and a curse in missions work. It is a curse because, if not worked through, it will eventually make it impossible for the missionary to reach his target people. It is a blessing because culture is the avenue through which the Gospel will be presented and the fruit of ministry will come.

MARCH 20

THERE IS A WAR GOING ON!

*"Five times I received from the Jews thirty-nine **lashes**. Three times I was beaten with rods, once I was stoned, three times I was shipwrecked, a night and a day I have spent in the deep."*
2 Corinthians 11:24-25

Some things just cannot be avoided. Christians who are active in their spiritual army—those "who desire to live godly in Christ Jesus"—surely "will be persecuted" (2 Tim. 3:12). A soldier must suffer because he is in "active service" (2 Tim. 2:4). War is not pleasant. For the Christian, spiritual war is the struggle against hell (Matt. 16:18). And so, Paul says, "Suffer hardship with *me*, as a good soldier of Christ Jesus. No soldier in active service entangles himself in the affairs of everyday life, so that he may please the one who enlisted him as a soldier" (2 Tim. 2:3-4).

It is inevitable when living a godly life that you will experience persecution and suffering. Another unavoidable thing is sacrifice. It would not be uncommon to hear a citizen of a country at war say, "We must sacrifice now because we are at war; sacrifice for the greater cause." Faith that costs nothing is worth nothing. The Gospel is free. You cannot buy a ticket to Heaven. It is costly because we try to keep what is not our own. We try to hold onto our lives and desires, instead of laying them down on behalf of the war effort. Soldiers must sacrifice. It is the nature of war.

Paul argued that his position as a soldier who served in the war was valid because of that which he sacrificed and suffered.

> Are they servants of Christ?—I speak as if insane—I more so; in far more labors, in far more imprisonments, beaten times without number, often in danger of death. Five times I received from the Jews thirty-nine *lashes*. Three times I was beaten with rods, once I was stoned, three times I was shipwrecked, a night and a day I have spent in the deep. *I have been* on frequent journeys, in dangers from rivers, dangers from robbers, dangers from *my* countrymen, dangers from the Gentiles, dangers in the city, dangers in the wilderness, dangers on the sea, dangers among false brethren; I have been in labor and hardship, through many sleepless nights, in hunger and thirst, often without food, in cold and exposure (2 Cor. 11:23-27).

Paul encouraged the Corinthian soldiers to *imitate* him (1 Cor. 4:16; 2 Tim. 2:3-4). Are you imitating Paul, who imitated Christ? Are you living the life of a soldier who is at war, or are you living the life of a civilian who does not participate? This does not necessarily mean that you are suffering, but it does mean that you are living a godly life. The General of your platoon requires obedience. The soldier must follow the directions of the leader if he is going to be successful.

A soldier must fight. The war is real. The enemy is real. Get in the fight. Be willing to "suffer hardship" and be a "good soldier of Christ Jesus" engaging in "active service" while not "entangling" yourself in the "affairs of everyday life" so that you "may please the one who enlisted" you "as a soldier" (2 Tim. 2:3-4).

MARCH 21

SPIRITUAL GIFTS SHOULD UNITE, NOT DIVIDE

"Now concerning spiritual gifts, brethren, I do not want you to be unaware."
1 Corinthians 12:1

The importance of the Holy Spirit and His ministry in and through the lives of His followers is obvious. It is the Spirit Who regenerates; "unless one is born of water and the Spirit he cannot enter into the kingdom of God" (John 3:5). It is the Spirit Who lives in believers (Rom. 8:11), anoints believers (1 John 2:20, 27), guides and convicts believers (John 16:8-11), teaches and comforts believers (John 14:26), and gives gifts to believers (1 Cor. 12:3-11).

Spiritual gifts are essential in our lives and ministries. Without them, we are limited. With them, the church goes forth equipped, enabled, and empowered. Paul promotes the significance of the gifts when he says, "Now concerning spiritual *gifts*, brethren, I do not want you to be unaware" (1 Cor. 12:1). Those who were unaware were called *idiotes*, a Greek word meaning "ignoramus" or "idiot." At least, according to Paul (1 Cor. 14:16, 22-24), spiritual gifts are very significant. We should not be ignorant of them.

In the Scriptures, there exist three types of spiritual gifts. First, there are the "manifestation gifts." These are the gifts of the Holy Spirit as described in 1 Corinthians 12:8-10:

> For to one is given the word of wisdom through the Spirit, and to another the word of knowledge according to the same Spirit; to another faith by the same Spirit, and to another gifts of healing by the one Spirit, and to another the effecting of miracles, and to another prophecy, and to another the distinguishing of spirits, to another *various* kinds of tongues, and to another the interpretation of tongues.

Next, there are the "functional gifts." These are the gifts of God's grace as described in Romans 12:6-8: "Since we have gifts that differ according to the grace given to us, *each of us* is to *exercise them accordingly*: if prophecy, according to the proportion of his faith; if service, in his serving; or he who teaches, in his teaching; or he who exhorts, in his exhortation; he who gives, with liberality; he who leads, with diligence; he who shows mercy, with cheerfulness."

In addition, there are the "equipping gifts." These are the gifts of Christ as described in Ephesians 4:11-12: "And He gave some *as* apostles, and some *as* prophets, and some *as* evangelists, and some as pastors and teachers, for the equipping of the saints for the work of service, to the building up of the body of Christ."

Spiritual gifts should unify the body of Christ. God does not give gifts to the Church to separate the Church. This would contradict His own goal and desire, which is to unify His people. Yet oddly enough, the gifts have sometimes been used to divide Christians. This is quite ironic since unity is the recurring theme that sets the context for all three major listings of spiritual gifts.

For example, the list of gifts of the Holy Spirit in 1 Corinthians 12:8-10 is preceded by a plea that there be unity in the taking of the Lord's Supper (1 Cor. 11:17-34). The list is then immediately followed by one of the great teachings on unity (1 Cor. 12:12-31). In addition, the emphasis of the verses that precede and follow the list is emphatically that of unity (1 Cor. 12:4-7, 11). One might note in these verses the repetition of words and phrases such as *same, common good,* and *all*.

Similarly, the list of gifts of God's grace in Romans 12:6-8 is immediately preceded by an explanation of the reality of unity (Rom. 12:5). It is followed by an emphasis on unity via various references to *love, devotion, preferring to one another, hospitality,* having the *same mind,* and *peace* (Rom. 12:9-10, 13, 16, 18).

In the same way, the list of gifts of Christ in Ephesians 4:11-12 is preceded by an emphatic call to unity as Paul encourages the Ephesians to be "showing tolerance for one another in love, being diligent to preserve the unity of the Spirit in the bond of peace. *There is* one body and one Spirit, just as also you were called in one hope of your calling; one Lord, one faith, one baptism, one God and Father of all who is over all and through all and in all" (Eph. 4:2-6). It should be noted that the word "one" is repeated seven times in these five short verses. The word "all" is repeated four times. Furthermore, followed by the list of the gifts of Christ is the explanation of their purpose—to bring unity (Eph. 4:13, 16).

And so, if your understanding of the spiritual gifts results in disunity with other Christians, maybe it is time to revisit the biblical teaching concerning those gifts. Maybe it is time to be challenged by the plea for unity that shows up in the context of all three of the lists so that Christians might be "all for one" and "one for all" (Eph. 4:2-6) "until we all attain to the unity of the faith" (Eph. 4:13). Gift-giving should unify people, not divide them!

MARCH 22

PERSPECTIVE IS EVERYTHING

"Come, and you will see."

John 1:39

Perhaps, the circumstances of our lives do not matter as much as how we see them. Perspective is everything. There are foundational principles of a Christian's life that give that life a real sense of purpose. These principles prompt Christians to view life through certain lenses—that is, through certain perspectives. "Come and you will see" (John 1:39). Look through these lenses.

One of those pair of lenses is the fact that I am chosen by God. When I look at life through this lens, I see my life as having value. This inspires me to live life to the fullest. Mediocrity is not an option. I am inspired toward excellence. The glass is always half full and never half empty. I have been chosen! I also understand that I am not chosen in the sense that someone else is excluded. I am chosen in order that others can be included. This is true because God has chosen to work through vessels. Thus, He must choose someone to work through in order to touch the lives of others. And so, I see life through the lenses of ministry. He chose me, in a very real sense, in order to choose others.

Another perspective through which to see life is that Jesus is the *only* way (John 14:6). My life gains clear direction when I consider the biblical fact that man cannot be saved without the Gospel (Acts 4:12). Thus, I see life as a dependent. In all that I do, I am dependent on God. I can do nothing without Him. Jesus says, "Apart from Me you can do nothing" (John 15:5). Thus, I must seek Him. Since I can do *nothing* apart from Him, then it only makes sense that I would seek Him in *all* my ways (Prov. 3:6).

An important perspective to apply to our lives is that good is the enemy of best. There might be a variety of "good" things to do and focus on in life. The question, however, still remains, "What is best?" A scribe came to Jesus and asked Him to tell him not what was a good thing to do but what was the best thing to do. Jesus said there were two things: love God and love others. My life must be built on the desire to love and know God. It must also be built on the desire to love others and make Him known to others. This is the pair of glasses through which to view life. Right lens equals knowing God. Left lens equals making God known. Put your glasses on!

It might be said that success in life comes from living according to proper perspectives. It might even be said that my life is built on logic. The Amplified translation of Romans 12:1 says that giving our lives to God is our "logical" service of worship. It is all very logical. There is a logical progression that I must recognize. If I really believe that Jesus did not lie when He said, "No one comes to the Father but through Me" (John 14:6), believe that the Gospel "is the power of God for salvation" (Rom. 1:16), know that hundreds of people right around me and billions of people all over the world do not yet know this salvation, understand that Jesus will not return until the Gospel is "preached in the whole world" (Matt. 24:14), and desire to see people saved and see Him return to establish His kingdom, then I will give my life to God by seeking to know Him and by making Him known.

Perspective is everything. It's all about the glasses. Without glasses, your vision may be blurry. But when you put the glasses on, everything suddenly clears up. You can see. Life makes sense. Perspective is everything!

MARCH 23

FAITH IS A PRESENT FUTURE

*"The assurance of **things** hoped for."*

Hebrews 11:1

What is faith? "Now faith is the assurance of *things* hoped for, the conviction of things not seen" (Heb. 11:1). The Greek term *upostasis* ("assurance") could be translated as "substance," "essence," "foundation," "guarantee," or "right of property." Faith is your guaranteed right of property—like a property deed—with respect to your place in eternity (2 Cor. 4:18). Faith is the belief in God without questioning His integrity or perfection (Heb. 11:6). Faith says, "We know that God causes all things to work together for good to those who love God, to those who are called according to His purpose" (Rom. 8:28).

This does not mean that all is clear sailing. Faith understands that the process may not be perfect. At times, the process may include things that are not "good." It is understood that the end result will be good (Heb. 11:39-40). Faith is oriented toward the future, but the action of faith is in the present. Faith must be based on the commandment of God. It must come from the desire to obey. Faith that is not based on the commandment of God is not faith; it is presumption.

Faith has two sides. One side has to do with the will. The other side has to do with the intellect. When Thomas transitioned from one who doubted to one who believed, he "answered and said to Him, 'My Lord and my God!'" (John 20:28). Faith surrenders one's will to the Lordship of Christ. It also proclaims the intellectual certainty that Jesus is God.

Faith is the combination of confidence and hope because faith is the mixing of the present and the future. It has confidence in the present. It has hope in the future. Faith is a present future; it is a confident hope. In "formulaic" terms: faith equals confidence plus hope.

Faith can be pictured as a series of activities. The mind trusts in God. The heart responds to the love of God. The will submits to the commands of God. The spirit obeys in the service of God. The entire person is involved (mind, heart, will, spirit). The person acts in active humility (trusts in, responds to, submits to, obeys in). The object of faith is God (love of God, commands of God, service of God.

The object of faith is not faith. To have faith in your faith is to have faith in yourself, not in God. The object of faith is not a desired answer to prayer. To have faith in your desire is to have faith in your own will, not God. A repeated declaration (while "welling up your faith") of a desired answer to your prayer is not faith; it is a form of superstitious incantation ("I will find $1000 . . . I will find $1000 . . . I will find $1000").

Faith sees ahead into places and situations that would, otherwise, not be visible. It sees God Who cannot be seen! By its very nature, faith is paradoxical. It sees "in the now" what God was, what God is, and what God always will be. What is faith? "Now faith is the assurance of *things* hoped for, the conviction of things not seen" (Heb. 11:1). Faith is a present future!

> By faith Noah, being warned *by God* about things not yet seen, in reverence prepared an ark for the salvation of his household, by which he condemned the world, and became an heir of the righteousness which is according to faith. By faith Abraham, when he was called, obeyed by going out to a place which he was to receive for an inheritance; and he went out, not knowing where he was going. By faith he lived as an alien in the land of promise, as in a foreign *land*, dwelling in tents with Isaac and Jacob, fellow heirs of the same promise; for he was looking for the city which has foundations, whose architect and builder is God. By faith even Sarah herself received ability to conceive, even beyond the proper time of life, since she considered Him faithful who had promised (Heb. 11:7-11).

MARCH 24

HEADLINE: HEY, THERE'S GOOD NEWS!

"To the weak I became weak, that I might win the weak; I have become all things to all men, so that I may by all means save some. I do all things for the sake of the gospel, so that I may become a fellow partaker of it."

1 Corinthians 9:22-23

In Journalism 101, one of the first things you are taught is how to write a news article in a newspaper. The news is very important. It is one of the pillars of our nation's founding and existence—the *freedom* of the *press*. There is another "news" that is even more important. It is the Good News that is the Gospel of Jesus Christ. It is the pillar of your new birth and existence—*freedom* from being op*press*ed. So, how do you write a news article in a newspaper? The lead paragraph must include the who, what, where, when, why, and how of the news story. Then the rest of the article expands on each separate aspect. What might the headline and the lead paragraph of a story about the sharing of the Good News look like?

The basic contents of the Gospel (what) should be shared with others through the use of various methods of communication (how). The Gospel needs to be shared frequently (when) with consideration of where people are at (where). Communicators of the Gospel must have the right motives (why) and be in the right position relative to other believers (who) when they share the good news.

The basic contents that we communicate are that people have a problem and that God has the solution. Of course, there are different ways to communicate this. But at the end of the day, it always comes back to the fact that people have a need; and God has the provision. People are sinners who are estranged from God, and God dies for those sins to mend the broken relationship. Now, that is good news!

The way we communicate must be considered. Basic communication theory tells us that as much as 90 percent of what is communicated to someone happens through non-verbal communication.

Thus, in sharing the Gospel (especially in public speaking types of contexts), we need to be very conscious of things like voice inflection, body language, facial expressions, and gestures.

The frequency with which we communicate the Gospel must be considered. Studies have shown that in the U.S., for example, it is common that a person—because of the existence of so many cultural filters that tend to block the message—hears the Gospel at least six times before he or she can understand it and make a real decision. Repetition, then, is critical.

The "place" in which we communicate the Gospel is also critical. Here we might speak of an "incarnational" evangelism. Jesus came to us to share the message and took on our "culture." He came to earth and became a Man (Phil. 2:7-8). He dwelled among us and identified with us. So, too, we must spend time with people if we are going to effectively share the message with them. We must, like Paul, be willing to "become all things to all men" (1 Cor. 9:22) if we are ever going to "get out of our own shoes" and put ourselves in their shoes in order to have compassion on them and relate to them.

Our motives with which we communicate the Gospel are essential. There are many important motives, but "the greatest of these is love" (1 Cor. 13:13). How do you communicate with love? You "LOVE YOUR NEIGHBOR AS YOURSELF" (Matt. 22:39). Treat people the way you would want to be treated. Who is my neighbor? As the story of the Good Samaritan teaches us, your neighbor is anyone who is in need (Luke 10:30-37). Thus, any unbeliever is your neighbor, since they are in desperate need of the good news. We must care enough to reach out to the needy. Those who are lost in their sin and separate from God need help. It is for this purpose that we share the Gospel message.

The position we are in relative to other believers will influence how our message will be received. Jesus makes it clear that successful evangelism is linked to unity among believers: "that they may all be one . . . that the world may believe that You sent Me" (John 17:21). Unity is a great witness. It testifies to the world that there is truly something special about this Good News that you are sharing with them. Conversely, when unity is not a reality, unbelievers smell hypocrisy and tend to see the Good News as *not* such good news. Moreover, the credibility of the one who is sharing the Good News nosedives into the muddy waters of inconsistency since "all men will know that you are My disciples, if you have love for one another" (John 13:35).

Extra, extra, read all about it! Did you hear the Good News? People need the Good News. So, let's get on our bikes and go on our delivery routes. Let's be the "newspaper boys and girls" that we are called to be (evangelistic children of God) and deliver the good news to everyone on our route.

MARCH 25

GOD SAVES OR MAN SAVES: TWO RELIGIONS

"It is no longer I who live, but Christ lives in me."

Galatians 2:20

How many religions are there? There is Christianity—the religion that believes in Jesus or "God saves." There is Humanism—the religion that believes in man or "man saves himself." Christianity's Bible claims that man cannot save himself; God must save man: "For by grace you have been saved through faith; and that not of yourselves, *it is* the gift of God; not as a result of works, so that no one may boast" (Eph. 2:8-9). The *Humanist Manifesto* claims that there is no God Who will save you; you must save yourself. There are only two religions—the religion that trusts in God to save and the religion that trusts in man to save himself. Christianity is the only religion that claims that God saves man. There are a multitude of religions—including Hinduism, Buddhism, Islam, Rabbinic Judaism, and many others—that claim to know how man can save himself. These religions may seem different, but they are really the same in that they all propose—using different methods—that man can save himself.

This fundamental distinction between religions may best be seen in how Eastern religions (especially Hinduism and Buddhism) understand "selflessness" and how Christianity understands it. Christianity requires death to self so as to live to Christ (Col. 1:27); I am emptied so Christ can live in me (Matt. 5:3). I have less of self so that there can be more of Christ (John 3:30). I am selfless not for the sake of self but for the sake of Christ—not to find self but to find Christ. "For through the Law I died to the Law, so that I might live to God. I have been crucified with Christ; and it is no longer I who live, but Christ lives in me; and the *life* which I now live in the flesh I live by faith in the Son of God, who loved me and gave Himself up for me" (Gal. 2:19-20).

Buddhism promotes selflessness as well. The purpose of self-denial for a Buddhist, however, is to find self, to come to a realization of self. Buddhism's selflessness is a tool to save oneself, whereas Christianity's selflessness is a prerequisite for God to save you.

Self-denial by itself, or for the sake of itself, yields no fruit. Repentance that only turns *away* from sin is not "repentance that leads to life" (Acts 11:18). Repentance must turn *away* from sin and turn *to* God (Acts 26:20). True repentance trusts in God for forgiveness. There are two religions—the religion that trusts in God for salvation (Christianity) and the religion that trusts in man for salvation (all other religions in the world). It is the difference between salvation by faith and salvation by works. Herein lies the power of the Gospel, the power of the Christian message. Other religions cannot offer their followers salvation because their salvation depends on their impotent good works. Christianity can offer salvation because it depends on the powerful work of God.

Other religions cannot offer assurance of salvation now because its recipients are waiting for their lives to end to see how their good works "weigh in" at judgment time; the jury is still out because the assessment cannot be made until all the possible works are in and counted. Christianity can offer assurance of salvation now because the assessment has already been made at the cross, and the work of Jesus was deemed to be enough. Jesus read the verdict Himself when He cried out, "It is finished" (John 19:30). Salvation has already been accomplished by another, so you can know it now. You do not have to wait. "So, for my part, I am eager to preach the gospel to you also who are in Rome. For I am not ashamed of the gospel, for it is the power of God for salvation to everyone who believes, to the Jew first and also the Greek" (Rom. 1:15-16).

MARCH 26

THE CHALLENGE OF THE VARIABLE TITHE

"'And test Me now in this,' says the Lord of hosts."

Malachi 3:10

The giving of a tithe to God (10 percent of your income) is a biblical concept. In fact, it is the only thing in the Bible that God references as something to test Him in.

"Will a man rob God? Yet you are robbing Me! But you say, 'How have we robbed You?' In tithes and offerings. You are cursed with a curse, for you are robbing Me, the whole nation of *you*! Bring the whole tithe into the storehouse, so that there may be food in My house, and test Me now in this," says the Lord of hosts, "if I will not open for you the windows of heaven and pour out for you a blessing until it overflows" (Malachi 3:8-10).

Materialism is a tendency to view money, possessions, and physical comfort as more important than spiritual values. Jesus was certainly denouncing materialism when He said, "No servant can serve two masters; for either he will hate the one and love the other, or else he will be devoted to one and despise the other. You cannot serve God and wealth" (Luke 16:13). A logical connection between the tithe and materialism would be that the tithe would tend to protect someone from, or move someone away from, materialism. However, a rigid understanding of the tithe can become a promoter of materialism, especially in a prosperous, consumer-oriented society. Although the tithe is a good place to begin in giving, it can actually put people in bondage and provide an excuse not to give more than they really could.

The tithe in the Old Testament was used for three things: to support the Levites (full-time ministers); to support the operations of God's house and ministry (tabernacle and temple); to provide for the needy (orphans, widows, aliens). New Testament tithes serve analogous purposes. The tithe was the minimum amount to give under the requirements of the law in the Old Testament. Although offering little evidence of the mandating of the tithe, the New Testament continues with and expands on the spirit of it. It offers much evidence of a practice of giving that goes beyond the tithe. New Testament people are no longer *under* the law—not because they are *exempt* from the law, but because in Christ they are now *over* the law. It is not that they do not have to observe the law. It is that they are more enabled to keep the law. "Do we then nullify the Law through faith? May it never be! On the contrary, we establish the Law" (Rom. 3:31). We can live and give *above* the minimum requirement of the tithe.

Instead of a rigid tithe, a "variable tithe" can be considered. Do our needs change when we are blessed with receiving more money? Is it a biblical principle that we *must* spend more money when we earn more money? Is the percentage of what we give simply to stay the same when we prosper? Should that percentage change with our increased earnings if our needs remain the same? It is a different way of thinking to realize that our needs should represent the constant or unchanged portion of our economic situation and that our giving can become the variable or changeable portion.

After our needs are defined and established—including our need to save and allowing for slight seasonal and situational changes in our spending—we can then increase that which we give, instead of increasing that which we keep. We can avoid the trap of materialism and, more importantly, we can steward more of our blessings to be more of a blessing. "It is more blessed to give than to receive" (Acts 20:35). Let us consider the "variable tithe."

MARCH 27

JUST CONFESS ALREADY!

"Confess with your mouth."

Romans 10:9

It is okay not to be perfect. It is okay to admit it. Because of the unnatural, it is natural to confess. Since our "image of God" nature has added a "sin nature," it is necessary that we confess. In order to not conform, we must be transformed so that we can be conformed to the nature in which God originally formed us. "And do not be conformed to this world, but be transformed by the renewing of your mind, so that you may prove what the will of God is, that which is good and acceptable and perfect" (Rom. 12:2). You should not be conformed to the world because you were not made in the image of the fallen world but in the image of the risen God.

Nevertheless, the fallen world and our fallen sin natures do exist. And so, we must be *trans*formed. Our form must change from the fallen form to the risen form; this is redemption. We were deemed one way originally, but then we polluted ourselves. God provides a way for us to be *re*deemed; to get back to the way we were first deemed.

How do we become transformed? What are the prerequisites? There is only one prerequisite. Confess! Your true identity is in Christ. The world and your sin nature try to cloud and confuse that identity. And so, your self-perception must be transformed. You need to be recalibrated, but you can only be recalibrated if you understand your need for it. You must confess your need.

God is not shocked by your sin. He is not all discombobulated because you need to be transformed. God hates sin (Prov. 6:16-19), but He is not tripped up by it. He is not mad when you confess your sin. He is pleased because that is the launching point for your transformation—to deem you again in His image. This is the very purpose for Christ's coming and dying on the cross and rising from the dead—to transform you because you need to be transformed.

You must be transformed "by the renewing of your mind." Your mind must become "new" again. It must make the transition from the sin nature's perspective ("I do not need") to the image-of-God perspective ("I need"). You must confess: "If you confess with your mouth Jesus *as* Lord, and believe in your heart that God raised Him from the dead, you will be saved; for with the heart a person believes, resulting in righteousness, and with the mouth he confesses, resulting in salvation" (Rom. 10:9-10).

God's job in our process of transformation is complete. Our job is minimal. We do nothing to achieve it; we only confess that we need it, and we need God to achieve it. God does the rest. Why, then, are we not transformed? Since there is only one prerequisite then there can only be one reason for failure: no confession. There has to be a "turning around," a repentance. But you cannot repent unless you first confess. If you define yourself as not needing God, then you judge yourself. "For God did not send the Son into the world to judge the world, but that the world might be saved through Him. He who believes in Him is not judged; he who does not believe has been judged already, because he has not believed in the name of the only begotten Son of God" (John 3:17-18).

It is not our best-case scenario, and we do not like it. And so, we struggle against the fact that we were made in the image of God, but we messed it up. But I do not want to feel like I am messed up. I refuse to admit it. I myself will "unmess" any bit of "mess" in me. I want to be the definer, and my definition of things says that I do not have to admit anything. I will not confess.

This is an absurd position. Everyone knows they are not perfect. Everyone knows they have done wrong things. Everyone knows they have messed things up at one point or another. "They have all turned aside, together they have become corrupt; there is no one who does good, not even one" (Psalm 14:3). "For all have sinned and fall short of the glory of God" (Rom. 3:23). Do not be absurd. Confess!

SINK OR SWIM, FAITH STILL WALKS... WITH JESUS!

"And Peter got out of the boat, and walked on the water and came toward Jesus. But seeing the wind, he became frightened, and beginning to sink, he cried out, 'Lord, save me!'"

Matthew 14:29-30

A man was climbing a mountain. He fell. He grabbed a branch. He desperately hung on to the branch and yelled for help. "Is there somebody up there?" Someone answered, "Yes, I am here." The man asked, "Who are You?" The answer, "I am the Lord." The man quickly begged, "Lord, please help me!" The Lord asked the man, "Do you trust Me?" The man claimed, "Yes, Lord. I trust You completely." The Lord instructed, "Very good. Now, let go of the branch." "What?" the man exclaimed. The Lord restated, "I said, 'Let go of the branch.'" After a long pause, the man inquired, "Is there anybody else up there?"

It is difficult to have faith sometimes. The implication of faith is that we will not have everything under our own control. The fact that faith is necessary suggests that we do not understand everything and that we are not able to do everything. If we could control, understand, and do all things, then we would not need faith. The truth is, however, that we do need faith. Still, at times, the way of faith may not seem like the best way. It may even seem like a crazy way. The life of faith is not easy but life without faith is impossible.

God is the Source of faith. Thus, the most foundational action of faith is to seek Him. "And without faith it is impossible to please *Him*, for he who comes to God must believe that He is and *that* He is a rewarder of those who seek Him" (Heb. 11:6). Since we are not the source of faith—we do not create it, nor do we produce it—the following are distorted understandings:

- I am "welling up" my faith;
- I will use "positive confession" to express my faith;
- Faith is a state of mind;
- Faith always produces positive, desirable, and "good" outcomes.

Faith is not man-sourced; it is God-sourced. It is "not of yourselves, *it is* the gift of God" (Eph. 2:8). It is "the fruit of the Spirit" (Gal. 5:22) and a gift of the Spirit (1 Cor. 12:9). Faith is "the work of God" (John 6:29).

Faith is reality-oriented, even as its Source, the "I AM" (Exod. 3:14), is primarily "real." Faith is not superficial; it is profound as it is housed in the heart. You are to "believe in your heart . . . for with the heart a person believes" (Rom. 10:9-10). Faith does not have to dwell in the land of self-delusion. It is not faith, if your arm is broken, to "positively confess" that your arm is not broken. To have faith, you do not have to negate reality in the present because "faith is the assurance of *things* hoped for, the conviction of things not seen" (Heb. 11:1). Faith believes today what is hoped for tomorrow. It is a present future!

Faith is most directly related to God. Therefore, there is faith without limits (John 11:39-44). There is perfect faith (James 2:22) and great faith (Matt. 8:10). Faith is holy (Jude 20). At the same time, faith is worked through an imperfect human vessel. So it is described as humble (Luke 7:6-7), little (Matt. 8:26, 17:20), and, at times, sincere (1 Tim. 1:5). As faith is worked through human vessels, it tends to knit those vessels together. There is a common faith (Titus 1:4), a mutual faith (Rom. 1:12), and a united faith (Mark 2:5).

It is hard to have faith. It involves risk. It can nudge you to walk on the water, or it can pull you up when you are sinking. Sink or swim, faith always points you to walk with Jesus.

> Peter said to Him, "Lord, if it is You, command me to come to You on the water." And He said, "Come!" And Peter got out of the boat, and walked on the water and came toward Jesus. But seeing the wind, he became frightened, and beginning to sink, he cried out, "Lord, save me!" Immediately Jesus stretched out His hand and took hold of him, and said to him, "You of little faith, why did you doubt?" (Matthew 14:28-31).

MARCH 29

CONTENTMENT AS AN ANTIDOTE TO MATERIALISM

"For I have learned to be content in whatever circumstances I am."
Philippians 4:11

Materialism can be a devastating disease that fights against spiritual health. Being bound to the material world can detach us from the spiritual world. This is not a surprise. Two thousand years ago, Jesus explained that it would be a terrible plague against the church and its mission. "And others are the ones on whom seed was sown among the thorns; these are the ones who have heard the word, but the worries of the world, and the deceitfulness of riches, and the desires for other things enter in and choke the word, and it becomes unfruitful" (Mark 4:18-19).

A balanced approach to this potential sickness is very important to employ. John Stott offers this description:

> We have looked at three options which confront all affluent Christians. Should we become poor? No, not necessarily. Though Jesus Christ still calls some like the Rich Young Ruler to a life of total voluntary poverty, it is not the vocation of all his disciples. Then, should we stay rich? No, this is not only unwise (because of the perils of conceit and materialism) but is actually impossible (because we are to give generously, which will have the effect of reducing our wealth). Instead of these two, we are to cultivate generosity on the one hand and simplicity with contentment on the other.[4]

The biblical doctrine of contentment can prove to be an effective starting place in the war against materialism. Here we are not talking about contentment with respect to shunning success, not working hard, being unproductive, or even with respect to refusing to make a lot of money. Contentment has nothing to do with being satisfied with mediocrity. It has to do with what you are going to do with success, working hard, being productive, and making a lot of money. It has to do with not being satisfied with the things of the world. "Do not love the world nor the things in the world. If anyone loves the world, the love of the Father is not in him" (1 John 2:15). The Bible does not so much advocate comfort as it promotes contentment (Luke 6:24).

The source of contentment is trust. "*Make sure* that your character is free from the love of money, being content with what you have; for He Himself has said, 'I WILL NEVER DESERT YOU, NOR WILL I EVER FORSAKE YOU'" (Heb. 13:5). Contentment is a learned trait. "Not that I speak from want, for I have learned to be content in whatever circumstances I am" (Phil. 4:11). Godliness is a result that is associated with contentment.

But godliness *actually* is a means of great gain when accompanied by contentment. For we have brought nothing into the world, so we cannot take anything out of it either. If we have food and covering, with these we shall be content. But those who want to get rich fall into temptation and a snare and many foolish and harmful desires which plunge men into ruin and destruction. For the love of money is a root of all sorts of evil, and some by longing for it have wandered away from the faith and pierced themselves with many griefs. But flee from these things, you man of God, and pursue righteousness, godliness, faith, love, perseverance *and* gentleness (1 Tim. 6:6-11).

Contentment is associated with repentance. After challenging the crowds of people who were listening to Him with the mandate to "bear fruits in keeping with repentance" (Luke 3:8), Jesus answers their question regarding what they should do:

And the crowds were questioning him, saying, "Then what shall we do?" And he would answer and say to them, "The man who has two tunics is to share with him who has none; and he who has food is to do likewise." And *some* tax collectors also came to be baptized, and they said to him, "Teacher, what shall we do?" And he said to them, "Collect no more than what you have been ordered to." *Some* soldiers were questioning him, saying, "And *what about* us, what shall we do?" And he said to them, "Do not take money from anyone by force, or accuse *anyone* falsely, and be content with your wages" (Luke 3:10-14).

Where do we begin in the fight against materialism? We begin by being honest with ourselves with respect to the temptation to live in excess and waste. We may need to redefine needs and to challenge ourselves to live more of a simple lifestyle. We begin by remaining balanced, so that our perspective does not end up being as extremely skewed (on the opposite end of the scale) as the perspective that we are trying to avoid. The answer to not living with too much is not to live with too little.

Where do we begin? We begin by following the biblical doctrine of contentment which will result in a healthy disinterest in worldly things. Instead of carrying an extreme focus on getting more and more stuff, we begin to foster more of a carefree attitude—an "it's not our focus" attitude—toward money and possessions that is the natural result of seeking first the kingdom of God (Matt. 6:33).

MARCH 30

COUNSELING AS A PROPHET AND KING

"Come to Me, all who are weary and heavy-laden, and I will give you rest. Take My yoke upon you and learn from Me, for I am gentle and humble in heart, and YOU WILL FIND REST FOR YOUR SOULS. For My yoke is easy and My burden is light."

Matthew 11:28-30

Sometimes, people need help. They need wisdom and advice. They need a helper or a counselor. When helping someone who needs to be counseled, there is a flow from a sort of priestly emphasis to what might be called a more prophetic style and, finally, to a more kingly type of approach. In general, this might be described as the movement from a more downward or relational phase, where the main goal is to build a bond, to a more upward or outward phase, where the main goal is to promote action. This "flow of counseling" can be used in more formal situations by "professional" counselors or in more informal situations by friends who want to help. In any case, helping someone work through his or her problems is the goal.

The goal of the prophetic helper is to help the person who is in need to better be able to define their problem—the root not simply the symptom. Jesus promises, "You will know the truth, and the truth will make you free" (John 8:32). This may have to include the use of "tough love;" speaking truth in love (Eph. 4:15). If there is sin involved, then "go and show him his fault in private; if he listens to you, you have won your brother" (Matt. 18:15). Even in this type of interaction, hope must be part of the prophetic equation: "Come to Me, all who are weary and heavy-laden, and I will give you rest. Take My yoke upon you and learn from Me, for I am gentle and humble in heart, and YOU WILL FIND REST FOR YOUR SOULS. For My yoke is easy and My burden is light" (Matt. 11:28-30). This prophetic combination of confrontation and hope can lead to confession and repentance as it did, for example, with Zaccheus: "Behold, Lord, half of my possessions I will give to the poor, and if I have defrauded anyone of anything, I will give back four times as much" (Luke 19:8).

And so, the prophetic helper looks to use the established trust in order to take risks. In one way or another, he is asking, "Do you wish to get well?" (John 5:6). Helping someone certainly starts in the arena of trust, but it then continues on the cliffs of risk. In this way, the prophetic counselor can be thought of as a confronter.

The goal of the kingly helper is to help the person in need to establish goals, adopt methods and plans, and create a format for evaluation. It is now time to help those who are being helped to act and to help themselves. There are a variety of methods the counselor can use here. He can share his own experiences. He can give "homework," even as Jesus told the man He was helping, "Go, wash in the pool of Siloam" (John 9:7). The kingly counselor can help set goals (1 Tim. 4:12-16) and stimulate and encourage the counselee to strive to meet those goals (Mark 11:23) through the use of, among other things, biblical positive thinking that focuses on God's abilities and not on man's abilities (Mark 10:26-27). Of course, one of the most important tools for the counselor is prayer. Therefore, "pray for one another so that you may be healed. The effective prayer of a righteous man can accomplish much" (James 5:16).

And so, the kingly helper looks to use the risks that have already been taken to move toward finding solutions. In one way or another, he is asking, "How can you do it? Have you succeeded?" Helping someone certainly starts in the arena of trust and then continues on the cliffs of risk, but then it ultimately finds its consummation on the mountaintop of success and security. In this way, the kingly counselor can be thought of as an equipper.

MARCH 31

IF IT'S NOT YOU, THEN WHO?

"And Jesus came up and spoke to them, saying, 'All authority has been given to Me in heaven and on earth. Go therefore and make disciples of all the nations, baptizing them in the name of the Father and the Son and the Holy Spirit, teaching them to observe all that I commanded you; and lo, I am with you always, even to the end of the age.'"

Matthew 28:18-20

When the church is more proper concerning how its religion is executed than it is passionate concerning its God-given mission, then the church becomes powerless. Jesus has one plan for the evangelization of the world. Historically, it has been called "the Great Commission." It is the name for Christ's redemptive mandate to His disciples. He commissioned them to faithfully reproduce themselves through sharing the Gospel message, as is seen in such passages as Matthew 28:18-20, which says, "And Jesus came up and spoke to them, saying, 'All authority has been given to Me in heaven and on earth. Go therefore and make disciples of all the nations, baptizing them in the name of the Father and the Son and the Holy Spirit, teaching them to observe all that I commanded you; and lo, I am with you always, even to the end of the age.'"

Having established this "commission" as *the* strategy by which Jesus' ongoing mission would be accomplished, there remains a glaring question: "What happens if those who have been mandated do not respond to the mandate?" Here is the haunting answer:

Jesus ascended to Heaven after His mission on earth was completed. The angels asked Him if He accomplished His goal. Jesus answered them with a victorious yes. Then the angels asked Him whether or not the entire world had heard of Him yet. Jesus answered no to that question. So the angels curiously asked Him what His plan was. Jesus answered with great confidence. He said that He had left twelve men and some other followers to spread the message throughout the whole earth. The angels looked a little concerned. They asked Jesus to tell them what His second plan was. Jesus said that there was no second plan.

The fact that the plan of God is to reach the whole world with the Gospel message through *you and me* is the essence of the Great Commission. There is no other plan. There is no Gospel airplane that is going to pull a banner behind it while it flies along the coastline so that all the people on the beach can read it. There is no satellite orbiting earth that is equipped with such a massive sound system that it can broadcast the Gospel message all over the world at the same time. The Great Commission is the *only* plan.

Ours is a lofty and vital mission. It is a heavenly mission. It is our collective mission as a Church, and it is our individual mission as followers of Christ. No single Christian is responsible for the collective mission, but each individual is responsible for his or her own mission. What sphere of influence do you live in? To whom is God calling you? The individual charge is the same as the collective charge—GO!

NOTES

April

APRIL 1

WHAT GOES IN THE "BLANK" OF YOUR LIFE?

"Follow Me, and I will make you fishers of men."

Matthew 4:19

I used to wonder what the idiomatic expression, "Get a life!" actually meant. Was there a store in the mall called "Lives 'R' Us" where you shop for and purchase a life? The more I heard the expression said in context, the more I came to understand that it was referring to something lacking in a person's life. Because you don't have _____ your life is deficient. What goes in the blank? I think what the expression is really referring to is the need for *purpose*. The phrase "Get a life!" means that you do not have a meaningful life. You need to fill in your blank with purpose. Life without purpose is no life at all.

Your sense of purpose is shaped by things you believe in and value. It is the motivation that drives you to do the things you do. It also helps you to get satisfaction from the things you do. Your sense of purpose actually organizes your life. It serves to help you set priorities, make plans, set and focus on goals, and persevere. The Bible teaches that, for the follower of Christ, there is a dual purpose of life. It is to know God and to make God known. Simeon spoke of this biblical dual purpose (Luke 2:29-32)—that which is "according to Your word"—when he said that he was at peace because he had seen God's salvation and then referenced the Gospel being shared with all peoples.

Jesus' life and teachings reveal this dual purpose. His disciples' lives were full of relationship with Him as He taught them and equipped them for ministry. Their lives were also full of spreading the Gospel as they followed Jesus and participated in His ministry. "When Jesus had finished giving instructions to His twelve disciples, He departed from there to teach and preach in their cities" (Matt. 11:1). Knowing God and making God known served as the dual purpose in the lives of Jesus' followers.

Jesus taught that the Bible proclaimed the dual purpose of life: He taught those who were at the temple, saying, "Is it not written, 'MY HOUSE SHALL BE CALLED A HOUSE OF PRAYER FOR ALL THE NATIONS'?" (Mark 11:17). The purpose of the temple was that people would know God, and God would be made known. Jesus' picture of His disciples is one of them being in relationship with Him and then, because they become like Him, going out to share the Gospel. Jesus explains that "it is enough for the disciple that he become like his teacher . . . and what you hear *whispered* in *your* ear, proclaim upon the housetops" (Matt. 10:25, 27). The dual purpose is seen in Jesus' explanation of why His followers might live sacrificial lives. He says it is "for My sake and for the gospel's sake" (Mark 10:29). It is to know Him and to make Him known.

There exists a progression within the dual purpose of life; one purpose follows the other. Jesus says to Peter and Andrew, "'Follow Me, and I will make you fishers of men'" (Matt. 4:19). They will be fishers of men; they will make God known. However, they must first follow Jesus; they must first know God. Relationship with God precedes laboring for God. He chose His disciples for a twofold purpose. "And He appointed twelve, *so that* they would be with Him and that He *could* send them out to preach, and to have authority to cast out the demons" (Mark 3:14-15). Why did He choose them? He chose them *so that* they would know Him and make Him known. He chose them to preach and to cast out demons, but His first purpose for them was simply that "they would be with Him."

Relationship with God precedes laboring for God. A man approached Jesus on the road to Jerusalem trying to express His desire to find purpose in his life through his dedication to Jesus. Jesus said to him, "'Follow Me . . . go and proclaim everywhere the kingdom of God'" (Luke 9:59-60). You cannot make God known without first knowing Him. Even Jesus Himself, in the midst of making

God known, spent time in relationship with His Father. "But the news about Him was spreading even farther, and large crowds were gathering to hear *Him* and to be healed of their sicknesses. But Jesus Himself would *often* slip away to the wilderness and pray" (Luke 5:15-16).

The importance of knowing God is unmistakable in the Scriptures. Just ask Mary and Martha. Mary "was seated at the Lord's feet, listening to His word. But Martha was distracted with all her preparations... But the Lord answered and said to her, 'Martha, Martha, you are worried and bothered about so many things; but *only* one thing is necessary, for Mary has chosen the good part, which shall not be taken away from her'" (Luke 10:39-42).

The importance of making God known is equally unmistakable in the Scriptures. "Now after this the Lord appointed seventy others, and sent them in pairs ahead of Him to every city and place where He Himself was going to come. And He was saying to them, The harvest is plentiful, but the laborers are few; therefore beseech the Lord of the harvest to send out laborers into His harvest'" (Luke 10:1-2).

The Bible clearly teaches that, for the follower of Christ, there is a dual purpose of life. It is to know God and to make God known. Are you living a purposeful life?

APRIL 2

BEATITUDES EQUALS ATTITUDES TO BE OF

"If anyone wishes to come after Me, he must deny himself, and take up his cross and follow Me."
Matthew 16:24

In Matthew 5-7, Jesus delivers the most powerful sermon ever. We call it the Sermon on the Mount. The introduction of the sermon consists of a list of nine beatitudes; these are "attitudes to be of" that form a person's character. The word "beatitude" means "blessed or happy." We could say that beatitudes are attitudes of those who are blessed.

The Sermon on the Mount paints a picture of life in the kingdom of God. This life is very different than life in the world. Those who enter into the kingdom must make a big change in how they live. There must be a transformation. "And do not be conformed to this world, but be transformed by the renewing of your mind, so that you may prove what the will of God is, that which is good and acceptable and perfect" (Rom. 12:2). There must be a renewing of the *mind*, a renewing of attitudes. It makes sense that the focus is on the mind, since it is the mind and its thoughts and attitudes that produce actions (Mark 7:20-23). Actions are a by-product of attitudes. If you want to know what someone will do, you must first know what someone will think.

What are we to think? What attitude should we be of? "Blessed are the poor in spirit, for theirs is the kingdom of heaven" (Matt. 5:3). It is only those who are poor in spirit—empty of themselves—who can live in the *kingdom* because it is only those people who are empty who can make room for the *King*. The word "kingdom" comes from the Greek term *basileia*, which can be translated as "a rule" or "a reign." Only those who empty themselves of their own rules are prepared to allow the King to make the rules for them; it is the "poor" who can live in the kingdom (the rule) of God. This is the first beatitude.

In some ways, those who say that it is impossible to fully live out the demands of the Sermon on the Mount are correct. That is the exact point that the first beatitude is making. We cannot, by ourselves, even begin to live according to such standards. Jesus is the only One Who can live like this. Thus, the only way we can live this sort of life is to let Jesus live it in us. That possibility necessitates being poor in spirit (emptied in order to be filled). Jesus says, "Therefore you are to be perfect, as your heavenly Father is perfect" (Matt. 5:48). The only way to be perfect is to allow Him Who is perfect to live in us.

The most efficient way to live in the kingdom of God is to pour yourself out. If there is a small container of polluted water and a large container of clean water, what is the most economical way to replace the polluted water with clean water? You can continuously pour the clean water into the polluted water until the polluted water is finally dispelled or diluted sufficiently. This takes time and can get messy. The alternative is to first empty the polluted water and then fill the empty container with clean water. This is much more efficient and effective. In other words, move over and let Jesus in!

The Beatitudes—and even the whole Sermon on the Mount—could be understood as a detailed commentary on Matthew 16:24-25: "Then Jesus said to His disciples, 'If anyone wishes to come after Me, he must deny himself, and take up his cross and follow Me. For whoever wishes to save his life will lose it; but whoever loses his life for My sake will find it.'" The Beatitudes challenge us to live by dying to ourselves in some way. As God gave, so we are called to give. The essence of each beatitude is that we give away something of ourselves. It is not surprising, then, that "i] is more blessed to give than to receive" (Acts 20:35). If you want more *beatitude,* then give!

APRIL 3

THE ROMANS 12 GIFT OF PROPHECY

"Since we have gifts that differ according to the grace given to us,
each of us is to exercise them accordingly: *if prophecy, according to the proportion of his faith."*
Romans 12:6

God equips His people with gifts for ministry. There exist various lists of gifts in the New Testament. One such list is found in Romans 12:6-8: "Since we have gifts that differ according to the grace given to us, *each of us is to exercise them accordingly*: if prophecy, according to the proportion of his faith; if service, in his serving; or he who teaches, in his teaching; or he who exhorts, in his exhortation; he who gives, with liberality; he who leads, with diligence; he who shows mercy, with cheerfulness" (Rom. 12:6-8).

The giver of these gifts is God the Father (Rom. 12:3). The gifts are called *charismata* (grace gifts). They are described as being "functional gifts" (Rom. 12:4) that are "effects" enacted by "God who works all things in all persons" (1 Cor. 12:6). The Romans 12 gifts are gifts that direct how a person functions; they determine the effects of a person's personality or tendencies. They are not so much gifts that a person is temporarily and situationally used in (as in the 1 Corinthians 12:8-10 gifts) or gifts that dictate a person's actual ministry (as in the Ephesians 4:11 gifts) as they are gifts that reside inside of a person and shape what that person is like. There is, then, for example, a "prophetic action" derived from the 1 Corinthians 12 list of gifts (an occasional use of a word of prophecy for a specific purpose), a "prophetic authority" derived from the Ephesians 4 list of gifts (more than a style of ministry, it is an actual ministry; it is more what a person is than what a person is like), and a "prophetic being" derived from the Romans 12 list of gifts (a prophetic style, tendency, emphasis, or personality).

How can the Romans 12 gift of prophecy be understood? Someone with this gift usually has a strong desire and tendency to identify error and evil; to improve, change or correct; and to speak the truth regardless of the consequences. This person places a strong emphasis on right and wrong and tends to see things as "black or white." Peter had this tendency (Acts 3:12-26). Of course, Jesus, Who was anointed in all ways, sometimes displayed this direct, no "beat around the bush" mentality (Luke 3:7-14).

People with this gift of prophecy have a need to express themselves verbally. They are willing to be transparent with others while having a tendency to be spontaneous and to respond quickly or be the first to speak up. Again, think of Peter (Matt. 14:28, 15:15). This person might be thought of as a bit of a "hard head" because they tend to be very direct and firm in their dealings with other people. The often-used phrase, "tough love," many times describes the stance they tend to take in confrontational situations.

Someone with the gift of prophecy tends to have the ability to persuade others with respect to right and wrong. Peter shows this ability (Acts 2:14-17), as does John the Baptist (Luke 3:3-20). More specifically, they are drawn to emphasizing the reputation and glory of God. "But when Peter saw *this*, he replied to the people, 'Men of Israel, why are you amazed at this, or why do you gaze at us, as if by our own power or piety we had made him walk?'" (Acts 3:12). Similarly, "John answered and said to them all, 'As for me, I baptize you with water; but One is coming who is mightier than I, and I am not fit to untie the thong of His sandals'" (Luke 3:16).

Just like any strength that has its correlated weaknesses, the gift of prophecy has its vulnerabilities or carnal tendencies that need to be avoided. If someone with this gift is not careful, he or she may become hypocritical, rebellious, judgmental, insensitive, impatient, or overly demanding of others. The person needs to beware of falling into having a negative attitude about life. Someone can be firm and direct while still remaining positive.

Here is the Romans 12 gift of prophecy. Life is absolute. The orientation is toward proclaiming right and wrong and perceiving evil and error. The person with this gift might be said to be a firm and direct type of person who puts an emphasis on speaking truth. People with the Romans 12 gift of prophecy would most definitely say about themselves, "We are people who tell it like it is!" Are you this person? Do you have the Romans 12 gift of prophecy?

APRIL 4

IF YOU BELIEVE, YOU WILL SEE

"Only believe."

Mark 5:36

Who or what is the object of your faith? Is your faith in a concept? "I believe in being nice to people." Is your faith in a cause? "I believe in animal rights." Is your faith in a movement? "I will keep the faith." Is your faith in an experience? "I have faith in my 9-iron." Is your faith in a person? "I have faith in my stockbroker."

For Christians, there is only one object of faith. Our faith must be in God (John 14:1; Gal. 2:16; Col. 2:5). Jesus says, "Everyone who lives and believes in Me will never die" (John 11:26). He does not say, "Everyone who believes in a concept or a cause or a movement or an experience or a person will never die." He does not even say, "Everyone who believes in their 9-iron will get a birdie on the eighteenth hole." Faith is in Jesus (John 20:31), the Word of God (John 5:46; Acts 26:27; Mark 1:15), and His promises (Rom. 4:21).

Since "whatever is not from faith is sin" (Rom. 14:23), you must have faith in all situations. Since "apart from Me you can do nothing" (John 15:5), you must "in all your ways acknowledge Him" (Prov. 3:6). The "when" and "where" of faith is *always* and *everywhere*.

How does faith work? It works within the context of three types of faith—limited faith, foundational faith, and unlimited faith.

> Martha then said to Jesus, "Lord, if You had been here, my brother would not have died. Even now I know that whatever You ask of God, God will give You." Jesus said to her, "Your brother will rise again." Martha said to Him, "I know that he will rise again in the resurrection on the last day." Jesus said to her, "I am the resurrection and the life; he who believes in Me will live even if he dies, and everyone who lives and believes in Me will never die. Do you believe this?" She said to Him, "Yes, Lord; I have believed that You are the Christ, the Son of God, *even* He who comes into the world . . . " Therefore, when Mary came where Jesus was, she saw Him, and fell at His feet, saying to Him, "Lord, if You had been here, my brother would not have died." When Jesus therefore saw her weeping . . . He was deeply moved in spirit and was troubled, and said, "Where have you laid him?" They said to Him, "Lord, come and see." Jesus wept. So the Jews were saying, "See how much He loved him? But some of them said, "Could not this man, who opened the eyes of the blind man, have kept this man also from dying?" So Jesus, again being deeply moved within, came to the tomb. Now it was a cave, and a stone was lying against it. Jesus said, "Remove the stone." Martha, the sister of the deceased, said to Him, "Lord, by this time there will be a stench, for he has been *dead* four days." Jesus said to her, "Did I not say to you that if you believe, you will see the glory of God?" So they removed the stone. Then Jesus raised His eyes, and said, "Father . . . I knew that You always hear Me; but because of the people standing around I said it, so that they may believe that You sent Me." . . . He cried out with a loud voice, "Lazarus, come forth." The man who had died came forth, bound hand and foot with wrappings, and his face was wrapped around with a cloth. Jesus said to them, "Unbind him, and let him go" (John 11:21-27, 32-44).

Martha had limited faith. Her faith ended when Lazarus died. She had faith that Jesus could heal Lazarus, but she did not have faith that Jesus could raise him from the dead. Faith with limits can restrain the power of Jesus as it did in Nazareth. "He did not do many miracles there because of their unbelief" (Matthew 13:58). Faith with limits is controlled by circumstances. It is motivated by the fear of failure.

Martha had undeveloped faith. She stated her intellectual knowledge of Christ, but this intellectual perspective resulted in faith that had limits. In response to this limited faith, "Jesus wept" (John 11:35). Intellectual knowledge of Christ is very important, but it is not sufficient. Faith must go beyond the mind and enter the heart, "for with the heart a person believes" (Rom. 10:10).

Martha had faith without limits. Finally, all of her restrictions were eliminated; her intellectual arguments were dismissed; and she agreed to remove the stone. "Jesus said to her, 'Did I not say to you that if you believe, you will see the glory of God?' So they removed the stone" (John 11:40-41).

The world says, "To see it is to believe it." Faith says, "To believe it is to see it." Faith comes before sight; "for we walk by faith, not by sight" (2 Cor. 5:7). If you want to see life come out of the tombs of your life, then you must remove the stones. Stones can only be removed by faith!

APRIL 5

TRUE PROSPERITY THEOLOGY

"So that he will have something to share with one who has need."
Ephesians 4:28

There is a prosperity theology that is biblical. However, its focus is the exact opposite of the focus of some strains of misguided "prosperity theology." The biblical focus is that "I receive in order to give." The carnal focus is that "I give in order to receive for me." True prosperity theology correctly understands that God has unlimited resources. It also understands that God wants to give in abundance to His children. The error in false prosperity theology is found in the answer to the question, "Why does God give to me?"

God gives to you because He wants to distribute His wealth and respond to the needs of others. To do this, He needs a faithful vessel. He blesses us, not so we can live a life of luxury, excess and waste, but so that we can be a blessing. This principle of distribution was the underlying dynamic of God's covenant with Abraham. He was not "blessed" only for himself. He was blessed "so you shall be a blessing" (Gen. 12:2). A faithful vessel is a conduit, not a closed system. "God be gracious to us and bless us, and cause His face to shine upon us that Your way may be known on the earth" (Psalm 67:1-2).

Why do I receive? I receive in order to be able to give. It is an opportunity. It is a privilege. I get to give. The Gospel is an "other-oriented" message. The essence of it is not built on selfishness; it is founded in selflessness. It is the Gospel of the cross of Jesus Christ. It is the Gospel of the love of God Who "*gave* His only begotten Son" (John 3:16). He gave *everything*!

The error of a faulty prosperity theology is not in the encouragement to expect a return on your giving. The error comes in the misunderstanding of the purpose of that return. When the motive to give simply becomes the desire to receive more for you, then the "prosperity" is no prosperity at all; it is excess and waste. I can expect a return on my giving as long as my motive is to receive in order to give. When I give, I receive more. When I receive more, I give more. The cycle should never stop. This is biblical stewardship; true prosperity theology!

This, in no way, is to deny, reject, or in any way limit the vastness of God's resources. The answer to materialism is not that Christians should live in poverty or that they should become unproductive. That is another example of faulty theology associated with the use of resources, money, and possessions. God is an abundant Supplier of needs, and He does operate His Divine business according to principles of reciprocity: "Give, and it will be given to you. They will pour into your lap a good measure—pressed down, shaken together, and running over. For by your standard of measure it will be measured to you in return" (Luke 6:38). This principle of reciprocity, however, must be understood in the context of the owner expecting His stewards to set their face toward a life of giving and not a life of taking, keeping, and hoarding. "It is more blessed to give than to receive" (Acts 20:35).

Thinking like this is not natural for those who live in a consumer society. They are bombarded with encouragement and rationale—even with proposed mandates—to spend more and more on themselves. Simplicity and contentment are inherently opposed to consumerism. The idea that "godliness" and "contentment" could be in the same verse in the Bible is somewhat appalling to certain "prosperity theologians."

But godliness *actually* is a means of great gain when accompanied by contentment. For we have brought nothing into the world, so we cannot take anything out of it either. If we have food and covering, we shall be content. But those who want to get rich fall into temptation and a snare and many foolish and harmful desires, which plunge men into ruin and destruction. "For the love of money is a root of all sorts of evil, and some by longing for it have wandered away from the faith and pierced themselves with many griefs. But flee from these things, you man of God, and pursue righteousness, godliness, faith, love, perseverance *and* gentleness" (1 Tim. 6:6-11).

Remember, simplicity is not unproductiveness. It is not so much focused on how much you produce but on why you produce it. To produce more is to give more. "He who steals must steal no longer; but rather he must labor, performing with his own hands what is good, so that he will have *something* to share with one who has need" (Eph. 4:28). Any call to simplicity should have three points of motivation: more time with God and His work, the avoidance of temptations that riches can bring, and having more to share with those in need. Simplicity must not be an end. It must be a means to an end. It is not "holy" to live a simple lifestyle. It is holy to live a simple lifestyle in order to get closer to God and to respond to the needs of others. The simple life is motivated by a desire to give. The materialistic life is motivated by a desire to possess.

As a follower of Christ, I am challenged to ask myself the question, "Did Jesus live a materialistic life?" Did He tend to keep, or did He tend to give? Did He come to be served or to serve? "For even the Son of Man did not come to be served, but to serve, and to give His life a ransom for many" (Mark 10:45). For Jesus, "prosperity" came in the form of giving, since God's love for the world came in the action of "He gave" (John 3:16). Go ahead and prosper. Give!

APRIL 6

CHRISTIAN CHARACTER DRIPS DOWN THE CROSS

"Have this attitude in yourselves which was also in Christ Jesus, who, although He existed in the form of God, did not regard equality with God a thing to be grasped."
Philippians 2:5-6

Perhaps the closest we can come to a one-word description of someone who exudes Christian character is that he or she is selfless. Selflessness is that part of a person's character that is able to forget about personal needs and desires in order to remember the needs and desires of others. Selflessness is the quality that allows Christ to live in me for "it is no longer I who live, but Christ lives in me" (Gal. 2:20).

Francis of Assisi, a monk who founded the Franciscan Order in the early thirteenth century, lived an exemplary life of selflessness. Selflessness leads to freedom, and freedom leads to joy. Selfishness leads to slavery, and slavery leads to depression. Francis told his followers that it was their own responsibility to be full of joy and to lift up the hearts of others. He was a man of joy because his selflessness was real. He did not force himself to die to himself. He died willingly because he wanted to be like Christ. "You also became imitators of us and of the Lord, having received the word in much tribulation with the joy of the Holy Spirit, so that you became an example to all the believers" (1 Thess. 1:6-7).

Francis of Assisi's suffering and discipline was done in joy (2 Cor. 8:2). Sincere selflessness is proven by a joyful spirit. Francis loved to fast. It was not a burden to him. He did not enjoy it because he was a masochist and enjoyed punishing himself. He enjoyed it because his motives to fast were sincere. A religious or selfish spirit leads to depression while a sincere or selfless spirit leads to joy.

It was the Spirit of selflessness that sent Christ to the cross. Even in the midst of suffering, there is freedom and joy in selflessness for "the Lord is the Spirit, and where the Spirit of the Lord is, *there is liberty*" (2 Cor. 3:17). Francis of Assisi asserted, "Above all graces and gifts of the Holy Spirit that Christ gave to the Church is to overcome oneself and willingly for the love of Christ endure pains and insults and shame and wants."[5] In referring to wisdom, simplicity, poverty, humility, love, and obedience as primary Christian virtues, Francis stated, "For it is from the Lord, most holy virtues, that you proceed. And there is not one among you that we may practice without being dead to self."[6]

There is One Who practiced perfect selflessness. Jesus came down from Heaven and laid aside His Divine privileges to become a Man. This God-Man is now our example. He shows us what it means to die to self:

> Do nothing from selfishness or empty conceit, but with humility of mind regard one another as more important than yourselves; do not *merely* look out for your own personal interests, but also for the interests of others. Have this attitude in yourselves which was also in Christ Jesus, who, although He existed in the form of God, did not regard equality with God a thing to be grasped, but emptied Himself, taking the form of a bond-servant, *and* being made in the likeness of men. Being found in appearance as a man, He humbled Himself by becoming obedient to the point of death, even death on a cross (Phil. 2:3-8).

APRIL 7

THE COUNSELOR MUST BE A LISTENER

"The eyes of the LORD are toward the righteous and His ears are open to their cry . . .
***The righteous** cry, and the LORD hears and delivers them out of all their troubles."*
Psalm 34:15, 17

Shepherds are good listeners. They are good observers. Most of what they do is watch; they watch over their sheep (Luke 2:8). The shepherd counselor must be a good communicator. This especially means that the counselor must be a good listener since as much as 90 percent of all communication includes different forms of listening. We are able to hear at a rate five times faster than we are able to speak (a person may be able to speak 120 words per minute, but that same person can hear six hundred words per minute). Maybe that comes from, in part, the fact that we have two ears but only one mouth.

If you want to help someone, you are going to have to listen to them. You must be listening, of course, for content; but you must also be listening for emphasis, emotion, voice fluctuation, intonation, tone, facial expressions, and non-verbal indicators, including body posture, gestures, and tension. You should even be listening for words not said.

All of this is necessary for counselors to maximize their ability to help people. It may be necessary, but it is not necessarily the natural or common way of communicating. Instead of listening, many people will daydream while someone else is talking or simply spend the time thinking about how they will respond to what the other person is saying. The counselor cannot afford to daydream. In order to help others, you have to first listen to them. God Himself—the Good Shepherd, the "Wonderful Counselor, Mighty God, Eternal Father, Prince of Peace" (Isa. 9:6)—is our prime example: "The eyes of the LORD are toward the righteous and His ears are *open* to their cry . . . *The righteous* cry, and the LORD hears and delivers them out of all their troubles" (Psalm 34:15, 17). What a great Counselor! What a great Listener!

When we try to help people but do not listen to them, we are in danger of engaging in foolishness for "he who gives an answer before he hears, it is folly and shame to him" (Prov. 18:13). Counselors who listen, however, are loved and sought out for they are those who can actually help others. "I love the LORD, because He hears my voice *and* my supplications. Because He has inclined His ear to me, therefore I shall call *upon Him* as long as I live" (Psalm 116:1-2).

Oh Lord, make us better listeners. Make us better counselors. Work in us so that we can help more people!

APRIL 8

THE WILDERNESS HELPS YOU SEE REALITY

"The LORD your God has led you in the wilderness ... that He might make you understand that man does not live by bread alone, but man lives by everything that proceeds out of the mouth of the LORD."

Deuteronomy 8:2-3

Just as it is in difficult times, we may be more likely to remember and look to God, so it is in times of prosperity we may be more likely to forget and ignore God. In the deserts and wildernesses of our lives, we naturally cry out to the Provider because our need of Him is so apparent. Prosperity can be a deceiver. In those seasons, though, we need God just as much then as at any other time, we can be fooled to think that we do not.

> Beware that you do not forget the LORD your God by not keeping His commandments and His ordinances and His statutes which I am commanding you today; otherwise, when you have eaten and are satisfied, and have built good houses and lived *in them,* and when your herds and your flocks multiply, and your silver and gold multiply, and all that you have multiplies, then your heart will become proud and you will forget the LORD your God who brought you out from the land of Egypt, out of the house of slavery. He led you through the great and terrible wilderness, *with its* fiery serpents and scorpions and thirsty ground where there was no water; He brought water for you out of the rock of flint. In the wilderness He fed you manna which your fathers did not know, that He might humble you and that He might test you, to do good for you in the end. Otherwise, you may say in your heart, 'My power and the strength of my hand made me this wealth.' But you shall remember the LORD your God, for it is He who is giving you power to make wealth, that He may confirm His covenant which He swore to your fathers, as *it is* this day. It shall come about if you ever forget the LORD your God and go after other gods and serve them and worship them, I testify against you today that you will surely perish (Deut. 8:11-19).

We can so easily become comfortable and lazy when everything is going well. Understanding this human tendency may be the only way that we can truly "exult in our tribulations, knowing that tribulation brings about perseverance; and perseverance, proven character; and proven character, hope" (Rom. 5:3-4). If testing in the wilderness produces fruit, then "consider it all joy, my brethren, when you encounter various trials, knowing that the testing of your faith produces endurance. And let endurance have *its* perfect result, so that you may be perfect and complete, lacking in nothing" (James 1:2-4).

The most important thing to focus on in a wilderness experience is the sovereignty of God. Sovereigns are in the business of using all resources for their purposes. *The* Sovereign God "causes all things to work together for good to those who love God, to those who are called according to *His* purpose" (Rom. 8:28). Sometimes in the wilderness, it is hard to understand what is going on around you. Even when it seems like there are no answers, you must trust that God knows what and why things are happening. Your focus must be to trust and obey Him, regardless of your outward circumstances.

The most important thing to learn from a wilderness experience is that success is from God and not self-created. "For who regards you as superior? What do you have that you did not receive? And if you did receive it, why do you boast as if you had not received it?" (1 Cor. 4:7). Sometimes it takes a little wandering in the wilderness to realize what God is always saying to us: "I am the vine, you are the branches; he who abides in Me and I in him, he bears much fruit, for apart from Me you can do nothing" (John 15:5).

The most dangerous response to a wilderness experience is idolatry. PWCD (Post Wilderness Comfort Disorder) can lull a previously alert follower of God into a spiritual sleep. The off-ramp from the wilderness highway leaves behind the hardships, but it may also leave behind the fruit that can come from those hardships. When it is not as clear as to how much you need God, then you become susceptible to worshipping other gods. "It shall come about if you ever forget the LORD your God and go after other gods and serve them and worship them, I testify against you today that you will surely perish" (Deut. 8:19).

Spirituality is sustained through experiencing the process in which death leads to life. The death of the wilderness or desert can turn into the fresh waters of an oasis. The cross turns into the resurrection. Walking in the wilderness prepares for and leads to the joy that comes when arriving at the oasis. That is no mirage! The pain and payment of Calvary prepares for and leads to the triumph and glory of the empty tomb. That is no mirage. He is risen, indeed!

APRIL 9

GOD DRAWS, WE RUN

*"Draw me after you **and** let us run together."*

Song of Songs 1:4

Jesus "did not come to abolish [the Law,] but to fulfill [it]" (Matt. 5:17). God's Law is not simply the outward show; it is the inward reality. "But if you had known what this means, 'I DESIRE COMPASSION, AND NOT A SACRIFICE,' you would not have condemned the innocent" (Matt. 12:7). The fullness of the Law is not found in its sacrificial aspect but in its heart aspect. Attitudes of the heart, more so than actions, are essential because actions are *subsets* of attitudes; they proceed from, are produced by, and become reflections of attitudes.

The words you speak, for example, do not cause you to be who you are. They are a reflection of who you are, "for the mouth speaks out of that which fills the heart" (Matt. 12:34). Since we are not creators, our words do not create. We are not magicians, nor should we see ourselves as having the incredible "powers" of one who practices superstition. No matter how loud we yell, "Abracadabra," we will not create with our words because we are not creators. No matter how correctly and consistently we sit in the "magic" chair, eating the right snacks at the right time of the game, and screaming the right words at the television with the same intonation as the last time we so powerfully influenced the game's outcome, we will not cause our team to win. Our words are just not that powerful because our words are only reflections of an actual substance. They are forms, and forms are things that *are* formed and not things *that* form. So, when the Scripture says, "For as he thinks within himself, so he is" (Prov. 23:7), it is not saying that your thoughts that produce your speech, in turn, create who you are. It is saying that your thoughts and your corresponding words reflect and confirm who you already are (Mark 7:20-23).

Spiritual disciplines or "means of grace" are those actions that are produced by and reflect spiritual substance. Fasting, for example, must proceed from appropriate attitudes—repentance, hunger for God, dependence on God—if it is to be meaningful and beneficial. Jesus' teaching concerning fasting includes a sharp rebuke with respect to wrong methods and wrong motives (Matt. 6:16-18). The manner had become externally focused and motivated by appearance before men. The methods were results of motives that were inconsistent with the very purpose and spirit of the practice. It is the humbling of man's soul before God, and not the act of fasting alone, which pleases God. It must be realized that the act of fasting itself is of less importance than the attitude of the heart. Only when the action of fasting is representative of the attitude is God's grace experienced. Only in this way can fasting be a means of grace.

Jesus rebukes the hypocrisy of the Pharisees not because they engage in forms but because they engage in forms without substance (Matt. 23:23). Jesus is careful to explain that fasting, for example, does not earn forgiveness of sins (Luke 18:9-14). His rebuke, however, does not invalidate the "penitential fast"; it only invalidates a fast that seeks to stake a claim on earning or deserving something from God. Biblical fasting is related to repentance as a handshake is related to friendship. It is an outward response to an inward reality. It is an expression of a reality which, if sincere, is an appropriate means of placing self rightly before God. It expresses the exact opposite attitude that accompanies the desire to earn forgiveness—the self-righteous attitude of one who does not see himself as needy. It expresses an attitude that accompanies a desperate need for forgiveness and, thus, is an appropriate means of grace.

To seek God does not, in itself, produce or create in you a desire for God. It is your desire for God that drives you to seek Him. Seeking is an *expression* of desire, not a source or cause of it. You cannot fake it until you make it. You cannot seek until you desire. Sometimes that is frustrating. Jesus says it this way, "Do not grumble among yourselves. No one can come to Me unless the Father who sent Me draws him" (John 6:43-44).

So, pray the most foundational prayer of all, "Draw me after you *and* let us run *together*! The king has brought me into his chambers" (Song of Songs 1:4). Draw me, God, so I will seek You. Bring me in, so I will run with You. Fill me with Your substance so I may become an expression of You (Gal. 2:20). What is that substance? It is God Himself.

What is your role in all this? What is required of you? The answer is in the question, "How much more will *your* heavenly Father give the Holy Spirit to those who ask Him?" (Luke 11:13). Ask Him to give you Him so that He can be your desire. This is what the psalmist means when he says, "Delight yourself in the LORD; and He will give you the desires of your heart" (Psalm 37:4). God draws you and you turn to Him, defer to Him, and ask Him for Him. He then lives in and through you. He is your beginning and your end, your Alpha and Omega, your "all in all" (Eph. 1:23).

APRIL 10

NO DOUBT THERE CAN SOMETIMES BE DOUBT

"I do believe; help my unbelief."

Mark 9:24

Can we believe but also doubt? Do Christians sometimes struggle with their faith? One person who was interacting with Jesus put it like this: "I do believe; help my unbelief" (Mark 9:24). Believers may sometimes find themselves having to fight off questions—or even doubts—about their faith or themselves. Questions like "What if I am not really saved?" or "What if Jesus was not really who He said He was?" or "What if I fail as a Christian?" can haunt a believer from time to time.

Doubt may rear its ugly head, especially in the context of situations that tend to produce feelings of loneliness or guilt. You might feel unseen, unloved, or unheard and begin to think that maybe even God has turned away from you. You may begin to measure God's love for you according to your perceived good standing with Him based on your "success" as a Christian. It can be easy to believe that God loves others no matter what they have done, but it may be more difficult to assess yourself in the same way.

All Christians have the potential to doubt what they know is true when they are tempted to measure themselves by themselves. This is both the problem and the solution. The problem is that God does not measure us according to our standards; so for us to measure differently limits our ability to see how things really are. Thankfully, God measures us according to Christ. This is what is real, whether we, in any given moment, see it that way or not.

We are called to live by faith. Even when it feels like we do not deserve God's grace, we believe that we do; that is the whole idea of grace. It is not that you deserve His favor or get it based on your actions. God's favor is based on *His* actions. Though you do not deserve His favor, Christ does deserve it; and you, then, "deserve" it in Him. This is the Gospel. This is truth. We may struggle to keep our eyes fixed on Jesus as we sometimes, instead, stare at ourselves. And so, this must be our prayer: "Perhaps more than anything else, almighty God, I ask that You constantly and increasingly reveal to me your truth; that You measure me by You and not by me. Help me to keep my eyes fixed on you" (Heb. 12:2).

The application of this revelation is that we say no to measuring ourselves according to ourselves, and we only measure ourselves according to God. When I see my *bad*, I say no to that as my measurement, but I let it magnify all the more my need for a yes to His *good* standard. His standard is perfection, and He stands over us showering that perfection on us. He says yes to Himself and His works and no to us and our works. In that declaration, we are measured in what is real. This true way to look at things leads to life instead of death and to faith instead of doubt. Indeed, He is "'the way, and the truth, and the life (John 14:6).

Even when we might not "feel" this truth, it is still true! It is what is real, so it eliminates the other "way" and says that the other way is false. This claim is not just philosophical or psychological jargon. It is as practical as it gets. It is as practical as when we are dealing in our minds and hearts with our own shortcomings, or even our own disappointments, that we, instead, consider the possibility that Christ stands there over us saying yes and not no. He says, "I receive you," not "I reject you."

Occasionally, doubt can creep in and wage war against truth. We believe, but we sometimes question. All those questions are answered by Jesus. He is our Help, and so we cry out to Him, "I do believe; help my unbelief" (Mark 9:24).

Therefore, since we have a great high priest who has passed through the heavens, Jesus the Son of God, let us hold fast our confession. For we do not have a high priest who cannot sympathize with our weaknesses, but One who has been tempted in all things as *we are, yet without sin*. Therefore let us draw near with confidence to the throne of grace, so that we may receive mercy and find grace to help in time of need (Heb. 4:14-16).

No doubt there can sometimes be doubt. There can be questions. Wrestling with your faith is not necessarily displeasing to God; in fact, God can use it to build up your "faith muscles." The question is not so much whether you will have questions. The question is who will you look to for the answers?

APRIL 11

OUR GOD IS THE LION; OUR GOD IS THE LAMB

"The Lion that is from the tribe of Judah, the Root of David, has overcome so as to open the book ... a Lamb standing, as if slain, having seven horns and seven eyes, which are the seven Spirits of God, sent out into all the earth. And He came and took the book out of the right hand of Him who sat on the throne."

Revelations 5:5-7

God is the King of the Kingdom. Sometime before God created mankind, He created the angels who were not humans but spiritual beings. And so, God was King over this spiritual kingdom and King over this human or earthly kingdom. In each kingdom, there was a rebellion. First, there was an angelic rebellion led by Lucifer or Satan (Isa. 14:12-14). Second, there was a human rebellion led by Adam and Eve (Gen. 3:5-7).

These two rebellions led to two major problems. First, a counterfeit kingdom was formed and led by Satan. Second, people—whom God loves—drew back into a fallen state. For God, this resulted in the establishment of two goals: first, to reclaim the usurped kingdom which might be called God's kingdom program; second, to provide salvation for mankind, which might be called God's redemptive program.

God provides one solution that will tend to the needs of both programs. This one solution—the crucifixion and resurrection of God's only Son—has two results. First, there is the victory over the counterfeit kingdom. Second, there is salvation for mankind. The use of this methodology—the sacrificial death of God Himself to serve as mankind's replacement and the ensuing resurrection with power to destroy death—is first seen very early on in the history of the kingdoms, their rebellions, and their subsequent problems.

"The LORD God said to the serpent, 'Because you have done this, cursed are you more than all cattle, and more than every beast of the field; on your belly you will go, and dust you will eat all the days of your life; and I will put enmity between you and the woman, and between your seed and her seed; He shall bruise you on the head, and you shall bruise him on the heel'" (Gen. 3:14-15).

The word *enmity* signifies a blood feud between her Seed, Jesus (Gal. 4:4), and the serpent, Satan (Rev. 20:2). It is the Seed Who will crush the head of the serpent—Christ's kingdom victory over Satan at the resurrection. It is the serpent who will bruise the heel of the seed—Christ's redemptive victory on the cross on behalf of mankind.

Historically, the two programs (victory over Satan and redemption for mankind) are represented by the covenants that God made with David and Abraham. The covenant with David reflects God's kingdom program. David is promised a kingdom and a royal seed (2 Sam. 7:12-16). This kingdom and seed would rule over Israel and the whole world forever (Amos 9:12; Zech. 14:9). The covenant with Abraham reflects God's redemptive program. Abraham is promised a seed that would bless all nations (Gen. 18:18). The seed, of course, is Jesus; and the blessing is redemption (Gal. 3:6-16).

More specifically, the two programs are portrayed in the lives of two sons: a son of David and a son of Abraham. Both Solomon and Isaac stand as a "type" or example that foreshows the future. Solomon became a type of Christ the King because the kingdom of Israel reached its greatest height under the rule of Solomon. Isaac portrayed a clear picture of Christ the Lamb when he walked up a mountain in the land of Moriah (Gen. 22:2) with wood on his back that was to be used for his own slaughter by his own father. This "only son" of Abraham portrays Jesus in an uncanny way as God, ultimately, calls out to Abraham not to kill his son because He would provide a lamb on that same mountain in the future (Gen. 22:14).

The two Divine programs are seen in the two animals that are related to David and Isaac as *types*; the lion represents the kingdom program (Gen. 49:9-10; Rev. 5:5), and the lamb represents the redemptive program (John 1:29; Isa. 53:7). Jesus is both the victorious Lion Who has overcome (Rev. 5:5) and the sacrificial Lamb "'Who [has taken] away the sin of the world'" (John 1:29).

These two monumental Divine programs reveal the purposes of God. They are distinct programs, yet they are related. They are joined together. It is, after all, a slain Lamb who receives power (Rev. 5:12). Moreover, God sovereignly uses the existence of the kingdom program to be the solution in the redemptive program. Satan hates people. God loves people and is sovereign over Satan. God actually uses Satan and his rebellion in a positive way. Satan fights back against God and tries to kill Him on the cross. God uses that death on the cross to pay the price for people's sins and reunite those He loves back to Himself. This is an incredible story. It is His story!

APRIL 12

SOME TIPS FOR PREACHERS AND TEACHERS

*"When Jesus had finished giving instructions to His twelve disciples,
He departed from there to teach and preach in their cities."*

Matthew 11:1

Those who preach and teach the Word of God are not only those who are in "professional" full time ministry. Bible study leaders, parents leading "family church," home group leaders, and speakers in a variety of other situations may preach and teach from time to time. The following tips for preachers and teachers of all kinds may be helpful.

One of the biggest misunderstandings regarding how to preach and teach effectively is that you should not repeat yourself. The truth is, most speakers do not repeat themselves enough. Do not be afraid of repetition. Use it. It is essential in the learning process. Repeat key themes or points in the message.

Be creative in how you repeat something. For example, you can use creativity with the contents of your message by explaining the same point from different angles or points of view. Certainly, you should repeat Scriptures or parts of Bible passages that are essential in your message. You can use creativity in the structure or form of the presentation by repeating words or phrases that connect different parts of the message together. For example, if you are teaching on the all-encompassing nature of the Great Commission, you could repeat the word "exhaustive" to tie your major points together: Exhaustive Authority, Exhaustive Audience, Exhaustive Assignment, Exhaustive Assistance, and Exhaustive Anticipation (the "Exhaustive 'A's'").

Another simple, yet very effective tip is to be specific. Use specific verses. Use fewer points with more details related to each point. Make applications specific and concrete. Develop a scenario in which people can place themselves. For example, instead of saying, "You must be honest," you could be more specific in your application and say, "You are walking down the road. What do you do when you see someone who is walking in front of you drop a ten-dollar bill?"

Remember that there are two phases of teaching and preaching. Both are essential. First is the process of preparing the message. What do I say? Second is the presentation of the message. How do I say it? It is important that you gain knowledge from other sources and learn how to be a better speaker by observing other speakers. At the same time, it is critical that you produce your own message and develop your own style of speaking. Francis Bacon, a sixteenth century philosopher said, "Some students never study but, like the spider, spin everything out from within, beautiful webs that never last. Some are like ants that steal whatever they find, store it away, and use it later. But the bee sets the example for us all. He takes from the many flowers, but he makes his own honey."[7]

Of course, preparation and presentation impact each other. A presentation without serious preparation is often a waste of time. The presentation may be done well, but there is not much to say. A strong presentation that is done without serious preparation is like a good-tasting medicine that has no healing medication in it. On the other hand, much preparation without a good presentation is often a waste of time, since there is much to say but the ineffective presentation negates the possible benefits for others. It is like having to take a potent medicine that appears and tastes so terrible that you are just not willing to take it.

Preaching and teaching the Word of God is what Jesus did, so this is what His followers do. "When Jesus had finished giving instructions to His twelve disciples, He departed from there to teach and preach in their cities" (Matt. 11:1). Let us be bearers of the Word of God, whether it be in the more "formal" and "official" settings or in the more informal and everyday situations. "Preach the word; be ready in season *and* out of season" (2 Tim. 4:2).

APRIL 13

FAITH, YOU MAY NOW KISS WORKS, YOUR BRIDE

"You see that faith was working with his works, and as a result of the works, faith was perfected."
James 2:22

One of the fundamental principles of the Gospel message is that salvation is not able to be attained by doing good works. It is impossible to save yourself. "For by grace you have been saved through faith; and that not of yourselves, it is the gift of God; not as a result of works, so that no one may boast" (Eph. 2:8-9). So then, why are you to "work out your salvation with fear and trembling?" (Phil. 2:12). You are to "work it out" because "it is God who is at work in you, both to will and to work for His good pleasure" (Phil. 4:12-13). Your works do not come out of you and save you. His work goes in you and saves you and then His works come out of you because He is in you. This is what James means when he says, "Even so faith, if it has no works, is dead, *being* by itself" (James 2:17). Works are not a cause of salvation; they are a result. In this way, salvation and sanctification are inextricably wed together. You cannot have sanctification without salvation, and you cannot have salvation without sanctification. Thus, James says, "I will show you my faith by my works" (James 2:18).

Faith is not your own. It is a gift from God. The Gospel rebukes us for our self-saving, self-sourced claims. "What do you have that you did not receive? And if you did receive it, why do you boast as if you had not received it? (1 Cor. 4:7). This self-reliant mentality is tantamount to slapping Jesus across the face. It is to stand at the foot of the cross and mock Jesus by saying something like, "What are You doing up there? It is certainly not necessary! You might as well come down." You stand right there with "the chief priests also, along with the scribes and elders . . . mocking *Him* and saying, 'He saved others; He cannot save Himself. He is the King of Israel; let Him now come down from the cross'" (Matt. 27:41-42).

Paul put it this way: "I do not nullify the grace of God, for if righteousness *comes* through the Law, then Christ died needlessly" (Gal. 2:21). The *Humanist Manifesto* is incorrect. Man cannot save himself. Salvation is from God. God is the Source of faith. God gifts it, and man receives it and then is saved by it. "A man can receive nothing unless it has been given him from heaven" (John 3:27).

There are four facets of faith: knowledge, assent, trust, and obedience. Knowledge is that part of faith that understands there is salvation through Jesus alone. "Then who can be saved? . . . With people this is impossible, but with God all things are possible" (Matt. 19:25-26). Jesus says, "I am the way, and the truth, and the life; no one comes to the Father but through Me'" (John 14:6). The name *Jesus* means "God saves." You must *know* that Jesus is the Way to salvation.

Knowledge is the foundational aspect of salvation, but it is not sufficient. "You believe that God is one. You do well; the demons also believe, and shudder" (James 2:19). Obviously, there needs to be something more than knowledge. This is where *assent* comes in to play. *Assent* means to say yes to the contents of the Gospel and to say yes to your need for the Gospel. It is not only to have knowledge of the Gospel, but it is also to agree with the Gospel. "And those are the ones on whom seed was sown on the good soil; and they hear the word and accept it" (Mark 4:20).

Knowledge and acceptance are critical components of faith, but it cannot stop there. Faith must include trust. You must trust in God and depend on Him. This requires dying to self so as not to trust in self. The trust component of faith enables you to say, "I have been crucified with Christ; and it is no longer I who live, but Christ lives in me; and the *life* which I now live in the flesh I live by faith in the Son of God" (Gal. 2:20).

After knowledge, assent, and trust comes obedience. Obedience is the proof of faith. It is the manifestation of true faith. "You see that faith was working with his works, and as a result of the works, faith was perfected" (James 2:2). Your faith is from God; that includes your works, which are also from God. "For we are His workmanship, created in Christ Jesus for good works, which God prepared beforehand so that we would walk in them" (Eph. 2:10).

Knowledge plus assent plus trust plus obedience equals faith. It is faith that pleases God (Heb. 11:6). So please God with your knowledge. Please God with your assent. Please God with your trust. Please God with your obedience. Please God with your faith!

APRIL 14

HUNGER GAMES

"'Blessed are those who hunger and thirst for righteousness, for they shall be satisfied.'"

Matthew 5:6

What are you hungry for? In the Sermon on the Mount, Jesus calls us to "hunger and thirst for righteousness." What is righteousness? Righteousness centers on the word "right." It has to do with that which is right, that which is correct, or that which is the way it was meant to be. To hunger and thirst for righteousness is to be passionately drawn to the things which are God-breathed, God-fashioned, and God-sanctioned. The vision is to be righteous or in right standing with God. The desire is to only approve of the things that God approves of and to disapprove of the things that God disapproves of. To hunger and thirst for righteousness is to deny personal and carnal desires in order to desire and pursue relationship with God, obedience to Him, and social justice for His creation. "'Blessed are those who hunger and thirst for righteousness, for they shall be satisfied'" (Matt. 5:6). Those who hunger and thirst for righteousness give of themselves and are satisfied via putting self-fulfillment on the cross and, thus, bearing the fruit of self-control.

Blessings are free. Like salvation, you cannot earn them (Eph. 2:8-10). That does not mean, however, that they are not costly. They are costly because we try to hang onto that which is not our own (1 Cor. 6:19-20). It is quite a challenge to relinquish your own desires and will and, instead, pursue the desires and will of another. Jesus is our Example. He hungered and thirsted not for His preference but for the preference of the Father. His desire for and understanding of what was right was based on the Father's will. Jesus proclaimed, "'For I have come down from heaven, not to do My own will, but the will of Him who sent Me'" (John 6:38)

We must die to self by giving away or letting go of self-fulfillment and our own desires. To hunger and thirst for these things is not a healthy lifestyle choice. You will likely become fat, lazy, and out of shape. If you get filled up with yourself, you will not be hungry for God. Those who live in the kingdom of God must die to the desires of the flesh and hunger for the desires of God.

The provision or blessing for those who hunger for God is that "they shall be satisfied." To be satisfied is to be full of joy. Jesus assures us, "'These things I have spoken to you so that My joy may be in you, and *that* your joy may be made full'" (John 15:11). With Jesus, it is satisfaction guaranteed! The fruit of the Spirit that corresponds to this beatitude is self-control. Self-control is where the "diet battle" is won or lost. Many New Year's resolutions—no sweets or no coffee—have met their demise in the arena of self-control. Hungering and thirsting for healthy food keeps us "in shape." Self-control helps us to get there.

The nature of the kingdom of God—relative to the kingdoms of this world—is backward; it is "flip flopped." Each beatitude in the Sermon on the Mount, therefore, is cloaked in irony. "Blessed are those who hunger and thirst for righteousness, for they shall be satisfied" (Matt. 5:6). "We must trade fleshly desires and fulfillments for godly desires, then we shall be fulfilled.

APRIL 15

THE POWER OVER DEATH IS DEATH ITSELF!

"That through death He might render powerless him who had the power of death, that is, the devil, and might free those who through fear of death were subject to slavery all their lives."
Hebrews 2:14-15

The power *over* death is death itself because the power *of* death is death itself. You cannot kill a dead man, so the power over death is to not be able to be killed. You can kill a living man and, so, the power of death is to be able to be killed. In Jesus' language, this truth goes something like this: "For whoever wishes to save his life will lose it, but whoever loses his life for My sake and the gospel's will save it" (Mark 8:35). There is something about death that *disarms* the power of death, and there is something about death that *arms* you with power over it.

How can we put to death the power of death? In the midst of talking to His disciples about His looming death, Jesus claims that there is no need to be afraid and that there can be supernatural peace. He speaks as though death has no power over Him and that it need not have power over them. He says, "The ruler of the world is coming, and he has nothing in Me" (John 14:30). What is it about death itself that makes it so it has "nothing in Me"?

The power over death is death itself. If I am already dead, what more can death do to me? It has lost its leverage, so it has lost its threat and its power. If I am already dead to myself in order to follow Jesus, then I have Christ. What more can I have when I have Him who is "all in all" (Eph. 1:23); the "Alpha and the Omega, the first and the last, the beginning and the end" (Rev. 22:13). Death has no power because I have already died. Death is only powerful to the degree that it could take something from me. If there is nothing of me left, then it has nothing it can take. Death speaks to death, "Go ahead. Take what you want. There is nothing here." The robber has no power over an empty house. What is he going to take—the paint on the walls?

You cannot kill a dead man! Death is frustrated and emasculated when it launches its threats at someone who is already dead. Death is only powerful to the degree that it can take what you hold on to. Death has no power over someone who has nothing left of himself of which he clings to, someone who realizes that "you are not your own" (1 Cor. 6:19) and, thus, can connect power to death in the same way Paul did when he said, "That I may know Him and the power of His resurrection and the fellowship of His sufferings, being conformed to His death; in order that I may attain to the resurrection from the dead" (Phil. 3:10-11).

Just as death has no power over someone who has nothing, death has no power over someone who has everything. Death is only powerful to the degree that it can take what you have gained in Christ. Death has no power over someone whose "everything" is eternally permanent for "he who loves his life loses it, and he who hates his life in this world will keep it to life eternal" (John 12:25). When you gain Christ, you gain that which is eternal (John 17:3). When you chose Jesus instead of yourself, you will have "chosen the good part, which shall not be taken away from [you]" (Luke 10:42).

Death has no power over someone who has everything, someone who realizes that "all things belong to you" (1 Cor. 3:21). When the worst thing your enemy can do to you is actually the best thing for you, then you have disarmed your enemy. "For to me, to live is Christ and to die is gain" (Phil. 1:21). The power of death is its threat to "end it all." When you understand that it does not *end* it all but, in fact, only *begins* the rest, then death has lost its sting. "But when this perishable will have put on the imperishable, and this mortal will have put on immortality, then will come about the saying that is written, 'DEATH IS SWALLOWED UP in victory. O DEATH, WHERE IS YOUR VICTORY? O DEATH, WHERE IS YOUR STING?'" (1 Cor. 15:54-55).

The power over death is death because death leads to life. "Truly, truly, I say to you, unless a grain of wheat falls into the earth and dies, it remains alone; but if it dies, it bears much fruit" (John 12:24). On God's calendar, Good Friday leads to Resurrection Sunday. The cross is followed by the resurrection. Death could not hold Him as "it was impossible for Him to be held in its power" (Acts 2:24). The power of death has become powerless. "Therefore, since the children share in flesh and blood, He Himself likewise also partook of the same, that through death He might render powerless him who had the power of death, that is, the devil, and might free those who through fear of death were subject to slavery all their lives" (Heb. 2:14-15).

Here we have the most fundamental issue in our battle against the power of death. "Do not be afraid; for I know that you are looking for Jesus who has been crucified. He is not here, for He has risen" (Matt. 28:5-6). Jesus is alive! The question is, "Is He alive in you?" If He is alive in you, then you have power over death. If He is still dead, then the story is over (1 Cor. 15:12-19); but if He is alive, well, then, that is another story!

A story is told of a man who became a Christian. His friends asked, "Why have you become a Christian?" He answered, "Suppose you were going down the road; and suddenly, the road forked in two directions, and you did not know which way to go. There at the fork were two men, one dead and one alive—who would you ask which way to go?" Christianity's God is alive. The power over death is that Jesus is alive. He is alive, indeed!

APRIL 16

THE ROMANS 12 GIFT OF EXHORTATION

"Since we have gifts that differ according to the grace given to us,
each of us is to exercise them accordingly*: . . . he who exhorts, in his exhortation."*
Romans 12:6, 8

God equips His people with gifts for ministry. There exist various lists of gifts in the New Testament. One such list is found in Romans 12:6-8: "Since we have gifts that differ according to the grace given to us, *each of us is to exercise them accordingly*: if prophecy, according to the proportion of his faith; if service, in his serving; or he who teaches, in his teaching; or he who exhorts, in his exhortation; he who gives, with liberality; he who leads, with diligence; he who shows mercy, with cheerfulness."

The giver of these gifts is God (Rom. 12:3). The gifts are called *charismata* (grace gifts). They are described as being "functional gifts" (Rom. 12:4) that are "effects" enacted by "God who works all things in all persons" (1 Cor. 12:6). The Romans 12 gifts are gifts that direct how a person functions; they determine the effects of a person's personality or tendencies. They are not so much gifts that a person is temporarily and situationally used in (as in the 1 Corinthians 12:8-10 gifts) or gifts that dictate a person's actual ministry (as in the Ephesians 4:11 gifts) as they are gifts that reside inside of a person and shape what that person is like. They are what are often called "motivational gifts."

How can the Romans 12 gift of exhortation be understood? People who have the gift of exhortation look for opportunities to encourage and stimulate others to think positively. Like Paul, they are likely to have a strong desire to urge others to excel, and they gravitate toward giving others advice (Phil. 3:17). Like Barnabas (Acts 4:36), they usually have the ability and desire to prompt vision in others.

Barnabas was sent off to the church at Antioch and "when he arrived and witnessed the grace of God, he rejoiced and *began* to encourage them all with resolute heart to remain *true* to the Lord" (Acts 11:23). Someone who has the gift of exhortation tends to be experience- and event-oriented. They are inclined to be very accepting of others. They are predisposed to being very personable people and lean toward being "people persons." They are not afraid of intimacy and personal relationships (Rom. 1:11-12; 2 Tim. 1:3-4). They are the ones who are apt to promote unity.

Just like any strength that has its correlated weaknesses, the gift of exhortation has its vulnerabilities or carnal tendencies that need to be avoided. If someone with this gift is not careful, he or she may become presumptuous in their dealing with others. In their insistence on seeing the "glass half-full," they may be blinded to important ways in which the glass is more than half-empty. In other words, they are vulnerable to oversimplifying things. Sometimes, not everything "comes up roses." When it does not, to simply ignore the weeds often results in the rationalizing of sin or error and the offering of fleshly advice.

Here is the Romans 12 gift of exhortation. Life is seen as being positive. The orientation is toward making progress. More than anything else, people with this gift view themselves as those who want everyone to see the good side of life. They are there to make sure everyone keeps going forward. They would say of themselves, "We are here to tell you that you can do it!" Are you this person? Do you have the Romans 12 gift of exhortation?

APRIL 17

TRYING TO TIE THINGS BACK

"He has made everything appropriate in its time. He has also set eternity in their heart, yet so that man will not find out the work which God has done from the beginning even to the end."

Ecclesiastes 3:11

Man is, by nature, religious. Cultures are defined and distinguished by their religion. The word "religion" is derived from the Latin, religio, meaning "to tie back." It is the nature of man to want to tie things back to where he came from. Where did it all come from? Who or what began everything? How did it all begin? Man, who has eternity in his heart—he is aware of the idea of pre-beginnings yet cannot fully comprehend it—is naturally drawn to these fundamental questions of reality (Eccl. 3:11). He is naturally drawn to religion. Of course, the very thing that draws him is his ultimate frustration. Who or what began everything? Okay, but who or what began that? Now there is frustration. The mathematician just puts a "line" over the last number and pretends to be satisfied with his inability to really answer the eternal equation: $1/3 = .33333333333$ forever.

These sorts of questions—"Who holds up the elephant?," and then after that is answered, "Who holds up the elephant holder?," or "What is on the other side of the end of the world?," and then after that is answered "What is on the other side of that?"—do have answers. The answer is the basis for religion. It is eternality. Whoever or whatever that Being, thing, or concept is defines your religion; it defines your God.

There exist three major worldviews that establish different understandings of "prime reality." Theists say that prime reality is an infinite, personal Being who alone exists forever and through whom exists all things. Who holds up the elephant? What is on the other side of the end of the world? God! Naturalists say that prime reality is the cosmos itself. Who holds up the elephant? What is on the other side of the end of the world? The World! Pantheists say that prime reality is the divine oneness that unifies all. Who holds up the elephant? What is on the other side of the end of the world? The concept of "allness" or "nothingness!" The world is not even there; all is "one" and the world is an illusion.

Hinduism is a pantheistic religion. It has no known founder and is, therefore, referred to as the "Sanatana Dharma" or the "eternal religion." Its authoritative texts are the Vedas, which are a collection of sacred hymns, the most ancient of which have an unknown origin. Brahman is the unknowable ultimate reality force or concept that is best defined as "oneness" or "allness." Anything that is perceived as being segmented (not "all") is "maya" or magic. It is not real, and the quest of the Hindu is to perceive things rightly—that is, come to a place of realization of allness. The goal of the Hindu is to achieve "moksha"—liberation from the limitations of space, time, and matter through the realization of "all." In order to do this, various forms of yoga are employed to "yoke" together what was otherwise falsely perceived to be separated. Hinduism is a religion of realization, not transformation. Nothing needs to be changed—it is already *all*—it just needs to be recognized.

Islam is a theistic religion. It was founded by Muhammad in 622 A.D. Islam means "submit to God," so a Muslim is one who submits to God. Its authoritative text is the Koran, which is the earthly center of Islamic faith. The sovereign, transcendent God is, for the most part, unknowable; but He still is understood to be a personal Being. Man is obligated to God in gratitude to Him and surrender to Him. The Day of Judgment results in the souls of men going to Heaven or Hell based on how thoroughly they have submitted to God and observed His commands, especially the "Five Pillars" of Islamic faith.

Buddhism is a pantheistic religion. It was founded by Sidhartha Gautama (the Buddha, which means "I am awake") in the sixth century B.C. The practice of the religion is based on the "four noble truths." First, life is *dukkha* (suffering) that can be relieved. Second, the cause of dukkha is *tanha* (desire for private fulfillment), which is inconsistent with the reality of "allness." Third, the cure for suffering is to overcome these selfish desires, to be released from the limits of self-interest into the vast expanse of universal life. The way to overcome selfish desires—the way out of captivity—is the "Eightfold Path," which can, ultimately, lead one into "nirvana" ("to extinguish" or "blow out"), which is a state of "nothingness" in which finite boundaries are extinguished.

All of these religions try to tie things back; they try to search for and define prime reality. Religions do that. That is why they exist. They ask these fundamental questions and offer a variety of answers. What is real? What's it all about? Each has its own soteriology that proposes: What is the problem? What is its solution? As a member of the human family, you are naturally drawn to these fundamental questions of reality. You have "eternity in your heart." You are, by nature, religious. Have you tried to tie things back? What do you think is real? Have you found the solution to your problem?

The great "I Am" (Yahweh) is, as indicated in His name (Exod. 3:14), real. There is nothing more real than God. Jesus, Whose name means "God saves," most clearly answers the question regarding "problem and solution." Our sin is the problem, and Jesus' payment for that sin is the solution. Everything is "tied back" to Jesus!

> In Him we have redemption through His blood, the forgiveness of our trespasses, according to the riches of His grace which He lavished on us. In all wisdom and insight He made known to us the mystery of His will, according to His kind intention which He purposed in Him with a view to an administration suitable to the fullness of the times, *that is*, the summing up of all things in Christ, things in the heavens and things on the earth (Eph. 1:7-10).

APRIL 18

LISTEN TO THE WIND BLOW

"The wind blows where it wishes and you hear the sound of it, but do not know where it comes from and where it is going; so is everyone who is born of the Spirit."

John 3:8

Not all cultures are reached with the Gospel in the same way. It is the same Gospel that goes to all cultures, but different methods to present that Gospel are more appropriate and effective in one culture than in another. Most people of the world who are not "Westernized" continue to live in a culture where community is more important than the individual. Individual evangelism may not be appropriate or effective. People tend to make decisions in groups. The Gospel is viewed as foreign, and individual converts are viewed as outcasts. It may be necessary to engage in group evangelism that results in "people movements."

Sometimes, the method of presenting the Gospel is as important as the Gospel message itself. This may not sound very "spiritual," but it certainly is very real and practical. If an evangelist shares the Gospel in Spanish to a Mandarin-speaking audience, then the method will negate the message. An ineffective or insensitive method can result in people never hearing the message. The family is a very powerful social force in Chinese culture. A strategy that uses families to evangelize families would be much more effective than a strategy that uses single women to evangelize families. Herein is an important principle for evangelistic endeavors. The Gospel spreads most effectively within the social structures that already exist. Although sometimes difficult to apply, individualistic Westerners must consider how they might share the Gospel while promoting group decisions. The Westerner reasons, "I think; therefore, I am." Many other people in the world would say, "I participate; therefore, I am." We often see in the Bible that families were both recipients and agents of evangelism:

"They said, 'Believe in the Lord Jesus, and you will be saved, you and your household.' And they spoke the word of the Lord to him together with all who were in his house. And he took them that very hour . . . having believed in God with his whole household" (Acts 16:31-34).

"Greet Prisca and Aquila, my fellow workers in Christ Jesus, who for my life risked their own necks, to whom not only do I give thanks, but also all the churches of the Gentiles; also *greet* the church that is in their house" (Rom. 16:3-5).

"How I did not shrink from declaring to you anything that was profitable, and teaching you publicly and from house to house" (Acts 20:20).

The use of effective evangelistic methods might also include understanding the distinction between the "social gospel" (an emphasis on responding to physical and social needs) and the "evangelical gospel" (an emphasis on meeting spiritual needs). These are not in conflict with each other; they can work together. Christ met physical and spiritual needs in His earthly ministry. The church must do the same. Many times, God uses the social gospel as an introduction to the evangelical gospel. A physical need is met, which results in an opportunity to share the Gospel message. We see this when Peter used the healing of the lame beggar in his most powerful sermon: "'In the name of Jesus Christ the Nazarene—walk!' . . . And all the people saw him walking and praising God . . . and they were filled with wonder and amazement at what had happened to him" (Acts 3:6, 9-10). As a result of Peter using this method, "Many of those who had heard the message believed; and the number of the men came to be about five thousand" (Acts 4:4).

The social gospel often opens the door for the evangelical gospel. In many countries, the only way for missionaries to initially enter is to engage in the social gospel. Providing relief and community development for people living in extreme poverty may provide a platform for the Gospel. Some common areas of need that have been successfully addressed by missionaries include the need for clean water, sanitation, food, fuel, healthcare, shelter and clothing, income production, education, communication, and transportation.

Evangelism is a mystery. The fruit of it is compared to a blowing wind (John 3:8). It is a mystery how God moves among people and changes them. Sometimes, the results can be seen, but the process is not clear. It is a mystery that God uses men to do this. Mysteries and planning do not seem to be compatible. Yet we must plan. We must be strategic with our methods and organized with our processes. Part of the mystery of evangelism is that the Holy Spirit can lead us in forming our plans. Both the message and the messenger—the contents and methods—can be holy and led by the Spirit.

APRIL 19

LET'S GO PLANT A CHURCH

"Then He said to His disciples, 'The harvest is plentiful, but the workers are few. Therefore beseech the Lord of the harvest to send out workers into His harvest.'"
Matthew 9:37-38

The church began to grow immediately. "So then, those who had received his word were baptized; and that day there were added about three thousand souls" (Acts 2:41). The Church is not a business or an organization; it is a body. It is made up of people who share life together—not just people who attend a meeting together—since it is based on relationships and not on programs. The successful planting of a church is based more on the quality of the work than on the quantity of the work or the pace at which it is accomplished. Quality will lead to quantity.

What does the planting of a church look like? The birth of a church happens in stages. The first stage might be called the conception stage. The team is formed. The ones who will eventually plant the church spend time together and form strong relationships. The vision and strategy are developed. The next stage of church planting is the prenatal stage. Evangelism is done. New disciples are organized into small groups and meet in houses. A public place of worship is not used yet. The next stage is the birth stage. The church begins to meet in a public place of worship. A philosophy and style of worship is implemented. People in the community are invited to attend the meetings. The sacraments—baptism and the Lord's Supper—should be performed in a public place. Specific areas of ministry should be offered, especially children's ministry.

The next stage of a church plant is its early life. Reproduction and multiplication of ministry begin. Leaders are trained, and authority and responsibility is shared. Training in small group leadership and evangelism are especially emphasized. Then follows the progression from adolescence to maturity. A permanent location is established. New ministries are formed. The focus is on leadership training, and a clear process of the multiplication of leaders and ministry is established. Church activities and ministry become increasingly organized and structured. The final stage is reproduction. The church begins to plant other churches and ministries. Evangelism and missions are emphasized. The church that was birthed now births its own "babies."

The most critical stage of church planting is the prenatal stage. This is when the initial evangelism is done to gain the converts who will make up the "infant" church. Without these converts, there will be no church. Especially in places where the soil is hard, this can be /very difficult to accomplish. Pray to the Lord of the harvest that He will bring in the harvest (Matt. 9:38). Practice hospitality. Invite people to your home. Have a neighborhood picnic. Offer home Bible studies on special topics of interest (marriage, raising children, and financial success) that would be especially relevant to those you are trying to reach. Organize special events for children. Engage in personal evangelism. Witness to those you meet in everyday situations.

Do door to door evangelism. Engage in street evangelism (in parks, on street corners, in "crusade" tents). Do follow-ups. Send a letter or visit those who have attended events you have organized in the past.

Because it is the body of Christ, the church is the "vehicle" through which God reveals Himself and advances His kingdom. The more the Church is multiplied, the more God is revealed in the world and the more the kingdoms of this world give way to the kingdom of God. Let's go plant a church!

APRIL 20

WHEN MONEY DEFINES US

"For the love of money is a root of all sorts of evil."

1 Timothy 6:10

Money seems to be directly associated with evil. In fact, it is said to be a foundation, a source, or a root of all other kinds of evil. This, of course, is a serious accusation that needs some further explanation.

> But godliness *actually* is a means of great gain when accompanied by contentment. For we have brought nothing into the world, so we cannot take anything out of it either. If we have food and covering, with these we shall be content. But those who want to get rich fall into temptation and a snare and many foolish and harmful desires which plunge men into ruin and destruction. For the love of money is a root of all sorts of evil, and some by longing for it have wandered away from the faith and pierced themselves with many griefs (1 Tim. 6:6-10).

More specifically, it is not money that is evil; it is the *love* of money that is denounced. It comes down to an issue of lordship. By definition, there can only be *one* Lord. There can only be *one* number one. You cannot have Jesus as your number One *and* money. Both cannot be on top; since for one to be on top, the other must be underneath.

> "No servant can serve two masters; for either he will hate the one and love the other, or else he will be devoted to one and despise the other. You cannot serve God and wealth." Now the Pharisees, who were lovers of money, were listening to all these things and were scoffing at Him. And He said to them, "You are those who justify yourselves in the sight of men, but God knows your hearts; for that which is highly esteemed among men is detestable in the sight of God" (Luke 16:13-15).

Only God can be in first place in our lives. We must not look to anything else before we look to God. This is the issue of lordship! Money may be desired not so much for the tangibles it gets us but for three intangibles that define us: success, security, and satisfaction. This is the danger regarding the love of money. It can become an idol when it stands in the place that should be only for God.

It can make us think we are successful. Yet only God can really define our success. Our relationship with God marks our success, not money. Money can also make us think we are secure. Yet only God can really generate our security. Our relationship with God produces security, not money. Money can also make us feel satisfied. Yet only God can really yield satisfaction. Our relationship with God produces satisfaction, not money. When something or someone other than God defines who we are, we live as if constantly attending a masquerade ball. We were not made by money, nor do we "live and move and exist" by money or for money. The warning about wealth is not necessarily with regard to generating it, having it, or using it. It is not about money in and of itself. It is about idolatry. It is about Lordship. It is about who God is and who He is not and, therefore, who you are and who you are not. All kinds of things, including money, can become our "unknown gods."

So Paul stood in the midst of the Areopagus and said, "Men of Athens, I observe that you are very religious in all respects. For while I was passing through and examining the objects of your worship, I also found an altar with this inscription, 'TO AN UNKNOWN GOD.' Therefore what you worship in ignorance, this I proclaim to you. The God who made the world and all things in it, since He is Lord of heaven and earth, does not dwell in temples made with hands; nor is He served by human hands, as though He needed anything, since He Himself gives to all *people* life and breath and all things; and He made from one *man* every nation of mankind to live on all the face of the earth, having determined *their* appointed times and the boundaries of their habitation, that they would seek God, if perhaps they might grope for Him and find Him, though He is not far from each one of us; for in Him we live and move and exist, as even some of your own poets have said, 'For we also are His children.' Being then the children of God, we ought not to think that the Divine Nature is like gold or silver or stone, an image formed by the art and thought of man. Therefore having overlooked the times of ignorance, God is now declaring to men that all *people* everywhere should repent, because He has fixed a day in which He will judge the world in righteousness through a Man whom He has appointed, having furnished proof to all men by raising Him from the dead" (Acts 17:22-31).

APRIL 21

THE SHADOW BEHIND THE GIFTS OF THE SPIRIT

"Therefore I make known to you that no one speaking by the Spirit of God says, 'Jesus is accursed'; and no one can say, 'Jesus is Lord,' except by the Holy Spirit. Now there are varieties of gifts, but the same Spirit. And there are varieties of ministries, and the same Lord. There are varieties of effects, but the same God who works all things in all persons."

1 Corinthians 12:3-6

Paul's reference to the gifts of the Holy Spirit in 1 Corinthians 12:1-11 stands as one of the most intriguing passages in all of the New Testament. Paul's description and explanation of the gifts is not without its own theological underpinnings. What stands behind the manifestation of these spiritual activities? There is a shadow that hovers over these gifts. Specifically, it is Jesus; and in general, it is the Trinity.

First and foremost, the emphasis is placed on the lordship of Christ. Paul makes it clear that it is only through the recognition of that lordship that the spiritual gifts can be manifested. The lordship of

Christ is directly linked to being in the Spirit, since "no one can say, 'Jesus is Lord,' except by the Holy Spirit" (1 Cor. 12:3). This connection is made before the list of the spiritual gifts is given. The lordship of Christ precedes the gifts of the Holy Spirit. There is a certain implied cause and effect relationship here. The important thing to notice is that the Spirit, as the Source, causes people to be able to make Christ their Lord; but it is then the lordship of Christ that, as the Source, causes the manifestation of the spiritual gifts.

That is to say that the pneumatic community is not so much a Spirit-centered community as it is a Christ-centered community. The focus is not the Spirit because the Spirit does not focus on Himself. The focus is on Jesus because the Spirit focuses on Him. Jesus explains, But when He, the Spirit of truth, comes, He will guide you into all the truth; for He will not speak on His own initiative, but whatever He hears, He will speak; and He will disclose to you what is to come. He will glorify Me, for He will take of Mine and will disclose it to you. All things that the Father has are Mine; therefore I said that He takes of Mine and will disclose it to you (John 16:13-15).

The real existence of the lordship of Jesus Christ results in the real existence of the movement and action of the Lord through the Spirit, Who manifests Himself through the gifts.

Even as, specifically, the lordship of Christ stands behind the gifts of the Spirit, more generally the Trinity shadows the manifestation of those gifts. The gifts of the Holy Spirit are listed in the context of unity within diversity. This foundational dynamic of the nature of the triune God is a dynamic that informs the use of the gifts. There are varieties of gifts, yet there is the same Source; unity in diversity is the very nature of the Trinity. This unity includes the members of the Trinity (Holy Spirit, Lord Jesus, God the Father): "Now there are varieties of gifts, but the same Spirit. And there are varieties of ministries, and the same Lord. There are varieties of effects, but the same God who works all things in all persons" (1 Cor. 12:4-6). This declaration of the Trinity with its unity in diversity terminology precedes the listing of the gifts.

It might even be noted here that the order of the Trinity in 1 Corinthians 12—Spirit (v. 4), Son (v. 5), Father (v. 6)—is consistent with the order in which they reveal each other; the Spirit reveals the Son, and the Son reveals the Father (John 16:13-15; John 1:18). And so, the gifts of the Spirit operate through the Trinity that stands behind the manifestation of the Spirit. More specifically, it is the lordship of Christ that fuels the gifts of the Spirit. The gifts of the Holy Spirit are a spiritual thing; more precisely, they are a God thing.

APRIL 22

SERVANTS KNOW STUFF

"If I then, the Lord and the Teacher, washed your feet, you also ought to wash one another's feet.
John 13:14

Servants are secure people. Secure people know *who* they are, *what* they have, and *why* they are here. Insecure people are not able to serve because they have to serve their own *who*, *what*, and *why*. Instead of serving others, they have to serve themselves. They have to spend their time, energy, and resources proving who they are, gaining what they do not think they have, and validating why they are here. All of this serves to hinder their service. Servants must be secure. They must know stuff!

God calls you to serve others. The Scripture says, "Through love serve one another" (Gal. 5:13). The fallen world and our fallen nature oppose such suggestions. To serve others, we must stop insisting on serving ourselves. Self must yield to selflessness, so serving others may take the place of serving self. This is not easy. There are always challenges that try to impede your service. Feelings of disappointment and dissatisfaction with others are challenges that need to be jumped over on the way to serving others.

To continue to serve, Jesus had to fight through feelings of disappointment. This is always true of servant leaders because people you serve will not always receive your service. "Then He began to denounce the cities in which most of His miracles were done because they did not repent. 'Woe to you, Chorazin! Woe to you, Bethsaida!'" (Matt. 11:20-21). This is the question for each of us: "Who are my Chorazins and Bethsaidas?"

Disappointment can be a stumbling block to continued service. You must be secure. "All things have been handed over to Me by My Father; and no one knows the Son except the Father; nor does anyone know the Father except the Son, and anyone to whom the Son wills to reveal *Him*" (Matt. 11:27). Jesus knew *what* He had ("all things"). He knew *Who* He was ("know the Father"). He knew *why* He was here ("the Son wills to reveal Him"). Security trumps disappointment and enables us to continue to serve. Because of His sense of security, Jesus, Who had every right to be heavy-laden with disappointment, did not succumb to it. Instead, He was able to serve those who were "weary and heavy-laden," offering them "rest" and the opportunity to "take My yoke upon you and learn from Me" (Matt. 11:28-29).

To multiply service, Jesus had to fight through dissatisfaction as "He became troubled in spirit" (John 13:21). This is often true of servant leaders because those they are leading tend to struggle along the way. The disciples struggled with their prideful misunderstanding of leadership. "And there arose also a dispute among them *as to* which one of them was regarded to be greatest" (Luke 22:24). Jesus was near the end of His service, so He needed to multiply those who would serve. He had been preparing twelve for the job; but now, at this most critical time, instead of serving, they were fighting over who was the greatest. Jesus was dissatisfied.

To enable others to be enablers themselves, you have to be secure enough to overcome being troubled. "Jesus knowing that His hour had come that He would depart out of this world to the Father ... knowing that the Father had given all things into His hands, and that He had come forth from God and was going back to God, got up from supper, and laid aside His garments; and taking a towel, He girded Himself" (John 13:1, 3-4).

Jesus knew why He was here ("knowing that His hour had come"). He knew what He had ("knowing that the Father had given all things into His hands"). He knew Who He was ("knowing that He had come forth from God"). This is when Jesus did the unthinkable. He got down on His hands and knees and did the lowliest act of service; He washed their feet. The Creator served the creation to show the creation that the Creator's service must be multiplied. Security turns back trouble. Service is multiplied. "If I then, the Lord and the Teacher, washed your feet, you also ought to wash one another's feet" (John 13:14).

Servants know stuff. They are secure in who they are, what they have, and why they are here. This enables them to begin serving, continue serving, and multiply serving. Invest in your ability to serve. Stock up on these securities!

APRIL 23

THE MEANS OF GRACE

"Delight yourself in the Lord; and He will give you the desires of your heart."
Psalm 37:4

God's grace flows toward us via various conduits. These may be called "means of grace." Fellowship with other believers is one such means. The action of fellowship, or *koinonia*, is to share. To fellowship with those who have Christ in them (Gal. 2:20) is, to some degree, to fellowship with Christ. Believers share the Word of God with each other and serve as mutual means of grace. Jesus said, "The one who listens to you listens to Me" (Luke 10:16). In our fellowship with each other, we hear Jesus because "whoever speaks, is to do so as one who is speaking the utterances of God" (1 Peter 4:11).

Especially in a culture that prides itself in its diversity and its lack of absolutes, we must stress biblical commonalties among believers. If our fellowship with each other is going to flourish, then we must protect ourselves from the societal effects of pluralism and relativism by stressing such commonalties as the fact that we are all sinners and we all "drink from the same cup," having the same desperate need for salvation and the same miraculous provision for it. The reality of common ground (things we share or fellowship around) points to our clear and distinct identity. This becomes a means of grace.

Means of grace can be found in biblical disciplines. Fellowship, Bible study, and prayer are foundational. "They were continually devoting themselves to the apostles' teaching and to fellowship, to the breaking of bread and to prayer" (Acts 2:42). The terminology "breaking of bread" is reflective of the Greek term *eucharisto*, which means "to give thanks." The picture here is the sharing that is done in the Lord's Supper. Remembering what Christ has done for us and giving Him thanks along with praise and worship serve as a means of grace. The flow of life is ultimately determined by God's quest to be glorified (John 14:13) and our quest to be satisfied (John 16:24). The life of praise satisfies both quests (Psalm 147:11); it serves as a means of grace.

Grace yields to pleasure. Pleasure is not evil; it has simply been polluted and redefined by sin. Redemption does not do away with pleasure. It allows us to have it in its pure form. It does not destroy it; it establishes and fulfills it. Moreover, the pursuit of pleasure is mandatory in order to truly worship God. "You will make known to me the path of life; in Your presence is fullness of joy; in Your right hand there are pleasures forever" (Psalm 16:11). Worship comes from more than the will. It comes from the heart. It comes from feelings: fearing Him, enjoying Him, admiring Him, hoping in Him, honoring Him, being in awe of Him, delighting in Him, being grateful to Him. "Be glad in the Lord and rejoice, you righteous ones; and shout for joy, all you who are upright in heart" (Psalm 32:11).

God's grace comes to us through a variety of means. It manifests itself through channels in which we point to, seek out, and glorify God. You can have anything you want when God is Who you want because He gives Himself to you. "Delight yourself in the Lord; and He will give you the desires of your heart" (Psalm 37:4).

What does it mean that there are means of grace? It is God's grace that He would give you "the desires of your heart." To "delight yourself in the Lord" is a means to that end.

APRIL 24

A HISTORY CHANNEL DOCUMENTARY

"[L]et it be known to all of you and to all the people of Israel, that by the name of Jesus Christ the Nazarene, whom you crucified, whom God raised from the dead—
by this name this man stands here before you in good health. He is the STONE WHICH WAS REJECTED by you, THE BUILDERS, but WHICH BECAME THE CHIEF CORNER stone. And there is salvation in no one else; for there is no other name under heaven that has been given among men by which we must be saved."

Acts 4:10-12

History, of course, is most pointedly His Story. If theology, in general, is the queen of the sciences, then soteriology, in particular, is the prince of the arts. The history of salvation is painted on a priceless canvass that hangs from Heaven and stretches down to earth. The painting depicts, in broad strokes, the entire story of salvation. What would such a "painting" look like that is titled, *The History of Salvation*? Let's take a look.

"In the beginning God created" (Gen. 1:1). He made mankind in His own likeness (Gen. 1:26-27). God desires relationship with mankind (Gen. 3:8). Sin entered the world when the first man and woman, Adam and Eve, disobeyed God (Gen. 3:1-6). Sin caused separation from God (Gen. 3:22-24). Sin leads to eternal death (Rom. 6:23). All mankind has inherited Adam's sinful nature (Rom. 5:12). Without God's help, all face eternal death (Heb. 2:9).

God sent His Son to save mankind (John 3:16). God the Son became a Man to identify with all people (Phil. 2:5-8). God in the flesh, Jesus, was sinless and perfect (2 Cor. 5:21). God placed the sin of the world upon Jesus (Isa. 53:6). He suffered on our behalf (1 Peter 3:18). Jesus was put to death by crucifixion on a cross (John 19:16). Jesus was buried in a tomb (Matt. 27:59-60). God raised Him from the dead (Acts 2:24). Jesus then appeared to many people (1 Cor. 15:5-8). The Son of God returned to Heaven to be with God the Father (Acts 1:9-11).

Eternal life with God has been made possible through Jesus (Rom. 5:20-21). God has given Jesus all authority in heaven and on earth (Matt. 28:18). Jesus will someday return to judge the living and the dead (Acts 10:42). Each person must turn away from sin to obtain eternal life (Acts 2:38-39). Each person must believe in Jesus to obtain eternal life (1 John 5:10-12). Salvation comes through faith (Eph. 2:8-10). Jesus commands us to tell others about eternal life (Mark 16:15).

And so, we see a "broad strokes" painting of the history of salvation starting from the beginning and ending with the scene in which the Good News of salvation is taken to all nations. Let's end with one more portrait that is made up of short wisps of salvation history.

APRIL 25

TO FLEE OR NOT TO FLEE

"And they all left Him and fled."

Mark 14:50

Spirituality is fueled by a correct perception of what we need. To the degree that we understand our need for God is the degree to which we will seek Him. Those who are full of pride cannot be spiritual because they cannot see their need for God. Spirituality assumes humility. Without humility, we only flee from God; we renounce spirituality.

The irony of man fleeing from the only One who can help him began immediately after the original sin was committed in the Garden of Eden.

> They heard the sound of the LORD God walking in the garden in the cool of the day, and the man and his wife hid themselves from the presence of the LORD God among the trees of the garden. Then the LORD God called to the man, and said to him, "Where are you?" He said, "I heard the sound of You in the garden, and I was afraid because I was naked; so I hid myself." And He said, "Who told you that you were naked? Have you eaten from the tree of which I commanded you not to eat?" The man said, "The woman whom You gave to be with me, she gave me from the tree, and I ate." Then the Lord God said to the woman, "What is this you have done?" And the woman said, "The serpent deceived me, and I ate" (Genesis 3:8-13).

God's desire to interact with Adam and Eve is contrasted with their desire to avoid Him. The "presence of the Lord" is contrasted with their response to that presence. They fled from the only One Who could help them. The opposite of spirituality is portrayed by those attitudes and actions of men that represent an attempt to hide from God in the midst of His creation. These attitudes and actions are prompted by sin, which separates us from God. We find ourselves fleeing from Him instead of seeking Him.

It was very early in the morning on the day that Jesus was crucified that Judas the betrayer led a group of men through the darkness to arrest Jesus. Jesus' best friends were by his side, but then "they all left Him and fled" (Mark 14:50). Those who walked, talked, laughed, cried, worked, slept, and ate with Him for three years left Him and fled. The ones who saw Him raise people from the dead, heal every kind of disease, cast out demons, multiply food, and walk on water abandoned Him and ran away. To be sure, they felt vulnerable. They sought refuge, security, and a covering. Specifically, "[a] young man was following Him, wearing *nothing but* a linen sheet over *his* naked *body*; and they seized him. But he pulled free of the linen sheet and escaped naked" (Mark 14:51-52). The result of fleeing from Jesus was that he was naked. He found no refuge, security, or covering. How ironic that he flees from the only One Who can help him. The picture in the Garden of Gethsemane is tragically similar to the one in the Garden of Eden (Gen. 3:7-21). Both pictures, sadly, can portray our own tendencies to flee from God.

Too often, we who are Jesus' friends flee from Him. We engage in the irony of needing Him and yet ignoring Him. We are naked, yet we could be covered (Psalm 17:7). There is a shelter, but we need to go there! "He who dwells in the shelter of the Most High will abide in the shadow of the Almighty. I will say to the LORD, 'My refuge and my fortress, my God, in whom I trust!' For it is He who delivers you from the snare of the trapper and from the deadly pestilence. He will cover you with His pinions, and under His wings you may seek refuge; His faithfulness is a shield and bulwark" (Psalm 91:1-4).

APRIL 26

QUITE A HANDY GOSPEL PRESENTATION

"It is no longer on the basis of works, otherwise grace is no longer grace."

Romans 11:6

All Gospel presentations should revolve around two major points: man has a problem, and God offers the solution to that problem. Man has a need, and God offers to provide for that need. Man is a sinner separated from God; and God pays for man's sin, which reunites him with God. This is the Gospel: sin and salvation, problem and solution, need and provision. Of course, there are different ways in which to present the basic contents of the Gospel. Some methods are more "packaged" and creative than others. One such method is the use of "the hand."

When sharing the Gospel, each finger is used to make a separate point. The thumb starts things off by saying, "Man is a sinner." There is no one who is exempt from this status, since it is true that all have sinned (Rom. 3:23) and that there is no person who has not sinned (1 Kings 8:46). The psalmist says of his own sin nature, "Behold, I was brought forth in iniquity, and in sin my mother conceived me" (Psalm 51:5). This sin nature entered into human existence through the first man, Adam, and spread to all men (Rom. 5:12). And so, "'THERE IS NONE WHO DOES GOOD, THERE IS NOT EVEN ONE'" (Rom. 3:12).

After the thumb makes its point, the index finger does its own pointing. It says, "God hates sin and must punish it." There are consequences to sin. Its wage is death (Rom. 6:23). God hates sin (Prov. 6:16). Sin separates man from God (Isa. 59:2). Moreover, sin must be punished (Exod. 32:34). A holy God is not able to approve of or show favor to sin (Hab. 1:13). The soul who sins must die (Ezek. 18:4).

After the index finger does its harsh pointing, the middle finger begins to point out that there is hope. It reveals that God loves man and does not want to punish him. He does not want anyone to perish (2 Peter 3:9). God wants to show us how much He loves us (Rom. 5:8). He has a plan that will make His kindness toward us and His great love for us actually appear to us (Titus 3:4). His love for us will result in eternal comfort and hope that we would, otherwise, never have (2 Thess. 2:16).

After the middle finger hints that there may be hope for man, the ring finger explains how that hope is accomplished. It asserts, "Jesus suffered and died for man." Man cannot escape from his sin. So, Jesus took man's sin and put it on Himself (2 Cor. 5:21). Jesus gave Himself up for man (John 3:16). Instead of man having to suffer and die for his sins, Jesus took responsibility for those sins and suffered and died in his place (Heb. 2:9). We were deemed as those who carried sin, but Jesus redeems us as those who no longer carry that sin since He carries it for us (1 Peter 2:24). We were estranged from God, but now we are brought back to God (2 Cor. 5:18; 1 Peter 3:18). The death of Jesus in our place is permanent; it is final and complete (Heb. 9:26; John 19:30).

After the ring finger explains God's provision of hope, the pinky directs man toward his required response to this provision. It declares, "Man cannot earn salvation; he must receive it." There is no boasting by man, since his salvation is unmerited and received by faith and not by his own works (Eph. 2:8-9; Titus 3:5; Rom. 4:2-4; Rom. 11:6; Isa. 64:6). God's part is to provide for and offer salvation, while man's part is to ask for and receive salvation. Man asks for it by confessing his need and declaring that Jesus Christ is his Lord. Man receives it by believing and trusting in the reality and efficacy of what Christ did for him on the cross and in the resurrection (Rom. 10:9, 13). Man's response, then, is twofold: repent or turn from his sin and believe in Jesus for his salvation (Mark 1:15). Since we could not do it, God had to do it Himself. God is our only hope (Gal. 2:21).

The presenter of the Gospel can use the hand both to package the Gospel contents and to apply those contents to the life of the listener. For example, the thumb can be used to explain what it means that man is a sinner and to ask the listener to consider ways that he or she has sinned against God, made mistakes in life, and done wrong things to other people. With the middle finger, it could be explained that God's love for each of us is where the problem (first two fingers) and the solution (last two fingers) come together. God loves us and wants to be with us; thus, He has a problem because the price of our sin is that we are separated from Him. God loves us and wants to be with us; thus, He comes up with a solution in which He pays the price for us to be brought back to Him. Then when the ring finger is introduced, the listener can be challenged with the picture of Christ—not winking at his sin as though it did not matter, but rather taking the punishment Himself. He can be directly confronted with the picture of Jesus dying on the cross in his place and taking his actual sins upon Himself.

The actual physical nature of the hand presentation can be taken advantage of by moving the fingers around. This can be especially effective when witnessing to children. The movement of the thumb might be to drop it down to characterize the fallen nature of man. The index finger can point as if to declare someone's guilt. The middle finger can cover the index finger to display God's love for man even though he is a sinner. The ring finger's ring can illustrate the crown of thorns placed on Christ's head as He suffered and died for our sins. Finally, the pinky can connect with the thumb to form an "A-OK" sign demonstrating that all is well.

APRIL 27

THERE MUST BE A DIFFERENCE

"So do not be like them."

Matthew 6:8

The Sermon on the Mount as seen in Matthew 5-7 is a practical teaching on how the kingdom of God is not of this world. It is not a political kingdom, and it is not a religious kingdom; thus, the political and religious leaders in the Roman Empire were inclined to come against Jesus. The kingdom of God represents a "counter-culture." Everything about the Sermon on the Mount is in contrast to the ways of the world. Its truths are not consistent with secularism or traditionalism.

The standards of the kingdom of God demand a life that is completely different from the life of the world. This kingdom life is not simply a different *form* of the life of the world; it is entirely different *from* the world. The Sermon on the Mount, therefore, does not promote the rebellious and violent aspects of "counter-culture." Yet, it does promote the idea of contrast. To live in the kingdom of God is to be in contrast to the world. It is not simply to be different. It is to be opposite, even as light is opposite of dark and righteousness is opposite of sin.

In its message of "counter-culture" the Sermon on the Mount challenges its listeners to consider the realities of the Christian life. It challenges us to count the cost of being a Christian, and it eliminates the prospect for "nominal" or "uncommitted" Christianity, which is Christianity *by name only*. Compared to the perspective of the world, there is nothing "nominal" about Christianity. It is very radical; it is like the difference between night and day. God proclaims His disgust for "nominalism" when He says, "So because you are lukewarm, and neither hot nor cold, I will spit you out of My mouth" (Rev. 3:16). There is really no such thing as *in-between* Christianity. Christianity, by its very nature, is either all or nothing at all!

Half-hearted Christianity is useless. Christianity in appearance only is not Christianity; it is hypocrisy. When God sees outward religious practice without inward commitment and devotion, He shouts, "Oh that there were one among you who would shut the gates, that you might not uselessly kindle fire on My altar!" (Mal. 1:10).

The nature of the kingdom of God is such that to live in it now in this world will seem like you are living the life of an alien. Jesus said, "I am not of this world" (John 8:23) and "My kingdom is not of this world" (John 18:36). Paul said, "For our citizenship is in heaven" (Phil. 3:20). The kingdom walk is a totally different walk: "Brethren, join in following my example, and observe those who walk according to the pattern you have in us" (Phil. 3:17). The two kingdoms and the two walks do not get along. Jesus said, "I have given them Your word; and the world has hated them, because they are not of the world, even as I am not of the world" (John 17:14).

Midway through the Sermon on the Mount appears a phrase that could be the sermon's title: "So do not be like them" (Matt. 6:8). These words summarize the message of the sermon and its purpose. This has been the purpose of God throughout all of history. He has sought to gather a people unto Himself. God's people have always been called to be holy (separate). They have always been called to be completely different. God said to the Israelites, "I am the LORD your God. You shall not do what is done in the land of Egypt where you lived, nor are you to do what is done in the land of Canaan where I am bringing you; you shall not walk in their statutes. You are to perform My judgments and keep My statutes, to live in accord with them; I am the LORD your God" (Lev. 18:2-4).

Is the Sermon on the Mount practical? Some theologians have argued that the sermon contains a series of statements that describe how life will be in Heaven and is not applicable to us now. This conclusion is rooted in a misunderstanding of the nature of the kingdom of God. The kingdom is already and not yet; it is applicable in the present and in the future. By living out the Sermon on the Mount, we can enjoy slices of Heaven in the here and now. When the kingdom comes in its fullness, we will be able to perfectly live out the Sermon on the Mount and enjoy the entire "heavenly pie." There is a "pie in the sky," after all. Start eating now!

APRIL 28

I CAN'T, BUT GOD CAN

"The LORD looked at him and said, 'Go in this your strength and deliver Israel from the hand of Midian. Have I not sent you?' He said to Him, 'O LORD, how shall I deliver Israel? Behold, my family is the least in Manasseh, and I am the youngest in my father's house.' But the LORD said to him, 'Surely I will be with you, and you shall defeat Midian as one man.'"

Judges 6:14-16

Even the humblest man "who was on the face of the earth" (Num. 12:3) struggled with pride. Moses' lack of humility resulted in his attempt to deliver Israel from the oppression of the Egyptians by murdering a Midianite who supervised the Hebrew slaves (Exod. 2:11-14). He got ahead of God and took matters into his own hands. His pride refused to trust in God's timing and sovereignty.

Saul also rejected God's timing when he refused to wait for Samuel (1 Sam. 13:8-14). His prideful action resulted in the loss of his kingdom. "Pride *goes* before destruction, and a haughty spirit before stumbling" (Prov. 16:18). Abraham's lack of humility resulted in an "Ishmael" (man's imperfect conception instead of God's perfect creation). Instead of trusting God, Abraham trusted in his own plan to produce an heir (Gen. 16:1-4, 15).

God ironically used Moses' lack of humility to force him into a situation that would teach him humility. After the murder, Moses, the great man of Egypt, fled into the wilderness and became a humble shepherd for the next forty years. "Whoever exalts himself shall be humbled; and whoever humbles himself shall be exalted" (Matt. 23:12). Humility is often produced by being hidden—or being led into the wilderness—for as ambition dies, humility grows.

After forty years in the wilderness, Moses comes out a different man. In his own eyes, he was no longer the special adopted son of the court of Pharaoh, who was able to deliver Israel from their enemies. He became the one who said, "Who am I?" when God commissioned him to deliver the Israelites (Exod. 3:10-11). Moses realized his own inadequacy. He understood and felt his helplessness that was created by the gap that existed between his personal ability and the mission that he was given. He humbly confessed that only God could fill that gap. God's calling upon one's life should produce humility, not pride. It should reveal the gap, as it did for Jeremiah (Jer. 1:6), Saul (1 Sam. 9:21), and Gideon (Judg. 6:15).

The humility of Moses still needed to mature. It is not enough for humility to say, "I cannot do it." Humility must complete that thought with the declaration, "God can do it." Moses was not yet humble enough to look away from his own weakness and inadequacy and look to God's strength and adequacy. Thus, "the anger of the LORD burned against [him]" (Exod. 4:14). Eventually, Moses' humility did mature. He learned to look to God's adequacy. Then, instead of God looking at Moses in anger, God looked at him with favor (Exod. 33:12-17).

Moses' humility was not immature because he recognized his own inadequacy. He did not recognize God's adequacy. Mature humility recognizes both parts, while false humility only recognizes one. Humility has more to do with how you think of God than how you think of yourself. Your "I can't" is necessary but only to the degree that it leads you to the "God can."

APRIL 29

JUSTICE

"He will have compassion on the poor and needy, and the lives of the needy he will save."
Psalm 72:13

A reference to the poor in the Bible is often coupled with the idea of justice. Although poverty can be associated with judgment (Prov. 6:10-11; Prov. 24:30-34), in the Old Testament the poor are most often referred to as being the victims of the sins of others. God's heart is to rectify this. And so, justice more than judgment is associated with the poor. "For he will deliver the needy when he cries for help, the afflicted also, and him who has no helper. He will have compassion on the poor and needy, and the lives of the needy he will save. He will rescue their life from oppression and violence" (Psalm 72:12-14).

The Hebrew word *sedaka* ("justice") refers to the positive actions of God to care for, preserve, and restore those who have been oppressed. The people of God were commanded to champion justice because He is a God of justice. "May he vindicate the afflicted of the people, save the children of the needy and crush the oppressor" (Psalm 72:4). This connection was understood to be so important that God equated it with knowing Him. "He pled the cause of the afflicted and needy; then it was well. Is not that what it means to know Me?' declares the LORD" (Jer. 22:16).

Jesus said that His own ministry was valid because He preached the Gospel to the poor (Luke 4:18-21). Jesus was with the needy (Luke 5:1-11). He ate with them (Luke 5:27-32). He comforted them

(Luke 12:22-34). He fed them (Luke 9:10-17). He healed them (Luke 5:12-16). He ministered to them (Luke 7:18-23). He taught His disciples to care for them (Luke 9:13).

Jesus' disciples put an emphasis on giving to the needy (Acts 4:32-35). Paul (Gal. 2:10), Tabitha (Acts 9:36-39), Barnabas (Acts 4:36-37), and Titus (2 Cor. 8:3-6) all exhibited a heart for the poor. This type of ministry is what is described in the New Testament as "pure and undefiled religion in the sight of our God and Father . . . to visit orphans and widows in their distress, *and* to keep oneself unstained by the world" (James 1:27).

The establishment of deacons as part of church government was the result of the understanding that the church had a responsibility to minister to the needy.

> Now at this time while the disciples were increasing *in number,* a complaint arose on the part of the Hellenistic *Jews* against the *native* Hebrews, because their widows were being overlooked in the daily serving of food. So the twelve summoned the congregation of the disciples and said, "It is not desirable for us to neglect the word of God in order to serve tables. Therefore, brethren, select from among you seven men of good reputation, full of the Spirit and of wisdom, whom we may put in charge of this task" (Acts 6:1-3).

The idea of justice being afforded to those in need was said to be the manifestation of true repentance.

> Therefore bear fruits in keeping with repentance, and do not begin to say to yourselves, "We have Abraham for our father," for I say to you that from these stones God is able to raise up children to Abraham. Indeed the axe is already laid at the root of the trees; so every tree that does not bear good fruit is cut down and thrown into the fire. And the crowds were questioning him, saying, "Then what shall we do?" And he would answer and say to them, "The man who has two tunics is to share with him who has none; and he who has food is to do likewise." And *some* tax collectors also came to be baptized, and they said to him, "Teacher, what shall we do?" And he said to them, "Collect no more than what you have been ordered to." *Some* soldiers were questioning him, saying, "And *what about* us, what shall we do?" And he said to them, "Do not take money from anyone by force, or accuse *anyone* falsely, and be content with your wages" (Luke 3:8-14).

"The crowds" (individuals) are to act justly by giving to those who are in need as they are able. It is the tax collectors (business) who are not to cheat but to be just. It is the soldiers (government) who are to act justly in the way they use their power. God is the God of justice, and His heart is toward the needy who have been oppressed.

APRIL 30

THE CURE FOR USELESS MEETINGS

"For which one of you, when he wants to build a tower, does not first sit down and calculate the cost to see if he has enough to complete it? Otherwise, when he has laid a foundation and is not able to finish, all who observe it begin to ridicule him, saying, 'This man began to build and was not able to finish.'"

Luke 14:28-30

Leaders, by definition, take initiative. A leader who does not initiate is like a driver who does not drive or a baseball player who does not swing the bat. Hitters swing. Drivers drive. Leaders lead.

They initiate. Leaders are, therefore, visionaries. They look ahead and point to destinations. In order to arrive at those destinations along with others, skilled "pointers" must be planners and organizers. They must be able to keep themselves organized and prompt others to be organized as well. This necessitates embracing the stereotypically dreaded meetings.

It is not uncommon to hear employees in the lunchroom complaining about meetings. "If I have to go to one more meeting this week, I think I am going to take a sick day!" Meetings are often perceived as being useless, if not evil. Participants in the meeting will either act like they are listening while they are, in fact, daydreaming; or they will try to escape, having come up with some bizarre excuse that everybody else knows is a desperate attempt to remove themselves from the misery. It does not have to be this way, though. Meetings can be very useful tools for the leader to organize those he is leading. And those who are being led can learn not only to accept meetings but also to look forward to them.

What is the secret? Leaders must organize meetings based on specifics (who, what, why, where, when, and how), not generalities (whoever, whatever, "whyever," wherever, whenever, and however). Starting with "why?" is very important. Without a specific and legitimate "why?," all involved will tend to check out since they will feel like there is no need for the meeting. Leaders should be able to clearly answer the question, "Why are we having this meeting?" Only when the "why?" question can be answered can the critical "what?" question be put forth. "What are we going to do and accomplish in this meeting?" If there is no answer to the "why?" question, then there is no clarity with respect to what to do. If you have no target to hit, you will miss every time.

Just as "why?" leads to "what?," so, too, does "what?" lead to "who?" There is nothing worse than being stuck in a meeting in which it is clear that there is absolutely no reason for you to be there. The goal of the meeting—*what* will be accomplished—will dictate *who* will be at the meeting. Who will do what by *when/where* is the sought after "what?" of the meeting that is rooted in the original "why?" that has birthed the meeting.

The only element that remains is the component of the meeting that is most critical; that is, the "how?" of the meeting. How will "who will do what by when/where" get accomplished? Sometimes, leaders miss the boat here. A very important aspect of leadership is release. Leaders must let go to let grow. Holding on too tightly is the self-destruction of many a leader. Control freaks are not good leaders. How will what we have organized in our meeting get done? Certainly, there can be some discussion during the meeting regarding methods and means. However, it should be done in such a way that what is clearly being screamed out by the leader is "You must take the ball and run with it. I authorize you to do this, and I trust you to do it."

Good meetings are essential to the health of an organization. "Why?" then "what?" then "who?" then "when/where?" all lead to "how?"—the crux of the meeting—which is going to lead to fruit. Fruitless meetings are what give them a bad name. Meetings that bear fruit are embraced. Fruit necessitates release. Leaders must multiply themselves for their organizations to grow. This requires giving away or letting go. In this sense, the most critical principle of leadership is found in 2 Timothy 2:1-2: "You therefore, my son, be strong in the grace that is in Christ Jesus. The things which you have heard from me in the presence of many witnesses, entrust these to faithful men who will be able to teach others also."

NOTES

May

MAY 1

LORD, I'M JUST DYING TO BE SAVED!

"For whoever wishes to save his life will lose it, but whoever loses his life for My sake, he is the one who will save it."

Luke 9:24

Someone hears the Gospel message for the first time. What do they do? How do they respond? They may simply not understand it and, therefore, just walk away. Alternatively, they may actually seem to grasp the message but only in a superficial way, and thus, just let go of it quickly. Another person might positively respond to the message only to have it overtaken by other seemingly more pressing issues in his or her life. Finally, there is one who hears the Gospel message, understands it, responds to it, and, hence, bears fruit. This is the person who is convicted and convinced, who repents and believes, and who responds with the response of life.

In so many ways, the Gospel is a paradox, a seeming contradiction. God becomes a man, which seems like a contradiction (Isa. 9:6). He who had no sin becomes sin seems like a contradiction (2 Cor. 5:21). He who is blind will see, but he who sees is blind seems like a contradiction (John 9:41). He who is last will be first seems like a contradiction (Matt. 19:30). The response of life is the response of death seems like a contradiction (Luke 9:23-24). To live, you must die!

The response to the Gospel message is to accept Jesus as Savior and Jesus as Lord (Rom. 10:9-10). Both of these responses involve dying to self, putting away and "dying" to your own desires, and submitting totally to Christ. In this sense, getting saved requires that you go to your own "funeral." This funeral results in the start of a new life—that is, the life of Christ, since "I have been crucified with Christ; and it is no longer I who live, but Christ lives in me" (Gal. 2:20). The initial funeral (your salvation) then results in an ongoing funeral (your sanctification) as you "work out your salvation" (Phil. 2:12). As you die to yourself, you make way for Jesus to become your Lord and Savior; and as you make Him Lord and Savior, you make way for further death to self. And so, one funeral leads to another funeral, which leads to another, which leads to another. A believer's life becomes one daily, ongoing funeral—one ongoing death to self. "And He was saying to *them* all, 'If anyone wishes to come after Me, he must deny himself, and take up his cross daily and follow Me. For whoever wishes to save his life will lose it, but whoever loses his life for My sake, he is the one who will save it'" (Luke 9:23-24). Now that is quite the paradox!

The Gospel is a gift. A gift must be received. To receive is to accept. First, we must accept Jesus as our Savior: "And there is salvation in no one else; for there is no other name under heaven that has been given among men by which we must be saved" (Acts 4:12). We must accept that the death and resurrection of Jesus is the *only* way to obtain eternal life. There is no forgiveness of sin, except through the blood of Jesus. There is no other religion, philosophy, or spiritual medium by which to gain eternal life. Most difficult, perhaps, is to give in to the stumbling block of the cross (1 Peter 2:4-8; Gal. 5:11)—that Jesus has done all of the work that is required for our salvation and that it is completely a gift of grace, not earned by us in any way (Eph. 2:8-9).

To receive is to accept. In addition to accepting Jesus as our Savior, you must accept Jesus as your Lord: "that if you confess with your mouth Jesus *as* Lord . . . you will be saved" (Rom. 10:9). You must accept that Jesus is the Master and Ruler of your life. You look to receive direction from Him. This especially includes the acceptance of the Bible as your guide for living. It also includes acceptance of the Church as your community of fellowship. Of course, it includes the acceptance of His purpose for your life and whatever mission He might call you to.

Death to self both launches and continues the reality of Jesus as Savior and Lord in your life (Matt. 16:24-25). Jesus as your Savior brings death to self. You must die to the desire to trust in yourself for salvation. You must die to your fallen inclination to be independent of God. Similarly, Jesus as your Lord brings death to self. You must die to the desire to control your own life. You must lay down what you feel are your rights. You must die to your fallen inclination to be your own definer and your own boss.

It must be stressed that Christianity is not only about death. It is equally about life. Even as the core of the Gospel message is about the cross and the resurrection, so, too, the core of the Christian life is about dying and living. Jesus did not simply die in order to die. He died in order to be resurrected. Christians do not simply die to themselves in order to die to themselves (that is something more akin to Buddhism). They die to themselves in order to live for Christ: "I have been crucified with Christ; and it is no longer I who live, but Christ lives in me" (Gal. 2:20). Death is for life; your death to self for His life in you!

The soteriological paradox is that the result of death is life: "Truly, truly, I say to you, unless a grain of wheat falls into the earth and dies, it remains alone; but if it dies, it bears much fruit. He who loves his life loses it, and he who hates his life in this world will keep it to life eternal" (John 12:24-25). The longer we live with Christ, the more areas of self that we still hold on to that will be exposed. Death to self, for a Christian, is an ongoing process (Phil. 3:12). So, be one who "bears much fruit." Be one who "falls into the earth and dies." Raise the white flag of surrender. Give up. Make your constant prayer, "Lord, take my life!"

MAY 2

LETTING GO IS THE HARDEST THING

"And now I commend you to God."

Acts 20:32

What is your "philosophy of ministry?" Missionaries should have a philosophy of ministry in which they go, give, and leave. *Go* is obvious. In order to "make disciples of all the nations" you must first go to them (Matt. 28:18-19). Abraham had to go (Gen. 12:1) so that "all the families of the earth will be blessed" (Gen. 12:3).

Of course, going is not the end goal. *Go* is obvious, and *give* is obligatory. "And as you go, preach, saying, 'The kingdom of heaven is at hand.' Heal *the* sick, raise *the* dead, cleanse *the* lepers, cast out demons. Freely you received, freely give" (Matt. 10:7-8). The greatest missions story is that God loved the world, so He *gave* (John 3:16).

Go is obvious, and *give* is obligatory. Perhaps not so obvious is that leaving is essential. Jesus left so that the Holy Spirit would come and complete the work (John 16:7). Paul left for the same reason. He knew that the natural process was for the Holy Spirit to mature the church. *"For I am* confident of this very thing, that He who began a good work in you will perfect it until the day of Christ Jesus" (Phil. 1:6). Leaving is a necessary ingredient in the recipe for reproduction. That understanding allows Paul to say, "The things which you have heard from me in the presence of many witnesses, entrust these to faithful men who will be able to teach others also" (2 Tim. 2:2). There is risk involved in leaving. It requires faith. "When they had appointed elders for them in every church, having prayed with fasting, they commended them to the Lord in whom they had believed" (Acts 14:23). To let go is to let grow. Leaving is an essential component in a biblical philosophy of missions.

Leaving is the most difficult part of the philosophy of missions and the most violated part. Sometimes, missionaries refuse to leave. They struggle to let go. It may happen because they are trying to build their own kingdoms. They may have a low opinion of the abilities of the nationals; they may feel that they cannot do the work correctly or that the nationals cannot do the work as good as the missionaries can do it. Another reason may be that missionaries do not have enough faith to let go and entrust the work to God or to trust that God is big enough to provide them with another mission. They may simply not want to lose their job.

The *leave* part of missions is often the most difficult part because missionaries must give away what they have worked so hard to start. They must understand that they *go* in order to *give*, and they *give* in order to *give away*. The *leave* part of missions is the most important part because it is that which allows churches to grow naturally. An indigenous-led church is a more naturally organized church.

Paul was able to implement the go, give, and leave philosophy of missions because he trusted the Holy Spirit to finish what He started. He placed his trust in God and was therefore able to say to the church at Ephesus, "Therefore be on the alert, remembering that night and day for a period of three years I did not cease to admonish each one with tears. And now I commend you to God and to the word of His grace, which is able to build *you* up and to give *you* the inheritance among all those who are sanctified" (Acts 20:31-32).

Go is obvious. *Give* is obligatory. *Leave* is essential. Missionaries who put this philosophy into practice will bear the most fruit!

MAY 3

STUDENTS OF CULTURE ARE FRIENDS OF CULTURE

*"And He made from one **man** every nation of mankind to live on all the face of the earth, having determined their appointed times and the boundaries of their habitation, that they would seek God, if perhaps they might grope for Him and find Him, though He is not far from each one of us; for in Him we live and move and exist, as even some of your own poets have said, 'For we also are His children.' Being then the children of God, we ought not to think that the Divine Nature is like gold or silver or stone, an image formed by the art and thought of man."*

Acts 17:26-29

Cross-cultural preachers and teachers of the Bible have a difficult job. They must communicate within the context of three different cultures: the biblical culture, their own culture, and the culture of their listeners. The missionary must take a message out of one culture and proclaim it to another culture without allowing his own culture to distort the message. This requires that the missionary be a "culture expert."

Missionaries must understand different worldviews in order to contextualize the Gospel. Worldview is the way people perceive reality. Contextualization is the process of communicating a message in a way that is consistent with the hearer's culture and, therefore, able to be understood and received by a particular culture. Contextualization does not change the message; it delivers the message in a way that can be understood.

Jesus adapted His message to funnel it through containers that facilitated cultural understanding. In the case of the rich young ruler, Jesus communicated on a level that he could certainly understand. He said to him, "'Sell all that you possess and distribute it to the poor, and you shall have treasure in heaven; and come, follow Me'" (Luke 18:22). In the case of the Samaritan woman at the well, Jesus explained, "'Everyone who drinks of this water will thirst again; but whoever drinks of the water that I will give him shall never thirst; but the water that I will give him will become in him a well of water springing up to eternal life'" (John 4:13-14).

Peter and Paul understood how to contextualize the Gospel message using the worldviews of their listeners. Peter preached two very different sermons—one to Jews in which he used the Psalms and the Prophets as a launching pad to present the Gospel (Acts 2:14-36) and one to Gentiles in which he emphasized the acts of Christ as a proof of His legitimacy (Acts 10:34-43). Paul also presented the Gospel message in two very different ways—one to Jews in which he focused on the history of Israel (Acts 13:16-41) and one to Greeks in which he spoke in more philosophical terms (Acts 17:22-31).

The basic content of the Gospel does not change; that is a constant (1 Cor. 2:2). The variable is the way in which it is presented; that will depend on the particular needs and worldview of the listeners. In one culture, it may be more effective to first focus on the idea of becoming a "new creation," while in another culture, it may be more appropriate to focus on the love and mercy of God.

Cross-cultural communicators must become relational and ideological "bridge-builders." Missionaries must adapt their message to their listeners. Once a missionary builds a relational bridge with the people, he will earn legitimacy and gain valuable knowledge regarding the culture. Then he will be ready to build ideological bridges. He will be able to use lifestyle examples, culturally sensitive metaphors, and iconic stories that will serve as conduits through which the Gospel message can travel.

A missionary who is a student of culture is more likely to be able to address the "felt needs" of those he is trying to reach. He will be more able to apply the message to the particular lives of his listeners. The missionary must try to speak to the heart of the person, to present the Gospel in a way that is relevant to the ears of his listeners. The cross-cultural communicator must not be afraid of culture. Culture must become his friend!

MAY 4

SAY WHAT YOU MEAN AND MEAN WHAT YOU SAY

"But let your statement be, 'Yes, yes' or 'No, no'; anything beyond these is of evil."
Matthew 5:37

Nehemiah was a great leader. He led a multitude of people in the massive project to rebuild the walls of Jerusalem in fifty-two days (Neh. 6:15). This kind of endeavor requires skillful leadership. The leader must embody certain character traits.

A leader must be able to exercise discretion when necessary. Proper judgment, especially when it comes to being discreet and not revealing information until the proper time, is often critical in leadership. When necessary, leaders should know how to keep a secret. Nehemiah exhibited great discretion:

> So I came to Jerusalem and was there three days. And I arose in the night, I and a few men with me. I did not tell anyone what my God was putting into my mind to do for Jerusalem . . . So I went out at night by the Valley Gate . . . Then I entered the Valley Gate again and

returned. The officials did not know where I had gone or what I had done; nor had I as yet told the Jews, the priests, the nobles, the officials or the rest who did the work (Neh. 2:11-16).

Integrity is one of those leadership traits that can be defined by short pithy statements. Say what you mean, and mean what you say. The seriousness of having integrity is soberly expressed by Jesus: "But let your statement be, 'Yes, yes' *or* 'No, no'; anything beyond these is of evil" (Matt. 5:37). Nehemiah was an integral leader, who also demanded integrity from those he was leading:

> So I called the priests and took an oath from them that they would do according to this promise. I also shook out the front of my garment and said, "Thus may God shake out every man from his house and from his possessions who does not fulfill this promise; even thus may he be shaken out and emptied. And all the assembly said, "Amen!" And they praised the Lord. Then the people did according to this promise (Neh. 5:12-13).

Leaders must be responsible people. A leader cannot afford to just "wing it." He has to be prepared. Before answering the king's question, Nehemiah prayed and prepared himself to respond (Neh. 2:4-5). Before approaching the Jews with a proposal to rebuild the walls of Jerusalem, Nehemiah went out and surveyed the situation so he could deliver a well-prepared presentation (Neh. 2:11-17).

A leader must be courageous. Nehemiah responded with courage when he was threatened: "He said, 'Let us meet together in the house of God, within the temple, and let us close the doors of the temple, for they are coming to kill you, and they are coming to kill you at night.' But I said, 'Should a man like me flee? And could one such as I go into the temple to save his life? I will not go in'" (Neh. 6:10-11).

Leaders need to be tactful in how they deal with people. Nehemiah exhibited this leadership trait (Neh. 2:5-8). At the same time, leaders need to be willing and able to confront people when necessary. Nehemiah exhibited righteous anger in a proper way.

> Then I was very angry when I had heard their outcry and these words. I consulted with myself and contended with the nobles and the rulers and said to them, "You are exacting usury, each from his brother!" Therefore, I held a great assembly against them. I said to them, "We according to our ability have redeemed our Jewish brothers who were sold to the nations; now would you even sell your brothers that they may be sold to us?" Then they were silent and could not find a word to say (Neh. 5:6-8).

What does a godly leader look like? He or she resembles someone who exhibits discretion, integrity, responsibility, courage, tactfulness, and righteous anger. More than any one thing—or even any one hundred things—a godly leader looks like Jesus.

MAY 5

WHO ARE THE POOR?

"And who is my neighbor?"

Luke 10:29

The Church is called to help the poor because the Church is most able to help the poor. The Church is the proclaimer of the Gospel, and it is the Gospel that meets people's needs. People need the Gospel and are helped by it. It provides hope to the hopeless, purpose to those who may not have a purpose, and a changed life to those who desperately need change.

There is a biblical mandate to help the poor. There are more than four hundred passages that include more than one thousand verses that mention the poor. In many of these cases, the emphasis is on the commandment of God to His people to unconditionally help the needy. "But whoever has the world's goods, and sees his brother in need and closes his heart against him, how does the love of God abide in him?" (1 John 3:17). The only condition is that the person is "in need."

What is the biblical definition of being "in need?" In the Old Testament, there are many different words that signify the "poor." There are the indigent—people who do not have the basic physical necessities of life. For the most part, the Old Testament pictures these people as being victims of the actions of others. There are the oppressed. These are people who have been victims of the injustice of society.

There are also the humble. These are the spiritually poor people who have complete confidence in God. Words that describe those "in need" include humble, weak, oppressed, powerless, helpless, hungry, thirsty, stranger, naked, sick, and prisoner. The common thread is found in the principle that God responds to real needs; if a need exists, then God will fill it. "So God heard their groaning . . . and God took notice of *them*" (Exod. 2:24-25). God does not turn away from the needy. The Psalmist declares, "A broken and a contrite heart, O God, You will not despise" (Psalm 51:17).

In the parable of the Good Samaritan, Jesus makes it clear that to be a neighbor is to help those in need. Your neighbor is anyone who is in need (Luke 10:29-37). Spiritually, the needy are the humble. They are those who understand, admit, and recognize their need. "And hearing *this*, Jesus said to them, '*It is* not those who are healthy who need a physician, but those who are sick; I did not come to call the righteous, but sinners'" (Mark 2:17). To be needy, you must see your need, say you are in need, and ask for help. "Ask and it will be given to you; seek, and you will find; knock, and it will be opened to you" (Matt. 7:7). Sometimes, people who have needs are not defined as needy because they do not recognize their needs. The Pharisees had the need to be saved from their sins like any other person. However, Jesus was not willing to give them much of His time because they were not willing to recognize and admit their needs.

And Jesus said, "For judgment I came into this world, so that those who do not see may see, and that those who see may become blind." Those of the Pharisees who were with Him heard these things and said to Him, "We are not blind too, are we?" Jesus said to them, "If you were blind, you would have no sin; but since you say, 'We see,' your sin remains" (John 9:39-41).

An alcoholic has obvious needs, but he is not truly needy until he is willing to recognize and admit that he is an alcoholic. The famous twelve-step program of Alcoholics Anonymous has as its first step the requirement to admit that you need help. The responsibility to help the alcoholic begins when he is able to say, "I am an alcoholic. I need help." Before this point, he is not able to be helped. The conditions for helping are not in the hands of the helper but in the hands of the one who needs help.

Ministry to the poor is a biblical mandate. There is no question about that. The question is, "Who are the poor that we are to help? Who is defined as 'in need?' Who is your neighbor?" Once that is understood, then you must "LOVE YOUR NEIGHBOR AS YOURSELF" (Matt. 22:39).

MAY 6

TRAITS OF GOOD COUNSELORS

"But the path of the righteous is like the light of dawn that shines brighter and brighter until the full day."

Proverbs 4:18

It might be said that wisdom is the single most important thing to be able to offer someone who needs counsel. So, it is no wonder that it is the book of Proverbs, the book of wisdom, that serves as the counselor's handbook. People who are able to help others are enabled to do so by certain "wisdom traits."

Those who walk a path of righteousness themselves, for example, are able to shine light on the problems that lurk in the lives of others (Prov. 4:18). It might be said, "If you want to be a good counselor, then be a good person." Good counselors are able to encourage people *and* be honest with them, not placate them. They can speak truth in love. "Oil and perfume make the heart glad, so a man's counsel is sweet to his friend" (Prov. 27:9). On the other hand, "He who says to the wicked, 'You are righteous,' peoples will curse him, nations will abhor him; but to those who rebuke the *wicked* will be delight, and a good blessing will come upon them. He kisses the lips who gives a right answer" (Prov. 24:24-26).

An effective counselor manages information well. For example, he knows how to keep a "secret." Counselors who ignore the importance of confidentiality tend to be counselors no longer. "He who goes about as a talebearer reveals secrets, but he who is trustworthy conceals a matter" (Prov. 11:13). By its very nature, the art of helping people must include engaging in the art of listening. "He who gives an answer before he hears, it is folly and shame to him . . . The mind of the prudent acquires knowledge, and the ear of the wise seeks knowledge" (Prov. 18:13, 15).

When offering advice, timing and tact with words are a counselor's friend. It has been said that 90 percent of stand-up comedy is timing. Maybe, 90 percent of counseling is timing as well. And so, "without consultation, plans are frustrated, but with many counselors they succeed. A man has joy in an apt answer, and how delightful is a timely word . . . The heart of the righteous ponders how to answer" (Prov. 15:22-23, 28).

Wisdom includes the use of objectivity and discernment, two traits that are critical to helping people. As it is said, "The first to plead his case *seems* right, *until* another comes and examines him" (Prov. 18:17). Similarly, it is a person of understanding who counsels effectively. Experiential wisdom is invaluable to the one who desires to help others. "A plan in the heart of a man is *like* deep water, but a man of understanding draws it out" (Prov. 20:5).

MAY 7

THE HOLY SPIRIT'S SHAKING OF HIS HANDS

"Therefore having been exalted to the right hand of God, and having received from the Father the promise of the Holy Spirit, He has poured forth this which you both see and hear."

Acts 2:33

Paul tells us that "to each one is given the manifestation of the Spirit for the common good" (1 Cor. 12:7). He Who cannot be seen becomes easy to perceive, readily viewable, clearly revealed, and plainly apparent. The word manifestation, phanerosis in Greek, refers to an "exhibition" or an "expression." The term, as it is derived from the Latin, is made up of two parts—*man* (hand) and *festus* (grab or shake). Thus, it can mean the "shaking of the hands." If we add the Spanish form of *festus (fiesta)*—party or celebration—we could define it as "a party or celebration of the hands." The Holy Spirit hovers over you and is shaking His hands; He is having a party or celebration with His hands. Now, that is a gift!

The Holy Spirit's activities are viewable. The term *manifestation* signifies a revelation of the Holy Spirit through a dynamic demonstration. This visible and audible demonstration flows through Christians. "Therefore having been exalted to the right hand of God, and having received from the Father the promise of the Holy Spirit, He has poured forth this which you both see and hear" (Acts 2:33). Certainly, among the nine gifts listed in 1 Corinthians 12:8-10, there are gifts that would be heard: "word of wisdom," "word of knowledge," "prophecy," "distinguishing of spirits," "*various* kinds of tongues," "interpretation of tongues." So, too, there are gifts that would be seen: "faith," "healing," "miracles."

The manifestation of the Spirit is not to say that the Spirit actually becomes incarnate or tangible. God in the flesh is reserved for Jesus alone. Nonetheless, Jesus sends the Spirit so that He might empower the body of Christ for service. One of the ways this is done is by the Spirit being manifested through followers of Christ. The demonstration of the power of the Holy Spirit is enacted through believers. When a light comes on, we do not see the source of power. We only see the demonstration of the power. The light is evidence of the existence and presence of the power source. In the same way, the gifts of the Holy Spirit are evidence of the presence of the Spirit.

It should be understood that the gifts of the Spirit are completely different than the fruit of the Spirit found in Galatians 5:22-23. The fruit of the Spirit is developed as a result of maturing in Christ. The growth of fruit implies that there is a process. The gifts of the Spirit are immediate expressions or demonstrations of the Spirit that are routed through human vessels who are open to His presence and power. They are occasional and situational activities that are not internal, but rather, are distributed "to each one individually just as He wills" (1 Cor. 12:11). The fruit of the Spirit is an outworking of that which is internal that stems from processes that are experienced over time.

It is true that very young Christians can be used in the gifts; this was true in the Corinthian church. Because of the immediate nature of the gifts, the Spirit only needs a willing vessel; whereas with the fruit of the Spirit, He needs a willing vessel and time, since it involves a process of maturation. At the same time, it should be understood that there is a certain learning process involved in being used in the gifts. The more a person is used, the more comfortable and effective he or she is in operating in the gifts of the Holy Spirit. In this context, it is interesting to note that Paul uses three separate Greek words to distinguish between three groups of people. He refers to those who believe, those who are unbelievers, and those who are "ungifted" or the *idiotes* (1 Cor. 14:16, 22-24). This Greek term means "unlearned" and seems to refer to those Christians who are not "aware" of the spiritual gifts (1 Cor. 12:1).

To a certain degree, there is an awareness and learning process that is associated with being used in the gifts of the Holy Spirit. Perhaps, it begins with a desire (1 Cor. 14:1; 12:31; 14:39) that can lead to a prayer (1 Cor. 14:13).

"God, I know that you distribute the gifts of the Holy Spirit to each one individually according to your will. I pray that you would use me in the gifts for your glory. Oh God, please shake your hands over me."

MAY 8

A DISCIPLE IS DISCIPLINED

"They were continually devoting themselves to the apostles' teaching and to fellowship, to the breaking of bread and to prayer."

Acts 2:42

A Christian is a disciplined disciple of Jesus Christ. The root of the word "discipline" is *disciple*. A disciple is a person who is motivated by a love for Christ to discipline himself or herself to follow and imitate Christ via the use of spiritual disciplines. There are a variety of spiritual disciplines that should be practiced by a Christian, including the study of the Word of God, prayer, thanksgiving and praise, and fellowship (Acts 2:42).

John Wesley, the founder of the Methodist movement, was a man of discipline. He was very methodical—from which came the name "Methodists"—in his walk with God. This is not to say that he was a legalist or a ritualist. His Christian life was not something he forced on himself. He did not engage in mere ritual for the approval of men; he engaged in relationship for the pleasure of God.

> When you pray, you are not to be like the hypocrites; for they love to stand and pray in the synagogues and on the street corners so that they may be seen by men. Truly I say to you, they have their reward in full. But you, when you pray, go into your inner room, close your door and pray to your Father who is in secret, and your Father who sees *what is done* in secret will reward you. And when you are praying, do not use meaningless repetition as the Gentiles do, for they suppose that they will be heard for their many words (Matt. 6:5-7).

Ritualists view discipline as an end in itself. They view spiritual disciplines as required tasks that are done for appearance's sake. Disciples view discipline as a means to an end and are motivated by their desire to grow in their relationship with God. The discipline is not simply a requirement, but it is an opportunity. It is not a surface/superficial practice but a profound/substantive experience.

John Wesley was a sincerely devout Christian. His Christian life and the disciplines that went with it were something that he did freely and joyfully. It was, more than anything else, a way to focus and organize the overflowing energy, commitment, and desire that he had for Christ. He organized a small group called the "Holy Club" that included fellow Christians of like mind. They practiced spiritual disciplines together. They fasted two times each week; had a time of praise, prayer, and Bible study together from 5:00 a.m. until 9:00 a.m. every morning; prayed for the poor from 6:00 p.m. until 7:00 p.m. every evening; and read devotional and theological books from 7:00 p.m. until 9:00 p.m. five nights each week.

The members of the Holy Club were very disciplined. However, they were not disciplined simply to be disciplined. Their discipline was motivated by their love for God and their burning desire to know Him. The structured discipline of early Methodism might be seen by some as bordering on legalism. However, the Methodist movement was not based on the disciplined ability of man, but on the inspiration of the Holy Spirit and a desire to fellowship closely with God. Discipline was practiced because of a desire for holiness. It was not an end. It was only a means to an end, which was to know God more fully. The focus of the discipline was not on forcing people to do something. It was on inviting people into a more consistent and fruitful relationship with Christ.

Discipline is not a cause of salvation; it is a result of it. It is a response to God that says, "I want to give you my whole life because you gave me your whole life." Discipline is a tool that can and should be used to "work out your salvation" (Phil. 2:12). Discipline is associated more with sanctification than it is with salvation. As we submit to the work of the Spirit to sanctify us, we will become more and more disciplined in all areas of our lives.

The focus of discipline in Christian character should be on holiness and relationship with God. A Christian must be disciplined to be able to control his flesh (1 Cor. 6:12-20). This discipline must be more than a "bodily discipline." It must be done in the context of godliness (1 Tim. 4:7-8). More than anything else, Christian character that includes discipline should be pointed toward spending time with God. We should discipline our minds to constantly be in the presence of God (1 Thess. 5:16-17). "Set your mind on the things above, not on the things that are on earth" (Col. 3:2).

A disciple of Jesus is one who *follows* Jesus. A disciple is disciplined to follow Jesus!

MAY 9

SO I PRAYED TO THE GOD OF HEAVEN

"Then the king said to me, 'What would you request?' So I prayed to the God of heaven."
Nehemiah 2:4

Leadership is essential to accomplish a mission. God's mission is to make Himself known to all people. In order to engage in this mission, God chooses a people through whom He can reveal Himself. His people, therefore, become leaders. They would be "the head and not the tail" (Deut. 28:13). They would be "a kingdom of priests" (Exod. 19:6), a nation that would be a mediator between God and other nations, leading them to be reconnected to God. When God's people failed to engage in God's mission—in effect, resulting in a worldwide catastrophe in which the leaders of the world became "blind guides of the blind" with the result that "if a blind man guides a blind man, both will fall into a pit" (Matt. 15:14)—He removed the leadership mantle from them and gave it "to a people, producing the fruit of it" (Matt. 21:43).

The church became the new world leaders, the new mediators, connectors, and proclaimers. "But you are A CHOSEN RACE, A royal PRIESTHOOD, A HOLY NATION, A PEOPLE FOR *God's* OWN POSSESSION, so that you may proclaim the excellencies of Him who has called you out of darkness into His marvelous light" (1 Peter 2:9). And so the church, like Israel, is called to "go" and bless all nations by leading them to God (Gen. 12:1-3; Matt. 28:18-19). God's people are called to be "the salt of the earth" (Matt. 5:13) and "the light of the world" (Matt. 5:14). The light goes "out in front of" and leads.

The book of Nehemiah is very much a book about leadership. Nehemiah was a great leader. He exhibited exceptional leadership skills. The setting of the book of Nehemiah revolves around the rebuilding of a nation. In 587 BC, the Babylonians sent Judah into exile. After Babylon fell to the Persians, Cyrus reversed the previous Babylonian policy and allowed the Jews to go back to Jerusalem in 538 B.C. The first Jews who returned to Jerusalem built an altar and rebuilt the temple (Ezra 1-6); however, the city remained unprotected. It had no wall. In 445 B.C., Nehemiah returned to Jerusalem to rebuild the city walls. In fifty-two days, the massive project was completed (Neh. 6:15). God used Nehemiah to lead the people of Israel to complete this enormous task. How did he do it? Most significantly, he stood in right relationship with God. Leadership is fueled by the leader's walk with his Leader.

The leader's default mode must be to rely on God. Nehemiah's initial response to the problem set before him was to seek God.

> They said to me, "The remnant there in the province who survived the captivity are in great distress and reproach, and the wall of Jerusalem is broken down and its gates are burned with fire." When I heard these words, I sat down and wept and mourned for days; and I was fasting and praying before the God of heaven. I said, "I beseech You, O LORD God of heaven, the great and awesome God, who preserves the covenant and lovingkindness for those who love Him and keep His commandments, let Your ear now be attentive and Your eyes open to hear the prayer of Your servant which I am praying before You now, day and night, on behalf of the sons of Israel Your servants" (Neh. 1:3-6).

Leaders have to make decisions. Decision-making is a skill that involves various components. Nehemiah was a skillful decision-maker. How did he make decisions?

> So the king said to me, "Why is your face sad though you are not sick? This is nothing but sadness of heart." Then I was very much afraid. I said to the king, "Let the king live forever. Why should my face not be sad when the city, the place of my fathers' tombs, lies desolate

and its gates have been consumed by fire?" Then the king said to me, "What would you request?" So I prayed to the God of heaven. I said to the king, "If it please the king, and if your servant has found favor before you, send me to Judah, to the city of my fathers' tombs, that I may rebuild it" (Neh. 2:2-5).

What are the most significant words in this passage with respect to decision-making? "So I prayed to the God of heaven." How do leaders make decisions? They must rely on God. It is difficult to lead others if you are not being led yourself. The leader must walk closely with *the* Leader.

MAY 10

HOARDING IS HIDING, NOT STEWARDING

*"But he who received the one **talent** went away,*
*and dug **a hole** in the ground and hid his master's money."*

Matthew 25:18

Prosperity theology often distorts the understanding of living a life of faith and victory. It says that victory *only* includes having no needs. This is not only illogical; it is not biblical. A need must first exist before God can supply it. "And my God will supply all your needs according to His riches in glory in Christ Jesus" (Phil. 4:19).We might say that needs are needed.

Philippians 4:19 is preceded by "I can do all things through Him who strengthens me" (Phil. 4:13). When Paul proclaims this, he says it in the context of being in need. "I know how to get along with humble means, and I also know how to live in prosperity; in any and every circumstance I have learned the secret of being filled and going hungry, both of having abundance and suffering need" (Phil. 4:12). What is the point? The point is that your material situation is not the point. This is the problem with prosperity theology teaching. The problem is not that it proposes that God will provide for us. The problem is that it makes that provision the primary thing. Jesus reminds us, "You cannot serve God and wealth" (Matt. 6:24). When you are ruled by stuff, you are not ruled by God. It is one or the other. You cannot serve both. There cannot be two number ones!

The hyper-prosperity theologian has a hard time reading, let alone agreeing with, many passages in the Scripture (2 Cor. 6:3-5; 2 Cor. 11:27; Heb. 11:35-39; Hab. 3:17-18). The following passage might be seen as revolting:

> For, I think, God has exhibited us apostles last of all, as men condemned to death; because we have become a spectacle to the world, both to angels and to men. We are fools for Christ's sake, but you are prudent in Christ; we are weak, but you are strong; you are distinguished, but we are without honor. To this present hour we are both hungry and thirsty, and are poorly clothed, and are roughly treated, and are homeless; and we toil, working with our own hands; when we are reviled, we bless; when we are persecuted, we endure; when we are slandered, we try to conciliate; we have become as the scum of the world, the dregs of all things, *even* until now (1 Cor. 4:9-13).

The point of this passage is not that it is somehow holy to be "both hungry and thirsty." The key phrase is "for Christ's sake." Paul is the one who said, "I can do all things through Him who strengthens me" (Phil. 4:13). The point is that it is neither right nor wrong, better or worse, righteous or unrighteous to have or not to have material things. Material things are not the point. They are not my ruler nor my treasure. Christ is!

Prosperity theology facilitates materialism by inverting scriptural principles. It advocates "giving to God, so that you will receive more." It focuses on and points toward *self* when it insists that God's management and stewardship plan merely exists so that *you* can gain. God becomes a formula. Plug Him in, and He works. We begin to embrace a sort of "Santa Claus God." God is not Santa Claus. He is a God of mission. He is a good Manager of His resources and, therefore, expects His workers to be good stewards. When stewards get more, they give more. Stewards do not waste. Stewards *use* what they get instead of burying it in their own hole (Matt. 25:18). Hoarding is hiding.

Stewards do not live in excess. Stewards give in excess. The Bible advocates "receiving blessing, so that you may give more to God." It focuses on and points toward God and His desire to give to others (John 3:16). God is an extravagant Giver; so there can be extravagant giving, not extravagant hoarding and wasting. Prosperity theology is not a stewardship theology; it is a theology of negligence. It is not a theology of multiplication; it is a theology of subtraction. So, live in kingdom prosperity. Be a multiplier!

MAY 11

WHAT OR WHO DO YOU FEAR?

"I, even I, am He who comforts you. Who are you that you are afraid of man who dies and of the son of man who is made like grass, that you have forgotten the LORD your Maker, who stretched out the heavens and laid the foundations of the earth, that you fear continually all day long because of the fury of the oppressor, as he makes ready to destroy? But where is the fury of the oppressor?."

Isaiah 51:12-13

There is a big difference between fearing God and being afraid of God. When I was a little boy, I remember thinking that my dad was so big; I was in awe of him. I respected him. I feared him, and it made me want to be close to him. That kind of fear made me want to jump up in the recliner and cuddle with him. If I was afraid of him, I would have simply wanted to get away from him. God does not want us to be afraid of Him. He wants us to fear Him. He does not want us to flee from Him. He wants us to come close to Him.

In the Garden of Eden, Adam and Eve "hid themselves" from the One Who was mercifully looking for them (Gen. 3:8-13). In the Garden of Gethsemane, Jesus' disciples "all left Him and fled" (Mark 14:43-50). We sometimes have our own gardens. We forget how much we need Jesus, and we ignore Him. We flee from the One we need. It may be because instead of *fearing* God, we are *afraid of* man.

> Immediately while He was still speaking, Judas, one of the twelve, came up accompanied by a crowd with swords and clubs, *who were* from the chief priests and the scribes and the elders. Now he who was betraying Him had given them a signal, saying, "Whomever I kiss, He is the one; seize Him and lead Him away under guard." After coming, Judas immediately went to Him, saying, "Rabbi!" and kissed Him. They laid hands on Him and seized Him. But one of those who stood by drew his sword, and struck the slave of the high priest and cut off his ear. And Jesus said to them, "Have you come out with swords and clubs to arrest Me, as *you would* against a robber? Every day I was with you in the temple teaching, and you did not seize Me; but *this has taken place* to fulfill the Scriptures." And they all left Him and fled (Mark 14:43-50).

We flee from Jesus when we are afraid of people and when we focus on temporal things. The disciples feared the darkness, soldiers, and weapons. They feared the multitude that seized Jesus. But they should have feared the One Who asked, "Or do you think that I cannot appeal to My Father, and He will at once put at My disposal more than twelve legions of angels?" (Matt. 26:53).

What or who do you fear? "Do not fear those who kill the body but are unable to kill the soul; but rather fear Him who is able to destroy both soul and body in hell" (Matt. 10:28). When all is said and done, we must fear the One Who has authority. Are you concerned about what others think of you or what God thinks of you? Do you fear the loss of material things, status, or reputation; or do you fear the loss of your soul? Do you have a temporal or eternal fear? If your fear is based on temporal things, you will leave the eternal One and flee from Him (Mark 14:50). Instead, fear the Father and cuddle up with Him in the recliner!

MAY 12

THE CREATOR DOES WINDOWS

"Wash me thoroughly from my iniquity and cleanse me from my sin ... Purify me with hyssop, and I shall be clean; wash me, and I shall be whiter than snow."

Psalm 51:2, 7

Repentance is the act of turning to your Creator, Who washes you. Yes, the Creator does windows! You are not your own creator nor are you your own window-washer. True repentance includes the understanding that God's cleansing is desperately necessary. It confesses, "I am unclean. I am dirty." Counterfeit repentance exhibits an attitude that says, "I will wait until I do enough good things that I feel clean enough to approach God." Repentance understands that you cannot wash yourself. It cries out, "God, please wash me!"

> Wash me thoroughly from my iniquity and cleanse me from my sin. For I know my transgressions, and my sin is ever before me. Against You, You only, I have sinned and done what is evil in Your sight, so that You are justified when You speak and blameless when You judge. Behold, I was brought forth in iniquity, and in sin my mother conceived me. Behold, You desire truth in the innermost being, and in the hidden part You will make me know wisdom. Purify me with hyssop, and I shall be clean; wash me, and I shall be whiter than snow (Psalm 51:2-7).

Peter had a counterfeit attitude. He apparently felt that God should not have to wash his dirty feet and that he should wash them himself. "'Lord, do You wash my feet?' Jesus answered and said to him, 'What I do you do not realize now, but you will understand hereafter.' Peter said to Him, 'Never shall You wash my feet!' Jesus answered him, 'If I do not wash you, you have no part with Me.'" (John 13:6-8). Jesus is the only One Who can make you "whiter than snow." We cannot clean ourselves, and we do not have to feel clean in order to come to God to be cleaned by Him. Repentance is the act of turning to your Creator who washes you. He cleans you and He creates in you. "Create in me a clean heart, O God, and renew a steadfast spirit within me" (Psalm 51:10).

True repentance includes the understanding that God is still at work in you. It says, "I am unfinished. I am imperfect." Counterfeit repentance does not include the understanding of the desperate need for God to continue to be at work in you. It exhibits the attitude that says, "I will wait until I have time to change myself so that I feel changed enough to approach God."

Have you ever set a date for when you would start being different? Meanwhile, you gorge yourself with your current lifestyle, filling yourself up with as much as possible before the "magical" date comes when you will change. You can set dates from here to eternity, but He is the only One Who can create something new in you. That is why you must repent; you must turn to God. You cannot change yourself. You do not have to feel changed in order to come to God to be changed by Him.

Do you "set dates" with respect to a sin area that keeps appearing in your life? Do you insist on washing yourself? Do you realize that if God does not wash you, you have no part with Him? Do you needlessly carry around the ball and chain of the imperfection and dirtiness of sin?

Repentance is the point of coming to the end of yourself and turning to God's ability. It is not so much the process of declaring your actions—"I will change"—as it is the process of asking to be acted upon. Change me, O God. Create anew in me. Wash my windows!

MAY 13

HE HUMBLES YOU TO SEE HIM

"For He has torn us, but He will heal us."

Hosea 6:1

What may or may not be self-imposed "wilderness experiences" can become God's platform that He uses to draw you to Himself. In a very real sense, in order to be comforted, you first must be uncomfortable (Matt. 5:4). Let us use this tautology: "Difficult times are not easy." Wandering through the wilderness is no fun. Difficult seasons of life are not what we look forward to. Nevertheless, God can use them for His own glory as He reminds us of our desperate need for Him and of His unmeasurable love for us.

This does not make discomfort desirable or good; but it does make it useful to a sovereign God, for "[He] is our refuge and strength, a very present help in trouble" (Psalm 46:1). The purpose of wilderness experiences is to bring us into a fuller realization that we must depend completely on God and not on ourselves. The result of wilderness experiences is an expansion of our spiritual lives through death to self; as more of you leaves, more of God is able to come in. "From where shall my help come? My help *comes* from the Lord" (Psalm 121:1-2).

> All the commandments that I am commanding you today you shall be careful to do, that you may live and multiply, and go in and possess the land which the LORD swore *to give* to your forefathers. You shall remember all the way which the LORD your God has led you in the wilderness these forty years, that He might humble you, testing you, to know what was in your heart, whether you would keep His commandments or not. He humbled you and let you be hungry, and fed you with manna which you did not know, nor did your fathers know, that He might make you understand that man does not live by bread alone, but man lives by everything that proceeds out of the mouth of the LORD. Your clothing did not wear out on you, nor did your foot swell these forty years. Thus you are to know in your heart that the LORD your God was disciplining you just as a man disciplines his son. Therefore, you shall keep the commandments of the LORD your God, to walk in His ways and to fear Him (Deut. 8:1-6).

In reference to their wilderness experience, God cautions the Israelites to be "careful," implying that they were previously *not* sufficiently careful. In order to sustain and grow our spiritual lives, we must learn from our mistakes and allow them to be a guide toward positive change instead of a source of discouragement. This does not entail forgetting about the wilderness—indeed, "you shall remember" and learn—but it does put the focus on "today" as opposed to yesterday. Do not fix yourself in the past so as to dwell negatively on your failings and become discouraged (Isa. 43:2, 18-19). Remember to forget yourself and do not forget God.

God repeats several ideas. First, His actions with regard to the wandering Israelites are "that He might humble you." How does He do this? He highlights two things: their need and His provision. To be humble is to be "poor," and it is the poor that realize God's kingdom (Matt. 5:3). Second, His actions are disciplinary, with the goal of producing obedience, so as "to walk in His ways and to fear Him." Nobody wants to enter the wilderness, but we all want to exit it with its fruit; we want to know God more fully. "Come, let us return to the LORD. For He has torn *us*, but He will heal us; He has wounded *us*, but He will bandage us. He will revive us after two days; He will raise us up on the third day, that we may live before Him. So let us know, let us press on to know the LORD. His going forth is as certain as the dawn; and He will come to us like the rain, like the spring rain watering the earth" (Hosea 6:1-3).

MAY 14

THAT'S WHAT SOVEREIGNS DO

"For the wrath of man shall praise You."

Psalm 76:10

Maybe you are the assistant manager. Maybe you are the vice president or the CEO. There are many roles and many titles. What is God's title? He is the Sovereign. He is not only the Monarch or King, He is the Absolute Monarch. He is the Sovereign.

A Sovereign creates, causes, and controls. If such a sovereign is loving and good, why do bad things happen? Bad things happen because there is another king who rules over another kingdom—a bad king and a bad kingdom. This king is not a sovereign. He is only a wannabe sovereign. He is a fake creator, fake causer, and fake controller with a counterfeit kingdom. When the bad that flows from a fake sovereign flies in the face of the good that surrounds a real sovereign, it is ultimately ineffective. God, the only true Sovereign, uses the bad for His own purposes.

In a fictitious boxing match, it might be imagined that a boxer knocks out his opponent with one punch; and so, he is deemed strong. In another match, the boxer withstands the blow of his opponent and then knocks him out with one punch; and so, he is deemed stronger. In one final match, he allows his opponent to throw the first punch; but somehow, with superior wisdom and creativity, he avoids the punch in such a way that the punch returns to his opponent and knocks him out. This means that the boxer is not just strong or stronger but that he is also sovereign. God is this "Boxer." He creates, causes, and controls. His control over His opponent results in His ability to use the opponent's punch to be the very one that knocks out the opponent! The Sovereign God uses "bad" for His own purposes.

Satan wanted Jesus dead. On Friday, it appeared as though he threw a knockout punch at Calvary. However, on Sunday, it was clear that it was Satan who had been knocked out by his own punch! That two-day-long party thrown by Satan in his demonic lair came to a terrorizing halt on the third day when "evil" was used for good. God is not only stronger than Satan; He is also sovereign over Him. "The LORD has established His throne in the heavens, and His sovereignty rules over all" (Psalm 103:19).

Why do bad things happen if there is a good God? They happen because that good God is Sovereign, and His control is so absolute that He is able to use His enemies' attempts to advance their own agendas to be, instead, the advancement of His holy agenda. In so doing, God magnifies Himself and extends His glory. The unholy is actually used for holy purposes. The sovereignty of God is so profound that He is able to make the wrath of men to praise Him and his enemies to serve Him (Psalm 76:10).

A kingdom is a realm. God has His realm, and man has his realm. God's realm is consistent with who He is; a Sovereign. He works in the realm of creating, causing and controlling. Man's realm is consistent with who he is; a subject of God's realm. Man works in the realm of receiving, responding, and relating. "But as many as received Him, to them He gave the right to become children of God, *even to those who believe in His name, who were born, not of blood nor of the will of the flesh nor of the will of man, but of God*" (John 1:12-13). Man receives and believes, while God creates and causes.

It is important to live in your own realm. If you live in the realm of receiving, responding, and relating, then you will be a fish out of water if you try to live in the realm of creating, causing, and controlling. Worry is nothing more than the fruit of insisting on living in a realm that is not your own. We worry because we are concerned with what is not our concern. "Martha, Martha, you are worried and bothered about so many things; but *only* one thing is necessary, for Mary has chosen the good part, which shall not be taken away from her" (Luke 10:41-42). We are not sovereign. "And which of you by worrying can add a *single* hour to his life's span? If then you cannot do even a very little thing, why do you worry about other matters?" (Luke 12:25-26). Why are you trying to live in God's realm? Live in your own realm. Why are you concerned about God's stuff? Concern yourself with your stuff!

More than anything else, our stuff is "Mary stuff." Mary was seated at the feet of Jesus and listened to His word (Luke 10:39). She was receiving, responding, and relating to Him. She was "seek[ing] first His kingdom" (Matt. 6:33). A challenging question for all of us is, "When is the last time you 'worried' about how much you were seeking God and spending time with Jesus?" Having asked this, we must remember that living in the realm of relationship does not negate other actions. Faith produces works (James 2:18-26). Actions confirm faith. The realm in which we live is not void of practical common sense. When Nehemiah's enemies approached, he prayed *and* set up a guard (Neh. 4:9).

It is true. There is evil in the world. Our response is to seek, trust in, obey, and act consistent with the Sovereign One. God, the only true Sovereign, will use the bad for His own purposes. That is what Sovereigns do!

MAY 15

DRIVING ON GRACE AVENUE

"O LORD God of hosts, hear my prayer; give ear, O God of Jacob! Behold our shield,
O God, and look upon the face of Your anointed. For a day in Your courts is better than
*a thousand **outside**. I would rather stand at the threshold of the house of my God*
than dwell in the tents of wickedness. For the LORD God is a sun and shield;
the LORD gives grace and glory; no good thing does He withhold from those who walk uprightly.
O LORD of hosts, how blessed is the man who trusts in You!"

Psalm 84:8-12

Spiritual disciplines are activities that should reflect the lifestyle of a follower of Christ. Prayer, for example, should be more of a practice or habit than a ceremony or afterthought. Activities like prayer, fasting, fellowship, worship, Bible study, and giving should represent disciplines that mark a Christian's way of life. These disciplines may also be referred to as a "means of grace." They are avenues through which God's grace flows. They have their purposes, and they have their results. Their practice includes proper motives and produces appropriate effects.

Fasting can be defined as the willful denial of an otherwise normal function for the sake of fervent spiritual activity. The ultimate direction of any means of grace is that relationship with God would be strengthened. Weeping and fasting were not uncommon in the life and experience of David (2 Sam. 1:12; 2 Sam. 12:16;). Fasting's connection to hunger is consistent with David's resolute desire to draw closer to God. David's spiritual discipline reflected his hunger for God; God called him "a man after His own heart" (1 Sam. 13:14). Means of grace are channels through which people experience and respond to the loving presence of God. Fasting is motivated by a response to the presence of God and has as its benefit the experience of the presence of God. In this sense, the motive is consistent with the effect. You are satisfied with what you hunger for just as "where your treasure is, there your heart will be also" (Matt. 6:21).

Fasting, as a means of grace, must include biblical motives on the part of the one who is fasting. In addition, it includes biblical effects as God takes what is directed to Him, uses it for His glory, and allows the effects to become blessings for the one who fasts. The actual benefit of fasting is not found in a particular result for self but in the blessing of the ramifications of Christ living in and operating through you. The grand motive of fasting—or of any other means of grace—is to want to make your life more available for God's use; it is to want to make more of a way for Christ to continue to walk the earth (Gal. 2:20).

To a certain degree, for Christians to insist that they will fast until they get what they want is dangerous. This sort of fasting is tantamount to a spiritual hunger strike. It does not understand the distinction between motive and effect. There are correct motives with which to engage in means of grace that are different from—yet consistent with—the effects of means of grace. When the Scripture exhorts "he who humbles himself will be exalted" (Luke 18:14), it does not mean to advocate humbling self simply for the purpose of lifting up self! That would be a misunderstanding of "humbling yourself." Rather, you humble yourself in response to your recognition of God and as a means to be more involved with Him. Less of you means more of Him (John 3:30). This is the actuality of receiving His grace.

Engaging in a means of grace like fasting should be your response to the grandeur of God and a means by which you can be more involved with Him. The humbling effect is that God lifts you up. This is grace. It is favor that you cannot earn; you can only drive on its avenue!

MAY 16

ARE YOU WILLING TO TESTIFY?

"So, having obtained help from God, I stand to this day testifying both to small and great, stating nothing but what the Prophets and Moses said was going to take place."

Acts 26:22

A lawyer who wants to win a court case hopes to have good witnesses who are willing to testify. A court case without witnesses is like a UFO sighting without anyone who claims to have seen it. The witness is important. His or her testimony builds credibility into the case. This is certainly true in the "Gospel trial." The Gospel messenger builds the case for Christ and His salvation when he shares his own personal testimony.

A personal testimony may be the single most effective way to reach unbelievers. No one can really dispute your personal experiences with God unless they just say that you are lying or that you are totally delusional. People relate to other people's life stories. Testimonies tend to prompt others to, at least, consider how God might also work in their lives. In a personal evangelism situation, the messenger might consider moving from casual conversation, to testimony, to Gospel presentation. Conversation can be used to walk up to Heaven's door. Testimony can then open that door. Gospel presentation might then result in the person walking through the door.

A great model is Paul's defense before King Agrippa (Acts 26:1-23). Your testimony can be thought of as consisting of three parts:

1. What was your life like before Christ (Acts 26:2-11)?

2. How did you meet Christ (Acts 26:12-18)?

3. What is your life like with Christ (Acts 26:19-23)?

What was your life like before Christ? Here, of course, you should focus on your need for Christ. What was going on in your life that showed your need for Him? Most people will be able to relate to some aspects of your situation. Sin is sin, and need is need. All people have that in common (Rom. 3:23). There is no need to exaggerate your problems, and you should, certainly, be careful not to glorify them.

How did you meet Christ? This is where you can most readily include the basics of the Gospel message. This will clarify for your listener what actually happens in order to become a Christian. Focus on the actual decision that you made. What did you have to decide? How did you express that decision? Your listener can relate to this in a specific and applicable way. Stay focused at this point and be sure to paint the actual picture of what happened.

What is your life like with Christ? Focus on how you have changed. Offer practical examples of how Christ is actually working in your life. Be genuine and honest. You certainly, for example, can testify how Christ has brought you success, peace, joy, and hope. You do not, however, have to feel that you must put yourself forward as a perfect person. So, for example, you should not suggest that you have no problems as a Christian. Rather, tell how Christ gives you strength to face your problems. Be careful of a common mistake in how testimonies are given—that is, testifying in extremes. Just like you do not need to paint yourself as an extreme sinner in the first part of your testimony, you also do not need to paint yourself as an extreme saint in the last part of your testimony. Be careful not to glorify your sin and be careful not to glorify your holiness. The only One Who is perfect in this story is Christ. Extremes, therefore, should be reserved for the second part of your testimony, where you can glorify Christ and His mercy, grace, love, and patience.

Testimonies should not be long. Keep your testimony brief. It might be between three and five minutes. Beware of using "Christianese." Don't say, "I had a check in my spirit that they were the frozen chosen, so I began fellowshipping where I felt the Spirit was really moving and had myself a real *kairos* moment as I just soaked in the presence that was so heavy." Not only will non-Christians not know what you are talking about, but they may also begin to feel less of a rapport with you. Also, beware of getting bogged down in unnecessary facts or details that might distract from your main points and especially be careful not to get lost by going down "rabbit trails" that take you away from those main points.

In a very real way, the Gospel is on trial. The witnesses are crucial to the direction that the trial will take. Are you willing to testify?

MAY 17

THE IMPORTANCE OF BEING OBEDIENT

"Not My will, but Yours be done."

Luke 22:42

Without obedience, there may as well be no commandments. Without commandments, there is no direction. Without direction, there is no purpose. Without purpose, there is no story. Without a story, there is no history. Without history, there is nothing. Obedience is indispensable!

Jesus remains the definitive Example of obedience. It was what fueled Him. "'My food is to do the will of Him who sent Me and to accomplish His work'" (John 4:34). Jesus understood it was not about Him and His desires. It was about the One Who sent Him: "'Father, if You are willing, remove this cup from Me; yet not My will, but Yours be done'" (Luke 22:42). Jesus was then able to say, "'I glorified You on the earth, having accomplished the work which You have given Me to do'" (John 17:4). Jesus was obedient until the end: "And Jesus, crying out with a loud voice, said, 'Father, INTO YOUR HANDS I COMMIT MY SPIRIT.' Having said this, He breathed His last" (Luke 23:46). Jesus' perfect obedience made Him perfectly successful and, therefore, perfectly exalted:

> Being found in appearance as a man, He humbled Himself by becoming obedient to the point of death, even death on a cross. For this reason also, God highly exalted Him, and bestowed on Him the name which is above every name, so that at the name of Jesus EVERY KNEE WILL BOW, of those who are in heaven and on earth and under the earth, and that every tongue will confess that Jesus Christ is Lord, to the glory of God the Father (Phil. 2:8-11).

His perfect exaltation that is rooted in His perfect obedience then results in Him having all authority: "And Jesus came up and spoke to them, saying, 'All authority has been given to Me in heaven and on earth. Go therefore and make disciples of all the nations'" (Matt. 28:18-19). The Command-follower then becomes the Command-giver. He becomes the One Who will build the entity through which His commands will be obeyed: "I will build My church; and the gates of Hades will not overpower it" (Matt. 16:18).

Immediately before Christ's ascension, He gives His mandate to the Church—that which is commonly called the Great Commission. This great commandment must be obeyed. The Church, the body of Christ, must now continue Christ's insistence on obedience. The Book of Acts records this obedience. Commandments come with privileges. Responsibilities come with resources. And so, the Commandment-giver is also the Resource-provider: "But you will receive power when the Holy Spirit has come upon you; and you shall be My witnesses both in Jerusalem, and in all Judea and Samaria, and even to the remotest part of the earth" (Acts 1:8).

After the mandate (be a witness to all nations) and the resource (the outpouring of the Holy Spirit) were issued, the remainder of the book of Acts serves to show how the early church responded to the mandate as they were equipped to do so. They witness in "Jerusalem" (Acts 1-7). Then they witness in "Judea and Samaria" (Acts 8-12). Finally, they spread the Gospel to "the remotest part of the earth" (Acts 13-28).

The Church is motivated to obey the Great Commission because of the return of Whom they are obeying. Jesus' disciples ask Him that all important question, "When will You return?" (Matt. 24:3; Acts 1:6). He answers this great question with the great mandate. I will return when the Gospel has gone to all nations (Matt. 24:14; Acts 1:8).

How important is our obedience to the Great Commission? Jesus certainly emphasizes its importance. The end depends on it. The Church must be able to say along with Jesus, "'not My will, but Yours be done'" (Luke 22:42).

MAY 18

HEY, MISSIONARY, LET CULTURE BE YOUR FRIEND

*"For though I am free from all **men**, I have made myself a slave to all, so that I may win more. To the Jews I became as a Jew, so that I might win Jews.*

1 Corinthians 9:19-20

Missionaries must understand the difference between spreading the Gospel and spreading their culture. The Great Commission does not call its agents to facilitate a *culture* transformation; it calls them to facilitate a *kingdom* transformation. Sometimes, the mistake has been made of trying to force culture upon the "natives." Missionaries must be careful to preach the Gospel of the Bible and not the Gospel of their culture. Only "the stumbling block of the cross" (Gal. 5:11) should be placed before people; culture should not be a stumbling block. If the Gospel is not effectively contextualized—using cultural ideas and practices of the audience—rejection of Christianity can actually be the rejection of the foreign culture.

What are acceptable and effective ways to contextualize the Gospel? The missionary must understand the difference between syncretism and indigenization. Syncretism uses a cultural form to express Christianity while retaining its corresponding faulty belief. This is not acceptable. Indigenization is acceptable. The new Christians deny the old belief while still using the cultural form. They fill the old cultural mold with new Christian beliefs as opposed to using a new Christian form and retaining the old belief.

People in animistic cultures might engage in the activity of cleaning their village of garbage and debris because they believe that the spirit world and the material world are inseparable. They believe that a spirit hides behind a garbage bag or a leaf, so they want to get rid of it. Syncretism would use that cultural practice to explain that there is a spiritual war in which God is victorious over Satan. It would not, however, correct and reject the animistic beliefs. Indigenization would use the "cleaning" cultural practice to explain the biblical idea of spiritual warfare. It would also teach theistic worldview and reject animistic worldview.

The missionary must be sensitive to unforeseen results of conversion. What should a missionary do when formerly animistic Christians no longer clean their village because their original incentive to throw away garbage—thinking that evil spirits hid in garbage—no longer exists?

What should a missionary do in places where polygamy is practiced? What happens to the three wives that a new Christian is ordered to give up? In many societies, they will become slaves or prostitutes or will be killed.

The complexities that come from the Gospel mixing with culture must not be underestimated. Often, the answers to these questions are found in the principle of substitution or replacement. Cultural substitutes must fill the void left by changed or eliminated cultural practices. It is now taught that there are no spirits hiding behind the garbage bags and leaves. New converts should still clean their villages—not because they will be sweeping away spirits but because God calls them to be good stewards of the resources He has given them. They should still war against evil spirits—not because those spirits are one and the same with all material things but because God has authority over them in Jesus' name.

Culture is both a blessing and a curse in missions work. It is a curse because, if not used effectively, it will eventually make it impossible for the missionary to reach his target people. It is a blessing because culture is the avenue through which the Gospel will be presented and the fruit of ministry will come. If the missionary is not "culturally stubborn" and keeps the prize before him, then he will be able to say along with Paul, "To the Jews I became as a Jew, so that I might win Jews" (1 Cor. 9:20). For missionaries, culture must be seen as their friend and partner and not their enemy and opponent.

MAY 19

IF YOU'RE NOT MARRIED, THEN DON'T ACT LIKE IT!

"This is now bone of my bones, and flesh of my flesh."

Genesis 2:23

How does our understanding of the biblical nature of marriage inform the way we look at something like dating? To understand what marriage is, is to understand what dating is not. Dating is not marriage. Marriage cannot fit into the structure of dating and a lack of a fit causes fits. So, if you are not married, then do not act like it; and if you do act like it, then get married. Counterfeits, by definition, are not pure. Impure things tend to be problematic. When dating acts as a fake marriage, problems are not far off. You cannot pretend to be married. You cannot practice being married without being married. If you try to practice basketball without actually playing basketball, it will not be very helpful. Fake is empty, and empty does not breed fullness.

Dating is informed by a "high view" of marriage. Marriage is established by God as the most foundational institution of human society. As soon as God created man, He declared, "'It is not good for the man to be alone; I will make him a helper suitable for him'" (Gen. 2:18). Man was incomplete, so God made for him his completion and then man said, "'This is now bone of my bones, and flesh of my flesh; she shall be called Woman, because she was taken out of Man'" (Gen. 2:23). He recognizes that they are *two* ("woman" and "man"), but he also recognizes that they are *one* ("bone of my bones and flesh of my flesh")—a singular plurality.

And so, immediately after Adam's singular plurality declaration in Genesis 2:23, we see the establishment of marriage: "For this reason a man shall leave his father and his mother, and be joined to his wife; and they shall become one flesh" (Gen. 2:24). A paraphrase might be: "Since God created them as a singular plurality and commanded them to multiply, the man shall leave family in order to multiply family by being joined to her who completes him; the two shall become one, the plural shall become singular." God, a Trinity, is a Singular Plurality—Three in One—Who created man in His singular plurality image (Gen. 1:26-27). Marriage means that two are one; they are a unity in diversity. There is equality without "sameness."

What does this have to do with dating? Perhaps the question is better worded, "What does dating have to do with this?" Marriage is a unique foundational relationship instituted by God. The distinction of the marriage relationship starts on the social level. It is rooted in its inception. It is descriptive of being "bone of my bones and flesh of my flesh" and then "cleaving" and becoming "one." On a social level, marriage is marked by *exclusivity*. She is his, and he is hers forever and ever. She is nobody else's, and he is nobody else's forever and ever. Sound familiar?

Only marriage holds this exclusive relationship. It is the very definition of what marriage is. When dating pretends to take on this social relationship dynamic, it causes problems. The exclusive social aspect necessarily fuels a deep, profound, and attached emotional aspect. That deep emotional aspect cannot help but trickle down into an involved physical aspect. When that stimulated physical aspect significantly develops, it ultimately leads to a spiritual aspect; one flesh physically is not void of one flesh spiritually. This is a mystery (Eph. 5:32) as it is experienced in marriage. When these same contents, however, are funneled through another structure, they are problematic. When dating acts like marriage, it is not God's design. When dating becomes the sort of social relationship that should only be expressed in marriage and leads to the sort of physical/spiritual relationship that is reserved for marriage and is the Divine definition of marriage (one flesh), then dating becomes a "fake marriage."

Is there no God-designed relationship between a young man and a young woman? Dating is just a word. It is not problematic just because it is called dating. It is problematic because people try to say they are married without being married. A young man and a young woman can be attracted to each other without yet being married to each other. They do not have to say to themselves and to others, "We are each other's, and we are nobody else's." They can be attracted to each other and spend time together getting to know each other without having to say they are in an exclusive relationship. This non-exclusive relationship (sometimes called friendship) does not have as much of a tendency to move from social intensity to emotional intensity to physical intensity to spiritual intensity (since the social intensity of non-exclusivity does not start the same avalanche as exclusivity does). Maybe we can call this "friending."

What happens next? Maybe we can bring back the word "date," but we can call it a "court date" or "courting/court dating" as in "on your way to the courthouse to get the marriage certificate." After "friendship" realizes that another social structure is needed and wanted, the non-exclusive relationship takes on an exclusive flavor in that it is agreed that the relationship is intentionally moving toward exclusivity. Guards are still held in place emotionally, physically, and spiritually as it is understood that the exclusive social role is anticipated but not yet realized. The claim that dating is necessary because something is needed between "friendship" and "court dating" should be challenged with the question, "What is it that you cannot do in a 'friendship' structure that you must do in a 'dating' structure?" The answer may very well be, "We cannot be married . . . even though we are not married!"

Marriage is serious. It is forever. The process of moving toward marriage is the process of finding your completion—finding the *one* you *own*, the one who is you, the one who is "bone of your bone and flesh of your flesh." It may sound wrong to go so far as to say "own." The Scripture does not think it is wrong: "The wife does not have authority over her own body, but the husband *does*; and likewise also the husband does not have authority over his own body, but the wife *does*" (1 Cor. 7:4). Dating cannot contain these contents, only marriage can. So, if you are not married then do not act like it and if you are acting like it then get married!

MAY 20

THE DEVOUT DEVOTES

"They were continually devoting themselves to."

Acts 2:42

In the early church, "they were continually devoting themselves to the apostles' teaching and to fellowship, to the breaking of bread and to prayer" (Acts 2:42). Bible study and prayer seem to stick out here along with fellowship and the taking of the Lord's Supper. More specifically, the elders of the Church focused on prayer and the ministry of the Word. "So the twelve summoned the congregation of the disciples and said, 'It is not desirable for us to neglect the word of God in order to serve tables . . . But we will devote ourselves to prayer and to the ministry of the word'" (Acts 6:2, 4).

Prayer and ministry of the Word cannot be separated. For those in "full-time ministry," the tendency can be to replace the emphasis on prayer and ministry of the Word with management and ministry of the Word. Pastoral renewal comes when pastors get back to the basics. Professional expectations sometimes influence ministers toward the "bigger" and more glamorous or high-profile activities. Common perceptions of the ministry do not lend themselves to encouraging ministers to devote themselves to prayer and to the ministry of the word because it requires perseverance in the commonplace and appreciation for the obscure. It would be quite an understatement to say that in today's high-pressure church, in which the pastor is expected to wear a variety of hats, there exists a need for a renewal of an emphasis on prayer as a foundational activity of his office.

This is true for all believers. Followers of Christ need a revival of prayer in their lives. Within the modern culture of the Church, so much emphasis has been placed on what we should get accomplished and how we should go about doing it that we can easily forget about the efficacy of prayer. With such an emphasis on "what and how to do it," it is quite easy to forget that God is more concerned with "who we are." For Jesus, the "how" is an issue mainly because it relates to relationship with Him which produces "who we are." It has been observed, for example, that Jesus never told His disciples how to get people to come to their church or how to make their church grow, but He did tell them how to pray. "Lord, teach us to pray" (Luke 11:1). "Pray, then, in this way" (Matt. 6:9).

This is not to say that Christians are not practitioners or hard workers. It is to say that followers of Christ must grow in the "rest" that comes from focusing and relying on God. Indeed, "rest" comes from reserving more of yourself and your time for the "means of grace" mentioned in Acts 2:42 and 6:2-4. Prayer and Bible study are key components of the Christian life. You give yourself to acknowledging God "in all your ways" (Prov. 3:6), and you proclaim, "Your word I have treasured in my heart" (Psalm 119:11).

This, of course, necessitates a clear understanding of the sovereignty of God. To increase and improve their ministry of the Word and prayer, Christians must trust in God enough to recognize that success in ministry does not rely on them accomplishing something but on Him accomplishing something through them. With this understanding, followers of Christ will give themselves more to the means by which He works through them; that is, they will give themselves more to the ministry of the Word and prayer.

Is there a balance? Perhaps the saying that is often attributed to Augustine is helpful here: "Pray as though everything depended on God. Work as though everything depended on you." Remember, "faith, if it has no works, is dead" (James 2:17) and works without faith "are worthless" (Isa. 41:29). Devote yourself to both! Let your "work" be your devotion (John 6:28), so your devotion results in your works.

MAY 21

GOD'S DESIRE MUST BECOME OUR PURPOSE

*"In those days ten men from all the nations will grasp the garment of a Jew, saying,
'Let us go with you, for we have heard that God is with you.'"*

Zechariah 8:23

Vessels have certain characteristics, the most fundamental of which is that they are created for a purpose. The potter makes the vessel for his own use that is consistent with his plan and what pleases him. God is the ultimate Potter. What pleases Him? If we understand the desires of the Potter, then we can understand the way in which His vessels will be used. If I want a drink of coffee, I do not use my mug for storing jellybeans. I use my mug for my desire. I fill it with coffee and drink it. So, let's look at God's desires, so we can see our purpose.

God has a great desire to reach the nations. God's heart for the nations is heard in the cry of the psalmist that "all peoples" would know the Lord and praise Him: "Praise the LORD, all nations; Laud Him, all peoples! For His lovingkindness is great toward us, and the truth of the Lord is everlasting. Praise the LORD!" (Psalm 117). God wants to reach all nations with the good news of the Gospel. He wants all people to know Him as Savior.

> Gather yourselves and come; draw near together, you fugitives of the nations; they have no knowledge, who carry about their wooden idol and pray to a god who cannot save. Declare and set forth *your case*; indeed, let them consult together. Who has announced this from of old? Who has long since declared it? Is it not I, the LORD? And there is no other God besides Me, a righteous God and a Savior; there is none except Me. Turn to Me and be saved, all the ends of the earth; for I am God, and there is no other. I have sworn by Myself, the word has gone forth from My mouth in righteousness and will not turn back, that to Me every knee will bow, every tongue will swear *allegiance* (Isa. 45:20-23).

Since God has a great desire to reach the nations, then God's purpose for Israel is to use them to reach the nations. The Potter makes the vessel for His own use that is consistent with His plan and what pleases Him. God has a great desire to show Himself to the nations. He will do this in whatever context is necessary.

> For this time I will send all My plagues on you and your servants and your people, so that you may know that there is no one like Me in all the earth. For if by now I had put forth My hand and struck you and your people with pestilence, you would then have been cut off from the earth. But, indeed, for this reason I have allowed you to remain, in order to show you My power and in order to proclaim My name through all the earth (Exod. 9:13-16).

God wants to show Himself to the nations so that they will seek Him and know Him:
> Thus says the LORD of hosts, "It will yet be that peoples will come, even the inhabitants of many cities. The inhabitants of one will go to another, saying, 'Let us go at once to entreat the favor of the LORD, and to seek the LORD of hosts; I will also go.'" So many peoples and mighty nations will come to seek the LORD of hosts in Jerusalem and to entreat the favor of the Lord. Thus says the Lord of hosts, "In those days ten men from all the nations will grasp the garment of a Jew, saying, 'Let us go with you, for we have heard that God is with you' (Zech. 8:20-23).

Since God has a great desire to show Himself to the nations then God's purpose for Israel is . . . to use them to show Himself to the nations. The potter makes the vessel for his own use that is consistent with his plan and what pleases him.

God has a great desire to provide a light to the nations. He expresses this when He says, "Behold, My Servant, whom I uphold; My chosen one *in whom* My soul delights. I have put My Spirit upon Him; He will bring forth justice to the nations . . . And I will appoint You as a covenant to the people, as a light to the nations" (Isa. 42:1, 6).

God has a great desire to offer salvation to the nations. "The LORD has made known His salvation; He has revealed His righteousness in the sight of the nations. He has remembered His lovingkindness and His faithfulness to the house of Israel; all the ends of the earth have seen the salvation of our God" (Psalm 98:2-3). "The LORD has bared His holy arm in the sight of all the nations, that all the ends of the earth may see the salvation of our God" (Isa. 52:10).

God is in the business of revealing Himself. As the ultimate Potter, His desire must become the ultimate purpose of His vessels. God's desire to reveal Himself to the nations must become our purpose. We find purpose in life to the degree to which we make God known to others.

MAY 22

WHAT YOU THINK IS WHAT YOU ARE

"For from within, out of the heart of men, proceed the evil thoughts."

Mark 7:21

Character is the reality of who you are and what you do. Character runs much deeper than personality, appearance, and reputation. It is the substance of what is in front of the personality. It is the reality of what is behind the appearance. It is the actuality that casts its shadow that is reputation. Personality, appearance, and reputation can be very dangerous things without godly character. Peter Kuzmic, in a speech at the Lausanne II International Congress on World Evangelization in Manila said, "Charisma without character leads to catastrophe."[8]

Your ideal is what you wish you were. It outdistances your character. Your reputation is what people say you are. It is but a shadow of your character. Your character is who you really are that results in what you really do. It is marked by who you are and what you do when you are alone, when no one is looking. It is who you are and what you do when things are not going your way, when you walk through the tough times of life. Christian character is Christ in you and, therefore, what Christ does through you.

Our character forms the direction of our lives. An old Chinese proverb states, "If we sow a thought, we reap an act. If we sow an act, we reap a habit. If we sow a habit, we reap character. If we sow character, we reap a destiny." The old biblical proverb states, "For as he thinks within himself, so he is" (Prov. 23:7). It starts with your thoughts. Thoughts are foundational, since actions are wrought out of thoughts. WWJD should be preceded by WWJT: "What Would Jesus Do" comes from "What Would Jesus Think." We cannot act like Jesus unless we first think like Jesus.

We reap what we sow. "Do not be deceived, God is not mocked; for whatever a man sows, this he will also reap" (Gal. 6:7). If we sow a thought, we will eventually reap an action. Our actions do not start by themselves; they are sourced by our thoughts. Mark 7:20-23 says, "That which proceeds out of the man, that is what defiles the man. For from within, out of the heart of men, proceed the evil thoughts, fornications, thefts, murders, adulteries, deeds of coveting *and* wickedness, *as well as* deceit, sensuality, envy, slander, pride *and* foolishness. All these evil things proceed from within and defile the man."

Eventually, thoughts of fornication will manifest the act of fornication. So, too, thoughts of thefts, murders, adulteries, and slanders will result in their corresponding actions. They do not begin, however, with evil actions but with evil thoughts, since "out of the heart come evil thoughts, murders, adulteries, fornications, thefts, false witness, slanders" (Matt. 15:19).

There is good news in the fact that actions, habits, and character find their source in thoughts. Have you ever tried to break a habit? It is very difficult. Just ask someone who has tried to stop smoking cigarettes or who has tried to put an end to their addiction to pornography. Habits are big walls to break down. An even bigger wall is your character. Have you ever tried to take down the wall of bad character and change who you are? That is a mountain. The good news is that you do not have to directly change your character by yourself. You do not even have to battle against those habits that seem so impossible to break. You only need to deal with the smallest of things. You just need to manage your thoughts. That is doable. It can be achieved by the power of the Holy Spirit in us.

The Spirit of God does the work of sanctification in us as He forms the Word of God in us. "God has chosen you from the beginning for salvation through sanctification by the Spirit and faith in the truth" (2 Thess. 2:13). The truth of the Word of God replaces the lies of the flesh—"Sanctify them in the truth; Your word is truth" (John 17:17)—as "the mind set on the flesh is death, but the mind set on the Spirit is life and peace" (Rom. 8:6).

With the help of the Holy Spirit, you can begin to "incline your ear and hear the words of the wise, and apply your mind to my knowledge" (Prov. 22:17). You can set your mind on righteous thoughts: "Therefore if you have been raised up with Christ, keep seeking the things above, where Christ is, seated at the right hand of God. Set your mind on the things above, not on the things that are on earth" (Col. 3:1-2). You can begin to say, "*We are* destroying speculations and every lofty thing raised up against the knowledge of God, and *we are* taking every thought captive to the obedience of Christ" (2 Cor. 10:5). Then you will "not be conformed to this world, but be transformed by the renewing of your mind, so that you may prove what the will of God is, that which is good and acceptable and perfect" (Rom. 12:2).

What you think is what you are, and what you are is your destiny. Let God shape your destiny. Be transformed by the renewing of your mind.

MAY 23

THE ROMANS 12 GIFT OF GIVING

"Since we have gifts that differ according to the grace given to us,
each of us is to exercise them accordingly:... *he who gives, with liberality."*
Romans 12:6, 8

God equips His people with gifts for ministry. There exist various lists of gifts in the New Testament. One such list is found in Romans 12:6-8: "Since we have gifts that differ according to the grace given to us, *each of us is to exercise them accordingly*: if prophecy, according to the proportion of his faith; if service, in his serving; or he who teaches, in his teaching; or he who exhorts, in his exhortation; he who gives, with liberality; he who leads, with diligence; he who shows mercy, with cheerfulness."

The Giver of these gifts is God the Father (Rom. 12:3). The gifts are called *charismata* (grace gifts). They are described as being "functional gifts" (Rom. 12:4) that are "effects" enacted by "God who works all things in all persons" (1 Cor. 12:6). The Romans 12 gifts are gifts that direct how a person functions; they determine the effects of a person's personality or tendencies. They are not so much gifts that a person is temporarily and situationally used in (as in the 1 Corinthians 12:8-10 gifts) or gifts that dictate a person's actual ministry (as in the Ephesians 4:11 gifts) as they are gifts that reside inside of a person and shape what that person is like. They are what are often called "motivational gifts."

How can the Romans 12 gift of giving be understood? People who have the gift of giving look for opportunities to give to others in need of material assistance. They tend to be very generous with their money and, in general, are willing to consume less in order to be able to give more (2 Cor. 8:1-5). They may often give secretly (Matt. 6:1-4). At the same time, they do have a desire to see what is given used effectively and efficiently.

People who have the gift of giving encourage others to also give. In the Bible, Dorcas seems to be one who surely had this gift of giving: "Now in Joppa there was a disciple named Tabitha (which translated *in Greek* is called Dorcas); this woman was abounding with deeds of kindness and charity which she continually did" (Acts 9:36).

Just like any strength that has its correlated weaknesses, the gift of giving has its vulnerabilities or carnal tendencies that need to be avoided. If someone with this gift is not careful, he or she may become impulsive and wasteful. At the same time, people who have this gift must be careful to maintain a "no strings attached" mentality lest their insistence on seeing fruit come from their giving results in frustration or an attempt to place themselves in a position of authority over other people that they really do not have. Frugality for the sake of having more to give may appear to be stinginess in the eyes of family members who may become bitter. Be ready to be misunderstood!

The Romans 12 gift of giving is that life is seen in terms of giving gifts. The orientation is toward needs. More than anything else, people with this gift view themselves as those who want to share. They especially want to redistribute material possessions in a way that meets material needs. They would say, "Do you need anything? We just love to give!" Are you this person? Do you have the Romans 12 gift of giving?

MAY 24

TOOLS IN THE COUNSELOR'S TOOLKIT

"Go, wash in the pool of Siloam."

John 9:7

People who are willing and able to help other people should have certain tools at their disposal. There exist tools that tend to be in a counselor's toolkit. One such tool is homework. This is where the counselor challenges the person to do something to help himself and to prove his desire to be helped. In other words, the person being helped is asked to take some responsibility. Some people want help but are not willing to make the effort to help themselves. They say that they want to change but do not show it by their actions. Giving an assignment to these people will help them to be involved in solving their problems. This seems to be what Jesus was doing with the man who was born blind when He gave him the assignment to "Go, wash in the pool of Siloam" (John 9:7).

Counselors should be consistent in the giving of their assignments. Homework could be given after each counseling session, and another session should not happen until the previous homework is completed. The first assignment should be brief and easy. All assignments should be specific. They should be able to be evaluated. A written assignment usually works well. The assignment should provide the person with a hope for change. For example, if the person has trouble with anger, then he could be given an assignment to study certain Scriptures that would challenge and encourage him.

Of course, a very important tool in a counselor's toolkit is the Bible since "all Scripture is inspired by God and profitable for teaching, for reproof, for correction, for training in righteousness" (2 Tim. 3:16). The Bible can be used to confront, teach, reprove, correct, instruct in righteousness, renew the mind, change habits, meditate, and comfort and encourage.

People who want to help other people must rely on the Holy Spirit. Counselors must depend on the Spirit as a tool that they use in their counseling. This only makes sense because He is "the Helper" (John 16:7) and the "Spirit of truth" Who guides us (John 16:13). The counselor can pray that the Holy Spirit will give him revelation, understanding, and discernment. In addition, the Spirit can give a counselor a sincere burden for the individual being helped. Love and caring are powerful tools since "perfect love casts out fear" (1 John 4:18). Counselors might also pray for the gifts of the Spirit that could be used to counsel others. Overall, the Holy Spirit can provide hope, confidence, truth, guidance, revelation, and solutions.

MAY 25

ALL THOSE QUESTIONS AND EXCUSES

*"But sanctify Christ as Lord in your hearts, always **being** ready to make a defense to everyone who asks you to give an account for the hope that is in you."*

1 Peter 3:15

A gospel messenger must, more than anything else, know how to present the Gospel message. At the same time, the bearer of good news must also be "ready to make a defense to everyone who asks you to give an account for the hope that is in you" (1 Peter 3:15). Readiness to answer common questions about salvation and thinking through your responses to potential excuses that someone might have to not make a decision about Christ are akin to putting more power tools in your evangelistic toolkit.

One of the more common questions that people ask about the Gospel is something like, "What *is* sin, anyway?" The Bible says that all unrighteousness is sin (1 John 5:17). So sin is anything that is not right. Have you ever done anything wrong? Well, you're just like me then. We are sinners.

Another popular question is "Why does God allow evil in this world?" That question seems to witness against God. However, it is not God's choice that is in question here. It is man's choice. Man chooses evil. God gives man a free will. God does not choose evil; He simply allows man to choose it or not. Perhaps, the question should be "Why does man choose evil?" That question, more correctly, seems to witness against man. God says, "I call heaven and earth to witness against you today, that I have set before you life and death, the blessing and the curse. So choose life in order that you may live, you and your descendants" (Deut. 30:19).

A question that is sometimes asked when bringing someone to a decision for Christ is, "Do I have to make my decision public?" How do you think God feels about that? How would your wife feel if you did not want anyone to know you were married? God says, "Therefore everyone who confesses Me before men, I will also confess him before My Father who is in heaven. But whoever denies Me before men, I will also deny him before My Father who is in heaven" (Matt. 10:32-33).

A somewhat less common question but, nonetheless, asked often enough is, "What about all the inconsistencies and contradictions in the Bible?" That question seems to assume that man is more intelligent than God. You assume that God is wrong. Is it not more rational to assume that man is wrong? God says, "For My thoughts are not your thoughts, nor are your ways My ways . . . For as the heavens are higher than the earth, so are My ways higher than your ways and My thoughts than your thoughts" (Isa. 55:8-9).

Another common question is, "How can I know that there is a God?" You actually have no excuse to not know that there is a God. The Scripture says, "That which is known about God is evident within them; for God made it evident to them. For since the creation of the world His invisible attributes, His eternal power and divine nature, have been clearly seen, being understood through what has been made, so that they are without excuse" (Rom. 1:19-20).

One more question might be something like, "Why do I need the blood of Jesus?" There is no forgiveness "without shedding of blood" (Heb. 9:22); so if it is not Jesus' blood, then it is going to have to be your own. He sheds His blood so that you don't have to shed your own (Rom. 5:8). Perhaps your question should be more of a statement: "I need the blood of Jesus."

When sharing the Gospel with others, it is not uncommon for people to make excuses for not wanting to make a decision about Christ. One popular excuse is "it is too late for me to change now." It is never too late. Actually, the fact that your excuse seems to imply that you would want to change if you could is an indicator that God is drawing you to Himself. Jesus says, "All that the Father gives Me will come to Me, and the one who comes to Me I will certainly not cast out" (John 6:37).

Another excuse is, "God is love. There is no danger of punishment." God is a holy God, Who gives man a free will. If He did not punish ungodliness, then that would make Him a sham and would make man's free will meaningless. In any case, it is not true that love and punishment cannot exist together. It is the exact opposite, and you and I should be very thankful for that. Because God loves us, He punished Himself so that we do not have to be punished. This is why Jesus died on the cross. It is because God is Love, and, thus, there was a very real danger of punishment. The Scripture says, "But God demonstrates His own love toward us, in that while we were yet sinners, Christ died for us" (Rom. 5:8).

Answering questions and responding to excuses is part of sharing the Gospel. The bearer of good news should be able to defend his answers. It has been said that defense wins games. So, go ahead and defend!

MAY 26

WHY YOU CAN'T OUTGIVE GOD

"So this joy of mine has been made full. He must increase, but I must decrease."

John 3:29

God is a Rewarder. "And without faith it is impossible to please *Him*, for he who comes to God must believe that He is and *that* He is a rewarder of those who seek Him" (Heb. 11:6). Are rewards a dead end? Does God reward just for the sake of rewards? Are rewards *God's* end goal and, therefore, our definer of ourselves? Another way to ask, "Are rewards a dead end?" is to ask, "Can faith be increased?"

The apostles said to the LORD, "Increase our faith!" And the LORD said, "If you had faith like a mustard seed, you would say to this mulberry tree, 'Be uprooted and be planted in the sea'; and it would obey you. Which of you, having a slave plowing or tending sheep, will say to him ... "Come immediately and sit down to eat? But will he not say to him, ... 'serve me ... and afterward you may eat and drink'? ... So you too ... say, 'We are unworthy slaves; we have done only that which we ought to have done'" (Luke 17:5-10).

If it is true that, as Hebrews 11:6 claims, faith manifested in seeking God pleases God and if He, in turn, rewards "those who seek Him," then rewards are not an end goal (a dead end) since if faith can increase then it would follow that rewards can increase.

The apostles came to Jesus and entreated, "Increase our faith!" Jesus' answer was interesting. He did not say, "Go and do more good works" or "Psyche yourselves up to put your mind into a hyper-positive confession state." He just said, "Get smaller." Your faith will *increase* when it yields a perspective of yourself that is *smaller* not bigger. Leave it to Jesus to turn the tables upside down. For your faith to increase, you must decrease: "He must increase, but I must decrease" (John 3:30). Increased faith is "mustard seed faith." When your faith is such that it is routed out of an attitude in which you see yourself as being smaller because you see Jesus as being bigger, then you will have increased faith; your tendency to seek the One Who is bigger than you will increase.

And so, Jesus tells a seemingly unconnected story right after He establishes this faith-growing principle of the mustard seed. Of course, it is not unconnected—Jesus is never a random storyteller—it is very connected. A servant is out in a field working. He comes inside only to continue serving his master. What is the servant's attitude? "I have been pulling more weight around here, so I should be first to eat" or "I have done all my work, so I have earned a place at the table"? No! The servant understands himself not by what he has achieved but by who he is, "'We are unworthy slaves; we have done *only* that which we ought to have done'" (Luke 17:10). He sees himself as "little"—not simply to belittle himself but to enlarge his Master. His attitude draws him to his Master and to his Master's requests of him. This is increased faith!

The ironic thing of all this, then, is that the servant is rewarded; he gets to sit down and eat. He worked because he had a correct view of himself. He sees himself as a servant of the Master; he decreases, and the Master increases. He is then rewarded by the Master, since the Master can trust him. The Master knows that the faith of the servant is such that he will not waste any resources given him that will enable him to accomplish his work. So he feeds him, so he can do more work which, of course, this kind of servant will do. The servant will inevitably receive even greater rewards so that he will be able to do even greater service. All of this is due to "increased faith." That is the incredible thing about faith as it relates to rewards. Reward is not an end in itself. It is a beginning!

This is why you cannot outgive God. It is because God calls you to be a steward, not just a servant. He calls you not just "to do" but to do in such a way as "to do again." You do not just "give to get"; you "give to get to get to give." Reward by itself only looks backward. Stewardship looks forward. God is not, most fundamentally, looking for people to reward. He is looking for people to use. He is not just the Owner. He is the skillful and effective Manager.

And so, you cannot outgive God. He gives you more—not simply because He is a Rewarder but because He is a Multiplier. His reward is not simply for you; it is for others who will be blessed because of His multiplication through you. And so, it is "more blessed to give than to receive" (Acts 20:35). The word *blessed* means "happy." Why is it a happier, more joyful thing to give than it is to receive? It is because giving puts you in your right place—the place of stewardship, the place of faith, the place of being used by your Maker in the way and for the purposes for which the Maker made you. This is why "He must increase, but I must decrease" is immediately preceded by, "So this joy of mine has been made full" (John 3:29-30).

Increased faith, increased stewardship, increased usefulness, increased satisfaction, and increased joy—God gives this increasing provision to those "mustard seeds" who are uniquely positioned to receive it. You cannot outgive God because it *is* more blessed for you to give. That giving is the very thing that moves God to give even more. Mustard seeds get the *greater* blessing, just like the weaker get the greater power, the last become first, the blind see, the poor become rich, and the servants become the leaders. This is God's flip-flopped kingdom. This is God's rule, God's dictionary. This is how God chooses to define things. What dictionary do you go by?

MAY 27

BEFORE, WHILE, AND AFTER HAVING A REASON

"So that, just as it is written, 'LET HIM WHO BOASTS, BOAST IN THE LORD.'"

1 Corinthians 1:31

Moses was a great man (Psalm 106:23; Matt. 17:3; Acts 7:22). At the same time, he was the humblest man "on the face of the earth" (Num. 12:3). How does humility mix with greatness? Humility does not seek after greatness; it seeks after the great One. Before having a reason to be proud, it does not seek for a reason. Another way to say this is that humility does not strive to lead; it strives to be led by God. Moses' life was a life full of doing what God told him to do. It was a life of being led. Moses was even led by God to his death (Deut. 32:48-50). "So Moses the servant of the LORD died there in the land of Moab, according to the word of the LORD" (Deut. 34:5).

Humility points a person away from himself in the midst of greatness. While having a reason to be proud, it gives the reason to God. We often want to focus on ourselves when we discuss our triumphs and victories, but humility points us to God. It does not reject praise and thanks from others—that is false humility—it gives it to God instead. Moses continuously pointed to God in the midst of his greatness. He avoided the temptation of giving himself credit for success. He certainly would have been tempted to impress his father-in-law with the amazing feats associated with the exodus. It would not have seemed out of order to hear him say something like, "I slapped those Egyptians with a few plagues and then crossed all my people through a raging sea and provided them with some food that I prayed down from Heaven." Moses' humility would not allow him to say those words. Instead, "Moses told his father-in-law all that the LORD had done to Pharaoh and to the Egyptians for Israel's sake, all the hardship that had befallen them on the journey, and how the LORD had delivered them" (Exod. 18:8).

Joseph exhibited this same kind of humility when he easily could have taken credit but instead pointed back to God. "Pharaoh said to Joseph, 'I have had a dream, but no one can interpret it; and I have heard it said about you, that when you hear a dream you can interpret it.' Joseph then answered Pharaoh, saying, 'It is not in me; God will give Pharaoh a favorable answer'" (Gen. 41:15-16).

Daniel shows this same kind of humility:

> Daniel answered before the king and said, "As for the mystery about which the king has inquired, neither wise men, conjurers, magicians *nor* diviners are able to declare *it* to the king. However, there is a God in heaven who reveals mysteries . . . and He who reveals mysteries has made known to you what will take place. But as for me, this mystery has not been

revealed to me for any wisdom residing in me more than in any *other* living man, but for the purpose of making the interpretation known to the king, and that you may understand the thoughts of your mind" (Dan. 2:27-30).

Humility does not selfishly take advantage of success. In the midst of Moses' success, he was offered an opportunity to become "a nation greater and mightier." However, he was more concerned with God's reputation among "the nations who have heard of thy fame" (Num. 14:12-17). Similarly, Daniel did not try to take advantage of his fame (Dan. 5:17) nor did Nehemiah (Neh. 5:14-15) or Paul (1 Cor. 9:1-15; 2 Thess. 3:8-9). The nature of humility leads people to look to God's fame, honor, reputation, and glory, instead of looking to their own self-interest.

Humility results in being almost oblivious to your importance. After having a reason to be proud, it is unaware of or unconcerned about the reason. Like John the Baptist (John 1:21) and Paul (1 Tim. 1:15), Moses was unconcerned with his own stature. He was unaware that his face was shining after being in God's presence (Exod. 34:29).

Humility is not a lack of esteem or confidence. Humility leads to a high "God-esteem" and "God-confidence" instead of a high "self-esteem" and "self-confidence." Confidence comes from a trust and reliance on God. Esteem comes from obedience to Him and an understanding of Who He is. Like low self-esteem, false humility is a manifestation of pride. It sometimes appears like humility but is actually a prideful response in that it focuses on self. A low self-esteem that only focuses on "I cannot do it" is the result of pride in that it focuses on self instead of God. Even Moses, the humblest man, was lured into a false humility. Moses' low self-esteem revealed his pride in that he focused on his own abilities instead of God's abilities (Exod. 4:10-13) and "the anger of the LORD burned against Moses" (Exod. 4:14).

Humility is the by-product of a full, true, and grand view of God, not an unhealthy view of a miniscule self. Humility, although including it, does not *focus* on saying, "I am nothing." It focuses on saying, "God is great!" It says, "I am something because He is in me." Self-image becomes a "vessel image." It is not so much that self is belittled as it is that God is enlarged. This happens by having the right beatitude. It is the poor in spirit and the meek and humble who get the kingdom of God and inherit the earth (Matt. 5:3,5). "I cannot" leads to "God can." That is the Gospel. That is Good News! "I need; He provides." That is the meaning of "Jesus"—God saves. That is how humility mixes with greatness!

MAY 28

SOMETIMES THE POOR ARE NOT THE POOR

"Do not give what is holy to dogs, and do not throw your pearls before swine."
Matthew 7:6

All people need Jesus. All people are needy and poor. And so, Jesus died for all people. "For God so loved the world, that He gave His only begotten Son, that whoever believes in Him shall not perish, but have eternal life" (John 3:16). God's heart is toward all people as He "is patient toward you, not wishing for any to perish but for all to come to repentance" (2 Peter 3:9).

Nevertheless, salvation is not unconditional. The conditions exist on the side of the receiver, not on the side of the Giver. Each person must receive that which was freely and unconditionally given. Still, many needy people do not receive—not because they are not needy but because they do not see themselves as needy. Is that because Jesus has not given? No, it is because they refuse to recognize their need and refuse to search for and ask for help. God's love is toward "the world" and is given to "whoever" (John 3:16). Jesus' love is not meant to judge anyone (John 3:17). It is meant to save everyone. We judge ourselves when we do not recognize our need for Jesus (John 3:18), our need for the name that means "God saves."

The fact that Jesus—God saves—provides for us is a clear statement of our need for Him. The lesser-known John 3:17-18 is just as important as the well-known John 3:16: "For God did not send the Son into the world to judge the world, but that the world might be saved through Him. He who believes in Him is not judged; he who does not believe has been judged already, because he has not believed in the name of the only begotten Son of God." When needy ones refuse to see who they are, they classify themselves as not needy and, in so doing, judge themselves. The Scripture refers to these self-judged ones as "dogs" and "swine" and asserts that nothing "holy" and no "pearls" can be given to them. The refusal to see your need is the definition of hypocrisy that results in a curse while the act of confession opens the door to blessing.

We avoid judging others by making sure we first look at ourselves. Then we realize that we are needy. Christ died for the needy (those who confess their need). He came to save, not judge. We are not judged, and so, we do not judge. Judgment is reserved for those who are not needy (those who do not confess their need). Those "dogs" and "swine" cannot be offered "holy pearls"—not because they are not needy but because they do not see and confess their need. In their "arrogant blindness" is their judgment. It is self-judgment!

> Do not judge so that you will not be judged. For in the way you judge, you will be judged; and by your standard of measure, it will be measured to you. Why do you look at the speck that is in your brother's eye, but do not notice the log that is in your own eye? Or how can you say to your brother, "Let me take the speck out of your eye," and behold, the log is in your own eye? You hypocrite, first take the log out of your own eye, and then you will see clearly to take the speck out of your brother's eye. Do not give what is holy to dogs, and do not throw your pearls before swine, or they will trample them under their feet, and turn and tear you to pieces. Ask, and it will be given to you; seek, and you will find; knock, and it will be opened to you. For everyone who asks receives, and he who seeks finds, and to him who knocks it will be opened (Matt. 7:1-8).

The people of God are called to help the poor. "Is this not the fast which I choose . . . to divide your bread with the hungry and bring the homeless poor into the house; when you see the naked, to cover him" (Isa. 58:6-7). Ministry to the poor is a complicated endeavor, partly because of the need to define, "Who are the poor?" In a discussion about who is "worthy" to be helped, Jesus instructs His disciples as He sends them out to do ministry, "Whoever does not receive you, nor heed your words, as you go out of that house or that city, shake the dust off your feet" (Matt. 10:14). Should Jesus' disciples respond to all people? How are truly needy people pictured here? How can we apply the principles of this verse to engaging in ministry to the poor? Should we continue to help a "poor" person if he does not want to be helped? Should we continue to help a poor person if he does not want to help himself? Who are the poor?

The biblical mandate given to God's people to participate in ministry to the poor is informed by three guiding principles used to define who are the needy:

1. Those who ask for and receive help (an alcoholic who is unwilling to admit he is an alcoholic is not needy; a beggar who is offered bread but will only accept money is not needy).To be needy, you must confess you are needy.

2. Those who cooperate with the help offered to them in such a way as to help themselves as well (a beggar who is offered a job but refuses to take it is not needy).

3. Those who are put before you in some way. Since poverty never ends (Matt. 26:11), it is understood that you will not help all the needy. There is a "led by the Spirit" component in ministry to the poor that may be discerned by what is put before you.

Sometimes, the poor are not the poor. Sometimes those who "see" are "blind" (John 9:39). No matter how blind someone is, you cannot help that person to see if he insists that he already sees. The needy are those who recognize and confess their need and ask for help. The people of God are called to help ones such as these.

MAY 29

BE CAREFUL WITH YOUR WORDS

"With the fruit of a man's mouth his stomach will be satisfied; he will be satisfied with the product of his lips. Death and life are in the power of the tongue, and those who love it will eat its fruit."
Proverbs 18:20-21

Wisdom and speech are necessarily linked together. Wisdom is to speech what a computer program is to a word-processed document. A proverb, by its very nature, is a practical expression of life. The book of Proverbs is a book of wisdom and, thus, full of practical suggestions for how to use your words. Proverbs teaches that wisdom will affect what you say and how you say it. A wise man understands that he is responsible for the words he says.

Speech is a significant aspect of life; it is significant in creation. We come from the one great speaker who *spoke* the world into being (Gen. 1:3, 6, 9, 11, 14, 20, 24). God *spoke* to man as soon as He made him (Gen. 1:28) and has never stopped speaking to him (2 Peter 1:21). Speech is significant in redemption. God speaks to us in His Son (Heb. 1:2). His Son is the **"Word"** of God (John 1:1).

Speech is significant in the book of Proverbs. In Proverbs 6:16-19, there is a list of seven things that are abominations to the Lord. This list represents the things that God hates! Three of the seven have to do with speech: a lying tongue, a false witness who utters lies, one who spreads strife among brothers. "There are six things which the LORD hates, yes, seven which are an abomination to Him: haughty eyes, a lying tongue, and hands that shed innocent blood, a heart that devises wicked plans, feet that run rapidly to evil, a false witness who utters lies, and one who spreads strife among brothers" (Prov. 6:16-19).

The power of the tongue is often underestimated. The use of too many words and a lack of restraint is an indicator of a lack of wisdom. The tongue must be used very carefully, for "death and life are in the power of the tongue" (Prov. 18:21). It can result in pain, or it can bring healing. "There is one who speaks rashly like the thrusts of a sword, but the tongue of the wise brings healing" (Prov. 12:18).

The release of words can be compared to a scorching fire that can separate intimate friends. "A worthless man digs up evil, while his words are like scorching fire. A perverse man spreads strife, and a slanderer separates intimate friends" (Prov. 16:27-28). Relationships suffer. "With *his* mouth the godless man destroys his neighbor" (Prov. 11:9).

At the same time, words can bring life and build relationships. They can feed others instead of starving them. "The lips of the righteous feed many" (Prov. 10:21). Good fruit can grow from wise words. "A man will be satisfied with good by the fruit of his words" (Prov. 12:14).

James tells us that "the tongue is a fire" (James 3:6). The wise man is careful with the use of his tongue. Perhaps, the most important thing to remember with respect to your words is to "think before you speak." "But everyone must be quick to hear, slow to speak" (James 1:19). The power of words does not always manifest itself in the most obvious way. We must be very careful. The influence of words can be very subtle. "With her many persuasions she entices him; with her flattering lips she seduces him" (Prov. 7:21). Similarly, "a man who flatters his neighbor is spreading a net for his steps" (Prov. 29:5). Words can cause us to make bad decisions and desire wrong things.

There is no question. Words are powerful. The question is, "What words will I use and how will I use them?" It is a question of life and death, since "death and life are in the power of the tongue" (Prov. 18:21). Be careful!

MAY 30

COME BEFORE GOD WITH AN HONEST HEART

*"When you pray, you are not to be like the hypocrites; for they love to stand and pray in the synagogues and on the street corners so that they may be seen by men. Truly I say to you, they have their reward in full. But you, when you pray, go into your inner room, close your door and pray to your Father who is in secret, and your Father who sees **what is done** in secret will reward you."*

Matthew 6:5-6

We say to God what He first said to us. Prayer is our response to what God has first said. God speaks through the Law and through the Prophets. The psalmist then responds to what God has said. In the Psalms, prayer does not necessitate being in the "proper state of mind." It is, instead, to engage with God in whatever state of mind you find yourself. The psalmist goes before God in both joy—"O come, let us sing for joy to the LORD, let us shout joyfully to the rock of our salvation. Let us come before His presence with thanksgiving, let us shout joyfully to Him with psalms" (Psalm 95:1-2)—and frustration

> O LORD, the God of my salvation, I have cried out by day and in the night before You. Let my prayer come before You; incline Your ear to my cry! For my soul has had enough troubles, and my life has drawn near to Sheol. I am reckoned among those who go down to the pit; I have become like a man without strength, forsaken among the dead, like the slain who lie in the grave, whom You remember no more, and they are cut off from Your hand. You have put me in the lowest pit, in dark places, in the depths. Your wrath has rested upon me, and You have afflicted me with all Your waves (Psalm 88:1-7).

Since God looks at the heart (1 Sam. 16:7), we need to offer heartfelt prayers. We must be honest with God. He wants our hearts, not our masks. Simply because we are being honest with God does not mean that we are accusing God. There is a difference between asking God honest questions and questioning God's integrity or holiness. When we pray with frustration or disappointment, we must always remember that God is never wrong. We must avoid Job's mistake.

Job was not wrong to speak openly with God or even to lament about his situation. He was wrong—and God became very angry with him—because in his frustration and groaning, he implied that it was God Who was wrong. In our honesty, we must keep a humble attitude before God that displays trust in Him and not greed, pride, or selfishness.

Building on the theme of offering heartfelt prayers, we should note that petition in the Bible is much more personal and involved than what might be more common generic forms of petition. As in Exodus 32, when Moses entreats the Lord in a sort of "case building" fashion, so, too, God would have us to not simply ask but to ask within a real and dynamic relationship. As with Moses, this might include such conversation as "debate" (done with respect, not rebellion) or bargaining (not to try to deceive selfishly, but to facilitate change selflessly). Additionally, it might include arbitrating (not to avoid, but to move toward God's will) or convincing (not to avoid God's best interests, but to realize them).

> The LORD said to Moses, "I have seen this people, and behold, they are an obstinate people. Now then let Me alone, that My anger may burn against them and that I may destroy them; and I will make of you a great nation." Then Moses entreated the LORD his God, and said, "O LORD, why does Your anger burn against Your people whom You have brought out from the land of Egypt with great power and with a mighty hand? Why should the Egyptians speak, saying, 'With evil *intent* He brought them out to kill them in the mountains and to destroy them from the face of the earth'? Turn from Your burning anger and change Your mind about *doing* harm to Your people. Remember Abraham, Isaac, and Israel, Your servants to whom You swore by Yourself, and said to them, 'I will multiply your descendants as the stars of the heavens, and all this land of which I have spoken I will give to your descendants, and they shall inherit it forever'" (Exod. 32:9-13).

There are three platforms from which Moses appeals to God: God's people, the world, and the Word. In each case, Moses is asking, not commanding. He comes before God in honesty; he is open and direct. He is, however, a straightforward servant before God and not a straightforward king. Moses appeals to God on behalf of His people as he asks Him to bless them. He then appeals on the basis of showing Himself rightly to the world. Finally, he appeals on the basis of the promises of God's Word. In each case, it is seen that the glory of God is the main issue and Moses' sincere motivation.

Honesty in prayer can expand our prayer lives. When we become more comfortable with God in the sense of being more able to come before God just as we are, we grow in relationship with Him. Petition may develop into lament, and thanksgiving may grow into praise and magnification. The point is that God is not so much interested in your many words (Matt. 6:7) as He is interested in your honest heart!

MAY 31

WHAT DOES IT MEAN THAT THE LAW IS FULFILLED?

> "Do not think that I came to abolish the Law or the Prophets; I did not come to abolish but to fulfill. For truly I say to you, until heaven and earth pass away, not the smallest letter or stroke shall pass from the Law until all is accomplished. Whoever then annuls one of the least of these commandments, and teaches others to **do** the same, shall be called least in the kingdom of heaven; but whoever keeps and teaches them, he shall be called great in the kingdom of heaven."
>
> Matthew 5:17-19

It stands as a grave theological error to think that the New Testament does away with the Old Testament or that Jesus does away with the Law. There is nothing further from the truth. Jesus does not negate or dissolve the Law. He substantiates and fulfills it. The New Testament does not reject or put an end to the Old Testament. It clarifies and continues it. The new covenant is not a *different* covenant. It is a *better* covenant (Heb. 7:22; 8:6) in that it continues, clarifies, and completes the old covenant. The two covenants are in no way mutually exclusive. They are inextricably linked, even as a less clear revelation of something is necessarily wed to a clearer revelation of the same thing.

Jesus alludes to this theological truth when He says to His disciples, "Do not think that I came to abolish the Law or the Prophets; I did not come to abolish but to fulfill" (Matt. 5:17). What does Jesus mean when He uses the word "fulfill"? The conjunction "but" establishes a direct contrast between the two infinitives, "to abolish" and "to fulfill." Thus, the definition of "fulfill" must be determined according to the definition of "abolish." The term "abolish" (*katalusai*) conveys the sense of dissolving or dismantling. It includes the idea of the destruction of something by separating it into pieces. It is the action of annulling, making invalid, or repealing. Now, we can better define "fulfill" (*plarosai*). It is to confirm, hold up, or validate.

Jesus fulfills the Law in the sense of confirming it, establishing it as valid, and restoring it to its originally intended full measure. The revelation in the Old Testament finds its validation and actual embodiment in Christ. "For the Law was given through Moses; grace and truth were realized through Jesus Christ" (John 1:17). This is not to say that the Law and "grace and truth" are two separate and entirely different things. It is to say that one is the realization of the other. Jesus is the perfect Law; He is everything the Law was always meant to be. The Law is not rejected by Christ. It is promoted.

The Law does not save us, but it does point us to salvation. In Christ, the Law exists and is accomplished. The application of this dynamic between Law and grace is that followers of Christ can take part in His accomplishment both for salvation and sanctification. We are saved by the One Who lived out the Law perfectly. We satisfy the requirements of the Law perfectly in Him as He becomes our Representative and Substitute. What we could not do with the Law, He did. In addition, we now live out the Law in our own lives—not because it saves us but because Christ lives in us (Gal. 2:20) and lives the Law through us. In the language of James, "Faith without works is dead" (James 2:26).

What does it mean that the Law is fulfilled? The great Methodist evangelist, John Wesley, understood Jesus' words regarding the Law in Matthew 5:17 to mean, "I have come to establish it in its fullness, in spite of all the changes of men. I have come to declare the truth and full importance of every part of it. I will show its length and breadth, and entire extent."[9] Christians must not understand themselves as having license to be law breakers or "law ignorers" (Rom. 6:1-7). They should understand themselves as being "law-doers!" "Do we then nullify the Law through faith? May it never be! On the contrary, we establish the Law" (Rom. 3:31).

June

JUNE 1

ONE AND DONE

"But seek first His kingdom."

Matthew 6:33

In the late 1960s, a band called Three Dog Night came out with a song titled, "One Is the Loneliest Number." Whether or not the number one is lonely, it is most definitely *only*. One sin condemns you. That is the *onlyness* of your problem. One way saves you. That is the *onlyness* of your solution. One worship consumes you. That is the *onlyness* of your focus.

You do not have a problem only if you have done more bad things than good things. You have a problem if you have done only one bad thing. The onlyness of your problem is that just one sin makes you unclean before God and separates you from Him. God says, "Whoever has sinned against me I will blot out of my book" (Exod. 32:33). It does not matter how many good things you have done. They cannot cancel out even one bad thing. The one bad thing is so disastrous because it alone separates you from God. The "onlyness of your problem" is devastating and seems insurmountable. "But your iniquities have made a separation between you and God, and your sins have hidden *His* face from you, so that He does not hear" (Isa. 59:2). No one is perfect. Everyone has done something wrong. You are not alone in the onlyness of your problem. In fact, everyone is in the same onlyness boat, "for all have sinned and fall short of the glory of God" (Rom. 3:23).

The exhaustive nature of man's problem necessitates the exhaustive nature of man's solution. "For God so loved the world, that He gave His only begotten Son, that whoever believes in Him shall not perish, but have eternal life" (John 3:16). Jesus died for *all* because "all have sinned" (Rom. 3:23). Just as only one sin condemns you, only one way saves you. Just as there is the onlyness of your problem, there is the onlyness of your solution. Jesus is the only Way. "I am the way, and the truth, and the life; no one comes to the Father but through Me" (John 14:6). Jesus is the "Good News;" He is the Gospel. There are not multiple gospels. There is only one Gospel, one solution. "I am amazed that you are so quickly deserting Him who called you by the grace of Christ, for a different gospel; which is *really* not another; only there are some who are disturbing you and want to distort the gospel of Christ. But even if we, or an angel from heaven, should preach to you a gospel contrary to what we have preached to you, he is to be accursed!" (Gal. 1:6-8).

It is this singular Gospel that saves you. "Now I make known to you, brethren, the gospel which I preached to you, which also you received, in which also you stand, by which also you are saved" (1 Cor. 15:1-2). The onlyness of your salvation is wrapped up in Jesus and His Gospel: "For whoever wishes to save his life will lose it, but whoever loses his life for My sake and the gospel's will save it" (Mark 8:35).

A "One worship" consumes those who are saved. The onlyness of their focus puts God first in all things. Only one can be first. "No servant can serve two masters" (Luke 16:13). By definition, there can only be one Lord in your life. There can only be one *final* authority. What consumes you? The "buck stops" where? God calls you to "seek first His kingdom and His righteousness" (Matt. 6:33). The idea of "first" here does not so much picture a "pecking order" type of dynamic as it depicts a singular response to all situations. You are to seek God's rule in everything you do and in all areas of your life. Then the rest of "these things will be added to you." The "rest of these things" are not in second, third, and fourth place. They are shaped by that which is in first place. There is no "top ten." There is only number one!

The exhaustive nature of your problem (all have fallen short) necessitates the exhaustive nature of your solution (Jesus is the only way for all) which results in the exhaustive nature of your response (give all of yourself to Him). Since you can do nothing without Him (John 15:5), you need to seek Him "in all your ways" (Prov. 3:6).

Jesus died for *all* because *all* sinned, so *all* is given to Him. Just as only one sin condemns you, only one way saves you; and only one worship consumes you. Just as there is the onlyness of your problem, there is the onlyness of your solution and the onlyness of your focus. Any other focus is useless. It is a waste. Any other building materials just do not count!

> For no man can lay a foundation other than the one which is laid, which is Jesus Christ. Now if any man builds on the foundation with gold, silver, precious stones, wood, hay, straw, each man's work will become evident; for the day will show it because it is *to be* revealed with fire, and the fire itself will test the quality of each man's work. If any man's work which he has built on it remains, he will receive a reward. If any man's work is burned up, he will suffer loss; but he himself will be saved, yet so as through fire (1 Cor. 3:11-15).

JUNE 2

HOLY DISSATISFACTION, BATMAN

"For we know that the whole creation groans and suffers the pains of childbirth together until now. And not only this, but also we ourselves . . . groan within ourselves."

Romans 8:22-23

God is in the business of making things right again. This implies that things were once right but are now wrong. God knows all about this. He originally made everything to work perfectly to work according to His purpose and plan. With His creation, He was satisfied. "God made the beasts of the earth after their kind, and the cattle after their kind, and everything that creeps on the ground after its kind; and God saw that it was good" (Gen. 1:25). After He made man, He was very satisfied. "God created man in His own image, in the image of God He created him; male and female He created them . . . God saw all that He had made, and behold, it was very good" (Gen. 1:27, 31).

Sadly, things did not stay "very good." Adam and Eve sinned and turned everything upside down. Nevertheless, that holy dissatisfaction did not turn Him away from man. It resulted in God going *to* man. "Then the LORD God called to the man, and said to him, 'Where are you?'" (Gen. 3:9). That is the thing about "holy" dissatisfaction. It does not give up. It moves forward. God's "dissatisfaction" with that which has been corrupted moves Him forward in making things uncorrupted. He does it for His glory. God's "holy dissatisfaction" has nothing to do with an emotional frustration. God, of course, cannot give up; and He cannot, in any way, be restricted or limited. Holy dissatisfaction has to do with His holiness and righteousness that cannot, and will not, allow that which is not righteous to stay "un-right." God is not satisfied with not being glorified because it is not right. It is not how He made everything, and it is not consistent with what is real. Things have to change.

We need to be changed. We must have a holy dissatisfaction. Change hurts. So there is a holy discomfort that comes along with our holy dissatisfaction. Change is edgy. So there is a holy disturbance that comes along with a holy dissatisfaction. Change is challenging. So there is a holy death to self that comes along with a holy dissatisfaction. Change is crucial. So there is a holy yearning and anticipation that comes along with a holy dissatisfaction.

For the creation was subjected to futility, not willingly, but because of Him who subjected it, in hope that the creation itself also will be set free from its slavery to corruption into the freedom of the glory of the children of God. For we know that the whole creation groans and suffers the pains of childbirth together until now. And not only this, but also we ourselves, having the first fruits of the Spirit, even we ourselves groan within ourselves, waiting eagerly for *our* adoption as sons, the redemption of our body. For in hope we have been saved, but hope that is seen is not hope; for who hopes for what he *already* sees? But if we hope for what we do not see, with perseverance we wait eagerly for it (Rom. 8:20-25).

Living out a Christian life in a fallen world means we must be content to be discontent. We must carry a holy discontent. It is that discontentment that produces greater contentment; discontentment with "you in you" leads to more of Jesus in you. When you take up your cross, you follow Him (Matt. 16:24). When you mourn, you are comforted (Matt. 5:4). Little by little, our holy dissatisfaction transforms us now.

Until He comes and makes everything perfectly right again, we must be wholly and holy dissatisfied. Here is our satisfaction. He is coming! "'Yes, I am coming quickly.' Amen. Come, Lord Jesus" (Rev. 22:20). Maranatha!

JUNE 3

WHO DO YOU WORK FOR?

"Whatever you do, do your work heartily, as for the Lord rather than for men, knowing that from the Lord you will receive the reward of the inheritance. It is the Lord Christ whom you serve."
Colossians 3:23-24

If it is true that "you get what you pay for," it is even truer that "to whom you serve is from whom you can expect your reward."

Beware of practicing your righteousness before men to be noticed by them; otherwise you have no reward with your Father who is in heaven. So when you give to the poor, do not sound a trumpet before you, as the hypocrites do in the synagogues and in the streets, so that they may be honored by men. Truly I say to you, they have their reward in full. But when you give to the poor, do not let your left hand know what your right hand is doing, so that your giving will be in secret; and your Father who sees *what is done* in secret will reward you. When you pray, you are not to be like the hypocrites; for they love to stand and pray in the synagogues and on the street corners so that they may be seen by men. Truly I say to you, they have their reward in full. But you, when you pray, go into your inner room, close your door and pray to your Father who is in secret, and your Father who sees *what is done* in secret will reward you (Matt. 6:1-6).

If you serve self, then self will reward you. If you serve man, then man will reward you. If you serve God, then God will reward you. Do everything, therefore, as unto God. "Slaves, in all things obey those who are your masters on earth, not with external service, as those who *merely* please men, but with sincerity of heart, fearing the Lord. Whatever you do, do your work heartily, as for the Lord rather than for men, knowing that from the Lord you will receive the reward of the inheritance. It is the Lord Christ whom you serve" (Col. 3:22-24).

To stay focused on serving God and not man, you must get in the habit of having an eternal mindset and not settle for a temporal mindset. "Set your mind on the things above, not on the things that are on earth" (Col. 3:2). In order to do this, "we look not at the things which are seen, but at the things which are not seen; for the things which are seen are temporal, but the things which are not seen are eternal" (2 Cor. 4:18).

In the context of various descriptions of "eternal living," the Scriptures instruct us to practice self-control (1 Cor. 9:25), as well as self-denial (1 Cor. 9:27), and to discipline ourselves for the purpose of godliness (1 Tim. 4:7-8). We are called into relationship with God. To know God is to practice eternal living (John 17:3). This relationship is not to be robotic and superficial but intimate and profound (Matt. 6:1, 4, 6, 18).

Futility is nowhere to be found in eternal living. Are you going for what counts? Will what you did today last throughout eternity? Or was it just a waste of time? At the Milan Cathedral, there are three huge doorways. Over the door on the right are the words, "All that pleases is but for a moment." Over the door on the left are the words, "All that troubles is but for a moment." Over the middle door are the words, "Nothing is important save that which is eternal." To some degree, you determine your situation in eternity today. Are you like a dog running after a train? Even if he catches it, what is he going to do with it? Does your life have purpose? Go for what counts!

> Ho! Everyone who thirsts, come to the waters; and you who have no money come, buy and eat. Come, buy wine and milk without money and without cost. Why do you spend money for what is not bread, and your wages for what does not satisfy? Listen carefully to Me, and eat what is good, and delight yourself in abundance. Incline your ear and come to Me. Listen, that you may live; and I will make an everlasting covenant with you, *according* to the faithful mercies shown to David (Isa. 55:1-3).

JUNE 4

WHAT IS YOUR "WHO SAYS?"

"My kingdom is not of this world."

John 18:36

What is your worldview? A practical way to answer this question is to ask another question: "What is your 'Who says?'" Your worldview is what you think is most real. It is the underlying authority structure that dictates what you believe, what you value, and what you do. It is what you perceive to be the ultimate authority—from what or whom everything else comes and answers to. It is what is first—what stands before and above all else. The English word "religion" comes from a Latin word that means "to tie back." Your religion or worldview is determined by what you think everything is tied back to. It is your final authority or your, "Who says." It is an issue of authority, allegiance, and subordination. If it is your ultimate authority, then it follows that it requires your undivided allegiance and places you in absolute subordination.

A very young child usually has a "Mommy and Daddy" worldview. When asked, "Why did you do that?," little Johnny may simply respond, "Because Mommy said so!" Mommy is the ultimate authority. She is what everything goes back to. There are many worldviews because there are many perceived ultimate authorities. A person who has a biblical worldview sees reality through the lens of the Bible. Everything is tied back to the Word of God.

You do not do things in a vacuum. Why did you steal that car? "There was no reason. It just happened." This response is, of course, ludicrous. Actions are rooted in something. You do what you consider to be good or desirable. What is good comes from what you think is true. What you think is true comes from what you deem to be authoritative. Your worldview births your beliefs, and your beliefs produce your values, which in turn result in your actions. You believe that Jesus is your Savior because the Bible says so. Since you believe that Jesus is your Savior, then you value His ability to meet your needs. Since you value His ability to meet your needs, then you pray and ask Him to meet your needs. Someone may ask, "Why do you pray?" Your answer is, "The Bible directs me to pray." You have a biblical worldview. Your "Who says?" is the Bible.

Worldview produces conflict. The tension comes from the idea of an "ultimate or final" authority. There can only be one "final" voice. Like the sign on President Truman's desk "THE BUCK STOPS HERE," final authority, by definition, has to stop and start somewhere. You cannot play for two teams at the same time, for you will either make one win and the other lose, or you will make one lose and the other win. Jesus said, "'No one can serve two masters; for either he will hate the one and love the other, or he will be devoted to one and despise the other. You cannot serve God and wealth'" (Matt. 6:24). The idea of Lordship is a very "optionless" concept. If there are viable options that can take the place of the One Who is said to be "Lord," then the use of the term "Lord" makes no sense; an "optional Lord" is no Lord at all. Since there can only be one "ultimate," then there is necessarily going to be tension. The conflict comes in the competition. Worldviews compete for your allegiance. Everybody wants to have the final say.

Does this mean that worldviews do not rub shoulders with each other? Jesus said, "My kingdom is not of this world" (John 18:36). He also said those in His kingdom are still in the world, even though they are not of the world (John 17:11). Those who live in the kingdom or "rule of God" cannot also live in the kingdoms of this world at the same time and in the same way. They can only live under one *final* rule.

Nevertheless, they still interact with the kingdoms of this world. The kingdom of God influences the kingdoms of this world while not allowing those kingdoms to influence it. After all, it is the *final* authority. The kingdom of God is the salt and light of the world (Matt. 5:13-14). It is the influencer, not the influenced. If the kingdom of God follower jumps ship and makes another kingdom his final authority, then he becomes ineffective; the salt becomes tasteless. "You are the salt of the earth; but if the salt has become tasteless, how can it be made salty *again*? It is no longer good for anything, except to be thrown out and trampled under foot by men" (Matt. 5:13).

What is your worldview? What kingdom do you live in? Who is your king? Do you have a biblical worldview? Is the Bible the underlying authority structure that dictates what you believe, what you value, and what you do? What is your "Who says?"

JUNE 5

IT'S A CULTURAL THING

"...I have become all things to all men, so that I may by all means save some."
1 Corinthians 9:22

Culture is the way a group of people organize their world. It includes the beliefs, values, traditions, and institutions that bind people together and result in a common identity. A culture has unwritten and unspoken rules regarding how people interact with each other. These rules cover a variety of different aspects of a society including language, religion, politics, customs, aesthetics, economy, geography, celebrations, community, communication, education, and history. Especially if you are a missionary, you must be a student of culture. You must understand the dynamics and importance of culture and cross-cultural communication.

Identification with the people you are trying to reach is essential. Jesus is our Model for identifying with people. "Therefore, He had to be made like His brethren in all things, so that He might become a merciful and faithful high priest in things pertaining to God, to make propitiation for the sins of the people. For since He Himself was tempted in that which He has suffered, He is able to come to the aid of those who are tempted" (Heb. 2:17-18).

Identification results in compassion and understanding for the people you are ministering to "for we do not have a high priest who cannot sympathize with our weaknesses, but One who has been tempted in all things as we are, yet without sin" (Heb. 4:15). The result of compassion and understanding is friendship and relationship. "Therefore let us draw near with confidence to the throne of grace, so that we may receive mercy and find grace to help in time of need" (Heb. 4:16).

There tend to be two extreme viewpoints with respect to how to minister in different cultures. First, there is ethnocentrism or cultural superiority. The missionary believes that his culture is superior to the culture of the people he is going to. The result can be a misguided focus on converting people to his own culture instead of converting people to Christ. Second, there is cultural rejection. In order to become like the people, the missionary rejects who he is and tries to live exactly like those he is ministering to. This extreme can result in engaging in sinful activities, or it can cause internal conflict because you cannot deny who you are by pretending to be someone else.

Jesus represents a balanced Model of identification. He identified fully with man. He became one of us. However, this did not mean that He rejected Who He was. He did not forfeit His deity. "Have this attitude in yourselves which was also in Christ Jesus, who, although He existed in the form of God, did not regard equality with God a thing to be grasped, but emptied Himself, taking the form of a bond-servant, *and* being made in the likeness of men" (Phil. 2:5-7).

The goal of identification is not to mimic all the customs, beliefs, and values of another culture. Imitating certain aspects of a culture can be a method of ministry, but it should not be the goal. The goal is to be effective in communication within another culture so that the Gospel message can be given and received.

> For though I am free from all *men*, I have made myself a slave to all, so that I may win more. To the Jews I became as a Jew, so that I might win Jews; to those who are under the Law, as under the Law though not being myself under the Law, so that I might win those who are under the Law; to those who are without law, as without law, though not being without the law of God but under the law of Christ, so that I might win those who are without law. To the weak I became weak, that I might win the weak; I have become all things to all men, so that I may by all means save some (1 Cor. 9:19-22).

It is Jesus Himself Who gives His followers an incarnational Model for ministry—a model that seeks to identify with those you are ministering to. Like Jesus, we must walk the "all things to all men" versus the "not becoming like all men" tightrope. In reaching out to a fallen world, we must get close enough to reach it while staying far enough away to not allow it to reach us. Even as God, in His nature, is both far (transcendent) and near (immanent), we in our ministry must practice separation and compassion. It is a cultural thing!

JUNE 6

GOD: THE SOURCE AND OBJECT OF FAITH

"Yet, with respect to the promise of God, he did not waver in unbelief but grew strong in faith, giving glory to God, and being fully assured that what God had promised, He was able also to perform. Therefore IT WAS ALSO CREDITED TO HIM AS RIGHTEOUSNESS. Now not for his sake only was it written that it was credited to him, but for our sake also, to whom it will be credited, as those who believe in Him who raised Jesus our Lord from the dead."

Romans 4:20-24

It is impossible to please God without faith (Heb. 11:6). Faith is life (John 17:3). Not all faith leads to life, however. There is a rare, powerful faith; and there is a common, impotent "faith." "Enter through the narrow gate; for the gate is wide and the way is broad that leads to destruction, and there are many who enter through it. For the gate is small and the way is narrow that leads to life, and there are few who find it" (Matt. 7:13-14).

There is a permanent, saving faith (Rom. 10:9-10). There is also a temporary faith: "Those on the rocky *soil are* those who, when they hear, receive the word with joy; and these have no *firm* root; they believe for a while, and in time of temptation fall away" (Luke 8:13). There is a non-acting, intellectual faith that is useless: "But someone may well say, 'You have faith and I have works; show me your faith without the works, and I will show you my faith by my works.' You believe that God is one. You do well; the demons also believe, and shudder. But are you willing to recognize, you foolish fellow, that faith without works is useless?" (James 2:18-20).

God is both the Source of faith (Eph. 2:8) and its object. We are not called to have faith in our faith. We are called to have faith in God. Jesus comforted His disciples by directing them to "believe in God, believe also in Me" (John 14:1). Faith is life; more specifically, faith in Jesus is life. "But these have been written so that you may believe that Jesus is the Christ, the Son of God; and that believing you may have life in His name" (John 20:31).

The Word of God is both the source of faith (John 20:30-31) and its object. Jesus declared that there should be faith in the writings of Moses (the Law). "For if you believed Moses, you would believe Me, for he wrote about Me. But if you do not believe his writings, how will you believe My words?" (John 5:46-47). There should be faith in the writings of the Prophets (Acts 26:27). We are also called to "repent and believe in the gospel" (Mark 1:15). Our faith is in God, His Word, and His promises (Rom. 4:20-21).

Where does faith come from? "For by grace you have been saved through faith; and that not of yourselves, it is the gift of God" (Eph. 2:8). Faith comes from God. We are built up in faith as we study the Word of God. "Therefore many other signs Jesus also performed in the presence of the disciples, which are not written in this book; but these have been written so that you may believe that Jesus is the Christ, the Son of God; and that believing you may have life in His name" (John 20:30-31). Similarly, faith comes from the preaching of the Word (John 17:20). Peter explained, "that by my mouth the Gentiles would hear the word of the gospel and believe" (Acts 15:7).

It is faith that brings life to an otherwise lifeless world. Jesus' disciples are mandated to make faith available by preaching the Word of God. "So faith *comes* from hearing, and hearing by the word of Christ" (Rom. 10:17). All Christians are "beautiful sent ones." How else could lifelessness be awakened? "How then will they call on Him in whom they have not believed? How will they believe in Him whom they have not heard? And how will they hear without a preacher? How will they preach unless they are sent? Just as it is written, 'HOW BEAUTIFUL ARE THE FEET OF THOSE WHO BRING GOOD NEWS OF GOOD THINGS!'" (Rom. 10:14-15).

JUNE 7

EXAMINING THE SCRIPTURES

"Now these were more noble-minded than those in Thessalonica, for they received the word with great eagerness, examining the Scriptures daily to see whether these things were so."

Acts 17:11

Biblical hermeneutics is the methodology of interpretation of the biblical text. How should we interpret the Word of God rightly? Should we view interpretation as something we do through our own lenses or through the lenses of the pages of Scripture?

The study of the Bible necessarily allows for both objectivism in which meaning is derived from the object or that which is being studied and subjectivism in which meaning is derived from the subject or the one who is doing the studying. Certainly, we should strive toward an inductive approach to the Scriptures and insist on being objective. Let the text say what the text says. At the same time, we should not negate the impact our own life experiences, mental tendencies, and motivational gifts bring to the text. Allow yourself—the subject involved in the hermeneutical process—to apply what the text says to your own life.

God is a "Unity in diversity." He is a Trinity. The Church is His body. It also is a "unity in diversity." "But now there are many members, but one body" (1 Cor. 12:20). These members are unified but different. "All are not teachers, are they?" (1 Cor. 12:29). Truth is truth. There is the same truth in the Word of God for the teacher as there is for the evangelist. However, the teacher may tend to apply that truth in a different way than the evangelist. In that sense, there is room for an objective and subjective hermeneutic.

The danger of "hyper-subjectivism" is obvious. The meaning of Scripture is not whatever you make it to be. The Bible is not true because you make it true with your own interpretation. It is true because of what it is. It is the Word of God. You cannot make it say what it means simply because you say it. No, it means what it says. This is the process of interpretation—to find what the Scripture means to say so that we can understand what it means and proclaim what it says. The balanced perspective of hermeneutics is that any given truth can be multifaceted in its purpose, use, or application but not in its content and Spirit.

Even as "hyper-subjectivism" and its postmodern tendencies lead to the errors of relativism, "hyper-objectivism" leads to dogmatism, an institutionalized rejection of diversity. The truth of Scripture can be applied in different ways. It will be applied differently by different people who come from different backgrounds and walk in different directions. A Bible interpreter in a materialistic culture might interpret Acts 4:12 in terms of the need to understand that your money cannot save you: "And there is salvation in no one else; for there is no other name under heaven that has been given among men by which we must be saved." —Whereas a Bible interpreter in an animistic culture might interpret that same verse in terms of the need to understand that a familiar spirit cannot save you. Both interpreters come to the same conclusion—that salvation is in Christ alone—with respect to the meaning of the Scripture (objective hermeneutics) while applying that truth in different ways (subjective hermeneutics).

The "one meaning and one intention" hermeneutic must be taken with a grain of salt; it must be insisted on, yet understood properly. It is true to say that we should search for the single meaning intended by the author. However, we need to understand that the "single" meaning can be applied in various ways that remain consistent with that single intention. A one-dimensional meaning hermeneutic does not deny a multi-dimensional application hermeneutic. By necessity, your interpretation of the Scripture is both objective and subjective.

JUNE 8

THE GIFTS OF THE SPIRIT

"And God, who knows the heart, testified to them giving them the Holy Spirit, just as He also did to us."
Acts 15:8

It is clear that the gifts listed in 1 Corinthians 12:8-10 are specifically gifts of the Holy Spirit. Paul specifies that he is writing about *pneumatikos* or "spiritual gifts." He then connects the idea of the gifts to the Holy Spirit and emphasizes that the Source of the gifts is the Holy Spirit (1 Cor. 12:1, 4, 11). Interestingly, Paul seems to refer to three different sets of gifts in 1 Corinthians 12:4-6. One set is linked to the Holy Spirit; another set is linked to the Lord Jesus; and a third set is linked to God the Father. There are three separate lists of gifts in the New Testament, and each is connected to one of the members of the Trinity (1 Cor. 12:1-11; Eph. 4:7-12; Rom. 12:3-8). It is the gifts found in 1 Corinthians 12:8-10 that are most directly linked to the Holy Spirit.

Why is Paul writing to the Corinthians about these spiritual gifts? It is important to realize that Paul was writing to the Corinthians about what they had already experienced. The Corinthian church had no lack of pneumatic (Holy Spirit-led) expression. The gifts of the Holy Spirit were in operation in abundance because the gift of the Holy Spirit had been poured out on them (1 Cor. 1:5-7; Acts 15:8). It is important to understand that an abundance of spiritual gifts implies that there is an abundance of the Spirit Himself. The two are inextricably linked. "You will be baptized with the Holy Spirit" (Acts 1:5) is linked to "you are not lacking in any gift" (1 Cor. 1:7). So, too, "distributing to each one individually just as He wills" is linked to "we were all made to drink of one Spirit" (1 Cor. 12:11, 13). The gifts of the Spirit are manifested in the context of the outpouring or baptism of the Spirit.

The Corinthians were very experienced in the gifts of the Spirit, yet they still needed instruction. In this sense, they were "unaware" (1 Cor. 12:1); they lacked understanding. Thus, they needed to learn how to allow the gifts to operate in an orderly and appropriate way. And so, Paul exhorts them, "Therefore, my brethren, desire earnestly to prophesy, and do not forbid to speak in tongues. But all things must be done properly and in an orderly manner" (1 Cor. 14:39-40).

Experience does not necessarily translate over to expertise. The Corinthians were not experts, but they were experienced. They did not need an orientation, but they did need guidance. Nevertheless, inasmuch as experience is the best teacher, the Corinthians were bound to move closer and closer to being proficient in the use of the gifts. With respect to being used in the gifts, there is no getting away from experience. Spiritual gifts, by their very nature, are experiential. It is futile to talk about the gifts of the Holy Spirit outside of a context of experiencing them and participating in them.

What are we to do then if we do not experience and participate in the gifts of the Holy Spirit? Some may say that it is wrong to desire them or ask for them. However, Paul actually tells us to "desire earnestly spiritual gifts" (1 Cor. 12:31, 14:1) and to "pray that" we may experience them (1 Cor. 14:13). In any case, it is most important to ask for and desire the Giver of the gifts; then you will experience the gifts that the Giver gives.

JUNE 9

GOOD NEWS: THERE IS VICTORY!

"How lovely on the mountains are the feet of him who brings good news."

Isaiah 52:7

The word *gospel* has an interesting historical background. In ancient days when armies went out to battle, people back home waited eagerly for any word from the battlefield regarding the outcome. A runner would be dispatched from the battlefield once the outcome was determined and return home to deliver the report. The runner would arrive and announce the good news, which would then result in jubilation and celebration. Isaiah paints this picture when he writes, "How lovely on the mountains are the feet of him who brings good news" (Isa. 52:7). This is the foundational meaning of the word *gospel*.

Jesus went far and wide proclaiming "the gospel of the kingdom" (Matt. 4:23). The essence of this gospel is victory over enemies. There is victory over death, victory over Satan, and victory over sin. Victory over death is God's ultimate victory as "the last enemy that will be abolished is death" (1 Cor. 15:26). This Good News is "already" and "not yet." It is already since it "now has been revealed by the appearing of our Savior Christ Jesus, who abolished death and brought life and immortality to light through the gospel" (2 Tim. 1:10). The good news is also not yet: "But each in his own order: Christ the first fruits, after that those who are Christ's at His coming, then comes the end, when He hands over the kingdom to the God and Father, when He has abolished all rule and all authority and power. For He must reign until He has put all His enemies under His feet. The last enemy that will be abolished is death" (1 Cor. 15:23-26).

There are two stages in the destruction of death because there are two stages in the coming of the kingdom. These two stages coincide with the two comings of Christ: His first coming (His incarnation) and His second coming (His return). "It is a trustworthy statement, deserving full acceptance, that Christ Jesus came into the world to save sinners" (1 Tim. 1:15). "Therefore be on the alert, for you do not know which day your Lord is coming" (Matt. 24:42). Death is abolished because Christ has come. That is good news. Death *will be* abolished completely and forever because Christ will return. That is also good news. That is the Gospel of the kingdom, the good news of the rule of God!

Victory over Satan is also part of the Gospel of the kingdom that is already and not yet. Satan has already been defeated: "Therefore, since the children share in flesh and blood, He Himself likewise also partook of the same, that through death He might render powerless him who had the power of death, that is, the devil" (Heb. 2:14). Satan will be defeated: "And the devil who deceived them was thrown into the lake of fire and brimstone, where the beast and the false prophet are also; and they will be tormented day and night forever and ever" (Rev. 20:10).

Victory over sin is also part of the good news. This victory, like the others, is already and not yet. Sin is already defeated: "For if we have become united with *Him* in the likeness of His death, certainly we shall also be *in the likeness* of His resurrection, knowing this, that our old self was crucified with *Him*, in order that our body of sin might be done away with, so that we would no longer be slaves to sin; for he who has died is freed from sin" (Rom. 6:5-7). Sin will be defeated:

> But when this perishable will have put on the imperishable, and this mortal will have put on immortality, then will come about the saying that is written, "DEATH IS SWALLOWED

UP in victory. O DEATH, WHERE IS YOUR VICTORY? O DEATH, WHERE IS YOUR STING?" The sting of death is sin, and the power of sin is the law; but thanks be to God, who gives us the victory through our Lord Jesus Christ (1 Cor. 15:54-57).

The Gospel of the kingdom, the good news, is God's message. His message proclaims victory over death, Satan, and sin. The victory is "already" and "not yet." Our enemies are already defeated and will be defeated completely and forever. We have read through the book and have gotten to the end. We won. We are winning. We will win. This is the good news. This is the Gospel. This is His victory!

JUNE 10

TOO MANY "I'S" ARE NOT GOOD

"Humble yourselves in the presence of the Lord, and He will exalt you."

James 4:10

The easiest way to understand humility is to understand its opposite—that is, pride. Pride is that which has to prove, promote, and proclaim self. Its focus and insistence on lifting up self results in a life lived on the proving grounds—"Don't you know who I am!" Self-promotion is the default mode—"You have not seen anything yet!" Proclamation is the repeated assertion, "I am the greatest!" Humility does not seek to prove, promote, or proclaim. It is the freedom *from* these things.

Pride is a one letter experience: "I," "I," "I," "I." Without humility, four "I's" are inevitable: **I**gnorance, **I**nsecurity, **I**solation, and **I**mpotence. Pride says, "I've arrived; I'm right; I know all." It can never be wrong. It must always be right. It does not need to be told anything. The ironic result is ignorance. When you say you know everything, you put yourself in a position to not learn. You are not teachable, and you are not one who repents or changes. The ironic thing is that the drive to prove, promote, and proclaim that you know everything ends up in the parking lot of ignorance—you know very little.

A professor reflected on his experience in earning his PhD. He said, "The most definite thing I have come to know is how much I do not know." Paul said, "If anyone supposes that he knows anything, he has not yet known as he ought to know" (1 Cor. 8:2). Pride thinks it is right, but the Scripture tells us "the way of a fool is right in his own eyes, but a wise man is he who listens to counsel" (Prov. 12:15). The pride versus humility contest is seen in the "counterfeit flip-flop" versus "kingdom flip-flop" competition. Ironically, pride wears its counterfeit flip-flops when its "I know" results in "I do not know." Realistically, humility wears its kingdom flip-flops when its "I do not know" becomes "I do know." Jesus said, "For judgment I came into this world, so that those who do not see may see, and that those who see may become blind... If you were blind, you would have no sin; but since you say, 'We see,' your sin remains" (John 9:39-41).

Pride says, "I have it all together; I am better than everyone else." It can never be tainted. It must compare favorably to everyone. It is secure in its view of itself as it uses a "give yourself the benefit of the doubt" reasoning to show off its relative superiority over the masses. The ironic result is insecurity and isolation. When your security is defined by comparing yourself to others, you inevitably feel the repercussions that come from constantly looking in the mirror; and you find yourself alone as you avoid others so as to avoid your insecurity. The ironic thing is that the drive to prove, promote, and proclaim that you have it all together and that you are better than anyone else ends up in the parking lot of insecurity and isolation. "For we are not bold to class or compare ourselves with some of those who commend themselves; but when they measure themselves by themselves and compare themselves with themselves, they are without understanding" (2 Cor. 10:12).

Pride thinks that it always has it together and that it stands out in the crowd, but the Scripture tells us that "the last shall be first, and the first last" (Matt. 20:16). The pride versus humility contest is again seen in the counterfeit flip-flop versus the kingdom flip-flop competition. Pride flip-flops ironically when its "I am well put together" results in "I am messed up." Humility flip-flops realistically when its "I am messed up" becomes "I am well put together." Jesus said, "Whoever exalts himself shall be humbled; and whoever humbles himself shall be exalted" (Matt. 23:12). Wisdom says, "A man's pride will bring him low, but a humble spirit will obtain honor" (Prov. 29:23).

Pride says, "I am able; I am sufficient." It can never be weak. It must always be strong. It does not need anyone's help. The ironic result is impotence. When you say you are able on your own, you necessarily forfeit the ability of another. You are not needy, and so you do not receive assistance. The ironic thing is that the drive to prove, promote, and proclaim that you can do it all ends up in the parking lot of helplessness—you are able to do very little.

Pride thinks it can achieve by itself, but Jesus says, "'I am the vine, you are the branches; he who abides in Me and I in him, he bears much fruit, for apart from Me you can do nothing'" (John 15:5). The pride versus humility contest is once again seen in the counterfeit flip-flop versus the kingdom flip-flop competition. Pride flip-flops ironically when its "I can" results in "I cannot." Humility flip-flops realistically when its "I am not able" becomes "I am able." Potency is preceded by impotence: "And He has said to me, 'My grace is sufficient for you, for power is perfected in weakness.' Most gladly, therefore, I will rather boast about my weaknesses, so that the power of Christ may dwell in me" (2 Cor. 12:9).

Herein lies the crux of the matter. When ignorance, insecurity, isolation, and impotence are the results of a faulty perception of self, then we are walking in pride. When they are, instead, launchers of a proper perspective of self in relation to God, then we are walking in humility. False humility sees its inability but then stops there. True humility flows in a cycle. You see God's ability, so you see your own inability, which in turn drives you to His ability. He must increase (John 3:30). When He increases, I necessarily decrease. When I decrease, then He increases all the more. What does humility look like? It looks like this cycle of true perception!

JUNE 11

LEADING OTHERS TO GOD IN PRAYER

"Let Your ear now be attentive and Your eyes open to hear the prayer of Your servant which I am praying before You now, day and night, on behalf of the sons of Israel Your servants, confessing the sins of the sons of Israel which we have sinned against You; I and my father's house have sinned."
                                                                                                Nehemiah 1:6

How can a leader lead unless he knows the Leader? Before any other attribute, a Christian leader must be someone who walks with God. He or she must be a man or woman of prayer. To be led by God may include waiting on God. Nehemiah was an accomplished leader, who was used by God to rebuild the walls of Jerusalem. He waited and prayed for four months before he acted. The month of Chislev (Neh. 1:1) to the month of Nisan (Neh. 2:1) is analogous to the month of December to the month of April. The character of a leader must enable him to persevere in prayer and wait on God. This is necessary because man's timing is not always God's timing.

A leader must seek the plan of God instead of trying to implement his own plan. Even his prayer is not one that he determines by himself in his own mind and will. Before praying for anything specific, he first prays to receive direction from God concerning what to pray and believe. Since his faith needs something to stand on, the leader prays the prayer of seeking God's will before he prays the prayer of faith. Nehemiah spent four months praying the prayer of seeking God's will (Ne. 1:1-10) before he prayed the prayer of faith (Neh. 1:11).

In prayer, a leader does not so much lead God toward those he is leading as much as he leads those he is leading toward God. He does not tell God what to do. He presents others to God, intercedes for them, and asks God to help them and lead them. He goes to God on behalf of his people. This implies that the leader identifies with those he is leading. It is unlikely someone will go to God on behalf of others if he does not identify with them.

Identification includes a sense of corporate responsibility (1 Cor. 12:26). A leader must identify with the sin and guilt of his people. He must be willing to bear others' burdens (Gal. 6:2) and mourn for their sins (1 Cor. 5:2). Nehemiah—like Abraham, Moses, Jeremiah, and Daniel—pleaded with God as an advocate for the people. In this way, the leader leads the people to God in prayer:

> When I heard these words, I sat down and wept and mourned for days; and I was fasting and praying before the God of heaven. I said, "I beseech You, O LORD God of heaven, the great and awesome God, who preserves the covenant and lovingkindness for those who love Him and keep His commandments, let Your ear now be attentive and Your eyes open to hear the prayer of Your servant which I am praying before You now, day and night, on behalf of the sons of Israel Your servants, confessing the sins of the sons of Israel which we have sinned against You; I and my father's house have sinned. We have acted very corruptly against You and have not kept the commandments, nor the statutes, nor the ordinances which You commanded Your servant Moses. Remember the word which You commanded Your servant Moses, saying, 'If you are unfaithful I will scatter you among the peoples; but *if* you return to Me and keep My commandments and do them, though those of you who have been scattered were in the most remote part of the heavens, I will gather them from there and will bring them to the place where I have chosen to cause My name to dwell.' They are Your servants and Your people whom You redeemed by Your great power and by Your strong hand" (Neh. 1:4-10).

The book of Nehemiah is full of Nehemiah's prayers (Neh. 1:3-11; 4:4-5; 5:19; 6:9, 14; 13:14, 22, 31). His prayers on behalf of his people included an expression of being jealous for God's reputation, the leader in relation to God. It also included a deep and sincere love for others, the leader in relation to others. Finally, it included an expression of selflessness, the leader in relation to self.

Leaders lead their people to God in prayer. Before praying for any specific request for their people, they pray for God's guidance and direction so they can then pray according to God's will. Sometimes, we think we are "storming the throne room"; but if we have not prayed the "prayer before the prayer," then we may be praying our own agenda and simply "storming our own room." Be sure to know what you are praying for!

JUNE 12

TOOLS TO USE TO HELP PEOPLE

"Again I say to you, that if two of you agree on earth about anything that they may ask, it shall be done for them by My Father who is in heaven. For where two or three have gathered together in My name, I am there in their midst."

Matthew 18:19-20

People who are willing and able to help other people should have certain tools at their disposal. There exist tools that tend to be in a counselor's toolkit. These tools should be used in the more formal settings in which "professional" counselors are helping counselees and in the more informal settings in which helpers are counseling friends who need help.

One such tool is prayer. Sometimes, that means praying with the person. There is, of course, great power in prayer. "Again I say to you, that if two of you agree on earth about anything that they may ask, it shall be done for them by My Father who is in heaven. For where two or three have gathered together in My name, I am there in their midst" (Matt. 18:19-20). There is healing in prayer: "Therefore, confess your sins to one another, and pray for one another so that you may be healed. The effective prayer of a righteous man can accomplish much" (James 5:16).

Sometimes, prayer is used to pray *for* the person being helped. Samuel prays on behalf of Israel against the Philistines who are coming against them (1 Sam. 7:5-11). Sometimes, it takes a counselor, one who comes alongside of someone else, to intercede against the "Philistines" or "giants" in others' lives. The counselor should never underestimate the power of prayer. It is in no way an overstatement to say, "To help is to pray!"

Another significant tool in a counselor's toolkit might actually sound counterintuitive but is very important—the tool of referral. Sometimes, it may be better for someone else to provide the counseling for a particular individual or regarding a particular situation. For example, it might not be appropriate for a man to be counseling a woman, especially with respect to certain topics. Sometimes, the wisest thing for a counselor to do is to not counsel.

So, just as in any other work in which someone uses tools, a counselor should consider what tools are necessary for the job. Are you helping someone? Don't forget your toolkit!

JUNE 13

INSPIRED TO INTERPRET

"For the word of God is living and active."

Hebrews 4:12

How do we know that the Bible was actually inspired by God and not just a collection of fictional stories that people made up? The question of Divine authorship or inspiration of the Bible is a question of ultimate authority. Since all questions of ultimate authority must answer to themselves, they cannot avoid becoming circular arguments. Little Johnny asks his mother, "Why do I have to do that?" Mommy answers, "Because I say so." Little Johnny presses the issue, "Why do you say so?" Mommy answers matter of fact, "Because I say so." And so goes the circular argument. How do I know the Bible is inspired by God? I know because the Bible says so. Why does the Bible say so? It says so because it is inspired by God.

The circular argument is actually a proof of the existence of God and His ultimate authority, inasmuch as God made man in such a way that man is aware of Him and the idea of ultimate authority: "He has also set eternity in their heart, yet so that man will not find out the work which God has done from the beginning even to the end" (Eccl. 3:11). Man, by nature, knows that ultimate authority exists. He is aware of the eternal. He cannot fully understand it, explain it, or "prove" it, but he is aware of it. That is why the argument for ultimate authority is inevitably circular. This "natural" call of God to humanity inevitably results in a circular argument for the inspiration of the Bible.

The evidence escapes from the circle with a "relational" call of God to me personally that produces a faith argument. How do I know the Bible is inspired by God? The answer, "I know because the Bible says so" is now expanded to "I know because God told me so." Circular arguments without faith arguments can only go so far. To run in a circle and not get dizzy, you need to have faith.

The faith argument is affirmed with an "experiential" call of God to history that produces an objective argument. Now the answer to the question of inspiration is "I know the Bible is inspired by God because the Bible says so, because God told me so, and because of the things I can observe in history." The unity in diversity of the Bible is remarkable. Written over a period of fifteen hundred years by more than forty different authors from various eras, cultures, backgrounds, and geo-political situations, the Bible stands as one unified book containing the same major themes from start to finish.

The accuracy and preservation of the Bible is astonishing. There is no proof that the Bible has any historical, prophetic, geographical, or scientific errors. The Bible's preservation is impressive. For such an expansive text (sixty-six books) to have been so meticulously kept for thousands of years is remarkable. The distribution and influence of the Bible is extraordinary. It is the bestselling book of all time and has been translated into seven hundred languages. There is no other book that has had more influence on more people. This objective evidence screams out, "What is this book? It seems like there's something behind it that goes way beyond man!"

Closely related to the question of inspiration is the question of interpretation. If the Bible is sacred, then how should we go about studying it? We are called by God to take this question seriously as the Scripture itself charges us, "Be diligent to present yourself approved to God as a workman who does not need to be ashamed, accurately handling the word of truth" (2 Tim. 2:15). Accurate handling is best achieved through proper attitudes and perspectives. How do you view yourself? As a Bible student, you should see yourself as an honest subordinate, a lover, a detective, a real estate agent, and an art critic.

As an "honest subordinate," you open the Bible thinking "inductive, inductive, inductive." Read it as if you had never read it before. Refuse to try to make it say what you want and insist on letting it say what it says. As a "lover," you approach the Bible feeling "passion, passion, passion." Read it like a love letter—slowly, counting every word, asking questions of the text, and affording it great value. As a "detective," you study the Bible, insisting on "observation, observation, observation." Look at the trees in the forest. Look at the branches on the trees. Look at the leaves on the branches. This is the hard labor of Bible study. It even includes the tedious work of observing grammar. This may not seem very "spiritual," but it should be remembered that it is God Who made the choice to give us the Bible through the agency of man and, thus, through the discipline of grammar. Detective work is spiritual.

As a "real estate agent," you evaluate the Bible repeating "location, location, location" or "context, context, context." Analyze it with a view toward what surrounds the text that is being studied. What precedes it, and what follows it? What context surrounds it, such as culture, history, geography, audience, author, and setting? Remember, actions, events, interactions, and ideas do not happen in a vacuum. As an "art critic," you understand the Bible, noticing "genre, genre, genre." Parables are different than poetry, proverbs, prophecy, history, law, doctrine, or apocalyptic literature. You do not interpret parables the same way you interpret doctrine. A parable is a metaphor. You do not look for a doctrinal principle in every part of a story. You are looking for the meaning of the story and how it "maps over" some doctrinal principle. This is often most readily found in the conclusion of the parable. Genre dictates hermeneutics.

How do we view the Bible? What is our attitude toward inspiration and interpretation? The Bible is the Word of God; so read it and be changed (Heb. 4:12). Inspired to interpret!

JUNE 14

COUNT YOUR WORDS

"When there are many words."

Proverbs 10:19

The most important math we might do is found in counting our words. In general, it is wise counsel to avoid an abundance of words. Too many words can lead to sin. "When there are many words, transgression is unavoidable, but he who restrains his lips is wise" (Prov. 10:19). The wisdom found in Ecclesiastes tells us that our words should be few. "Do not be hasty in word or impulsive in thought to bring up a matter in the presence of God. For God is in heaven and you are on the earth; therefore let your words be few" (Eccl. 5:2).

You are called to be a good steward of your mouth. You must guard your mouth. "He who guards his mouth and his tongue, guards his soul from troubles" (Prov. 21:23). It is an issue of self-protection. "The one who guards his mouth preserves his life; the one who opens wide his lips comes to ruin" (Prov. 13:3). This self-protection requires self-discipline. "When there are many words, transgression is unavoidable, but he who restrains his lips is wise" (Prov. 10:19).

There is wise speech, and there is foolish speech. Patience is associated with wisdom. "Do you see a man who is hasty in his words? There is more hope for a fool than for him" (Prov. 29:20). It is better to put a hand over your mouth than to put your foot in your mouth. "If you have been foolish in exalting yourself or if you have plotted *evil, put your* hand on your mouth" (Prov. 30:32). Count your words. Use a door and a bolt on your mouth. Weigh your words. Put them on balances and scales and understand their weight. Be careful not to speak cheap words. Consider the worth of a word *before* it is spoken. Be wise and be disciplined!

When I was a child, my grandfather always would tell me not to speak too much. He would reason with me by explaining that I only had a certain amount of words that I could say in my life and that I would want to save as many as I could for when I was older and would need them more. Of course, his primary purpose in this exhortation was to keep me quiet so as not to bother him. Nevertheless, there was an element of wisdom that he conveyed to me. Count your words. Use your words as if you had a limit on the number you could speak. Choose them carefully. Be a good steward of your words!

Many pithy, metaphorical sayings are available to us to remind us of the importance of being wise with our words. Count your words. Silence is golden. Think before you speak. God gave us two ears and only one mouth. Talk is not cheap. David Wright sums up these ideas:

> We think much about physical resources and guard these jealously. According to Solomon, our word resources must be just as jealously guarded, just as wisely used. There is a right

and a wrong way to spend this precious commodity. God is vitally interested in what pours forth from our lips because, like the desire for fellowship, this power of language is an expression of His image in us. Language is not to be taken lightly; talk is not cheap."¹⁰

JUNE 15

CRISIS GOES BACK TO BASICS

"For I determined to know nothing among you except Jesus Christ, and Him crucified."
1 Corinthians 2:2

We had a plan, but things changed. We were sailing in one direction, but a storm blew us off course. We thought one thing was going to happen, but a completely different thing happened. We were comfortably accustomed to a certain way of life, but then another uncomfortable way of life was imposed upon us. This is the essence of crisis! We all find ourselves in some level of crisis from time to time. Those experiences shake us up. Sometimes, we might even experience a major crisis. Those experiences shake our world!

Crises do not usually happen overnight. There is a buildup. People, events, technology, health, economy, philosophies, worldviews, and changes in culture are but a few of the significant potential builders. Little by little, things change. Then the ball starts rolling down the proverbial hill and gains more and more momentum until, "Boom!" there is a crisis. This can happen in any area of a person's individual life, and it can happen in most any aspect of society.

There is, for example, a crisis in education. The answer, to a large degree, revolves around two builders: technology and worldview. Technological changes over the past generation have been awesome. In many ways, they have improved our lives. They also have changed people. Specifically, they have changed students' ability to focus. This attention deficit disorder results in a crisis in education. Students have become bound to images. There is an implicit desire, need, and demand for more appearance and less content, more superficiality and less of the profound, and more fluff and less substance. Students may spend more time staring at their phones while in class than listening to the teacher and taking notes. Another builder of the crisis in education is changing worldview. For decades, Western culture has been inundated with postmodernism and its implicit rejection of authority. Authority is out, and "I make my own reality" is in. This results in a crisis in the classroom. Students act like they are the teacher and refuse to acknowledge that the teacher is the teacher. This picture is one that cries out, "There is a crisis in education!"

One of the most important principles in crisis management may seem to be counterintuitive. We must get "back to the basics." More than ever, crisis solutions necessitate fundamentals: foundational principles and practices. Crises naturally drive us there. It is a natural (and wise) human response to seek out the beginnings when things seem to be moving toward the endings. In crisis, families pull together. Husbands and wives reflect on their vows made many years ago. Sayings like, "Remember what is important and what will last," ring out when stock markets crash, businesses fail, and people stand on death's doorstep. The crisis experience naturally cries out, "Let us get back to basics."

How do educators respond to the kind of crisis that has emerged in the midst of changing technology/culture, and the resultant changing synapses in students' brains? Educators must reject the cultural temptation to look to entertain at the expense of the content of education. Certainly, teaching can be contextualized so as to take advantage of delivery systems that are consistent with their students' experiences; but the "cart must not come before the horse," and "form must follow substance." Back to the basics is back to the substance and not just back to the methods. If you put on a show and that is all it is, then you will ultimately have nothing to show for it. Similarly, teachers must get back to the basics with respect to authority. They must refuse to cower to the absurd idea that students rule the classroom and implement, once again, the practice of taking authority through taking responsibility. Back to the basics!

Paul was in the midst of an ecclesiastical crisis when he penned 1 Corinthians. There were debilitating divisions in the Corinthian church, and some were trying to preach other gospels. How did Paul respond to this crisis? He went back to the basics—nothing more, nothing less. "For I determined to know nothing among you except Jesus Christ, and Him crucified" (1 Cor. 2:2). Built into this "church crisis" is the ultimate crisis. Man is always desperately in need of God. This soteriological crisis is solved by the very expensive, yet completely foundational, provision of the cross of Christ.

A major crisis can shake our world. The world was shaken in the Garden of Eden when the crisis of separation from God began. The solution is the most foundational Being that exists—God. It is Jesus, which literally means, "God saves." So, Paul says, "I respond to the crisis by getting back to the most basic truth in the universe; God saves, and God saves by dying for me." Crisis goes back to basics!

JUNE 16

LET'S GET REAL!

"I am the vine, you are the branches; he who abides in Me and I in him, he bears much fruit, for apart from Me you can do nothing."

John 15:5

Why do we not pray more? It may be due to a lack of understanding of reality—the reality of "since nothing, then all." What is real is that apart from Jesus, "you can do nothing" (John 15:5) so "[i]n all your ways acknowledge Him" (Prov. 3:6). The degree to which we think we do not need God is the degree to which we lack in prayer. We ask when we need. We need when we realize we are not sufficient. We realize we are not sufficient when we live in reality. Let's get real; let's pray!

This tendency to escape from reality can be rooted in our own experiences of success, the technology and tools we have at our disposal, and the philosophies that inundate our culture. They can all deceive us into thinking that we do not need God. Deism is a worldview—a way to view reality—that says that, to one degree or another, God is a Creator Who is no longer involved in His creation. We do not need God because God is not available. He has left us on our own to do His work. This attitude can sneak in unknowingly through the door of faulty theology. When the "closing of the Canon" is effectually translated into the closing of God's mouth—He no longer communicates with His people in a dynamic way—then we are in danger of incipient deism. And deism, by its nature, leads its followers *away* from God, not toward Him.

People who pray—who trust, depend on, and seek God—must avoid the "Ishmael syndrome." As was with Abraham, Sarai, and Hagar (Gen. 16:1-4), this occurs when we feel we must and can take it upon ourselves to cause and create. It tends to occur because our focus is on *doing* instead of *being* and on a worldly success—utilitarianism or pragmatism—instead of a holy success rooted in obedience to, faith in, and relationship with God. It comes into its fullness when we perceive ourselves as being sufficient to make things work. Those at Babel were so full of themselves that they lived in the false reality that nothing would be impossible for them (Gen. 11:6). They were not ones who sought God.

When we or our ministries become Ishmaels who dwell in Babel, we cease to pray. The reality is that no matter what we think we can do on our own, we still can do nothing without Him.

After visiting the United States and preparing to return to the Congo, a church leader from Africa reflected on his observations of the American church and innocently stated, "It is amazing what you people can accomplish without the Holy Spirit." When we accomplish things in our own power, we may be building but we are not really achieving (Luke 6:47-49). "Though Edom says, 'We have been beaten down, but we will return and build up the ruins'; thus says the LORD of hosts, 'They may build, but I will tear down'" (Mal. 1:4). To avoid the Ishmael syndrome, we must return to being experts in *being* (we seek and know God) in order that the only true Expert can be an expert in *doing* (God works through us). We must return to defining our goals in terms of facilitating God's work instead of creating or manufacturing it. To do this, we must return to a focus on involving ourselves in "means of grace" (like prayer) that point us to our dependence on God.

Prayer is very real. We are to be real with God when we talk with Him. For David, this even included "arguing" with God. This type of arguing was not designed to make, cause, convince, or guilt God into doing something; but it was done to agree with and facilitate His work. To argue in prayer with God is to be His tool to advance His cause with respect to His people, the world, and His Word.

Prayer for God's People

Father God, your people need faithful shepherds; they need to eat meat instead of milk. Protect them from heresy. Give them a model to inspire them, for they need a shepherd who loves them.

Prayer for the World

Almighty God, the world needs a prophetic voice; someone needs to stand in the gap for sinners. I need to remain separate from the world, while offering a biblical response to current social issues and being a missiological blessing to the nations. Provide the world with a prophetic voice.

Prayer for God's Word

Lord, You promised to transform me. You promised to complete what You began in me. You promised to be at work in me to will and to do Your good pleasure. You promised that I would do great exploits. Fill me with Your Spirit to do Your work.

The most foundational truths are that we need God, and God provides for us. This is good news; it is "gospel." When you pray, you declare that you understand and agree with this good news, this definition of reality. So, let's get real. Let's pray!

JUNE 17

DON'T HIDE YOUR TALENT; MULTIPLY IT!

*"But he who received the one talent went away,
and dug a hole in the ground and hid his master's money."*

Matthew 25:18

God is not One Who divides. He is not One Who subtracts. He is not One Who adds. God is a *Multiplier*. He is like the master in the parable of the talents who was "reaping where you did not sow and gathering where you scattered no *seed*" (Matt. 25:24). That master expected someone else to do something with what he gave so as to multiply the original quantity. He commended the multipliers and rebuked the one who did nothing to multiply (Matt. 25:14-30). Multiplication is God's strategy, and it should be the strategy of God's workers.

In kingdom work, reproduction is normal (Matt. 13; Mark 4:26-29; John 15:1-6). Multiplication principles should be used in all facets of ministry. To do this, there must be a willingness to let go of ministry and to work oneself out of a job. Instead of holding on and building your own ministry, you are letting go and equipping the ministries of others. "The things which you have heard from me in the presence of many witnesses, entrust these to faithful men who will be able to teach others also" (2 Tim. 2:2). Paul gave to Timothy and then encouraged Timothy to give to others, who would then give to "others also." The name of the game in multiplication and reproduction is *release*. The opposite of this is to hold on to and hide. That is like the one who "went away, and dug *a hole* in the ground and hid his master's money" (Matt. 25:18). There is no multiplication in hiding!

A church is a body, it is not a building. It should grow naturally. A missionary with a multiplication mentality will be willing to plant a basic church and then leave it to the trained local leaders. The apostle Paul was able to do this because he was not planting a building; he was planting a body of believers, and he trusted God for their natural growth. His strategy of "go, give, leave" refused to hide his talent in the ground and facilitated multiplication. Hiders build their own kingdoms by holding on and maintaining control and by not reproducing themselves; conveniently, they are the only ones who can do the job.

Respect for the autonomy of the local church is critical to reproductive ministry. *Release* is to multiply. *Control* is to stagnate. Apostolic authority is natural; it is not institutional. Planted churches need to be independent of their "mothers" so that they do not become handicapped children. The goal of the multiplying missionary is a self-governing, self-supporting, and self-propagating church or ministry. Planters must release what they have planted, and they must multiply that releasing mentality. The missionary does not become the head of a new denomination, and the church that is planted does not build its own denomination. In the New Testament, the autonomy of the local church is seen in the fact that each church had its own leadership (Acts 14:23, 15:4, 20:17; Phil. 1:1). Certainly, churches can, and should, have relationships with each other, but their relationships must not infringe upon the autonomy of each individual church. This will keep the church from becoming institutionalized, and it will promote the natural growth of a body.

Very important to multiplication is to understand the importance of vision. Of course, you can have no vision by simply not having vision. If you do not have a vision for multiplication, then you are probably not going to do it. You can also not have vision by having a vision for everything. If you have a vision for everything, then you will probably just be adding and not multiplying. Reproduce yourself and your ministry. Catch the vision! Multiply!

JUNE 18

LET'S GET RADICAL!

"THIS PEOPLE HONORS ME WITH THEIR LIPS, BUT THEIR HEART IS FAR FROM ME. BUT IN VAIN DO THEY WORSHIP ME, TEACHING AS DOCTRINES THE PRECEPTS OF MEN."

Matthew 15:8-9

What is radical Christianity? Sometimes, the phrase "radical Christian" is misleading. People can think that there is a choice between being an "average" Christian and a "radical" Christian. The term "radical" intimidates some into not being all they are called to be in Christ because they do not see themselves as extraordinary. The term "average" excuses others because they argue that being average is enough. Ironically, the term "radical," by definition, is the opposite of extraordinary. It refers to things that are basic and fundamental. Its focus is on that which arises from the root or source of a thing. To be a "radical" Christian is to get back to basics; it is to do the fundamental things that the Bible sets forth. Perhaps, instead of saying, "Let's get radical," we should encourage each other by saying, "Let's get normative." To be a radical Christian is to be a biblical Christian. It is to get back to the source. Radical is normal!

Sometimes, our traditional and cultural models or images of Christianity distort the biblical models or images that our faith is rooted in. How is the praise and worship portion of a church service perceived? After the service, one person says to another, "Praise and worship were not very good today." What does that mean? Does it mean that people were not exalting, adoring, honoring, and glorifying God? How do you know? Or does it mean that you did not feel exhilarated, tingly, and inspired by the song choices? Do I worship God so that I can have a good experience for myself (traditional/cultural model), or do I worship God because He is worthy (biblical model)? Do I worship God because of what I need and want or because of who *God* is and what He does?

How do we view the Church? Is the church an organization or is it an organism? Is it a corporation or business run by CEOs and businessmen (traditional/cultural model), or is it a body or family run by God through chosen and anointed spiritual leaders (biblical model)? How do we view the church's activities and fellowship? Is it program-oriented or relationship-oriented? Are we involved in conducting events together (traditional/cultural model) or living out the life of Christ together (biblical model)? How do we measure church growth? Do we focus on adding numbers simply for the sake of numbers (traditional/cultural model), or do we focus on multiplying, reproducing, and discipling (biblical model)? Are we satisfied with a superficial effect on many, or do we insist on a more profound impact on people regardless of the numbers?

How do we move forward in our faith? How do we accomplish things? Do we rely on our own abilities and expertise (traditional/cultural model), or do we focus on prayer and other means of grace (biblical model)? How do we determine success? What criteria do we use to say something is achieved? Is it determined by results and the world's perception of what constitutes quantity and progress (traditional/cultural model), or is it determined by obedience to God (biblical model)?

Of course, these things are not mutually exclusive. Worship and a positive experience for the worshipper can live together. A model of church growth that focuses on multiplying, reproducing, and discipling does not have to reject adding numbers. The question is not one or the other. It is more of a question of what is the root or source? What is primary? The root of worship is worship. How you worship—standing, kneeling, raising your hands—is the method. Methods cannot be the root or contents.

Sources and contents are different from results and methods. They are not necessarily separated from each other. The problem of faulty models or images comes in the way in which they invert things. A desirable personal experience becomes the source or contents, and the actual worship becomes the result or method. Form must follow function. When the form is put in first place, it then *becomes* the function. This is called hypocrisy. When the appearance or superficial comes first, then the contents, or that which is actual, gets hidden and lost. You can have contents without methods—although it is better to have both—but you cannot have methods without contents. That is just fake. It is not radical!

Woe to you, scribes and Pharisees, hypocrites! For you tithe mint and dill and cumin, and have neglected the weightier provisions of the law: justice and mercy and faithfulness, but these are the things you should have done without neglecting the others. You blind guides, who strain out a gnat and swallow a camel! Woe to you, scribes and Pharisees, hypocrites! For you clean the outside of the cup and of the dish, but inside they are full of robbery and self-indulgence. You blind Pharisee, first clean the inside of the cup and of the dish, so that the outside of it may become clean also (Matt. 23:23-26).

JUNE 19

A FAST WAY TO MINISTER

"And after He had fasted forty days and forty nights."

Matthew 4:2

The idea of the use of fasting in the context of ministry preparation is not without Scriptural support. Jesus' ministry was launched with power after fasting forty days in the wilderness; Paul and Barnabas' missionary ministry was inaugurated with fasting; and the appointment of elders in the churches was done after having prayed with fasting. Similarly, throughout church history, ministry leaders have testified of the role fasting played in their preparation for ministry.

Fasting may become a part of preparation for ministry inasmuch as it is a discipline consistent with self-denial, and someone who serves other people must be able to deny himself to put the needs of others first. More importantly, fasting facilitates an expression of reliance upon God. Reliance upon God is a foundation stone for ministry.

Jesus' fasting during His wilderness temptation experience (Luke 4:1-2) immediately preceded the launching of His empowered ministry. "When the devil had finished every temptation, he left Him until an opportune time. And Jesus returned to Galilee in the power of the Spirit, and news about Him spread through all the surrounding district. And He *began* teaching in their synagogues and was praised by all" (Luke 4:13-15). It also could be said, logically and experientially, that Satan attacks a ministry directly when it is first beginning, at its most vulnerable time. In the midst of this early attack, fasting can be a means of preparation inasmuch as it is an expression and means of focusing upon the need to rely on God. As Jesus' fasting highlighted His physical reliance upon the Father, it also prepared Him to express His spiritual reliance. In fact, all three of His responses to the "tempter" emphasized that reliance (Matt. 4:4, 7, 10).

In Acts 13:1-3, it is "when they had fasted and prayed and laid their hands on them" that they proceeded to commission Paul and Barnabas as missionaries and send them away. This occasion of fasting is clearly associated with preparation for ministry. In preparing themselves to send and be sent, they fasted. Similarly, in Acts 14:23, the decisions made in the appointment of elders were of a critical nature, and they were not entered into without "having prayed with fasting." In commissioning those chosen, fasting became part of their preparation for ministry.

Fasting is a biblical spiritual discipline. It is useful as a means of grace for a variety of purposes. One of those purposes may be to prepare oneself for ministry. Success in ministry is fueled by being empowered by the Spirit of God. It is the Spirit Who led Jesus into the wilderness to be tempted. He fasted. Then He began His public ministry in the power of the Spirit.

Jesus, full of the Holy Spirit, returned from the Jordan and was led around by the Spirit in the wilderness for forty days, being tempted by the devil. And He ate nothing during those days, and when they had ended, He became hungry. And the devil said to Him . . . When the devil had finished every temptation, he left Him until an opportune time. And Jesus returned to Galilee in the power of the Spirit, and news about Him spread through all the surrounding district. And He *began* teaching in their synagogues and was praised by all. And He came to Nazareth, where He had been brought up; and as was His custom, He entered the synagogue on the Sabbath, and stood up to read. And the book of the prophet Isaiah was handed to Him. And He opened the book and found the place where it was written, "THE SPIRIT OF THE LORD IS UPON ME" (Luke 4:1-3, 13-18).

Jesus fasted as a preparation for ministry. Perhaps, we should fast also. Are you prepared? Our preparation should focus on nothing less than seeking God. Fasting does not by itself equal seeking God, and it is certainly not mandatory that we fast in order to seek God; nevertheless, it can be an aid to that end. So, seek, fast, prepare, minister!

JUNE 20

WHICH ROMANS 12 GIFT DO YOU HAVE?

"Since we have gifts that differ according to the grace given to us,
each of us is to exercise them accordingly."

Romans 12:6

God equips His people with gifts for ministry. There exist various lists of gifts in the New Testament. One such list is found in Romans 12:6-8: "Since we have gifts that differ according to the grace given to us, *each of us is to exercise them accordingly*: if prophecy, according to the proportion of his faith; if service, in his serving; or he who teaches, in his teaching; or he who exhorts, in his exhortation; he who gives, with liberality; he who leads, with diligence; he who shows mercy, with cheerfulness."

The Giver of these gifts is God the Father (Rom. 12:3). The gifts are called *charismata* (grace gifts). They are described as being "functional gifts" (Rom. 12:4) that are "effects" enacted by "God who works all things in all persons" (1 Cor. 12:6). The Romans 12 gifts are gifts that direct how a person functions; they determine the effects of a person's personality or tendencies. They are not so much gifts that a person is temporarily and situationally used in (as in the 1 Corinthians 12:8-10 gifts) or gifts that dictate a person's actual ministry (as in the Ephesians 4:11 gifts) as they are gifts that reside inside of a person and shape what that person is like. They are what are often called "motivational gifts" or "inclinational gifts" because they form people's tendencies, unction, emphases, inclinations, and personalities. They establish a default mode in terms of how someone, almost automatically, thinks and then tends to act. They even could be said to be undercurrents that shape a person's personality and what they are like in their interactions with others.

Each member of the body of Christ has at least one gift. The following descriptions of someone's tendencies may help to determine what gift that person might have (of the first three gifts listed in Romans 12). Of course, the descriptions cannot give you the gift—only God does that—but they can indicate or confirm your gift(s). Read each paragraph and consider to what degree you resonate with that description and to what degree those statements tend to describe you. If reading the paragraph tends to make you say, "Yes, that seems like me," then perhaps you have that gift.

The Gift of Prophecy

I am able to identify error easily. I have a great desire to motivate others to change when they are involved in error. I have a strong desire to speak the truth. I tend to emphasize what is right and wrong about an issue. Other people sometimes think I am a "hard" person because I can be so direct in my interaction with them. I view the issues of life as "black and white" and "right and wrong." I can be impatient with others who do not agree with my position in a matter. Even at the risk of personal rejection, I am inclined to speak out when something wrong is said or done. God sometimes uses me to shake up lives and ministries that are stagnant.

The Gift of Service

I enjoy helping others in practical ways. I find fulfillment in assisting others in their ministries. I like to be involved in short-term projects that have more immediate goals and results. I enjoy helping others as long as my help is appreciated. I am very loyal and committed to those I work with. I will do things myself instead of recruiting others to help, even if it results in my being overworked. I view life as a series of activities in which I help others. I am very active in my church, always looking for opportunities to help others. I do not mind doing menial tasks especially when it frees up others to more significant ministry. I tend to not be able to say no to people who need help.

The Gift of Teaching

I enjoy doing research and discovering truth. I tend to categorize information and define truth in a systematic way. When studying the Bible, I feel that details and individual words are very important. When I listen to others teach, I tend to analyze and evaluate what they are saying and check it with the Bible. I focus more on theology than practice, and I tend to be more objective than subjective in my view toward issues of truth. I am fulfilled when I am involved in activities that rely heavily on the use of the mind. I view life as a collection of information in which truth is defined. I tend to repeat myself often when I want someone to understand something I am saying. I am concerned about the accuracy of what I believe and proclaim it even to the smallest detail. I am able to explain difficult Bible passages to others in a way in which they are able to understand.

So do you have the gift of prophecy, the gift of service, or the gift of teaching? Perhaps you have one of them, or perhaps you have two, or perhaps you have all three. Perhaps you have none of these gifts, but you might have the gift of exhortation or giving or leading or showing mercy. In any case, the most important thing is that we use our gift(s) and, even more, that we use our gifts to glorify God. May God be glorified in whom He made us to be!

JUNE 21

WHAT DOES A MINISTER DO?

*"Shepherd the flock of God among you, exercising oversight not under compulsion, but voluntarily, according to **the will of** God; and not for sordid gain, but with eagerness; nor yet as lording it over those allotted to your charge, but proving to be examples to the flock. And when the Chief Shepherd appears, you will receive the unfading crown of glory."*

1 Peter 5:2-4

What is the most common image of a minister? What do they actually do for their "job?" The way you perceive what a minister does will probably depend on your background, experience, and exposure to church culture. When some people think of a minister, they think of someone who is like an entertainer or salesman they might see on television. Others might picture a monk who spends most of his time in a secluded and solitary small room communing with God. There are many different images of a minister. Eugene Peterson, the translator of The Message Bible, views the minister as one who prays, studies the Scripture, and gives spiritual direction to others. He summarizes his image of a minister by saying, "The pastor's responsibility is to keep the community attentive to God."[11] Peterson refers to the minister as a "spiritual director" as he reflects on what the common image of the minister used to include. Spiritual direction is a fading image of the work of ministers because of their busy schedules and the busyness of those they shepherd, which tends to yield both a lack of supply and demand for spiritual direction.

What are some biblical images that point to the activities of a minister? A minister is a preacher. He proclaims the Word of God and, in so doing, encourages and motivates his listeners. When this image becomes the only way in which a pastor is viewed, the danger is that he becomes only a *public* speaker and loses an *interpersonal* connection with his sheep. He may forfeit "doing" for speaking.

Similarly, the minister can be seen as a teacher. This image puts forth the pastor as an authority figure who directs, protects, and disciples his people. The minister who only sees himself in this way is vulnerable to foregoing his own study and taking on false doctrines. He may forfeit "being" for teaching.

Another image of who a minister is and what he does is that he is a leader. Pastors are called to be people of vision, order and focus who protect and equip their sheep. There is a danger for the sheep in having an excess of this perception. Followers can begin to look to leaders instead of God. They can also become lazy by putting all authority and responsibility on the leader. The minister who allows this may forfeit "humility" for power.

Understanding biblical leadership, we can say that it is very closely tied to service. The minister as a servant is another image of a minister. The servant is supportive and approachable. The pastor is a "doer." An exaggeration of this role can lead to unwittingly encouraging those he is serving to not serve. The pastor will do it. The minister may forfeit "equipping and releasing" for burnout.

The role of the minister, by definition, is a relational one. It is not surprising that two common images of the minister revolve around roles found in the family—parent and sibling. The minister can be seen as a father or mother. He or she is a credible authority figure who offers security and nurturing. A corruption of this model causes the minister to be feared instead of respected. He or she can become distant and inflexible. The minister may forfeit "intimacy" for distinction. The minister can also be seen as a brother or sister who is approachable, not feared, and able to relate to others. The vulnerability of having this as an exclusive image is that the minister can become less authoritative and less credible to his or her people. The minister may forfeit "authority" for the ordinary.

Sometimes, the minister is seen as a counselor. A pastor can be viewed as a wise shepherd who leads the sheep toward reconciliation with God, themselves, and others. A minister shows personal concern for his sheep and offers them guidance. This image must not be overemphasized. It can lead to the pastor being overwhelmed with other people's problems. An imbalance here can also lead to the tendency of people to ignore seeking God's guidance themselves. The minister may forfeit "God giving people rest" for too little rest for himself.

A compelling image of a minister is that he is a healer. He is one who facilitates restoration by the supernatural power of God. The warning here is obvious. Be careful that people do not begin to look to you instead of God and try to make you an idol. The minister may forfeit "pointing to God" for others pointing to him.

These different perspectives of a minister do not, in any way, change the actuality of what the minister is and does. The minister is who he is regardless of different perspectives. A particular image of a minister promotes an understanding of a piece of his nature and activities. The minister is a preacher, teacher, leader, servant, father/mother, brother/sister, counselor, and healer. He is also much more. One biblical image of the minister helps us see the minister rightly as long as we understand there are many other biblical images of the minister.

Jesus assembles these images. "And He gave some *as* apostles, and some *as* prophets, and some *as* evangelists, and some *as* pastors and teachers" (Eph. 4:11). Jesus says, "I will build My church" (Matt. 16:18).

JUNE 22

THANK YOU, THANK YOU, THANK YOU

"We give thanks to You, O God, we give thanks."

Psalm 75:1

A culture of entitlement results in a poverty of thankfulness. Entitled people are not prone to being thankful since they see their blessings in a more matter-of-fact sort of way. When your tendency is to say "You owe me," you will not tend to say, "I thank you." It is all about perception. Jesus knew this and tried to make sure His disciples understood it also, so He told them this story:

"A moneylender had two debtors: one owed five hundred denarii, and the other fifty. When they were unable to repay, he graciously forgave them both. So which of them will love him more?" Simon answered and said, "I suppose the one whom he forgave more." And He said to him, "You have judged correctly." Turning toward the woman, He said to Simon, "Do you see this woman? I entered your house; you gave Me no water for My feet, but she has wet My feet with her tears and wiped them with her hair. You gave Me no kiss; but she, since the time I came in, has not ceased to kiss My feet. You did not anoint My head with oil, but she anointed My feet with perfume. For this reason I say to you, her sins, which are many, have been forgiven, for she loved much; but he who is forgiven little, loves little" (Luke 7:41-47).

How do you perceive your blessings from God? How much have you been forgiven? You may have many blessings from God, and you may have been forgiven much; yet if you do not see those blessings, then you will not be thankful for them. It is all about perception. Everyone has been forgiven the same amount—completely forgiven. It is not the amount of forgiveness that is different; it is the perception of forgiveness that is the variable in the equation. Some people realize that and are thankful. Others fail to realize it and are not thankful; in fact, their lack of thankfulness often turns into bitterness.

It is all about perception. Moreover, there is a "momentum" of perception—a movement from before to now to later. This "past-present-future" aspect of thankfulness shows up in all kinds of situations in our lives. When someone has done something for you—no matter how small or common—and you recognize it and are thankful, that enables you to be thankful now. When you are thankful now, you set yourself up to be thankful later on. If you fail to be thankful in the past, then you will more likely not be thankful in the present; and you will not be set up to be thankful in the future.

When you fail to be thankful for your parents' sacrifice in providing for you as a child, then you are less likely to be thankful for a gift they give you now as an adult; and you will not anticipate being thankful for any blessing from them in the future. The downward momentum starts in your attitude toward the past. You do not express your thankfulness to your parents for what they have given you. Maybe it is because you think that they already know you are grateful, or maybe you do not want to bother them. Maybe you plan to do it later, or maybe you think that one of your brothers or sisters has already done it and has represented you. Maybe you feel like it does not really matter, or maybe you just forgot. Maybe you think that what your parents did is only what they were supposed to do, or maybe you just do not value it much.

Failure to be a thankful person for past blessings lends itself to never being a thankful person. Thanking God breeds thankfulness. Not thanking God breeds dissatisfaction. The ungrateful person is the miserable person. There is a reason why we are encouraged to "count our blessings." It is so we will truly be blessed (a word that means "happy"). The most unhappy people in the world are those who are not thankful.

How often do you thank your husband or wife, your parents or children, your co-workers or friends, or even the stranger who opened the door for you? How often do you thank God? Is it 90 percent of the time, 60 percent of the time, 30 percent of the time, or maybe only the leprous 10 percent of the time? Jesus healed ten lepers, but only one came back to thank Him: "Now one of them, when he saw that he had been healed, turned back, glorifying God with a loud voice, and he fell on his face at His feet, giving thanks to Him" (Luke 17:15-16).

Consider how God has blessed you. Now, "turn back" and thank God in prayer. That is how you become a more thankful person. When you are thankful for what God has already done, then you will be thankful for what God is doing and will do. Start there. Thank You, God, for what You have already done. Thank You. Thank You. Thank You!

JUNE 23

THE ART OF FINDING THE ONE AND ONLY

"This is now bone of my bones, and flesh of my flesh."

Genesis 2:23

Finding "the one" is informed by a high view of marriage. Marriage is established by God as the most foundational institution of human society. As soon as God created man, He declared, "It is not good for the man to be alone; I will make him a helper suitable for him" (Gen. 2:18). Man was incomplete, so God made for him his completion. And the man said, "'This is now bone of my bones, and flesh of my flesh; she shall be called Woman, because she was taken out of Man'" (Gen. 2:23).

When Adam says, "This is now bone of my bones," he is saying, "She is me, and I am her." It is not surprising, then, that the Scripture instructs, "So husbands ought also to love their own wives as their own bodies. He who loves his own wife loves himself; for no one ever hated his own flesh, but nourishes and cherishes it" (Eph. 5:28-29). When husbands love their wives, they love themselves because the wife is the husband; they are "one." It is an exclusive relationship. The "bone of my bones" reality results in mutual ownership. "Each man is to have his own wife, and each woman is to have her own husband. The husband must fulfill his duty to his wife, and likewise also the wife to her husband. The wife does not have authority over her own body, but the husband *does*; and likewise also the husband does not have authority over his own body, but the wife *does*" (1 Cor. 7:2-4).

Because of the way God created, Adam immediately recognized that they are *two* ("woman" and "man"), and he also recognized that they are *one* ("bone of my bones and flesh of my flesh"). They are a singular plurality. The two are one; they are a unity in diversity. There is equality without being the same. And so, immediately after Adam's singular plurality declaration in Genesis 2:23, we see the establishment of marriage: "For this reason a man shall leave his father and his mother, and be joined to his wife; and they shall become one flesh" (Gen. 2:24). A paraphrase might be: "Since God created them as a singular plurality and commanded them to multiply, the man shall leave family in order to multiply family by being joined to her who completes him; the two shall become one, the plural shall become singular." God, Who is a singular plurality—in the Trinity, He is Three in One—created man in His singular plurality image (Gen. 1:26-27). A high view of marriage is based on the fact that God institutes it in His own image. Marriage reflects Him.

Out of this comes discussion with regard to the nature of marriage roles. Simply because husband and wife are equal does not mean they are the same, and simply because they are not the same does not mean they are not equal. And out of this comes discussion with regard to finding a mate. Since according to God, the couple is "one," there must be certain "non-negotiables"—certain "oneness" assumptions must be made and insisted on—that can become flashlights or indicators. Since according to God, the couple is "two," there should be certain "negotiables"—certain "distinction" assumptions can be made and allowed—that should not be differences that are thought to be disqualifiers.

What are some of the "oneness" indicators? If you are "the one" who is me, then you will be composed of recognizable physical, social, emotional, mental, and spiritual leanings. Physically, you will be attracted to each other. Socially, you will see each other as being each other's and nobody else's, and you will want to form a new family together. Emotionally, you will have a similar vision for the multiplication of that family—how many children you want and what your philosophy of parenting is. Mentally, you will have a similar vision for the desired lifestyle of that new family—how career, money, and possessions are viewed. Spiritually, you have a similar degree of intensity with which you would say, "As for me and my house, we will serve the LORD" (Josh. 24:15).

What are some of the "distinction" indicators? If you are "the one" who is part of our two, then you will be quite different than me in ways that are not part of our holy "oneness" but part of our equally holy "twoness." It is okay that he or she is different from you in these "negotiable" ways. In fact, it is natural and to be expected (and, thus, not thought of as disqualifiers). Some differences are inherent to the very nature of men and women. Men need to be wanted, desired, and needed. They need to be seen as heroes. Women need to be valued, cherished, and prized. They need to be seen as treasures. Other differences are simply personality or motivational distinctions. Some people are more optimists or pessimists, realists or idealists. Some are more task-oriented, and others are more relational. Some focus on efficiency (let's put the pedal to the metal and get it done) while others focus on the process (let's talk through this). Some people's style of conflict management is to "fight," while others are bent toward "flight." Some are more adventurous, while others tend to be more careful. Some are very comfortable with showing affection, and others are more comfortable with very little touching. Some people are more pragmatic, while others are more aesthetic.

The art of finding "the one and only" is founded on the Founder Himself. What is the nature of marriage as it is created by God? To understand this is to understand what you are looking for and what you are not looking for. Your "one and only" is "you who is not you." What does that look like? You will know it when you see it!

JUNE 24

THE NEVERNESS OF GOD

"... The Everlasting God, the LORD, the Creator of the ends of the earth does not become weary or tired."

Isaiah 40:28

God is eternal. He never began, and He never ends. Do not think about that too long. It will fry your brain! His eternality is the most fundamental aspect of His nature. Thus, His most foundational name is "I Am."

> Then Moses said to God, "Behold, I am going to the sons of Israel, and I will say to them, 'The God of your fathers has sent me to you.' Now they may ask me, 'What is His name?' What shall I say to them?" God said to Moses, "I AM WHO I AM"; and He said, "Thus you shall say to the sons of Israel, 'I AM sent me to you.'" God, furthermore, said to Moses, "Thus you shall say to the Israelites, 'The LORD, the God of Abraham, the God of Isaac and the God of Jacob, has sent me to you.' This is My name forever, and this is My memorial-name to all generations" (Exod. 3:13-15).

An "I Am" is both never and always. He is never because He is always. For example, He is Jehovah Shammah (Ezek. 48:35); He is "always there." Because He is always there, He is never gone. He is like your shadow. You cannot get away from Him. He never leaves you (Heb. 13:5). When you are at your lowest point, He is there. The "neverness" of God is comforting!

The "always God" is never rushed. As the only eternal Being, He has no time. "But do not let this one fact escape your notice, beloved, that with the Lord a day is like a thousand years, and a thousand years like a day. The Lord is not slow about His promise, as some count slowness, but it patient toward you" (2 Peter 3:8-9). The timeless God is never hurried. He is never in a rush. He never runs out of time. For example, He is "slow to anger" (Psalm 103:8). The "neverness" of God gives us hope!

God is never weary. The eternal One never runs out of energy. "Do you not know? Have you not heard? The Everlasting God, the LORD, the Creator of the ends of the earth, does not become weary or tired" (Isa. 40:28). His "always power" means He is never unable. He is never without an answer or the ability to enact that answer. God never fails. "Not one of the good promises which the Lord had made to the house of Israel failed; all came to pass" (Josh. 21:45). The "neverness" of God is encouraging!

God is never learning new things. He is not in process. He never matures. He is already perfect (Psalm 18:30). He is never needy. He never lacks. "Who has directed the Spirit of the LORD, or as His counselor has informed Him? With whom did He consult, and *who* gave Him understanding? And *who* taught Him in the path of justice and taught Him knowledge and informed Him of the way of understanding?" (Isa. 40:13-14). God's independence, and dependence on no one, makes Him available as the One to completely depend on. The "neverness" of God directs us!

God is never wrong. He is never confused or in a panic. No matter how hard it is to understand things that are happening to you, it is never God's "fault." Job's sin did not cause his problems. Job's sin came in the way he analyzed his problems. When he could not understand what was happening to him, he began to blame God. God rebuked him: "Would you discredit my justice? Would you condemn me to justify yourself?" (Job 40:8). In whatever way things in this fallen world are assessed, one thing is always true. God is never wrong! The "neverness" of God informs us!

God is eternal. He is always and never. His "never nature" means that we are never without comfort and encouragement. We are never without direction, hope, and information. We can say of Him, "Always, always, always"; and we can say of Him, "Never, never, never." He never began, and He never ends. He is "the Alpha and the Omega" (Rev. 22:13). Praise be to God!

JUNE 25

IS YOUR PALACE BUILT ON THE KING?

"You are God's field, God's building. According to the grace of God which was given to me, like a wise master builder I laid a foundation."

1 Corinthians 3:9-10

Have you ever experienced something in your life that "rocked your world," that shook you to your very foundations? Life and major storms have a funny way of meeting up with each other. Storms will come. If your foundation is not strong, then things can begin to fall apart.

Therefore everyone who hears these words of Mine and acts on them, may be compared to a wise man who built his house on the rock. And the rain fell, and the floods came, and the winds blew and slammed against that house; and *yet* it did not fall, for it had been founded on the rock. Everyone who hears these words of Mine and does not act on them, will be like a foolish man who built his house on the sand. The rain fell, and the floods came, and the winds blew and slammed against that house; and it fell—and great was its fall (Matt. 7:24-27).

You are "God's building" (1 Cor. 3:9). Thus, it is your life that must have a strong foundation. What is your life's foundation? A Christian life must be built on the kingdom of God and, thus, the King of that kingdom.

Ultimately, we must build our lives on Jesus. Paul explains this when he writes, "According to the grace of God which was given to me, like a wise master builder I laid a foundation, and another is building on it. But each man must be careful how he builds on it. For no man can lay a foundation other than the one which is laid, which is Jesus Christ" (1 Cor. 3:10-11). Since Jesus' self-proclaimed purpose was to preach the Gospel (Mark 1:14, 38; Luke 4:43) and since "it is no longer I who live, but Christ lives in me" (Gal. 2:20), then my life must be built on the foundation of sharing the Gospel with others. Certainly, my life must become the extension of the life of Christ. This exact dynamic is what makes up the book of Acts. The people of God, especially Peter, Philip and Paul, *act* on behalf of Christ. The book of Acts shows the extension of Jesus' ministry through His disciples.

How will His ministry be extended through me? It will happen through a relationship with Him. The more intimately I know Him, the more successfully I can make Him known. I must know

Him as Lord. Nothing has meaning apart from Christ. Everything has meaning in Christ. He is Lord. Everything finds its value and meaning as it relates to Him. I must know Him as the Word of God. I must make decisions according to the Bible. It directs my life. I must know Him as Savior. He is my only Hope. The cross represents my salvation. I must build my life on the victory of the cross. I must also accept and follow its method. Thus, my life is built on my death. And so, Jesus says to us, "'If anyone wishes to come after Me, he must deny himself, and take up his cross and follow Me. For whoever wishes to save his life will lose it; but whoever loses his life for My sake will find it'" (Matt. 16:24-25).

Finally, I must know Him as my Authority. I do not live for myself or by myself. I live for Christ and under Christ. I do not minister in my own authority. I minister in His authority (Matt. 28:18-19). I am an ambassador. I am a messenger for a King. In summary, my life must be built on a foundation that is made up of knowing Jesus as Lord, the Word of God, Savior, and my Authority.

Can you picture yourself as "God's building?" What does the foundation look like? Does it look like Jesus? He is the "corner *stone*, in whom the whole building, being fitted together, is growing" (Eph. 2:20-21). With Him as the Foundation and cornerstone of our buildings, even when the storms come—and they will come—we will not fall.

JUNE 26

WHAT IS SPIRITUAL IS REALLY JUST LOGICAL

"The sons of Israel would see the face of Moses, that the skin of Moses' face shone. So Moses would replace the veil over his face until he went in to speak with Him."

Exodus 34:35

Humility has a certain look. It looks away from self. A lack of humility lends itself to pointing *to* self, boasting about yourself. People boast about who they are and what they have done. They also brag about who they *think* they are and what they *think* they have done. They use their false perceptions to paint an ideal picture of themselves for others to see. This portrait is often painted with words. Humility drives us to the world of wisdom instead of to the world of fantasy. It helps us to count our words and not be loose with our lips, for "when there are many words, transgression is unavoidable, but he who restrains his lips is wise" (Prov. 10:19). Humility steers us away from the exaggerations of a puffed-up mind and prompts us to pray, "Deliver me, O LORD, from lying lips, from a deceitful tongue" (Psalm 120:2). Embellishment is the tool of the one who boasts as "the fool multiplies words" (Eccl. 10:14).

Moses did not fall to this temptation of pointing to himself. His humility (Num. 12:3) kept him from taking glory for himself when it obviously belonged to God. After the crossing of the Red Sea, Moses sang a beautiful song of victory. We might ask the question, "Where is Moses' name in this song?" The answer is that it is not there (Exod. 15:1-18). Most of us would have stuck our name in there *somewhere*. There are forty six references to God in the victory song, yet there are no references to Moses. Moses' humility allowed him to understand that he was but an instrument in God's hand. An instrument only plays the song; it is not the song itself!

Humility is a logical, rational, and reasonable response to reality. If you understand the nature of God—what is real and true—then it will seem logical to walk in humility and very irrational to boast. "For who regards you as superior? What do you have that you did not receive? And if you did receive it, why do you boast as if you had not received it?" (1 Cor. 4:7). Your boasting makes absolutely no sense. Stop pointing to yourself and start pointing to God. It is only logical! "Therefore I urge you, brethren, by the mercies of God, to present your bodies a living and holy sacrifice, acceptable to God, *which is* your spiritual service of worship" (Rom. 12:1). The word *spiritual* comes from the Greek word *logikos*, which can be translated (as in the King James Version) *logical, rational,* or *reasonable.* Point to God instead of yourself? It is the most rational, logical, and reasonable thing you can do. It is the most *spiritual* thing you can do. It just . . . makes sense!

A lack of humility results in projecting glory for yourself. Pride is a showoff. It wants to shine its face upon other people. "But whenever Moses went in before the LORD to speak with Him, he would take off the veil until he came out; and whenever he came out and spoke to the sons of Israel what he had been commanded, the sons of Israel would see the face of Moses, that the skin of Moses' face shone. So Moses would replace the veil over his face until he went in to speak with Him" (Exod. 34:34-35). Moses used his humility to cover up his pride's desire. He does realize his face is shining. He does not try to pretend. He is not faking it; his is not a false humility. He does not try to negate reality. He covers reality so as not to bring the focus on himself but to leave the focus on God.

This is, perhaps, the greatest challenge of the life of humility; consciously covering up self, so as to focus more on God. Cover up your shine, so as to unveil the shine of God. It only makes sense!

JUNE 27

GET A HANDLE ON THE WORD

"Be diligent to present yourself approved to God as a workman who does not need to be ashamed, accurately handling the word of truth."

2 Timothy 2:15

Variety is the spice of Bible study. All it may take to spice up your study of Scripture is to be more diverse hermeneutically. Because of your training, gifting, and personal preference, you may, for example, have a propensity toward a thematic or topical interpretive style (systematic theology). In order to expand your methods of study, you can take more of a historical analysis approach (biblical theology) and study the text with more of a literary analysis consideration.

When studying the Bible from a historical perspective, you can look at the Bible as a mirror and categorize the truth while also looking at the Bible as a window through which to view the life situation of the text and get a fuller understanding of its meaning. Your ability to apply the Word can improve via such processes. The fruit of such study can facilitate a "mapping" or "matching" the application for the original audience to the application for the contemporary audience.

With literary analysis — consideration of the literary genre of the text and its author's motives in writing it — you can interpret the text relative to its literary form. Parables, for example, should not be interpreted in the same way as genealogies. Parables are meant to make one major point. There may be a multitude of specific descriptions within the story of a parable, but they all serve to move toward one conclusion—the lesson or teaching of the parable. Genealogies, on the other hand, should be interpreted according to each individual piece of information, for that is the nature of that sort of genre of literature.

Literary analysis can also take into account the author's motive. Bible text that is meant to record a historical event must be interpreted as such, as opposed to text that is meant to prophesy future events. Who was the author writing to? What was the situational context? Why was the author writing to these particular people at this particular time and in this particular way? Engaging in literary analysis can expand your understanding of Scripture.

Bible students naturally become Bible preachers and teachers. Perhaps you already preach regularly, or maybe you will soon be asked to teach a Sunday school class or share the Word at a home group. In any case, it can be helpful to consider an expository preaching approach, in which you will fashion your message around the "one thing" the text says.

Your introduction can hook the listener as it creatively alludes to the single point to be made and promises the listener that this point will lead to a certain application. The explanation portion of your message can reveal and explain the process of interpretation that led to this ultimate point being made. The illustration section of your teaching can then use storytelling to place the point into an appropriate story that your listeners can relate to. The application segment of an expository message can more easily utilize the "fallen condition focus" of the text. Felt needs are the same for all of us. They revolve around the human problems that are a result of the fall of man. This type of focus in applying the text is very impactful.

After explaining, illustrating, and applying the text, it is time for your conclusion. Go back to the introduction. What did you propose? What did you promise your listeners? Conclude with a clear and concise way to reiterate that proposition and strengthen your promise.

Messages are given by messengers, which they get from their study of the Word of God. Study the Word. Proclaim the Word. Study the Word more! "Be diligent to present yourself approved to God as a workman who does not need to be ashamed, accurately handling the word of truth" (2 Tim. 2:15). Engage in different methods of Bible study, and you will be more apt to preach and teach with more creativity. Do not be ashamed. Work hard at it. Get a handle on it. God approves!

JUNE 28

SPIRITUALITY IS ALL ABOUT PRIORITIES

"'The kingdom of heaven is like a treasure hidden in the field, which a man found and hid again; and from joy over it he goes and sells all that he has and buys that field.
Again, the kingdom of heaven is like a merchant seeking fine pearls,
and upon finding one pearl of great value, he went and sold all that he had and bought it.'"

Matthew 13:44-46

Spiritual people live in spiritual realms. God's kingdom is such a realm; it is "not of this world" (John 18:36). It is a spiritual kingdom (Romans 14:17). Spirituality is measured by the degree to which you seek that kingdom. And so, when we talk about spirituality, we must talk about priorities. A priority is that which comes first. It is a preference in an order of importance. Spiritual people must understand how to set and live out priorities.

Determination is used to set priorities, and discipline is used to live out priorities. Determination helps us to clearly set as our priority the kingdom of God (Matt. 6:33). Spiritual people are determined to stand firm in their decisions and resolute in their persistence (Luke 11:8-9). "No one, after putting his hand to the plow and looking back, is fit for the kingdom of God" (Luke 9:62). Elisha was a very determined person. Elijah suggests to him three separate times to not follow him any longer, but Elisha responds three times in the same way, "As the LORD lives, and as you yourself live, I will not leave you" (2 Kings 2:6). Determination sets priorities.

Discipline is used to live out the priorities that are set by determination. Discipline includes mental and moral training that result in obedience to rules. What are often referred to as "spiritual disciplines"—for example: Bible study, prayer, fellowship, worship—are such because they help us act on the prioritization of spiritual things. Paul was a spiritual man because he was a disciplined man.

Do you not know that those who run in a race all run, but *only* one receives the prize? Run in such a way that you may win. Everyone who competes in the games exercises self-control in all things. They then *do it* to receive a perishable wreath, but we an imperishable. Therefore I run in such a way, as not without aim; I box in such a way, as not beating the air; but I discipline my body and make it my slave, so that, after I have preached to others, I myself will not be disqualified (1 Cor. 9:24-27).

Dedication is used to set priorities, and decision-making is used to live out priorities. Dedication is the attitude of devotion toward something that is set aside or marked for a specific purpose or use. "Therefore I urge you, brethren, by the mercies of God, to present your bodies a living and holy sacrifice, acceptable to God, *which is* your spiritual service of worship. And do not be conformed to this world, but be transformed by the renewing of your mind, so that you may prove what the will of God is, that which is good and acceptable and perfect" (Rom. 12:1-2). We dedicate ourselves to God and set His kingdom as our priority as we deprioritize "this world."

Decision-making is used to live out the priorities that are set by dedication. Decision-making includes the process by which we determine to follow a certain course of action. Sometimes, we are afraid or reluctant to make decisions. Perhaps that is because we sometimes fear determination, discipline, and dedication. Decision-making requires faith (Heb. 11:1-31).

To live a life of spirituality, priorities must be set and lived out. In order to die to self, we must be determined and disciplined to reject self-sufficiency and seek God's sufficiency. We must be dedicated and able to make decisions that deny self and lift up Christ. A priority is that which comes first. Christian spirituality recognizes that Christ comes first. It utilizes determination, discipline, dedication, and decision-making to set Christ as the priority and to live out that priority. For God says, "You shall have no other gods before Me" (Exod. 20:3). Yes, true spirituality is walked out on a very narrow path!

JUNE 29

THE ROMANS 12 GIFT OF LEADERSHIP

"Since we have gifts that differ according to the grace given to us,
each of us is to exercise them accordingly *... he who leads, with diligence."*

Romans 12:6, 8

God equips His people with gifts for ministry. There exist various lists of gifts in the New Testament. One such list is found in Romans 12:6-8: "Since we have gifts that differ according to the grace given to us, *each of us is to exercise them accordingly*: if prophecy, according to the proportion of his faith; if service, in his serving; or he who teaches, in his teaching; or he who exhorts, in his exhortation; he who gives, with liberality; he who leads, with diligence; he who shows mercy, with cheerfulness."

The Giver of these gifts is God the Father (Rom. 12:3). The gifts are called *charismata* (grace gifts). They are described as being functional gifts (Rom. 12:4) that are effects enacted by "God who works all things in all persons" (1 Cor. 12:6). The Romans 12 gifts direct how a person functions; they determine the effects of a person's personality or tendencies. They are not so much gifts that a person is temporarily and situationally used in (as in the 1 Corinthians 12:8-10 gifts) or gifts that dictate a person's actual ministry (as in the Ephesians 4:11 gifts) as they are gifts that reside inside of a person and shape what that person is like. They are what are often called "motivational gifts."

How can the Romans 12 gift of leadership be understood? People who have the gift of leadership look for opportunities to initiate action among people and organize those people and the tasks that are necessary to engage in those activities. The gift of leadership prompts those who have it to receive and implement vision. When Nehemiah heard about the problems in Jerusalem, he went to the king and said, "'If it please the king, and if your servant has found favor before you, send me to Judah, to the city of my fathers' tombs, that I may rebuild it'" (Neh. 2:5). People with the gift of leadership have a propensity toward effectively matching needs and resources. Nehemiah had a vision for the building of the wall in Jerusalem. He organized his resources to meet his needs and, thus, requested of the king,"'If it please the king, let letters be given me for the governors *of the provinces* beyond the River, that they may allow me to pass through until I come to Judah, and a letter to Asaph the keeper of the king's forest, that he may give me timber to make beams for the gates of the fortress which is by the temple, for the wall of the city and for the house to which I will go'" (Neh. 2:7-8).

Leaders have the ability to delegate effectively. When Nehemiah became aware of the dangers in building the wall, he "stationed *men* in the lowest parts of the space behind the wall, the exposed places, and stationed the people in families with their swords, spears and bows" (Neh. 4:13). Those who have the gift of leadership are apt to be very goal oriented and able to recruit and train other leaders.

Just like any strength that has its correlated weaknesses, the gift of leadership has its vulnerabilities or carnal tendencies that need to be avoided. If someone with this gift is not careful, he or she may become prideful, insensitive to others' feelings, and impatient with others who are less able to keep up. Oftentimes, because of the sense of self-imposed pressure that leaders might put upon themselves to be successful, they may begin to struggle with insecurity. This insecurity can then set the stage for other vulnerabilities in a leader's life like becoming judgmental of others; being bound up by fear; and struggling with jealousy, depression, and self-pity. These things, of course, need to be avoided.

In the Romans 12 gift of leading, life is seen in terms of organizing others. The orientation is toward accomplishing goals. More than anything else, people with this gift view themselves as those who want to, and are able to, manage people and tasks well. They especially want to provide guidance for those people and tasks. They would say of themselves, "If people do not know where to go and what to do, then they can just follow me!" Are you this person? Do you have the Romans 12 gift of leadership?

JUNE 30

HOW WILL THEY HEAR WITHOUT A PREACHER?

"...And how will they hear without a preacher? How will they preach unless they are sent."
Romans 10:14-15

There are steps on the road to salvation. People get saved; however, there is a process that must take place in order to eventually arrive at that glorious outcome. Unbelievers will get saved because they "CALL ON THE NAME OF THE LORD" (Rom. 10:13). They get saved because they believe in Him (Rom. 10:14). They believe in Him because they have heard (Rom. 10:14). They hear because someone preached (Rom. 10:14). Someone preached because they were sent (Rom. 10:15).

And so, the finish line is someone's salvation; however, the starting gate is someone being sent to share the Gospel message. Who is sent to do such a thing? It must be the clergy. Or maybe it is the traveling evangelists. Although fulltime ministers and crusade evangelists may share the Gospel message, it must be understood that all Christians are called and sent by God to be messengers for Christ: "And He ordered us to preach to the people and solemnly to testify that this is the One who has been appointed by God to be judge of the living and the dead" (Acts 10:42). When we have excuses to not share the Gospel, He says to us, "'As for you, go and proclaim everywhere the kingdom of God'" (Luke 9:60).

He sends us out as witnesses: "'You will receive power when the Holy Spirit has come upon you; and you shall be My witnesses both in Jerusalem, and in all Judea and Samaria, and even to the remotest part of the earth'" (Acts 1:8). Since we are sent by the One Who has all authority, we should not be ashamed or timid to share the Gospel. Jesus says to us, "'All authority has been given to Me in heaven and on earth. Go therefore and make disciples'" (Matt. 28:18-19) and "do not be ashamed of the testimony of our Lord" (2 Tim. 1:8).

There are various reasons why we fail to share the Gospel with others. We simply may not care enough, or we may be too busy to take the time. We may feel it is not our job, so we pass it off on someone else. We may feel unprepared and, therefore, afraid to be rejected, to fail, or to just look stupid. In any case, none of these reasons cancel out the most basic issue—that is, that He sends us out as witnesses.

The biggest hindrance to evangelism occurs simply when we fail to share the Gospel with lost people. The Gospel is powerful to save. However, its power to save will not save if it is not proclaimed. It will not be written in the sky with wisps of clouds. It will have to be spoken in family rooms and coffee shops and schools with words of life poured through holy vessels (2 Tim. 2:21). In order to reach the finish line, there must first be a starting line. How will they hear without a preacher? So, let's get in the starting blocks and run the race, and we will see the finish line of salvation.

NOTES

July

JULY 1

WHAT'S IT ALL ABOUT?

"This is eternal life, that they may know You, the only true God, and Jesus Christ whom You have sent."
John 17:3

Essentials are things you cannot do without. You have to make sure you bring the essentials with you and be careful to accomplish the essential goals first. They are vital, crucial, fundamental, and, yes, indispensable. Essentials are what we are referring to when we use the expression, "Give me the bottom line."

What is the bottom line with respect to life? What are those things that will give my life purpose because there is nothing else more foundational, nothing else more essential? Perhaps, we should begin with "the essential question," which just might lead us to "the essential truth," which may prompt us to consider "the essential mystery," which will then point us to "the essential definition" that will ultimately yield "the essential understanding."

The essential question is rather obvious. Why am I alive? What is my purpose in life? What gives my life meaning? This is a question that, for many, only produces frustration and depression. The prevailing philosophy in Western culture, existentialism, necessarily lends itself to this frustration and depression. When it is understood that all that is real is bottled up in a moment of time, then yesterday is gone; and tomorrow never comes. There is nothing to look back to, and there is nothing to look forward to. More than anything else, there is no purpose, no meaning. Why am I alive? What is my purpose in life? What gives my life meaning? This is the essential question.

In order to answer this essential question, we must consider the essential truth. Reality is not just a moment. It is actually as opposite of that as you can get. Reality is eternity. This life, however, is but a split-second relative to eternity. For the sake of making a calculation, allow us to say that eternity is eight billion years long, though after eight billion years in eternity, you're still only eating breakfast! Now let us say that you are blessed with a very long life, and you live to be a hundred years old. Using these numbers, your life compared to eternity would only be a fraction of a second (1/30 of a second). Your life would end before you could say "me."

These calculations illustrate an essential truth. Our lives are here today and gone tomorrow. A split second can only find purpose as it positively affects the rest of time. It is not big enough to find purpose in itself. This is the essential truth. Purpose in life can only be found in eternity; our lives in this world can only find purpose as they positively affect our lives to come. If the split second can be used to move us toward eternity, then, and only then, does it have a purpose. This is the essential truth.

This essential truth leaves us with an essential mystery. Purpose in this life is found in eternal life. This seems counterintuitive. It is somewhat enigmatic. This is a mystery to many people who try to find purpose in temporal things. The frustration of man comes from this misunderstanding of eternal purpose. He tries various ways to find purpose. They are all temporal: money, sex, drugs, alcohol, power, influence, education, and so on. Some of these things are "good" things, and some are "bad." In any case, they all fail to provide a lasting sense of fulfillment because they all try to pretend that the "split second" is longer than it really is. This is the essential mystery.

If the essential mystery is that purpose is found in eternal life, then the essential definition is the definition of eternal life. If I can know what eternal life is, then I can know where to find purpose. Jesus defines eternal life for us in very plain terms. It is not sitting on a cloud wearing a bleach white robe and playing a harp. It is not, as the Buddhists say, "nothing." Neither is it, as the Hindus say, "all."

It is as Jesus says, "This is eternal life, that they may know You, the only true God, and Jesus Christ whom You have sent" (John 17:3). Eternal life is to know God. This is the essential definition.

This essential definition brings us to the essential understanding. Why are we alive? We are alive to know God and to make God known. We are eternal beings. Eternity is within us. It is how we were made. "He has made everything appropriate in its time. He has also set eternity in their heart, yet so that man will not find out the work which God has done from the beginning even to the end" (Eccl. 3:11). And if eternal life is to know God, then we exist in order to know God and to make God known. We are alive to live eternal life and to help others to live it also. This is the essential understanding.

A wise proverb might be, "Leave what is unessential to be unessential and what is essential to be essential." In other words, do what counts. Do what matters. Does anything else make sense?

JULY 2

GOD IS CALLING YOU OUT

"That you may proclaim the excellencies of Him who has called you out of darkness into His marvelous light."

1 Peter 2:9

God calls you out over and over again. He continually works in your life. The New Testament word for "Church" is *ekklesia*. The word *ek* means "out," and the word *kaleo* means "to call." The Church is the gathering together of the "called out ones." God is calling you out from new birth to new Heaven. First, He calls you out in that He points to your sin and your need for His salvation. Second, He calls you out in that He calls you out of the world for sanctification. Third, He calls you out in that He sends you out into the world and uses you to call out others through evangelization. Finally, He calls you out in that He receives you into Heaven for glorification.

You are a called-out one. God calls you out on your sin. He does not let you go your own way as if to say it is all fine. He convicts you. If He did not call you out, then you would have no chance of being saved. Jesus explained this when He declared, "No one can come to Me unless the Father who sent Me draws him" (John 6:44). Repentance is required for salvation: "Therefore repent and return, so that your sins may be wiped away, in order that times of refreshing may come from the presence of the Lord" (Acts 3:19). Conviction is required for repentance, and conviction comes when God calls you out. "And He, when He comes, will convict the world concerning sin and righteousness and judgment" (John 16:8). This God-sourced conviction is efficacious; it results in a new birth via the call to "be out." "I now rejoice, not that you were made sorrowful, but that you were made sorrowful to *the point* of repentance; for you were made sorrowful according to *the will of* God, so that you might not suffer loss in anything through us. For the sorrow that is according to *the will of* God produces a repentance without regret, *leading* to salvation, but the sorrow of the world produces death" (2 Cor. 7:9-10).

You are a called-out one. God calls you out of the world. He does not allow you to remain the same. He changes you by separating you and making you holy. If He did not change you, then you would have no chance of being sanctified. Sanctification is a process; you are continually being called out of the world and being made holy. (Heb. 10:14) The process moves toward completion. He who began to call you out will call you out to the end as "He who began a good work in you will perfect it until the day of Christ Jesus" (Phil. 1:6). God does not stop calling you out until the work is done. "Now may the God of peace sanctify you entirely, and may your spirit and soul and body be preserved complete, without blame at the coming of our Lord Jesus Christ" (1 Thess. 5:23). Sanctification prepares you for ministry as you are "sanctified, useful to the Maste, prepared for every good work" (2 Tim. 2:21). You are set apart for a new lifestyle via the call to "live out."

You are a called-out one. God calls you out to send you out. Salvation and sanctification result in evangelization. You are saved to serve others, give to others, and share with others; you are called out to go out (Matt. 28:19), not to stay in. "But you are A CHOSEN RACE, A royal PRIESTHOOD, A HOLY NATION, A PEOPLE FOR God's OWN POSSESSION, so that you may proclaim the excellencies of Him who has called you out of darkness into His marvelous light" (1 Peter 2:9). You are called out to go out, not to hide under. "You are the light of the world. A city set on a hill cannot be hidden, nor does *anyone* light a lamp and put it under a basket, but on the lampstand, and it gives light to the whole house"" (Matt. 5:14-15). You come out of the world ready to go into the world, "always *being* ready to make a defense to everyone who asks you to give an account for the hope that is in you, yet with gentleness and reverence" (1 Peter 3:15). You are given a new mission via the call to "go out."

You are a called-out one. God will ultimately call you out forever. When the trumpet sounds (1 Cor. 15:52), you will be transformed, resulting in your glorification. "Those He called, he also justified; those he justified, he also glorified" (Rom. 8:30). When the One Who calls you appears, you hear Him and see Him, and it changes you. "Beloved, now we are children of God, and it has not appeared as yet what we will be. We know that when He appears, we will be like Him, because we will see Him just as He is" (1 John 3:2). Your glorification is forever. "And when the Chief Shepherd appears, you will receive the unfading crown of glory" (1 Peter 5:4). You are brought into the new Heaven and earth via the call to "stay out."

God calls you to be out, live out, go out, and stay out. He calls you to salvation, sanctification, evangelization, and glorification. You are the Church, the *ekklesia*, the "called out ones." God is calling you out! Do you hear Him?

JULY 3

FRIDAY IS, INDEED, GOOD!

"I have been crucified with Christ; and it is no longer I who live, but Christ lives in me."
Galatians 2:20

The Christian holy day commemorating the brutal death of Jesus Christ on the cross is called Good Friday. This is an expression of the flip-flopped nature of the kingdom of God. What seems so bad is, in fact, exceedingly good. And so, the term *gospel* means "good news." The method of the Gospel is the cross. The method of good news is death. Throughout the Scriptures, there is one clear methodology used to live in the kingdom of God—death to self. The words "broken," "empty," and "yield" describe a sort of progression that is necessary for living the good life of the cross.

First, you must be broken in order to make room for God to work through you. "For You do not delight in sacrifice, otherwise I would give it; You are not pleased with burnt offering. The sacrifices of God are a broken spirit; a broken and a contrite heart, O God, You will not despise" (Psalm 51:16-17). God desires and responds to your brokenness, for there is something about the death found in brokenness that brings forth life (2 Cor. 8:9). "Truly, truly, I say to you, unless a grain of wheat falls into the earth and dies, it remains alone; but if it dies, it bears much fruit" (John 12:24). God blesses brokenness, since it is brokenness that places you in the kingdom of God. "Blessed are the poor in spirit, for theirs is the kingdom of heaven" (Matt. 5:3). Walls that are broken down are then rebuilt (2 Chron. 32:5; Neh. 2:17).

Second, you must be emptied in order to be filled with God's Spirit, for it is "'not by might nor by power, but by My Spirit', says the Lord of hosts" (Zech. 4:6). The "leprosy" in our lives must be emptied out or removed before it can be refilled, replaced, and cleansed (Lev. 14:33-42). If we are not emptied of self, then our "aroma" will not change: "And he has not been emptied from vessel to vessel . . . therefore he retains his flavor, and his aroma has not changed . . . I will send to him those who tip *vessels*, and they will tip him over, and they will empty his vessels and shatter his jars" (Jer. 48:11-12).

Finally, on this road that leads from death to life, you must yield to God in order to walk in His desire to give to you, for you will receive from Him by surrendering to Him. "Now do not stiffen your neck like your fathers, but yield to the LORD and enter His sanctuary which He has consecrated forever, and serve the LORD your God" (2 Chron. 30:8). The question is, "Who do you present yourself to?" To yield to God is to present yourself to Him, as you are called to "not go on presenting the members of your body to sin *as* instruments of unrighteousness; but present yourselves to God as those alive from the dead, and your members as instruments of righteousness to God" (Rom. 6:13). Another way to ask this question is, "Whose agenda are you following?" You must yield to His agenda (Acts 16:6-10).

The good life of the cross is described by these three words: broken, empty, and yield. This is consistent with asking God to melt me, mold me, fill me, and use me. Our activity in the kingdom of God (use me) begins with the idea of brokenness (melt me), continues with the idea of becoming empty of self (mold me), and ends with the idea of yielding to and receiving from Him (fill me).

Simplicity is essential in living this type of life. To focus on Christ instead of self, you need to view life from an orientation of simplicity. You must realize your status and abilities relative to God. You are not sovereign; you cannot create, cause, or control. You must realize that God does not call you to these complex dynamics but to the simpler dynamics of looking to Him Who creates, causes, and controls via your own brokenness, emptying of self, and yielding to Him.

What are your priorities and concerns? Do you realize that worry is usually nothing more than being concerned over things that are, in fact, not your concern. We have a singular concern. It is to seek God's kingdom before all else (Matt. 6:33). Seeking God is good. It is good news. It is Gospel. The method of the Gospel is death to self and, so, brokenness, emptiness, and yielding lead to life. They lead to life because they all pull away from self and lead to God, Who is life (John 14:6). Instead of me, it is Jesus; and the way to get there is the cross. "I have been crucified with Christ; and it is no longer I who live, but Christ lives in me" (Gal. 2:20). Friday is, indeed, good!

JULY 4

FREE WILL—DON'T COUNT ON IT!

*"So then it **does** not **depend** on the man who wills or the man who runs, but on God who has mercy."*
Romans 9:16

You have a free will. You are not a robot because God is not a robot, and you are made in "the image of God" (Gen. 1:27). At the same time, you are not God. Equally as significant is that you and your free will are fallen. Your free will cannot create because you are not God, and your free will cannot save you because you are fallen. As much as you may want to stress that you have a free will, you also must remember that you cannot count on it!

If returning to God depended on your free will, you would never see God again. Your sin nature is such that you freely stay away from and reject God. Your free will by itself will not say yes to God;

it will only say no. This is where the sovereignty of God comes in. Sometimes, these two attributes are pitted against each other in theological debates as if they cannot live together. How can man have a free will if God is sovereign? Free will cannot be free in the midst of sovereignty. There is nothing further from the truth. Not only *can* they live together, but they also *must* live together. In fact, free will apart from God's sovereignty cannot be free at all because without God, it would have no choice; and without choice, it is not free.

God, in His mercy, sovereignly affords the free will of man a choice—to choose Him or not to choose Him. Without God's mercy, man's free will directs itself in one way only—away from God. With God's mercy, man's free will has the ability not to create its own choice and save itself but to receive God's choice and be chosen. To be chosen is to choose God's choice (Matt. 22:11-14). Man cannot create, cause, or control choice, for that is not in his nature; he is not God. He can freely receive it because that is in his nature. He can only have a free will consistent with Who He is, not with Who He is not.

> There was the true Light which, coming into the world, enlightens every man. He was in the world, and the world was made through Him, and the world did not know Him. He came to His own, and those who were His own did not receive Him. But as many as received Him, to them He gave the right to become children of God, *even* to those who believe in His name, who were born, not of blood nor of the will of the flesh nor of the will of man, but of God (John 1:9-13).

You cannot work your way to Heaven. You will not free will yourself back to God. Only God can provide you with a choice and, in so doing, enact your free will—a free will that can then choose God. God is Sovereign in all of this, and man has a free will in it as well. The two are not enemies. They are necessarily wedded together. When we understand this, we do not question God and accuse Him of injustice. Oppositely, we thank God and proclaim His glory.

> What shall we say then? There is no injustice with God, is there? May it never be! For He says to Moses, "I WILL HAVE MERCY ON WHOM I HAVE MERCY, AND I WILL HAVE COMPASSION ON WHOM I HAVE COMPASSION." So then it *does* not *depend* on the man who wills or the man who runs, but on God who has mercy. For the Scripture says to Pharaoh, "FOR THIS VERY PURPOSE I RAISED YOU UP, TO DEMONSTRATE MY POWER IN YOU, AND THAT MY NAME MIGHT BE PROCLAIMED THROUGHOUT THE WHOLE EARTH." So then He has mercy on whom He desires, and He hardens whom He desires. You will say to me then, "Why does He still find fault? For who resists His will?" On the contrary, who are you, O man, who answers back to God? The thing molded will not say to the molder, "Why did you make me like this", will it? Or does not the potter have a right over the clay, to make from the same lump one vessel for honorable use and another for common use? What if God, although willing to demonstrate His wrath and to make His power known, endured with much patience vessels of wrath prepared for destruction? And *He did so* to make known the riches of His glory upon vessels of mercy, which He prepared beforehand for glory, *even us*, whom He also called, not from among Jews only, but also from among Gentiles (Romans 9:14-24).

As much as you may want to stress that you have a free will at the expense of God's Sovereignty, you also must remember that you cannot count on your free will! We should not be insulted by or opposed to God's Sovereignty. We should rejoice in it. "So then it does not depend on the man who wills or the man who runs, but on God who has mercy" (Rom. 9:16).

LEAD ON!

"Then I said to them, 'You see the bad situation we are in, that Jerusalem is desolate and its gates burned by fire. Come, let us rebuild the wall of Jerusalem so that we will no longer be a reproach.'"
                                                                                                     Nehemiah 2:17

Nehemiah was a great leader. He led a multitude of people in the massive project to rebuild the walls of Jerusalem in fifty-two days (Neh. 6:15). This kind of endeavor requires skillful leadership; the leader must embody certain character traits.

In order to lead others, leaders must know where to go. They have to be knowledgeable and have a natural bent toward acquiring knowledge. Nehemiah was naturally inquisitive: "I asked them concerning the Jews who had escaped *and* had survived the captivity, and about Jerusalem" (Neh. 1:2). Leaders look to gain knowledge, so they can better lead their people. This "informed leadership style" resulted in Nehemiah reporting, "So I went up at night by the ravine and inspected the wall" (Neh. 2:15). Leaders just know! It is like when you were a child and your mother would say to you, "Your mother knows everything!"

Leaders must also have great discernment. The ability to judge well is a critical character trait for a leader to possess. Deception is a constant enemy of the leader. Discernment is his weapon. Nehemiah used his weapon when he "perceived that surely God had not sent him, but he uttered *his* prophecy against me . . . He was hired for this reason, that I might become frightened and act accordingly and sin, so that they might have an evil report in order that they could reproach me" (Neh. 6:12-13). Seeing into things protects the leader and those he is leading.

Leaders must be action-oriented people. Doers are leaders. Talkers are dreamers. It is a superficial or cheap imitation of leadership that does not act. Leadership, by definition, is portrayed by a person who is a "go-getter," as opposed to a person who is lazy. Leaders are entrepreneurial at heart. Nehemiah was prone to take initiative: "Then I said to them, 'You see the bad situation we are in, that Jerusalem is desolate and its gates burned by fire. Come, let us rebuild the wall of Jerusalem so that we will no longer be a reproach'" (Neh. 2:17).

Leaders tend to be very practical people. What is more practical than getting people to rebuild the section of the wall that is in front of their house? This is exactly what Nehemiah did. "After him Meremoth the son of Uriah the son of Hakkoz repaired another section, from the doorway of Eliashib's house even as far as the end of his house . . . After them Benjamin and Hasshub carried out repairs in front of their house. After them Azariah the son of Maaseiah, son of Ananiah, carried out repairs beside his house" (Neh. 3:21, 23).

Leaders persevere. They do not give up, and they are willing to do whatever it takes to complete their mission. Nehemiah led his people in this way:

> So we carried on the work with half of them holding spears from dawn until the stars appeared. At that time I also said to the people, "Let each man with his servant spend the night within Jerusalem so that they may be a guard for us by night and a laborer by day." So neither I, my brothers, my servants, nor the men of the guard who followed me, none of us removed our clothes, each *took* his weapon *even to* the water (Neh. 4:21-23).

What does a godly leader look like? He or she resembles someone who is knowledgeable, discerning, action-oriented, practical, and willing to persevere. Calling all leaders! Lead on!

JULY 6

DON'T LET THE SUN GO DOWN ON ME!

"The law of the LORD is perfect, restoring the soul; the testimony of the LORD is sure, making wise the simple. The precepts of the LORD are right, rejoicing the heart; the commandment of the Lord is pure, enlightening the eyes."

Psalm 19:7-8

As we move from the Old Testament to the New Testament, some may say that we move from the Law as the focal point to grace which is highlighted. They might say that the dawning of the New Covenant brought in the setting of the Law. Yet the Old Testament prophets do not promise an annulment of the demand of the Law. They promise an Enabler and the power needed to obey. The Spirit gives life and ethical ability. "I will put My Spirit within you and cause you to walk in My statutes, and you will be careful to observe My ordinances" (Ezek. 36:27).

The fulfilling of the Law that Jesus speaks of is not that which changes it but that which satisfies its requirements on behalf of others and equips others to better keep it.

Do not think that I came to abolish the Law or the Prophets; I did not come to abolish but to fulfill. For truly I say to you, until heaven and earth pass away, not the smallest letter or stroke shall pass from the Law until all is accomplished. Whoever then annuls one of the least of these commandments, and teaches others *to do* the same, shall be called least in the kingdom of heaven; but whoever keeps and teaches *them*, he shall be called great in the kingdom of heaven (Matt. 5:17-19).

The doing of the Law is not something we do in our own power. The enabling grace is manifested in the sending of the Holy Spirit. To claim otherwise is foolishness: "Are you so foolish? Having begun by the Spirit, are you now being perfected by the flesh?" (Gal. 3:3).

Puritan ethics understood that there was a supernatural grace that enabled believers to fulfill the Law. This occurred in the following four ways: the new life (a prerequisite to enabling grace), forgiveness of sins (sanctification arises from justification), the indwelling of Christ (the power for keeping the Law is found in our union with Christ), the work of the Holy Spirit who conforms us (the work of sanctification). The most basic Puritan question and answer was: "What is the chief end of man? It is to glorify God."

To a large degree, the Puritan ethic that was based on an adherence to authoritative commands is replaced today with a set of ethics based on inner compulsions. The objective has been replaced by the subjective. Ethics are in the eye of the beholder. This postmodern humanistic relativism is even sometimes seen as being "spiritual." However, the leading of the Spirit must always be consistent with the Spirit of God's Word. The absolute nature of God's Laws must not be ignored. It is true that we may sometimes not "feel led" to love our neighbor, but that does not mean for that instance that it is not God's Law. The Spirit does not oppose His own Law; and the Law is not invented by the Law-receiver, for it can only exist in the Law-giver.

God's law has not set on the eastern horizon. It is perfect (Psalm 19:7-8), and it will never go away. "The works of His hands are truth and justice; all His precepts are sure. They are upheld forever and ever" (Psalm 111:7-8).

WHICH SPIRITUAL GIFTS ARE WE TALKING ABOUT?

"Now there are varieties of gifts, but the same Spirit. And there are varieties of ministries, and the same Lord. There are varieties of effects, but the same God who works all things in all persons."
1 Corinthians 12:4-6

The idea of spiritual gifts covers quite a variety of distinctions. There are three separate and self-defined lists of gifts found in the New Testament. They are not the same. And so, for us to understand what they are, we must be study them within their own contexts. It cannot simply be assumed that one list of gifts can be explained and understood in the same way as another list of gifts. The three different types of gifts, for example, are each associated with a different member of the Trinity. The Spirit, God the Father, and Christ are named as Givers of their specific list of gifts. Moreover, Paul seems to be referring to this distinction when he writes, "Now there are varieties of gifts, but the same Spirit. And there are varieties of ministries, and the same Lord. There are varieties of effects, but the same God who works all things in all persons" (1 Cor. 12:4-6). Each set of gifts has its own distinct nature and purpose. To not study the lists of gifts separately is to do them a disservice and is to put ourselves in danger of misunderstanding them. Different lists of gifts must point us to the realization of different gifts.

The list of nine gifts found in 1 Corinthians 12:8-10 include "word of wisdom," "word of knowledge," "faith," "gifts of healing," "miracles," "prophecy," "distinguishing of spirits," "*various* kinds of tongues," and "interpretation of tongues." The Giver of these gifts is the Holy Spirit (1 Cor. 12:7, 11). These gifts are what are called *pneumatikos* (spiritual gifts or "spirituals"). They are described as being a "manifestation of the Spirit" (1 Cor. 12:7) that "are varieties of gifts" (1 Cor. 12:4).

The seven gifts found in Romans 12:6-8 include: prophecy, serving, teaching, exhorting, giving, leading, and showing mercy. They are described as being functional gifts (Rom. 12:4) that are effects enacted by "God who works all things in all persons" (1 Cor. 12:6).

The list of five gifts found in Ephesians 4:11 include: apostles, prophets, evangelists, pastors, teachers. The Giver of these gifts is Christ (Eph. 4:7). These gifts are called *domata* (gifts). They are described as being "equipping gifts" (Eph. 4:12) that are "ministries" (1 Cor. 12:5).

Certainly, there are some similarities in the nature of each of the three lists of gifts. Even though it is only the list of gifts in Romans 12 that are specifically called *charismata*, it is true that all gifts are, in a sense, *charismata*; all are based on God's grace, and none are earned. "But one and the same Spirit works all these things, distributing to each one individually just as He wills" (1 Cor. 12:11). "Since we have gifts that differ according to the grace given to us, *each of us is to exercise them accordingly*" (Rom. 12:6). "But to each one of us grace was given according to the measure of Christ's gift" (Eph. 4:7).

So there are, of course, similarities across all three lists, since they are all lists of gifts. Nevertheless, in order to fully understand what these gifts are and how they function, it is critical to understand that they are different lists of gifts. The 1 Corinthians 12 manifestation gift of prophecy, for example, is not the Romans 12 functional gift of prophecy, nor is it the Ephesians 4 equipping gift of prophet. The 1 Corinthians 12 gift is a manifestation ("a shaking of the hands") of the activity of the Holy Spirit—a display or demonstration of His presence. It is not so much a gift that resides inside of a person as it is a gift that a person is temporarily and situationally used in. The Romans 12 gift is a gift that directs how a person functions; it determines the effects of a person's personality or tendencies. It is not so much a gift that a person is temporarily and situationally used in as much as it is a gift that resides inside of a person and shapes what a person is like. The Ephesian 4 gift is an actual ministry or "office"; it places someone into a position in which they equip others for ministry. It is not so much a gift that resides inside of a person or a gift that someone is temporarily used in as it is a gift that establishes a ministry focus or placement around someone's life.

And so, the 1 Corinthian 12 gifts are "outside" their recipients, while the Romans 12 gifts are "inside" their recipients and the Ephesians 4 gifts are "around" their recipients. There is, then, a "prophetic action" (an occasional use of prophecy for a specific purpose), a "prophetic being" (a prophetic style, tendency, emphasis, or personality), and a "prophetic authority" (more than a style of ministry, it is more what a person is than what a person is like). And so, since there are different lists of gifts, there are different kinds of gifts that function in different ways.

JULY 8

AND I WILL BLESS YOU!

*"Nebuchadnezzar the king to all the peoples, nations, and **men of every** language that live in all the earth: 'May your peace abound! It has seemed good to me to declare the signs and wonders which the Most High God has done for me."*

Daniel 4:1-2

Why did God choose Israel? Why did He not choose the Chaldeans or the Akkadians or the Babylonians? Actually, why did He have to choose anyone at all? The answer to this question has to do with how God's business works. God is in the business of revealing Himself to people. He has a main strategy for how He operates His business. He actually employs a large workforce to get His message out there. That is the way He runs His business.

God chooses Israel so that others can be chosen through them. God chooses Israel as a missionary nation. When God makes His covenant with Abraham, He tells him that He is going to bless him (choose him). This blessing is not, however, simply for the purpose of blessing *him*. God tells Abraham why He is going to bless him (choose him) when He says, "And so you shall be a blessing; and I will bless those who bless you, and the one who curses you I will curse. And in you all the families of the earth will be blessed" (Gen. 12:2-3). God blesses (chooses) Israel *so that* Israel will be a blessing to others (others will be chosen).

God told Israel, "I will make you a great nation, and I will bless you, and make your name great" (Gen. 12:2). The purpose for Israel being chosen (receiving blessings) is clear throughout the Old Testament. God made Israel a great nation. Its land was fertile, and its location was strategic. Israel was a strong and influential country.

The missiological purpose for this is clearly seen in Solomon's prayer:

> Also concerning the foreigner who is not from Your people Israel, when he comes from a far country for Your great name's sake and Your mighty hand and Your outstretched arm, when they come and pray toward this house, then hear from heaven, from Your dwelling place, and do according to all for which the foreigner calls to You, in order that all the peoples of the earth may know Your name, and fear You as *do* Your people Israel, and that they may know that this house which I have built is called by Your name (2 Chron. 6:32-33).

God told Israel He would make them a great nation *so that* "all the peoples of the earth may know your name, and fear you." God blessed Israel. He blessed her people. For example, God blessed Joseph "in order to bring about this present result, to preserve many people alive" (Gen. 50:20). God blessed Joseph *in order to* bless others. Similarly, God blessed Solomon *so that* His name would be known among the people of Sheba. When the Queen of Sheba heard about how the God of Israel had blessed Solomon, she traveled to Israel. There she saw with her own two eyes the blessings of God. She returned to Sheba with a great testimony of God's greatness: "Now when the queen of Sheba heard about the fame of Solomon concerning the name of the LORD, she came . . . Then she turned and went to her own land together with her servants" (1 Kings 10:1, 13).

In a similar situation, the blessings of God upon Daniel's life resulted in King Darius' evangelistic writings to all peoples: "Then Darius the king wrote to all the peoples, nations and men of every language who were living in all the land: 'May your peace abound! I make a decree that in all the dominion of my kingdom men are to fear and tremble before the God of Daniel; for He is the living God and enduring forever, and His kingdom is one which will not be destroyed, and His dominion *will be* forever'" (Dan. 6:25-26).

Over and over again, God blesses His people in the book of Daniel *so that* the nations would come to know Him (Dan. 2:46-49; 3:28-30; 4:1-3, 34-37).

God made Israel a great nation, and He blessed her people *so that* other nations would be blessed. He also made Israel's name great for the same purpose. It was the reputation of Israel that drew the Queen of Sheba to Solomon's side and then sent her back to her own people with convincing testimonies of the greatness of God. Also, it was the "name" of Israel's God that gave Solomon reason to believe that people from far-off countries would come to Jerusalem and come to know Him. Israel's name became great *so that* God would be known in the nations.

God is a good businessman. He does not waste resources. He does not invest in something simply for the sake of investing. He is a God of purpose. He is a missionary God. He has a plan. His plan includes blessing a chosen people so that they can be a blessing to other people, who can then be chosen. That is His business. His "bottom line" is not made up of numbers; it is made up of people. "For God so loved the world" (John 3:16).

JULY 9

WHO'S BOSS?

"No servant can serve two masters; for either he will hate the one and love the other, or else he will be devoted to one and despise the other. You cannot serve God and wealth."

Luke 16:13

Jesus tells a story in Luke 16:1-9 about an "unrighteous manager" who gets praised by his master, seemingly, for being irresponsible, deceptive, and dishonest. If this steward is so unrighteous with regard to the way in which he represents his master, then why does the master congratulate him and approve of his actions? Money, like anything else, only has worth as it relates and points to God and His kingdom. The point of the parable is that the correct perspective of money is that it is a means to an end, not an end in itself. Money becomes a means for being received "into the eternal dwellings" (Luke 16:9). It is not that we buy our salvation. It is that our perspective of money is consistent with our understanding and application of the value and preeminence of that salvation. Knowing God and living in His kingdom is superior to all else. Money only finds value in the degree to which it remains subordinate to the King and His kingdom.

We are called to "seek first His kingdom" (Matt. 6:33). The kingdom of God must take such priority in our lives that it makes everything else seem inconsequential. "The kingdom of heaven is like a treasure hidden in the field, which a man found and hid *again*; and from joy over it he goes and sells all that he has and buys that field. Again, the kingdom of heaven is like a merchant seeking fine pearls, and upon finding one pearl of great value, he went and sold all that he had and bought it"(Matt. 13:44-46).

From the perspective of the "unrighteous steward," the relative worthlessness of money found its importance in terms of how it moved him closer to the relative superiority of Heaven. For this he was praised and gained approval. "And I say to you, make friends for yourselves by means of the wealth of unrighteousness, so that when it fails, they will receive you into the eternal dwellings" (Luke 16:9).

The parable is obviously not meant to be a lesson on integrity in business. At the same time, we should understand that it is not somehow making the unbiblical point that we can earn our salvation through a correct perspective of money. It is a parable about the importance of salvation and how money should be viewed in light of that supreme importance. This becomes clearer when we observe the connection that is made between the present and the future. What I do here on earth now will affect my situation in eternity in the future. Therefore, all that I do now—including how I use my money—finds value and purpose relative to how it moves me toward a positive situation in eternity.

The steward who is praised for his actions says, "I know what I shall do" so that "people will welcome me into their homes" (Luke 16:4). Then it is suggested that you "make friends for yourselves" so that "they will receive you into the eternal dwellings" (Luke 16:9). Then in Luke 16:11-12, temporal value ("unrighteous wealth") is put up against eternal value ("true riches"), and temporal stewardship ("that which is another's") is compared to eternal stewardship ("that which is your own"). The parable is not about how the steward uses money. It is about how the steward views money. Is money understood to be subordinate because of knowing God is the Master?

Parables must be understood by their conclusions or summaries. Jesus wraps up the parable of the unrighteous steward when He says, "'No servant can serve two masters; for either he will hate the one and love the other, or else he will be devoted to one and despise the other. You cannot serve God and wealth'" (Luke 16:13). Is what you do with wealth dependent upon God and his purposes? If it is, then you make God and His purposes unconditional. Money becomes conditional with respect to God. God is the Master. Is what you do with God and His purposes dependent upon money? If it is, then you make money unconditional. God and His purposes become conditional with respect to money. Money is the master. This is idolatry!

What is supreme? What comes before all else? God calls us to a radical perspective. All is subordinate to Him and His kingdom. We must call Him Lord and live out His Lordship (supremacy) in our lives. Anything less and we break the first commandment, "You shall have no other gods before Me" (Exod. 20:3). Avoid idolatry!

JULY 10

YOU ARE FREE TO GIVE TO THE WORK OF GOD

"For by your standard of measure it will be measured to you in return."

Luke 6:38

The word *tithe* means "a tenth" and points us toward giving 10 percent of our income to God and His work. "Bring the whole tithe into the storehouse, so that there may be food in My house" (Mal. 3:10). This is a command of God, but does the command require that we give *no more* than 10 percent? Instead of a rigid tithe, a variable tithe can be considered. Do our needs change when we are blessed with receiving more money? Is it a biblical principle that we *must* spend more money when we earn more money? Is the percentage of what we give simply to stay the same when we prosper? Should that percentage change with our increased earnings if our needs remain the same?

It is a different way of thinking to realize that our needs should represent the constant or unchanged portion of our economic situation and that our giving can become the variable or changeable portion. After our needs are defined and established—including our need to save and allowing for slight seasonal and situational changes in our spending—we can then increase that which we give, instead of increasing that which we keep. We can avoid the trap of materialism, and more importantly, we can steward more of our blessings to be more of a blessing. "It is more blessed to give than to receive" (Acts 20:35).

A couple determines that their needs are represented by one hundred units of money, and their salary is only one hundred units of money. They will be challenged to tithe in this situation. When they do tithe ten units by faith, God blesses and prospers them. "Bring the whole tithe into the storehouse, so that there may be food in My house, and test Me now in this . . . if I will not open for you the windows of heaven and pour out for you a blessing until it overflows" (Mal. 3:10). God continues to promise, "'Give, and it will be given to you. They will pour into your lap a good measure—pressed down, shaken together, and running over. For by your standard of measure it will be measured to you in return'" (Luke 6:38).

Later, the couple receives 150 units of money as their salary. Do their needs change simply because they receive more money? No, therefore, they can give fifty units of money because their needs are still represented by one hundred units of money. Note that what they can give is the changing portion or the variable. Their needs are the unchanging portion or the constant. Originally, they gave 10 percent (the minimum). Now they are able to give 33 percent of their income.

They are able to do this because they are not slaves to the concept of the tithe. They do not use the tithe as an excuse to not give what they could give. They understand the idea of a variable tithe, instead of a rigid tithe.

If they did not consider the possibility of a variable tithe, then they would have only given fifteen units of money. They would have then had 135 units of money left for themselves. Yet their needs would still be represented by one hundred units of money. What happens to the extra thirty-five units of money? The answer to this question is often the beginning of materialism. Suddenly, they "need" extra things. Little by little, their lifestyle becomes more and more luxurious until, finally, they are very sick. They have been infected with the disease called materialism. Christians must be challenged to ask themselves some hard questions. Are we fooling ourselves with our convenient terms and concepts? Are we being honest with ourselves? The question should be, "How much can we give?" not simply, "How much do we have to give?"

These ideas should be considered while staying aware of the risk of being either overly simplistic (it is understood that needs can significantly change as life moves forward) or brutally legalistic (it is understood that giving is a matter of the heart, not a matter of a calculator). The fact that "it is more blessed to give than to receive" (Acts 20:35) in no way means it is not blessed to receive. The variable tithe is not a mandate; it is a challenge. Moreover, it should be seen as an opportunity enacted in freedom and not a threat enacted in bondage. "Each of you should give what you have decided in your heart to give, not reluctantly or under compulsion, for God loves a cheerful giver" (2 Cor. 9:7). Balance and wisdom must be wrapped up in this challenge.

John Wesley, the pioneer of the Methodist revivals in England in the 1700s, seemed to have understood the concept of the variable tithe. Wesley believed and practiced that an increase in income should result in a rise in the standard of giving as opposed to a rise in the standard of living. Wesley lived his life in this way. His general needs did not change. The amount he gave changed. He lived a simple life and gave away anything that was extra.

> The directions which God has given us, touching the use of our worldly substance, may be comprised in the following particulars. First, provide things needful for yourself: food to eat, clothes to wear, whatever nature moderately requires for preserving the body in health and strength. Secondly, provide these for your wife, your children, your employees, or any others who pertain to your household. If, when this is done, there be an excess left, then do good to them that are of the household of faith. If there be an over plus still, as you have opportunity, do good unto all men. In so doing, you give all you can. In a real way you give all you have.[12]

JULY 11

HOPE FOR THE POOR

"Now we who are strong ought to bear the weaknesses of those without strength ... For whatever was written in earlier times was written for our instruction, so that through perseverance and the encouragement of the Scriptures we might have hope."

Romans 15:1, 4

God calls His people to minister to the poor, but it is not an easy ministry. Sometimes, a poor person simply needs to be helped. Sometimes, however, a poor person needs to be helped to see that he needs help. The poor often need to see their need by seeing their need to be willing to be helped along with their need to help themselves.

Pertinent to this type of ministry is the need for "tough love." Confrontation is often necessary in ministry to the poor. A poor person may need to be confronted with some hard questions. What are you doing to provide for yourself? In what ways have you shown responsibility this past week? When the answer, "You just do not understand my situation," becomes synonymous with the assertion, "I do not have need," the challenge and confrontation has to become more direct and firm. If the person does not have need, then you certainly cannot help to provide for that non-existing need. To be the needy, you have to have need. Another way to say this is, "You cannot be helped if you do not want to be helped."

Poor people need hope. They need to be encouraged. The most important tool for those who minister to the poor is the Bible:

Now we who are strong ought to bear the weaknesses of those without strength and not *just* please ourselves. Each of us is to please his neighbor for his good, to his edification. For even Christ did not please Himself; but as it is written, "THE REPROACHES OF THOSE WHO REPROACHED YOU FELL ON ME." For whatever was written in earlier times was written for our instruction, so that through perseverance and the encouragement of the Scriptures we might have hope. Now may the God who gives perseverance and encouragement grant you to be of the same mind with one another according to Christ Jesus, so that with one accord you may with one voice glorify the God and Father of our Lord Jesus Christ (Rom. 15:1-6).

The Scripture can be used to offer teaching, training, reproof, and correction. "All Scripture is inspired by God and profitable for teaching, for reproof, for correction, for training in righteousness; so that the man of God may be adequate, equipped for every good work" (2 Tim. 3:16-17). Reading, studying, and meditating on the Word of God can aid in reforming the poor person's system of ethics and habits. A renewed mind can result in a renewed lifestyle.

There is what some call "the cycle of poverty." Poverty culture or poverty lifestyle breeds more poverty. Within an individual, this cycle can be devastating. A poor person can become comfortable in his poverty. He can begin to become used to and satisfied with a life of minimal accountability and work. He can begin to refuse to take responsibility for his own situation and, in effect, make himself one who is not needy and not able to be helped, hence, the "cycle."

The root cause of this is fear. The poor person can become a slave of fear. He may never even try to help himself. He may have a tremendous fear of failure. Thus, he may have a fear of making decisions. This lack of ability to make decisions will lead to a lack of discipline. The lack of discipline will lead to a lack of commitment. The lack of commitment will lead to a rejection of responsibility.

Ministry to the poor is a difficult and complicated ministry. God calls His people to engage in this difficult ministry because He is the God Who turns problems into solutions. He turns death into life, condemnation into forgiveness, and poverty into provision. There is hope!

JULY 12

REVELATION IS LIFE, BUT BE CAREFUL

"Man lives by everything that proceeds out of the mouth of the LORD."
Deuteronomy 8:3

Revelation is life! Without it, death reigns; for "where there is no vision, the people are unrestrained" (Prov. 29:18). They perish. Food is important for survival, but even more critical is God's revelation of Himself. "He humbled you and let you be hungry, and fed you with manna which you did not know, nor did your fathers know, that He might make you understand that man does not live by bread alone, but man lives by everything that proceeds out of the mouth of the LORD" (Deut. 8:3). Jesus put it this way when He explained it to His disciples: "It is the Spirit who gives life; the flesh profits nothing; the words that I have spoken to you are spirit and are life" (John 6:63). Revelation is life.

Revelation is powerful, and so we must be careful. The same revelation that moves us toward life can also move us toward death. We are prone to sin, and so we are prone to twist what we see.

Six days later, Jesus took with Him Peter and James and John, and brought them up on a high mountain by themselves. And He was transfigured before them; and His garments became radiant and exceedingly white, as no launderer on earth can whiten them. Elijah appeared to them along with Moses; and they were talking with Jesus. Peter said to Jesus, "Rabbi, it is good for us to be here; let us make three tabernacles, one for You, and one for Moses, and one for Elijah." For he did not know what to answer; for they became terrified. Then a cloud formed, overshadowing them, and a voice came out of the cloud, "This is My beloved Son, listen to Him!" All at once they looked around and saw no one with them anymore, except Jesus alone (Mark 9:3-8).

It was an incredible revelation event. Jesus was transfigured before them. Peter, James, and John understood that this was "good for us to be here." It was life! Yet they were not exempt from twisting that which was life into something that was not so good. Peter was ready to engage in idolatry. He wanted to make a tabernacle for Moses and Elijah. God immediately corrected them. He pointed them toward the uniqueness of Christ and back to basics. "You shall have no other gods before Me" (Exod. 20:3). And so, they saw "Jesus alone."

Peter again showed his tendency to easily mix life and death in the midst of Divine revelation. Alarmingly, God-sourced revelation was immediately followed by Satan-sourced "revelation."

He said to them, "But who do you say that I am?" Simon Peter answered, "You are the Christ, the Son of the living God." And Jesus said to him, "Blessed are you, Simon Barjona, because flesh and blood did not reveal *this* to you, but My Father who is in heaven. I also say to you that you are Peter, and upon this rock I will build My church; and the gates of Hades will not overpower it. I will give you the keys of the kingdom of heaven; and whatever you bind on earth shall have been bound in heaven, and whatever you loose on earth shall have been loosed in heaven." Then He warned the disciples that they should tell no one that He was the Christ. From that time Jesus began to show His disciples that He must go to Jerusalem, and suffer many things from the elders and chief priests and scribes, and be killed, and be raised up on the third day. Peter took Him aside and began to rebuke Him, saying, "God forbid it, Lord! This shall never happen to You." But He turned and said to Peter, "Get behind Me, Satan! You are a stumbling block to Me; for you are not setting your mind on God's interests, but man's" (Matt. 16:15-23).

Awakenings can lead to cults because the incredible life that is experienced in revival can so easily be expanded, distorted, and skewed. For example, out of the Second Great Awakening of the early 1800s came Mormonism. Why does this happen? What can keep this from happening? It is important to understand what revival produces. It produces hunger. This is a good thing, unless no food is available. Hungry people can become desperate when there is a shortage of food. Starving people are not picky eaters. They will eat anything that is put before them. False teaching needs to be made irrelevant by the availability of biblical teaching.

So the answer to the question of how to "keep this from happening" has to do with food. Revivals need to be fed. They need to be taught (like God taught Peter at the Transfiguration). Revelation is life, but an awakening needs to eat if it is going to avoid falling back to sleep. Jairus' daughter was raised from the dead (Mark 5:35-42). In an incredible exhibit of seeing God's power, Jesus directs people to feed the risen girl (Mark 5:43). Revelation makes us hungry for God. We need to make sure in the midst of God revealing Himself to us that we continue to eat from the Bread of Life and so satisfy our hunger, since "man lives by everything that proceeds out of the mouth of the Lord" (Deut. 8:3).

GRACE, FAITH, AND LAW LIVE IN THE SAME HOUSE

"Do we then nullify the Law through faith? May it never be! On the contrary, we establish the Law."
Romans 3:31

Some theologians argue that the Christian life and obedience to the Law are mutually exclusive issues. Often, this erroneous way of thinking is rooted in a misunderstanding of grace. Grace is not to be understood as that which excuses us from doing the Law but as that which enables us to do the Law. Far from making the Law non-applicable to Christian lives, grace makes the Law extremely relevant (Rom. 7:15-25). Through Christ the Lawmaker and Law-accomplisher, His followers live out the Law as He lives it out in them (Gal. 2:20).

The Law does not justify sinners. It does not have the power to save. The Law points us to the Savior, Who saves us by His grace that is highlighted by His perfect enacting of and acting out of the Law. Christ did not achieve this in order to exempt us from the Law. He did it to both save us and sanctify us. Our salvation from the curse of the Law becomes our being set apart to embrace it. "Do we then nullify the Law through faith? May it never be! On the contrary, we establish the Law" (Rom. 3:31).

Grace includes two major aspects. First, it frees us from the burden of sin. Second, it frees us to seek and follow God and live by His Law. Grace delivers people from the dominion of sin and from the ramifications of the transgression of the Law.

> But thanks be to God that though you were slaves of sin, you became obedient from the heart to that form of teaching to which you were committed, and having been freed from sin, you became slaves of righteousness . . . For just as you presented your members as slaves to impurity and to lawlessness, resulting in *further* lawlessness, so now present your members as slaves to righteousness, resulting in sanctification. For when you were slaves of sin, you were free in regard to righteousness. Therefore what benefit were you then deriving from the things of which you are now ashamed? For the outcome of those things is death. But now having been freed from sin and enslaved to God, you derive your benefit, resulting in sanctification, and the outcome, eternal life (Rom. 6:17-22).

Grace delivers us from sin, and that same grace then becomes our deliverance to holiness and righteousness. Grace does not exempt someone from the demands of the Law; rather, it establishes the character and status of a person that enables him or her to respond positively to those demands.

In terms of ethics and Christian living, grace must be seen not as excuser but as enabler. It is not because I accomplish the Law but because Christ accomplishes the Law in me. Paul reports, "And He has said to me, 'My grace is sufficient for you, for power is perfected in weakness'" (2 Cor. 12:9). This is a spiritual transaction walked out in faith. Grace and faith work together. "For by grace you have been saved through faith; and that not of yourselves, *it is* the gift of God; not as a result of works, so that no one may boast. For we are His workmanship, created in Christ Jesus for good works, which God prepared beforehand so that we would walk in them" (Eph. 2:8-10). Grace by faith produces works or the doing of the Law. It is the formula for Christian ethics. We are the workmanship *of* the Lawmaker and do good works *in* the Law-accomplisher. God does not "grace us from the Law." He graces us to do the Law. This is Christian ethics.

Grace and Law live together "so that the requirement of the Law might be fulfilled in us, who do not walk according to the flesh, but according to the Spirit" (Rom. 8:4). Grace is active, not passive. It is alive, not dead. It is enabler, not exempter. It "is Christ in you, the hope of glory" (Col. 1:27).

JULY 14

A DISHONORABLE CHURCH

"When you are invited by someone to a wedding feast, do not take the place of honor, for someone more distinguished than you may have been invited by him, and he who invited you both will come and say to you, 'Give your place to this man,' and then in disgrace you proceed to occupy the last place. But when you are invited, go and recline at the last place, so that when the one who has invited you comes, he may say to you, 'Friend, move up higher'; then you will have honor in the sight of all who are at the table with you. For everyone who exalts himself will be humbled, and he who humbles himself will be exalted."

Luke 14:8-11

What does a dishonorable church look like? It looks like a church that looks more like a business than a ministry. It looks like something that is led by someone who looks more like a CEO than an anointed minister of the Word of God. It looks like something that looks more like "what it looks like" than "what it actually is." When "excellence" is defined by appearance and methods instead of reality and contents, then form does not follow function but, instead, becomes the function itself. This is generally called hypocrisy and ultimately leads to dishonor.

A picture of putting form ahead of function is seen in the "seating fiasco" story told by Jesus in Luke 14:8-11. There can be great embarrassment in presumption. By way of deception, misunderstanding, assumption, or presumption, you can try to take a place that is not actually there for the taking. Forcing yourself into these kinds of situations can result in very awkward experiences; they can lead to disgrace and shame. It is important to know how to seat yourself. The most important tip that will help you get better at this skill is to never seat yourself in front of God. Don't put your form in front of His function or your appearance in front of His reality.

Jesus tells a parable about a man who was invited to a wedding feast. His advice for how he should conduct himself is, "'Do not take the place of honor'" (Luke 14:8). Jesus then describes how the problem with taking the place of honor is that "someone more distinguished than you" may come, and then you will have to give up your seat in disgrace (Luke 14:8-9). When it is God Who is the "more distinguished" One and we are those who try to seat ourselves in front of Him, then it is not only awkward but also is idolatrous.

When the image of the Church and its leaders is to make a platform for the advancement of "my ministry, business or kingdom," dishonor is not far off. When it is all about us and our personal elevation, then we are increasing, and He is decreasing (John 3:30). The next thing you know "in disgrace you proceed to occupy the last place" (Luke 14:9). Sadly, we have seen too many times that when the Church has insisted on seating itself in the front, it has been told to move to the back. Scandals have erupted exposing this faulty "me theology." There has been embarrassment, disgrace, and dishonor. There has been a reduction in credibility. Historically, ministers were usually considered the most respected, well-known, and influential people in a town. When ministry is viewed as an avenue for self-advancement, disgrace is right around the corner; and this historical perception suffers.

The problem is not found in the actuality of sitting up front. It is found in the problem of seating yourself up front. Only God can elevate you. Seat yourself and your ministry behind the one Who *is* seated up front, and then He can pull you up. "For everyone who exalts himself will be humbled, and he who humbles himself will be exalted" (Luke 14:11). Be honorable. Allow yourself or your ministry to be seated. Do not be dishonorable. Do not insist on seating yourself!

JULY 15

VESSEL THEOLOGY

"He will be a vessel for honor, sanctified, useful to the Master, prepared for every good work."
2 Timothy 2:21

What might be called "vessel theology" is rooted in the realization that God works through people. The implications of the Scriptural idea of "Christ in you" (Col. 1:27) are at the core of such a theology. As tools are to a carpenter, so are Christians in the hands of *the* Carpenter from Nazareth (Mark 6:3). And so, a definition of vessel theology is this: God works through vessels, and His vessels are His people. God works through His people.

A man was walking down a road when he saw from a distance what looked like a small boy vigorously pumping a handle up and down. The man could also see that water was flowing out of a spigot. As he came closer, the man could not believe his eyes. The boy had been pumping for five minutes at an incredible rate of speed and showed no sign of slowing down, yet he appeared to be the size of a five-year-old. Suddenly, he realized that the "boy" was a wooden caricature that was being pumped by a motorized handle.

So, too, you are empowered by God to the degree that your works are not your own. They are God's works as He works His works through you. You are a vessel, not the contents. Your "work" is God at work in you both to want to do His work and to be able to do His work. "So then, my beloved, just as you have always obeyed, not as in my presence only, but now much more in my absence, work out your salvation with fear and trembling; for it is God who is at work in you, both to will and to work for His good pleasure" (Phil. 2:12-13). God is actually doing the pumping, and it appears as though we are doing the work.

If we do not base our theology on this kind of "vessel theology," we will be in danger of working in our own strength. In 1979, a young man flew a pedal-powered plane twenty-two miles across the English Channel. Certainly, this was an incredible accomplishment with respect to man-powered flight. However, that type of flight is not practical. Man cannot maintain the necessary output of energy for extended flights. In the same way, we only deceive ourselves when we think we can live the Christian life in our own power.

According to Jesus, we can do nothing apart from Him (John 15:5). Vessel theology touts the clear implications of this fact. To be a worker for God, then, our vessels must be emptied and cleansed so that the pure contents of the Word of God can flow through them. "Now in a large house there are not only gold and silver vessels, but also vessels of wood and of earthenware, and some to honor and some to dishonor. Therefore, if anyone cleanses himself from these *things*, he will be a vessel for honor, sanctified, useful to the Master, prepared for every good work" (2 Tim. 2:20-21). The "vessel for honor" must rid itself of contaminates and make itself available for that which is pure (1 John 3:3). This necessitates death. "I have been crucified with Christ; and it is no longer I who live, but Christ lives in me" (Gal. 2:20). The fruit of good works can only come through death to self because there is no life apart from death; and there are no works apart from Christ, and there is no Christ apart from getting rid of self to make room for Him. "Truly, truly, I say to you, unless a grain of wheat falls into the earth and dies, it remains alone; but if it dies, it bears much fruit" (John 12:24).

The attitude of someone who adheres to a vessel theology comes from the understanding that "every good thing given and every perfect gift is from above, coming down from the Father of lights" (James 1:17). Anything good must come from God. This attitude results in a yearning for God, a hunger for righteousness and a sense of reliance upon grace to experience that righteousness. It is an attitude that says, "God, I want to make myself available for your use. I want to be a vessel for your activity. Work through me. Make me a vessel!"

JULY 16

TWO MOUNTAINS AND A BRIDGE

*"For Christ did not enter a holy place made with hands, a mere copy of the true one, but into heaven itself, now to appear in the presence of God for us; nor was it that He would offer Himself often, as the high priest enters the holy place year by year with blood that is not his own. Otherwise, He would have needed to suffer often since the foundation of the world; but now once at the consummation of the ages He has been manifested to put away sin by the sacrifice of Himself. And inasmuch as it is appointed for men to die once and after this **comes** judgment, so Christ also, having been offered once to bear the sins of many, will appear a second time for salvation without reference to sin to those who eagerly await Him."*

Hebrews 9:24-28

All Gospel presentations should revolve around two major points. Man has a problem, and God offers the solution to that problem. Man has a need, and God offers to provide for that need. Man is a sinner who is separated from God, and God pays for man's sin which reunites him with God. This is the Gospel—sin and salvation, problem and solution, need and provision. Of course, there are different ways in which to present the basic contents of the Gospel. There is, for example, the "Scripture passage" method, and there is the "story" method.

One such Scripture passage is Hebrews 9:24-28. It can be readily used to present the basic contents of the Gospel. The passage includes descriptions of three appearances of Christ and explains how each appearance is related to the reality of sin. First, there is the incarnation. Christ appears on earth. This includes His birth, death, and resurrection (1 Cor. 15:21). This appearance of Christ results in the destruction of the penalty and punishment of sin by His sacrifice on the cross. "Otherwise, He would have needed to suffer often since the foundation of the world; but now once at the consummation of the ages He has been manifested to put away sin by the sacrifice of Himself" (Heb. 9:26).

Second, there is the ascension. After His resurrection, Christ ascends and appears in Heaven. This includes being seated at the right hand of the Father. This appearance of Christ results in the destruction of the power of sin by His glorification (1 Cor. 15:55-57). "For Christ did not enter a holy place made with hands, a mere copy of the true one, but into heaven itself, now to appear in the presence of God for us" (Heb. 9:24).

Third, there is the return of Christ. After His ascension, angels proclaim that Christ will come again (Acts 1:9-11). This includes His creation of the new Heaven and the new earth (Rev. 21:1). This appearance of Christ results in the destruction of the existence of sin by the establishment of His

Kingdom. "Christ also, having been offered once to bear the sins of many, will appear a second time for salvation without reference to sin, to those who eagerly await Him" (Heb. 9:28).

Alternatively, the story method of presenting the Gospel can also be a powerful way in which to share the good news. One such story might be titled, "Two Mountains and a Bridge." God is holy. He lives on the mountain called Holy. Man is a sinner. He lives on the mountain called Sin. The two mountains were separated by a very big valley. God sent His Son to fill the valley with His love. This love touched Mount Holy and Mount Sin at the same time. The Son remained God, but He also became Man. He remained Holy, but He also became Sin. Hence, He served as the only connection between the two mountains. The love of God was so great that it refused to let go. Finally, it died as it held on to both mountains. Therefore, now there is a bridge that connects them. It goes over the valley of separation. The death of the Son of God enabled man to have a relationship with God. This bridge, named Jesus Christ, provides the only way to go from one mountain to the other.

Whether a "Scripture passage" method, a "story" method, or any other method is used to present the Gospel, it always carries the same content—Jesus, which means "God saves!"

JULY 17

DEAD FAITH IS NO FAITH AT ALL

*"What use is it, my brethren, if someone says he has faith but he has no works? Can that faith save him? If a brother or sister is without clothing and in need of daily food, and one of you says to them, 'Go in peace, be warmed and be filled,' and yet you do not give them what is necessary for their body, what use is that? Even so faith, if it has no works, is dead, **being** by itself."*

James 2:14-17

Martin Luther's Reformation stood on *sola fide* (faith alone). Salvation is by faith and not by works. So then, why are you to "work out your salvation with fear and trembling"? (Phil. 2:12). You are to "work it out" because "it is God who is at work in you, both to will and to work for His good pleasure" (Phil. 2:12-13). Your works do not come out of you and save you. His work goes in you and saves you, and then His works come out of you because He is in you. This is what James means when he says, "Even so faith, if it has no works, is dead, *being* by itself" (James 2:17). Works are not a cause of salvation; they are a result. In this way, salvation and sanctification are inextricably wed together.

Faith has two sides. There is the use of the intellect, and there is the use of the will. There is theory, and there is practice. There is doctrine, and there is action. There is trust, and there is obedience. There is belief, and there is repentance (Mark 1:15). There is faith, and there is works. There is salvation, and there is sanctification. Just as there needs to be fruit with repentance (Matt. 3:8), there needs to be action with faith (James 2:14-26).

A house is on fire. There is a little girl on the second floor who cannot escape. A big man yells, "Jump! I will catch you." It is one part of faith that the girl knows that the man is there (knowledge). It is another part of faith that the girl believes that the man is strong (assent) and that he is able to catch her (trust). Nevertheless, the essence of faith is that the girl actually jumps (action/obedience)!

Faith and works are inseparable. They are like the sun and the light of the sun. Faith is the sun. Works are the rays. The sun produces rays. When there are no more rays, the sun is dead. True and living faith produces works. "For just as the body without *the* spirit is dead, so also faith without works is dead" (James 2:26).

A man says, "I have faith without works." He is like a man who builds the foundation but never builds his house. Another man says, "I have works without faith." He is like a man who does not build his house upon a good, solid foundation.

Therefore everyone who hears these words of Mine and acts on them, may be compared to a wise man who built his house on the rock. And the rain fell, and the floods came, and the winds blew and slammed against that house; and *yet* it did not fall, for it had been founded on the rock. Everyone who hears these words of Mine and does not act on them, will be like a foolish man who built his house on the sand. The rain fell, and the floods came, and the winds blew and slammed against that house; and it fell—and great was its fall (Matt. 7:24-27).

Intellectual knowledge and obedient action are like the two chemical ingredients in salt. Salt consists of sodium and chloride. Both sodium and chloride are poisonous. Sodium, if ingested, will kill a human. Chloride will also kill you. However, when sodium and chloride are combined, they produce salt, which is essential to life. The same is true with faith and works. The one without the other is like a poison; but together, they produce life.

JULY 18

THE HEART OF GOD IS TOWARD THE NEEDY

"For the LORD hears the needy."

Psalm 69:33

Jesus did not come into this world and die on a cross to forgive people of their sins, even though they did not need forgiveness of sins. That would be absurd! God did not leave Heaven and sacrifice Himself to provide for people's needs when there was actually no need to do it. Paul expresses how absurd this is when he writes, "I live by faith in the Son of God, who loved me and gave Himself up for me. I do not nullify the grace of God, for if righteousness *comes* through the Law, then Christ died needlessly" (Gal. 2:20-21). The fact is we cannot provide for our own need. We need God!

God has favor on people with needs. He does not have favor on people without needs. If you do not need Him, then you will not get Him. You judge yourself "for God did not send the Son into the world to judge the world, but that the world might be saved through Him. He who believes in Him is not judged; he who does not believe has been judged already, because he has not believed in the name of the only begotten Son of God" (John 3:17-18). Of course, everyone needs God. However, some people see that need, and some people do not. Only those who see their need are, in fact, needy.

God has favor on those who recognize their needs. He has favor on the sick, not the healthy. He has favor on the humble, not the proud. He has favor on the poor, not the rich. Jesus did "not come to call the righteous, but sinners" (Mark 2:17). The truth is that "everyone who exalts himself will be humbled, but he who humbles himself will be exalted" (Luke 18:14). Jesus continuously explained this principle to His followers: "And turning His gaze toward His disciples, He *began* to say, 'Blessed *are* you *who are* poor, for yours is the kingdom of God . . . but woe to you who are rich, for you are receiving your comfort in full'" (Luke 6:20, 24).

Is Jesus against people who have a lot of money? No, His favor is not toward those who do not recognize their need for Him. Is Jesus for people who have very little money? No, His favor is toward those who recognize their need for Him. Need moves God. "'Because of the devastation of the afflicted, because of the groaning of the needy, now I will arise,' says the LORD; 'I will set him in the safety for which he longs'" (Psalm 12:5). Those who confess their need for God walk in hope "for the LORD hears the needy" (Psalm 69:33). Need turns into provision. "The LORD raises up those who are bowed down" (Psalm 146:8). Jesus' eyes are toward the poor. His heart is with the needy. When He began His ministry, His first message to those who would listen came from the book of Isaiah: "THE SPIRIT OF THE LORD IS UPON ME, BECAUSE HE ANOINTED ME TO PREACH THE GOSPEL TO THE POOR. HE HAS SENT ME TO PROCLAIM RELEASE TO THE CAPTIVES, AND RECOVERY OF SIGHT TO THE BLIND, TO SET FREE THOSE WHO ARE OPPRESSED, TO PROCLAIM THE FAVORABLE YEAR OF THE LORD" (Luke 4:18-19).

The heart of God is toward the needy. Another way to say this is, "God came to man because man could not get to God." Man truly needs God. God knows that and loves man. And so, God's heart is toward man. This is the good news. This is the Gospel! Do you see it?

JULY 19

ALL IS NOT WELL IN THE WORLD

"For the creation was subjected to futility, not willingly, but because of Him who subjected it, in hope that the creation itself also will be set free from its slavery to corruption into the freedom of the glory of the children of God. For we know that the whole creation groans and suffers the pains of childbirth together until now."

Romans 8:20-22

All is not well in the world. Things have been corrupted. This is not satisfying. There is what might be called a "holy dissatisfaction." This holy dissatisfaction must become a vision producing discontentment in us. Things are not right. They are not right in us. They are not right in others, and they are not right in the world. Things are shattered. That is what happens when there is a fall. Things break. It is not a holy thing to be satisfied with that. A holy dissatisfaction wants things to be put back together. We are put back together when we are together again with God. The difference between "unholy dissatisfaction" and "holy dissatisfaction" is the difference between running away from God and running to Him. Dissatisfaction with that which is not right drives us to seek God and motivates us to see Him glorified.

Holy dissatisfaction is to despise what is broken and wrong. The "Preacher" of Proverbs says it this way: "The fear of the LORD is to hate evil" (Prov. 8:13). Holy dissatisfaction is a healthy "fear of the Lord." In a sense, to get sick of yourself (your sin) is to gain a desire for God. To understand that there are a ridiculous multitude of options, opportunities, and manifestations of broken stuff available apart from God is to understand that the only reasonable response to our holy dissatisfaction is to seek God. The following verses show how:

- "But seek first His kingdom and His righteousness" (Matt. 6:33).
- "I beseech you therefore, brethren, by the mercies of God, that ye present your bodies a living sacrifice, holy, acceptable unto God, which is your reasonable service" (Rom. 12:1, KJV).
- "I am the vine, you are the branches; he who abides in Me and I in him, he bears much fruit, for apart from Me you can do nothing" (John 15:5). "In all your ways acknowledge Him, and He will make your paths straight" (Prov. 3:6).

Holy dissatisfaction recognizes that things must change. We must be saved, and we must be sanctified. This transformation is fueled by holy dissatisfaction. Change is God's story. It is because the fallen world is not satisfactory. The history of change—God's work in changing His creation back to what He originally intended it to be—will come to a triumphant culmination in our complete transformation. "Beloved, now we are children of God, and it has not appeared as yet what we will be. We know that when He appears, we will be like Him, because we will see Him just as He is" (1 John 3:2). This is what God is doing in His holy dissatisfaction. "He who began a good work in you will perfect it until the day of Christ Jesus" (Phil. 1:6). Dissatisfied people must remember that God is not done yet!

Change hurts, so there is a holy discomfort that comes along with a holy dissatisfaction. Change is edgy, so there is a holy disturbance that comes along with a holy dissatisfaction. Change is challenging, so there is a holy death to self that comes along with a holy dissatisfaction. Change is crucial, so there is a holy yearning and anticipation that comes along with a holy dissatisfaction. "Come, Lord Jesus" (Rev. 22:20). Maranatha!

> For the creation was subjected to futility, not willingly, but because of Him who subjected it, in hope that the creation itself also will be set free from its slavery to corruption into the freedom of the glory of the children of God. For we know that the whole creation groans and suffers the pains of childbirth together until now. And not only this, but also we ourselves, having the first fruits of the Spirit, even we ourselves groan within ourselves, waiting eagerly for *our* adoption as sons, the redemption of our body. For in hope we have been saved, but hope that is seen is not hope; for who hopes for what he *already* sees? But if we hope for what we do not see, with perseverance we wait eagerly for it (Rom. 8:20-25).

JULY 20

SPIRITUALITY LEAKS

"'I am the Alpha and the Omega,' says the Lord God,
'who is, and who was, and who is to come, the Almighty.'"

Revelations 1:8

There is something about us that defaults to fizzling out. We attend a spiritually charged conference or a weekend retreat, and we are on fire for God the next week. Then it seems to fade away. The Israelites are literally revived in experiencing one of the great miracles of the ages (Exod. 14:21-22) only to make an idol for worship at Sinai (Exod. 32:1-4) one month after the parting of the Red Sea.

We leak! This dynamic translates over into society. The level of spirituality in a society tends to decline. The revival movements of yesterday become the dead institutions of today. The chosen becomes the frozen chosen. Contents move toward process, and the profound moves toward the superficial. Reality morphs into the mere appearance of reality, and in so doing, a disappearance of authentic spirituality is realized.

The process of the decline of spirituality in a culture might be described in historical terms. Our forefather's faith was their actual experience. Then our fathers received their faith as an inheritance. For us, our faith has become a mere convenience. When it comes to our children, their faith may just be a nuisance.

Fallen man has a tragic way of receiving life from God and, over time, converting it into death. Humanity has a tendency to engage in this type of progression on a societal level, religious movement level, and individual level. It is on the individual level that we must tackle this nemesis with our number one weapon. The revived life is eternal life, and eternal life is relationship with God (John 17:3). Our weapon against spiritual lethargy is our consistent implementation of our walk with God.

Spirituality can be defined as the proper attitudes and actions that are based on the recognition of Who God is and, therefore, who man is not. In short, it is the proper human response to the reality of God. The opposite of true spirituality is superficiality. The very nature of the idea of true spirituality is based on the implications of such Scriptures as 1 Samuel 16:7: "God sees not as man sees, for man looks at the outward appearance, but the LORD looks at the heart."

We are reminded of the hypocrisy of the Pharisees. Spirituality is not based on appearance.

> Woe to you, scribes and Pharisees, hypocrites! For you are like whitewashed tombs, which on the outside appear beautiful, but on the inside they are full of dead men's bones and all uncleanness. So you, too, outwardly appear righteous to men, but inwardly you are full of hypocrisy and lawlessness (Matt. 23:27-28).

Spirituality is based on internal reality. It is not based on form, but substance.

> "The Pharisees and the scribes asked Him, "Why do Your disciples not walk according to the tradition of the elders, but eat their bread with impure hands?" And He said to them, "Rightly did Isaiah prophesy of you hypocrites, as it is written: 'THIS PEOPLE HONORS ME WITH THEIR LIPS, BUT THEIR HEART IS FAR AWAY FROM ME. IN VAIN DO THEY WORSHIP ME, TEACHING AS DOCTRINE THE PRECEPTS OF MEN.' Neglecting the commandment of God, you hold to the tradition of men" (Mark 7:5-8).

Christian spirituality consists of those attitudes and actions that spring forth from the changed heart of a redeemed believer who has as their central focus a desire for a dynamic, intimate, and profound relationship with God through Jesus Christ. True spirituality can only be as pure as the purity of one's understanding of Who God is. It must begin with this knowledge because it is both sourced by it and directed to it. Jesus is the "Alpha and the Omega" (Rev. 1:8) of Christian spirituality.

JULY 21

MOTIVATION IS MEDICINE FOR DISCOURAGEMENT

"You see the bad situation we are in, that Jerusalem is desolate and its gates burned by fire. Come, let us rebuild the wall of Jerusalem so that we will no longer be a reproach"

Nehemiah 2:17

An effective leader must be able to motivate others. Discouragement can be a leader's worst enemy. If you take away the motivation to pursue the goal, it is like driving a car with a flat tire.

In Nehemiah's case, discouragement came upon his workers through a loss of strength, vision, and confidence. "The strength of the burden bearers is failing, yet there is much rubbish; and we ourselves are unable to rebuild the wall" (Neh. 4:10). Nehemiah was leading people who had a keen sense of a loss of security: "Our enemies said, 'They will not know or see until we come among them, kill them and put a stop to the work'" (Neh. 4:11).

The people who were building the wall in Jerusalem under Nehemiah's leadership had become discouraged and were in need of a large dose of motivation. How did Nehemiah respond to this situation? He unified his worker's efforts toward a common goal (Neh. 4:13). "'They will come up against us from every place where you may turn,' then I stationed *men* in the lowest parts of the space behind the wall, the exposed places, and I stationed the people in families with their swords, spears and bows" (Neh. 4:12-13). He directed their attention to the Lord: "When I saw *their fear*, I rose and spoke to the nobles, the officials and the rest of the people: 'Do not be afraid of them; remember the Lord who is great and awesome, and fight for your brothers, your sons, your daughters, your wives and your houses'" (Neh. 4:14).

Leaders can combat discouragement and motivate their people, as Nehemiah did, by leading them back to work; "then all of us returned to the wall, each one to his work" (Neh. 4:15). There may need to be a reorganizing of tasks in response to the source of discouragement (Neh. 4:16); in any case, work itself can serve as a remedy to discouragement. In response to discouragement, leaders may also look to determine and define a "rallying point" so people who otherwise might feel separated from each other can gain the strength that comes with unity. Nehemiah concluded, "The work is great and extensive, and we are separated on the wall far from one another. At whatever place you hear the sound of the trumpet, rally to us there. Our God will fight for us" (Neh. 4:19-20).

Nehemiah also encouraged and organized ways for the people to help each other. "So we carried on the work with half of them holding spears from dawn until the stars appeared. At that time I also said to the people, 'Let each man with his servant spend the night within Jerusalem so that they may be a guard for us by night and a laborer by day" (Neh. 4:21-22).

An effective leader motivates others by setting a good example (Neh. 4:23). You cannot move a string by pushing it. It must be pulled. So, too, good leaders do not push from behind; they go in front and pull by providing a good example to follow. Jesus did not push His disciples into washing feet, but He gave them a reason to do it, saying, "For I gave you an example that you also should do as I did to you" (John 13:15). Nehemiah set an example of compassion and selflessness (Neh. 5:14-15). He set an example of sacrifice (Neh. 5:16) and hard work (Neh. 4:23).

An effective leader motivates others through building strong, personal relationships. Nehemiah knew his people. His knowledge of their names and the work which they had accomplished showed his awareness of and connection to them (Neh. 3:11, 19-30). This type of personal recognition from the leader is very important in dismantling discouragement as it creates a sense of belonging and a sense of security within the followers. Commendation and appreciation are necessary elements of motivation.

An effective leader learns how to motivate with internal motivations. External motivation (money, other material benefits) only motivates temporarily. Internal motivation (job satisfaction, a sense of purpose and fulfillment) motivates continuously. Nehemiah used internal motivation when he appealed to the workers' personal pride and national honor. "Then I said to them, 'You see the bad situation we are in, that Jerusalem is desolate and its gates burned by fire. Come, let us rebuild the wall of Jerusalem so that we will no longer be a reproach'" (Neh. 2:17).

Nehemiah, in that one statement, encouraged his people to "behold, build, and believe." The leader as motivator must present the task, promote the action, and provide a sense of hope. He must motivate his people to move from reality to action to faith. Skilled leaders who specialize in motivation always seek this outcome: "Then they said, 'Let us arise and build.' So they put their hands to the good *work*" (Neh. 2:18).

DID PILATE INVENT PILATES?

"Pilate said to them, 'Shall I crucify your King?'"

John 19:15

Have you ever done Pilates? These can be effective exercises to develop flexibility. There was a ruler in Rome during the time of Christ named Pilate. Although he is not the one who invented Pilates, you could say he had a similar philosophy: flexibility based on what he thought people wanted to hear or on what he wanted for himself. It resulted in what could be called a "Pilate theology" with regard to how he viewed Jesus as he presided over His trial. Pilate did not say much. He mainly asked questions.

His man-made theology can, in some ways, be seen to be representative of many people's theology of Jesus. What do we see in Pilate's twelve questions?

Question #1: "What accusation do you bring against this Man?" (John 18:29).

Pilate is expressing his indifference here. He may have simply said, "Why are you bothering me with this?" This theology—that which views God as a bother—expresses the depth of man's fallen nature. It reveals a heart that says, "I could care less about God!"

Question #2: "Are You the King of the Jews?" (John 18:33).

Sarcasm! Pilate is expressing his low view of Jesus; he is mocking Him. He says, "Look at You. You are a joke, all beat up and bound up by the very people who You rule. You would never see me like that!" This is the theology that builds oneself up at the expense of God. Mockery makes someone else smaller, so you can feel bigger. God is not mocked. "He must increase, but I must decrease" (John 3:30).

Question #3: "I am not a Jew, am I?" (John 18:35).

Challenge! Pilate is expressing his view that Jesus does not know what He is talking about. He is saying to Jesus, "What's the matter with You? Don't give me that nonsense!" This theology is that which assumes God is wrong, since you must be right. It is the attitude in Bible study, for example, that concludes that the Bible must be wrong when you do not understand it, instead of assuming the opposite.

Question #4: "Your own nation and the chief priests delivered You up to me; what have You done?" (John 18:35).

Self-defense! Pilate is expressing his lack of guilt. He may have simply said, "I am not to blame. It is your own fault!" This theology implicitly blames God in order to throw guilt off of self. The problems in my life are not mine; they are God's!

Question #5: "So You are a king?" (John 18:37).

Disagreement! Pilate is expressing an opposing view. He may have simply said, "You obviously do not know what it means to be a king!" This theology expresses the depth of man's pride. It rejects the idea that God's ways are higher than man's ways (Isa. 55:9) and boldly states, "My ways are superior to God's inferior ways."

Question #6: "What is truth?" (John 18:38).

Skepticism! Pilate is expressing his subjective epistemology here. He may have simply said, "There is no such thing as truth! I am my own definer." This theology expresses man's desire to be God. It says, "Truth is whatever I say it is because I say it is. There is no other truth but my own because there is no other god but me."

Question #7: "Do you wish then that I release for you the King of the Jews?" (John 18:39).

Apathy! Here, Pilate is expressing his boredom. He may have simply said, "I am not into this. You take Him." This theology expresses man's spiritual bankruptcy. It reveals a heart that says, "The things of God bore me. I just want to do something else."

Question #8: "Behold, the Man!" (John 19:5).

Indecisiveness! This proclamation implies a clear question posed by Pilate: "Do you not see that I cannot decide what to do?" This theology—that which prefers a neutral response to God—expresses the laziness that comes from sin. It is so much easier to just stay on the sidelines with respect to how you stand with God.

Question #9: "Where are you from?" (John 19:9).

Self-preservation! Pilate is expressing his fear. He is saying, "Just in case there is something to this God thing, I better check it out." This theology may draw one toward God but in an "anti-Gospel" sort of way. Instead of coming to God for Him to provide for your need, you "come to" God superstitiously. You merely want to cover your bases, instead of being covered by His blood!

Question #10: "You do not speak to me? Do You not know that I have authority to release You, and I have authority to crucify You?" (John 19:10).

Threat! Pilate is really confused. He is saying, "Who is the man? I am the man! I have authority over the final authority." This absurd theology tries to tell God that He has to obey His creation. It is completely nonsensical!

Question #11: "Behold, your King!" (John 19:14).

Fear of man! This proclamation implies a clear question posed by Pilate, "Do you see that I am not against Caesar? You will not make that assertion against me, right?" This theology—that which fears man at the expense of fearing God—expresses the depth of man's worldliness; he desires the wrong kingdom.

Question #12: "Shall I crucify your King?" (John 19:15).

Rejection! Pilate is expressing his adherence to the Jews' rejection of Jesus. He is finally saying, "Okay, if you want to reject God, then I will go along with you and reject Him also." People influence each other to abandon God. All man-made theology eventually leads here, even the "flexible" theology of Pilate(s)!

JULY 23

DIFFERENT QUESTIONS, SAME ANSWER

*"Then Darius the king wrote to all the peoples, nations and **men of every** language who were living in all the land: 'May your peace abound! I make a decree that in all the dominion of my kingdom men are to fear and tremble before the God of Daniel.'"*

Daniel 6:25-26

Why did God choose Israel? Why did God allow the exile of the Jews to Babylon? These questions, although seemingly very different, both have the same answer. These things were done because "God so loved the world" (John 3:16). God is a missionary God because God loves all people and wants them to come to know Him. He desires that His salvation would go "TO THE END OF THE EARTH" (Acts 13:47). And so, God chose Israel to be a conduit through which He could reveal Himself to "all the families of the earth" (Gen. 12:3). It is because God loves Israel and because God loves the world through His missionary people Israel being used to make Him known to them (Deut. 7:8). God did not start loving the world when John penned that well-known verse (John 3:16). God has always loved the world and so has always sought to reveal Himself to all people.

Why did God permit the Babylonian exile? First of all, let's ask, why did God rescue Israel from their first exile experience in Egypt? According to God, He involved Himself in those matters so that Pharaoh and the Egyptians "may know that there is no one like Me in all the earth" (Exod. 9:14). More specifically, God said that it was "in order to show you My power and in order to proclaim My name through all the earth" (Exod. 9:16). God rescues His people out of Egypt and eventually brings them into the promised land so that "all the peoples of the earth may know that the hand of the LORD is mighty, so that you may fear the LORD your God forever" (Josh. 4:24). The exodus of the Jewish people from Egypt to Israel is used by God to reveal Himself to all the nations. Israel then settles in the Promised Land and continues to be used by God in the same way because "God so loved the world" (John 3:16).

And so, missions is the reason why God got Israel out of exile. But why did God then permit Israel to be taken into exile by the Babylonians? The main way in which Israel fulfilled its calling as a missionary nation was to provide a clear witness for God by following and obeying Him and, thus, being blessed to such a degree that even the nations would be drawn to Him. This is seen, for example, when Solomon's blessings are so well-known that it prompts the Queen of Sheba to want to know His God (1 Kings 10:1-13). When Israel rejected their responsibility as a missionary nation—when they did not follow and obey God and, therefore, did not provide a good witness—then God would have to discipline them to get things back on track. For example, God references Israel's disobedience in the context of naming Himself "the God of hosts" and says, "'Therefore, I will make you go into exile beyond Damascus,' says the LORD, whose name is the God of hosts" (Amos 5:27).

If God's chosen vessels do not obey the missions mandate voluntarily, then God will "help" them—as He did with Jonah and His desire to make Himself known in Nineveh—to obey it involuntarily. God really does love the world. And so, even if it takes a whale, God will make Himself known. The witness of a disobedient Israel could actually begin to work against the missionary plan of God. If Israel stopped being a blessing, then they would have to stop being blessed. When their positive witness ceased from building up and shouting out the reputation of God—and, in that sense, they stopped "going" to the nations—then God was able to "send" them to the nations by way of the exile, forcing them to function as a missionary nation.

God's people have been exiled to places all over the world. Naturally, this has a great missiological impact. For example, consider the missiological results of Daniel's life in exile. The book of Daniel can certainly be viewed as a book full of the missionary activity of God and His people. As many as eight times in the book of Daniel, we see the Revelation 5:9 missiological expression referencing peoples, nations, and tongues and/or foreign rulers proclaiming the glory of God (Dan. 2:46, 3:4-7, 3:28-29, 4:1-3, 4:37, 5:19, 6:25-27, 7:14). Nebuchadnezzar, for example, sees God's power and responds, "Therefore I make a decree that any people, nation or tongue that speaks anything offensive against the God of Shadrach, Meshach and Abed-nego shall be torn limb from limb and their houses reduced to a rubbish heap, inasmuch as there is no other god who is able to deliver in this way" (Dan. 3:29).

God can use any situation for His glory. Even if He has to use a whale in your life to get you to your "Nineveh," where He can be made known through you, He will do it. If you refuse to be used the first way (usually the easier way), then God is able to use the second way (usually the more difficult way): "Then the LORD commanded the fish, and it vomited Jonah up onto the dry land. Now the word of the LORD came to Jonah the *second* time, saying, 'Arise, go to Nineveh the great city and proclaim to it the proclamation which I am going to tell you'" (Jonah 2:10-3:2, emphasis added). Why would God do this? "God so loved the world" (John 3:16).

JULY 24

GOD, PLEASE GRACE ME!

"Therefore let us draw near with confidence to the throne of grace,
so that we may receive mercy and find grace to help in time of need."

Hebrews 4:16

To truly repent means to turn to a Person. It is not simply turning to a way but turning to *the Way*. Jesus Christ is "the way, and the truth, and the life" (John 14:6). To repent is to turn to the abilities of Jesus Christ. It is not so much the process of declaring your actions as it is the process of asking to be acted upon. We must cry out to God, "Please grace me!"

> Be gracious to me, O God, according to Your lovingkindness; according to the greatness of Your compassion blot out my transgressions. Wash me thoroughly from my iniquity and cleanse me from my sin. For I know my transgressions, and my sin is ever before me. Against You, You only, I have sinned and done what is evil in Your sight, so that You are justified when You speak and blameless when You judge (Psalm 51:1-4).

The psalmist introduces his repentant discussion with "Be gracious to me, O God." True repentance includes the understanding that God's grace is necessary. God's actions on my behalf are unmerited. I am unworthy. Counterfeit repentance does not include the understanding of the desperate need for God's grace. It exhibits an attitude that tries to earn or deserve the right to come to God. It says, "I feel unworthy, so I will wait until I do enough good things that I feel worthy enough to come to God." We forget the good news! Jesus graciously came to us to die in our place and conquer sin on our behalf. He gets it! He sits on the throne of grace so that we can turn to Him.

> Therefore, since we have a great high priest who has passed through the heavens, Jesus the Son of God, let us hold fast our confession. For we do not have a high priest who cannot sympathize with our weaknesses, but One who has been tempted in all things as *we are*,

yet without sin. Therefore let us draw near with confidence to the throne of grace, so that we may receive mercy and find grace to help in time of need (Heb. 4:14-16).

Someone might say, "Before I repent, I want to get my life right." That is like saying, "Before I start exercising and eating less, I want to lose weight." First, you must start exercising and eating less. Then you can lose weight. So, too, first you must repent. Then God can begin to "get your life right." This is the essence of repentance; turning to God's abilities. Repentance is not getting yourself right. It is turning to the only One Who is able to get you right!

Do you do that sometimes? Do you try to drink the milk without first milking the cow? Do you try to solve your sin problem without first going to the only One Who is able to solve it? Do you needlessly carry around the ball and chain of the unworthiness (guilt) of sin?

Repentance is the point of coming to the end of yourself and turning to God's ability. It is not so much the process of declaring your actions—I will become worthy—as it is the process of asking to be acted upon. God, please grace me!

JULY 25

THE CHRISTIAN CAUSE IS THE CAUSE OF CHRIST

"I do all things for the sake of the gospel."

1 Corinthians 9:23

Is there a biblical case for a call to social concern? Are Christians mandated to get involved in matters of social justice? The short answer is yes. The expanded answer is, "Yes, but not simply for the sake of the cause." The cause may be just, but that does not mean that we serve the cause. True social justice, or "whatever you do" for that matter, is only just in the name of the "just One." Christians engage in social justice with a view toward spiritual justice. "Whatever you do, do your work heartily, as for the Lord rather than for men, knowing that from the Lord you will receive the reward of the inheritance. It is the Lord Christ whom you serve" (Col. 3:23-24). The cause of the Christian is the cause of Christ.

> Then the King will say to those on His right, "Come, you who are blessed of My Father, inherit the kingdom prepared for you from the foundation of the world. For I was hungry, and you gave Me *something* to eat; I was thirsty, and you gave Me something to drink; I was a stranger, and you invited Me in; naked, and you clothed Me; I was sick, and you visited Me; I was in prison, and you came to Me." Then the righteous will answer Him, "Lord, when did we see You hungry, and feed You, or thirsty, and give You *something* to drink? And when did we see You a stranger, and invite You in, or naked, and clothe You? When did we see You sick, or in prison, and come to You?" The King will answer and say to them, "Truly I say to you, to the extent that you did it to one of these brothers of Mine, *even* the least of *them*, you did it to Me" (Matt. 25:34-40).

For the Christian, there is but one cause: the cause of Christ. There may be many areas of social justice that he or she engages in, but there can only be one focus: Christ and the Gospel. Christians are involved in many "movements," but all of them result in the same movement: the movement toward Christ and the Gospel. "I do all things for the sake of the gospel, so that I may become a fellow partaker of it" (1 Cor. 9:23).

> Submit yourselves for the Lord's sake to every human institution, whether to a king as the one in authority, or to governors as sent by him for the punishment of evildoers and the praise of those who do right. For such is the will of God that by doing right you may silence the ignorance of foolish men. *Act* as free men, and do not use your freedom as a covering for evil, but *use it* as bondslaves of God. Honor all people, love the brotherhood, fear God, honor the king (1 Peter 2:13-17).

What does it mean to care for people who are hurting and in need? It means that we help them. What does help look like? How is it done? How far do we go, and how much do we help? This is where wisdom in social justice comes into play. We may need to use different methods when we try to address different needs and different situations. Sometimes, we must simply help those who cannot help themselves. In other situations, it might be better to help others to help themselves. Other circumstances necessitate more of a helping others not to hurt themselves. Sometimes it is wise to see that you should help one's own to help their own. In general, we should seek to help society to help itself.

In any case, the help we offer is not a "generic" sort of help. Social justice must be spiritual justice, lest it be superficial justice. And so, the greatest way to help society to help itself is to declare that it cannot help itself; it needs Jesus. This is the Gospel message, the greatest social justice movement ever. The cause of the Christian is the cause of Christ, and the change agent for mankind is the Gospel message.

JULY 26

EAGLES SOAR INTO THE HEAVENS—FREEDOM!

"I said, 'Oh, that I had wings like a dove! I would fly away and be at rest.'"

Psalm 55:6

Perhaps the closest we can come to a one-word description of someone who exudes Christian character is that he or she is "selfless." Selflessness is that part of a person's character that is able to forget about personal needs and desires in order to remember the needs and desires of others. Selflessness is the quality that allows Christ to live in me, for "it is no longer I who live, but Christ lives in me" (Gal. 2:20).

Francis of Assisi, a monk who founded the Franciscan Order in the early thirteenth century, lived an exemplary life of selflessness. His greatest desire was to be free of himself through an imitation of the life of Christ. His life was a revived life because he embraced the Spirit, which led Christ to the cross. He died to self so as to live to Christ. "For whoever wishes to save his life will lose it; but whoever loses his life for My sake will find it" (Matt. 16:25).

Freedom is to selflessness what slavery is to selfishness. Selfishness makes us slaves of ourselves. Selflessness makes us free from ourselves and free to serve God and others. Francis of Assisi gained freedom through his selflessness. As he was considering the freedom of a bird, he followed it onto the roof of a house. He walked slowly toward the edge of the roof where the bird was standing. Then the bird flew away. The bird was free. Francis was determined to fly also. He wanted to be free. He understood that in order to fly, he had to be very light. He had to free himself of the heavy burdens he was carrying. He had to die to himself.

This metaphorical picture of selflessness is captured more succinctly in Jesus words, "'Come to Me, all who are weary and heavy-laden, and I will give you rest. Take My yoke upon you and learn from Me, for I am gentle and humble in heart, and YOU WILL FIND REST FOR YOUR SOULS. For My yoke is easy and My burden is light'" (Matt. 11:28-30). What are easy yokes and light burdens? They are summed up in one thing—the cross. It was the Spirit of selflessness that sent Christ to the cross. There is freedom in selflessness, for "the Lord is the Spirit, and where the Spirit of the Lord is, *there* is liberty" (2 Cor. 3:17).

Freedom is not that which justifies or rationalizes sins of commission or sins of omission. That kind of "freedom" is rooted in selfishness, not selflessness. We are not free *from*; we are free to. We are not exempt *from* the Law of God and free from sin; we are enabled *to* do the Law of God and free to serve. "For you were called to freedom, brethren; only *do* not *turn* your freedom into an opportunity for the flesh, but through love serve one another" (Gal. 5:13). Freedom is not liberalism's excuse for sin. It is the Spirit's impetus for righteousness. "*Act* as free men, and do not use your freedom as a covering for evil, but *use it* as bondslaves of God" (1 Peter 2:16).

Jesus' selflessness—His emptiness (Phil. 2:7)—enabled Him to do and fulfill God's will. His selflessness freed Him to be fueled to do only that which "'He sees the Father doing'" (John 5:19). Jesus proclaimed, "'My food is to do the will of Him who sent Me and to accomplish His work'" (John 4:34). Selflessness results in obedience and is, therefore, a pillar of Christian character.

> Do not think that I came to abolish the Law or the Prophets; I did not come to abolish but to fulfill. For truly I say to you, until heaven and earth pass away, not the smallest letter or stroke shall pass from the Law until all is accomplished. Whoever then annuls one of the least of these commandments, and teaches others *to do* the same, shall be called least in the kingdom of heaven; but whoever keeps and teaches *them*, he shall be called great in the kingdom of heaven (Matt. 5:17-19).

JULY 27

PRIVILEGE AND RESPONSIBILITY ARE A COUPLE

"From everyone who has been given much, much will be required."
Luke 12:48

Privilege got together with Responsibility and they really hit it off. They were so compatible that they finally got married. What a wedding! You never saw two mates so perfect for each other.

It is a biblical principle that privilege and responsibility must flow in tandem with each other. "From everyone who has been given much, much will be required; and to whom they entrusted much, of him they will ask all the more" (Luke 12:48). God is the Owner of all things (Psalm 50:10-12). He is a God of mission. He is a very effective Manager of His resources. And so, privilege and responsibility line up with each other. If you have more of the Owner's resources that He wants to manage for His mission, then you will have to do more with those resources as they pertain to accomplishing His mission.

The book of Ephesians has six chapters. The first three chapters include the privileges of believers. The final three chapters describe the responsibilities that are connected to those privileges. Similarly, the Abrahamic covenant includes three ways that God's people will be blessed and three ways that God's people will be a blessing (Gen. 12:2-3).

Each person has responsibility toward other people because each person has the privilege of being one of those people. You are your brother's keeper, most fundamentally, because you are a brother. You have responsibility toward others because of the value of each person that is a mutual value. This is why the heart of the law is to "love your neighbor as yourself" (Lev. 19:18). Each person is a life created by the same Creator, the same Owner and Manager. This is the biblical rationale for ministry to the poor. "He who oppresses the poor taunts his Maker, but he who is gracious to the needy honors Him" (Prov. 14:31). My responsibility to those in need is founded on our commonality. "If I have despised the claim of my male or female slaves when they filed a complaint against me, what then could I do when God arises? And when He calls me to account, what will I answer Him? Did not He who made me in the womb make him, and the same one fashion us in the womb?" (Job 31:13-15). We can view our responsibility toward the needy in terms of our responsibility toward the creation of God and God the Creator.

Responsibility to help the poor is a correct response to God, Who has already helped us. He has been our "Jehovah Jireh" (God our Provider), so we now carry a responsibility to multiply that provision to others. "You shall not pervert the justice due an alien *or* an orphan, nor take a widow's garment in pledge. But you shall remember that you were a slave in Egypt, and that the LORD your God redeemed you from there; therefore I am commanding you to do this thing" (Deut. 24:17-18).

We give to others because He first gave to us. "We love, because He first loved us" (1 John 4:19). Jesus puts it this way: "'*Freely* you received, freely give'" (Matt. 10:8). Givers are imitators of God because giving is what God has done. "Therefore be imitators of God, as beloved children; and walk in love, just as Christ also loved you and gave Himself up for us, an offering and a sacrifice to God as a fragrant aroma" (Eph. 5:1-2). This "just as" motivation and sense of obligation to give are not produced by the question, "What must I do?" but by the question, "What has God done for me?" Our motivation should pour out of the bowl of gratitude and not out of the bowl of legalism.

This proper understanding of our responsibility being founded on our privilege helps us to avoid a self-righteous attitude toward the needy. Some people are unwilling to give to the poor because they think they have earned what they have. The poor have not earned anything. Why should anything be given to the poor? Be thankful that God does not have this attitude. If He had that attitude, then we would all be going to Hell (2 Cor. 8:9; Rom. 5:6-8). Instead, it should be that "no one of you will become arrogant in behalf of one against the other. For who regards you as superior? What do you have that you did not receive? And if you did receive it, why do you boast as if you had not received it?" (1 Cor. 4:6-7).

This kind of self-righteous attitude borders on idolatry. God had to give to the ultimate need, but do we not need to give to lesser needs? Are we higher than God? That, of course, is the wrong response to God. The correct response to God, Who has given to us freely, is that of sincere gratitude. This gratitude should manifest itself in giving to others.

Let us go back to the wedding ceremony. Privilege marries Responsibility. You never saw two mates so perfect for each other. They are naturally linked together. What happens when you tear them apart? Divorce! When privilege divorces responsibility, it buries itself in the ground; it digs its own grave (Matt. 25:18). God hates that (Matt. 25:26-30; Mal. 2:16).

JULY 28

GOAL!

*"Forgetting what **lies** behind and reaching forward to what **lies** ahead,
I press on toward the goal for the prize of the upward call of God in Christ Jesus."*

Philippians 3:13-14

Broadcasters for Argentinian soccer games get very excited about the end result. When a goal is scored, the commentator will shout, "Goal!" This emphatic statement will last for a few minutes or until the commentator runs out of breath. It is exciting. The goal has been reached. It is the highlight of the game.

Goals are very important. You have to know your goal in order to work toward reaching your goal so that you might, ultimately, be successful. How can a missionary be successful? He must know his goal. What is the goal of the Great Commission? "And Jesus came up and spoke to them, saying, 'All authority has been given to Me in heaven and on earth. Go therefore and make disciples of all the nations, baptizing them in the name of the Father and the Son and the Holy Spirit, teaching them to observe all that I commanded you; and lo, I am with you always, even to the end of the age'" (Matt. 28:18-20).

Is the goal to *go*? No, that is a participle that would be better translated *going*. A participle indicates more of a method than a goal. Is the goal to *baptize*? No, that is a participle that would better be translated *baptizing*. Is the goal to *teach*? No, that is a participle that would better be translated *teaching*. The main verb in the commandment and, thus, the goal of the mission is to *make disciples*.

Going, baptizing, and teaching are all methods that should be used to arrive at the goal. A serious danger for one who is engaged in a mission is to confuse methods and goals. If a missionary goes somewhere and thinks that is the goal, then he will not have success. He will be content to simply be there. We must remember that the work of missions must have a mission. The goal is not to go or to baptize or to teach; the goal is to make disciples.

What does it mean to make disciples? A disciple is a follower of Christ. "As He passed by, He saw Levi the son of Alphaeus sitting in the tax booth, and He said to him, 'Follow Me!' And he got up and followed Him. And it happened that He was reclining at the table in his house, and many tax collectors and sinners were dining with Jesus and His disciples; for there were many of them, and they were following Him" (Mark 2:14-15).

One who becomes a follower exhibits a changed life and changed priorities (Acts 2:41-42; John 13:35). So how do we know when the ball has gone into the net? It is when we see people following Jesus.

JULY 29

GOOD CULTURE, BAD CULTURE

*"God created man in His own image, in the image of God He created him; male and female
He created them. God blessed them; and God said to them, 'Be fruitful and multiply,
and fill the earth, and subdue it; and rule over the fish of the sea and over the birds of the sky
and over every living thing that moves on the earth."*

Genesis 1:27-28

Since God created man in His own image, aspects of human culture are good and beautiful. Since man rebelled against God, all of human culture is affected by sin and evil. Culture is a mix of right and wrong, good and bad. It reflects all that is good about man. It portrays all that is sinful about man as it becomes twisted and prone to corruption.

The foundation of culture was set with God's first words to man: "Be fruitful and multiply, and fill the earth, and subdue it; and rule over the fish of the sea and over the birds of the sky and over every living thing that moves on the earth" (Gen. 1:28). These commands establish creativity and productivity as the pillars of human culture. With the fall of man, these pillars get corrupted and infuse debauchery and exploitation into culture. As soon as God drove man out from the Garden of Eden, we see good aspects of culture developing as well as bad aspects:

> And it came about when they were in the field, that Cain rose up against Abel his brother and killed him . . . When you cultivate the ground, it will no longer yield its strength to you . . . Then Cain went out from the presence of the LORD, and settled in the land of Nod, east of Eden. Cain had relations with his wife and she conceived, and gave birth to Enoch; and he built a city, and called the name of the city Enoch, after the name of his son. Now to Enoch was born Irad, and Irad became the father of Mehujael, and Mehujael became the father of Methushael, and Methushael became the father of Lamech. Lamech took to himself two wives: the name of the one was Adah, and the name of the other, Zillah. Adah gave birth to Jabal; he was the father of those who dwell in tents and have livestock. His brother's name was Jubal; he was the father of all those who play the lyre and pipe. As for Zillah, she also gave birth to Tubal-cain, the forger of all implements of bronze and iron (Gen. 4:8, 12, 16-22).

Immediately, we see developing outside of the Garden of Eden a culture of violence, poverty, and godlessness. At the same time, we see the development of a culture of family values, development, innovation, lifestyle, work productivity, and the arts. Culture is the patterned way in which people function together. It is the way a group of people organize their world. It includes the beliefs, values, traditions, and institutions that bind people together and result in a common identity. A culture has unwritten and unspoken rules regarding how people interact with each other. These rules cover a variety of different aspects of a society, including language, religion, politics, customs, aesthetics, economy, geography, celebrations, community, communication, education, and history. Culture provides for a basic human need, the need for a sense of identity and security. The good aspects of culture, based on God's creation of man in His image, enhance man's sense of identity and security. The bad aspects of culture, based on the fall of man, corrupt man's sense of identity and security.

This is the power of the Gospel. It can change culture. It can move an individual from darkness to light, from being lost to being found. It can move a society from relying on twisted and perverted unwritten and unspoken rules regarding how its people interact with each other to a healthy pattern of living that satisfies people's need for a sense of identity and security. It can move bad culture to good culture by untwisting that which was twisted; the power of the Gospel takes the twist out of society!

THE ONE THING—THE ULTIMATE ALL-INCLUSIVE!

"What shall we do."

John 6:28

Life seems complicated. It *is* complicated for a "non-puzzlemaker." For a sovereign God, however, puzzles are meant to be put together. It is when we try to take God's place and insist on being our own puzzlemakers that life seems so difficult. We were never meant to be our own sovereigns who are able to figure out everything. In fact, one thing takes care of all things. One thing is the ultimate all-inclusive. Life is not so complicated!

What is this one thing? Jesus was challenging people who were following Him to consider what they should do with their lives. They asked Him to cut to the quick and give them the bottom line: "'What shall we do, so that we may work the works of God?'" (John 6:28). Jesus answered, "'This is the work of God, that you believe in Him whom He has sent'" (John 6:29). Is it that simple? You just have to believe?

The word "believe" is a translation of the Greek word *pistis*. This is the same word that is often translated as "faith." The action of "believe" or "faith" is to seek or to come to God. "And without faith it is impossible to please *Him*, for he who comes to God must believe that He is and *that* He is a rewarder of those who seek Him" (Heb. 11:6). References to "faith" and "believe" are directly linked to "come to" and "seek Him."

What is the bottom line? Does life have an "ultimate"? The ultimate of anything is its furthest point. The furthest point of "life" is *eternal* life. What is eternal life? Jesus continued the conversation with those who had asked the original question by explaining that they did not have to "eat" everything. They did not have to be culinary puzzlemakers. It was not complicated. They only needed to eat one thing. "'Do not work for the food which perishes, but for the food which endures to eternal life'" (John 6:27). He explained, "'Whoever eats my flesh and drinks my blood has eternal life'" (John 6:54). What is the one food that is linked to eternal life? "'For this is the will of My Father, that everyone who beholds the Son and believes in Him will have eternal life'" (John 6:40). Here it is again. This idea of "believe" is the thing you have to eat. It is the response to the provision that is offered by the culinary puzzlemaker. "'Truly, truly, I say to you, he who believes has eternal life'" (John 6:47).

Give me the bottom line. What is the one thing? What is eternal life? "'Now this is eternal life: that they know you, the only true God, and Jesus Christ, whom you have sent'" (John 17:3). This is the bottom line. It is that out of which everything else flows. In that sense, it is the *only* thing necessary.

Now as they were traveling along, He entered a village; and a woman named Martha welcomed Him into her home. She had a sister called Mary, who was seated at the Lord's feet, listening to His word. But Martha was distracted with all her preparations; and she came up to Him and said, "Lord, do You not care that my sister has left me to do all the serving alone? Then tell her to help me." But the Lord answered and said to her, "Martha, Martha, you are worried and bothered about so many things; but only one thing is necessary, for Mary has chosen the good part, which shall not be taken away from her" (Luke 10:38-42).

And so, it is relationship with God—spending time with God, coming to God, seeking God, depending on God, trusting God—that is the action of "believe" and "faith." It is this action that is the bottom line; the one thing we are called to "eat." Does this mean that nothing else matters? Does it mean that we are to be involved in nothing else? No, the "onlyness" of seeking God is not exclusive but inclusive. "'But seek first His kingdom and His righteousness, and all these things will be added to you'" (Matt. 6:33). Seeking God is the singular action in the sense that all things include that action. It is not a "totem pole" idea in which God is first, then family, then work, then friends, then country, etc. It is an "inner circle/outer circle idea" in which the inner circle of seeking God informs, directs, and impacts all other outer circle activities.

Seek God first—not so much chronologically, but primarily and exhaustively—and everything else will fall into place (Matt. 6:33). The bottom line is not exclusive, it is inclusive. It is an all-inclusive! "Trust in the LORD with all your heart and do not lean on your own understanding; in all your ways acknowledge Him, and He will make your paths straight" (Prov. 3:5-6). The ultimate is "all your heart." The bottom line is "all your ways." Then everything else will fall into place, and "he will make your paths straight." Everything comes together when everything is submitted to Him.

Life is not complicated. It really comes down to only one thing. It is simple but not easy. It is not easy because we want to reject simplicity. We want to reject doing the one thing and, instead, do the many things without the one thing. We tend to need a little more Mary and a little less Martha. "Martha, Martha, you are worried and bothered about so many things, but *only* one thing is necessary, for Mary has chosen the good part which shall be not taken away from her" (Luke 10:41-42). Uncomplicate your life. Get to the bottom line of things. Seek God!

JULY 31

RUN FROM THE DEVIL

"Then Jesus was led up by the Spirit into the wilderness to be tempted by the devil. And after He had fasted forty days and forty nights, He then became hungry. And the tempter came."

Matthew 4:1-3

When we fast, we do not make God do anything. We facilitate; we do not create. That is the idea of any of the "means of grace" like prayer, fellowship, meditation, or fasting; it is a means, not an end. It is a spiritual discipline that we can engage in to express our need for God and to facilitate the flow of His provision. Could the biblical practice of fasting be a means of grace for resisting temptation? Can a spiritual discipline strengthen us in areas of our lives in which we might lack physical discipline? The lust for food is sometimes associated in Scripture with a lack of discipline and falling into sin. In fact, the whole war started when Eve was tempted by the fruit: "When the woman saw that the tree was good for food" (Gen. 3:6). It is not simply the food that is the problem. It is the lust of the flesh. Fasting can express a fight against that flesh.

This war against the flesh and its association with the lust for food is seen throughout Scripture. Noah fell into a trap (Gen. 9:20-21); Esau sold his birthright (Heb. 12:16-17); Isaac picked Esau as his favorite (Gen. 25:28); the people of God murmured (Exod. 16:3; Num. 11:4-5, 21:5); and the priests were rebuked (1 Sam. 2:29). Scripture calls its followers to make the body the servant of the spirit (1 Cor. 9:24-27). Discipline in eating is fundamental, and fasting develops fundamentals of discipline.

Elijah fasted for forty days on his way to Mount Horeb (1 Kings 19:8). Fasting can express and facilitate an attitude of dependence upon God. In the midst of Elijah's temptation to abandon his ministry, it took this type of attitude to receive from God the necessary equipping to overcome the temptation. God revealed Himself to him and strengthened him. Fasting became a means of grace, a facilitator of being prepared to receive Divine guidance and encouragement to overcome temptation.

Prior to Jesus being tempted by the devil in the wilderness, He "fasted forty days and forty nights" (Matt. 4:1-2). In this incredible account of spiritual warfare, fasting is certainly associated with an ability to resist temptation. Once Jesus denied self, He was better prepared to resist temptation because temptation appeals to lifting up self. The physical discipline of fasting, then, became a means of expressing and establishing the type of attitude that led to victory.

John the Baptist had a ministry that called people to resist temptation and turn from sin (Matt. 3:1-3). He came "eating no bread and drinking no wine" (Luke 7:33). This type of partial fast is reminiscent of the Nazarite vow (vow of separation) seen in Numbers 6:3-4. In this sense, we see fasting associated with separation from sin. Fasting can be a means to express that separation.

Any "means of grace" is a means, not an end. It is a spiritual discipline that we can engage in to express our need for God and to facilitate the flow of His provision. Fasting does not make you a victor in the fight; it makes room for the Victor to win the fight in you. All means of grace—if they actually are means of grace—work to get rid of you, not to boast of you. Fasting is not a "good work" in which the practitioner earns something. Any result of fasting is "not as a result of works, so that no one may boast" (Eph. 2:9). Fasting "works" not because of *your* works but because it facilitates Christ's works in you, even as you are called to "work out your salvation with fear and trembling for it is God who is at work in you" (Phil. 2:12-13).

The degree to which fasting aids in resisting temptation is the degree to which fasting establishes that "I have been crucified with Christ; and it is no longer I who live, but Christ lives in me" (Gal. 2:20). Yes, "Christ in you [is] the hope of glory" (Col. 1:27), not fasting. But fasting can make room for that glorious One to work. So, let the Warrior in to win your war.

NOTES

August

AUGUST 1

LET'S HAVE A HEART TO HEART

"But I say to you that everyone who looks at a woman with lust for her has already committed adultery with her in his heart."

Matthew 5:28

The iconic Sermon on the Mount must have left its original listeners speechless. Every line stands as a profound nugget of truth. The heart of the sermon comes when Jesus sets the standards for those living in the kingdom of God. These standards are rooted in what is real, not simply in what things look like. Appearance is not enough. Actuality is demanded. Moreover, appearance without actuality is judged: "'Woe to you, scribes and Pharisees, hypocrites! For you are like whitewashed tombs which on the outside appear beautiful, but inside they are full of dead men's bones and all uncleanness'" (Matt. 23:27).

The standards that are set by "religiosity"—the practice of outward religious appearance only—are false standards. The Law is not by the letter or by appearance but by reality and the Spirit. It is not *superficial*; it is *profound*. To be of use, standards must be based on the *heart* of the Law and not on its *skin*.

> For indeed circumcision is of value if you practice the Law; but if you are a transgressor of the Law, your circumcision has become uncircumcision . . . For he is not a Jew who is one outwardly, nor is circumcision that which is outward in the flesh. But he is a Jew who is one inwardly; and circumcision is that which is of the heart, by the Spirit, not by the letter; and his praise is not from men, but from God (Rom. 2:25, 28-29).

Man gravitates toward the superficial. It does not satisfy but man is deceived into being content with it. God and His standards are very different. "'God *sees* not as man sees, for man looks at the outward appearance, but the LORD looks at the heart'" (1 Sam. 16:7).

First, there is the standard for hatred. Certainly, murder is an extreme expression of hatred. Most people have never taken anyone else's life, and so they feel that they can say, "I have not broken the Law. I have never killed anybody." Jesus, however, turns the tables upside down (Matt. 21:12-13) as He sets a new standard.

> You have heard that the ancients were told, "YOU SHALL NOT COMMIT MURDER" and "Whoever commits murder shall be liable to the court." But I say to you that everyone who is angry with his brother shall be guilty before the court; and whoever says to his brother, "You good-for-nothing," shall be guilty before the supreme court; and whoever says, "You fool," shall be guilty *enough to go* into the fiery hell (Matt. 5:21-22).

Next is the standard for adultery. Someone once famously claimed, "I did not have sexual intercourse with that woman." Jesus responds, "'You have heard that it was said, *YOU SHALL NOT COMMIT ADULTERY*; but I say to you that everyone who looks at a woman with lust for her has already committed adultery with her in his heart'" (Matt. 5:27-28).

God hates divorce (Mal. 2:16). He has high standards for marriage. Divorce is a "high ramification" operation.

> *Some* Pharisees came to Jesus, testing Him and asking, "Is it lawful *for a man* to divorce his wife for any reason at all?" And He answered and said, "Have you not read that He who created *them* from the beginning MADE THEM MALE AND FEMALE, and said, 'FOR THIS REASON A MAN SHALL LEAVE HIS FATHER AND MOTHER AND BE JOINED TO HIS

WIFE, AND THE TWO SHALL BECOME ONE FLESH'? So they are no longer two, but one flesh. What therefore God has joined together, let no man separate" (Matt. 19:3-6).

Many people understand divorce as a necessary, and even a helpful, option. They say, "It is best for everyone involved." No, it is not! But in Matthew 5:31-32, we read, "'Now it was said, WHOEVER SENDS HIS WIFE AWAY, LET HIM GIVE HER A CERTIFICATE OF DIVORCE; but I say to you that everyone who divorces his wife, except for *the* reason of unchastity, makes her commit adultery; and whoever marries a divorced woman commits adultery'" (Matt. 5:31-32).

Each standard that Jesus sets in the Sermon on the Mount is introduced with the words, "You have heard that it was said . . . but I say to you . . . " Jesus is saying, "You have embraced one standard, but I am giving you another." He was not changing or destroying the Law (Matt. 5:17). He was going beyond the common, religious understanding of the Law in order to capture the heart of the Law. Jesus' standards are a matter of the heart!

AUGUST 2

WE GET TO GIVE

*"Each one **must do** just as he has purposed in his heart, not grudgingly or under compulsion, for God loves a cheerful giver."*

2 Corinthians 9:7

Why is it "more blessed to give than to receive" (Acts 20:35)? It is because of the significance of love. God is Love, and *give* is the action. Thus, the essence of love is "'For God so loved the world, that He gave His only begotten Son, that whoever believes in Him shall not perish, but have eternal life'" (John 3:16). There is life and blessing in *giving* because when you give, you reach the heart of God.

The name "Rockefeller" is synonymous with wealth like the name "Hitler" is synonymous with evil or the name "Babe Ruth" is synonymous with baseball. John D. Rockefeller is widely considered to have been one of the richest people of all time. Midway through his life and already having gained his billions, Rockefeller fell deathly ill. Doctors gave him little hope. Then he began to give away his money. He was healed miraculously and understood his healing to be connected to his giving. He was, it could be said, "more blessed."

Someone who is in need of revival in their life needs only to start giving. It has been said that giving is the shortest route to glory. Indeed, we are told to be "cheerful giver[s]" (2 Cor. 9:7). If it is really giving that you are doing, then you cannot help but be cheerful. It is a *blessed* thing.

I remember the first time that I became completely aware of this truth. We had bought some food for a family from Poland who were living in the United States. The man could not find a job, and he was having trouble feeding his family. We decided to secretly put the bags of food by their front doorstep. As we passed their window, we saw the mother praying on her knees in the bedroom. Her oldest child was also praying, and her two youngest children were crying.

We put the food by the door, knocked, and ran away. As we watched from behind a tree, the mother opened the door. When she saw the food, she immediately began to shout praises to God. The children ran out in their pajamas and started dancing around the bags of food. That night, they filled their stomachs; and we were filled with an overwhelming joy. The word *revival* would be an understatement. This is the reality and opportunity in giving.

Somehow on his death bed, Rockefeller came to understand the purpose of his wealth in a different way than he had previously. He began to see giving as the purpose of receiving as opposed to seeing receiving as an end in itself. The Bible is consistent. Whenever there is a command, there is a promise. In other words, whenever there is an obligation, there is an opportunity. The opposite is also true. Whenever there is a promise, there is a command. In other words, whenever there is an opportunity, there is an obligation.

First, we must realize that we must receive from God in order to give back to God. We have nothing in ourselves (John 15:5). "What do you have that you did not receive? And if you did receive it, why do you boast as if you had not received it?" (1 Cor. 4:7). It is like the five-year-old boy who wants to get his father a present for Christmas. He has no money to buy the present, so he asks his father to give him money. He then buys his father a present with his father's own money.

We are like that five-year-old boy. We give to God using what is already His. We receive from God so as to be used by God for His glory. We are meant to be conduits. The reason that we are supplied by God is to equip others (Eph. 4:11-12). We are blessed to be a blessing (Gen. 12:1-3). We receive so that we can give. Although it is a biblical statement to say that when we give, we get (Luke 6:38), it is incomplete to stop at "we get." It is not so much that we give to get as it is that we get to give. It is "more blessed to give than to receive" (Acts 20:35).

AUGUST 3

BUT IT'S NOT WHAT I EXPECTED

"Faith is the assurance of things hoped for."

Hebrews 11:1

The conversation went something like this:

Simon: "Did you see that?"

Ananias: "See what?"

Simon: "Don't you know what that is?"

Ananias: "I have no idea. Were we expecting something?"

Simon: "Yes, we were expecting Him."

Ananias: "Well, He is certainly not what I was expecting."

Expectations can frame your understanding. In this sense, expectation and preparation are synonyms. Faulty expectations result in faulty preparation, which then leads to faulty interpretation. We often miss things or misunderstand what is happening around us because we do not carry accurate expectations. Expectations are like containers. They form the parameters by which contents are able to be held. Without proper expectations, contents tend to spill out; and we miss what we might otherwise have seen.

This explains the paradoxical response to Jesus during what we now call Holy Week. On Palm Sunday in the midst of the crowd, Jesus rode into Jerusalem triumphantly on a donkey only to be condemned by the crowds less than five days later on Good Friday.

> Most of the crowd spread their coats in the road, and others were cutting branches from the trees and spreading them in the road. The crowds going ahead of Him, and those who

followed, were shouting, "Hosanna to the Son of David; BLESSED IS HE WHO COMES IN THE NAME OF THE LORD; Hosanna in the highest!" (Matt. 21:8-9).

But the chief priests and the elders persuaded the crowds to ask for Barabbas and to put Jesus to death. But the governor said to them, "Which of the two do you want me to release for you?" And they said, "Barabbas." Pilate said to them, "Then what shall I do with Jesus who is called Christ?" They all said, "Crucify Him!" And he said, "Why, what evil has He done?" But they kept shouting all the more, saying, "Crucify Him!" (Matt. 27:20-23).

What was going on? From Sunday to Friday, contents were spilling out everywhere because of unmet expectations. Jews were waiting for the Messiah, yet many missed Him because they were *expecting* a geopolitical Messiah Who would deliver them "militarily" from their Roman oppressors. He came into Jerusalem with a reputation that they could force into that sort of box—hence, the "hosannas." He was preaching the kingdom and rule of God, and He was known to do powerful acts. Certainly, He could be the Deliverer.

However, as Sunday came to an end without any fireworks, they all went back to their homes a bit dismayed, trying to convince themselves that their pigeonholed Messiah must be drawing up battle plans in His bunker. As Monday went on with no call to fight, they put it off to the possibility that the delay was strategic. By Tuesday, frustration began to mount; and after Wednesday, a full dose of doubt began to set in. By Thursday, expectations were clearly not being met, which set up the showdown on Friday.

Salvation is missed when expectations are flawed. When you expect to save yourself, you miss your Savior (Gal. 2:21). To see your need for a Savior is to have the expectation that only a Savior can meet that need (John 9:41). Thus, you are more inclined to knock on the door of salvation and have it opened (Matt. 7:7). If we are honest with ourselves and true to who we are, we should expect that we are in need of help. We are not perfect. We are inclined toward sin (Gal. 5:19-21). That is our nature (Rom. 3:23).

Sanctification is missed when expectations are flawed. It is God Who makes us holy and uses us for His glory. These sorts of expectations direct us to view the world around us differently. What is going on? I expect it has something to do with God using me for His glory; and thus, I look at situations as opportunities toward that end. It is all about Him. It is not about us. If we are honest with ourselves and true to who we are, we should expect that there is a God and, therefore, that we are not Him. God has made us with eternity in our hearts (Eccl. 3:11). We are aware of God. We know we are not Him. We are without excuse (Rom. 1:20). What do you expect?

Expectation is faith. "Now, faith is the assurance of things hoped for, the conviction of things not seen" (Heb. 11:1). Faith is the certainty of what you are expecting. A life of no expectation is a life of no faith. A life of faulty expectation is a life of faulty faith. A life of biblical expectation is a life of biblical faith. What do you expect?

AUGUST 4

WISE COUNSEL MAY HELP YOUR MARRIAGE

"A fool always loses his temper, but a wise man holds it back."
Proverbs 29:11

Many times, a divorce is the result of a lack of good communication in a marriage. A lack of communication either yields wrong perceptions of your partner or non-vented and bottled-up correct perceptions. Both of these unhealthy dynamics cause a growing bitterness and irritation with your partner. Eventually, mutual respect is damaged. Due to this tendency toward poor communication in a marriage, counselors should focus on getting couples to communicate more effectively. Counselors can use a variety of methods to encourage, challenge, and correct a couple's communication.

Husbands and wives should be reminded of the power of the tongue: "Death and life are in the power of the tongue, and those who love it will eat its fruit" (Prov. 18:21). They should be encouraged to consider the efficacy of words. "*Like* apples of gold in settings of silver is a word spoken in right circumstances" (Prov. 25:11). Sometimes, a husband or wife just does not realize how hurtful words can be; and he or she needs to picture the other saying, "How long will you torment me and crush me with words?" (Job 19:2). The wound can grow deeper until the couple agrees to not be "returning evil for evil or insult for insult" (1 Peter 3:9). Some marriages come to the point where unless the fire is put out, the entire "forest" will burn to the ground: "See how great a forest is set aflame by such a small fire! And the tongue is a fire" (James 3:5-6).

Marriage counselors can encourage husbands and wives in a variety of ways with respect to how they communicate with each other. For example, be careful to guard your words since "he who guards his mouth and his tongue, guards his soul from troubles" (Prov. 21:23). Think before you speak, as "the heart of the righteous ponders how to answer" (Prov. 15:28). "Do you see a man who is hasty in his words? There is more hope for a fool than for him" (Prov. 29:20). So "be quick to hear, slow to speak and slow to anger" (James 1:19).

The marriage counselor should emphasize the importance for the couple to listen to each other. Be sure to allow the other person to finish before you give your response, since "he who gives an answer before he hears, it is folly and shame to him" (Prov. 18:13). Do not use silence to frustrate the other person. Be mature. "Speaking the truth in love, we are to grow up" (Eph. 4:15). Try not to exaggerate. Avoid phrases like "You always . . . " or "We never . . . " Avoid arguing. It is possible to disagree without arguing. "The beginning of strife is *like* letting out water, so abandon the quarrel before it breaks out" (Prov. 17:14). Be wise in your marriage, knowing that "keeping away from strife is an honor for a man, but any fool will quarrel" (Prov. 20:3). Do not respond with anger. "He who is slow to anger has great understanding, but he who is quick-tempered exalts folly" (Prov. 14:29). And remember, "a gentle answer turns away wrath, but a harsh word stirs up anger" (Prov. 15:1).

Many problems in a marriage can be solved by simply admitting when you are wrong and asking for forgiveness (James 5:16). When the other person asks to be forgiven, be sure to forgive, forget, and do not mention it again (Prov. 17:9). Do not nag. Do not criticize. "Encourage one another and build up one another" (1 Thess. 5:11). Always try to understand and show interest in the other person's opinion and, in so doing, follow the command to "not *merely* look out for your own personal interests, but also for the interests of others" (Phil. 2:4).

Sometimes, the marriage is so damaged that divorce is looming. This is a crisis situation. There are, of course, other crisis situations—for example, a financial collapse or a runaway child or out of control substance abuse—in which counseling may be necessary. There are a variety of practical points that can be made when engaging in crisis counseling. First of all, it should be understood that there are negative ways for a person to confront a crisis situation. These include denying that the problem exists; trying to avoid the problem; refusing help; hiding feelings of anger, guilt, and fear; refusing to think about the crisis; or even trying to just forget about it. Other negative responses include refusing to consider practical solutions, blaming others and waiting for them to provide the solution, avoiding friends and family, and trying to convince yourself that the crisis is the punishment of God.

Positive ways for a person to confront a crisis situation include accepting that there is a problem; trying to understand the situation better; accepting help from family and friends; acknowledging feelings of anger, guilt, and fear; trying to resolve the problem; distinguishing between what can be changed and what cannot be changed; and accepting what cannot be changed. Other positive responses include considering practical solutions, taking small steps initially to work toward a solution, accepting your own responsibility for the problem, drawing close to family and friends, and praying and depending on the sovereignty of God.

The marriage relationship is the most foundational human relationship. It is, therefore, the relationship most to be cherished and protected. Invest into it your most valuable words. Cherish it! Protect it! Keep it!

AUGUST 5

CALLING ALL LEADERS: STAND FIRM

"Stand firm therefore."

Ephesians 6:14

Opposition to leadership can come from outside or inside of the ranks. Leaders must be skilled in handling opposition because it is inevitable, and it will not go away easily. If a leader never gets criticized, it probably means that he is not doing his job correctly. Jesus warned, "'Woe *to you* when all men speak well of you, for their fathers used to treat the false prophets in the same way'" (Luke 6:26). At the same time, opposition often accompanies success; the greater the success, the greater the opposition. Leaders must be able to respond to any type of opposition with wisdom.

Nehemiah led the Jews in a great task. They set out to rebuild the walls of Jerusalem and were having great success. Of course, opposition arose against them, but Nehemiah skillfully responded to it:

> Now when it was reported to Sanballat, Tobiah, to Geshem the Arab and to the rest of our enemies that I had rebuilt the wall, and *that* no breach remained in it, although at that time I had not set up the doors in the gates, then Sanballat and Geshem sent *a message* to me, saying, "Come, let us meet together at Chephirim in the plain of Ono." But they were planning to harm me. So I sent messengers to them, saying, "I am doing a great work and I cannot come down. Why should the work stop while I leave it and come down to you?" They sent *messages* to me four times in this manner, and I answered them in the same way. Then Sanballat sent his servant to me in the same manner a fifth time with an open letter in his hand. In it was written, "It is reported among the nations, and Gashmu says, that you and the Jews are planning to rebel; therefore you are rebuilding the wall. And you are to be their king, according to these reports. You have also appointed prophets to proclaim in Jerusalem concerning you, 'A king is in Judah!' And now it will be reported to the king according to these reports. So come now, let us take counsel together." Then I sent a *message* to him saying, "Such things as you are saying have not been done, but you are inventing them in your own mind." For all of them were *trying* to frighten us, thinking, "They will become discouraged with the work and it will not be done." But now, *O God*, strengthen my hands (Neh. 6:1-9).

Nehemiah discerned the source of the opposition (as opposed to simply believing rumors). He then discerned their motive. He did not allow the actions and threats of the opposition to intimidate him and distract him or his workers. They moved ahead with their eyes on their goal and not on the opposition. They stayed focused on the mission.

Nehemiah used some of the tools in his leadership toolkit to effectively come against his opposition. First, he used prayer. He responded to the attempt to scare and discourage his people with the prayer, "But now, O God, strengthen my hands." This was a common response to opposition. Nehemiah would lead his people in prayer crying out, "Hear, O our God" (Neh. 4:4). They would not cower before their enemies, "but we prayed to our God" (Neh. 4:9). Another tool Nehemiah used to combat opposition was his ability to motivate his people. Instead of being "demoralized," they "had a mind to work" (Neh. 4:5-6). Effective leaders are, by default, persistent prayers and, by ability, skilled motivators.

Nehemiah used common sense in response to opposition. If you think that someone might break into your car, you pray and trust God to protect it. You also lock the doors! Nehemiah did not have presumptuous faith. He was a man of prayer and action. "But we prayed to our God, and because of them we set up a guard against them day and night" (Neh. 4:9). Action does not negate faith; it is a very important component of it.

Opposition to leadership comes from a variety of places. It may come from the inside—the negative people from inside the church who love to complain and try to "whisper" (Psalm 41:7) their way to gain a following. It may come from outside—the "Sanballats" of the world who try to destroy God's work. It may come from another realm—the spiritual warfare that goes on around us that must be fought with spiritual weapons (2 Cor. 10:3-4).

Wherever it comes from, one thing is assured: opposition *will* come. "Indeed, all who desire to live godly in Christ Jesus will be persecuted" (2 Tim. 3:12). Leaders must be willing and able to respond to opposition effectively. Leaders must "be able to stand firm . . . having done everything, to stand firm" (Eph. 6:11-14). The instruction given to the leader is, "Be on the alert, stand firm in the faith, act like men, be strong" (1 Cor. 16:13). Stand firm!

AUGUST 6

TO THE JEW AND TO THE GREEK— TO ALL NATIONS

"To the Jew first and also to the Greek."

Romans 1:16

Jesus referred to Himself most often as the Son of Man: the Divine Representative for mankind. This title of Deity is used by both Ezekiel and Daniel. Ezekiel, as the "son of man," (Ezek. 2:3, 3:17) becomes a "type" of Christ, whose ministry is to the nations: "My holy name I will make known in the midst of My people Israel; and I will not let My holy name be profaned anymore. And the nations will know that I am the LORD, the Holy One in Israel" (Ezek. 39:7). This Divine title, the Son of Man, is also used by Daniel and is set within the context of an eternal kingdom in which all peoples and nations will serve Him:

> I kept looking in the night visions, and behold, with the clouds of heaven One like a Son of Man was coming, and He came up to the Ancient of Days and was presented before Him. And to Him was given dominion, glory and a kingdom, that all the peoples, nations and *men of every* language might serve Him. His dominion is an everlasting dominion which will not pass away; and His kingdom is one which will not be destroyed (Dan. 7:13-14).

Jesus' self-proclaimed purpose was to preach this eternal kingdom to *both* Jew and Gentile (Luke 4:43). Perhaps, this is why His title is "Son of Man" and not "Son of Israel" (Luke 9:51-56). There exists, however, a sort of missiological process in which the messengers of the Son of Man would take the Gospel "to the Jew first and also to the Greek" (Rom. 1:16). As soon as Jesus appointed the Twelve—twelve Jews representing the twelve tribes of Israel—He sent them out to "the house of Israel." This was done for strategic purposes. A Jew could understand the Gospel. It was the ancient message of God to mankind that was expressed in their Scriptures of which they were guardians (Rom. 9:4). There is also a situational priority, since judgment would first come upon the Jews (Rom. 2:9).

The ministry of the Son of Man is directed toward both the Jew and the Gentile. Even as the Twelve were sent initially to the house of Israel, the Seventy were sent to the Gentiles: "Now after this the Lord appointed seventy others, and sent them in pairs ahead of Him to every city and place where He Himself was going to come" (Luke 10:1). The "cities" represent the Gentiles, and the "seventy" represent the seventy descendants of Noah that formed the nations (Gen. 10).

Jesus' ministry to all people can be seen in general terms, as well as in specific situations. Jesus ministers to the *Roman* centurion (Matt. 8:5-13). Obviously, this *Roman* is not Jewish. Jesus references the Gentiles—"many will come from east and west"—as those who will receive the Gospel. After using irony to make a point to His disciples that all people are welcome to the Gospel—a common cultural method of teaching used by Jesus in other situations as well (Matt. 12:1-3; John 10:31-32)—Jesus heals the *Canaanite* woman's daughter (Matt. 15:21-28). Obviously, this *Canaanite* is not Jewish.

Jesus' ministry is toward all people. Jesus makes this point again to His disciples when they haughtily threaten the *Samaritans*. Jesus corrected this prejudicial spirit and redirected their attitudes toward a non-biased Gospel. "You do not know what kind of spirit you are of; for the Son of Man did not come to destroy men's lives, but to save them" (Luke 9:55-56).

Jesus offers the Gospel to "anyone" for He "will draw all men" to Himself (John 12:20-21, 26, 32). It will ultimately be "a great multitude which no one could count, from every nation and *all* tribes and peoples and tongues" (Rev. 7:9) who will be saved. The Gospel goes to the Jew and to the Gentile. The ancient Scriptures declare it, Jesus makes it His Great Commission, and the Spirit is sent to empower it. "Thus it is written, that the Christ would suffer and rise again from the dead the third day, and that repentance for forgiveness of sins would be proclaimed in His name to all the nations, beginning from Jerusalem" (Luke 24:46-47). So, as Mark 16:15 says, "Go into all the world and preach the gospel to all creation" (Mark 16:15). But you do not have to do this on your own. "But you will receive power when the Holy Spirit has come upon you; and you shall be My witnesses both in Jerusalem, and in all Judea and Samaria, and even to the remotest part of the earth" (Acts 1:8).

AUGUST 7

THE KINGDOM OF GOD IS NOT A LAWLESS SOCIETY

"Do we then nullify the Law through faith? May it never be! On the contrary, we establish the Law."

Romans 3:31

Jesus, of course, was a master teacher and preacher. The Sermon on the Mount stands as the single most comprehensive message that He preached while He walked this earth. The Sermon is a discourse on the kingdom of God. The introduction is made up of a series of principles called "Beatitudes" that describe the character of those who live in the kingdom. Once that is established, Jesus moves on to explain the kingdom standards that are set for kingdom-dwellers.

These standards, most importantly, are based on reality and not simply on appearance. The King of the kingdom "'*sees* not as man sees, for man looks at the outward appearance, but the LORD looks at the heart'" (1 Sam. 16:7). The standards that were held by those who were only *outwardly* religious in appearance were not consistent with life in the kingdom. Many who heard were certainly shocked when Jesus proclaimed, "'For I say to you that unless your righteousness surpasses *that* of the scribes and Pharisees, you will not enter the kingdom of heaven'" (Matt. 5:20). The seemingly holy standards of the Pharisees were, in fact, false standards. They were fake and empty! And so, Jesus repeatedly called those who were stuck in religiosity *hypocrites* (Matt. 15:7, 23:23). He addresses them with ominous words: "'Woe to you, scribes and Pharisees, hypocrites! For you are like whitewashed tombs which on the outside appear beautiful, but inside they are full of dead men's bones and all uncleanness. So you, too, outwardly appear righteous to men, but inwardly you are full of hypocrisy and lawlessness'" (Matt. 23:27-28).

It should be pointed out that the Pharisees' problem was not their focus on the Law. In fact, their hypocrisy is directly connected to their *lack* of focus on the Law (their "lawlessness"). The Law is not by the letter or by appearance but by reality and the Spirit. Kingdom standards are based on the heart of the Law.

> For indeed circumcision is of value if you practice the Law; but if you are a transgressor of the Law, your circumcision has become uncircumcision. So if the uncircumcised man keeps the requirements of the Law, will not his uncircumcision be regarded as circumcision? And he who is physically uncircumcised, if he keeps the Law, will he not judge you who though having the letter *of the Law* and circumcision are a transgressor of the Law? For he is not a Jew who is one outwardly, nor is circumcision that which is outward in the flesh. But he is a Jew who is one inwardly; and circumcision is that which is of the heart, by the Spirit, not by the letter; and his praise is not from men, but from God (Rom. 2:25-29).

Jesus was not changing or doing away with the Law. He was going beyond the common, religious understanding of the Law in order to capture its heart. Outward religion tends to make the doing of the Law an external show. Jesus was revealing that the doing of the Law was not an outward display but an internal reality. With a greater revelation of the Law Himself came a higher standard. He did not come to *exempt* kingdom-dwellers from doing the Law. He came to *empower* them to do the Law (Jer. 31:33).

> Do not think that I came to abolish the Law or the Prophets; I did not come to abolish but to fulfill. For truly I say to you, until heaven and earth pass away, not the smallest letter or stroke shall pass from the Law until all is accomplished. Whoever then annuls one of the least of these commandments, and teaches others *to do* the same, shall be called least in the kingdom of heaven; but whoever keeps and teaches *them*, he shall be called great in the kingdom of heaven (Matt. 5:17-19).

Jesus goes on to describe the kingdom standards. They are not different standards. They are unpolluted standards. They are the pure standards that God has always had for His people but were often corrupted and mocked. Jesus repeats the formula, "'You have heard that it was said . . . but I say to you'" (Matt. 5:27-28) as He sets the real standards for hatred, adultery, divorce, vows, retribution, and love (Matt. 5:21-48).

And so, it must be understood by those who desire to live in the kingdom of God, that grace and faith (Eph. 2:8) do not stand in opposition to the Law and works. "For sin shall not be master over you, for you are not under law but under grace" (Rom. 6:14). You are not under the Law—not because you have nothing to do with the Law but because you are enabled to do the Law. You are *over* it, not *under* it. "Do we then nullify the Law through faith? May it never be! On the contrary, we establish the Law" (Rom. 3:31).

The righteous live by faith (Rom. 1:17)—not because faith has nothing to do with righteousness but because the righteous, by definition, are empowered by faith, grace, and salvation unto righteousness. This righteousness does not save them, but their being saved results in righteousness. Grace puts them over the Law, instead of under it. Grace, faith, and salvation empower them to do the Law; not exempt them from it.

No Law for the Christian? May it never be! Christians *establish* the Law! Fake Christians mock the Law in their superficiality. Christians are not perfect; but instead of mocking the Law, they find grace to do the Law. Unlike hypocrites, they are not "lawless."

AUGUST 8

WITHOUT WAX

"Treasures on earth . . . treasures in heaven."

Matthew 6:19-20

There are two apple vendors in the old country market. One vendor is "without wax," and the other vendor is "with wax." From which one should you buy your apples? In order to not get cheated, you should go to the "without wax" vendor.

The word *sincere* is derived from two Latin parts—"sin," meaning "without," and "cere," meaning "wax." To be sincere is to be "without wax." This is why you want to buy your apples from the "without wax" vendor. He is sincere. The other vendor is "insincere"; he is "with wax." He drills holes in his half-pound counterbalance weights and fills them with wax. The wax weighs much less than the stone or iron that he drilled out; so instead of weighing a half pound, it weighs something less. When you put your four pounds of apples up on the scale and he puts what appears to be four pounds of counterweight on the other side, the apples still seem to weigh more. The insincere vendor then puts another halfpound weight on the scale, and it then counterbalances the weight of the apples. You pay for four-and-a-half pounds of apples, even though you are only getting four pounds.

Insincere, "with wax" vendors are hypocrites. Their weights are weights in appearance only. Sincere, "without wax" vendors are integral. What you see is what you get! In the Sermon on the Mount, Jesus warns against hypocrisy. The repeated way in which He structures His sermon reveals His message: when you do something, do not do it publicly for men but secretly for God. Your reward will come from who you did it for.

> So when you give to the poor, do not sound a trumpet before you, as the hypocrites do in the synagogues and in the streets, so that they may be honored by men. Truly I say to you, they have their reward in full. But when you give to the poor, do not let your left hand know what your right hand is doing, so that your giving will be in secret; and your Father who sees *what is done* in secret will reward you. When you pray, you are not to be like the hypocrites; for they love to stand and pray in the synagogues and on the street corners so that they may be seen by men. Truly I say to you, they have their reward in full. But you, when you pray, go into your inner room, close your door and pray to your Father who is in secret, and your Father who sees *what is done* in secret will reward you . . . Whenever you fast, do not put on a gloomy face as the hypocrites do, for they neglect their appearance so that they will be noticed by men when they are fasting. Truly I say to you, they have their reward in full. But you, when you fast, anoint your head and wash your face so that your fasting will not be noticed by men, but by your Father who is in secret; and your Father who sees *what is done* in secret will reward you (Matt. 6:2-6, 16-18).

Hey, hypocrites! Listen up, you who are insincere and "with wax." Stop drilling holes in your religion. Stop putting on a show and acting like you are something that you are not. The only thing that you will get out of it is what you put into it. Your reward will come from the one you did it for. Appearance for appearance's sake is empty. Disappearance for the sake of God is full. Secrecy is consistent with intimate relationship. It indicates pure motives. Publicity is consistent with hypocrisy. It reveals ulterior motives. Where is your treasure?

> Do not store up for yourselves treasures on earth, where moth and rust destroy, and where thieves break in and steal. But store up for yourselves treasures in heaven, where neither moth nor rust destroys, and where thieves do not break in or steal; for where your treasure is, there your heart will be also . . . No one can serve two masters; for either he will hate the one and love the other, or he will be devoted to one and despise the other. You cannot serve God and wealth. (Matt. 6:19-21, 24).

If you do things for man, then your reward will come from man; and the real reward is stolen. If you do things for God, then your reward will come from God; and it cannot be stolen. You cannot do things for God (sincere, authentic worship) *and* for man (hypocritical, insincere worship). Your treasure is how you are fulfilled or satisfied. Are you fulfilled by the rewards of men? Or is your treasure the rewards that God gives? For whom do you do things? God is warning against giving your heart to men by making their rewards your treasures. When appearance is your treasure, hypocrisy is your action. Flee from hypocrisy. Pursue God. Get rid of the wax!

AUGUST 9

THE ROMANS 12 GIFT OF SERVICE

*"Since we have gifts that differ according to the grace given to us,
each of us is to exercise them accordingly ... if service, in his serving."*

Romans 12:6-7

God equips His people with gifts for ministry. There exist various lists of gifts in the New Testament. One such list is found in Romans 12:6-8:

> Since we have gifts that differ according to the grace given to us, each of us is to exercise them accordingly: if prophecy, according to the proportion of his faith; if service, in his serving; or he who teaches, in his teaching; or he who exhorts, in his exhortation; he who gives, with liberality; he who leads, with diligence; he who shows mercy, with cheerfulness.

How can the Romans 12 gift of service be understood? A person who has the gift of service is drawn toward helping and assisting others in practical ways. They are genuinely fulfilled as they engage in their gift finding joy and satisfaction simply in serving others. Because they are people who see life through the lens of specific acts of service, they tend to be more comfortable with setting short-term goals. People with this gift of service tend to shy away from leadership and do not, in general, like to be the one who takes charge while working in a group. A person who has this gift tends to be very loyal and committed both to those they are serving and to the service itself. Examples of people in the Bible who seem to have had this gift are Martha (John 12:2), Timothy (Acts 19:22), Stephen (Acts 6:1-5), and Phoebe (Rom. 16:1).

Just like any strength that has its correlated weaknesses, the gift of service has its vulnerabilities or carnal tendencies that need to be avoided. If someone with this gift is not careful, he or she may become overworked as they tend to not delegate well. They would rather do the task themselves than spend the time and effort to get someone else to do it. The person also needs to beware of falling into self-pity and withdrawing from other people if and when their service is not recognized by others. Another vulnerability of this gift is to become judgmental of others who do not seem to be willing to serve.

Here is the Romans 12 gift of service. Life is seen as a series of activities. The orientation is toward others. More than anything else, people with this gift view themselves as helpers. People with the gift of service would most definitely say about themselves, "We are here to help you!" Are you this person? Do you have the Romans 12 gift of service?

AUGUST 10

GOD'S SOVEREIGNTY IN EVANGELISM

*"And He, when He comes, will convict the world concerning sin and righteousness and judgment;
concerning sin, because they do not believe in Me; and concerning righteousness,
because I go to the Father and you no longer see Me; and concerning judgment,
because the ruler of this world has been judged."*

John 16:8-11

God oversees His operations. Of course, His operations exist within the business of evangelism. God reveals Himself to people, and people come to know Him. He uses His people to be the conduits through which the revelation of Himself travels. These evangelistic endeavors require that people share the message—that is, the Gospel. They also require that God's power and Sovereign influence are involved. God is Sovereign in evangelism.

Sometimes, that sovereignty is as specific as what is currently going on in a person's life when the message is being shared with them. For example, people, in general, are more responsive to the Gospel when they are in the midst of crisis events. These extreme situations might include death events or birth events. When people or things are taken away or when people or things are newly introduced, potential receivers of the Gospel tend to be more open to it. God can sovereignly piece these pieces of the puzzle together—messenger, hearer, and situation—so as to produce fruit in an evangelistic event. The messenger is necessary, but the messenger is not responsible for the results. This is certainly true, since the messenger cannot control the results. Only God, through the work and power of the Holy Spirit, can do that. God sovereignly produces the fruit. He is "the Lord of the harvest" (Matt. 9:38).

God is sovereign in revival. He is the Lord of the really big harvests. It was the Lord Who "was adding to their number day by day those who were being saved" (Acts 2:47), even as many as "three thousand souls" (Acts 2:41). Again, the Spirit can sovereignly work through circumstances and situations. Sometimes, revival comes in the midst of overcoming disunity (Acts 6:1-7). Revival may come in the context of persecution (Acts 8:1-9:31). Other times, revival may come against the backdrop of government resistance (Acts 12:1-24). Revival may also come in the midst of demonic activity and spiritual warfare (Acts 19:13-20). So, too, great harvests and a pouring out of the Holy Spirit's power on the Church can be associated with intercession (Acts 4:24-31). In all cases, God is Sovereign and sovereignly uses circumstances and situations to bring forth fruit in evangelism.

The Holy Spirit must bring understanding to the mind of the unbeliever. This is necessary, since "the god of this world has blinded the minds of the unbelieving so that they might not see the light of the gospel of the glory of Christ" (2 Cor. 4:4). Minds are veiled; "but whenever a person turns to the Lord, the veil is taken away. Now the Lord is the Spirit, and where the Spirit of the Lord is, *there* is liberty" (2 Cor. 3:16-17). Spiritual matters require the involvement of the Spirit, since "a natural man does not accept the things of the Spirit of God, for they are foolishness to him; and he cannot understand them, because they are spiritually appraised" (1 Cor. 2:14). The Holy Spirit nudges minds.

The Holy Spirit must convict the heart of the unbeliever. The messenger must speak the message, but the Spirit must move the person: "Now when they heard *this*, they were pierced to the heart, and said to Peter and the rest of the apostles, 'Brethren, what shall we do?'" (Acts 2:37). When the Spirit moves, the Philippian jailers of the world say, "'Sirs, what must I do to be saved?'" (Acts 16:30). The Holy Spirit nudges hearts.

The Holy Spirit must influence the will of the unbeliever. People are stubborn. We all have a little bit of the Prodigal Son in us. We want what we want. Nevertheless, God can sovereignly use our circumstances so as to shake our will in such a way that we eventually say, "I will get up and go to my father, and will say to him, 'Father, I have sinned against heaven, and in your sight'" (Luke 15:18). The Holy Spirit nudges wills.

The Holy Spirit is Sovereign in evangelism. He nudges minds, hearts, and wills. He convicts the world concerning sin, righteousness, and judgment (John 16:8-11). God is the Lord of the harvest. "Therefore beseech the Lord of the harvest to send out laborers into His harvest" (Luke 10:2). "O LORD, save Your people" (Jer. 31:7).

AUGUST 11

WHAT DO YOU MEAN I AM A SLAVE?

*"And if you are willing to accept **it**."*

Matthew 11:14

Only servants can serve. Character sources actions. The choice to be a servant is a character issue, while the choice to serve is an action issue. A river does not flow without a source. Service does not happen without a servant. Slavery does not happen without a slave. There is nothing "glamorous" about slavery. It is not service or slavery that is the greatest; but "whoever wishes to become great among you shall be your servant, and whoever wishes to be first among you shall be your slave" (Matt. 20:26-27). It is all about who or what you are a slave to. Everybody is a slave to something. The great ones are slaves to Christ.

When we choose to serve, we may still remain in charge of who, when, why, where, and how we will serve. This necessarily limits our service and also makes it possible to feel manipulated and used by others. We can easily get offended and stop serving. When we choose to be servants, we give up the "right" to be in charge of those factors. There are no limits to our service in Christ, and we cannot feel manipulated or used because we have already given up our rights; there are no rights left to manipulate or violate. We cannot get offended, and so our service continues. It is who we *are*, not simply what we *do*.

Like a slave, a servant lays down his or her rights. Holding on to rights and giving up rights is the difference between one who serves and one who is a servant. Jesus exemplifies this in that "although He existed in the form of God, did not regard equality with God a thing to be grasped, but emptied Himself, taking the form of a bond-servant" (Phil. 2:6-7). He emptied Himself of His rights and privileges and became a *doulos*: a "bond-servant" or a slave.

There are many radical claims and obligations put forth in the Bible. Perhaps the most bothersome requirement for those who live in democratic, free market cultures is this command to lay down your rights. Democracies are built on the emotional demand to protect one's rights. To have rights is to live; and therefore, people are willing to die to keep them. The credo of the democratic culture is, "I *do* have certain rights!" This, of course, has some traction relative to biblical principles of government and social interaction. However, with regard to individual interaction with Christ, the "rights argument" is not able to be supported. In fact, followers of Christ are called to lay down their rights (Phil. 2:5). This is not so much because of what we are called to do but because of who we are called to be.

> Which of you, having a slave plowing or tending sheep, will say to him when he has come in from the field, "Come immediately and sit down to eat"? But will he not say to him, "Prepare something for me to eat, and *properly* clothe yourself and serve me while I eat and drink; and afterward you may eat and drink"? He does not thank the slave because he did the things which were commanded, does he? So you too, when you do all the things which are commanded you, say, "We are unworthy slaves; we have done *only* that which we ought to have done" (Luke 17:7-10).

Jesus spoke this parable in response to His disciples' request to increase their faith. Faith is dependent on how you view yourself. Do you view yourself like a slave? Slaves have no rights. They do not do their work in order to get something in return. They have no rights or privileges, and their work cannot earn for them rights or privileges. Jesus calls His disciples to have the same attitude. This is radical. This is hard to accept! No rights just does not seem to be right.

There is some balance that comes with this radical call, lest it be irresponsibly radical. Surely, we are not to do anything that anyone tells us we must do. The balance comes in the emphasis of who we are slaves to; we are slaves to Christ. We are answerable to Him. That which brings balance to this radical call is nothing less than that which makes it so radical: complete and total resignation to Jesus Christ alone. To abandon yourself to the One necessarily implies the lack of abandonment to any other. To say yes to Christ will mean saying no to others. "Whether it is right in the sight of God to give heed to you rather than to God, you be the judge; for we cannot stop speaking about what we have seen and heard" (Acts 4:19-20). The balance of the command to lay down your rights comes in the understanding that you lay them down only at the feet of Jesus. "We must obey God rather than men" (Acts 5:29).

Paul viewed himself as a slave (Rom. 1:1). Timothy viewed himself as a slave (Phil. 1:1). How do you view yourself? We are called to be "slaves of Christ" (Eph. 6:6).

AUGUST 12

THE "SO THAT" KIND OF PEOPLE

*"God be gracious to us and bless us, **and** cause His face to shine upon us ... That Your way may be known on the earth, Your salvation among all nations."*

Psalm 67:1-2

After the tower of Babel fiasco in Genesis 11, God began to work His plan through chosen instruments. We might call this "vessel theology." Since the nations were now spread out, He chose a missionary nation through which He could reach them. Israel was selected to be that missionary nation. Israel was not selected in order to exclude others. Rather, Israel was selected in order to include others. And so, we can understand the Old Testament better when we study it from three different viewpoints: Israel's opportunity, Israel's obligation, Israel's response.

The Abrahamic covenant is a missionary covenant. Through it, Israel is promised the resources, ability, and blessings to be a blessing to all the families of the earth (Gen. 12:3). Israel received great authority and opportunity that came with great responsibility and obligation.

> Now the LORD said to Abram, "Go forth from your country, and from your relatives and from your father's house, to the land which I will show you; and I will make you a great nation, and I will bless you, and make your name great; and so you shall be a blessing; and I will bless those who bless you, and the one who curses you I will curse. And in you all the families of the earth will be blessed" (Gen. 12:1-3).

Just as there are three separate statements of being blessed (Gen. 12:2), there are three separate statements of being a blessing: you shall be a blessing; bless/curse those who bless/curse you; "in you all the families of the earth will be blessed."

God expects us to use that which He has given us. In fact, "freely you received, freely give" (Matt. 10:8) and "from everyone who has been given much, much will be required, and to whom they entrusted much, of him they will ask all the more" (Luke 12:48). God expected Israel to use His blessings to bless the nations. In other words, God insists that there be an obligation that matches up with the opportunity.

Israel had two different kinds of obligations. First, they had a passive obligation. Israel blessed the world by being a conduit through which the Messiah would come. They provided the genetic line for the birth of Christ. Second, Israel had an active obligation. They were to take an aggressive and active role in God's missionary activity. Israel was in covenant with God. The stronger the commitment of each member of the covenant to complete its part, the stronger the covenant would be. God's obligation was to bless Israel. Israel's obligation was to be a blessing to the nations.

The covenant is repeated to Abraham in Genesis 17. It is then repeated to Isaac in Genesis 26:4 and to Jacob in Genesis 28:14-15. It is the Great Commission as it is played out in the Old Testament. There are uncanny similarities of the wording in Matthew 28:18-20 and the wording in Genesis 12:1 and Genesis 28:14-15.

God speaks of His missionary covenant. "Now then, if you will indeed obey My voice and keep My covenant, then you shall be My own possession among all the peoples, for all the earth is Mine; and you shall be to Me a kingdom of priests and a holy nation" (Exod. 19:5-6). Israel will be God's "own possession" (blessing), and they will be that in the midst of "all the peoples" (be a blessing). They shall be a "kingdom of priests"—mediators (priests) between God and the nations who would minister to the world. Israel was to be "a holy nation" so that as they were set apart in obedience to God, the nations could have a witness of the greatness of God as He blessed Israel for their obedience. In Psalm 67, God makes His missionary heart very clear as He repeatedly specifies that there are blessings *so that* they will be used to reach the nations:

> God be gracious to us and bless us, *and* cause His face to shine upon us—*Selah*. That Your way may be known on the earth, Your salvation among all nations. Let the peoples praise You, O God; let all the peoples praise You. Let the nations be glad and sing for joy; for You will judge the peoples with uprightness and guide the nations on the earth. *Selah*. Let the peoples praise You, O God; let all the peoples praise You. The earth has yielded its produce; God, our God, blesses us. God blesses us, that all the ends of the earth may fear Him" (Psalm 67).

God thinks in *so thats*. He is a *so that* God. What have you been given? Whatever it is, it is not just to be buried in a hole in the ground (Matt. 25:18). It is to be used for something. You have it *so that* somebody else can be blessed, especially with the Good News of the Gospel.

AUGUST 13

CHOOSE FAITH. CHOOSE LIFE!

"For the things which are seen are temporal, but the things which are not seen are eternal."
2 Corinthians 4:18

Faith is a paradox; it tends to reach *beyond* reason. Faith believes without necessarily understanding why. Faith sings at midnight and praises God while in jail (Acts 16:25). What is the expected response to tribulation, hardships, and rough times? It might be complaining, moaning, or withdrawing. In any case, it would not be celebrating unless, of course, faith is paradoxical. "And not only this, but we also exult in our tribulations, knowing that tribulation brings about perseverance; and perseverance, proven character; and proven character, hope; and hope does not disappoint, because the love of God has been poured out within our hearts through the Holy Spirit who was given to us" (Rom. 5:3-5).

Faith chooses to endure mistreatment. "By faith Moses, when he had grown up, refused to be called the son of Pharaoh's daughter, choosing rather to endure ill-treatment with the people of God than to enjoy the passing pleasures of sin" (Heb. 11:24-25). Faith is able to see as advantageous what would otherwise be seen as negative situations.

> Now I want you to know, brethren, that my circumstances have turned out for the greater progress of the gospel, so that my imprisonment in *the cause of* Christ has become well known throughout the whole praetorian guard and to everyone else, and that most of the brethren, trusting in the Lord because of my imprisonment, have far more courage to speak the word of God without fear (Phil. 1:12-14).

Faith is a perception. It is to perceive as reality that which is not revealed to the senses. It "is the assurance of *things* hoped for, the conviction of things not seen" (Heb. 11:1). Faith enables us to not lose heart when we find ourselves in heart-wrenching situations.

> Therefore we do not lose heart, but though our outer man is decaying, yet our inner man is being renewed day by day. For momentary, light affliction is producing for us an eternal weight of glory far beyond all comparison, while we look not at the things which are seen, but at the things which are not seen; for the things which are seen are temporal, but the things which are not seen are eternal (2 Cor. 4:16-18).

Perhaps, the most specific way to define something is to identify its opposite. What is good? It is what is not bad. What is dark? It is what is not light. What is the opposite of faith? "Whatever is not from faith is sin" (Rom. 14:23). Faith is natural, according to the plan of God. "By faith we understand that the worlds were prepared by the word of God, so that what is seen was not made out of things which are visible" (Heb. 11:3).

Sin, however, is *not* natural, according to the plan of God. "For this reason God gave them over to degrading passions; for their women exchanged the natural function for that which is unnatural, and in the same way also the men abandoned the natural function of the woman and burned in their desire toward one another, men with men committing indecent acts" (Rom. 1:26-27).

And so, the result of faith is life—"you have been saved through faith" (Eph. 2:8)—while the result of sin is death. "For the wages of sin is death, but the free gift of God is eternal life in Christ Jesus our Lord" (Rom. 6:23). Choose life! Choose faith!

AUGUST 14

THE ESSENCE OF MARRIAGE IS UNITY

> *"Then God said, 'Let Us make man in Our image, according to Our likeness...'*
> *God created man in His own image, in the image of God He created him; male and female*
> *He created them... For this reason a man shall leave his father and his mother,*
> *and be joined to his wife; and they shall become one flesh."*
>
> Genesis 1:26-27; 2:24

The essence of the Trinity is perfect unity set forth in perfect love. It is not surprising, then, that the essence of marriage is unity based in love. It is an "Us" (Trinity) Who created a "them" (male and female) in "Our" image. "God said, 'Let Us make man in Our image, according to Our likeness'" God created man in His own image, in the image of God He created him; male and female He created them" (Gen. 1:26-27).

Even before the fall of man, we see the first marriage. It was holy and pure. Even within the realm of the sexual, there was purity and innocence; "and the man and his wife were both naked and were not ashamed" (Gen. 2:25). Certainly, in the first wedding ceremony, we can see very plainly the "essence" of marriage—that is, unity. "For this reason a man shall leave his father and his mother, and be joined to his wife; and they shall become one flesh" (Gen. 2:24). With respect to God's instituting of marriage, we see His reason for it, man's response to it, and its godly result.

The marriage event starts off with the words, "For this reason." What is God's reason? It is whatever came before that statement: "'This is now bone of my bones, and flesh of my flesh; she shall be called Woman, because she was taken out of Man'" (Gen. 2:23). The reason for marriage is that God Himself "fashioned into a woman the rib which He had taken from the man, and brought her to the man" (Gen. 2:22). It is God's doing. It is God's bringing together what He originally created as a "together." It is God Who initiates and sources. This is God's reason for marriage.

Man's response is that "a man shall leave his father and his mother." God sources the union, and then man takes the initiative to prepare for the new union. He initiates the leaving of one bond to form a new bond. He responds to God's reason. He agrees with God's action of taking from him and applies it by leaving and retaking. This is man's response to marriage.

The result is that the husband is "joined to his wife, and they shall become one flesh." God has His reason for the union; man responds to that reason for the union; and the result is union, the essence of marriage. The man and the woman were one—just as the rib and the body were one—that is, "bone of my bones and flesh of my flesh." And so, the husband and wife return to what they were originally—one flesh. This is the result of marriage.

How does this truth get applied to a marriage? Another way to ask this question is what makes for a more unified marriage? One definite answer is prayer; praying together results in staying together. Many marriages end in divorce. Married couples who pray together, however, have a greater chance of not getting divorced. Prayer is productive. With respect to marriage, it produces the right result and the right resource.

The right result of marriage is unity. The marriage relationship should continually be growing into a more actualized "one flesh" reality. This is, of course, God's plan and desire as it is He Who "brought her to the man." He created them to be one flesh. Prayer can move toward this, since it is the nature of prayer to bind people together. "These all with one mind were continually devoting themselves to prayer" (Acts 1:14). Disunity can be the result of a lack of communication and the lack of honesty. Oppositely, unity can be the result of the honest communication that is experienced in praying together.

The right resource of marriage is power. God said, "'It is not good for the man to be alone; I will make him a helper suitable for him'" (Gen. 2:18). One by itself is limited. But one plus one equals two, a much more powerful number. The one can "complete" the other (which is a proper translation for "helper").

> Two are better than one because they have a good return for their labor. For if either of them falls, the one will lift up his companion. But woe to the one who falls when there is not another to lift him up. Furthermore, if two lie down together they keep warm, but how can one be warm *alone*? And if one can overpower him who is alone, two can resist him. A cord of three *strands* is not quickly torn apart (Eccl. 4:9-12).

A husband and a wife united with God— a prayer-driven marriage—is the "cord of three strands." It is very pleasing to God when we "dwell together in unity" (Psalm 133). God loves a unified marriage, but He hates its opposite—divorce (Mal. 2:16).

The essence of marriage is unity based in love because that is the essence of Him Who created marriage in His image. God loves unity in marriage, and He hates disunity in marriage. Praying together builds unity. So build unity and please God. Pray together!

AUGUST 15

THE KEY THAT OPENS THE DOOR

*"Devote yourselves to prayer, keeping alert in it with **an attitude** of thanksgiving; praying at the same time for us as well, that God will open up to us a door for the word, so that we may speak forth the mystery of Christ, for which I have also been imprisoned; that I may make it clear in the way I ought to speak."*

Colossians 4:2-4

A key opens a door. The door might be the way through which to present the Gospel. The key might be a redemptive analogy that can be used by a missionary to communicate cross-culturally. Concept fulfillment occurs when a concept, idea or story that is part of a particular culture is realized by the Gospel message. These "redemptive analogies" and "concept fulfillments" help missionaries cross cultures and present the Gospel "that God will open up to us a door for the word . . . that I may make it clear in the way I ought to speak" (Col. 4:3-4).

For the Jews, the fact that Jesus was the Lamb of God fulfilled their concept of animal sacrifice for the forgiveness of sins. The Karen tribe in Burma has experienced incredible church growth. It all began with "concept fulfillment." The tribe had a legend that one day a teacher of truth would come. The legend said that this teacher would carry a black book under his arm. When the first missionary came to the Karen tribe, he had a black Bible that he carried it under his arm. When he began to speak what he claimed to be truth, the people eagerly listened.

Concept fulfillments or redemptive analogies are not always so dramatic. Missionaries must come to know the culture, so they might be able to pick out the more subtle fulfillments or analogies. What is it that could serve as the connection from one culture to another and bring understanding? What is it that will "open their eyes so that they may turn from darkness to light and from the dominion of Satan to God, that they may receive forgiveness of sins"? (Acts 26:18).

Jesus crossed cultures when He came into Samaria to share the Gospel. He used an eye-opening introduction to His message when He told a Samaritan woman to "'give Me a drink'" (John 4:7). This certainly caught the woman's attention, since "Jews have no dealings with Samaritans" (John 4:9). Jesus used a cultural issue to move His way forward toward presenting the Gospel. He then used a relevant redemptive analogy—eternal Living Water that will fulfill the temporal water that she must retrieve every day—to claim that He could be her eternal Provision. Jesus began to turn the woman from darkness to light by first using her culture to prompt an eye-opening moment.

Paul began to turn the Athenians from darkness to light by using a cultural eye-opener. He spoke to them on their level, recognizing that they were "very religious in all respects" (Acts 17:22). He used their philosophical culture to be a launching pad for his Gospel presentation:

"For in Him we live and move and exist, as even some of your own poets have said, 'For we also are His children.' Being then the children of God, we ought not to think that the Divine Nature is like gold or silver or stone, an image formed by the art and thought of man. Therefore having overlooked the times of ignorance, God is now declaring to men that all *people* everywhere should repent, because He has fixed a day in which He will judge the world in righteousness through a Man whom He has appointed, having furnished proof to all men by raising Him from the dead" (Acts 17:28-31).

A key opens a door. So let us pray "that God will open up to us a door for the word" (Col. 4:3) and that we will be able to see Him turn people in our mission fields from darkness to light.

AUGUST 16

BUT THE BAR IS SET SO HIGH

"'Man looks at the outward appearance, but the LORD looks at the heart.'"
1 Samuel 16:7

The iconic Sermon on the Mount must have left its original listeners speechless. Every line stands as a profound nugget of truth. The heart of the sermon comes when Jesus sets the standards for those living in the kingdom of God. These standards are rooted in what is real, not simply in what things look like. Appearance is not enough. Actuality is demanded. Man gravitates toward the superficial. It does not satisfy, but man is deceived into being content with it. God and His standards are very different. Kingdom of God standards do not concern themselves with what something looks like; they are concerned with what something actually is. It is all about God, the great "I Am." It is all about reality—that which is. There is nothing really "super" about *super*ficiality. It only serves to deceive.

And so, for example, in the list of standards set in the Sermon on the Mount is the standard for hatred. Certainly, murder is an extreme expression of hatred. Most people have never taken anyone else's life, so they feel that they can say, "I have not broken the Law. I have never killed anybody." This, however, is a very superficial statement relative to the reality of hatred that is manifested in everyday life. Jesus turns the tables upside down (Matt. 21:12-13) as He sets a new or a more real standard.

> You have heard that the ancients were told, "YOU SHALL NOT COMMIT MURDER" and "Whoever commits murder shall be liable to the court." But I say to you that everyone who is angry with his brother shall be guilty before the court; and whoever says to his brother, "You good-for-nothing," shall be guilty before the supreme court; and whoever says, "You fool," shall be guilty *enough* to go into the fiery hell (Matt. 5:21-22).

These are very high standards. A low, superficial standard allows so much wiggle room that a person can easily deceive themselves and others into thinking that they have met the standard when, in fact, they have not met it at all. Expectations are so low that anyone can jump over the bar. It is easy, for example, to love those who love you. But what happens when you are called to love those who give you no reason to love them? Do you have to love those people? If so, how can it be done? You would have to be *perfect*! Since there is only One Who is perfect (Mark 10:18), you can only achieve these standards by reflecting and channeling the Perfect One.

> "You have heard that it was said, 'YOU SHALL LOVE YOUR NEIGHBOR and hate your enemy.' But I say to you, love your enemies and pray for those who persecute you, so that you may be sons of your Father who is in heaven; for He causes His sun to rise on *the* evil and *the* good, and sends rain on *the* righteous and *the* unrighteous. For if you love those who love you, what reward do you have? Do not even the tax collectors do the same? If you greet only your brothers, what more are you doing *than others*? Do not even the

Gentiles do the same? Therefore you are to be perfect, as your heavenly Father is perfect" (Matt. 5:43-48).

As Jesus states in the very beginning of His sermon, "'Blessed are the poor in spirit, for theirs is the kingdom of heaven'" (Matt. 5:3). Those who are poor or empty of themselves are able to live out standards that only God can live out because God achieves the standards through you. That is the only way. It must be "no longer I who live, but Christ lives in me" (Gal. 2:20).

The bar is set as high as it could possibly be set. Who can meet such a standard? Only the Standard Setter is able. And so, to live in the kingdom of God, one must not try to live *like* a king. You must live *with* the King in you—"Christ in you, the hope of glory. We proclaim Him, admonishing every man and teaching every man with all wisdom, so that we may present every man complete in Christ" (Col. 1:27-28).

AUGUST 17

BE A WHOLESALER

"But when you are invited, go and recline at the last place,
*so that when the one who has invited you comes, he may say to you, **Friend, move up higher**;*
then you will have honor in the sight of all who are at the table with you.
For everyone who exalts himself will be humbled, and he who humbles himself will be exalted."

Luke 14:10-11

You walk into a large room, where there is a meeting. There are no ushers. Where should you sit? Jesus says, "'Go and recline at the last place'" (Luke 14:10). Apparently, it is not right to seat yourself up front. "He must increase, but I must decrease" (John 3:30). Do you seat yourself up front? Do you view life through your own lenses focusing on *your* needs and rights? Do you live out a Christian life primarily for what you can and should get from it? Or do you recognize that Jesus is to sit up front and, thus, seat yourself in the back? Do you view life through His lenses, focusing on His desires and glory? Do you live out your Christian life for what He can and should get from you? Who is increasing?

Paul was a wholesaler. He wrote, "I have been crucified with Christ; and it is no longer I who live, but Christ lives in me" (Gal. 2:20). Do you seat yourself as a "retailer" in which Christ is near you but separate from you? In a metaphorical sense, there is then a huge "mark-up," which results in you getting the direct glory while God is only glorified indirectly? Or do you seat yourself as a wholesaler in which Christ is in you? There is no "mark-up," which results in God getting all the glory directly.

Is it "God helps me" or "God is my help"? Is it "God helps me to be righteous" or "God is my righteousness"? Is it "God helps me to live" or "God lives in me"? We seat God last when we think that He should get behind our plans, instead of Him *being* our plans. It is not what you are doing through God but, rather, what God is doing through you. We do not set the agenda; He does. His work is not done according to our desires or goals; it is done according to His!

If you are in need of encouragement and uplifting, then the best thing you can do is sit in the back and lift up God, for "then you will have honor in the sight of all who are at the table with you" (Luke 14:10). It is important to understand the difference between our purpose and the results associated with that purpose. Our purpose is to glorify God (seat Him up front), while the result is that we are blessed (He brings us up front).

The Bible includes many descriptions of this dynamic:

- "In Your presence is fullness of joy" (Psalm 16:11);
- "Delight yourself in the LORD; and He will give you the desires of your heart" (Psalm 37:4);
- "'Give, and it will be given to you'" (Luke 6:38);
- "And I, if I am lifted up from the earth, will draw all men to Myself" (John 12:32);
- "'But seek first His kingdom and His righteousness, and all these things will be added to you'" (Matt. 6:33).

Notice that in each description, God is the focus. God comes first. "For from Him and through Him and to Him are all things. To Him *be* the glory forever. Amen" (Rom. 11:36).

By no means am I saying that we should not receive from God. We *must* receive from God. It is not an "either or" issue (either I get from God, *or* I give to God). It is an issue of understanding the proper order and progression. In order to receive what we need from God, we must first give ourselves to God. We must seat ourselves in the back and allow God to bring us forward. We must humble ourselves and allow God to exalt us.

We must give everything to God, holding nothing back. Yes, we must be wholesalers. Retailers take a cut for themselves. This is not the way we are called to do "business" with God. He must get all the glory! "Whatever you do, do all to the glory of God" (1 Cor. 10:31).

AUGUST 18

AM I MY BROTHER'S KEEPER?

"Then the LORD said to Cain, 'Where is Abel your brother?' And he said, 'I do not know. Am I my brother's keeper?'"

Genesis 4:9

God calls His people to a high standard of social responsibility. The ethics of social concern is in no way a topic foreign to the Scriptures. There is a biblical hierarchy of concern that moves from a responsibility for one's own to a responsibility for all people. Proper conduct toward oneself and toward others is the application of obedience toward God.

Advocacy for social ethics began right away in the human story. With God's very first words to man in Genesis 1:28 to "'be fruitful and multiply, and fill the earth, and subdue it,'" God establishes the mandate of responsibility that is upon mankind. He is to be productive as he uses God's resources responsibly. Then comes His first question to him. After Adam and Eve sin, God asks them, "'Where are you?'" as He rhetorically points to the reality of human self-responsibility (Gen. 3:9). But then, after murdering his brother, Abel, Cain asks, "'Am I my brother's keeper?'" (Gen. 4:9). Cain is arguing that he does not have to be socially responsible, but God's implied answer is the very opposite.

The Scripture clearly and repeatedly argues that responsibility for others is rooted out of responsibility for self. Indeed, the second greatest commandment is, "'YOU SHALL LOVE YOUR NEIGHBOR AS YOURSELF'" (Mark 12:31). This ethical responsibility is nothing less than logical, "for no one ever hated his own flesh, but nourishes and cherishes it" (Eph. 5:29). It is social responsibility inasmuch as taking care of yourself is being considerate of others when you "make it your ambition to lead a quiet life and attend to your own business and work with your hands, just as we commanded you, so that you will behave properly toward outsiders and not be in any need" (1 Thess. 4:11-12). Irresponsible people are not only detrimental to themselves but to society as a whole.

Part of responsibility to one's own is the social responsibility that is inherent to living in a family. To negate familial responsibilities is a serious offense. "But if anyone does not provide for his own, and especially for those of his household, he has denied the faith and is worse than an unbeliever" (1 Tim. 5:8). There is a reason we use the word "dependents" to describe those we are responsible for; they depend on us because they can depend on no one else. "If any woman who is a believer has *dependent* widows, she must assist them and the church must not be burdened, so that it may assist those who are widows indeed" (1 Tim. 5:16).

Another part of responsibility to one's own is the social responsibility that comes with living in the family of God. This is a priority. "So then, while we have opportunity, let us do good to all people, and especially to those who are of the household of the faith" (Gal. 6:10). This spiritual responsibility comes in the form of both spiritual and material resources.

> For this reason I have often been prevented from coming to you; but now, with no further place for me in these regions, and since I have had for many years a longing to come to you whenever I go to Spain—for I hope to see you in passing, and to be helped on my way there by you, when I have first enjoyed your company for a while—but now, I am going to Jerusalem serving the saints. For Macedonia and Achaia have been pleased to make a contribution for the poor among the saints in Jerusalem. Yes, they were pleased *to do so*, and they are indebted to them. For if the Gentiles have shared in their spiritual things, they are indebted to minister to them also in material things (Rom. 15:22-27).

Concern for those in the family of God is not only a logical response to what God did to get each member into the family, but it is an expression of the love that is indicative of that family (John 13:35). "We know love by this, that He laid down His life for us; and we ought to lay down our lives for the brethren. But whoever has the world's goods, and sees his brother in need and closes his heart against him, how does the love of God abide in him?" (1 John 3:16-17). To a certain degree, a person who claims to be in the family of God also agrees to be socially responsible for that family. "What use is it, my brethren, if someone says he has faith, but he has no works? Can that faith save him? If a brother or sister is without clothing and in need of daily food, and one of you says to them, 'Go in peace, be warmed and be filled,' and yet you do not give them what is necessary for their body, what use is that?" (James 2:14-16).

Like Cain, when we leave the garden of sin and make our way through the wilderness of the fallen world, our struggle with selfishness makes us want to ignore and reject our social responsibility toward others. We would rather rhetorically ask, "'Am I my brother's keeper?'" than responsibly declare, "Of course, I will help you; you are family!" We must remember that it is the blood of Christ that has bought social responsibility. Blood brothers forever!

AUGUST 19

TRUTH AND THE MYTH OF NEUTRALITY

"'Everyone who is of the truth hears My voice'... Pilate said to Him, 'What is truth?'"
John 18:37-38

A young college student sat in her political science course trying to make sense out of the senseless things that were being said. The basic objective of that day's class session was to describe, proclaim, and convince students that truth is relative. The professor was following the lead of Pontius Pilate, who sarcastically challenged Jesus when he asked Him, "'What is truth?'" (John 18:36). Pilate and the professor of the political science course both claimed that truth is neutral; it is in no way objective and certainly not absolute. Its nature is that it lacks definition and takes no sides. It is all true, and nothing is false. Live, and let live; I'm okay, and you're okay. To say anything else is immoral because to be moral, you must be amoral.

The college student, who could throw away logic no longer, could not contain herself and blurted out, "If everything is true, can anything be true?"

Finally, a statement that did not outright insult the first three laws of logic was offered to the class. The professor mostly just ignored the student and continued on in her nonsensical assertions by repeating in one way or another, "I agree with everything, and I agree with nothing because what is truth, anyway?"

The question is not what is true? That question is for other kinds of debates. The question here is what is truth? What is the nature of truth? Postmodernism has answered that question for us—albeit erroneously—by asserting that truth is so relative that it somehow has no definition. In fact, it is the lack of definition that makes it truth. Of course, this is a myth—the myth of neutrality. It is a myth because it is not possible. It could be called the myth of "definition-less" definitions. It is a contradiction. Truth, by definition, must have options—this or that—otherwise, it cannot be truth. Neutrality is void of definition; and thus, it cannot be truth. The very nature of truth is such that neutrality is absurd.

Can morality be legislated? No, it cannot in the sense that a law, by itself, cannot change someone's heart. Yes, it can in the sense that the nature of truth requires it to be legislated—morality, necessarily, will be legislated. By definition, "law" must express morality—something is good or bad, right or wrong—lest it not be a law. The question is not can morality be legislated? The question is whose morality will be legislated? The idea that nobody's morality or a "neutral" morality is what will make a law is akin to saying that no definition will make a definition or no law will make a law. This is indicative of the absurd proposal of having a "definition-less" definition, or a "law-less" law. Can you drink "milk-less" milk? Can you breathe "air-less" air? No! That is absurd. Even more absurd is to advocate for "truth-less" truth.

Even if somebody says that the "definition" (or morality) used to draft a law is neutral, that particular definition, in itself, *is* a definition and, thus, not neutral. This is the hypocrisy of the myth of neutrality. Somebody's "neutral" definition is still imposed on others, even if they say it is neutral. Otherwise, it is not a law! A law, in order to be a law, must be enforced; but something that is undefined cannot be enforced and, thus, cannot be a law. Everybody has a position, even if their position is to have no position. Neutrality is a myth, and it reeks of hypocrisy!

Neutral truth is oxymoronic, even as a positionless position or a definitionless definition is oxymoronic. It makes no logical sense because it rejects the basic laws of logic. God is not a myth. God is real ("I AM," Exod. 3:14) and has created everything with real definitions (Gen. 1-2). As the Definer, His reality has established the nature of truth as objective, not neutral. Jesus is "'the way, and the truth, and the life'" (John 14:6), making the ultimate definition very clear and making it very clear that there is a choice—Jesus or something else—and that a choice must be made. Because there is a choice and a free will, there is no neutrality. Neutral truth would necessitate a neutral God, which is impossible because the concept of God is the concept of a final or *highest* authority, which means there are other authorities that exist. Once there is an "est," there is no longer neutrality.

The most significant application for the argument against neutrality is the challenging question of what you are going to do with Jesus (Matt. 27:22). There is no neutral blank in that question—"What are you going to do with _____?" The philosophically wimpy application for those who hold to the myth of neutrality is to always afford yourself with the easy way out. How convenient, for example, to have a neutral position on abortion. Then you do not have to do anything about it, or you can do whatever you want about it. You may be for abortion or against abortion, but one thing you cannot be is neutral. Neutrality is the evil that irresponsibility hides behind. To understand truth as having definition, position, choice, and conviction is tantamount to saying, "I accept responsibility."

And so, Jesus calls us to one definition ("hot") or the other ("cold") but not to no definition (neutrality or "lukewarmness"). Revelation 3:15-16 is a sharp rebuke of our irresponsible, easy-way-out, illogical, hyper-subjective postmodernism and its moronic or oxymoronic myth of neutrality. Jesus says very clearly, "'He who is not with Me is against Me'" (Matt. 12:30). There is no neutrality! He does not say like Buddha, "He who is neutral is neutral." Of course, Buddha's supposed neutrality is still not neutral, since his suggested and defined position regarding truth is to be neutral (which is a defined position).

Here is the problem. If you think that you are, or can be, neutral, then you do not have to answer the Jesus question. However, if truth is not neutral, then, what are you going to do with Jesus? What is truth? Jesus is Truth!

AUGUST 20

THE JOY OF BEING PERSECUTED

"'Blessed are those who have been persecuted for the sake of righteousness, for theirs is the kingdom of heaven.'"

Matthew 5:10

Have you ever heard such a powerful sermon that you could not forget it? Surely, Jesus' disciples never forgot the Sermon on the Mount. Jesus' introduction in that sermon included a series of assertions called Beatitudes, or blessings. The last beatitude is, perhaps, the most memorable:

"Blessed are those who have been persecuted for the sake of righteousness, for theirs is the kingdom of heaven. Blessed are you when *people* insult you and persecute you, and falsely say all kinds of evil against you because of Me. Rejoice and be glad, for your reward in heaven is great; for in the same way they persecuted the prophets who were before you" (Matt. 5:10-12).

To be persecuted for the sake of righteousness is to be insulted and accused falsely. It includes physical and emotional discrimination and slander. It is to share in the sufferings of Christ. Paul refers to "the fellowship of His sufferings, being conformed to His death" (Phil. 3:10). This persecution is inevitable for the godly. "Indeed, all who desire to live godly in Christ Jesus will be persecuted" (2 Tim. 3:12). John explains it this way:

"If you were of the world, the world would love its own; but because you are not of the world, but I chose you out of the world, because of this the world hates you. Remember the word that I said to you, 'A slave is not greater than his master.' If they persecuted Me, they will also persecute you; if they kept My word, they will keep yours also. But all these things they will do to you for My name's sake, because they do not know the One who sent Me" (John 15:19-21).

To be persecuted, insulted, and slandered is to lose your reputation or your "glory" for Christ's sake. You give of yourself and receive the kingdom of heaven and its rewards via putting self-reputation on the cross and, thus, bearing the fruit of joy.

Blessings are free and they are costly because we try to hang onto that which is not our own (1 Cor. 6:19-20). The beatitude (blessing) includes a challenge or an obligation, a cost. It is quite a challenge to endure persecution and lay down your glory. Jesus is our Example. He emptied Himself of His privileges (Phil. 2:7). He laid down His Divine glory and became a Man. Then He took it back again. "'Now, Father, glorify Me together with Yourself, with the glory which I had with You before the world was'" (John 17:5).

You must die to self by giving up or letting go of self-reputation. You must be willing to be put to shame in the eyes of the world for the cause of the Gospel. This can occur in the context of normal, everyday activities. For example, taking a stand for righteousness in your neighborhood or witnessing to co-workers can be a way to risk being put to shame. It is not easy to always be "the weird guy." There is, however, a momentum dynamic in this process. Once you begin the practice of dying to your reputation, it gets easier and easier because you have less and less to defend.

The provision or blessing for those who are persecuted for the sake of righteousness is to be in the kingdom of God; it is to receive the rewards of the kingdom and to obtain the glory or reputation of Jesus. "It was for this He called you through our gospel, that you may gain the glory of our Lord Jesus Christ" (2 Thess. 2:14). The fruit of the Spirit that corresponds to this beatitude is joy (Gal. 5:22). If we are willing to swallow our pride and maybe even feel a little bit awkward when we stand up for Jesus in public, then He is willing to stand up for us in front of the Father. What could be more joyous than that? Anything less is the essence of sadness. "'Therefore everyone who confesses Me before men, I will also confess him before My Father who is in heaven. But whoever denies Me before men, I will also deny him before My Father who is in heaven'" (Matt. 10:32-33).

The nature of the kingdom of God—relative to the kingdoms of this world—is backward. Each beatitude in the Sermon on the Mount, therefore, is cloaked in irony. "'Blessed are those who have been persecuted for the sake of righteousness, for theirs is the kingdom of heaven. Blessed are you when *people* insult you and persecute you, and falsely say all kinds of evil against you because of Me. Rejoice and be glad, for your reward in heaven is great'" (Matt. 5:10-12). In other words, we must give away our glory and reputation with men; then we will obtain glory and reputation with God.

AUGUST 21

HELPING THOSE WHO ARE GRIEVING

"'You will grieve, but your grief will be turned into joy.'"

John 16:20

Sometime or another in this life, most of us will have to endure a grievous situation. When that time comes, it is very important that someone is by your side to help you through the mourning and grieving process. Mourning is the natural way of healing in situations in which there is an extreme sense of loss. It is a process that the one who has experienced the loss must go through. It is healthy when the grieving person is able to express deep feelings. A counselor can help the person go through this process.

A skilled counselor understands that there are phases of mourning that will normally be experienced. In the first phase, the conflict event (the loss), people typically express denial and manifest lethargy as if to say, "I don't know what's going on." In the second phase, there tends to be a longing for that which was lost. There may be an expression of anger and feelings of pain or guilt. The one who has suffered the loss might say, "Why did God let this happen?"

In the next phase, the person may exhibit a lack of organization and extreme despair. Typically, during this third phase there is a sense of struggle, strife, and uncertainty; and the person might say, "I cannot go on." Finally, in the last phase, those who are grieving begin to look to reorganize their lives and try to determine how they might replace that which has been lost with something else. At this point, the healing process begins as attention and love are directed toward others.

This process does not happen overnight. A counselor should realize that the mourning process can last for several years. Generations ago, the anticipation of a lengthy time period for mourning was built into the culture. Widows, for example, would wear black for one year. Especially in the initial phase, the counselor should listen, even when the person is repeating the story over and over. The best way to counsel someone in this phase of mourning is to say nothing and to just listen. Again, it is a long process so try to be patient.

Do not become too worried if the person seems to be unable to control himself immediately after the death or the loss. Comfort and protect him or her. Be careful to allow the person to express anger and guilt, even if you feel it is not an appropriate response. It is part of the process. The person must express these emotions as a means to release the power that they hold and to ease the stress that has built up. And so, for example, do not say, "Don't cry." Instead, give the person permission to cry and even cry with them.

A counselor can use the situation to discuss spiritual things. Many people are much more open to talk about God when there has been irreversible loss such as death, the loss of employment, or a severe life-altering sickness or injury. Counselors should strongly discourage the making of big decisions and the implementing of major life changes, especially during the first year of mourning.

Children must also go through the process of mourning. Allow and assist children to go through the grieving process. It is very dangerous to allow a child to deny a death or to create a fantasy that replaces the reality.

In general, in the beginning, more than anything else, the counselor can help simply by being present and by being a good listener. In the end, after considerable time has passed, the counselor can help by providing spiritual understanding with respect to the loss. The counselor can also use the situation to challenge the person to grow spiritually. Of course, when all is said and done, "'you will grieve, but your grief will be turned into joy'" (John 16:20). There is hope in Christ!

CHARACTER TRAITS OF NEHEMIAH THE LEADER

"So I prayed to the God of heaven."

Nehemiah 2:4

Nehemiah was a great leader. He led a multitude of people in the massive project to rebuild the walls of Jerusalem in fifty-two days (Neh. 6:15). This kind of endeavor requires skillful leadership; the leader must embody certain character traits.

First, and foremost, Nehemiah was a man of faith. He led his people to God using his faith to build up their faith. "When I saw *their fear*, I rose and spoke to the nobles, the officials and the rest of the people: 'Do not be afraid of them; remember the Lord who is great and awesome, and fight for your brothers, your sons, your daughters, your wives and your houses . . . Our God will fight for us'" (Neh. 4:14, 20).

Godly leaders do not rely on themselves. Nehemiah was a man of prayer. His default response to a difficult situation was to seek God in prayer. "When I heard these words, I sat down and wept and mourned for days; and I was fasting and praying before the God of heaven" (Neh. 1:4).

When he needed direction, he did not initially consult with himself but immediately looked to God. "Then the king said to me, 'What would you request?' So I prayed to the God of heaven" (Neh. 2:4). Nehemiah did not simply say a prayer; he had a lifestyle of prayer. He would cry out, "Hear, O our God" (Neh. 4:4) and then proclaim, "But we prayed to our God" (Neh. 4:9). Then he would request, "Remember me, O my God" (Neh. 5:19) and entreat, "But now, *O God*, strengthen my hands" (Neh. 6:9). Finally, he would ask, "Remember, O my God" (Neh. 6:14). Nehemiah relied on God.

A very important attribute for a leader to possess is the ability to be sensitive to other people's needs. Godly leaders must exhibit compassion. Sometimes, the way this is applied is in having the wisdom to not "speak out of turn." Divulging information ahead of time may confuse, scare, or upset others. The wise leader is sensitive enough to know when to speak. Nehemiah exhibited such wisdom. "And I arose in the night, I and a few men with me. I did not tell anyone what my God was putting into my mind to do for Jerusalem" (Neh. 2:12).

Leaders need to be informed. They need knowledge. "The fear of the LORD is the beginning of knowledge" (Prov. 1:7). Nehemiah challenged his people to walk in the fear of the Lord: "Again I said, 'The thing which you are doing is not good; should you not walk in the fear of our God'" (Neh. 5:9). Leaders are able to obey God and not go astray when they consider Who God is and what He is able to do. Nehemiah proclaimed, "But I did not do so because of the fear of God" (Neh. 5:15).

Godly leaders are those who steadfastly depend on God. They need to trust God for a variety of things, not the least of which are monetary resources and building materials. Nehemiah knew Jehovah Jireh, God the Provider. He depended on Him for what was needed to complete the mission that he was leading. He sent "a letter to Asaph the keeper of the king's forest, that he may give me timber to make beams for the gates of the fortress which is by the temple, for the wall of the city and for the house to which I will go. And the king granted them to me because the good hand of my God was on me" (Neh. 2:8). Nehemiah's dependence on God fueled his leadership and motivated those he was leading: "I told them how the hand of my God had been favorable to me and also about the king's words which he had spoken to me. Then they said, 'Let us arise and build.' So they put their hands to the good *work*" (Neh. 2:18).

What does a godly leader look like? He or she resembles someone who has a strong faith in God, is a person of prayer, is sensitive toward others, walks in the fear of God, and lives life in dependence upon God. Those who are in the "School of Leadership" have an assignment: have faith, pray, be sensitive, walk in the fear of God, and live in dependence upon Him. Lead on!

AUGUST 23

YOU CAN'T FAKE HIM OUT

"'A good tree cannot produce bad fruit, nor can a bad tree produce good fruit. Every tree that does not bear good fruit is cut down and thrown into the fire. So then, you will know them by their fruits.'"

Matthew 7:18-20

The Sermon on the Mount is the greatest sermon ever preached. Jesus challenges His listeners to live in the "flip-flopped kingdom." To say that Jesus turned the tables upside down is an understatement. The upside-down dynamic is seen in the fact that what is real is opposite of that which is false. The emphasis throughout Jesus' sermon is on the contrast between that which is real, authentic, and profound (from the heart), and that which is fake, hypocritical, and superficial (merely a show).

Enter through the narrow gate; for the gate is wide and the way is broad that leads to destruction, and there are many who enter through it. For the gate is small and the way is narrow that leads to life, and there are few who find it. Beware of the false prophets, who come to you in sheep's clothing, but inwardly are ravenous wolves. You will know them by their fruits. Grapes are not gathered from thorn *bushes* nor figs from thistles, are they? So every good tree bears good fruit, but the bad tree bears bad fruit. A good tree cannot produce bad fruit, nor can a bad tree produce good fruit. Every tree that does not bear good fruit is cut down and thrown into the fire. So then, you will know them by their fruits. Not everyone who says to Me, "Lord, Lord," will enter the kingdom of heaven, but he who does the will of My Father who is in heaven *will enter.* Many will say to Me on that day, "Lord, Lord, did we not prophesy in Your name, and in Your name cast out demons, and in Your name perform many miracles?" And then I will declare to them, "I never knew you; DEPART FROM ME, YOU WHO PRACTICE LAWLESSNESS." Therefore everyone who hears these words of Mine and acts on them, may be compared to a wise man who built his house on the rock. And the rain fell, and the floods came, and the winds blew and slammed against that house; and *yet* it did not fall, for it had been founded on the rock. Everyone who hears these words of Mine and does not act on them, will be like a foolish man who built his house on the sand. The rain fell, and the floods came, and the winds blew and slammed against that house; and it fell—and great was its fall (Matt. 7:13-27).

Jesus ends His sermon alluding to a variety of contrasts. Each one paints a different picture of that which is real versus that which is fake or that which is sincere versus that which is hypocritical. First, He references two different gates. Next, Jesus contrasts those who are truly of God and those who are not. There are the false prophets and the true prophets, the good fruit and the bad fruit, and those who never really knew God (although it *appeared* as though they did) and those who do really know God. Finally, we see a contrast between two types of houses. One is built on the things that remain, while the other is built on the things that will disappear.

God cannot be fooled or deceived (Gal. 6:7). Although it may seem that reality can be hidden temporarily, it will eventually reveal that which is false. God is reality. His kingdom is the real kingdom. There is nothing fake about it, and there can be nothing fake about those who live in it. Reality always wins the day!

The response of Jesus' listeners to this kingdom teaching is interesting. "When Jesus had finished these words, the crowds were amazed at His teaching; for He was teaching them as *one* having authority, and not as their scribes" (Matt. 7:28-29). They perceived two very different styles of teaching. There was Jesus' teaching, and there was the scribes' teaching. The hypocrisy of the scribes did not allow them to speak with authority. Authority is the result of a genuine living out of that which you are speaking. Jesus spoke with authority because His kingdom was real. He spoke with authority because His life was real. He spoke as God because He was really God.

Perhaps the greatest challenge in the Sermon on the Mount is that if we want to speak with the authority of those who live in the kingdom of God, then we must actually live in that kingdom. There is no other way. You cannot fake Him out!

AUGUST 24

THE SUBORDINATION OF MONEY

"'And I say to you, make friends for yourselves by means of the wealth of unrighteousness, so that when it fails, they will receive you into the eternal dwellings.'"

Luke 16:9

Jesus tells a story about an unrighteous manager who gets praised by his master, seemingly, for being irresponsible, deceptive, and dishonest. If this steward is so unrighteous with regard to the way in which he represents his master, then why does the master congratulate him and approve of his actions? Jesus tells the parable to his disciples:

> There was a rich man who had a manager, and this *manager* was reported to him as squandering his possessions. And he called him and said to him, "What is this I hear about you? Give an accounting of your management, for you can no longer be manager." The manager said to himself, "What shall I do, since my master is taking the management away from me? I am not strong enough to dig; I am ashamed to beg. I know what I shall do, so that when I am removed from the management people will welcome me into their homes." And he summoned each one of his master's debtors, and he *began* saying to the first, "How much do you owe my master?" And he said, "A hundred measures of oil." And he said to him, "Take your bill, and sit down quickly and write fifty." Then he said to another, "And how much do you owe?" And he said, "A hundred measures of wheat." He said to him, "Take your bill, and write eighty." And his master praised the unrighteous manager because he had acted shrewdly; for the sons of this age are more shrewd in relation to their own kind than the sons of light. And I say to you, make friends for yourselves by means of the wealth of unrighteousness, so that when it fails, they will receive you into the eternal dwellings (Luke 16:1-9).

The manager basically cheats his employer, and the boss gives him an exceptional end of the year performance review! Is the five-star review based on his lack of integrity? No, it is based on something else. The parable is not about the weak character of the steward. It is about the steward's perspective of money—or anything else, for that matter—as it relates to salvation and drawing close to God. To have a proper perspective on the value of money and your desire for it, it must be seen as subordinate to the value of salvation and your desire for God.

This parable is put forth by Jesus within the context of soteriological teachings. A series of parables that repeatedly declare the value of salvation and knowing God precedes the parable of the unrighteous steward. This series of salvation parables begins with the dinner parable that serves to point to the value of God's invitation to know Him (Luke 14:16-24). The "count the cost" parable then depicts the preeminence of salvation (Luke 14:25-35). Next, the parable of the lost sheep declares the supremacy of salvation from God's perspective (Luke 15:1-7). The parable of the lost coin (Luke 15:8-10) reiterates the primacy of right relationship with God. The parable of the prodigal son emphasizes how our returning to God is viewed by Him as more important than anything else (Luke 15:11-32).

Immediately after offering this long string of parables—all of which focus on the same theme—Jesus then puts forth another parable to strengthen the point being made. No matter what scenario we are talking about, there is nothing that sits higher in importance and value than salvation and knowing God.

The unrighteous steward's interest in God did not depend on his interest in money. His interest in money depended on his interest in God. "'No servant can serve two masters; for either he will hate the one and love the other, or else he will be devoted to one and despise the other. You cannot serve God and wealth'" (Luke 16:13). He had a perspective of money that defined its value with respect to whether or not it could get him closer to God. "'And I say to you, make friends for yourselves by means of the wealth of unrighteousness, so that when it fails, they will receive you into the eternal dwellings'" (Luke 16:9).

The unrighteous steward must understand the importance and value of "eternal dwellings" if he is to come to God. His perspective of money does not save him. He is unrighteous. His perspective of money is required for him to not get entangled in its vying for first place in his life. It must not be an end. It must only be a means to an end. Like the woman and the lost coin, salvation and knowing God is such a priority that all else seems inconsequential. My focus and desire is not on money because my desire is for God. To the degree that money can move me toward that end, then and only then does it have worth. I serve God. I do not serve man.

AUGUST 25

TO IMITATE GOD IS TO DIE TO SELF

"Therefore be imitators of God, as beloved children; and walk in love, just as Christ also loved you and gave Himself up for us, an offering and a sacrifice to God as a fragrant aroma."

Ephesians 5:1

Rich Little used to do a great Johnny Carson imitation. You could close your eyes and listen, and you would think you were watching Carson doing his monologue on *The Tonight Show*. Rich Little was spot-on. The timber of the voice, the inflection, the timing, and the facial expressions were more like Carson's than Carson! Rich Little was the premier impersonator of his generation. He could, seemingly, imitate anyone.

To imitate Johnny Carson is one thing, but to imitate God is a whole other matter. It does not seem like a thing that should be said. Imitate *God*? The Bible does not simply suggest that this can be done; it commands that it must be done. "Therefore be imitators of God" (Eph. 5:1). How is this done? What is the nature of the content of this imitation? Who is the active force behind the imitation?

The idea of imitation is presented in the Law. "You shall be holy, for I the LORD your God am holy" (Lev. 19:2). It is important to note that the Scripture does not say "You shall be holy because of your ability to imitate Me who is holy." Rather, it introduces the explanation or justification of imitation with the connector word ""or," as it points directly to God Himself as the Source of "you shall be holy." The very reason why they can be holy is that God is holy and because they are a chosen people and a people set apart for His holiness (Lev. 18:29-30). Thus, imitation is rooted in the very existence and abilities of God, not in the existence and abilities of man. It is God's holiness that "en-holies" them; God imitates Himself through them.

Various translations use "followers" instead of "imitators" in Ephesians 5:1. This is consistent with the God-sourced idea of imitation; in following Him by faith, He lives through us (Gal. 2:20). Paul uses terminology in 1 Thessalonians 1:6 that is also reflective of this dynamic: "You also became imitators of us and of the Lord." The verb "became" (*genathata*) is in the passive voice and can be translated "were made," establishing God as the logical subject. In this way, "became imitators" is not simply a matter of chance or solely a matter of active seeking but is directly under God's causing and controlling.

In other words, the imitation of God has less to do with our ability to mimic Him and more to do with His ability to live in us. The focus in the imitation-example relationship is on Christ as the One Who gives and not on man as the one who attains. Man, by his own right, power, or works cannot be as God. The imitation of God is a by-product of surrender and fellowship, as opposed to the more active process that would include those acts, which produce a likeness. Christ is the active Force Who enables us to imitate His ethical example; He lives His ethics through us.

What, then, is man's part in all of this? The key word is "surrender." The best description of the work associated with the imitation of Christ is nothing less than the best description of the work of Christ Himself, the work of the cross, or the work of selflessness. It is to this end that Christ calls us most fundamentally, "'If anyone wishes to come after Me, he must deny himself, and take up his cross and follow Me'" (Matt. 16:24). For this reason, when asked what to do so as to do the "works of God," Jesus answers, "'This is the work of God, that you believe in Him whom He has sent'" (John 6:28-29). To imitate Christ is to imitate the way of the cross because only through getting rid of self will you have room for Him (Matt. 5:1). In every reference to the imitation of Christ in the New Testament, the immediate context places the emphasis on dying to self (Eph. 5:1-2, 2 Thess. 3:7-9). Only then can we imitate God because that imitation is "Christ in you, the hope of glory" (Col. 1:27), not you acting like the hope of your *own* glory.

The John 6:29 good work of believing in Jesus is the only good work necessary (Luke 10:38-42) to do all good works because it is the good work that will "'MAKE READY THE WAY OF THE LORD, MAKE HIS PATHS STRAIGHT!'" (Matt. 3:3) to do *His* good works by being His workmanship (Eph. 2:10). To let your light shine so as to do good works (Matt. 5:16) is nothing less than to let the "'Light of the world'" (John 8:12) do His works through you. Ultimately, this leads to an alternative understanding of ethics or good works. The Christian ethic is a cross ethic or an ethic of selflessness because the Christian's ethic is not his own ethic but the ethic of God. To God be the glory for "whatever you do, do all to the glory of God" (1 Cor. 10:31).

Rich Little may be able to imitate a great Johnny Carson. His imitation of Carson and others is spot-on because of his own skills in mimicking them. This is not the idea in the imitation of God. That "imitation" is purer than simply performing polished mimicking skills. The only one who can imitate God is God Himself. When we let Him in, God imitates a great God through us! And so, to imitate God is to die to self.

AUGUST 26

IMAGES OF THE CHURCH

"'I will build my church, and the gates of Hades will not overcome it.'"

Matthew 16:18

Police at an accident scene try to interview as many witnesses as possible in an attempt to ascertain what happened when the cars ran into each other. Witnesses of the accident may have had a slightly different perspective based on where they were, what hampered their vision, and how much of the event they saw. These different perspectives do not, in any way, change what actually happened. What happened is what happened, regardless of different perspectives. A particular perspective serves to see a piece of what happened. Similarly, people can see the church from different perspectives. These images can be derived from particular theological emphases and lead to certain ministerial applications. They can also, if exaggerated, result in distorted views of the Church.

The church might be seen as an "army." This image is rooted in the theology of warfare. The church is called to fight the good fight (1 Tim. 6:12).

> "Finally, be strong in the Lord and in the strength of His might. Put on the full armor of God, so that you will be able to stand against the schemes of the devil. For our struggle is not against flesh and blood, but against the rulers, against the powers, against the world forces of this darkness, against the spiritual *forces* of wickedness in the heavenly *places* (Eph. 6:10-12).

Ministerial applications for this image of the church include an emphasis on strong leadership, a focus on the implementation of authority, and the training of its soldiers. Distortions of this image include legalistic attitudes and a lack of compassion or gentleness.

The Church may also be seen as a "mystical communion." This image may be rooted in a theology of unity, freedom, and the supernatural. When applied to the life of the church, there is an emphasis on sharing, love, relationships, fellowship, and the use of the gifts of the Holy Spirit. "What is *the outcome* then, brethren? When you assemble, each one has a psalm, has a teaching, has a revelation, has a tongue, has an interpretation. Let all things be done for edification" (1 Cor. 14:26). When exaggerated, this image can result in an inward church carried away in emotionalism.

Another way in which people see the Church is as the "mouthpiece of God." The Church is seen as the proclaimer of God's Word that evangelizes and teaches people. "Go therefore and make disciples of all the nations, baptizing them in the name of the Father and the Son and the Holy Spirit, teaching them to observe all that I have commanded you; and lo, I am with you always, even to the end of the age" (Matt. 28:19-20). Revival services, the use of media, the teaching of Bible courses, and a robust missionary program may be utilized. A vulnerability of this sort of image of the Church is a superficial response to the tangible needs of people.

The Church can be seen as a "healing community." Practical ministry, coupled with the power of God, is the theology behind this image. The ministries of counseling, deliverance, and healing are emphasized. "Jesus summoned His twelve disciples and gave them authority over unclean spirits, to cast them out, and to heal every kind of disease and every kind of sickness" (Matt. 10:1). These emphases, if not kept in check, can result in a neglect of the ministry of the Word and an ingrown Church.

These different perspectives of the Church do not, in any way, change the actuality of what the Church is and does. A particular image of the Church promotes an understanding of a piece of its nature and activities. The Church is an army, a mystical union, a mouthpiece of God, and a healing community. It is also much more. One biblical image of the Church helps us see it rightly, as long as we understand there are many other biblical images of the Church. Jesus assembles these images. He says, "I will build My church" (Matt. 16:18).

AUGUST 27

THE PHYSICAL DYNAMICS OF FASTING

"And after He had fasted forty days and forty nights, He then became hungry."
Matthew 4:2

Fasting is a commended biblical discipline that, like all biblical disciplines, serves as a means of grace, a form through which Divine substance might flow. To fast is to express one's desperate need for God (means) and to more readily realize and experience God's faithful provision of Himself (grace). Fasting, more than any other spiritual discipline, is a physical activity. It directly and emphatically engages the body via its disengagement; it deprives the body of its physical fuel. Of course, this depletion of food impacts the body physically.

It is most important to understand fasting as a spiritual practice, to appreciate its spiritual purposes and benefits. However, it can be useful to recognize the physical dynamics of fasting as well. In a somewhat counterintuitive way, fasting can improve physical health. The most concise way to explain why fasting may be beneficial to one's health is to describe the process of detoxification. Fasting gives the digestive system a break and allows time for the body to renew itself as it burns away its "rubbish." During a prolonged fast, the body lives on surplus fat while it burns up its waste and decaying tissues. Only when this refining process is complete does it begin to consume its healthy cells. That is when physical—not just psychological—starvation begins (typically between twenty-one and forty days). When Scripture says of Jesus that "after He had fasted forty days and forty nights, He then became hungry" (Matt. 4:2), it is not using understated or sarcastic humor. Jesus began to feel the pain of physical hunger, the body eating itself.

Fasting includes various physical stages. During the first one or two days, a craving for food is present (psychological not physiological). During the next two or three days, the craving for food subsides; but there can be a feeling of weakness or faintness. The end of this second stage comes as poisons and toxins are eliminated from the body. During the next stage, there is a growing sense of physical strength with less concern for food. Termination of this phase comes when a painful sense of hunger (physical starvation) begins (generally, between twenty-one and forty days).

There are two practical points of information that are linked to what could be called the "three-day rule." First, never engage in an absolute fast (no food or drink) for more than three days. The body cannot function without water for more than three days. Second, normal fasts of more than three days should be broken slowly. This is the most difficult time in fasting—and also the most critical. In a longer fast the stomach shrinks and the digestive organs that normally assimilate food do not operate at full force. They must be given sufficient time to become efficient again. A full meal should not be eaten immediately but should be worked up to over a period of time. The longer the fast, the more critical is this process. Initially, after a four- or five-day fast, a light meal should be taken mainly consisting of fruits and vegetables. With fasts that last longer than five days, the first several meals taken should consist of juices and soups. With a fast that lasts longer than twenty-one days, it may be necessary to take up to a week before full, regular meals can be taken.

Fasting is not for everyone. It should not be done by diabetics, pregnant women, heart patients, extremely thin people, or young children. Others who want to begin a discipline of fasting should work their way into it. The first time someone fasts should not be for a prolonged period of time. Start with one meal. Then, try a one-day fast. Eventually, a prolonged fast can be attempted.

Some say fasting should consist of only water being consumed. Others advocate drinking juices when fasting. Do not allow yourself to be bound by such arguments of methodology. Remember, the issue in biblical fasting is not methodology. It is motive. The supreme motive in fasting is to glorify God. This is the picture we see when Jesus fasted for forty days in the wilderness temptation event (Luke 4:1-17). He glorified God while Satan attacked Him.

Satan may try to come against you as well while you are fasting. It can become a spiritual war. He may attack by using discouragement. Praise can become your most important weapon during a fast. Lift God up! Glorify Him, and your fast will serve as a means of His grace.

AUGUST 28

VESSEL THEOLOGY

"Or does not the potter have a right over the clay, to make from the same lump one vessel for honorable use and another for common use."

Romans 9:21

"Then I went down to the potter's house, and there he was, making something on the wheel. But the vessel that he was making of clay was spoiled in the hand of the potter; so he remade it into another vessel, as it pleased the potter to make" (Jer. 18:3-4). Vessels have certain characteristics, the most foundational of which is that they are created for a purpose. The potter makes the vessel for his own use that is consistent with his plan and what pleases him. God has a master plan. He is pleased to make vessels for His purposes. His purpose is that He would be revealed to all people who would then come to know Him and be saved from only knowing themselves. God reveals Himself to others by first revealing Himself to His chosen vessels. He blesses (chooses) someone so that someone else can be blessed (chosen). This is the plan that is laid out for Abraham in Genesis 12:1-3. God will bless Abraham so that in Abraham, "'all the families of the earth will be blessed.'"

This is what might be called "vessel theology." God has chosen to work *through* a chosen people in order to reach the entire world. The foundational idea of vessel theology is that preaching needs a preacher. "How will they hear without a preacher?" (Rom. 10:14). The active dynamic of this theology is that God lives and works inside and through His vessel. In this sense, vessel theology's defining biblical statement is, "I have been crucified with Christ; and it is no longer I who live, but Christ lives in me" (Gal. 2:20). The vessel can only be a productive vessel because the Vessel-maker stands with it and works through it. This type of biblical principle—"we love, because He first loved us" (1 John 4:19), and we are holy because He is holy (Lev. 19:2)—highlights the sovereignty of the Vessel-maker. God's chosen people are His witnesses who are called to proclaim His truth to the nations (Isa. 43:9-10). They are His vessels *through* whom He makes Himself known.

Sometimes, perhaps because of our use of the phrase "*Great* Commission," we may think that God's missionary plan did not begin until just before Jesus ascended into Heaven (Matt. 28:18-20). Of course, this is not true. God's missionary plan began as soon as that missionary plan was needed, immediately after the fall of man. It began with the declaration that was made in Genesis 3:14-15 that God would redeem mankind via His own death on a cross.

In the first eleven chapters of Genesis, we see the fall of man, the Flood, and the increase of evil that comes to a head at the Tower of Babel. Prior to this time, people lived relatively close to each other. There were no separate nations or even different languages. Thus, the missiological declaration of Genesis 3:14-15 would have been common knowledge. That language dynamic ended, however, at the Tower of Babel when the nations were formed. That's why it is called "Babel." "Come, let Us go down and there confuse their language, so that they will not understand one another's speech. So the LORD scattered them abroad from there over the face of the whole earth, and they stopped building the city" (Gen. 11:7-8). Since there is a scattering of nations, there then had to be a "going" to the nations with the message of God's provision for salvation. Hence, the Abrahamic covenant (Gen. 12:1-3). What happened? Did God become frustrated and abandon His universal plan of redemption referred to in Genesis 3:14-15? Did He become angry with the world and choose a favorite to appease Himself? No! He simply began to use his plan that is based on *vessel theology*. He chose a missionary nation and enacted a missionary covenant. Abraham would be blessed so that all the nations could be blessed.

Vessels are created for a purpose. A potter shapes the pot on the potter's wheel in such a way that satisfies His purposes. God is the Master Potter, and we are His obedient vessels. God's missionary plan is to use us to make Himself known to the world. Let this be our prayer: "God thank you for making me your vessel. Please make me 'a vessel for honor, sanctified, useful to the Master, prepared for every good work'" (2 Tim. 2:21).

AUGUST 29

STEWARDS ARE NOT OWNERS

"Yours, O LORD, is the greatness and the power and the glory and the victory and the majesty, indeed everything that is in the heavens and the earth; Yours is the dominion, O Lord, and You exalt Yourself as head over all."

1 Chronicles 29:11

Money and possessions are a big part of our lives. What is the purpose of money and possessions? It is no different than anything else. Their purpose is to glorify God. The right purpose of money is that it be used in a way that glorifies and points to God. God is reality. Therefore, the value of anything is measured relative to Him. Money and possessions must point to that reality if they are to have any value at all. "For from Him and through Him and to Him are all things. To Him *be* the glory forever. Amen" (Rom. 11:36).

The value of anything is measured in terms of whether or not it brings us closer to God. We must understand the difference between ownership and stewardship. We are not owners. There is only one Owner, and that is God. We are stewards. This understanding helps us to properly answer the question, "What is the purpose of money and possessions?" The Christian does not receive from God in order to *have* for God (an ownership type of mentality). The Christian receives from God in order to *give* for God (more of a stewardship-type of mentality).

We can understand the concept of stewardship through a study of the parable of the talents:

> For *it is* just like a man *about* to go on a journey, who called his own slaves and entrusted his possessions to them. To one he gave five talents, to another, two, and to another, one, each according to his own ability; and he went on his journey. Immediately the one who had received the five talents went and traded with them, and gained five more talents. In the same manner the one who *had received* the two *talents* gained two more. But he who received the one talent went away, and dug *a hole* in the ground and hid his master's money. Now after a long time the master of those slaves came and settled accounts with them. The one who had received the five talents came up and brought five more talents, saying, "Master, you entrusted five talents to me. See, I have gained five more talents." His master said to him, "Well done, good and faithful slave. You were faithful with a few things, I will put you in charge of many things; enter into the joy of your master." Also the one who *had received* the two talents came up and said, "Master, you entrusted two talents to me. See, I have gained two more talents." His master said to him, "Well done, good and faithful slave. You were faithful with a few things, I will put you in charge of many things; enter into the joy of your master." And the one also who had received the one talent came up and said, "Master, I knew you to be a hard man, reaping where you did not sow and gathering where you scattered no seed. And I was afraid, and went away and hid your talent in the ground. See, you have what is yours." But his master answered and said to him, "You wicked, lazy slave, you knew that I reap where I did not sow and gather where I scattered no *seed*. Then you ought to have put my money in the bank, and on my arrival I would have received my *money* back with interest. Therefore take away the talent from him, and give it to the one who has the ten talents." For to everyone who has, *more* shall be given, and he will have an abundance; but from the one who does not have, even what he does have shall be taken away. Throw out the worthless slave into the outer darkness; in that place there will be weeping and gnashing of teeth (Matt. 25:14-30).

A steward is not an owner. The master is the owner. "The earth is the LORD'S, and all it contains" (Psalm 24:1). A steward is entrusted with things. A steward owes everything. He must give everything to God. His motives to do this must come from his love for God and his gratitude for His provision. Jesus says, "'Give, and it will be given to you'" (Luke 6:38). This is not optional, nor is it a one-time act. It is a command that calls for an ongoing lifestyle. A steward invests for multiplication. He does not simply conserve what has been given to him. He uses it and multiplies it. He is more of a giver than a keeper.

What is the purpose of money and possessions? Its purpose is to glorify God. Right actions come from right attitudes. The attitude of a steward lends itself not to burying and storing but to using and multiplying. Money and possessions are not so much for self-comfort as they are for God-mission. What are you doing with your money and possessions?

AUGUST 30

FAITH IS A PRESENT FUTURE

*"Now faith is the assurance of **things** hoped for, the conviction of things not seen."*
Hebrews 11:1

Leaders must be people of faith. They must believe in something lest they lead their people nowhere. Jesus alludes to these "leaders" when He says, "'They are blind guides of the blind. And if a blind man guides a blind man, both will fall into a pit'" (Matt. 15:14). Leaders with no faith are hypocrites. They claim to be leading people somewhere, but they are going nowhere themselves. "'But woe to you, scribes and Pharisees, hypocrites, because you shut off the kingdom of heaven from people; for you do not enter in yourselves, nor do you allow those who are entering to go in'" (Matt. 23:13-14).

Nehemiah was a godly leader, a man of great faith. He was a positive thinker. "I said, 'I beseech You, O LORD God of heaven, the great and awesome God, who preserves the covenant and lovingkindness for those who love Him and keep His commandments" (Neh. 1:5). His positive thinking sort of faith was based on three things.

First, it was based on his firm belief that his God was able to meet his need—faith starts with Who God is—and so his prayer began with a focus on God's ability—"the great and awesome God." Second, Nehemiah's positive thinking was based on his firm belief that his God was faithful and willing to answer his prayer. Faith continues with the belief that God is for you, not against you. And so Nehemiah believes that God is a God of justice and love "who preserves the covenant and lovingkindness." Third, Nehemiah's positive thinking was based on his confidence that he was in the right position. Faith includes an understanding of who you are. Nehemiah's prayer ended with a description of those who God was willing to help. They were the ones who had a relationship with God and walked with Him in obedience—"those who love Him and keep his commandments."

Nehemiah's "positive thinking" is different than the "pop culture" type of positive thinking that too often seeps into the Church. Biblical positive thinking focuses on the promises of God and what God has already said. Pop culture positive thinking focuses on the desires of man and what man says. Biblical positive thinking retains a balanced view of God's sovereignty and man's free will and sees itself as a result, not a cause. Pop culture positive thinking exhibits a faulty view of God's sovereignty and man's free will and sees itself as the cause, not the result. This places positive thinking in the category of creator—use your faith to create your own world—and borders on being idolatrous.

Faith can wait on God. A twisted understanding of faith stresses the idea of immediate gratification. It encourages people to "name it and claim it." A biblical understanding of faith is more consistent with the encouragement to "believe it and receive it." In these two very different perspectives of faith there is the difference between arrogance and humility. To say that my faith causes reality instead of saying that it is the result of it, is tantamount to saying, "I can create reality." It is not surprising that in our postmodern culture, this has become equivalent to "faith."

Biblical teaching on faith often stresses the process of faith and the waiting—maybe even the suffering—that is involved.

> And what more shall I say? For time will fail me if I tell of Gideon, Barak, Samson, Jephthah, of David and Samuel and the prophets, who by faith conquered kingdoms, performed *acts of* righteousness, obtained promises, shut the mouths of lions, quenched the power of fire,

escaped the edge of the sword, from weakness were made strong, became mighty in war, put foreign armies to flight. Women received *back* their dead by resurrection; and others were tortured, not accepting their release, so that they might obtain a better resurrection; and others experienced mockings and scourgings, yes, also chains and imprisonment. They were stoned, they were sawn in two, they were tempted, they were put to death with the sword; they went about in sheepskins, in goatskins, being destitute, afflicted, ill-treated (*men* of whom the world was not worthy), wandering in deserts and mountains and caves and holes in the ground (Heb. 11:32-38).

While waiting, faith can see ahead without having to deny the reality of the present since "faith is the assurance of *things* hoped for, the conviction of things not seen" (Heb. 11:1). It is a present future, a present confidence of a future reality.

To have faith that God *will* heal your broken arm does not require you to deny that your arm *is* broken. That is not faith; that is absurd. On your perceived road to create your own reality, you keep shouting, "My arm is not broken; my arm is not broken; my arm is not broken!" Meanwhile, someone grabs you to shake the hand of your self-proclaimed "unbroken" arm; and you now keep shouting, "Ouch, ouch, ouch!" Absurdity is not faith, and faith is not absurd!

AUGUST 31

DO YOU WISH TO GET WELL?

"He raises the poor from the dust, He lifts the needy from the ash heap."

1 Samuel 2:8

Jesus calls His followers to minister to the poor. How do you do that? A general model of ministry to the poor includes three stages: the identification stage, the encouragement and challenge stage, and the service stage.

The identification stage may be the most important. The poor person may be apathetic. He or she might not trust you. He may be skeptical of your motives to help him. Before you can be effective in your ministry to the poor, you must build a good relationship and a strong sense of trust. Compassion and empathy go a long way to that end. The minister must show in some way that he can identify with the poor person. Even though it may be true that the minister has never been unemployed for a period of two years, he may still be able to identify with the emotions of frustration and boredom.

Success in the identification stage naturally leads to the encouragement and challenge stage. The minister is able to begin to respond to the root problems of many poor people: the lack of hope, the lack of encouragement, and the lack of motivation. In many cases, a poor person has been influenced by his past experiences to think in a negative way. It is difficult for him to motivate himself to change. His past failures hang over his head like a heavy rain cloud. He needs to be encouraged. He needs to receive a vision for change. Encouragement includes much more than merely saying, "You can do it." It includes providing information, instruction, challenge, and vision. It may even include stern correction with the Bible as the authority. People who have been in a poverty condition for a long time may have developed a "poverty mentality." They do not necessarily want to be helped. They do not want to help themselves. This needs to be challenged because to be needy, you must first see your need. To be helped, you must first want to be helped and be willing to help yourself. Do not do everything for the poor person. Instead, help him to help himself.

A man was there who had been ill for thirty-eight years. When Jesus saw him lying *there*, and knew that he had already been a long time in that condition, He said to him, "Do you wish to get well?" The sick man answered Him, "Sir, I have no man to put me into the pool when the water is stirred up, but while I am coming, another steps down before me." Jesus said to him, "Get up, pick up your pallet and walk" (John 5:5-8).

The encouragement and challenge stage makes its way to the service stage. Now the person must be helped to help himself and, ultimately, to help others. A plan must be developed that will be used to complete specific goals. To start, the goals should be easy to accomplish. You need to build momentum. Poor people generally do not have confidence in what they can accomplish.

Step by step, they can build a sense of confidence. The pattern of a lack of ability to achieve goals—whether it is due to the fault of the poor person himself, the fault of other people, or the injustice of society—must be broken. Here, the minister to the poor must have patience. A slow momentum toward success is to be expected as the poor person gains much needed confidence and encouragement. Initially, accomplishing easier goals can lead to the accomplishment of more difficult goals later on. For many reasons—emotional, psychological, and practical—helping the poor person to get a job is most important. Most critical, however, is spiritual transformation through exposure to and teaching of the Word of God. If there is not a spiritual change that forms Christian character, then habits of laziness, irresponsibility, and lack of discipline may not be changed, and the person will probably lose their new job after a short period of time.

As soon as possible, the minister should encourage the poor person to help others. The progression of "help" moves from admitting your need for help, being helped, helping yourself, and, ultimately, helping others. God helps those who ask for help to help themselves to help others. This is what breaks the "cycle of poverty."

NOTES

September

SEPTEMBER 1

BECAUSE GOD SO LOVED THE WORLD

"This is good and acceptable in the sight of God our Savior, who desires all men to be saved and to come to the knowledge of the truth. For there is one God."

1 Timothy 2:3-5

Why did God choose Israel? Why did God allow the exile of the Jews to Babylon? Why did God send His Son? Why did God reject the Jews? Why did God choose the church? Why did God choose you? All of these questions have a common answer: "For God so loved the *world*" (John 3:16, emphasis mine). God is a missionary God. He wants to "draw *all* men" to Himself (John 12:32, emphasis mine) because as the Savior of the world, He "desires *all* men to be saved and to come to the knowledge of the truth" (1 Tim. 2:4, emphasis mine). His basic plan for accomplishing this worldwide evangelism revolves around His people. Those who know Him will make Him known to others. God does all those things we asked about so that He will be made known to *all* people.

God chooses Israel as a missionary nation (Gen. 12:1-3). He blesses them so that "in them all the families of the earth will be blessed." He allowed the exile of the Jews to Babylon so that His people would be a more effective witness to the nations (Amos 5:27). In the same way, God allowed Jonah to be swallowed by a whale so that he would be the evangelist to Nineveh that God always wanted him to be (Jonah 2:10-3:2). Job came to understand this *principle of the whale*—God can use anything to achieve His purposes. "I know that You can do all things, and that no purpose of Yours can be thwarted" (Job 42:2).

God sent His Son because He loves the *world* (John 3:16). He wants to draw all people to Himself (John 12:32), He wants all men to be saved (1 Tim. 2:4), and He does not want any to perish (2 Peter 3:9). He has a missiological plan in which He will use those who know Him to make Him known to others.

God rejected the Jews for the same reason that He chose them: because He loves the world, and His mission is to make Himself known to all people. It is in the context of Jesus telling a parable about the Jewish leaders (Matt. 21:33-45), who failed to deliver the landowner's "produce," that He proclaims, "'Therefore I say to you, the kingdom of God will be taken away from you and given to a people, producing the fruit of it'" (Matt. 21:43). The Jews rejected Christ and their missionary obligation to the nations. Thus, God rejected them.

The parable references "the harvest" and "vine-growers." Jesus' missiological plan is highlighted with similar words, "the harvest" and "workers." "Then He said to His disciples, 'The harvest is plentiful, but the workers are few. Therefore beseech the Lord of the harvest to send out workers into His harvest'" (Matt. 9:37-38). God's plan is to reach the nations because He loves the world. Israel disagreed with this plan, so they were rejected.

God chooses the Church because His plan is to use a people who know Him to make Him known to others. In this sense, the Church became the new Israel, the new missionary nation. "But you are A CHOSEN RACE, a royal PRIESTHOOD, A HOLY NATION, for a PEOPLE FOR *God's* OWN POSSESSION, so that you may proclaim the excellencies of Him who has called you out of darkness into His marvelous light" (1 Peter 2:9).

This "body of Christ" is now the vessel through which God continues His missionary plan (Matthew 28:18-20).

Of course, all of these questions and answers are important as they pertain to God's plans and purposes. Perhaps, the most important question and answer, however, is "Why did God choose you?"

God chose you because He loves you and because He loves the world. He wants you to know Him, and He wants you to make Him known. He wants to transform you into a vessel that He can use for His own glory and for His own missionary purposes. So, go! Go to those in your house, in your neighborhood, in your school, at your place of work, in your social circles, and on your map. Go to all people. That is where God is, "for God so loved the world" (John 3:16).

SEPTEMBER 2

HE HAS HIGH STANDARDS

"'But I say to you, love your enemies and pray for those who persecute you, so that you may be sons of your Father who is in heaven...'"

Matthew 5:44-45

The iconic Sermon on the Mount must have left its original listeners speechless. Every line stands as a profound nugget of truth. The heart of the sermon comes when Jesus sets the standards for those living in the kingdom of God. These standards are rooted in what is real, not simply in what things look like. Appearance is not enough. Actuality is demanded. Moreover, appearance without actuality is judged. "'Woe to you, scribes and Pharisees, hypocrites! For you are like whitewashed tombs which on the outside appear beautiful, but inside they are full of dead men's bones and all uncleanness'" (Matt. 23:27).

Jesus sets a standard for integrity. To be *integral* is to be *sincere*. The word "sincere" comes from two Latin words which, when combined, are translated "without wax." Merchants who were insincere (with wax) would drill holes in their weights that were used to counterbalance the scale in order to determine the price to be paid. Wax was then placed in the holes and covered up so that it would take more weights to counterbalance the weight of the product on the other scale. This would result in the vender getting more money out of the transaction than he should have. The sincere vender (without wax) uses true weights and does not rob his customer. Sincerity or integrity is the character trait that allows your *yes* to be *yes* and your *no* to be *no*.

What you see is what you get. It is what it is! Jesus explained it this way:

Again, you have heard that the ancients were told, "YOU SHALL NOT MAKE FALSE VOWS, BUT SHALL FULFILL YOUR VOWS TO THE LORD." But I say to you, make no oath at all, either by heaven, for it is the throne of God, or by the earth, for it is the footstool of His feet, or by Jerusalem, for it is THE CITY OF THE GREAT KING. Nor shall you make an oath by your head, for you cannot make one hair white or black. But let your statement be, "Yes, yes" *or* "No, no"; anything beyond these is of evil (Matt. 5:33-37).

Perhaps, the most difficult standard to live up to is the standard for retribution. It includes such a big cross to die on that it almost seems impossible to achieve. Of course, that is the crux of the matter. You cannot achieve it; it can only be achieved by Christ (Gal. 2:20). Kingdom of God standards are set high because they assume that the Standard-Setter is standing in for you.

You have heard that it was said, "AN EYE FOR AN EYE, AND A TOOTH FOR A TOOTH." But I say to you, do not resist an evil person; but whoever slaps you on your right cheek, turn the other to him also. If anyone wants to sue you and take your shirt, let him have your coat also. Whoever forces you to go one mile, go with him two. Give to him who asks of you, and do not turn away from him who wants to borrow from you (Matt. 5:38-42).

The standard for retribution may be the most difficult, but the standard for love is definitely the most important and all-encompassing. God is love (1 John 4:8). God's children are known by their love (John 13:35). Love never fails (1 Cor. 13:8).

> You have heard that it was said, "YOU SHALL LOVE YOUR NEIGHBOR and hate your enemy." But I say to you, love your enemies and pray for those who persecute you, so that you may be sons of your Father who is in heaven; for He causes His sun to rise on *the* evil and *the* good, and sends rain on the righteous and the unrighteous. For if you love those who love you, what reward do you have? Do not even the tax collectors do the same? If you greet only your brothers, what more are you doing *than others*? Do not even the Gentiles do the same? (Matt. 5:43-47).

Each standard that Jesus sets in the Sermon on the Mount is introduced with the words, "You have heard that it was said . . . but I say to you . . ." Jesus is saying, "You have embraced one standard, but I am giving you another." He was not changing or destroying the Law (Matt. 5:17). He was going beyond the common, religious understanding of the Law in order to capture the heart of the Law. Jesus' standards are a matter of the heart!

Outward religion tends to make the doing of the Law an external show. Jesus was showing that the doing of the Law is not a show, but an internal reality. With the coming of Christ and the New Covenant, there is now a greater revelation of the Law, and so, there is a higher standard. "'Behold, days are coming,' declares the LORD, 'when I will make a new covenant . . . I will put My law within them and on their heart I will write it; and I will be their God, and they shall be My people'" (Jer. 31:31, 33).

SEPTEMBER 3

NO PAIN, NO GAIN

"He learned obedience from the things which He suffered."

Hebrews 5:8

One of the great questions of life is the question of pain and suffering. All people everywhere throughout all history have asked, "Is there a solution to pain and suffering?" The Buddhists call it "dukkha"—life is suffering—and say it comes from "tanha," or "desire," which is eliminated by reaching "nirvana" ("nothingness" or "extinguishing the flame"). Whether you run toward *nothing* or run toward *something*, you will try to run *from* suffering. What is your *painkiller*?

Your painkiller may be something good. You may run from your pain by running to the love of your family or to the love of your work. Your painkiller may also be something bad. You may run from your pain by running to illicit sex or drug and alcohol abuse. These destinations may prove to serve as temporary painkillers. Surely, they must work to some degree, or people would not run to them. This may be true but, the key word here is *temporary*. This temporary dynamic yields a double whammy for its practitioner. First, the soothing does not last. Second, it is a deceiver, since the very way it seems to be helping is the same way in which it causes more pain and suffering. People who "drown their sorrows" in a bottle end up having more sorrows as their bodies begin to deteriorate, their relationships begin to fall apart, and their finances begin to dissolve. So where can we find comfort? Almost unbelievably, we find comfort within the suffering itself.

> In the days of His flesh, He offered up both prayers and supplications with loud crying and tears to the One able to save Him from death, and He was heard because of His piety.

> Although He was a Son, He learned obedience from the things which He suffered. And having been made perfect, He became to all those who obey Him the source of eternal salvation (Heb. 5:7-9).

This is a fascinating picture. Jesus the Man experienced real temptation and fought against it, suffered through it, and beat it; He did not sin. Moreover, "He learned obedience from the things which He suffered." The battle against sin is just that—a battle; it is a war! There is a reason why something is tempting. It is because you desire it. It must be told no! It has to be nailed to the cross and put to death—and that hurts. "Therefore, since Christ has suffered in the flesh, arm yourselves also with the same purpose, because he who has suffered in the flesh has ceased from sin" (1 Peter 4:1).

Jesus won the war, so run to Jesus! "For since He Himself was tempted in that which He has suffered, He is able to come to the aid of those who are tempted" (Heb. 2:18). Jesus is a much better solution than sex, drugs, and alcohol, and even the love of your family or your love for your work. "For we do not have a high priest who cannot sympathize with our weaknesses, but One who has been tempted in all things as *we are, yet* without sin. Therefore let us draw near with confidence to the throne of grace, so that we may receive mercy and find grace to help in time of need" (Heb. 4:15-16).

Christ is our Comforter. "He Himself is our peace" (Eph. 2:14). Suffering may not be desirable—and it certainly is not coveted—but it can be useful. Without your own suffering, you would not be as able to "suffer with" (the word "compassion" is made up of "con" and "pati" or "suffer with"). Compassion is a major attribute of God that He can work in you to make Him known to others and for you to know Him more fully. It is sometimes in the deepest of suffering that we find the depth of God. "Deep calls to deep" (Psalm 42:7) in the Psalm of despair and suffering. No pain, no gain.

> Blessed *be* the God and Father of our Lord Jesus Christ, the Father of mercies and God of all comfort, who comforts us in all our affliction so that we will be able to comfort those who are in any affliction with the comfort with which we ourselves are comforted by God. For just as the sufferings of Christ are ours in abundance, so also our comfort is abundant through Christ. But if we are afflicted, it is for your comfort and salvation; or if we are comforted, it is for your comfort, which is effective in the patient enduring of the same sufferings which we also suffer; and our hope for you is firmly grounded, knowing that as you are sharers of our sufferings, so also you are *sharers* of our comfort (2 Cor. 1:3-7).

Painkillers are only as good as the degree to which they actually kill pain. Jesus is the ultimate Painkiller. "The LORD is near to the brokenhearted and saves those who are crushed in spirit" (Psalm 34:18). Of course, the ultimate "pain-free zone" is the new Heaven and earth. This is where the great Painkiller "will wipe away every tear from their eyes; and there will no longer be *any* death; there will no longer be *any* mourning, or crying, or pain; the first things have passed away" (Rev. 21:4).

How do we get to that place? Is there a solution to pain and suffering? Is there a painkiller that really works? The answer is found in the paradox of the Gospel. The "Good News" answer is to run to the cross; it is to run to the suffering. We do this by running to Jesus. "Fixing our eyes on Jesus, the author and perfecter of faith, who for the joy set before Him endured the cross, despising the shame, and has sat down at the right hand of the throne of God" (Heb. 12:2). Hey, sufferer, run!

SEPTEMBER 4

A DISEASE CALLED MATERIALISM

"For the love of money is a root of all sorts of evil, and some by longing for it have wandered away from the faith and pierced themselves with many griefs."

1 Timothy 6:10

Materialism can be a devastating disease. Being bound to the material world can detach us from the spiritual world. This is not a surprise. It is expected. Two thousand years ago, Jesus explained that it would be a terrible plague against the church and its mission. "'And others are the ones on whom seed was sown among the thorns; these are the ones who have heard the word, but the worries of the world, and the deceitfulness of riches, and the desires for other things enter in and choke the word, and it becomes unfruitful'" (Mark 4:18-19).

The Church in the Western world sometimes seems to be obsessed with the material world and depressed in the spiritual world. Much of the power of the disease comes in its deceitfulness. Many Western Christians whose walk with the Lord has been affected by this plague do not even recognize that they are sick. The normal way of defining what is a need versus what is desired has become exaggerated. Jack Taylor provides the following statistics to show how this exaggeration has become unmanageable: "Sociologists reported a few years ago that at the beginning of the 20th century the average American wanted 72 things and considered 18 of them important. Fifty years later the want list had risen to 496 of which 96 were considered necessary to happiness."[13]

The deceitfulness of riches can be rooted in a false hope, a false security, and a false joy that money and possessions offer. It also can be associated with the inability to distinguish between being provided for and being wasteful. It is the deceitfulness that so easily fools a spoiled child who just wants more and more. A spoiled child is never satisfied.

How we view money and possessions is a very important topic. Jesus was not reluctant to speak about it. It has been shown that as much as 25 percent of His teachings in the Gospel of Luke focused on the topic of money and possessions. It might be said that the financial picture in someone's life illuminates their spiritual picture.

Luxurious living may be said to be tantamount to promoting waste. Of course, the measurement of such things is subjective. How much is too much? At what point does extra become excess? Regardless of what criteria are used to form that definition, we can confidently say that excess has alternative uses. "But whoever has the world's goods, and sees his brother in need and closes his heart against him, how does the love of God abide in him?" (1 John 3:17). This is the main argument against waste. It is not so much that it is wrong to consume more than you need. It is more that it is right to give to those in need.

Another way to consider this challenge is found in the biblical principle that the more privilege you have, the more responsibility you have. In other words, your excess is not to be held in excess but is to be distributed. "From everyone who has been given much, much will be required; and to whom they entrusted much, of him they will ask all the more" (Luke 12:48). Of course, there is a need for balance here. Both luxurious living in excessive waste and living in poverty are not recommended. Each has its own pitfalls. "Keep deception and lies far from me, give me neither poverty nor riches; feed me with the food that is my portion, that I not be full and deny You and say, 'Who is the LORD?' Or that I not be in want and steal and profane the name of my God (Prov. 30:8-9).

The opposite of living in luxury is living according to what one actually needs. The Bible seems to advocate this for two reasons: to avoid the temptations of riches and to be able to give more to others who are in need. Giving to those in need is not for the purpose of being in need yourself—there is nothing holy about being poor—but for the purpose of using your excess for someone else's want. "And all those who had believed were together and had all things in common; and they *began* selling their property and possessions and were sharing them with all, as anyone might have need" (Acts 2:44-45).

Just as there is nothing holy about poverty, there is nothing evil about money in and of itself. It is the love of money that results in the disease of materialism. Luxurious living that includes excess and waste—however that is defined—puts someone into a precarious position. The disease of materialism can be extremely debilitating.

> But those who want to get rich fall into temptation and a snare and many foolish and harmful desires which plunge men into ruin and destruction. For the love of money is a root of all sorts of evil, and some by longing for it have wandered away from the faith and pierced themselves with many griefs. But flee from these things, you man of God (1 Tim. 6:9-11).

SEPTEMBER 5

OLD TESTAMENT PERSPECTIVES ON COUNSELING

"And His name will be called Wonderful Counselor, Mighty God."

Isaiah 9:6

What is counseling according to the Old Testament? It might be said that counseling is consistency in putting forth godly principles. Concerning the use of His words and, therefore, the practice of biblical counseling, God says "You shall teach them to your sons, talking of them when you sit in your house and when you walk along the road and when you lie down and when you rise up" (Deut. 11:19).

Counseling is directly associated with successful planning. "Without consultation, plans are frustrated, but with many counselors they succeed" (Prov. 15:22). Not all counsel ends in success. There is a type of counsel that leads to turmoil and should be avoided. And so, the psalmist cries out, "Hide me from the secret counsel of evildoers, from the tumult of those who do iniquity" (Psalm 64:2). On the other hand, godly counsel results in an increase in learning, since "a wise man will hear and increase in learning, and a man of understanding will acquire wise counsel" (Prov. 1:5). It also results in peace and joy. "Deceit is in the heart of those who devise evil, but counselors of peace have joy" (Prov. 12:20).

What are the benefits of counseling? Counseling can help to relieve anxiety. "Anxiety in a man's heart weighs it down, but a good word makes it glad" (Prov. 12:25). Counseling leads to success, since "where there is no guidance the people fall, but in abundance of counselors there is victory" (Prov. 11:14). Some of that success may come from better planning that can be the result of good counsel. We are encouraged to "prepare plans by consultation" (Prov. 20:18).

Counseling in the Old Testament is often associated with wisdom. First, "a wise man is he who listens to counsel" (Prov. 12:15). Second, "wisdom is with those who receive counsel" (Prov. 13:10). Third, we are strongly encouraged to "listen to counsel and accept discipline, that you may be wise the rest of your days" (Prov. 19:20).

Ultimately, perhaps, godly counseling leads to healing. The struggles of life and the inevitable painful residue produced by this fallen world often result in various forms of suffering. Wise counsel can help bring healing to that pain. "There is one who speaks rashly like the thrusts of a sword, but the tongue of the wise brings healing" (Prov. 12:18).

Unfortunately, not all people are wise enough to receive godly counseling. There are those who simply reject the truth. This is done at their own peril, since "he is *on* the path of life who heeds instruction, but he who ignores reproof goes astray" (Prov. 10:17). Sometimes, people refuse counsel simply because they want to be the only one who speaks; they are not willing or able to listen. It is true that "a fool does not delight in understanding, but only in revealing his own mind" (Prov. 18:2). Some people are just so angry that they do not want to change. "A *man of* great anger will bear the penalty, for if you rescue *him*, you will only have to do it again" (Prov. 19:19).

Then there are those who simply despise and undervalue the truth. God's instruction regarding such ones is, "Do not speak in the hearing of a fool, for he will despise the wisdom of your words" (Prov. 23:9). Such a person may even try to avoid righteous confrontation with his rage or laughter. "When a wise man has a controversy with a foolish man, the foolish man either rages or laughs, and there is no rest" (Prov. 29:19). This kind of person may simply not address the problem or issue and "will not be instructed by words alone; for though he understands, there will be no response" (Prov. 29:19).

Certainly, the Old Testament has quite a bit to say about counseling. Most importantly, we need to recognize that our Counselor is always available. He is none other than God Himself. And so, we are in good hands, "for a child will be born to us, a son will be given to us; and the government will rest on His shoulders; and His name will be called Wonderful Counselor, Mighty God, Eternal Father, Prince of Peace" (Isa. 9:6). Praise God!

SEPTEMBER 6

HUMAN ACTIVITY IN SPIRITUAL GIFTS

"But to each one is given the manifestation of the Spirit for the common good... But one and the same Spirit works all these things, distributing to each one individually just as He wills."

1 Corinthians 12:7, 11

The gifts of the Holy Spirit are extraordinary. They are extra (beyond ordinary) yet, at the same time, they are ordinary; they include both Divine and human activity. People are involved in spiritual activity. This is God's way. He has chosen to use vessels through which He will do His work. His vessels are people. And so, activation of the gifts of the Holy Spirit requires human activity.

Paul declares that "to each one is given the manifestation of the Spirit for the common good" (1 Cor. 12:7). A person is the recipient of the gift. It is the person who must use the gift. For example, in Acts 2:4, we see that it was those who were filled with the Holy Spirit who "began to speak with other tongues." They had to speak. They had to act. The gifts are not manifested automatically or forced upon someone. In this sense, the human factor does exist in its fullness; the abilities, talents, and experience of the vessel affects the manifestation. The manifestation of the Spirit does not depend on these human variables, but He can use them.

The idea here is that the human is the vessel. Whether or not the vessel will be used is based on the preparation and availability of that vessel. The vessel can be better prepared and, therefore, more available through study, practice, and experience. Again, the source does not depend on these things, but the source can and will use these things.

This principle of spiritual gifts of the Divine working through humanity is not a foreign concept in the Bible. It is consistent with how God used humans to produce the inspired Scripture itself, "for no prophecy was ever made by an act of human will, but men moved by the Holy Spirit spoke from God" (2 Peter 1:21). It is not a matter of the human will; the Spirit (the Source) did not depend on man (the vessel) to initiate. Yet it is man (the vessel) who is moved by the Spirit (the Source) to act. The implication is that the final result of the use of the gift will be affected by the vessel, since it is poured through the vessel.

This is the reason why there are four gospels. It is the Spirit working through four different men to produce four somewhat different results. The Spirit did not depend on the specific backgrounds, perspectives, characteristics, abilities, personalities, or talents of the four gospel writers. Yet He did use those different variables for His purposes while maintaining the Scripture's infallibility. With respect to the manifestation of spiritual gifts, however, this dynamic of Divine activity mixed with human activity can result in errors. The vessels can allow their human nature to interfere with what the Spirit is doing. The result can be disorder and confusion as it was, to some degree, in the Corinthian church.

The gifts of the Spirit do not reside in people; the human activity with respect to spiritual gifts is not permanent. The Spirit is "distributing to each one individually just as He wills" (1 Cor. 12:11). Different people are used on different occasions. A gift of the Spirit is not a ministry "office" or appointment. It is, rather, a situational and temporary enablement that meets an immediate need or is used for a specific purpose (1 Cor. 12:7; 14:26, 31). These gifts are not possessions. The Spirit moves freely (John 3:8) and according to His own choice as it is applied to a particular situation and occasion (1 Cor. 12:11). The gift is *given* (1 Cor. 12:7). It is for the present. It is not the result of a gift that has been given in the past and has been stored for future use.

What does that mean for you and me? At any time and in any situation, the Spirit may choose to use us in any of the gifts. And so, we must make sure that we are prepared and available.

SEPTEMBER 7

STAY OUT OF THE POT

"I will stand on my guard post and station myself on the rampart; and I will keep watch to see what He will speak to me."

Habakkuk 2:1

It is those who are pure in heart who will see God (Matt. 5:8). Vision is clearly connected to obedience. "Where there is no vision, the people are unrestrained, but happy is he who keeps the law" (Prov. 29:18). A lack of vision is clearly connected to disobedience and disaster. How is vision lost? It is a slow process. It happens gradually because it is enacted via deception. Glaucoma and macular degeneration are tragic physical examples of this spiritual dynamic. These diseases gradually reduce your vision. They have no early symptoms and therefore are called "silent thieves of sight." It is like the proverbial frog in a boiling pot. It is not boiling at first, lest he just hop out. It starts off warm and gradually gets hotter and hotter until it is too late for the frog.

Even as the pure in heart see God more and more, the impure (disobedient) see God less and less. There is a deception because of the slow process. You think you can see, so you do not see your problem; and the next thing you know, you are blind.

For judgment I came into this world, so that those who do not see may see, and that those who see may become blind. Those of the Pharisees who were with Him heard these things and said to Him, "We are not blind too, are we?" Jesus said to them, "If you were blind, you would have no sin; but since you say, 'We see,' your sin remains" (John 9:39-41).

How do you stay out of the pot? How do you keep your sight? How do you keep from becoming "unrestrained" by losing your vision?

I will stand on my guard post and station myself on the rampart; and I will keep watch to see what He will speak to me, and how I may reply when I am reproved. Then the LORD answered me and said, "Record the vision and inscribe it on tablets, that the one who reads it may run. For the vision is yet for the appointed time; it hastens toward the goal and it will not fail. Though it tarries, wait for it; for it will certainly come, it will not delay" (Hab. 2:1-3).

You need to get yourself in position—"station" yourself—and "keep watch" in order to see farther and clearer. The position of prayer is the proper position. Jesus said, "'So, you *men* could not keep watch with Me for one hour? Keep watching and praying'" (Matt. 26:40-41). Watch out for the pot! Prayer is how you watch. "In the morning, O LORD, You will hear my voice; in the morning I will order *my prayer* to You and *eagerly* watch" (Psalm 5:3). One way to keep your sight is to *put your watch on.*

To have a greater vision for God's work, you need to have a greater vision for God. "We love, because [God] first loved us" (1 John 4:19). How can our love grow for others? God loves us. Then we love others. So if we can increase God's love for us, then we can increase our love for others. Can God's love increase? No, but our revelation of God's love for us can increase. So, then, what is the answer? How can our love grow for others? This is where the position of prayer comes into play again. Paul prays for the Ephesian church, "[T]hat you, being rooted and grounded in love, may be able to comprehend with all the saints what is the breadth and length and height and depth, and to know the love of Christ which surpasses knowledge, that you may be filled up to all the fullness of God" (Eph. 3:17-19).

To have a greater vision of your love for others, you need to have a greater vision of God's love for you. This is a very important principle in the Christian life. Pray for God to reveal Himself to you. The more clearly you see His love, holiness, goodness, and kindness, the more vision you will have to show love, holiness, goodness, and kindness toward others. Revelation is life (John 17:3)!

SEPTEMBER 8

LOOKING TO ETERNITY

"'And I say to you, make friends for yourselves by means of the wealth of unrighteousness, so that when it fails, they will receive you into the eternal dwellings.'"

Luke 16:9

One of the most misunderstood parables of Jesus is the parable of the unrighteous steward (Luke 16:1-13). Sometimes, it is understood as a teaching to direct its hearers away from poor character and poor business practices. This interpretation, however, makes no sense because the unrighteous steward is actually praised and congratulated for his seemingly deceptive and dishonest actions.

Parables must be understood by their conclusions or summaries. Jesus wraps up the parable of the unrighteous steward when He says, "'No servant can serve two masters; for either he will hate the one and love the other, or else he will be devoted to one and despise the other. You cannot serve God and wealth'" (Luke 16:13). Is what you do with wealth (money and possessions) dependent upon God and His purposes? If it is, then you make God and His purposes unconditional. Money becomes conditional with respect to God. God is the Master. Is what you do with God and His purposes dependent upon money? If it is, then you make money unconditional. God and His purposes become conditional with respect to money. Money is the master. This is idolatry! God calls us to a radical perspective. All is subordinate to Him and His kingdom. We must call Him Lord and live out His Lordship (supremacy) in our lives. Anything less and we break the first commandment, "You shall have no other gods before Me" (Exod. 20:3).

The unrighteous steward is praised, not because he hides from the here and now but because he looks to the not-yet. The temporal is informed by the eternal. The purpose of money is consistent with the purpose of life. Is the purpose of my life here on earth to be as comfortable as possible? Many people answer yes to this question because they see this life as the main attraction and the centerpiece of eternity. Their lives are formed by the implied philosophies of such existential sayings as "You only live once in life" and "Live for the moment." They do not believe in life after death. They are existentialists who are lost in a lack of hope. What other choice is there but hopelessness for someone who does not believe in life after death? If there is nothing after death, then what purpose could there be to this life? Without eternity, there is utter hopelessness because without something ahead, hope cannot be defined.

To obey God with respect to money, one must be a firm believer in eternity. Paul had a very different attitude about life. His focus was on what would come after this life. "For to me, to live is Christ and to die is gain" (Phil. 1:21). My life now on earth should be an extension of the life of Christ. "I have been crucified with Christ; and it is no longer I who live, but Christ lives in me" (Gal. 2:20). Purpose in this life is not based on this life itself but on the life to come. With an eternally based purpose in life, giving of one's wealth is understood as an opportunity to express desire for God and to know God. "'He pled the cause of the afflicted and needy; then it was well. Is not that what it means to know Me?' declares the LORD" (Jer. 22:16). Jesus says to us, "'For I was hungry, and you gave Me *something* to eat . . . to the extent that you did it to one of these brothers of Mine, *even the least of them*, you did it to Me'" (Matt. 25:35, 40).

The point of the parable of the "unrighteous steward" is that the correct perspective of money is that it is a means to an end, not an end in itself. It is a perspective that looks toward eternity. Money becomes a means for being received "into the eternal dwellings" (Luke 16:9). It is not that we buy our salvation. It is that our perspective of money is consistent with our understanding and application of the value and preeminence of that salvation. Knowing God and living in His kingdom is superior to all else. Money only finds value in the degree to which it remains subordinate to the King and His kingdom.

SEPTEMBER 9

WHAT USE IS THAT?

"Learn to do good; seek justice, reprove the ruthless, defend the orphan, plead for the widow."
Isaiah 1:17

One of the least addressed responsibilities given by God to His people is their responsibility to seek justice for the oppressed and the needy. God often warns His people who do not respond to this responsibility. He expresses anger and disgust when He refers to this sort of situation. The consequences are terrible. Rejecting God's heart for the needy can result in God not hearing the prayers of the offenders.

"What are your multiplied sacrifices to Me?" says the LORD. "I have had enough of burnt offerings of rams and the fat of fed cattle; and I take no pleasure in the blood of bulls, lambs or goats. When you come to appear before Me, who requires of you this trampling of My courts? Bring your worthless offerings no longer, incense is an abomination to Me. New moon and sabbath, the calling of assemblies—I cannot endure iniquity and the solemn assembly. I hate your new moon *festivals* and your appointed feasts, they have become a burden to Me; I am weary of bearing *them*. So when you spread out your hands *in prayer*, I will hide My eyes from you; yes, even though you multiply prayers, I will not listen. Your hands are covered with blood. Wash yourselves, make yourselves clean; remove the evil of your deeds from My sight. Cease to do evil, learn to do good; seek justice, reprove the ruthless, defend the orphan, plead for the widow" (Isa. 1:11-17).

God's warning to His people with regard to not taking up their responsibility also includes His promises of blessing when they do pay attention to their responsibility to care for and enact justice for the needy.

Cry loudly, do not hold back; raise your voice like a trumpet, and declare to My people their transgression and to the house of Jacob their sins . . . . "Why have we fasted and You do not see . . . Behold, on the day of your fast you find *your* desire, and drive hard all your workers. Behold, you fast for contention and strife and to strike with a wicked fist . . . Will you call this a fast, even an acceptable day to the LORD? Is this not the fast which I choose, to loosen the bonds of wickedness, to undo the bands of the yoke, and to let the oppressed go free and break every yoke? Is it not to divide your bread with the hungry and bring the homeless poor into the house; when you see the naked, to cover him; and not to hide yourself from your own flesh? Then your light will break out like the dawn, and your recovery will speedily spring forth; and your righteousness will go before you; the glory of the LORD will be your rear guard" . . . If you remove the yoke from your midst, the pointing of the finger and speaking wickedness, and if you give yourself to the hungry and satisfy the desire of the afflicted, then your light will rise in darkness and your gloom *will become* like midday (Isa. 58:1-10).

Addressing needs is connected to useful faith. "If a brother or sister is without clothing and in need of daily food, and one of you says to them, 'Go in peace, be warmed and be filled,' and yet you do not give them what is necessary for *their* body, what use is that? Even so faith, if it has no works, is dead, *being* by itself" (James 2:15-17).

What use is it to not be a responsible follower of the One you are following? "He who shuts his ear to the cry of the poor will also cry himself and not be answered" (Prov. 21:13). Those who are merciful shall receive mercy (Matt. 5:7). Those who meet the needs of others will have their needs met, but those who do not meet the needs of others will not have their needs met. What use is that?

SEPTEMBER 10

GOD'S FAVORITE THING TO DO

"'Rejoice with me, for I have found my sheep which was lost!'"

Luke 15:6

Our spirituality is based on God's desire to be in relationship with us. We desire God because He first desired us. "We love, because He first loved us" (1 John 4:19). We are holy because He is holy (Lev. 19:2). We choose God because He first chose us (John 15:16). We seek God because He first sought us.

"What man among you, if he has a hundred sheep and has lost one of them, does not leave the ninety-nine in the open pasture and go after the one which is lost until he finds it? When he has found it, he lays it on his shoulders, rejoicing. And when he comes home, he calls together his friends and his neighbors, saying to them, 'Rejoice with me, for I have found my sheep which was lost!' I tell you that in the same way, there will be *more* joy in heaven over one sinner who repents than over ninety-nine righteous persons who need no repentance" (Luke 15:4-7).

God's favorite thing to do is to spend time with us to reveal Himself to us. It is to find us and walk with us "in the garden in the cool of the day" (Gen. 3:8). God delights in us (Prov. 8:31, 11:20, 12:22). "He also brought me forth into a broad place; He rescued me, because He delighted in me" (2 Sam. 22:20). God delights in us knowing Him; "the prayer of the upright is His delight" (Prov. 15:8). He longs for us. "You have made my heart beat faster, my sister, *my* bride; you have made my heart beat faster with a single *glance* of your eyes, with a single strand of your necklace" (Song of Songs 4:9). This is God's favorite thing to do. It is what He delights in. "For I delight in loyalty rather than sacrifice, and in the knowledge of God rather than burnt offerings" (Hosea 6:6). God wants to be *with us;* and so "He appointed twelve, so that they would be with Him" (Mark 3:14). All of history is moving toward knowing God. "For the earth will be full of the knowledge of the LORD as the waters cover the sea" (Isa. 11:9).

How do we respond to this desire of God? Sometimes, we act like we are too important to spend time with God. Yet, God is the Creator (Gen. 1:1). He is "'the Alpha and Omega,'" the beginning and the end (Rev. 1:8). He is the King of kings and Lord of lords (1 Tim. 6:15). He is *the* important One. Yet as important as God is, His greatest desire is to spend time with you. God Almighty wants to be your Friend. He wants to abide in you, and He wants you to abide in Him (John 15:5). How will you respond?

Sometimes, we act like we have too many important things to do to spend time with God. Yet as "busy" as God is—He "upholds all things" (Heb. 1:3)—He makes time for us. God is "busy" doing so many *important things.* He takes your burdens and sustains you; and so, you can cast "all your anxiety on Him, because He cares for you" (1 Peter 5:7). He is busy doing important things. He makes nations rise and fall (Job 12:23). Yet as many important things as there are that God has to do, His most important is to spend time with you. The One Who holds the world together wants to be alone with you in secret. "But you, when you pray, go into your inner room, close your door and pray to your Father who is in secret" (Matt. 6:6). How will you respond?

We want to spend time with God because He first wanted to spend time with us. Based on this "formula," for our desire for Him to increase, His desire for us must increase. However, God's desire for us cannot increase. It is already full. Therefore, the only way to a stronger relationship with God is that our revelation of God's desire for us increases. When we see more of God's desire for us, we are drawn to Him more; we are changed. "Beloved, now we are children of God, and it has not appeared as yet what we will be. We know that when He appears, we will be like Him, because we will see Him just as He is. And everyone who has this hope *fixed* on Him purifies himself, just as He is pure" (1 John 3:2-3). In this, God is glorified. He is glorified in His desire for you to desire Him! He delights in you to delight in Him. "Delight yourself in the LORD; And He will give you the desires of your heart" (Psalm 37:4).

SEPTEMBER 11

ONE FOR ALL AND ALL FOR ONE

"For just as we have many members in one body and all the members do not have the same function, so we, who are many, are one body in Christ, and individually members one of another. Since we have gifts that differ according to the grace given to us, **each of us is to exercise them accordingly**.*"*

Romans 12:4-6

As the body of Christ, why is it true that we are better when we are together? Why can we accomplish so much more together than we can by ourselves? Is it just the power of synergy? No, it is much more fundamental than that. It goes all the way back to the way in which we were created. "Then God said, 'Let Us make man in Our image, according to Our likeness . . .' God created man in His own image, in the image of God He created him; male and female He created them" (Gen. 1:26-27). God, Who is a "singular plurality" (the Trinity), created man in His image; one God, Who is an "Us," created a "man," who is a "them."

The initial and most foundational example of this singular plurality is marriage. "For this reason a man shall leave his father and his mother, and be joined to his wife; and they shall become one flesh" (Gen. 2:24). Two are one, a unity in diversity. This singular plurality is also seen in the body of Christ. There is one body with many members (1 Cor. 12:20). This unity in diversity promotes the proper and effective working of the Church as "the whole body, being fitted and held together by what every joint supplies, according to the proper working of each individual part, causes the growth of the body for the building up of itself in love" (Eph. 4:16).

To be made in the image of God means that we can use our individual gifts—the individual ways in which God created us—to "complete" each other. This, in fact, is the meaning of the Hebrew word *neged*, which is used to describe how the one part (woman) will "complete" the other part (man) so that *they* can become *one*. The *one* body of Christ works best when its individual *parts* (gifts) work together. Teamwork is not only best, but it is necessary. Christianity cannot be lived out on an island. We are to love one another, be devoted to one another, and give preference to one another (John 15:12, Romans 12:10). The Greek term *allelon* is used over forty times in the New Testament to mandate the kind of actions that we are to engage in with *one another*. We need each other in order to obey God and use our gifts.

Circles are better than rows. Connection is the key. Those who do not stay connected put themselves in danger. This is why Paul instructed the Corinthians to not associate with the man who was engaging in extreme immorality. It had to do with the power of connection and the danger of disconnection. To disconnect the man was to "throw him to the wolves" and make him vulnerable to the enemy. This was a last-ditch effort in the process of church discipline to persuade the man to repent and get reconnected. Even Satan could be used as a tool in this endeavor; so Paul says, *"I have decided* to deliver such a one to Satan for the destruction of his flesh, so that his spirit may be saved in the day of the Lord Jesus" (1 Cor. 5:5).

Apart from each other, we are weak; but together, we are strong. The body of Christ works properly when its parts work together. It is who we are. It is how we were created. We are a singular plurality, a unity in diversity. Stay connected!

SEPTEMBER 12

HAVING A KINGDOM ATTITUDE

"'Do not judge so that you will not be judged. For in the way you judge, you will be judged; and by your standard of measure, it will be measured to you.'"

Matthew 7:1-2

Keep your eyes on God, not on men. It is easier said than done. In any case, it is the practice that will help us in the game of life. It will determine whether we are ones who judge or ones who pray. When we have a judgmental attitude, our minds are set on men and their problems. When we have a prayerful attitude, our minds are set on God and His solutions.

> Do not judge so that you will not be judged . . . Why do you look at the speck that is in your brother's eye, but do not notice the log that is in your own eye . . . Ask, and it will be given to you; seek, and you will find; knock, and it will be opened to you. For everyone who asks receives, and he who seeks finds, and to him who knocks it will be opened . . . (Matt. 7:1-7).

A judgmental attitude is a hypocritical attitude. Hypocrisy is always pitted against sincerity. That which is fake comes up against that which is real. That which is worldly is always contrasted with that which is heavenly. Living in the kingdom of God is living in a "counterculture." It is to live an alternative lifestyle. Instead of having a judgmental attitude, kingdom-dwellers are called to have a prayerful attitude.

So much time is wasted with a judgmental attitude. The inefficiencies of judging can be replaced with the efficiencies of praying. God will answer if you would only ask. Prayer is effective. "The effective prayer of a righteous man can accomplish much" (James 5:16). Judgment is ineffective (James 4:11-12). The ineffective judging of an unrighteous man accomplishes nothing!

Nobody asks someone else to judge them, but people do ask others to pray for them. "In everything, therefore, treat people the same way you want them to treat you" (Matt. 7:12). Instead of judging people, pray for them because this is what you would want them to do for you. This is the kingdom attitude!

SEPTEMBER 13

THE FOUNDATION OF MARRIAGE

"What therefore God has joined together, let no man separate."

Matthew 19:6

It is not a stretch to view the marriage relationship as the most fundamental and intimate bond between human beings. The institution of marriage is foundational to the definition of society.

> The man gave names to all the cattle, and to the birds of the sky, and to every beast of the field, but for Adam there was not found a helper suitable for him. So the LORD God caused a deep sleep to fall upon the man, and he slept; then He took one of his ribs and closed up

the flesh at that place. The LORD God fashioned into a woman the rib which He had taken from the man, and brought her to the man. The man said, "This is now bone of my bones, and flesh of my flesh; she shall be called Woman, because she was taken out of Man." For this reason a man shall leave his father and his mother, and be joined to his wife; and they shall become one flesh (Gen. 2:20-24).

Since marriage is the most foundational relationship found in society and the most intimate relationship between individuals, the breaking of that relationship is a very serious and ruinous act, ruinous for society and ruinous for individuals. When a wife "leaves the companion of her youth" (Prov. 2:17a), she is leaving her intimate friend. When a wife "forgets the covenant of her God" (Prov. 2:17b), she is separating what "God has joined together" (Matt. 19:6). The stability and permanence of marriage is critical to the strength of any society because it is fundamental to society. It is critical to individuals because it is the essence of human intimacy. And so, God says, "I hate divorce" (Mal. 2:16).

Such words as oneness, faithfulness, unity, loyalty, devotion, and "onlyness" serve to describe the sanctity of marriage. The respected "Proverbs 31 woman" is a wife who is faithful to her husband, whereas the "Proverbs 9 woman" is a foolish wife who is not faithful to her husband. "The woman of folly is boisterous, *she is* naive and knows nothing. She sits at the doorway of her house, on a seat by the high places of the city, calling to those who pass by, who are making their paths straight: 'Whoever is naive, let him turn in here'" (Prov. 9:13-16).

The wife either creates a home or destroys the household. "The wise woman builds her house, but the foolish tears it down with her own hands" (Prov. 14:1). Wives are seen as collaborators with their husbands in the training of their children. They speak with one voice. "Hear, my son, your father's instruction and do not forsake your mother's teaching" (Prov. 1:8). Wives are "one" with their husbands.

Husbands are "one" with their wives. The wife is the "one and only" of the husband. Husbands are called to be faithful, loyal, and devoted to their wives. Devotion should be the cause and the result of mutual satisfaction in the marriage relationship.

> Drink water from your own cistern and fresh water from your own well. Should your springs be dispersed abroad, streams of water in the streets? Let them be yours alone and not for strangers with you. Let your fountain be blessed, and rejoice in the wife of your youth. *As* a loving hind and a graceful doe, let her breasts satisfy you at all times; be exhilarated always with her love. For why should you, my son, be exhilarated with an adulteress and embrace the bosom of a foreigner? (Prov. 5:15-20).

True intimacy is lost without the ribbon of loyalty that wraps up the gift of marriage. The abuse of the sexual urge affects the family and family relationships. A husband can destroy himself and his family. "The one who commits adultery with a woman is lacking sense; he who would destroy himself does it" (Prov. 6:32). Sanctity in marriage is suggested for our own benefit. It is logical and sensible to listen to this suggestion. It is wisdom and knowledge that follow it. Lips that drip with knowledge counter lips that drip with honey.

> My son, give attention to my wisdom, incline your ear to my understanding; that you may observe discretion and your lips may reserve knowledge. For the lips of an adulteress drip honey and smoother than oil is her speech; but in the end she is bitter as wormwood, sharp as a two-edged sword. Her feet go down to death, her steps take hold of Sheol. She does not ponder the path of life; her ways are unstable, she does not know *it* (Prov. 5:1-6).

The ways of the unstable are dangerous. The stability and permanence of marriage is critical to the strength of any society because it is fundamental to society. It is critical to individuals because it is the essence of human intimacy. We must have a "high view" of marriage. It must be cherished!

SEPTEMBER 14

"JESUS" MEANS "GOD SAVES"

*"I have come **as** Light into the world, so that everyone who believes in Me will not remain in darkness. If anyone hears My sayings and does not keep them, I do not judge him; for I did not come to judge the world, but to save the world."*

John 12:46-47

God created man in His image (Gen. 1:26). God is Spirit (John 4:24). Man, who is created in God's image is, therefore, created as a spiritual being, even as God breathed into his nostrils the breath or spirit of life (Gen. 2:7). When Adam and Eve fell to sin in the Garden of Eden, they died (Gen. 3:3). They would die—not only physically, but spiritually also (Gen. 3:8). Man, as a spiritual being, needs to be redeemed. His spirit needs to be "born again"" or born from above. Only God can accomplish this redemption; only God can make man spiritually alive again.

Man's spirituality began with God, and it has to be redeemed by God. Fallen man's spirituality begins with the fact that "God saves." Names have meanings. For example, the name "Judah" means "let God be praised." "Jesus" means "God is salvation" or "God saves." In Hebrew, the name is "Yeshua." In Spanish, it is "Jesús," while in French, it is "Jésus." And in the Congolese language of Lingala, it is "Yésu." Regardless of what language is used, "Jesus" means "God saves." The name emphasizes both that God *saves,* and *God* saves.

God does not create the world and all that is in it only to leave it in order to watch from a distance and require that it operate without Him. This type of deistic thinking misunderstands the nature of God. He is Sovereign and loving. God *saves* the world; He does not leave it to its own doom. Jesus means "God saves," not "God leaves" or "God ignores."

Neither does Jesus mean "God judges." God is not so consumed by anger over your sin that He wants nothing to do with you. God's desire is your salvation. "This is good, and acceptable in the sight of God our Savior, who desires all men to be saved and to come to the knowledge of the truth" (1 Tim. 2:3-4). He wants to "draw all people" to Himself (John 12:32), and does not want "anyone to perish" (2 Peter 3:9). He is the God Who sent Jesus; He sent "God *saves.*"

It is not the church that saves you. It is certainly not drugs, alcohol, or money that saves you. It is not what family you were born into that saves you (John 3:3-7). It is not even how good you are that saves you. "For by grace you have been saved through faith; and that not of yourselves, *it is* the gift of God; not as a result of works, so that no one may boast" (Eph. 2:8-9).

Jesus means "*God* saves" because *only* God can save. It is God, the Alpha and Omega, Who saves you. He has redeemed you, "for you have been bought with a price" (1 Cor. 6:20). We are in need, and He provides for our need. He is the answer!

Jesus means "God saves." This is the way it must be. There is no other way, for He is the only Way. He says, "'I am the way, and the truth, and the life; no one comes to the Father but through Me'" (John 14:6). It is the name of Jesus that saves. What a name! "And there is salvation in no one else; for there is no other name under heaven that has been given among men by which we must be saved" (Acts 4:12).

SEPTEMBER 15

PLEASE GOD, GET IN MY WAY

*"And He who searches the hearts knows what the mind of the Spirit is, because He intercedes for the saints according **to the will of** God. And we know that God causes all things to work together for good to those who love God, to those who are called according to **His** purpose."*

Romans 8:27-28

God draws us to Himself. Jesus said, "'No one can come to Me unless the Father who sent Me draws him" (John 6:44). It is God Who makes our relationship with Him a possibility. Moreover, God is constantly intervening in our lives. The fact that God keeps "getting in the way" can serve as a profound definition or description of the idea that God is a God of mercy and grace. If God is not directly involved with you this very second, you would instantly evaporate. "If He should gather to Himself His spirit and His breath, all flesh would perish together, and man would return to dust" (Job 34:14-15). God is constantly involved with us for our own benefit. This is good news. Please, God, get in my way!

The constancy of Divine intervention in our lives includes God's constant Divine favor. When the writer of Hebrews tells us that Jesus "always lives to make intercession for them," it is not saying that Jesus is praying for us. It means that He is constantly intervening in all our affairs for our benefit. "Therefore He is able also to save forever those who draw near to God through Him, since He always lives to make intercession for them" (Heb. 7:25). According to Marvin Vincent, "The idea is not intercession, but intervention. It includes every form of Christ's identifying himself with human interests."[14]

Similarly, in Romans 8:26, it is not that the Spirit pleads on our behalf but that He involves Himself in our situation; He takes part in it. He is intervening, and *we* are praying. This is His constant grace. "For we do not have a high priest who cannot sympathize with our weaknesses, but One who has been tempted in all things as we are, yet without sin. Therefore let us draw near with confidence to the throne of grace, so that we may receive mercy and find grace to help in time of need" (Heb. 4:15-16).

Picture, if you will, a scene in Heaven. You have just gotten yourself in a difficult situation because of your ignorance, negligence, or even because of your own sin. The case is brought before God. The question goes forth, "Is there anyone here who can put in a good word for this guy?" All eyes turn to Jesus. He nods his head in a sign of support. The command goes forward, "Bless him, help him, show him favor." It is not what you know but Who you know. It is not what you did but what He did. It is not you making your way but Him getting in your way!

Sometimes, we feel all alone. No one is on our side. We may even feel that no one should be on our side. We may feel that we do not deserve favor and that no one should help us. The good news is that Jesus sits at the right hand of the Father to intervene for us (Rom. 8:34). He entered Heaven to "appear in the presence of God for us" (Heb. 9:24). He is our Representative. He is for us. We have an Advocate (1 John 2:1). Since we are always in need—we can "do nothing" without Him (John 15:5)—we "do all things through [Christ] who strengthens [us]" (Phil. 4:13). This strength is the constancy of the grace of God.

There is no peace in deism. God is *not* an absentee landlord. Praise God that He truly is involved with His creation. He intervenes constantly. In His intervention, we are shown favor; and He becomes our peace, rest, and hope. "Trust in the LORD with all your heart and do not lean on your own understanding. In all your ways acknowledge Him, and He will make your paths straight" (Prov. 3:5-6). Please, God, get in my way!

SEPTEMBER 16

THE IDOLATRY OF FAITH IN FAITH

"I can do all things through Him who strengthens me."

Philippians 4:13

What is faith? Some people think it is a certain type of result, a certain category of outcomes that are defined by desirable criteria. This type of theological understanding says that faith only includes the "positive" scenarios that are consistent with what someone wants. Faith, whatever it is, must be more profound than this, since by faith, some "escaped the edge of the sword" (Heb. 11:34) and by that same faith, others were "put to death with the sword" (Heb. 11:37). Faith goes deeper than a certain set of circumstances.

> Not that I speak from want, for I have learned to be content in whatever circumstances I am. I know how to get along with humble means, and I also know how to live in prosperity; in any and every circumstance I have learned the secret of being filled and going hungry, both of having abundance and suffering need. I can do all things through Him who strengthens me (Phil. 4:11-13).

The point is that circumstances are not the point. If they are not the essence of faith, then what or who is? Paul can do all things and be content in all circumstances through Christ. Most fundamentally, faith has something to do with relationship with Jesus.

Some people think faith is simply a positive confession, a certain category of desired results that can be spoken into being. Faith becomes a creator. This is actually idolatry. You are not a creator, and your faith cannot create, lest you and your faith become God. Faith is not your *ability* or *non-ability* to get anything you want. It is your *availability* to engage in any circumstances that may be put before you and be able to "do all things"—not because you can create whatever situation you want but because you can be victorious in Christ in whatever situation comes your way. You cannot do "all those things" because you create them or make them happen but because you do them "through Christ who strengthens you." Your faith does not create; it relates. Your faith is not in faith; it is in God. Your faith is not exercised by exerting your faith. It is exercised by really engaging in relationship with a very real God.

The challenge of faith (really engaging in relationship with God) is the very essence of faith (believing that God is real and is really there). God's most fundamental nature is revealed in His memorial-name (Exod. 3:15) that He gave to Moses at the burning bush.

> Then Moses said to God, "Behold, I am going to the sons of Israel, and I will say to them, 'The God of your fathers has sent me to you.' Now they may say to me, 'What is His name?' What shall I say to them?" God said to Moses, "I AM WHO I AM"; and He said, "Thus you shall say to the sons of Israel, 'I AM has sent me to you'" (Exod. 3:13-14).

God's name is I AM. Most fundamentally, He is real! God is Jehovah Shammah. He is really there (Ezek. 48:35). Do you have faith? Do you really believe I AM is I AM, that He is real? Do you act on your faith? Do you really believe that God is there and, therefore, seek Him, come to Him, look to Him, set your mind on Him, acknowledge Him, and obey Him?

Superficial faith can lead to idolatry. Faith cannot simply be in faith. Watered-down Christianity can lead to living as a "Christian" but not really believing that God is there and, therefore, acting like He is not. Faith is "seeing real" and then "being real" by responding to what you see. And so, we cry out to God, "'Help my unbelief'" (Mark 9:24). And we pray, "God help me to see!" When we see, we will be changed (1 John 3:2). This is the power of revelation!

SEPTEMBER 17

SOLDIER ON!

*"No soldier in active service entangles himself in the affairs of everyday life,
so that he may please the one who enlisted him as a soldier."*

2 Timothy 2:4

Should I not live a luxurious lifestyle? Perhaps, the answer to that question is not so much, "Why you *should* not," as it is "Why not?" It is more about "alternatives" than "right" and "wrong." The answer does not hinge on what you must or must not do with money. It centers on what you could do with money *instead* of doing something else. Alternatives to living in luxury may include having more money to give, more time to spend with God, and more availability to minister. Another alternative is to live more like a "soldier" who avoids temptations.

Is it peacetime or wartime? Do we still live in a fallen world, or is this Heaven? Are there oppressed poor people around us, or does the world provide for an equitable system of opportunity for its distribution of resources? Should we be living the life of a soldier or the life of a prince? "Suffer hardship with *me,* as a good soldier of Christ Jesus. No soldier in active service entangles himself in the affairs of everyday life, so that he may please the one who enlisted him as a soldier" (2 Tim. 2:3-4). The question of living luxurious lifestyles is not one of right and wrong. It is an issue of opportunity and missed opportunity. It is an issue of alternatives. The soldier could live an easy life. However, it would not be consistent with his work. It would not be consistent with the reasons why he is a soldier. So, he lives a simple life. He is at war. He must not be tempted by worldly things. He must stay "ready for battle."

As soldiers of Christ, we are asked to "suffer hardship" due to the existence of an alternative. The alternative is that we "may please the one who enlisted him as a soldier." Living a simpler lifestyle means that we can give more to those in need. This pleases God. Living a simpler lifestyle means that we can have more time for and concentration on the things of the kingdom of God. We can have more time for God and with God. This pleases God. Living a simpler lifestyle means that we are not entangled in an abundance of worldly things. We separate ourselves from the temptations of riches. This pleases God. It is important to understand that it is not suffering hardship that is sought after. It is the alternative benefit that might come from sacrifice or suffering that is sought after. We do not live simpler lives because it is somehow holy in and of itself. This is a misunderstanding. We live simpler lives because of the alternative benefits it includes.

All of this is not to say that Christians should be lazy and unproductive. Christians who live a simpler lifestyle and understand the correct motives to live a simpler lifestyle should be the most productive people in the world. They are productive at work because of the greater incentive—greater than the incentive of working for yourself—to be able to give to others in need. "He who steals must steal no longer; but rather he must labor, performing with his own hands what is good, so that he will have *something* to share with one who has need" (Eph. 4:28). They are productive with and for God because they have extra time to concentrate on the things of the kingdom. They are productive in life, in general, because they are not weighed down by the cares and temptations of this world.

Jesus' disciples are not referred to as "civilians of Christ." They are pictured as "soldiers of Christ." This picture and its implications are quite challenging but also quite promising.

Nowhere in the universe is there a better model of the worth and workability of God's plan of economy than in the Person of Christ. Jesus was here on business! He would not be deterred or distracted. His face was set. No less are you and I on business here. When you are prepared to be to Jesus, what Jesus was to the Father, Jesus is prepared to be to you, what the Father was to Him.¹⁵

What is the point? Should I live in luxury or not? It is not a matter of "should." It is a matter of "could." Throw off the vanity of the love of riches (Eccl. 5:10) and, instead, put on the wisdom of giving more, spending more time with God, spending more time in ministry, and living more like a soldier so as to better avoid temptations.

SEPTEMBER 18

NOW CONCERNING SPIRITUAL GIFTS

*"Now concerning spiritual **gifts**... to one is given the word of wisdom through the Spirit... and to another the distinguishing of spirits, to another **various** kinds of tongues, and to another the interpretation of tongues."*

1 Corinthians 12:1, 8, 10

The gifts of the Spirit are wondrous things. Not the least of these wonders is the gift of the distinguishing of spirits, the gift of various kinds of tongues, and the gift of the interpretation of tongues (1 Cor. 12:10).

Why is such a gift as the distinguishing of spirits necessary? The most basic answer to this question is that there are a variety of spirits. The distinguishing must occur between human, demonic, angelic, and divine spirits. Sometimes, for example, we engage in spiritual warfare against evil spirits when we should be battling against our flesh. Sometimes, we are laboring to deny and resist our flesh when we should be waging war against the powers of darkness. The distinguishing of spirits is very useful here, since you cannot crucify a demon, and you cannot cast out the flesh. To be successful, you have to be fighting in the right war. Warriors need eyes to see the battlefield rightly.

Now when the attendant of the man of God had risen early and gone out, behold, an army with horses and chariots was circling the city. And his servant said to him, "Alas, my master! What shall we do?" So he answered, "Do not fear, for those who are with us are more than those who are with them." Then Elisha prayed and said, "O LORD, I pray, open his eyes that he may see." And the LORD opened the servant's eyes and he saw; and behold, the mountain was full of horses and chariots of fire all around Elisha (2 Kings 6:15-17).

There was a missionary ministering in Zaire prior to the breakout of a civil war. Each day that he left his house to go to his place of ministry, the violence in the streets grew increasingly dangerous. Daily, he had to leave behind his wife and two small children in order to travel to his ministry locations. He began to ask God if he and his family should leave the country. He did not know if they were safe there. Then, in the middle of the night, he abruptly woke up and sprang up in his bed to an almost tangible sense of peace and tranquility. Sitting across the room on his bedroom dresser were two angels. He prayed, "God, what is this?" God answered, "You have been concerned for the safety of your family. These angels are here to protect you. Moreover, I have hundreds of these encamped around the perimeter of your house. Do not fear."

The use of this gift is certainly seen in the Scriptures (Acts 5:1-3, 13:9-10). For example:
Following after Paul and us, she kept crying out, saying, "These men are bond-servants of the Most High God, who are proclaiming to you the way of salvation." She continued doing this for many days. But Paul was greatly annoyed, and turned and said to the spirit, "I command you in the name of Jesus Christ to come out of her!" And it came out at that very moment (Acts 16:17-18).

Other passages of Scripture show the importance of this gift (1 Tim. 4:1): "Beloved, do not believe every spirit, but test the spirits to see whether they are from God, because many false prophets have gone out into the world" (1 John 4:1).

Another spiritual gift is the gift of various kinds of tongues. Paul says, "Now I wish that you all spoke in tongues" (1 Cor. 14:5). Speaking in tongues is praying with the Spirit. "For if I pray in a tongue, my spirit prays, but my mind is unfruitful. What is *the outcome* then? I will pray with the spirit and I will pray with the mind also" (1 Cor. 14:14-15). Herein, we might speak of having a "prayer language" (Eph. 6:18; Jude 20).

The gift of tongues, when used in the community of believers, should be followed by the gift of the interpretation of tongues. Although tongues are spoken to God, its interpretation (note, it is not a translation) should be addressed to people. Inasmuch as prophecy is referred to as a "greater gift" (1 Cor. 12:31, 14:5), tongues and its interpretation together are also classified this way: "Now I wish that you all spoke in tongues, but even more that you would prophesy; and greater is one who prophesies than one who speaks in tongues, unless he interprets, so that the church may receive edifying" (1 Cor. 14:5).

Of course, as is the case with all gifts, it is critical to use the gifts in a proper and orderly way. "Therefore, my brethren, desire earnestly to prophesy, and do not forbid to speak in tongues. But all things must be done properly and in an orderly manner" (1 Cor. 14:39-40). And so, the gifts must not be forbidden, but they must also not be abused.

SEPTEMBER 19

DISAPPOINTMENT TO SECURITY TO MINISTRY

"And being in agony He was praying very fervently; and His sweat became like drops of blood, falling down upon the ground."

Luke 22:44

When disappointment or heaviness finds security, then ministry is not far off. Another way to say this is, "When things are rough, remember what you know; and then you'll be able to grow and go." Remembering your appointment turns back your disappointment. Disappointment and/or feelings of heaviness are inevitable experiences when living in this fallen world. When we take it to God and rehearse what we know about Him and Who He is in us, the resulting feeling of security enables us to turn our own heaviness into serving and helping others who are also experiencing heaviness. Our own security enables us to serve others who, in turn, can then serve others. This multiplication of life is the fruit of God's sovereignty over death. He does not ignore your heaviness; He uses it. God uses all things for His glory. He turns death into life. This is His way!

"Hope deferred makes the heart sick" (Prov. 13:12). *Dis*appointment comes when your appointment has been "dissed." How do you remedy that heavy situation? You must remind yourself of your appointment. *In*security comes when there is no security. (The Latin word for "in" is a negating prefix). When you gain security, you get rid of the "in," overcome the disappointment, and make the heart healthy instead of sick. That security, even for Jesus, turned disappointment into ministry.

> Then He began to denounce the cities in which most of His miracles were done, because they did not repent. "Woe to you, Chorazin! Woe to you, Bethsaida! For if the miracles had occurred in Tyre and Sidon which occurred in you, they would have repented long ago in sackcloth and ashes." At that time Jesus said, "I praise You, Father, Lord of heaven and earth, that You have hidden these things from *the* wise and intelligent and have revealed them to infants. Yes, Father, for this way was well-pleasing in Your sight. All things have been handed over to Me by My Father; and no one knows the Son except the Father; nor does anyone know the Father except the Son, and anyone to whom the Son wills to reveal *Him*. Come to Me, all who are weary and heavy-laden, and I will give you rest" (Matt. 11:20-21, 25-28).

Jesus' disappointment with the response from the people of Chorazin and Bethsaida is countered with praise, declaring Who God is, and rehearsing what He knows. Praise reminds Him of Who the Father is, and His declaration of God's Sovereignty reminds Him of how God works. Jesus reminds Himself of what He has from the Father, Who He is in the Father, and what He is called to by the Father. The security that comes from His appointment turns back His disappointment, and He is then able to minister to those who are "weary and heavy-laden."

In order to serve others—to get down on your knees and wash others' feet—you have to be secure in what you have, who you are, and where you are going. You have to know what you know, lest you consume yourself with trying to attain that which you do not know. When you are consumed with yourself, you cannot offer yourself to others.

> Now before the Feast of the Passover, Jesus knowing that His hour had come that He would depart out of this world to the Father, having loved His own who were in the world, He loved them to the end. During supper, the devil having already put into the heart of Judas Iscariot, *the son* of Simon, to betray Him, *Jesus*, knowing that the Father had given all things into His hands, and that He had come forth from God and was going back to God, got up from supper, and laid aside His garments; and taking a towel, He girded Himself. Then He poured water into the basin, and began to wash the disciples' feet and to wipe them with the towel with which He was girded (John 13:1-5).

The "heaviness" upon Jesus in those hours just before the Cross is seen very clearly in the Garden of Gethsemane (Luke 22:44). How could He serve others when He was so heavy? He knew what He knew. He knew what He had: that the Father had given Him all things. He knew Who He was: that He came from God. He knew where He was going: that He was returning to God. Security freed Him up to wash feet, to go to the cross, and to multiply service. "'If I then, the Lord and the Teacher, washed your feet, you also ought to wash one another's feet. For I gave you an example that you also should do as I did to you'" (John 13:14-15).

In the midst of your heaviness, ask yourself, "What do I already have in Christ? Who am I in Christ? Where am I going in Christ?" When you know what you know, know what you have, know who you are, and know where you are going, then you do not have to attain or earn those things. The heavy burden is off your shoulders, and you are available to invite others who are "heavy-laden" to "come unto" Jesus. Disappointment leads to security, and security leads to ministry. Turn death into life!

SEPTEMBER 20

AMBASSADORS ARE VESSELS OF TREASURE

"But we have this treasure in earthen vessels."

2 Corinthians 4:7

As Christians, "we are ambassadors for Christ" (2 Cor. 5:20). We do not represent ourselves; we represent Him. We do not live from, through, or to ourselves; "for from Him and through Him and to Him are all things" (Rom. 11:36). As an ambassador, you are not your own; for if you were, then by definition, you would not be an ambassador. This is the essence of the "ambassadorial principle" of Christian ministry. The ambassadorial principle guides Christianity. It defines Christian calling and identity. The Christian life is only understood within its parameters. Attitude, character, walk, and ministry all flow out of its reality.

Christians are God's ambassadors in that they are representatives of *His* kingdom and not their own (John 18:36); and in that, they have been "approved by God to be entrusted with the gospel" (1 Thess. 2:4). Due to the nature of his position, an ambassador must have certain traits—selflessness, submission, obedience, faithfulness, loyalty, and flexibility—so as to "become all things to all men" (1 Cor. 9:22) while remaining in the world but not of it (John 17:11, 13-16). The essence of the "ambassadorial principle" is the idea of being entrusted with someone else's identity, authority, resources, and talents. The one who accepts the ambassadorial assignment acts on and uses that authority on behalf of the provider. The one who rejects it hides the authority for his own purposes.

> For *it is* just like a man *about* to go on a journey, who called his own slaves and entrusted his possessions to them. To one he gave five talents, to another, two, and to another, one, each according to his own ability; and he went on his journey. Immediately the one who had received the five talents went and traded with them, and gained five more talents. In the same manner the one who *had received* the two *talents* gained two more. But he who received the one *talent* went away, and dug *a hole* in the ground and hid his master's money (Matt. 25:14-18).

The theology behind this ambassadorial principle is what might be called "vessel theology." The ambassador is not the contents; he is only the container. He is not the source; he is only the channel through which the source flows, a conduit for power. He is the temple, not the power in the temple, and, therefore, is not his own. "Or do you not know that your body is a temple of the Holy Spirit who is in you, whom you have from God, and that you are not your own?" (1 Cor. 6:19). The vessel is not the Vine; he is only the branch (John 15:5). When he is securely connected to the Vine, "he will be a vessel for honor, sanctified, useful to the Master" (2 Tim. 2:21).

Ambassadors are vessels. They are formed and ordained by the one they are to represent (Psalm 139:14-16). They are the Potter's clay shaped for His purposes (Isa. 64:8). It is the Potter, then, Who provides what the ambassador needs. "But we have this treasure in earthen vessels, so that the surpassing greatness of the power will be of God and not from ourselves" (2 Cor. 4:7). What He commits to the vessel is that which the vessel uses. "He has committed to us the word of reconciliation. Therefore, we are ambassadors for Christ, as though God were making an appeal through us; we beg you on behalf of Christ, be reconciled to God" (2 Cor. 5:19-20).

The work that the vessel does is actually the work of the Vessel-maker (Phil. 2:13). In fact, the Vessel-maker lives in the vessel (Gal. 2:20), and the vessel can do nothing without Him (John 15:5).

What a privilege! What an honor! To be a vessel and an ambassador of Christ is to represent Him in the most intimate of ways. It is to be "one" with Him. "But the one who joins himself to the Lord is one spirit *with Him*" (1 Cor. 6:17). Rejoice, you vessels as it is "Christ in you, the hope of glory" that is the joy of the ambassador (Col. 1:27).

SEPTEMBER 21

THE ABSURDITY OF RACISM

*"When you come together as a church, I hear that divisions exist among you . . .
Therefore when you meet together, it is not to eat the Lord's Supper."*

1 Corinthians 11:18, 20

Although they may be identified by different names, prejudice and discrimination exist as cancers in all societies. It is often called racism in the United States, apartheid in South Africa, the caste system in India, tribalism in much of Africa, denominationalism or sectarianism within religions, gangs in inner cities, teenage cliques in high schools, and economic class systems all over the world. These cancers are absurd, illogical, and destructive—nowhere more so than in the Church of Jesus Christ, for it is the Church that is the carrier of that which can heal this disease. What is it about the Church and its Gospel message that might be said to be the only sure answer and antidote for racism? It is the cross!

The cross is at the heart of the Church's message, the message of the Gospel. Jesus died on the cross to take upon Himself our shame and penalty for sin. He sacrificed Himself to pay for our sin and then told us to take up our own cross daily and follow Him (Luke 9:23). The cross is the answer to racism, since its power destroys its roots: selfishness, pride, and insecurity. Selfishness withers away before the selflessness of the cross. Pride is dug out with the shovel of humility that shines from the cross. Insecurity is turned upside down by the security of the cross. The cross takes away the "fuels" that spark the fires of racism by dousing them with its fire retardants.

To take up your cross is to die to yourself (Matt. 16:24). Selfishness turns you inward, while the cross turns you outward. When we are *consumed* in considering ourselves, we do not make room for considering others. The racist is an inconsiderate person, but taking up the cross allows him or her to take down that inconsideration and be considerate of others. Pride lifts you up and tells you to look down on others. The cross humbles you and insists that you look up to God. We begin to see ourselves rightly, so we stop seeing others wrongly. Insecurity pushes you down and scares you into thinking that you must bring others down with you. The cross lifts you up as it affirms your worth and eternal position in Jesus. This security enables you to not have to try to fabricate your status at the expense of others.

The practice and meaning of the Lord's Supper provides a picture for how and why racism can be abolished (1 Cor. 11:17-34). The Gospel puts us all in the same boat. We "all have sinned" (Rom. 3:23), yet God loves and provides for us all (John 3:16). When we have a mutual understanding that we all have the same problem (we are all burdened with the same predicament) and that we all have the same solution (we are all freed by the same resolution), then we understand that racism is completely and utterly absurd. Its practice is not only wrong, but it is embarrassingly illogical.

Racism, like any form of prejudice and discrimination, is a humanity issue. It is not one group's issue. We are all racists, and we can all be freed from racism in the same way. Herein is how the Lord's Supper paints a picture of its destruction. Since *"all* have sinned" (Rom. 3:23, emphasis mine), then "we *all* partake of the one bread" (1 Cor. 10:17, emphasis mine). Whether we like it or not, we are *all* caught in the same problem and have no choice but to *all* look to the same solution. It is when we admit this that we stop deceiving ourselves into thinking that we are better than others; we climb out of the lie that is racism. Honest humans must proclaim, "I cannot be a racist. It makes no sense."

Within the Church, which is the proclaimer of the Gospel, there should be no racism. The Church should be the model for society. If we all have the same problem and solution, then how can one person be better than the other? We are all on the same level. The cross is the great equalizer. This presents the Church in the United States with an obvious challenge. What are we going to do about the possibility that the most segregated time of the week is Sunday morning? Church leaders must become more intentional about reversing this possibility; for just as the Church is the salt of the earth (Matt. 5:13), so, too, does judgment begin in the house of God (1 Peter 4:17).

> Therefore whoever eats the bread or drinks the cup of the Lord in an unworthy manner, shall be guilty of the body and the blood of the Lord. But a man must examine himself, and in so doing he is to eat of the bread and drink of the cup. For he who eats and drinks, eats and drinks judgment to himself if he does not judge the body rightly (1 Cor. 11:27-29).

Within society, the Church—the proclaimer of the Gospel and the salt and light of the world—must abhor racism and lead the charge to dissolve it. Christians, by definition, should not be racists. Even if some people have not yet received the "common solution" of the Gospel, all people still have the "common problem." A racist Christian is an oxymoron, since that person denies his or her own doctrine and beliefs by implicitly declaring, "I do not have the problem, so I do not need the solution." This denial of the Gospel is a denial of the faith! This presents the Church with an obvious challenge. What are we going to do about our witness and testimony with regard to racism? Christians must search their hearts and repent when necessary, and church leaders must teach on this topic.

Yes, racism is destructive, illogical, and absurd. If I am somebody today, and I spray paint myself another color tonight, then am I somebody else tomorrow? Racism's pervasiveness in society highlights the need for healing. What is the medicine? It is the cross, the message of the Gospel!

SEPTEMBER 22

SEE YOUR BROTHER THROUGH YOUR FATHER

> *"If, however, you are fulfilling the royal law according to the Scripture,*
> *'YOU SHALL LOVE YOUR NEIGHBOR AS YOURSELF,'*
> *you are doing well. But if you show partiality, you are committing sin."*
>
> James 2:8-9

In order to be a spiritual people, we must know that we need God and His abilities. We need to properly relate to God. Beyond this, we must know that in order to properly relate to others, we must first properly relate to God. The quality of our spirituality with others depends on the quality of our spirituality with God. For a domino at the end of the line to fall, the dominos in the front of the line must first fall. If I want to have strong relationships with others, I must first have a strong relationship with God. If I want to be a better family member of the body of Christ, I must first be a better child of God.

Fellowship with others is based on fellowship with God. This is true because it is God Who loves others through us. It is no longer I who relate properly to others, but Christ who relates properly to others through me (Gal. 2:20). John clearly made this connection when he told his readers "that you too may have fellowship with us; and indeed our fellowship is with the Father, and with His Son Jesus Christ" (1 John 1:3). In his gospel, John argues that to abide in Christ (John 15:1-11) is a prerequisite to loving others (John 15:12-17).

The two "greatest commandments" follow this same progression as "love God" precedes "love others" (Matt. 22:37-39). Jesus' high priestly prayer requests this flow for His disciples as "keep them in Thy name" paves the way for "they may be one" (John 17:11). Jesus closes out His prayer proclaiming "I in them," which leads to "they may be perfected in unity" (John 17:23).

To a large degree, how you treat others is determined by the security and health of your relationship with God. When you struggle in your relationship with God, you will also tend to struggle in your relationship with others. The quality of your fellowship with others depends upon the degree to which you understand that your relationship with God is a shared relationship. We all have a common problem and a common solution. "Is not the cup of blessing which we bless a sharing in the blood of Christ? Is not the bread which we break a sharing in the body of Christ? Since there is one bread, we who are many are one body; for we all partake of the one bread" (1 Cor. 10:16-17).

Relationship with God is based on the understanding that my need for Him is only satisfied by His provision for me. Relationship with others is based on the understanding that everyone is in the same boat. I treat my neighbor as myself because I understand that I am no better or worse than my neighbor. And so, for example, prejudice and discrimination should be anathema in the church (1 Cor. 11:27-29). We are not to show favoritism to one person over another, based on *worldly* criteria. We are to treat others as we would want to be treated based on our common *spiritual* status (James 2:1-9).

Your commitment to fellowship with others in the body of Christ depends on the degree to which you are committed to your relationship with God. Christian fellowship must be based on, motivated by, and developed within a mutual loyalty to God. You must see your brother through your Father. You must see your Father rightly to see your brother rightly. Fellowship is spiritual!

SEPTEMBER 23

GIFTS FOR ALL

"But to each one is given the manifestation of the Spirit for the common good."
1 Corinthians 12:7

It seems that gift-giving, by its very nature, is usually an individualistic exercise. One person gives a gift to another person. Spiritual gifts are quite different. Gifts of the Holy Spirit are given "for the common good" (1 Cor. 12:7). They are to be used for the good of the community of believers. Although a gift may be manifested through an individual and can be directed toward an individual, its ultimate purpose is to benefit the whole community.

The gifts of the Holy Spirit enable believers to minister effectively one to another. They are given for the building up or edification of the body of Christ. Paul instructs one of the members of the Corinthian church, "Since you are zealous of spiritual *gifts*, seek to abound for the edification of the church" (1 Cor. 14:12). He tells others who spend their time in that pneumatic community to "let all things be done for edification" (1 Cor. 14:26). He then offers an entire discourse on the use of the gifts that has as its entire focus an appeal to use them for the benefit of everyone in the church (1 Cor. 14:4-19). For Paul, the focus is not so much on the gifts themselves as it is on the edification of the body of Christ.

The gifts of the Holy Spirit edify the whole community in two ways: all receive from the gifts (1 Cor. 14:4-5, 12), and all are used in the manifestation of the gifts—"to *each one* is given" (1 Cor. 12:7, emphasis mine). Paul's vision is that each member of the community should be involved. Each member should participate, not just the leaders or the "extra spiritual" ones. This vision points to the importance of small group meetings. There needs to be the larger, more public temple church meetings as well as the smaller, more private and intimate house church meetings, where it may be more likely that everyone would be able to participate. The members of the New Testament church organized themselves in this way as they were "continuing with one mind in the temple, and breaking bread from house to house" (Acts 2:46).

This exhaustive nature of the use of the gifts assumes that all hold a certain amount of responsibility with respect to the manifestation of the gifts. A member must not suppress a gift when the Holy Spirit leads and prompts him or her to manifest it. All members are responsible, and all members are necessary; "for the body is not one member, but many" (1 Cor. 12:14). So, too, all gifts are necessary. Thus, we should not despise any gifts. And so, Paul warns, "Do not quench the Spirit; do not despise prophetic utterances" (1 Thess. 5:19-20).

Since each one is *given* the manifestation of the Spirit, it is not valid that anyone should boast with respect to being used in the gifts. "For who regards you as superior? What do you have that you did not receive? And if you did receive it, why do you boast as if you had not received it?" (1 Cor. 4:7). Pride has no place in the use of the gifts of the Holy Spirit. People who are perceived as being "more gifted" or gifted in the "greater gifts" should not be shown any more respect than anyone else. A true and pure response to the operation of the gifts of the Spirit should place man in the background and leave God up front to be the only one who can be glorified. The gifts may be for all, but all the glory must go to Him!

SEPTEMBER 24

THE MANDATE, MESSAGE, METHOD, AND MOTOR

"They are not of the world ... I also have sent them into the world."

John 17:16, 18

The Bible gives us the mandate, message, method, and motor for world evangelization. The mandate is clear: "Go!" (Matt. 28:19). There is a reason it is called the Great Commission or the Great Mandate. It is God's mandate to His people that, if followed, will fill God's ultimate mold to mold people into the image of Christ (Rom. 8:29).

The Bible gives us the message for world evangelization. This message is called the Gospel or the Good News. Its contents do not change; however, the ways to present the Gospel can change. Methods change (contextualization), while contents remain the same (biblical dogma). It is important, but sometimes difficult, to maintain a balance between these two aspects of evangelization. The method of presentation may depend on the culture and specific needs of the listeners, while the content is not dependent on any factor.

Extremes (lack of balance) in each aspect of evangelization must be avoided. Too much emphasis on contextualization without consideration of biblical dogma, for example, can result in utilitarian approaches, new gospels, or syncretism. The missionary may find himself smoking a peace pipe, getting drunk on moonshine, or sleeping with the chief's daughter in order to gain an opportunity to preach the Gospel. Remember, the end does not necessarily justify the means. In these cases, there is just not enough insistence on biblical dogma. Similarly, too much emphasis on biblical dogma without consideration of contextualization can result in being impractical or irrelevant while attempting to impose your own cultural Gospel. The Western missionary, for example, may find himself insisting on presenting a prosperity gospel message to people living in the third world. Youth workers may insist on still using organs to lead their high school worship services. In these cases, there is just not enough contextualization.

Contextualization is the process of planting the Gospel within a different culture. It is very important to understand that the Gospel is not North American or European. The Gospel transcends culture. We must adapt the presentation of the Gospel to specific cultures. We must "become all things to all men" (1 Cor. 9:22), while at the same time, we must avoid preaching "a different gospel" (Gal. 1:6-9). We must avoid the utilitarian temptation to contextualize to such a degree that the content of the message is sacrificed. At the same time, we must avoid the pride that can lead us to be so inflexible with our dogma that our Gospel presentation is perceived as impractical and irrelevant. The balance in evangelism is found in the balance between contextualization and dogma (sound doctrine). The method changes, but the contents stay the same.

The Bible gives us the model or example' for world evangelization. It is found in the Incarnation—that is, in God becoming man. In the Incarnation, there is identification without the loss of identity. Jesus was completely Man and completely God. In His humanity, He identified with us. In His divinity, He did not lose His identity. Identification means that to reach a people, we must relate to them. We must have compassion for them. We must, if necessary, suffer with them and be willing to walk in their shoes. For those who share the Gospel with others, no loss of identity means that we must live our lives as Christians. In identifying with lost people, we cannot lose our Christian standards and values. Balance means that we must become one of them without losing who we are.

This is very similar to the balance between contextualization and biblical dogma. We must be flexible while remaining true to ourselves. We must be in the world but not of the world (John 17:14-18). If we maintain this balance, then we will be able to present Jesus Christ as the true Stumbling Block, the Barrier that must be dealt with for someone to come to salvation. However, if we do not identify with our listeners, then they may not accept the Gospel because they may not accept us. In this case, we become the stumbling block instead of Jesus. On the other hand, if we identify with the people to the extent of losing our Christian identity, then we may never be able to present Jesus as the true stumbling block because we have lost credibility. In this case, we are the stumbling block again because the messenger is seen as being inconsistent with the message.

The Bible gives us the *motor* for world evangelization. There is *power*. There is both authoritative power (*exousia*, as in Matthew 28:18) and dynamic power (*dunamis*, as in Acts 1:8 and Romans 1:16). The one who shares the Gospel with others does not do so in his or her own power. No, there is a definite motor under the evangelistic hood:

- "All *authority* has been given to Me in heaven and on earth. Go therefore and make disciples of all the nations" (Matt. 28:18-19, emphasis mine).
- "But you will receive *power* when the Holy Spirit has come upon you; and you shall be My witnesses both in Jerusalem, and in all Judea and Samaria, and even to the remotest part of the earth" (Acts 1:8, emphasis mine).
- "For I am not ashamed of the gospel, for it is the *power* of God for salvation to everyone who believes, to the Jew first and also to the Greek" (Rom. 1:16, emphasis mine).

SEPTEMBER 25

THE CHALLENGES OF LIVING IN THE KINGDOM

"You have heard that it was said ... but I say to you."

Matthew 5:27-28

The Sermon on the Mount stands as the most comprehensive single message that Jesus preached. It is a discourse on the kingdom of God. The introduction is made up of a series of principles called "beatitudes" (blessings) that describe the character of those who live in the kingdom. Once that is established, Jesus moves on to explain the kingdom standards that are set for kingdom-dwellers, including standards for hatred, adultery, divorce, vows, retribution, and love (Matt. 5:21-48).

Jesus knew the hypocritical and deceptive heart of man. Therefore, He avoided playing with words, beating around the bush, or allowing for any confusion about His message. He was direct and very clear. Jesus always went right to the root of the matter. He refused to let people hide behind their masks. He had ways of exposing the otherwise-hidden underlying issues. So, when He set the kingdom standards, He did not set them based on outward acts. He set each standard according to its inward reality.

It is one thing to commit the act of adultery. That is an outward act. It is another thing to lust after a woman in your *heart*. That is the *internal* reality. "'You have heard that it was said, YOU SHALL NOT COMMIT ADULTERY; but I say to you that everyone who looks at a woman with lust for her has already committed adultery with her in his heart'" (Matt. 5:27-28). Even if the act is not committed, the standard is broken if the heart is guilty. Jesus set each kingdom standard deep down inside a man's soul and therefore did not allow for hypocrisy to pass as righteousness.

The action of the incarnation sets the kingdom standards. The moment that God laid down His rights in order to become a man (Phil. 2:7), the standards of living were radically changed. The children cannot claim a higher privilege than the parent. Children of God cannot cling to their rights when their God did not cling to His.

Especially with respect to the standard for retribution (Matt. 5:38-42), it must be understood that Jesus was talking about laying down your rights. He was speaking about dying to yourself. He was not talking about allowing others to harm your family while you stand back and watch. He was talking about laying down your rights for the sake of others. He challenged us to surrender ourselves in order to show love, kindness, patience, and mercy. It is not just the act of selflessness. It is the purpose for it and the result of it.

> You have heard that it was said, "AN EYE FOR AN EYE, AND A TOOTH FOR A TOOTH." But I say to you, do not resist an evil person; but whoever slaps you on your right cheek, turn the other to him also. If anyone wants to sue you and take your shirt, let him have your coat also. Whoever forces you to go one mile, go with him two. Give to him who asks of you, and do not turn away from him who wants to borrow from you (Matt. 5:38-42).

What is actually surrendered? What rights are laid down? A slap in the face is an insult. Jesus is challenging kingdom-dwellers to be willing to surrender their "rights" to their reputations. Having a "coat" was considered an inalienable right (Exod. 22:26). Jesus is saying, "Are you willing to lay down your most basic fundamental rights?" Go two miles when someone is already forcing you to go one?

That cuts across the grain of my sense of fairness and justice. Jesus says, "Can you lay down your right to fairness for the sake of the kingdom?" This is very challenging!

> Does any one of you, when he has a case against his neighbor, dare to go to law before the unrighteous and not before the saints? Or do you not know that the saints will judge the world? If the world is judged by you, are you not competent *to constitute* the smallest law courts? Do you not know that we will judge angels? How much more matters of this life? So if you have law courts dealing with matters of this life, do you appoint them as judges who are of no account in the church? I say *this* to your shame. *Is it so, that* there is not among you one wise man who will be able to decide between his brethren, but brother goes to law with brother, and that before unbelievers? Actually, then, it is already a defeat for you, that you have lawsuits with one another. Why not rather be wronged? Why not rather be defrauded? On the contrary, you yourselves wrong and defraud. *You do* this even to *your* brethren (1 Cor. 6:1-8).

Perhaps the most difficult challenge of all is to surrender your right to say no to those in need. This brings up all kinds of questions. "'Am I my brother's keeper?'" (Gen. 4:9). "'Who is my neighbor?'" (Luke 10:29). How do I know if someone is really in need? Jesus says, "Give to him who asks of you." He says, "You are your brother's keeper." He says, "Your neighbor is anyone who is in need." He says, "Follow me. Give. Do the action of love. Live in the kingdom." Selflessness is most famously described, "Greater love has no one than this, that one lay down his life for his friends" (John 15:13). No wonder the King of the kingdom challenges kingdom-dwellers to lay down their right to not give. The kingdom is a kingdom of crosses. Jesus says, "Get on your cross!" "Then Jesus said to His disciples, 'If anyone wishes to come after Me, he must deny himself, and take up his cross and follow Me. For whoever wishes to save his life will lose it; but whoever loses his life for My sake will find it'" (Matt. 16:24-25).

SEPTEMBER 26

THE KINGDOM ALREADY, THE KINGDOM NOT YET

> *If Satan casts out Satan, he is divided against himself; how then will his kingdom stand . . .*
> *But if I cast out demons by the Spirit of God, then the kingdom of God has come upon you."*
> Matthew 12:26, 28

Jesus says, "The kingdom of God has come upon you." It is "at hand" (Matt. 10:7) or "in your midst" (Luke 17:21). The kingdom of God has already come (Matt. 6:10), yet it has not yet come:

> When the hour had come, He reclined *at the table,* and the apostles with Him. And He said to them, "I have earnestly desired to eat this Passover with you before I suffer; for I say to you, I shall never again eat it until it is fulfilled in the kingdom of God." And when He had taken a cup *and* given thanks, He said, "Take this and share it among yourselves; for I say to you, I will not drink of the fruit of the vine from now on until the kingdom of God comes" (Luke 22:14-18).

The kingdom is already and not yet. It has already come in Christ, but it has not yet come in its fullness. For those who live in the "kingdom already"—the rule of God through the victory of Christ in the power of the Holy Spirit—the obvious question is, "When will the 'kingdom not yet' come?" The Bible is very clear on this matter. Of course, "of that day and hour no one knows" (Matt. 24:36); nevertheless, there will be signs that will point to the return of Jesus and the consummation of His kingdom.

When will the kingdom come? "'This gospel of the kingdom shall be preached in the whole world as a testimony to all the nations, and then the end will come'" (Matt. 24:14). It is the kingdom already that will usher in the kingdom not yet. The kingdom will come in its fullness after the Good News of that kingdom is proclaimed to all the nations.

This is great news for those who live in the *kingdom now* and yearn for the *kingdom to come*. Kingdom-dwellers have the resources at their disposal now to move into their future kingdom dwelling. The resource is the Good News of the kingdom. It must be preached to all people. Good news implies that there is bad news, just as the source and bearer of good news implies that there is a source and bearer of bad news. The source of the Good News is God. The source of the bad news is Satan. These two sources rule two different kingdoms and war against each other. The fact that the "kingdom of God already" is victorious over the kingdom of Satan assures that the "kingdom of God not yet" will come. "'But if I cast out demons by the finger of God, then the kingdom of God has come upon you'" (Luke 11:20). It is this power that is available to kingdom-dwellers that equips them to preach the Gospel to all nations so that, then, the end will come. "But you will receive power when the Holy Spirit has come upon you; and you shall be My witnesses both in Jerusalem, and in all Judea and Samaria, and even to the remotest part of the earth" (Acts 1:8).

What does all of this mean for me and you? Well, if our first desire is for the kingdom of God (Matt. 6:33), then we will do everything possible to complete the requirement for the kingdom to come in its fullness. The requirement is to preach the Gospel to all the nations. Thus, missions must be a priority for every Christian. Some people will witness in their Jerusalem, others in their Judea and Samaria, and some to the nations. Some will help financially, while others will help by praying.

What is the main purpose of living in a kingdom that has not yet arrived in its fullness? It is to live in a way that will help usher in that kingdom. We know God so that we can make God known. This has been God's strategy since the enacting of the Abrahamic covenant (Gen. 12:1-3). The kingdom that is "already" exists in order to move to the kingdom that is "not yet."

So, let's move! Let's pray, "'Your kingdom come'" (Matt. 6:10). Let's be "looking for and hastening the coming of the day of God" (2 Peter 3:12). Let's go! (Matt. 28:19).

SEPTEMBER 27

IT'S A BIT UNCOMFORTABLE

"Therefore we do not lose heart, but though our outer man is decaying,
yet our inner man is being renewed day by day. For momentary,
light affliction is producing for us an eternal weight of glory far beyond all comparison."
2 Corinthians 4:16-17

Can you imagine how it would feel to throw your staff down at someone's feet and see it turn into a snake (Exod. 7:9-10)? How awesome would you feel to tell someone that when you strike the river with your staff, it is going to turn to blood (Exod. 7:15-17)? You strike the dust of the earth, and it becomes gnats (Exod. 8:16). You lift up your staff and "thunder and hail, and fire ran down to the earth" (Exod. 9:23). Then you bring upon your enemy frogs, lice, pestilence, wild animals, boils, locusts, darkness, and finally, death. As if that is not enough, then you casually walk up to a huge body of water, stretch out your hands, and part the sea (Exod. 14:21). This is all well and good, but there is a big problem. Pride and self-reliance could easily overtake you.

It is difficult to imagine how Moses could *not* have become prideful. He needed some immediate help. God brought him into a situation at Rephidim that pressed him to consider his own inadequacy. In the midst of almost being stoned to death (Exod. 17:4), Moses was reminded of his total dependence upon God. He grew in humility as he saw how much he needed God. Moses came to the end of himself and arrived at the beginning of God.

God humbled and tested the Israelites by making them a little uncomfortable and allowing them to suffer hardship so that they might learn to trust in Him (Deut. 8:16). "He humbled you and let you be hungry, and fed you with manna which you did not know, nor did your fathers know, that He might make you understand that man does not live by bread alone, but man lives by everything that proceeds out of the mouth of the LORD" (Deut. 8:3). The entire process of wandering in the wilderness and being completely helpless produced humility in the Israelites. It included suffering. Suffering and humility often go together. The meaning of the Hebrew word *anav* (translated as "humility" in Numbers 12:3) includes both ideas. Suffering produces humility.

Sometimes, we complain about uncomfortable and hard times in our lives, yet these experiences may be necessary for us to learn to depend on God. Whether this is viewed as a "good" or "bad" thing depends on our perspective. If we have an "eternal" perspective (Col. 3:2), then what is "bad" can be seen as "good." We can rejoice in our sufferings (Col. 1:24). We may not rejoice *for* it, but we can rejoice *in* it (1 Thess. 5:16-18). If we have a temporal perspective, then it can be "bad," even though it is "good."

> Therefore we do not lose heart, but though our outer man is decaying, yet our inner man is being renewed day by day. For momentary, light affliction is producing for us an eternal weight of glory far beyond all comparison, while we look not at the things which are seen, but at the things which are not seen; for the things which are seen are temporal, but the things which are not seen are eternal (2 Cor. 4:16-18).

Suffering is a teacher. We should not want to suffer or make ourselves suffer. Nevertheless, suffering is inevitable. "Indeed, all who desire to live godly in Christ Jesus will be persecuted" (2 Tim. 3:12). It is not a question of whether or not you will ever be uncomfortable or go through hard times or suffer. It is a question of what will be done with that suffering. "And not only this, but we also exult in our tribulations, knowing that tribulation brings about perseverance; and perseverance, proven character; and proven character, hope" (Rom. 5:3-4). Having an eternal attitude allows us to say, "Consider it all joy, my brethren, when you encounter various trials, knowing that the testing of your faith produces endurance. And let endurance have *its* perfect result, so that you may be perfect and complete, lacking in nothing" (James 1:2-4).

Of course, having this eternal attitude is easier said than done. The trick is to look ahead. Jesus, "who for the joy set before Him endured the cross" (Heb. 12:2), is our example. We are people who are looking for another kingdom. "'Blessed are those who have been persecuted for the sake of righteousness, for theirs is the kingdom of heaven'" (Matt. 5:10). When life gets a bit uncomfortable (and it will), "'lift up your heads, because your redemption is drawing near'" (Luke 21:28). Look beyond suffering by looking up and looking ahead. He is always there!

SEPTEMBER 28

WHAT ARE YOU DOING WITH YOUR BLESSINGS?

"'From everyone who has been given much, much will be required; and to whom they entrusted much, of him they will ask all the more.'"

Luke 12:48

After the tower of Babel fiasco in Genesis 11, God began to work His plan *through* chosen instruments. We might call this vessel theology. Since the nations were now spread out, He chose a missionary nation through which He could reach them. Enter Abraham and the nation of Israel. Israel was selected as a missionary nation. Israel was not selected in order to exclude others. Rather, Israel was selected in order to include others—hence, the term "missionary nation." And so, we can understand the Old Testament better when we study it from three different viewpoints: Israel's opportunity, Israel's obligation, and Israel's response.

The Abrahamic covenant is a missionary covenant. Through it, Israel is promised the resources, ability, and blessings to be a blessing to all the families of the earth (Gen. 12:3). Israel received great authority and opportunity, in that sense, but it came with great responsibility or obligation. "Now the LORD said to Abram, 'Go forth from your country, and from your relatives and from your father's house, to the land which I will show you; and I will make you a great nation, and I will bless you, and make your name great'" (Gen. 12:1-2). Just as there are three separate statements of being blessed, there are three separate statements of being a blessing: you shall be a blessing; those who bless/curse you shall be blessed/cursed; and in you all the families of the earth will be blessed (Gen. 12:3).

God does not expect us to do what He does not equip us to do (Matt. 25:15; 1 Cor. 10:13). God did not expect Israel to be able to bless the nations unless He first blessed them. In other words, God provided the opportunity to keep the obligation. For example, the location of Israel attracted many people. It was a fertile land. Moreover, it was located in the center of three continents. It was a strategic crossroads of the world. God said that He would make Israel a great nation. This *greatness* gave Israel the opportunity to keep their obligation.

The location of Israel also served as an obvious strategic location from which to send out missionaries. Without much effort, Israel could go out to many areas and many peoples. And so, throughout the Old Testament, we see messengers who are "sent" to other nations to be a blessing. For example, Joseph went to Egypt; Daniel went to Babylon; Esther went to Persia; Jonah went to Nineveh; and many "oracles" went to the nations as seen in the prophetic books.

The knowledge of God was Israel's greatest blessing. "But as for me, the nearness of God is my good; I have made the Lord GOD my refuge, that I may tell of all Your works" (Psalm 73:28). Israel had an obligation to bring that knowledge to others. Holding the message meant that they were required to distribute it. Israel was blessed with the message of salvation: "He has told you, O man, what is good; and what does the LORD require of you but to do justice, to love kindness, and to walk humbly with your God?" (Micah 6:8). Israel had an intimate knowledge of God and, thus, a profound obligation to share that knowledge (Exod. 3:13-14).

Do you have an opportunity? Then you have an obligation. Do you have more privileges than others? Then you have more responsibilities. In fact, "freely you received, freely give" (Matt. 10:8); and "from everyone who has been given much, much will be required; and to whom they entrusted much, of him they will ask all the more" (Luke 12:48). What are you doing with your blessings?

SEPTEMBER 29

CAPITALISTIC SHARING

"And all those who had believed were together and had all things in common."

Acts 2:44

The Bible does not advocate socialism or communism. In many ways, the Scripture promotes and respects the correlation between individual authority and responsibility that is the backbone of capitalistic and democratic philosophies. Even when Scripture seemingly depicts the sort of "sameness" mentality that is the hallmark of such philosophies as socialism and communism, it only does it in the context of freedom. Sharing with others who do not have as much as you is not communism if it is done via your own free decision; it is Holy Spirit-empowered *koinonia* (fellowship or sharing).

Everyone kept feeling a sense of awe; and many wonders and signs were taking place through the apostles. And all those who had believed were together and had all things in common; and they *began* selling their property and possessions and were sharing them with all, as anyone might have need. Day by day continuing with one mind in the temple, and breaking bread from house to house, they were taking their meals together with gladness and sincerity of heart, praising God and having favor with all the people (Acts 2:43-47).

Even in incredible cases when people were selling their property in order to share with others, the capitalistic foundation of individual ownership was not condemned or negated. It was, in fact, validated and respected.

For there was not a needy person among them, for all who were owners of land or houses would sell them and bring the proceeds of the sales and lay them at the apostles' feet, and they would be distributed to each as any had need ... But a man named Ananias, with his wife Sapphira, sold a piece of property, and kept back *some* of the price for himself, with his wife's full knowledge, and bringing a portion of it, he laid it at the apostles' feet. But Peter said, "Ananias, why has Satan filled your heart to lie to the Holy Spirit and to keep back *some* of the price of the land? While it remained *unsold*, did it not remain your own? And after it was sold, was it not under your control?" (Acts 4:34-5:4).

Various Old Testament directives to the people of Israel were designed to promote the sharing of resources. The charging of interest was forbidden (Exod. 22:25). The taking of clothing as a loan pledge was negated (Exod. 22:26). Bribery was condemned (Exod. 23:8). Every seventh year, slaves were to be released (Exod. 21:2). The institution of the sabbatical year (Deut. 15:7-11), the year of Jubilee (Lev. 25), and the dividing of the land (Num. 26:52-56) all served to promote more of a sharing of resources and less of a hoarding of excess resources. In any case, the emphasis in Scripture is not the defense of any particular form of government but the encouragement of mercy, justice, generosity, faithfulness, sharing, and giving (Matt. 23:23). This proposed giving is to reflect God. He provides for our needs. God invites us to voluntarily engage in this business of meeting needs as well.

Now, brethren, we *wish to* make known to you the grace of God which has been given in the churches of Macedonia, that in a great ordeal of affliction their abundance of joy and their deep poverty overflowed in the wealth of their liberality. For I testify that according to their ability, and beyond their ability, *they gave* of their own accord, begging us with much urging for the favor of participation in the support of the saints . . . But just as you abound in everything, in faith and utterance and knowledge and in all earnestness and in the love we inspired in you, *see* that you abound in this gracious work also . . . For if the readiness is present, it is acceptable according to what *a person* has, not according to what he does not have. For *this* is not for the ease of others *and* for your affliction, but by way of equality—at this present time your abundance *being a supply* for their need, so that their abundance also may become *a supply* for your need, that there may be equality; as it is written, "HE WHO *gathered* MUCH DID NOT HAVE TOO MUCH, AND HE WHO *gathered* LITTLE HAD NO LACK" (2 Cor. 8:1-15).

SEPTEMBER 30

MAKE THE MOST OF YOUR TIME WITH GOD!

"For no man can lay a foundation other than the one which is laid, which is Jesus Christ."
1 Corinthians 3:11

The Scripture commands us to make "the most of our time" (Eph. 5:16). How can we do that? We must be sure to spend it on things that count. In the end, the things that will not burn are the things that were built on the foundation of Christ. These things will "count." And so, the best way to make the most of your time is to spend time with Jesus.

According to the grace of God which was given to me, like a wise master builder I laid a foundation, and another is building on it. But each man must be careful how he builds on it. For no man can lay a foundation other than the one which is laid, which is Jesus Christ. Now if any man builds on the foundation with gold, silver, precious stones, wood, hay, straw, each man's work will become evident; for the day will show it because it is *to be* revealed with fire, and the fire itself will test the quality of each man's work. If any man's work which he has built on it remains, he will receive a reward. If any man's work is burned up, he will suffer loss; but he himself will be saved, yet so as through fire (1 Cor. 3:10-15).

Sometimes, we may feel like we just do not have enough time for God; too many things to do, places to go, people to see. Comparatively, God is everywhere at all times (Psalm 139:7-12). He is in Russian prayer meetings at the same time He's protecting people in China. Yet as many places as God resides, His greatest desire is to be with you where you are right now. We too often say to God, "I am not able to be with You now." He says, "'I am with you always'" (Matt. 28:20). God's delight is to spend time with you. "For I delight in loyalty rather than sacrifice, and in the knowledge of God rather than burnt offerings" (Hosea 6:6). Our reasonable and spiritual response (Rom. 12:1) should be, "Come, let us worship and bow down, let us kneel before the LORD our Maker. For He is our God" (Psalm 95:6-7).

What is your favorite thing to do? What is God's favorite thing to do? The incredible Creator Who holds all things together, Who is everywhere at one time and at all times, and Whose purposes and methods are critical and complex, delights in spending time with us. God delights in us knowing Him; "the prayer of the upright is His delight" (Prov. 15:8). Certainly, we must be humbled by this reality. We must respond to God and spend time with Him. "For the earth will be full of the knowledge of the LORD as the waters cover the sea" (Isa. 11:9).

The way to a stronger relationship with God is that our revelation of God's desire for us "increases." When we see more of God's desire for us, we are drawn to Him more; we are changed. "We know that when He appears, we will be like Him, because we will see Him just as He is. And everyone who has this hope fixed on Him purifies himself, just as He is pure" (1 John 3:2). Redeem the time by making the most of your time. Spend time with Jesus!

NOTES

October

OCTOBER 1

I CAN'T—HE CAN—I CAN!

"Blessed are the poor in spirit, for theirs is the kingdom of heaven."

Matthew 5:3

Why are the poor blessed? "Blessed *are* you *who are* poor" (Luke 6:20). Are they blessed simply because they do not have much money? No, the beatitude is not referring to *material* poverty; it is speaking of *spiritual* poverty. You can be spiritually poor whether you have five dollars in your bank account or five million dollars. Those who are poor in spirit—who empty themselves of self—give of themselves and receive the kingdom of God via putting self-reliance on the cross, and thus, bear the fruit of faithfulness.

Blessings are free. Like salvation, you cannot earn them (Eph. 2:8-10). That does not mean, however, that they are not costly. They are costly because we try to hang onto that which is not our own (1 Cor. 6:19-20). The beatitude (blessing) includes a challenge or an obligation. It is quite a challenge; but in order to say "hello" to Jesus, you have to say "goodbye" to yourself. To be poor in spirit is to be empty of yourself—you reach in your pocket, and there is no "money." It is to confess your spiritual bankruptcy—you go to the bank, and there are no "funds." It is the opposite of being self-sufficient—you walk down the street, and you humble yourself to accept money from a stranger. Spiritual poverty confesses complete spiritual need—you come to the end of yourself and beg on a corner, no more self-reliance.

This does not mean that you become lazy and irresponsible. It does mean that you realize and admit your all-inclusive need. It is then that you bear fruit.

> Abide in Me, and I in you. As the branch cannot bear fruit of itself unless it abides in the vine, so neither *can* you unless you abide in Me. I am the vine, you are the branches; he who abides in Me and I in him, he bears much fruit, for apart from Me you can do nothing. If anyone does not abide in Me, he is thrown away as a branch and dries up; and they gather them, and cast them into the fire and they are burned. If you abide in Me, and My words abide in you, ask whatever you wish, and it will be done for you. My Father is glorified by this, that you bear much fruit, and so prove to be My disciples. Just as the Father has loved Me, I have also loved you; abide in My love. If you keep My commandments, you will abide in My love; just as I have kept My Father's commandments and abide in His love. These things I have spoken to you so that My joy may be in you, and *that* your joy may be made full (John 15:4-11).

Letting go of self-reliance and receiving the kingdom of God (Matt. 5:3) is a *joyful* thing (Rom. 14:17). It is often associated with *sadness* because we often do not realize the reality of our helplessness until we are thrust into disastrous situations, when we find ourselves in situations that are clearly out of our control. Someone in the eye of a Category 5 hurricane has no trouble feeling helpless!

Admitting your helplessness—so as to accept Jesus' help—is not easy. It seems so costly. It costs us our pride. Jesus helps us with this stumbling block. Jesus is not only our Helper; He is also our Example. "Therefore Jesus answered and was saying to them, 'Truly, truly, I say to you, the Son can do nothing of Himself, unless *it is* something He sees the Father doing; for whatever the Father does, these things the Son also does in like manner'" (John 5:19).

Jesus would later say to the Father, "'Not My will, but Yours be done'" (Luke 22:42). When you lay down the noose of self-reliance, you are more inclined to pick up the mantle of obedience. You obey who you rely on.

And so, the fruit of the Spirit that corresponds to this beatitude is "faithfulness" (Gal. 5:22). A person who just got fired from his job leaves the office, saying, "Now I don't have to do what you say, since I do not rely on your salary anymore." Pharaoh "left the office," saying, "'Who is the LORD that I should obey His voice to let Israel go? I do not know the LORD'" (Exod. 5:2). Self-reliance must be nailed to the cross for beatitudes to be released.

The nature of the kingdom of God—relative to the kingdoms of this world—is backward. Each beatitude in the Sermon on the Mount, therefore, is cloaked in irony. "'Blessed are the poor in spirit, for theirs is the kingdom of heaven'" (Matt. 5:3) equals "You must confess that you are not able to do anything without Jesus; then you will become able to do all things through Jesus. Irony can be very powerful!"

OCTOBER 2

THE POWER OF SIGHT

"We know that when He appears, we will be like Him, because we will see Him just as He is."

1 John 3:2

The Gospel is often described as "the Good News." For there to be good news, there must have been bad news. The Gospel is Good News because there *is* bad news. It is bad news that *necessities* good news. God so desperately provides (which is the good news) because we so desperately need (which is the bad news). Our bad news (our sin) necessitates God's good news (His payment for that sin).

To take part in the Good News, we must first *see* our bad news. It all starts with our need, but there is no need unless we see it. And we cannot see it unless God reveals it to us. Jesus says, "'No one can come to Me unless the Father who sent Me draws him'" (John 6:44). And so, to receive any aspect of the Good News, we must first have the bad news revealed to us by God. This is called "conviction." Jesus says of the Holy Spirit, "'And He, when He comes, will convict the world concerning sin'" (John 16:8). I see my need for God. I receive His provision. I am able to offer His provision to others. This is the Gospel. This is the proclamation and multiplication of the Gospel.

I cannot proclaim or give what I have not received. I cannot receive what I do not need. I do not need what I do not see that I need. I do not see what I need unless my need for it is revealed to me. This is the Gospel. The bad news turns into good news because God reveals the bad news to people who need the good news. God exposes sin and then pays for it Himself—with Himself! God addresses man's fall into death with His own rise from death. This is the Good News!

It all ends with God. He is proclaimed. It all begins with God. He convicts. There is an incredible power in conviction and its response of confession. It is confession that leads to seeing; and seeing leads to receiving; and receiving leads to giving and, thus, multiplying. *"It is more blessed to give than it is to receive"* (Acts 20:35), but you have to confess before you can arrive at the "more blessed." Confession triggers all of it; it is the "key to the kingdom" (Matt. 16:13-19). It is as powerful as the fact that the blind will *see* (John 9:39-41), the poor will *see* the kingdom of God (Matt. 5:3), the pure will *see* God (Matt. 5:8), and the weak will *see* strength (2 Cor. 12:10). The key that is confession yields powerful results, and it all starts with revelation: "'Blessed are you, Simon Barjona, because flesh and blood did not reveal *this* to you, but My Father who is in heaven'" (Matt. 16:17).

What do we see? Do we see ourselves in need of God? When we do, then we pray. When we do not, then we do not seek Him. Do we see our sin? When we do, then we happily accept His righteousness. When we do not, then we stubbornly claim self-righteousness. Do we see our need for salvation? When we do, then we repent and trust in His grace. When we do not, then we unapologetically trust in our own works.

Seeing is powerful. Paul understood this, so He prayed for the Ephesians that they would "be able to comprehend with all the saints what is the breadth and length and height and depth, and to know the love of Christ which surpasses knowledge" (Eph. 3:18-19). He prayed this because he understood another principle: "We love, because He first loved us" (1 John 4:19). If this is true, then how can we love more? God has to love us more. Can God love us more? No, His love is perfect and "surpasses knowledge." If God's love cannot increase, then what can increase? Our revelation of His love for us can increase. Paul prays for the Ephesians that they would be able to see more of God's love. Seeing is believing because seeing is receiving and receiving is giving—or, in this example, receiving is loving. We love because He loves. So, when you see more of His love, you will love more. Seeing is powerful.

The ultimate power in our lives is revelation because that is where it all starts for someone who is blind. Revelation is life! The ultimate life transformation will come with the ultimate revelation—the revelation of Jesus Christ. "Beloved, now we are children of God, and it has not appeared as yet what we will be. We know that when He appears, we will be like Him, because we will see Him just as He is" (1 John 3:2). Perfect seeing yields perfect transformation. Seeing is powerful!

OCTOBER 3

THAT WAS A REALLY "DUM" THING TO SAY

*"So also the tongue is a small part of the body, and **yet** it boasts of great things. See how great a forest is set aflame by such a small fire!"*

James 3:5

Sometimes, we disappoint ourselves with regard to how we speak to others. We might respond, "That was a really *dumb* thing to say!" We try to be wise with our words, but sometimes, we are "dum." Three unwise styles of speech make up this *dum* style: "d" is the *d*estructive style, "u" is the *u*ndisciplined style, "m" is the *m*anipulative style. Although each one of us may be more prone to one of these styles than the other two, we all need to avoid all three and replace them with a wise style of speech. This is how we will become better "speakers."

The first *dum* style of speech is the *d*estructive style. This is the treacherous, hostile, and violent way. Like the manipulative style, its goal is to destroy. However, instead of being deceptive, it is brutally direct. "With *his* mouth the godless man destroys his neighbor" (Prov. 11:9).

The treacherous speaker is harsh and rude. "There is one who speaks rashly like the thrusts of a sword" (Prov. 12:18). These words do hurt! "A worthless man digs up evil, while his words are like scorching fire" (Prov. 16:27). When the destructive speaker is more withdrawn as a "whisperer," it is only for the purpose of fueling a fire and feeding strife. "For lack of wood the fire goes out, and where there is no whisperer, contention quiets down" (Prov. 26:20). The tongue has the potential to be a very negative part of the body. "So also the tongue is a small part of the body, and *yet* it boasts of great things. See how great a forest is set aflame by such a small fire! And the tongue is a fire, the *very* world of iniquity; the tongue is set among our members as that which defiles the entire body, and sets on fire the course of *our* life, and is set on fire by hell" (James 3:5-6).

The fiery tongue dabbles in boasting, which can be destructive, since "*like* clouds and wind without rain, is a man who boasts of his gifts falsely" (Prov. 25:14). The lying tongue, in its motivation, is destructive. "A lying tongue hates those it crushes" (Prov. 26:28). Lies are in direct opposition to truth; they are the enemy of God. "Lying lips are an abomination to the LORD" (Prov. 12:22).

The fiery tongue establishes itself as a false witness: "*like* a club and a sword and a sharp arrow is a man who bears false witness against his neighbor" (Prov. 25:18). Similarly, where there is gossip (Prov. 11:13), there is danger. "He who goes about as a slanderer reveals secrets, therefore do not associate with a gossip" (Prov. 20:19).

The destructive tendency of a "backbiter" is associated with anger. "The north wind brings forth rain, and a backbiting tongue, an angry countenance" (Prov. 25:23). Behind the scenes, the deceptive nature of a "flatterer" is destructive (Prov. 29:5). "A lying tongue hates those it crushes, and a flattering mouth works ruin" (Prov. 26:28). The superficiality of flattery yields emptiness. "He who rebukes a man will afterward find *more* favor Than he who flatters with the tongue" (Prov. 28:23).

The wise way is the opposite of the destructive way. The destructive style is a violent, harsh, and hostile style. The wise style is a gentle style. A wise man speaks with a "cool spirit" (Prov. 17:27), giving him time to listen (Prov. 18:13) and allowing tempers to cool when necessary (Prov. 15:1). Destructive, harsh speech is ineffective and impotent while wise, gentle speech is effective and powerful. "By forbearance a ruler may be persuaded, and a soft tongue breaks the bone" (Prov. 25:15). The wise style of speech serves to edify (Prov. 12:25) and to heal. The opposite of destruction is construction: "the tongue of the wise brings healing" (Prov. 12:18). "My son, give attention to my words; incline your ear to my sayings. Do not let them depart from your sight; keep them in the midst of your heart. For they are life to those who find them and health to all their body" (Prov. 4:20-22). Based on personality, experience, and relational orientation, you might be prone to using more of a destructive style of speech than an undisciplined or manipulative style. Being aware of this is half the battle. You must try to be more attentive to your words. You must make it a habit to ask yourself some challenging questions. Am I using words to edify and to heal? Are my intentions to hurt or to help? Do I often fall to the temptation of speaking poorly of another person? Do my words hurt other people? Should I be more patient with others? Can I be gentler in my approach? Am I being wise with my words?

Of course, we can only hope to gain in wisdom through the power of the Holy Spirit. Ask God to help you to not be so *dum* with your words. "God, I ask you to help me to replace *d*estructive words with wise words. Amen."

OCTOBER 4

CHANNELS FOR GOD TO FLOW THROUGH

"I am the vine, you are the branches; he who abides in Me and I in him, he bears much fruit, for apart from Me you can do nothing."

John 15:5

The attitude of someone who adheres to vessel theology comes from the understanding that "every good thing given and every perfect gift is from above, coming down from the Father of lights" (James 1:17). Anything good must come from God. This attitude results in a yearning for God; a hunger for righteousness, and a sense of reliance upon grace to experience that righteousness.

The idea of "means of grace" is implicit to vessel theology. If Good (God) is going to flow through me (a vessel), then there must be a way for that flow to be enacted. The means of grace are those biblical actions that facilitate God's activity in a person's life. They are used by God as instruments of His grace. Often, these "means" are called "spiritual disciplines" and include such activities as prayer, Bible study, fellowship, worship, and fasting.

The essence of biblical fasting is the idea that there would be a willful denial of an otherwise normal function (eating food) for the sake of fervent spiritual activity. This definition is preferred, since it recognizes the idea of self-denial as a necessary dynamic of fasting and focuses on the existence of a spiritual purpose without which fasting loses its divinely intended meaning.

Fasting, as with other means of grace, can make way for a variety of acts of grace that are imparted to the vessel-receiver. Not the least of these acts is Divine guidance.

> Now there were at Antioch, in the church that was there, prophets and teachers: Barnabas, and Simeon who was called Niger, and Lucius of Cyrene, and Manaen who had been brought up with Herod the tetrarch, and Saul. While they were ministering to the Lord and fasting, the Holy Spirit said, "Set apart for Me Barnabas and Saul for the work to which I have called them." Then, when they had fasted and prayed and laid their hands on them, they sent them away (Acts 13:1-3).

Somehow, the fasting experience seems to have provided a context in which guidance from the Holy Spirit was communicated. Whether we are more comfortable with saying, "God spoke" or "God illumined" is neither here nor there. The point is that He clearly provided guidance. This is not to say that guidance cannot come from means other than fasting or that fasting is an automatic guarantee for guidance, but it is to say that fasting—or any other biblical means of grace—seems to put us into a position to receive from God more readily. Another way to understand this spiritual dynamic is to say that "those who fast are placing themselves in a situation through which the Holy Spirit has an easier access to them."

There is nothing good (Psalm 14:3) in fallen man by which he can make himself more godly. Only God can make a person godlier. He must be our Perfecter (Heb. 12:2) because only He is perfect (1 John 3:5). It is this combination of truths—our total depravity and His singular perfection—that require divinely appointed means of grace to be that which serves to prepare the way for God in our lives. "Abide in Me, and I in you. As the branch cannot bear fruit of itself unless it abides in the vine, so neither *can* you unless you abide in Me. I am the vine, you are the branches; he who abides in Me and I in him, he bears much fruit, for apart from Me you can do nothing" (John 15:4-5).

OCTOBER 5

GIFTS OF THE SPIRIT: DIVINE AND HUMAN ACTIVITY

"And they were all filled with the Holy Spirit and began to speak with other tongues, as the Spirit was giving them utterance."

Acts 2:4

The gifts of the Holy Spirit are extraordinary. They are extra (beyond ordinary) yet, at the same time, they are ordinary; they include both Divine and human activity. The extra ordinary works through the ordinary. It is a God thing that is also a man thing. These activities are sourced in God and received by man. They are *gifts* of the *Holy Spirit.*

The gifts of the Spirit are manifestations of God Himself. In this sense, they are supernatural. They are extraordinary. The gifts of the Spirit are not simply an advanced expression of a person's natural talents or trained abilities. They are not simply the working of the Spirit that causes a person's talents and abilities to be more effective. No, the gifts of the Spirit are distributed by the Spirit "just as He wills" (1 Cor. 12:11). Thus, the Spirit can operate in a person regardless of his or her talents, natural abilities, or experience. The use of the gifts does not depend on education and training. Being filled with the Holy Spirit, for example, is linked to speaking with boldness (Acts 4:31). That same Spirit-generated speaking with boldness is then linked to "uneducated and untrained men" (Acts 4:13).

Having established the fact that the use of the gifts of the Holy Spirit requires Divine activity, it should also be acknowledged that the use of the gifts requires human activity as well. According to 1 Corinthians 12:7, "To each one is given the manifestation of the Spirit." It is a person who is the recipient. It is the person who acts. It is the person through whom the gift operates.

This concept of God activity mixed with human activity mirrors the same paradoxical dynamic that has been argued among theologians for centuries: is God sovereign or does man have a free will? The very structure of this question, however, reveals its misunderstanding. It is not an "either/or" issue; rather, it is a "both/and" dynamic. God is Sovereign. He is the Divine Source. Man has a free will. He is the human receiver. We sometimes get this wrong because we try to put each trait in the wrong realm; for example, we try to put man's free will in the realm of source and God's sovereignty in the realm of receiver.

To understand the paradox is to understand the nature of both God and man—what God is and is not and what man is and is not. God does not receive, and man does not source. God sources, and man receives. God is Sovereign, and man has a free will. Man's free will cannot be placed in the realm of the source. Man cannot will himself to be or do anything he determines. He is not a source; thus, his free will cannot be applied to or explained by that realm. He is a receiver; thus, his free will must be applied in *that* realm. He has a free will to receive or not receive. In that sense, man's question is, "To receive or not to receive?"

Similarly, God's sovereignty cannot be placed in the realm of the receiver. God is not limited by what he receives or by what others do. He is not a receiver; thus, His Sovereignty cannot be applied to or explained by that realm. He is the Source; thus, His sovereignty must be applied in *that* realm. He is Sovereign to create or not create, to cause or not cause, to control or not control. In that sense, God's question is, "To source or not to source?"

Perhaps, this "both/and" dynamic is best seen in John 1:12-13: "But as many as received Him, to them He gave the right to become children of God, *even* to those who believe in His name, who were born, not of blood nor of the will of the flesh nor of the will of man, but of God." Man has a free will, *and* God is Sovereign. Man has a free will to "receive Him" without canceling out the Sovereignty of God. He is not born "of the will of man, but of God." Similarly, God is Sovereign to source people with "the right to become children of God" without canceling out the free will of man; it is to "as many as received . . . even to those who believe."

And so, Divine activity can, and does, mix with human activity. The gifts of the Holy Spirit are both God-sourced and man-received. So, for example, in Acts 2:4, we see that it was those who were filled with the Holy Spirit who "began to speak with other tongues," while it was the Spirit who "was giving them utterance." The Spirit did not do the speaking. People spoke. The Spirit gave the speaker the words to speak. The Spirit gave them utterance.

Of course, when Divine activity mixes with human activity, there is room for error. Thus, the perfect gift can result in an imperfect use of that gift. Spiritual activity can be wrapped up in false manifestations. Someone can be "led astray" and possibly say "Jesus is accursed" (1 Cor. 12:2-3). How can the Christian community know if a manifestation is from the Holy Spirit or from some other source? First, a manifestation of the Spirit will glorify Jesus since the Spirit Himself glorifies the Lord (John 16:14). Second, a manifestation of the Spirit will be consistent with the Word of God, since the Spirit is the Author of the Scripture and will not contradict Himself (2 Peter 1:20, 2 Timothy 3:16). Third, a manifestation of the Spirit will be confirmed in the spirits of believers, since it is the Spirit Who lives in them (1 Cor. 14:29).

That there exists the possibility for error when Divine activity mixes with human activity should in no way deter God's people from desiring and expecting to engage in such activity (1 Cor. 12:31). To be sure, it is God's Sovereign choice to work this way. To reject the mixing is to reject the Mixer. So, by all means, expect to be mixed and to mix!

OCTOBER 6

FAITH CAN REALLY COME IN HANDY

"For indeed we have had good news preached to us, just as they also; but the word they heard did not profit them, because it was not united by faith in those who heard."

Hebrews 4:2

Do you have faith? What do you use your faith for? In general, the Christian uses his or her faith to *live*. "For I am not ashamed of the gospel, for it is the power of God for salvation to everyone who believes, to the Jew first and also to the Greek. For in it *the* righteousness of God is revealed from faith to faith; as it is written, 'BUT THE RIGHTEOUS *man* SHALL LIVE BY FAITH'" (Rom. 1:16-17).

Faith is used to live. More specifically, it is used to *maintain* and *overcome*. Prayer and faith go hand in hand. Unbelieving prayer is an oxymoron. "'And all things you ask in prayer, believing, you will receive'" (Matt. 21:22). Christians are in a spiritual war against the powers of darkness, the flesh, and the world. Faith is used as a weapon in this spiritual war. "But since we are of *the* day, let us be sober, having put on the breastplate of faith and love, and as a helmet, the hope of salvation" (1 Thess. 5:8). Christians are called to "fight the good fight" using their faith. "This command I entrust to you, Timothy, *my* son, in accordance with the prophecies previously made concerning you, that by them you fight the good fight, keeping faith and a good conscience, which some have rejected and suffered shipwreck in regard to their faith" (1 Tim. 1:18-19).

Since the war is real, our faith must be real. It must be used to turn back the advance of the evil one: "In addition to all, taking up the shield of faith with which you will be able to extinguish all the flaming arrows of the evil *one*" (Eph. 6:16).

Our faith must be used to fight against the flesh as we "draw near with a sincere heart in full assurance of faith, having our hearts sprinkled *clean* from an evil conscience and our bodies washed with pure water" (Heb. 10:22). Christians are called to overcome the world by their faith. "I have written to you, young men, because you are strong, and the word of God abides in you, and you have overcome the evil one. Do not love the world nor the things in the world" (1 John 2:14-15). By faith, Christians are victorious: "For whatever is born of God overcomes the world; and this is the victory that has overcome the world—our faith" (1 John 5:4).

Faith is used to *maintain* and *overcome*. It is used to *live*. It is even used to *die*. Faith is that which allows Christians to look at death differently than others. Death is not the end that is dreaded; it is the beginning that is welcomed.

> All these died in faith, without receiving the promises, but having seen them and having welcomed them from a distance, and having confessed that they were strangers and exiles on the earth. For those who say such things make it clear that they are seeking a country of their own. And indeed if they had been thinking of that *country* from which they went out, they would have had opportunity to return. But as it is, they desire a better *country*, that is, a heavenly one. Therefore God is not ashamed to be called their God; for He has prepared a city for them (Heb. 11:13-16).

What could be more important than pleasing your Father in Heaven? The only way to please God is by faith. "And without faith it is impossible to please *Him*, for he who comes to God must believe that He is and *that* He is a rewarder of those who seek Him" (Heb. 11:6). Faith enables us to walk in relationship with God and to seek Him. That is what pleases God. Faith is used for many things, but the most important use of faith is to please God!

OCTOBER 7

IS "GOOD" EVEN A POSSIBILITY FOR US?

"There is no one who does good, not even one . . . no one is good except God alone."
Psalm 14:3; Mark 10:18

Can sinful man be ethical or good in terms of the biblical understanding of the term "good?" The answer is an emphatic NO! Sinful man can in no way be good by his own doing. Paul explains it this way: "For I know that nothing good dwells in me, that is, in my flesh; for the willing is present in me, but the doing of the good *is* not" (Rom. 7:18).

A born-again nature provided by Jesus Christ is a prerequisite to Christian ethics. This is true because it is actually the new nature in man that does good, not the old nature. More specifically, it is Christ in us doing good, not us in us doing good. Christ's fulfillment of the Law had extenuating circumstances for us. We can now ask Christ into our hearts and, by faith, experience Christ accomplishing the Law through us.

Jesus clearly calls us to do the Law (Matt. 5:17-20). The immediate context of this passage supports the conclusion that the only way for us to be law-abiding heavenly citizens is for Jesus to abide in us (John 15:4-5). "'Let your light shine in such a way that they may see your good works, and glorify your Father who is in heaven'" (Matthew 5:16). Jesus is the Light (John 8:12). The Son glorifies the Father (John 17:1). Our good works are found in Christ (Eph. 2:10).

The Law has not changed, but the doer of the Law has changed. We are mere flesh, but God is Spirit. The flesh no longer strives hopelessly to do the Law. Now, it is the Spirit Who does it. That is what has changed!

> For what the Law could not do, weak as it was through the flesh, God *did*: sending His own Son in the likeness of sinful flesh and *as an offering* for sin, He condemned sin in the flesh, so that the requirement of the Law might be fulfilled in us, who do not walk according to the flesh but according to the Spirit. For those who are according to the flesh set their minds on the things of the flesh, but those who are according to the Spirit, the things of

the Spirit. For the mind set on the flesh is death, but the mind set on the Spirit is life and peace, because the mind set on the flesh is hostile toward God; for it does not subject itself to the law of God, for it is not even able *to do so,* and those who are in the flesh cannot please God. However, you are not in the flesh but in the Spirit, if indeed the Spirit of God dwells in you. But if anyone does not have the Spirit of Christ, he does not belong to Him. If Christ is in you, though the body is dead because of sin, yet the spirit is alive because of righteousness. But if the Spirit of Him who raised Jesus from the dead dwells in you, He who raised Christ Jesus from the dead will also give life to your mortal bodies through His Spirit who dwells in you (Rom. 8:3-11).

Certainly, we should understand Christ's obedience to the Law in terms of His accomplishing atonement for us; but we should also understand it in terms of our own sanctification, holiness, and ethical ability. The Holy Spirit causes the believer to grow in likeness and obedience to Christ. He does this "until Christ is formed in you" (Gal. 4:19).

At first glance, the picture does not look good for man. The Scripture is clear. There is no one who is good, and "'no one is good except God alone'" (Mark 10:18). When we catch another glimpse, however, it becomes clear that *goodness* is achievable—not because we climbed up to Heaven but because God lowered Himself down to us. In so doing, He interacts with us and steps into our shoes. His goodness fills our steps, as the only One Who is good continues to be good in us (Gal. 2:20).

OCTOBER 8

RICHES: BE CAREFUL!

"But those who want to get rich fall into temptation . . . the love of money is a root of all sorts of evil . . . flee from these things, you man of God."

1 Timothy 6:9-11

Are money and possessions inherently evil? No, it is the love of money that is evil (1 Tim. 6:10). Unfortunately, many Christians answer the question correctly but then make the wrong application. They try to justify having an excessive amount of money and possessions that go way beyond their needs, as if there is no danger in riches.

Christians who live a lifestyle of excessive luxury and waste take a fresh and honest look at how their view of riches might be affecting their walk with God. The Bible does not say that money and possessions are inherently evil. However, it repeatedly refers to our fallen nature (Psalm 51:5), so it warns against the temptations associated with the desire for riches. "But those who want to get rich fall into temptation and a snare and many foolish and harmful desires which plunge men into ruin and destruction" (1 Tim. 6:9).

Possessions and riches can hinder people from coming to God. Jesus explained, "'It is hard for a rich man to enter the kingdom of heaven. Again I say to you, it is easier for a camel to go through the eye of a needle, than for a rich man to enter the kingdom of God'" (Matt. 19:23-24). In an almost shocking way, Jesus repeatedly instructs people to sell their possessions (Luke 12:33, 14:33). "'If you wish to be complete, go *and* sell your possessions and give to *the* poor, and you will have treasure in heaven; and come, follow Me'" (Matt. 19:21). A materialistic mentality to life is definitely not encouraged.

The definition of materialism, however, is not come by easily. It is a complicated discussion. For example, the call to give does not negate the responsibility to take care of your own obligations. "But if anyone does not provide for his own, and especially for those of his household, he has denied the faith and is worse than an unbeliever" (1 Tim. 5:8). There is a balance in the discussion regarding how much we should give versus how much we should keep. Both luxurious living in excessive waste and living in poverty are not recommended. Each has its own pitfalls. "Keep deception and lies far from me, give me neither poverty nor riches; feed me with the food that is my portion, that I not be full and deny *You* and say, 'Who is the LORD?' Or that I not be in want and steal and profane the name of my God" (Prov. 30:8-9).

At the very least, materialistic Christians must begin to recognize and respond to the New Testament emphasis on the danger of riches and the emphasis to avoid them. The disease of materialism can be debilitating.

> But those who want to get rich fall into temptation and a snare and many foolish and harmful desires which plunge men into ruin and destruction. For the love of money is a root of all sorts of evil, and some by longing for it have wandered away from the faith and pierced themselves with many griefs. But flee from these things, you man of God (1 Tim. 6:9-11).

OCTOBER 9

WHICH ROMANS 12 GIFT DO YOU HAVE?

"Since we have gifts that differ according to the grace given to us,
each of us is to exercise them accordingly..."

Romans 12:6

God equips His people with gifts for ministry. There exist various lists of gifts in the New Testament. One such list is found in Romans 12:6-8:

> Since we have gifts that differ according to the grace given to us, *each of us is to exercise them accordingly*: if prophecy, according to the proportion of his faith; if service, in his serving; or he who teaches, in his teaching; or he who exhorts, in his exhortation; he who gives, with liberality; he who leads, with diligence; he who shows mercy, with cheerfulness.

These gifts are often called "motivational gifts" or "inclinational gifts" because they form people's tendencies, unction, emphases, inclinations, and personalities. They establish a default mode in terms of how someone, almost automatically, thinks and then tends to act. They even could be said to be undercurrents that shape a person's personality and what they are like in their interactions with others.

Each member of the body of Christ has at least one gift. The following descriptions of someone's tendencies may help to determine what gift that person might have (of the last four gifts in the list only). Of course, the descriptions cannot give you the gift—only God does that—but they can indicate or confirm your gift(s). Read each paragraph and consider to what degree you resonate with that description and to what degree those statements tend to describe you. If reading the paragraph makes you say, "Yes, that seems like me," then perhaps you have that gift.

The Gift of Exhortation

I am able to get others to think positively about life. I have a strong desire to see others excel in what they do. I am able to prompt vision in others. I am consistently involved in giving others counsel and advice. I view life in a positive way and am oriented toward making progress. I am more concerned about the application of the truth than the research of the truth. I tend to urge people toward growth and progress in their lives. I tend to be an optimist, looking at the bright side of situations. I have the ability to discern a person's level of spiritual growth and encourage them toward the next level. I have a strong desire to promote unity among Christians.

The Gift of Giving

I feel a sense of great fulfillment when I am able to give in order to meet the physical needs of people. I am motivated to consume less of myself in order to give more to others. I am deeply concerned that what I give financially is used effectively and efficiently. Along with my own personal giving, I enjoy encouraging others to give. I am pulled toward meeting physical needs of others. I look for ways in which I can make a difference through financial giving. I tend to give beyond my tithe. I tend to be aware of the physical needs of others before most people. I am bothered by high-pressure, emotional appeals for money. I tend to be involved in projects that require material resources to be completed.

The Gift of Leading

I will initiate action in a group when it is needed, even if I am not the official person in charge. I am able to organize groups of people and am comfortable initiating activities. I have the ability to receive vision from God and communicate it to others. I am able to effectively match needs with resources. I am motivated and able to delegate responsibilities to others in an effective way. I am a very goal-oriented person. I tend to be impatient with those who lack ability to accomplish the task at hand. I am comfortable in offering guidance to others before most people. I tend to be one people follow more than one who follows others. I am willing and able to take charge of situations.

The Gift of Showing Mercy

I am very sensitive to the pain of others. I often feel deep compassion for other people and their problems. I am not firm or direct with others, unless it will clearly help them to avoid more problems. I do not like to argue with people. I have a great desire to defend those who are oppressed. I am more concerned about the needs and feelings of people than accomplishing tasks. I am often too easy on others who need to be confronted and challenged. I am fulfilled in ministries that involve comforting and caring for others. I desire to minister to those who are neglected by others. I enjoy visiting people in hospitals, prisons, and nursing homes.

Do you have the gift of exhortation, giving, leading, or showing mercy? Perhaps you have one of them, or perhaps you have two or three. Perhaps you have none of those gifts, but you might have the gift of prophecy, service, or teaching. In any case, the most important thing is that we use our gifts(s) and, even more, that we use our gifts to glorify God. May God be glorified in who He made us to be!

OCTOBER 10

CURSES BECOME BLESSINGS SO OTHERS ARE BLESSED

*"It will come about that just as you were a curse among the nations,
O house of Judah and house of Israel, so I will save you that you may become a blessing."*

Zechariah 8:13

After the tower of Babel fiasco in Genesis 11, God began to work His plan through chosen instruments. Since the nations were now spread out, He chose a missionary nation through which He could reach them. Israel was selected to be that missionary nation. Israel was not selected in order to exclude others but, rather, to *include* others.

God greatly blessed Israel so that Israel could greatly bless "all the families of the earth" (Gen. 12:2-3). They were blessed with knowing God in order to make God known to others. They had an *opportunity*, but that came with an *obligation*. This, of course, would warrant a response, be it positive or negative. Israel's response was not positive. God blessed them, but they rebelled and practiced idolatry. This led to them becoming a bad witness to the peoples around them. And so, they did not fulfill their obligation.

God allowed them to have a king. That resulted in more idolatry. Finally, the kingdom was divided (1 Kings 11:1-13). Israel did not respond to the mercy of God or His discipline (Jer. 3:1-14). Nevertheless, God would restore a remnant (Ezek. 20:30-38). Israel responded in idolatry, rebellion, and ethnic selfishness. She resisted her obligation to be a witness to the nations. This was exemplified very clearly and specifically in the case of Jonah, who refused to go to Nineveh to bring them God's Word. Thus, God "helped" Jonah to obey the mandate to go to the nations by using a whale. If the chosen vessels of God do not obey the missions mandate voluntarily, then they will complete their obligation involuntarily.

Israel's tainted witness—due to her disobedience, idolatry, and apathy—was beginning to have a significant negative effect on God's mission plan. They were not being a blessing. Therefore, they stopped being blessed and became an involuntary blessing. This was manifested in the form of two exiles. The ten tribes that made up the Northern Kingdom were exiled to Assyria in 722 B.C. The two tribes that made up the Southern Kingdom were exiled to Babylon in 587 B.C. It is from the remnant—those who survived and remained faithful—that God began to activate His missionary plan again. In exile, the Jews spread the Word of God throughout Babylon and Persia. Then, later, they spread the word of God in Greece and Rome as emigrating Jews settled in different places (they had no country until 1948).

In summary, God chose to work His mission plan through a vessel (Israel). A covenant was made. God would bless them so that they could bless others. In this way, the nations could have a witness of God and His salvation message. The witness would be given, in word and deed, by an obedient Israel. God blessed Israel; however, Israel did not use those blessings to be a blessing to other nations. God withdrew the blessings, which resulted in exile. Thus, the mission plan of God through Israel continued involuntarily. "It will come about that just as you were a curse among the nations, O house of Judah and house of Israel, so I will save you that you may become a blessing" (Zech. 8:13).

This, of course, is history. Yet history remains as current events. The principles are still the same, and the principles now apply to me and you. Here is the ancient "principle": if it be given to you, then you must give, lest it be taken away from you. There is an obligation because there is an opportunity.

Greater opportunity requires greater obligation. Obligation fulfilled yields opportunity retained and, even more, opportunity given. What have you been given by God? What do you, then, give to others? The following verses show us what to do with what we have been given:

- "'Give, and it will be given to you. They will pour into your lap a good measure—pressed down, shaken together, *and* running over. For by your standard of measure it will be measured to you in return'" (Luke 6:38).
- "You ask and do not receive, because you ask with wrong motives, so that you may spend *it* on your pleasures" (James 4:3).
- "'Therefore take away the talent from him, and give it to the one who has the ten talents. For to everyone who has, *more* shall be given, and he will have an abundance; but from the one who does not have, even what he does have shall be taken away'" (Matt. 25:28-29).

OCTOBER 11

LET'S GET REAL

> "'I AM WHO I AM . . . you shall say to the sons of Israel, I AM has sent me to you.'"
>
> Exodus 3:14

What is the most fundamental aspect of the nature of God? What one name would you use if someone who knew nothing said to you, "Who is your God? What is His name?" Who is it that you are going to say sent you?

> Then Moses said to God, "Behold, I am going to the sons of Israel, and I will say to them, 'The God of your fathers has sent me to you.' Now they may say to me, 'What is His name?' What shall I say to them?" God said to Moses, "I AM WHO I AM"; and He said, "Thus you shall say to the sons of Israel, 'I AM has sent me to you'" (Exod. 3:13-14).

God's name is "YHWH" or "I AM." Most fundamentally, He is real! God is "Jehovah Shammah" or "The LORD is there" (Ezek. 48:35). Do you have faith? Do you really believe I AM is I AM? Do you act on your faith? Do you really believe that God is there and, therefore, seek Him, come to Him, look to Him, set your mind on Him, acknowledge Him, and obey Him? Let's get real!

Do we really believe? Do we really have faith? Do we really want to please God? "And without faith it is impossible to please *Him*, for he who comes to God must believe that He is and *that* He is a rewarder of those who seek Him" (Heb. 11:6). The essence of faith is to believe that God is actually there. The challenge of faith is that you come to Him and seek Him and respond to the reality of His "thereness."

We respond to what we believe to be real. Philosophers call this "worldview." Out of your worldview (what you see as real) comes your beliefs; and out of your beliefs come your values; and out of your values come your actions. The essence of faith corresponds to your worldview, and the challenge of faith corresponds to your actions. Do you really think God is real? If you do, then you will acknowledge Him and look to Him. You will engage in relationship with Him. This is the challenge of faith. When there is no faith, there is no acting on that faith. When God is not real, then we respond to Him as if He is not even there.

If God is real, then what kinds of responses to Him should we naturally have? "Trust in the LORD with all your heart and do not lean on your own understanding. In all your ways acknowledge Him, and He will make your paths straight" (Prov. 3:5-6). If He is real and always there, then trust Him, look to Him, and acknowledge Him in all your ways. "Rejoice always; pray without ceasing; in everything give thanks; for this is God's will for you in Christ Jesus" (1 Thess. 5:16-18).

It is because God is there that we turn from sin. Would you really do what you did or say what you said if you really thought the holy God of the universe was standing right there watching you? "'Repent, for the kingdom of heaven is at hand'" (Matt. 4:17). This literally means that God is "in your midst" or "right there." The question is not so much whether we believe enough to do the right thing. The question is whether we really believe that "God is" (YHWH) and that He is there (Jehovah Shamah). When we believe He is "at hand," then we repent; we turn to Him. This is faith. It is turning to Him, coming to Him, seeking Him, acknowledging Him, setting our minds on Him (Col. 3:2), talking to Him, and being in relationship with Him (Hosea 6:3). Faith is knowing God!

Revival comes when we apply this truth. When we believe God is there and act like He is there, we are revived. We are transformed when we see Him (1 John 3:2). "You will seek *Me* and find Me when you seek Me with all your heart" (Jer. 29:13).

God, reveal Yourself to us that we would know that You are really there. God, stir in us to seek You, since you are really there. God, may You be pleased!

OCTOBER 12

SOMETIMES SILENCE IS GOLDEN— IT CAN PAY OFF!

"Give attention that you may gain understanding."

Proverbs 4:1

Sometimes, silence is golden. It can be a very valuable commodity in the arena of a multitude of words. It can display wisdom in two ways: in what we do not say and in what we listen to. Shutting your mouth is often the wisest thing you can do. Job appeals to his friends to embrace this sort of wisdom when he pleads, "'O that you would be completely silent, and that it would become your wisdom!'" (Job 13:5). Silence can protect us from ourselves and others. "I will guard my ways that I may not sin with my tongue; I will guard my mouth as with a muzzle while the wicked are in my presence. I was mute and silent" (Psalm 39:1-2). Sometimes, the wisest thing we can say is *nothing*. "Even a fool, when he keeps silent, is considered wise" (Prov. 17:28). We might call this the irony of wise silence!

Just as silence can display wisdom in what we do not do, it can also display wisdom in what we do. Silence displays wisdom in what we listen to. The less we say, the more we can listen. The more we listen, the more we can learn. We are exhorted to "be quick to hear, slow to speak" (James 1:19). It is not, of course, that we never speak. It is just that there is "a time to be silent and a time to speak" (Eccl. 3:7). You cannot consider wise speech until you consider wise listening, for then you can "give attention that you may gain understanding" (Prov. 4:1). Paying attention pays off!

Listening is the function that should consume more of our time in the process of communication. We do have twice as many ears as mouths! An ear is inextricably linked to a mouth. The mouth needs the ear to hear it, and the ear needs the mouth to speak to it. "My son, give attention to my words; incline your ear to my sayings" (Prov. 4:20). If silence is golden, listening is like diamonds! "Heed instruction and be wise, and do not neglect *it*" (Prov. 8:33). It is wise to listen. "The way of a fool is right in his own eyes, but a wise man is he who listens to counsel" (Prov. 12:15).

Listening is not simply the passive side of communication. It is active. Listening must be selective. "He whose ear listens to the life-giving reproof will dwell among the wise" (Prov. 15:31). It is just as wise to *not* listen to words that kill and destroy. The wise, active listener selects what to listen to and then must be receptive to it, for only "if you will receive my words and treasure my commandments within you" will you benefit from it (Prov. 2:1). In order to get the "payoff," you have to pay attention: "My son, give attention to my wisdom, incline your ear to my understanding" (Prov. 5:1). Ultimately, the words of the wise must be followed and held onto. "Now then, *my* sons, listen to me and do not depart from the words of my mouth" (Prov. 5:7).

It is a challenge. It is so much easier to be lazy with our mouths and ears, to say whatever we want whenever we want and to be an inactive listener. It is hard work to discipline our mouths and our ears, but it is worth it. It pays off!

OCTOBER 13

WHAT ELSE CAN I DO WITH MY MONEY?

"He who loves money will not be satisfied with money."

Ecclesiastes 5:10

It is my money! I do not think God has a problem with me enjoying that money. I also do not think that it is "wrong" to live a luxurious lifestyle. Should I turn away from that sort of life? Perhaps, the answer to that question is not so much, "Why you should," as it is "Why not?"

It is more about "alternatives" than "right" and "wrong." Even if we were to conclude that it is wrong to live a luxurious lifestyle, especially if it is associated with senseless waste, we would have to admit that the definition of "luxury" and "waste" is subjective. One man's luxury is another man's necessity. The answer does not hinge on what you must or must not do with money. It centers on what you could do with money *instead* of doing something else.

The first alternative to luxury or waste is to have more money to give. To live more simply—according to your needs—in order to have more to give to people in need is not a matter of right and wrong but a matter of opportunity and missed opportunity. It is not a matter of legalistic burden but a matter of merciful privilege. Moreover, "it is more blessed to give than to receive" (Acts 20:35). When someone justifies his luxurious living by saying, "It is a blessing from God," he may be speaking words of truth. Yet he may miss out on an opportunity.

Of course, "more" is a relative word. It is not that "receiving" is wrong. Even if we are willing to give, we must first receive. Just as "we love because He first loved us" (1 John 4:19), we give because He first gave to us. Whether you give or receive is not a matter of right or wrong; it is simply *better* to give. All of our works will be put through the fire. Some of it will not count. We will still be saved, but we will suffer the lost *opportunity* to have more "rewards."

> For no man can lay a foundation other than the one which is laid, which is Jesus Christ. Now if any man builds on the foundation with gold, silver, precious stones, wood, hay, straw, each man's work will become evident; for the day will show it because it is *to be* revealed with fire, and the fire itself will test the quality of each man's work. If any man's work which he has built on it remains, he will receive a reward. If any man's work is burned up, he will suffer loss; but he himself will be saved, yet so as through fire (1 Cor. 3:11-15).

Another alternative to luxury or waste is to have more time for God and His work. It is certainly not wrong to be rich. Money is not evil. It is "the love of money" that is "a root of all sorts of evil" (1 Tim. 6:10). How do you remain rich? When it is at the expense of your time with God and your time for God, there may be a missed opportunity. If in order to live a luxurious lifestyle, you have to work twelve-hour days, six days a week, then you might consider living less luxuriously and having more time to spend with God and more time to minister. "Do not weary yourself to gain wealth, cease from your consideration of *it*" (Prov. 23:4). If making more and more money becomes an obsession, then "money is not evil" transitions to "the love of money," which is evil. The alternative is to love money less and love God and the Gospel more. It would be to live a simpler life (Matt. 6:25-32) and to "seek first His kingdom and His righteousness, and all these things will be added to you" (Matt. 6:33).

Should I live in luxury or not? It is not a matter of "should." It is a matter of "could." Listen to the wisdom of the preacher: "He who loves money will not be satisfied with money, nor he who loves abundance *with its* income. This too is vanity" (Eccl. 5:10). Throw off the vanity of the love of riches and, instead, put on the wisdom of giving more, spending more time with God, and spending more time in ministry.

OCTOBER 14

FAITH EQUALS CORRECT SEEING AND SEEKING

"For now we see in a mirror dimly, but then face to face; now I know in part, but then I will know fully just as I also have been fully known."
1 Corinthians 13:12

What is faith? What is the essence of faith? Faith is to come to God. It is to seek Him. "And without faith it is impossible to please *Him*, for he who comes to God must believe that He is and *that* He is a rewarder of those who seek Him" (Heb. 11:6). Faith pleases God. Coming to God and seeking God pleases Him. The essence of faith is relationship with God; it is to "come to God" and to "seek Him."

God's most personal name is YHWH ("I AM"). The essence of faith is to believe that He is real. Both demons (James 2:19) and deists (God is an absentee landlord) believe this, but that understanding alone does not please God for He is Jehovah Shammah; He not only "is," but "He is there" (Ezek. 48:35). He is not only real, but He is *really* there. Demons and deists do not believe He is needed or that He should be or can be sought. Hence, they do not turn to God, seek Him, or repent, since God is not there; He is not in their midst or at hand.

The motivation to turn to God comes from faith that He is there actually interacting with us. "Or do you think lightly of the riches of His kindness and tolerance and patience, not knowing that the kindness of God leads you to repentance?" (Rom. 2:4). When "He is" is not also "He is there" and is not also "He is pertinent or necessary or involved," then it yields a non-relational and non-interactive "faith" which is no faith at all. Faith without works is dead (James 2:17). The "works" of faith are to believe or know God (John 6:29).

Faith that seeks is faith that sees. Correct seeing leads to correct seeking, even as YHWH leads to Jehovah Shammah. Faith is to see myself rightly so as to not seek myself. It is to see God rightly so as to seek God. "The apostles said to the Lord, 'Increase our faith!' And the Lord said, 'If you had faith like a mustard seed'... So you too, when you do all the things which are commanded you, say, 'We are unworthy slaves; we have done *only* that which we ought to have done'" (Luke 17:5-6, 10).

The request to "increase our faith" is answered with the instruction to make your faith consistent with a mustard seed—to see yourself as small so as to see God as big and to seek not yourself so as to seek God.

Jesus offers a parable to explain this "mustard seed faith." The slave sees Himself as one who does not deserve, is not entitled, and is not self-sufficient. He sees himself as being small, like a mustard seed. Subsequently, he sees his master as worthy, boss, sufficient—large. Your faith in God increases when you decrease. You come to God when you do not come to yourself. You see God correctly when you see yourself correctly. You seek God when you do not seek yourself. You seek God *more* when you get out of your own *smaller* way.

"He must increase, but I must decrease" (John 3:30). He increases because when I do not seek myself, then I seek Him. "Little I" naturally seeks "Big Him," even as a small child naturally seeks his or her big dad (Luke 18:16-17). The decreasing is in how I look to and at myself as *not* being adequate, able, or creator. The increasing is in how I look to and at the One Who is adequate, able, and Creator. That sort of seeing and seeking is faith. When I realize I can do nothing without Him (John 15:5), then I realize that I must acknowledge Him in all my ways (Prov. 3:5-6). The Hebrew word *yada* ("acknowledge") signifies an experiential, interactive, and intimate relationship (Gen. 4:1). Faith is a profound seeking of God.

This is faith. It is seeking God, coming to God, interacting with God, developing relationship with God, knowing God; it is eternal life. "This is eternal life, that they may know You, the only true God, and Jesus Christ whom You have sent" (John 17:3). Whatever is not of faith is sin (Rom. 14:23). In eternity, there will be no sin; there will only be faith. If eternal life is knowing God, then faith is knowing God. Heaven is perfect relationship with God (1 Cor. 13:9-12, 1 John 3:2).

Faith is relationship with God. Everything else comes from this (Matt. 6:33), is built or torn down on this (1 Cor. 3:11-15), and is made beautiful or ugly in this (Rom. 14:23). Relationship with God as the essence of faith is the "bottom line" of life (John 6:29, Luke 10:39-42) because it is the "finish line" of life (Matt. 25:12-13; 7:21-23).

> Not everyone who says to Me, "Lord, Lord," will enter the kingdom of heaven, but he who does the will of My Father who is in heaven *will enter*. Many will say to Me on that day, "Lord, Lord, did we not prophesy in Your name, and in Your name cast out demons, and in Your name perform many miracles?" And then I will declare to them, "I never knew you; DEPART FROM ME YOU WHO PRACTICE LAWLESSNESS" (Matt. 7:21-23).

Faith is to come to God. It is to seek Him because "He is" and because "He is there." Do you see and, therefore, seek the YHWH who is Jehovah Shammah? God, make us people of faith. Cause us to seek You!

OCTOBER 15

WHAT DOES "MEANS OF GRACE" MEAN?

"But as many as received Him . . . who were born, not of . . . man, but of God."

John 1:12-13

The theological idea of "means of grace" is implicit to vessel theology. If God is going to flow through me, then there must be a way for that flow to be enacted. The means of grace are those biblical actions that facilitate God's activity in a person's life. Fundamental to this dynamic is the understanding that God is the Source, and man is a receiver. The part played by man involves the idea of "means." A creation does not cause. He can only receive, for that is who he is. Only God can cause; thus, the phrase is not "causes of grace."

The idea of "means" or "instruments" allows for man to be involved. The idea of "grace" insists that God must be involved. The foundational theology is clear. Man cannot change his own heart (for God is the Source), but he can engage himself in means of grace via which God changes hearts (man can receive). Jesus says, "'No one can come to Me unless the Father who sent Me draws him'" (John 6:44). At the same time, we know that both Bartimaeus and Zaccheus intentionally positioned themselves along the path of grace (Mark 10:46-52, Luke 19:1-10). God is the "Causer," and man is the "receiver." Man comes, and God draws.

One might ask, "If God sovereignly chooses, does man really have a free will?" God is 100 percent sovereign, *and* man has a 100 percent free will; "for many are called, but few *are* chosen" (Matt. 22:14). According to the parable of the wedding feast, to be "chosen" is to choose God's choice (Matt. 22:1-14). Man receives what God causes or provides.

> There was the true Light which, coming into the world, enlightens every man. He was in the world, and the world was made through Him, and the world did not know Him. He came to His own, and those who were His own did not receive Him. But as many as received Him, to them He gave the right to become children of God, *even* to those who believe in His name, who were born, not of blood nor of the will of the flesh nor of the will of man, but of God (John 1:9-13).

It is only God's right to give the right. At the same time, it is only man who can receive that right. In other words, God must act, and so must man. God's actions are those of a Source, while man's actions are those of a receiver. Means of grace, then, simply become ways in which to receive from God.

Vessel theology is that which is concerned with facilitating God's unchangeable decrees. It understands that man must be involved in what God has ordained. Biblical thinking is not fatalistic thinking. In a somewhat paradoxical sense—established by the fact that man tries to understand God's perspective on eternal things within a framework of space and time when God, Himself, is not bound by those parameters—man may "change" or impact that which God is doing, since man, by his own decision, may or may not be involved in what God is doing.

Since man does have a clear part to play, a theology of God's grace cannot include the idea that it is automatic. God's grace is appropriated, in large measure, according to man's actions. God must be the first cause. Nevertheless, man can be seen to be the "second cause." Christian growth is not accidental. It is not involuntary. The pursuit of holiness is an intentional undertaking. The "means of grace" are sourced by God and directed toward Him. They are practiced by men.

OCTOBER 16

PRAYER AND FASTING: FRIENDS FOREVER!

"And I was fasting and praying before the God of heaven."

Nehemiah 1:4

When we pray, we do not tell God what to do. We ask; we do not instruct. When we fast, we do not make God do anything. We facilitate; we do not create. That is the idea of any "means of grace" like prayer or fasting; it is a *means*, not an end. It is a spiritual discipline that we can engage in to express our need for God and to facilitate the flow of His provision.

Prayer and fasting are often seen together in Scripture. Moses intercedes for his people with fasting (Deut. 9:9-29). The idolatrous Israelites turn to the Lord with prayer and fasting (1 Sam. 7:5-6). David fasted and prayed for his sick child (2 Sam. 12:15-23). Inasmuch as fasting is a form that facilitates a sincere expression of need, it is effective as an aid to prayer. With a massive army quickly approaching, Jehoshaphat realized his desperate need for God. He proclaimed a fast; and all the people prayed and sought God, and God responded.

> Jehoshaphat was afraid and turned his attention to seek the LORD, and proclaimed a fast throughout all Judah. So Judah gathered together to seek help from the LORD; they even came from all the cities of Judah to seek the LORD . . . "O our God, will You not judge them? For we are powerless before this great multitude who are coming against us; nor do we know what to do, but our eyes are on You . . . Listen, all Judah and the inhabitants of Jerusalem and King Jehoshaphat: thus says the LORD to you, 'Do not fear or be dismayed because of this great multitude, for the battle is not yours but God's . . .'" Jehoshaphat bowed his head with *his* face to the ground, and all Judah and the inhabitants of Jerusalem fell down before the LORD, worshiping the LORD. The Levites, from the sons of the Kohathites and of the sons of the Korahites, stood up to praise the LORD God of Israel, with a very loud voice (2 Chron. 20:3-4, 12, 15, 18-19).

God responds to a humble and needy people. Prayer and fasting are expressions of that humility and need, and so they are commonly and naturally linked together as means of grace. Ezra understood this dynamic and led his people in its practice.

> Then I proclaimed a fast there at the river of Ahava, that we might humble ourselves before our God to seek from Him a safe journey for us, our little ones, and all our possessions. For I was ashamed to request from the king troops and horsemen to protect us from the enemy on the way, because we had said to the king, "The hand of our God is favorably disposed to all those who seek Him, but His power and His anger are against all those who forsake Him." So we fasted and sought our God concerning this *matter*, and He listened to our entreaty (Ezra 8:21-23).

Many biblical figures utilized the combination of prayer and fasting. Nehemiah prayed and fasted for the inhabitants of Jerusalem (Neh. 1:4). In response to the evil intentions of his enemies, David prayed and fasted (Psalm 35:13). Daniel expressed his need for God's mercy (Dan. 9:3) and direction (Dan. 10:2) with prayer and fasting. Joel's response to Israel's need for deliverance is prayer and fasting (Joel 1:14, 2:12). God responded favorably to the newly converted people of Nineveh after they fasted and prayed (Jonah 3:5-9). The leaders of the church at Antioch engaged in prayer and fasting for the purposes of receiving direction from God and commissioning others for His work (Acts 13:1-3). Similarly, Paul and Barnabas prayed and fasted in conjunction with the appointing of elders in all the churches (Acts 14:23).

Any "means of grace"—like prayer or fasting—is a *means*, not an end. It is a spiritual discipline that we can engage in to express our need for God and to facilitate the flow of His provision. Let the good friends, prayer and fasting, become your friend as you use them to express your need for God, Who calls you His friend (John 15:14).

OCTOBER 17

JESUS' VISION STATEMENT FOR THE FUTURE

"This gospel of the kingdom shall be preached in the whole world as a testimony to all the nations, and then the end will come."

Matthew 24:14

Do you have a vision for the future? Before going to the cross, Jesus shared His vision for the future with His disciples. As if He was saying to them, "Picture this," Jesus explained to His disciples that, "'This gospel of the kingdom shall be preached in the whole world as a testimony to all the nations, and then the end will come'" (Matt. 24:14). What a beautiful painting! It is the masterpiece that depicts the wondrous Gospel message inserted into all cultures and societies that will culminate with the return of Christ. Just picture that!

Jesus' vision statement for the future includes the message, the mission, and the motive that are necessary to bring the vision to pass. The message is "this gospel of the kingdom." The *Gospel* is Good News," and the *kingdom* is "God's rule." The "gospel of the kingdom," then, is the Good news of God's rule. The message is that there is now, and in the future, victory over enemies. These enemies include death, Satan, and sin. Death is defeated; for it "has been revealed by the appearing of our Savior Christ Jesus, who abolished death and brought life and immortality to light through the gospel" (2 Tim. 1:10). Satan is defeated. "Since the children share in flesh and blood, He Himself likewise also partook of the same, that through death He might render powerless him who had the power of death, that is, the devil" (Heb. 2:14). Sin is defeated. "Our old self was crucified with *Him*, in order that our body of sin might be done away with, so that we would no longer be slaves to sin; for he who has died is freed from sin" (Rom. 6:6-7).

In each of the three previous passages, the same Greek word is used to express the idea of defeat ("abolished death," "render powerless . . . the devil," "sin might be done away with"). This term, *katargeo*, means to render inoperative, useless, ineffective, or impotent. The same Greek term is used in 1 Corinthians 15:24-26 to describe the future victory ("abolished") over all enemies: "Then *comes* the end, when He hands over the kingdom to the God and Father, when He has abolished all rule and all authority and power. For He must reign until He has put all His enemies under His feet. The last enemy that will be abolished is death."

This is the message of God's vision statement for the future: The good news of God's reign is that He has already abolished, and that He will abolish completely and forever, His enemies. It is an "already and not yet" statement because it is an "already and not yet" Gospel of the kingdom.

Jesus' vision statement for the future includes the message, the mission, and the motive that are necessary to bring the vision to pass. The mission is that the message "shall be preached in the whole world as a testimony to all the nations" (Matt. 24:14). This has been going on since the beginning when God's statement in Genesis 3:15 proclaimed the Gospel. His story is God's history of the revelation of Himself and His Good News for all people as it is proclaimed by His people. And so, Israel was chosen as a missionary nation (Gen. 12:1-3). Israel rejected her *active* responsibility to be a testimony to the nations through her words and deeds. Israel fulfilled her passive responsibility via the birth of Christ. Israel rejected Christ. The mission was taken away from Israel (Matt. 21:43) and given to a new nation, the Church (1 Peter 2:9). And so, the Church became the new missionary nation (Matt. 28:19-20) that would take on the mission of preaching the message "in the whole world as a testimony to all the nations."

Jesus' vision statement for the future includes the message, the mission, and the motive that are necessary to bring the vision to pass. The motive is "and then the end will come." Do you want to see the return of Christ? Do you want to see the fullness of the kingdom? Are you looking for the new heavens and the new earth? The desire to see these coming events motivate Christians to engage in and complete world evangelization.

Disciples of Christ should be "looking for and hastening the coming of the day of God" (2 Peter 3:12). The end will not come until the Gospel has been preached to all nations. Missions is not an option for the one who cries out, "Come, Lord Jesus" (Rev. 22:20); it is a mandate!

OCTOBER 18

WHAT RULES YOU?

*"But **wanting** to have their ears tickled, t
hey will accumulate for themselves teachers in accordance to their own desires."*

2 Timothy 4:3

The disease of materialism is clearly described by Jesus when He declares, "'You cannot serve God and wealth'" (Matt. 6:24). The gaining of wealth is put forth by "prosperity theology" teaching as a sort of God-given right for disciples of Jesus who must take hold of that right by faith. This teaching, although including an element of truth that is realized in God's promise to bless His people, often promotes living in excess and waste and paints it as a picture of holiness and righteousness. Prosperity theology, in its extreme and unbalanced forms, provides a supposed "biblical" rationalization for materialistic Christianity. It is a theology that was developed to feed and defend our carnal desires. Interestingly, Paul seems to have predicted that these sorts of things would happen! "For the time will come when they will not endure sound doctrine; but *wanting* to have their ears tickled, they will accumulate for themselves teachers in accordance to their own desires and will turn away their ears from the truth and will turn aside to myths" (2 Tim. 4:3-4).

Prosperity theology defends itself by distorting Scripture. Living in excess and waste is justified because we are "king's kids," since we are children of God the King. However, this materialistic focus is not consistent with the nature of the kingdom of that King; "for the kingdom of God is not eating and drinking, but righteousness and peace and joy in the Holy Spirit" (Rom. 14:17). Prosperity theology tries to connect the kingdom of God to having an excess of money and possessions. However, Jesus makes the opposite connection. He connects the kingdom of God to giving away money and possessions. "Do not be afraid, little flock, for your Father has chosen gladly to give you the kingdom. Sell your possessions and give to charity" (Luke 12:32-33).

Prosperity theology becomes a facilitator of materialism when it produces Christians who are afraid of being perceived by others as not having an abundance of material things. Its teaching implies that Christians are out of the will of God if they are in need. It teaches that if you have a need, then you must lack faith. Prosperity Christians become afraid of needs. They respond by keeping and guarding money and possessions as a kind of "righteousness insurance," since they are told that they are unrighteous if they have a need.

Prosperity theology often distorts the understanding of living a life of faith and victory. It says that victory *only* includes having no needs. This is illogical; it is also not biblical. God's supply flows toward needs. A need must first exist before God can supply it. "And my God will supply all your needs according to His riches in glory in Christ Jesus" (Phil. 4:19). At some point, a Christian *must* be in need for God to be able to supply that need. It is a logical and theological impossibility to say we should have no needs. Actually, we should say that needs are needed. A more general way to say this is to say that a victory without a battle is no victory at all. The existence of a victory necessarily implies the existence of a battle. Prosperity theology often negates these types of biblical principles. It promotes materialism and actually hinders the flow of God's resources. A "denial of need" and a "desire to keep" tend to do that.

As we reconsider the principle of Philippians 4:19, we see that it is set in the context of another often-quoted verse: "I can do all things through Him who strengthens me" (Phil. 4:13). When Paul proclaims this, he says it in the context of being in need. "I know how to get along with humble means, and I also know how to live in prosperity; in any and every circumstance I have learned the secret of being filled and going hungry, both of having abundance and suffering need" (Phil. 4:12).

Paul understood that God could and would supply his needs. Yet that did not mean that Paul would *never* be in need. It did mean that God would supply him with the strength to live in whatever conditions that he found himself in while spreading the Gospel.

The point is that your material situation is not the point. This is the problem with prosperity theology teaching. The problem is not that it proposes that God will provide for us. The problem is that it makes that provision the primary thing—that which stands above all else. Jesus reminds us, "'You cannot serve God and wealth'" (Matt. 6:24). When your prosperity becomes your focus and you begin to live in excess and waste, you begin to live in another kingdom. When you are ruled by stuff, you are not ruled by God. It is one or the other. You cannot serve both.

OCTOBER 19

PAUL'S MISSIONARY METHODS

*"So that from Jerusalem and round about as far as Illyricum I have fully preached the gospel of Christ. And thus I aspired to preach the gospel, not where Christ was **already** named."*
Romans 15:19-20

Paul was called as an apostle—one who is sent. The Latin form of the Greek term *apo stello* is "missio" or "missionary." As a missionary, Paul was sent to the Gentiles and directed to use certain methods to reach them: "'I am sending you, to open their eyes so that they may turn from darkness to light and from the dominion of Satan to God, that they may receive forgiveness of sins and an inheritance among those who have been sanctified by faith in Me'" (Acts 26:17-18).

First, Paul was told "to open their eyes." This would imply that he would have the ability to contextualize the Gospel. He would have the ability to make the Gospel practical and apply the Gospel to real needs. Second, Paul was to turn them "from darkness to light." Thus, he would hone the ability to point others to the Light, Jesus. Paul was also told to turn the Gentiles "from the dominion of Satan to God." This would include the ability to lead someone to repentance—to submission to the Lordship of Christ. It may also include the ability to minister deliverance, if necessary.

Paul was sent to the Gentiles "that they may receive forgiveness of sins." Paul would have the ability to lead people into new life through faith and then lead them toward assurance of salvation. Also, Paul was told to minister to people in such a way that they may receive "an inheritance among those who have been sanctified by faith." And so, Paul would have the ability to disciple a new believer and to lead him or her toward participation in the life of the body of Christ.

Paul used certain methods and strategies in his missionary work. For example, he always worked in a missionary team; he never worked alone (Acts 13:2, 5, 13 15:36, 40, 18:2-5; Philippians 4:3). He focused on unreached areas always keeping his eyes fixed on the frontiers (Rom. 15:20).

Perhaps, the most concise way to describe Paul's missionary methods and strategies would be to call it a strategy of "go, give, leave." He would go to an unreached area and give of his ministry until a "baby" church was birthed. After some nurturing—the longest time of which was spent in Ephesus for three years—Paul would then leave in order to go to another unreached area (Rom. 15:14-25). Paul was able to leave because he never lost his vision to go to the unreached, and he trusted in the Holy Spirit to continue and finish the work that was started (Phil. 1:6, 1 Thessalonians 5:23-24, 2 Thessalonians 3:3). The result of this strategy was that strong, non-dependent churches were established instead of weak, dependent churches, and the Gospel was able to go to all known parts of the earth.

> For I will not presume to speak of anything except what Christ has accomplished through me, resulting in the obedience of the Gentiles by word and deed, in the power of signs and wonders, in the power of the Spirit; so that from Jerusalem and round about as far as Illyricum I have fully preached the gospel of Christ. And thus I aspired to preach the gospel, not where Christ was *already* named, so that I would not build on another man's foundation (Rom. 15:18-20).

OCTOBER 20

HELPING OTHERS TO BE IN COURAGE(D)

*"Just as you know how we **were** exhorting and encouraging and imploring each of you as a father **would** his own children, so that you would walk in a manner worthy of the God who calls you into His own kingdom and glory."*

1 Thessalonians 2:11-12

Where do you stand? Do you reside in fear? Do you sit in despair? Do you stand in courage? Perhaps your answer is that of the Ethiopian eunuch, who said to Philip, "'Well, how could I, unless someone guides me?'" (Acts 8:31). Sometimes, in order to stand in courage, you need someone else to encourage you. In order for us to stand tall and be courageous, we need to "encourage one another and build up one another" (1 Thess. 5:11). We all need someone to come alongside to help us to be *in courage[d]!*

How can we encourage others? The most all-inclusive word to describe the action of encouragement is *inclusion*. The seventh-grade boy who sits alone and dejected at the lunchroom table receives encouragement when five of the "cool kids" invite him to sit at their table. He is included. He is encouraged. To encourage someone can be to simply recognize them because to recognize is to include. Showing approval, appreciation, and affirmation encourages others because it includes them.

Leaders must understand the nature of encouragement. Encouragement is not the act of bashing and verbally beating people in order to scare or intimidate them toward change. This is abuse, not encouragement. It tends to cause people to retreat, not move forward. Dwight D. Eisenhower said, "Pull the string, and it will follow wherever you wish. Push it, and it will go nowhere at all."[16] Leaders whose default style of motivation is to be harsh with those they are leading tend to be insecure leaders; they want to keep people down. Leaders who motivate those they are leading by lifting them up are secure in their leadership; they are willing to raise people up to their level.

In many ways, the most important arena for encouragement to take place is in the family. Many people need to learn a new vocabulary once they are adults if they are going to be able to encourage others. They were not raised with a vocabulary of encouragement. Words like "awesome," "amazing," "together," "try," "congratulations," and "vision" are words that some people never heard growing up. Parents need to build up their children and cast vision into their lives so as to alleviate the natural hesitancy to move forward that comes with never having been there before.

Similarly, husbands need encouragement from their wives. Their natural need to be admired—to be the "hero husband"—needs to be met by their wives, since they can easily question their impact without it. Wives need encouragement from their husbands. Their natural need to be valued—to be the "treasure wife"—needs to be met by their husbands, since they can easily question how others view them.

There is a reason why young people join gangs. They feel encouraged. They feel included. The courage that comes from inclusion is that which enables new gang members to act in ways they never would have before. This is the risk associated with of a lack of encouragement in families. When people do not get encouragement from where they should, they often look for it in other places. This is dangerous for children, husbands, and wives.

Of course, the greatest source of encouragement comes from God. It is true that "the people who know their God will display strength and take action" (Dan. 11:32). The most important job of the encourager is to encourage others to seek God. This is the ultimate inclusion that changes everything! Encouragement is powerful. We all need someone to come alongside of us to help us to be *in courage[d]*, so we can be like David who "encouraged himself in the LORD his God" (1 Sam. 30:6).

OCTOBER 21

BEWARE OF THE "BERTHA BUT BOOGIE"

"Be merciful, just as your Father is merciful."

Luke 6:36

It is not an overstatement to say that life is all about relationships. How do you relate to society? How do you relate to people? How do you relate to God? God sums up what He requires of man by alluding to these three relationships: "He has told you, O man, what is good; and what does the LORD require of you but to do justice, to love kindness, and to walk humbly with your God?" (Micah 6:8). Three relationship dynamics sum it up: justice, kindness, and walking humbly. Another way to express these three dynamics is: relating *across*, relating *to*, and relating *with*. We are to do justice; we are to relate *across* society in upright ways in which we insist on being advocates of justice. We are to love mercy; we are to relate *to* others in our common human plight and, therefore, have mercy on and show compassion to our neighbors. Finally, and most preeminently, we are to relate *with* God by walking with Him in humility.

Relating with God may be the most significant dynamic of the three—inasmuch as all else flows from that dynamic—yet relating *to* others may be the most difficult to do, since pride is our most natural inclination, especially when it comes to how we view ourselves relative to others. When we get ready to judge someone instead of showing them mercy, we begin to say things like, "Well, I could understand if they did this. Even I have done that. And I could understand if they did that, since I have also done that. *But, but, but.* I cannot show them any mercy if they have done the thing I have not done. I am better than they, so I can judge them!" Pride does not relate *to* others and can show no mercy to others.

To wallow in self-condemnation or self-righteousness is human, but to rejoice in mercy or grace is Divine. Mercy and grace are siblings. Mercy is grace looking backward, and grace is mercy looking forward. Mercy is not getting what you do deserve, and grace is getting what you do not deserve. Man's tendency is, foolishly, not toward mercy. People like to "dig their own graves" as they fall into the pit of irony. They claim for themselves the thing they really do not want as their self-incriminating judgments grow out of their appointment of themselves as judges.

> Therefore you have no excuse, everyone of you who passes judgment, for in that which you judge another, you condemn yourself; for you who judge practice the same things. And we know that the judgment of God rightly falls upon those who practice such things. But do you suppose this, O man, when you pass judgment on those who practice such things and do the same *yourself*, that you will escape the judgment of God? Or do you think lightly of the riches of His kindness and tolerance and patience, not knowing that the kindness of God leads you to repentance? (Rom. 2:1-4).

What does God require of us? He does not want us to despise mercy; He wants us to love it. He wants us to be like Him, Who delights in mercy (Micah 7:18). How can we *delight* in mercy? We do not even like it a little bit! Let us work things backward. You cannot give something to someone else unless you first possess it yourself. You cannot possess it unless you have first received it. And you will not receive it unless you first understand and confess that you need it. Here is the key that unlocks or keeps locked all else. When we receive mercy from God—admitting that we need it—we then become carriers of it and are equipped to be givers or multipliers of it.

Mercy is powerful; it is efficacious (Heb. 4:16, Rom. 2:4). Just as "we love, because God first loved us" (1 John 4:19) and we are holy because God is holy (1 Peter 1:16), so we, too, can show others mercy because God has shown mercy to us (Luke 6:36). The crux of the matter, however, is located at the floodgates as all else flows out from there. Do we see our need for God's mercy or not. When our answer is "yes"—which we can only arrive at by God's mercy (John 16:8)—then the floodgates open, and the waters of mercy begin to flow. When the answer is no, then the floodgates remain shut; so we look for it in other places.

Instead of looking to God, we begin to look at others; we compare ourselves to others. The problem with this is that there will always be people who are "worse" than you and still others who are "better" than you. When you compare yourself to others who are worse than you, then you birth self-righteousness. When you compare yourself to others who are better than you, then you birth self-condemnation. In each case, one way or the other, you compete in the arena of "works"; and works do not mesh well with grace and mercy. Without God's grace, there is only self-righteousness (Gal. 2:21); and without God's mercy, there is only self-condemnation. Each road leads to a hellish life. The grace (Gal. 2:21) and mercy (Rom. 8:1) road leads to Heaven (Titus 3:5).

All begins with God. His grace and mercy wrapped up in His love make for a powerful antidote to the fallen world and our fallen nature. All ends with God. His grace and mercy wrapped up in His love make all that is fallen to be transformed into all that is risen. It is a different kind of "Bertha But Boogie": "And you were dead . . . But God, being rich in mercy, because of His great love with which He loved us, even when we were dead in our transgressions, made us alive together with Christ (by grace you have been saved)" (Eph. 2:1, 4-5). So, choose grace and choose mercy!

OCTOBER 22

THAT WAS A HARD TEST!

*"When He heard that he was sick, He then stayed two days **longer**
in the place where He was."*

John 11:6

Faith is not optional in the Christian life. God commands His people to have faith. Regarding the quality of their faith, disciples of Christ are called to be firm in their faith (1 Cor. 16:13, Col. 1:23), to continue in their faith (Acts 14:22, 1 Tim. 1:19), and to be strong in their faith (Rom. 4:20-24). Regarding the quantity of their faith, followers of Jesus are called to abound in faith (2 Cor. 8:7) and to pray for more faith (Luke 17:5).

Faith is very important. It is such a critical factor in a person's life that "whatever is not from faith is sin" (Rom. 14:23). How important is faith? This question can be answered with another question. How important is it to please God? "And without faith it is impossible to please *Him*, for he who comes to God must believe that He is and *that* He is a rewarder of those who seek Him" (Heb. 11:6).

Faith is so important that it is the basis for meaning in life. "For we through the Spirit, by faith, are waiting for the hope of righteousness. For in Christ Jesus neither circumcision nor uncircumcision means anything, but faith working through love" (Gal. 5:5-6). Faith is of primary importance in a Christian's walk with God. Without faith, prayer is ineffective. "But he must ask in faith without any doubting, for the one who doubts is like the surf of the sea, driven and tossed by the wind. For that man ought not to expect that he will receive anything from the Lord" (James 1:6-7).

So, beware of obstacles! Sometimes, even disciples of Christ can be an obstacle to faith:

And a Canaanite woman from that region came out and *began* to cry out, saying, "Have mercy on me, Lord, Son of David; my daughter is cruelly demon-possessed" . . . And His disciples came and implored Him, saying, "Send her away, because she keeps shouting at us" . . . And He answered and said, "It is not good to take the children's bread and throw it to the dogs." But she said, "Yes, Lord; but even the dogs feed on the crumbs which fall from their masters' table." Then Jesus said to her, "O woman, your faith is great; it shall be done for you as you wish." And her daughter was healed at once (Matt. 15:22-28).

If the Canaanite woman would have allowed Jesus' disciples to be an obstacle to her faith, her daughter would not have been healed. Faith screams, "Obstacles get out of my way" (Luke 5:18-19). Religiosity and worldliness can try to interrupt your faith. They try to tell you that there is no use in following Jesus; there is no hope. "While He was still speaking, they came from the *house of* the synagogue official, saying, 'Your daughter has died; why trouble the Teacher anymore?'" (Mark 5:35). Jesus' response to that obstacle was "'Do not be afraid *any longer*, only believe'" (Mark 5:36).

Obstacles to faith can be incredibly ridiculous. Unbelief is ridiculous! Jesus healed a blind man. The religious folk did not like that. They tried to roll an obstacle in front of the blind man's faith. The blind man jumped over the obstacle. "So a second time they called the man who had been blind, and said to him, 'Give glory to God; we know that this man is a sinner.' He then answered, 'Whether He is a sinner, I do not know; one thing I do know, that though I was blind, now I see'" (John 9:24-25). They commanded, "Give glory to God by ignoring your faith in Him."

A similar situation included an equally absurd demand: "Get back in your wheelchairs!" At a Crusade in Zaire, an evangelist prayed for the sick. The power of God moved, and many were healed. Former paralytics were dancing before God in praise to Him. The local priests chastised them and told them to get back in their wheelchairs, or they would not help them anymore. The ones who were healed refused to get back in their wheelchairs and told the priests, "Thank you very much, but we no longer need your help." They leaped over the obstacle.

God may test your faith in order to grow it. A test may come in the form of a delay; you may have to wait for God's answer (John 11:3-6). Other tests may come in the form of requirements that are difficult to understand. It is odd to march around a city, shout, and blow trumpets in order to conquer it (Josh. 6:3). It is quite awkward to have to lay on your side for 430 days while playing with a virtual doll house and cooking over human and cow dung (Ezek. 4:1-17). Tests and obstacles may make it difficult to have faith sometimes. Nevertheless, we must be strong in our faith and press on. George Müller, a nineteenth-century evangelist and great man of faith, said:

> God wants to increase the faith of His children. However, many times his people do not want more faith because there is a great price to pay. There are tests and trials before the victory and there are delays before the end. We need to be willing to receive them from the hand of God. It is God's way of increasing our faith. This is the experience of the life of faith: trials, obstacles, difficulties, and at times defeats. God uses all of them as the food of faith."[17]

OCTOBER 23

OH MY WORDS

"For to one is given the word of wisdom through the Spirit,
and to another the word of knowledge according to the same Spirit."

1 Corinthians 12:8

In a very curious portion of Scripture, Paul lists nine gifts of the Holy Spirit. He explains that "there are varieties of gifts, but the same Spirit" (1 Cor. 12:4), Who distributes the gifts "to each one individually just as He wills" (1 Cor. 12:11).

> For to one is given the word of wisdom through the Spirit, and to another the word of knowledge according to the same Spirit; to another faith by the same Spirit, and to another gifts of healing by the one Spirit, and to another the effecting of miracles, and to another prophecy, and to another the distinguishing of spirits, to another *various* kinds of tongues, and to another the interpretation of tongues (1 Cor. 12:8-10).

The phrase "to another" is repeated eight times. Two times, the phrase is translated from the Greek word *heteros*, meaning "another of a different kind"; and six times, it is translated from the Greek word *allos*, meaning "another of the same kind." *Heteros* appears between the gift of the word of knowledge and the gift of faith. It also appears between the gift of distinguishing of spirits and the gift of various kinds of tongues. *Allos* appears between the remaining gifts of the Spirit. Thus, for example, the listing of the initial gifts would better be translated, "For to one is given the word of wisdom through the Spirit, and to another of the same kind the word of knowledge according to the same Spirit; to another of a different kind faith by the same Spirit, and to another of the same kind gifts of healing by the same Spirit."

In this way, the list of spiritual gifts can be organized into three groups. The first group might be called the "rational" gifts. Included in this group are the word of wisdom and the word of knowledge. A second group might be called the "action-spectacular" gifts. Included in this group of gifts are faith, gifts of healings, the effecting of miracles, prophecy, and the distinguishing of spirits. The final group might be called the "supra-rational" gifts. Included in this group of gifts are various kinds of tongues and interpretation of tongues.

So what exactly are these "rational" gifts? What is the word of wisdom and the word of knowledge? First and foremost, to understand these gifts is to understand that God possesses perfect wisdom and perfect knowledge. "Oh, the depth of the riches both of the wisdom and knowledge of God! How unsearchable are His judgments and unfathomable His ways! FOR WHO HAS KNOWN THE MIND OF THE LORD" (Rom. 11:33-34). Certainly, we are speaking of Jesus Christ "in whom are hidden all the treasures of wisdom and knowledge" (Col. 2:3).

These "mental" gifts express the mind of the Lord, which is somehow and to some degree transferred over to the human mind. The gift is not wisdom or knowledge. It is a word, utterance, or statement of a piece of wisdom or knowledge; it is a *word* of wisdom or a *word* of knowledge. It is not wisdom and knowledge themselves. The actuality of the gift does not mean that the recipient becomes the giver. The recipient does not become wisdom or knowledge; he or she only becomes a vessel through which a piece of wisdom or knowledge flows.

How do these gifts work? These are "mental" or "rational" gifts. Thus, the Spirit works through the mind of the receiver of the gift, and the receiver then translates those thoughts into words—thus, a *word* of wisdom and a *word* of knowledge. "Now we have received, not the spirit of the world, but the Spirit who is from God, so that we may know the things freely given to us by God, which things we also speak, not in words taught by human wisdom, but in those taught by the Spirit, combining spiritual *thoughts* with spiritual *words*" (1 Cor. 2:12-13).

In order to get an idea of what a word of wisdom might look like, consider how it may have been used in the following situations to offer advice with respect to the government and mission of the church (Acts 6:1-6, 13:1-3, 15:28-31). Also consider how, in the following passages, the word of wisdom might have been used to confound an opponent (Luke 12:11-12, Matt. 22:15-46, Acts 6:8-10). A minister stood praying for a man, and the Spirit revealed to him an answer to a problem that plagued the man for some time. This might come forth as a word of wisdom.

Since the Christian faith is the knowledge of Divine truth, a word of knowledge is primarily a declaration of that truth. Thus, words of knowledge are especially important in the teaching ministry (1 Cor. 14:26). Certainly, a word of knowledge can include facts that are past, present, and future (Acts 5:1-11). A minister stood praying for a woman, and the Spirit nudged him to encourage her concerning her low self-esteem that she had carried with her for years due to being bullied in school. This is a word of knowledge.

A Chinese proverb says, "If you wish to know the mind of a man, listen to his words." Perhaps we could also say, "If you wish to know the spiritual mind of a man, listen to his words of wisdom and words of knowledge." Don't take my *word* for it. Take God's *Word* for it, which says that the Spirit combines "spiritual thoughts with spiritual words" (1 Cor. 2:13).

OCTOBER 24

GOD WANTS YOU TO BE A LIQUID ASSET ACCOUNT!

"Now He who supplies seed to the sower and bread for food will supply and multiply your seed for sowing and increase the harvest of your righteousness; you will be enriched in everything for all liberality."

2 Corinthians 9:10-11

Hoarded wealth is no wealth at all because wealth that is buried in the ground and not used is not beneficial (Matt. 25:18) and, thus, ceases to be true wealth. Indeed, the action of love is to give (John 3:16), and love is never love until you give it away. Wealth must remain in circulation to continue. We might say that Jesus was the Wealth of God in circulation, distributed to all people. "For you know the grace of our Lord Jesus Christ, that though He was rich, yet for your sake He became poor, so that you through His poverty might become rich" (2 Cor. 8:9).

The principle of distribution is seen in the laws of nature. Divine nature naturally gives and distributes. The sun gives its light. The trees give oxygen. Fallen nature naturally keeps and hoards. It can be scientifically proven that there are no shortages of necessary resources in the world. There is only greed and selfishness. The "eyes of the LORD move to and fro throughout the earth" (2 Chron. 16:9) looking for those who will act as distributors of blessings. God is a Master Investor. He does not want to deposit his money in a thirty-year bond. He wants to establish a liquid asset account. He wants to *distribute* His provision to people who have needs. What kind of account are you? When God finds a "liquid" account, He keeps that account supplied for ongoing liquidity.

> Now this *I say*, he who sows sparingly will also reap sparingly, and he who sows bountifully will also reap bountifully. Each one *must do* just as he has purposed in his heart, not grudgingly or under compulsion, for God loves a cheerful giver. And God is able to make all grace abound to you, so that always having all sufficiency in everything, you may have an abundance for every good deed; as it is written, "HE SCATTERED ABROAD, HE GAVE TO THE POOR, HIS RIGHTEOUSNESS ENDURES FOREVER." Now He who supplies seed to the sower and bread for food will supply and multiply your seed for sowing and increase the harvest of your righteousness; you will be enriched in everything for all liberality (2 Cor. 9:6-11).

God wants to distribute resources. He is searching the earth for vessels who have two doorways in their lives. The first doorway is faith. It is used for the resources to enter. The second doorway is compassion. It is used for the resources to leave. God is looking for good stewards who will use, multiply, and distribute His resources. In order for Him to entrust His resources to you, He must first trust you to use them properly, for it "is required of stewards that one be found trustworthy" (1 Cor. 4:2). The Divine Owner/Manager must trust you to give and not to hoard. Hoarders and wasters are not useful to the manager. Givers are useful; that is why one of His company's core values is "it is more blessed to give than to receive" (Acts 20:35).

God, the efficient and effective cosmic Manager of all resources, is looking for lovers. To love is to give—your time, talents, gifts, physical and spiritual resources. God is looking for good stewards, distributors who are like liquid asset accounts. As stewards, we are called to be responsible employees of our employer. "'From everyone who has been given much, much will be required; and to whom they entrusted much, of him they will ask all the more'" (Luke 12:48). Are you being responsible with what God has entrusted to you? Are you a distributor or a hoarder?

OCTOBER 25

WHEN ALL HAS BEEN SAID AND DONE

"The conclusion, when all has been heard, **is***:*
fear God and keep His commandments, because this **applies** *to every person."*
Ecclesiastes 12:13

The Bible consistently makes mention of a dual purpose of life. The way in which this dual purpose is described may be a little bit different depending on the context of Scripture in which it is found; but like a biblical thread, it always connects the same two purposes: know God and make God known. We will look at an example of this dual purpose of life as it is described in each of the five major categories of Bible literature: the Law, the Prophets, Writings, Gospels, and Epistles.

The dual purpose of life shows up in the Law. God says to Abraham, "'I will make you a great nation, and I will bless you, and make your name great; and so you shall be a blessing; and I will bless those who bless you, and the one who curses you I will curse. And in you all the families of the earth will be blessed'" (Genesis 12:2-3). There are two parts or purposes that make up this Abrahamic covenant. In the first half of the covenant, we see three privileges that relate to Israel being blessed. Since Abraham's greatest blessing was to know God, then we can conclude that to know God was the essence of the blessings. In the second half of the covenant, we see three responsibilities that relate to Israel being a blessing to others. The essence of this responsibility was to make God known. Here is an example of the dual purpose of life as it is found in the Law.

The dual purpose of life also shows up in the Prophets. God says to His people:

"You are My witnesses," declares the LORD, "and My servant whom I have chosen, so that you may know and believe Me and understand that I am He. Before Me there was no God formed, and there will be none after Me. I, even I, am the LORD, and there is no savior besides Me. It is I who have declared and saved and proclaimed, and there was no strange *god* among you; so you are My witnesses," declares the LORD, "And I am God" (Isa. 43:10-12).

In this passage in which God is declaring to His people Who He is and explaining to them why He chose them, we see the word "so" used two times to introduce the purposes in their lives. There are two distinct purposes. First, "so that you may know and believe Me," and second, "so you are My witnesses." The Israelites are to know God and to make Him known so that the nations would "hear and say, 'It is true'" (Isa. 43:9). Here is an example of the dual purpose of life as it is found in the Prophets.

The dual purpose of life also shows up in the Writings. The author of Ecclesiastes struggled through an entire book to finally come up with the universal purpose of life. Nothing else made sense but the two purposes that he finally arrived at: "The conclusion, when all has been heard, *is*: fear God and keep His commandments, because this *applies* to every person" (Eccl. 12:13). The first purpose is to "fear God." To fear God is to know Him (Psalm 34:9-10, Prov. 2:5). For example, Solomon says, "In order that all the peoples of the earth may know Your name, and fear You as *do* Your people Israel" (2 Chron. 6:33). The second purpose is to "keep His commandments." Since the making of the Abrahamic covenant, God made it clear that His Great Commission was for His people to make Him known. And so, in the Writings, we see the dual purpose of life.

The dual purpose of life is easily found in the Gospels. A scribe approaches Jesus and wants to know "the bottom line." He asks:

> "What commandment is the foremost of all?" Jesus answered, "The foremost is, 'HEAR, O ISRAEL! THE LORD OUR GOD IS ONE LORD; AND YOU SHALL LOVE THE LORD YOUR GOD WITH ALL YOUR HEART, AND WITH ALL YOUR SOUL, AND WITH ALL YOUR MIND, AND WITH ALL YOUR STRENGTH.' The second is this, 'YOU SHALL LOVE YOUR NEIGHBOR AS YOURSELF.' There is no other commandment greater than these" (Mark 12:28-31).

The first purpose is to love God. Certainly, to love God is to seek Him, build a relationship with Him, and know Him. The second purpose is to love your neighbor. The most direct way to love other people is to share love with them. God is Love (1 John 4:8). To love others is to share God with them—that is, to make God known. The dual purpose of life is found in the Gospels.

The dual purpose of life is found in the Epistles. For example, Paul writes to the Philippians explaining his purpose in life. He says, "I count all things to be loss in view of the surpassing value of knowing Christ Jesus my Lord, for whom I have suffered the loss of all things ... that I may know Him" (Phil. 3:8, 10). Then, in a passage in which Paul is grappling with the advantages of either living or dying, he concludes, "If I am to live on in the flesh, this will mean fruitful labor for me . . . to remain on in the flesh is more necessary for your sake. Convinced of this, I know that I will remain and continue with you all for your progress and joy in the faith" (Phil. 1:22-25).Paul finds purpose in this life in continuing to make God known among the Philippians. The dual purpose of life is found in the Epistles.

The Bible is clear as to the purpose of life. If you want to live a life of meaning and fulfillment, then know God and make God known. "This is eternal life, that they may know You, the only true God, and Jesus Christ whom You have sent" (John 17:3).

OCTOBER 26

WHAT FAITH IS NOT

"I have learned the secret of being filled and going hungry."

Philippians 4:12

What is the nature of faith or the essence of faith? Sometimes, this question is answered superficially as it is couched in terms of man attaining his own desires. This tendency results in what has been called prosperity theology—a "name it and claim it" or "positive confession" type of "hyper-faith" theology. We must begin by addressing, "What faith is not!"

Faith is not a certain category of desired results. In the Scripture, faith is associated with a variety of "results." Some are good, and some are not good; some are more desirable, and some are less desirable. In the "Hall of Fame of Faith" in Hebrews 11, we see that some people by faith conquered kingdoms, while others by the same faith were tortured. By the same faith, some escaped the edge of the sword; and others were put to death with the sword. Whatever faith is, it is not simply a certain category of results.

> Who by faith conquered kingdoms, performed *acts* of righteousness, obtained promises, shut the mouths of lions, quenched the power of fire, escaped the edge of the sword, from weakness were made strong, became mighty in war, put foreign armies to flight.

Women received back their *dead* by resurrection; and others were tortured, not accepting their release, so that they might obtain a better resurrection; and others experienced mockings and scourgings, yes, also chains and imprisonment. They were stoned, they were sawn in two, they were tempted, they were put to death with the sword; they went about in sheepskins, in goatskins, being destitute, afflicted, ill-treated (*men of whom the world was not worthy*) wandering in deserts and mountains and caves and holes in the ground (Heb. 11:33-38).

These were the great people of faith. By their faith, they "gained approval" (Heb. 11:2). People like Abel, Enoch, Noah, Abraham, Sarah, Joseph, Moses, and Rahab all acted in faith. This faith was situated in a variety of settings and ended with a variety of results. The settings and the results themselves were not "the faith," since by the same faith, they all engaged in different settings and experienced different kinds of results.

Faith is not a certain kind of situation or circumstance. It is not a particular lifestyle or desirable definition of "success."

> Not that I speak from want, for I have learned to be content in whatever circumstances I am. I know how to get along with humble means, and I also know how to live in prosperity; in any and every circumstance I have learned the secret of being filled and going hungry, both of having abundance and suffering need. I can do all things through Him who strengthens me (Phil. 4:11-13).

Paul, the man of faith, explains that he is content with plenty or in lack. "I can do all things *through* [Christ] who strengthens me" (emphasis mine). The point is that it is a relational thing ("through") not a creational thing. "I can do all things," not because I create them (positive confession) but because I am enabled to do them. My being "in Christ" (2 Cor. 5:17) and Christ being in me (Gal. 2:20) is the actual positive confession. Faith is not naming and claiming whatever you want. It is not someone's own desired definition of success or prosperity. Faith is not waving your magic wand and making things happen. Faith is much more profound than that!

OCTOBER 27

IRONIC GARDENS

"Let us be alert and sober."

1 Thessalonians 5:6

Tragically, gardens can be full of irony. Both in the Garden of Eden and in the Garden of Gethsemane, the irony of man fleeing from the only One Who can help him is clearly seen. In Eden, Adam and Eve "hid themselves" from the One Who was mercifully looking for them (Gen. 3:8-13). In Gethsemane, Jesus' disciples—His followers—"all left Him and fled" (Mark 14:50).

We sometimes have our own gardens. We forget how much we need Jesus, and we ignore Him. We flee from the One we need. Why do we leave Him and flee? To some degree, it is simply a lack of preparation. In the Garden of Gethsemane, Jesus told His disciples to do three things in preparation for avoiding the temptation to flee: wait, watch, and pray.

> They came to a place named Gethsemane; and He said to His disciples, "Sit here until I have prayed." And He took with Him Peter and James and John, and began to be very distressed and troubled. And He said to them, "My soul is deeply grieved to the point of

death; remain here and keep watch." And He went a little beyond them, and fell to the ground and *began* to pray that if it were possible, the hour might pass Him by. And He was saying, "Abba! Father! All things are possible for You; remove this cup from Me; yet not what I will, but what You will." And He came and found them sleeping, and said to Peter, "Simon, are you asleep? Could you not keep watch for one hour? Keep watching and praying that you may not come into temptation; the spirit is willing, but the flesh is weak" (Mark 14:32-38).

Jesus told His disciples to "sit" and "remain." Waiting upon Jesus is necessary to avoid falling into temptation. As we spend time with Him and wait for His direction and guidance, we prepare ourselves to be strong in the hour of temptation. However, like the disciples, we sometimes sleep instead!

Followers of Christ are admonished to "not sleep as others do, but let us be alert and sober" (1 Thess. 5:6). Jesus told His disciples to "keep watch." Watching is necessary to avoid falling into temptation. As we remain ready through discipline, self-control, and discernment, we prepare ourselves to be strong in the hour of temptation. However, like the disciples, we sometimes sleep instead!

Jesus encouraged His disciples to "keep praying." Prayer includes the act of asking for God's help with the attitude of depending on God. It is necessary to avoid falling into temptation. As we walk in the Spirit through engaging in conversation with God, we prepare ourselves to be strong in the hour of temptation. However, like the disciples, we sometimes sleep instead!

Without the preparation of waiting, watching, and praying, we will not be spiritually awake people; and we may fall to the temptation to flee from Jesus, even as His disciples did. "And they all left Him and fled" (Mark 14:50). Jesus warned them three times (Mark 14:41), and He warns us now. Are you waiting? Are you watching? Are you praying? Warning, warning, warning! Are you prepared? If not, when temptation comes, you, too, will leave Him and flee. Prepare yourself. Be ready. Be rooted! "In a similar way these are the ones on whom seed was sown on the rocky *places*, who, when they hear the word, immediately receive it with joy; and they have no *firm* root in themselves, but are *only* temporary; then, when affliction or persecution arises because of the word, immediately they fall away" (Mark 4:16-17).

OCTOBER 28

GET IN THE RACE AND RUN FOR THE PRIZE

*"Do you not know that those who run in a race all run, but **only** one receives the prize? Run in such a way that you may win."*

1 Corinthians 9:24

"'Blessed are the poor in spirit for theirs is the kingdom of heaven'" (Matt. 5:3). "'Blessed are the pure in heart for they shall see God'" (Matt. 5:8). Why is being "poor in spirit" or "pure in heart" desirable? It is "blessed" because of its outcome. The "kingdom of heaven" and "seeing God" are worthwhile results. They are worthy conclusions. They are worth it! The question that looms in such a short life (relative to eternity) is, "What counts?" If you drive a fast car and get to your destination sooner than everyone else only to arrive at the wrong place anyway, then what difference does it make? Alternatively, if you get the "kingdom of heaven" and get to "see God," then what you have done really counts. It counts because it *remains*, instead of perishing.

Do you not know that those who run in a race all run, but *only* one receives the prize? Run in such a way that you may win. Everyone who competes in the games exercises self-control in all things. They then *do it* to receive a perishable wreath, but we an imperishable. Therefore I run in such a way, as not without aim; I box in such a way, as not beating the air; but I discipline my body and make it my slave, so that, after I have preached to others, I myself will not be disqualified (1 Cor. 9:24-27).

Kingdom-of-God-dwellers do not have their rewards determined by the rules of this world (John 18:36). Theirs is a different criteria, a spiritual world criteria. They are being built up as a spiritual temple and, therefore, live in accord with the purposes of that sort of "house."

And coming to Him as to a living stone which has been rejected by men, but is choice and precious in the sight of God, you also, as living stones, are being built up as a spiritual house for a holy priesthood, to offer up spiritual sacrifices acceptable to God through Jesus Christ. For *this* is contained in Scripture: BEHOLD, I LAY IN ZION A CHOICE STONE, A PRECIOUS CORNER stone, AND HE WHO BELIEVES IN HIM WILL NOT BE DISAPPOINTED. This precious value, then, is for you who believe; but for those who disbelieve, THE STONE WHICH THE BUILDERS REJECTED, THIS BECAME THE VERY CORNER stone, and, A STONE OF STUMBLING AND A ROCK OF OFFENSE; for they stumble because they are disobedient to the word, and to this *doom* they were also appointed. But you are A CHOSEN RACE, A royal PRIESTHOOD, A HOLY NATION, A PEOPLE FOR God's OWN POSSESSION, so that you may proclaim the excellencies of Him who has called you out of darkness into His marvelous light (1 Peter 2:4-9).

What are the purposes of those who live in the "spiritual house?" One purpose is "to offer up spiritual sacrifices acceptable to God through Jesus Christ." This may include sacrifices of justice and righteousness (Psalm 4:5), praise (Psalm 27:6), thanksgiving (Psalm 107:22), and a broken spirit (Psalm 51:17). Another purpose is being obedient to the word as opposed to those who "stumble because they are disobedient to the word." Those who live in the spiritual house have as their purpose to "proclaim the excellencies of Him who has called you." These purposes point to activities that will count in the end. It only makes sense to do things that count toward something!

The philosophies of this world deem Christianity vain at best and senseless at worst. Paul uses the idea of a race—"do you not know that those who run in a race all run"—to declare that he is not a Christian for nothing. He is not a participator in futility. He wants to go for what counts. He is not running simply for the sake of running. No, he runs to win a prize!

When running in a race, you only do those things that propel you toward the finish line. If something does not move you closer to the reward, then you do not do it. "By faith Moses, when he had grown up, refused to be called the son of Pharaoh's daughter, choosing rather to endure ill-treatment with the people of God than to enjoy the passing pleasures of sin, considering the reproach of Christ greater riches than the treasures of Egypt; for he was looking to the reward" (Heb. 11:24-26).

Runners in a race are single minded. They have a goal, and everything is directed toward it. Are you running the race? Are you running in such a way as to receive that "imperishable wreath"? Are your eyes fixed on Jesus, or are you looking toward other finishing lines? "Therefore, since we have so great a cloud of witnesses surrounding us, let us also lay aside every encumbrance and the sin which so easily entangles us, and let us run with endurance the race that is set before us, fixing our eyes on Jesus, the author and perfecter of faith" (Heb. 12:1-2).

OCTOBER 29

WHAT'S ON THE AGENDA OF YOUR WORDS?

"With her many persuasions she entices him; with her flattering lips she seduces him."
Proverbs 7:21

Sometimes, we disappoint ourselves with regard to how we speak to others. We might respond, "That was a really *dumb* thing to say!" We try to be wise with our words; but sometimes, we are "dum"

The third *dum* style of speech is the *m*anipulative style. The way of the manipulator mimics the style of a crafty and deceptive salesman or prostitute. She uses words in a creative style. However, she is insincere. "For the lips of an adulteress drip honey and smoother than oil is her speech; but in the end she is bitter as wormwood, sharp as a two-edged sword" (Prov. 5:3-4).

The manipulative speaker is an expert in the use of flattery and persuasion. They are her two greatest weapons.

> That they may keep you from an adulteress, from the foreigner who flatters with her words. For at the window of my house I looked out through my lattice, and I saw among the naive, *and* discerned among the youths a young man lacking sense, passing through the street near her corner; and he takes the way to her house, in the twilight, in the evening, in the middle of the night and *in* the darkness. And behold, a woman *comes* to meet him, dressed as a harlot and cunning of heart. She is boisterous and rebellious, her feet do not remain at home; *she is* now in the streets, now in the squares, and lurks by every corner. So she seizes him and kisses him and with a brazen face she says to him: "I was due to offer peace offerings; today I have paid my vows. Therefore I have come out to meet you, to seek your presence earnestly, and I have found you. I have spread my couch with coverings, with colored linens of Egypt. I have sprinkled my bed with myrrh, aloes and cinnamon. Come, let us drink our fill of love until morning; let us delight ourselves with caresses. For my husband is not at home, he has gone on a long journey; he has taken a bag of money with him, at the full moon he will come home." With her many persuasions she entices him; with her flattering lips she seduces him (Prov. 7:5-21).

The adulteress first attempts to establish personal credibility (v. 14). Then she tries to convince others of personal superiority (v. 15). The manipulator uses her words to take advantage of the weakness of others and makes offers "they cannot refuse" (vv. 16-21).

You do not have to be a car salesman or a prostitute to use this style of speech. All of us are prone to using manipulation to get our way, and engaging in it can be very subtle. It can even be used without realizing it. And so, we must challenge ourselves. Do we use this style of speech? Do we use our ability to persuade others to get what we want? Do we use flattery to prepare the person to be persuaded? Do we really care about our listeners? Or do we only care about our own personal interests and agendas?

The wise way of speech is the opposite of the manipulative way, even as truth is the opposite of deception. "He who speaks truth tells what is right, but a false witness, deceit" (Prov. 12:17). Honesty is nowhere to be found in the insincere, manipulative style of speech, whereas honesty—especially honesty with oneself—is the cornerstone of the wise style of speech. Wisdom steers us away from deception. "Put away from you a deceitful mouth and put devious speech far from you" (Prov. 4:24). Manipulation is subtle. It is more of a motive than an outward action. It is difficult for someone else to know for sure that it is being used. Wisdom is that "check" in your heart that only you can know as it challenges you to admit to yourself, "This is what I am actually doing, and I must stop!" You must be honest with yourself.

Based on personality, experience, and relational orientation, you might be prone to using more of a manipulative style of speech than a destructive style or undisciplined style. Being aware of this is half the battle. You must try to be more attentive to your words. You must make it a habit to ask yourself some challenging questions: Do I use words to "set people up"? Do I have a hidden agenda when I speak? Am I using my words to deceive? Do I use flattery only to advance my own cause? Do I have the best interests of the other person in mind, or do I only have my own interests in front of me? Am I being wise with my words or am I being *dum*?

OCTOBER 30

IT DOES NOT CUT EASILY

"So they are no longer two, but one flesh. What therefore God has joined together, let no man separate."

Matthew 19:6

The family is the foundation of society. When society begins to fall apart, it is because the family unit has already fallen apart. Marriage is the foundation of the family. When the family unit begins to fall apart, it is because marriages and the definition of marriage have already fallen apart. The individual male and female are the foundation of marriage. When marriages begin to fall apart, it is because individual males and females and their definitions have already fallen apart. What happens to a society when 50 percent of marriages break apart? What happens when the definition of two becoming one—"For this reason a man shall leave his father and his mother, and be joined to his wife; and they shall become one flesh" (Gen. 2:24)—becomes a definition of many different identifications becoming some other classification.

The only hope when foundations crumble is that they are put back together again. God hates the breaking apart: "'I hate divorce,' says the LORD" (Malachi 2:16).

> Have you not read that He who created *them* from the beginning MADE THEM MALE AND FEMALE, and said, "FOR THIS REASON A MAN SHALL LEAVE HIS FATHER AND MOTHER AND BE JOINED TO HIS WIFE, AND THE TWO SHALL BECOME ONE FLESH"? So they are no longer two, but one flesh. What therefore God has joined together, let no man separate (Matt. 19:4-6).

Although divorce is common, it is never easy. Two lives have been joined together by God. To separate that union is not done without difficulties. The bond that is broken is very strong. The covenant that is broken is not only with each other, but it is with God. "To deliver you from the strange woman, from the adulteress who flatters with her words; that leaves the companion of her youth and forgets the covenant of her God; for her house sinks down to death" (Prov. 2:16-18). The result of divorce is disaster. The "house" or family "sinks down to death." The broken covenant creates a mess and produces pain. When something so intimate is "torn apart" (Matt. 19:6), it does not cut easily. The man that the woman is said to leave is called "the companion of her youth" (Prov. 2:17). The word "companion" comes from the Hebrew word *alluph*, which points to closeness and can be translated as "intimate friend" (Prov. 17:9). Cutting up best friends is devastating. Breaking apart families is life-altering. Fracturing society is culture-shifting.

We must return to a high view of marriage. It is not flippant. It is not temporary. It is a serious matter. It is a permanent endeavor. A prenuptial agreement attached to a marriage covenant is an oxymoronic document. Plans for dissolution before something is entered into that is, by its nature, indivisible, are nonsensical plans. Marriage is between one man and one woman and is entered into for life. It is defined by God and not simply whatever we define it to be. Commit to His definition. Set the foundation. Humanity depends on it!

OCTOBER 31

NO, NO, NO! MAY IT NEVER BE!

"Do we then nullify the Law through faith? May it never be! On the contrary, we establish the Law."
Romans 3:31

An experience that is extremely enjoyable to someone might be described as "heaven on earth." This actually does exist; it is called life in the kingdom of God. Followers of Christ are called to live in the kingdom of God and enjoy its benefits. This life also has significant responsibilities. Kingdom people must be "the salt of the earth" and the "light of the world" (Matt. 5:13-14). The light is for "all who are in the house" (Matt. 5:15). To what extent do the responsibilities of kingdom-dwellers extend? Salt goes into *all* the earth; light is of *all* the world and is for *all* in the house. That is pretty exhaustive!

Jesus brought the kingdom of God to earth and called His people to live and work in it. This work includes fulfilling the Law. *Nothing* of the Law will be omitted, and *all* will be accomplished. Those who keep and teach the Law will be the great ones in the kingdom. Again, words like *nothing* and *all* and *great* are all-encompassing words.

> Do not think that I came to abolish the Law or the Prophets; I did not come to abolish but to fulfill. For truly I say to you, until heaven and earth pass away, not the smallest letter or stroke shall pass from the Law until all is accomplished. Whoever then annuls one of the least of these commandments, and teaches others *to do* the same, shall be called least in the kingdom of heaven; but whoever keeps and teaches *them*, he shall be called great in the kingdom of heaven (Matt. 5:17-19).

Kingdom-dwellers are called to be holy; they are called to be "separate." Those who have the responsibility to serve and those who are the recipients of that service are two distinct groups of people. There are those who live on the earth and who are of the world. There are those who are the salt of the earth and the light of the world. Kingdom-dwellers are "not of the world" while still remaining in the world. They are separate while not being separated from those they are serving. "I do not ask You to take them out of the world, but to keep them from the evil *one*. They are not of the world, even as I am not of the world" (John 17:15-16).

Kingdom-dwellers are called to be active. Salt must act. It must preserve the meat. At the same time, it must promote or encourage others to eat the meat by making the meat tasty. Christians, through their social actions, must try to be a preservative for a decaying, sinful world. At the same time, through their evangelistic actions, Christians must encourage others to act by making this life taste a little better. Light must act. It must shine and drown out the darkness. At the same, it must provide light for others to walk in. Christians must invade the darkness of the world with their own actions. They must also make things brighter and clearer for others and encourage them to act. Christians must obey. They must try to keep all of the commands. At the same time, they must encourage others to act; they must teach the commands. Kingdom-dwellers live in the kingdom and guide others toward it.

Kingdom-dwellers are called to be multipliers. Talents must be used and multiplied. Three men were given five, two, and one talent, respectively. The ones given five and two talents did something with them and multiplied what was given to them. The one who was given one talent did nothing with it and did not multiply what was given to him. The ones who multiplied were applauded, while the one who did not was judged. Kingdom-dwellers cannot be "lazy" and hide their talents "in the ground" (Matt. 25:14-30). They must multiply their talents. Evangelists and teachers must not only evangelize and teach, but they must also equip others to evangelize and teach (Eph. 4:11-12).

Kingdom-dwellers are not ones who are exempt. They are ones who fulfill. "Do not think that I came to abolish the Law or the Prophets; I did not come to abolish but to fulfill" (Matt. 5:17). Christians live by grace, but this in no way excuses them from the responsibilities of the Law. Jesus was not excused from the responsibilities of the Law. He did not destroy or ignore the Law. He did the Law. He lived the Law perfectly. He fulfilled the requirements of the Law; and now, through living in us by His Spirit (Gal. 2:20), He enables us to do the Law as well. "For what the Law could not do, weak as it was through the flesh, God *did*: sending His own Son in the likeness of sinful flesh and *as an offering* for sin, He condemned sin in the flesh, so that the requirement of the Law might be fulfilled in us, who do not walk according to the flesh but according to the Spirit" (Rom. 8:3-4).

It is true that kingdom-dwellers are not "under Law" (Rom. 6:14). This does not mean, however, that they are excused from doing the Law. It means that they are "over the Law" in the sense that they are enabled to do it. "Do we then nullify the Law through faith? May it never be! On the contrary, we establish the Law" (Rom. 3:31). We are not saved *by* works, but we are saved *to* works (James 2:17). Are kingdom-dwellers called to be lazy and unproductive? May it never be!

NOTES

November

NOVEMBER 1

WE'VE ONLY DONE WHAT WE SHOULD HAVE

*"We are unworthy slaves; we have done **only** that which we ought to have done."*
Luke 17:10

For the same reason it is a challenge to live the Christian life in general, it can be really hard to forgive people who have really hurt us. It is hard because we think too much of ourselves; we compare ourselves, situations, or experiences to other people, their situations, or their experiences. We do this so that we can place ourselves, relatively, on top as ones who have earned, and deserve, and are owed. We see ourselves as mulberry trees instead of mustard seeds. "And if he sins against you seven times a day, and returns to you seven times, saying, 'I repent,' forgive him." The apostles said to the Lord, "Increase our faith!" And the Lord said, "If you had faith like a mustard seed, you would say to this mulberry tree, 'Be uprooted and be planted in the sea'; and it would obey you" (Luke 17:4-6).

In order to avoid the "me-focus" mentality, we have to be people of faith. It takes faith to forgive. Faith is that which moves us to seek God because we understand Who He is (the Lord Who provides), and therefore, we understand who we are relative to Him (the servant who needs). This faith is like a mustard seed. A "mustard seed" is to "small" what "faith" is to "seeing yourself as small" (in need, not owed, not deserving, not having earned). In other words, "He must increase, but I must decrease" (John 3:30). This is faith.

Faith is putting God in His rightful place (over you) and putting yourself in your rightful place (under God). The natural result of doing that is to seek Him, to look to Him, and to compare yourself to Him; it is to come to Him. "And without faith it is impossible to please *Him*, for he who comes to God must believe *that* He is and that He is a rewarder of those who seek Him" (Heb. 11:6). Faith does not create. It is more profound than the act of "naming it and claiming it." Faith relates. It is manifested in the depths of relationship with God. "Faith like a mustard seed," that which describes the proper way to look at yourself and that which frees you up to do things like serve and forgive, is pictured in the story Jesus uses to answer His disciples' request to "increase" their faith.

> Which of you, having a slave plowing or tending sheep, will say to him when he has come in from the field, "Come immediately and sit down to eat"? But will he not say to him, "Prepare something for me to eat, and *properly* clothe yourself and serve me while I eat and drink; and afterward you may eat and drink"? He does not thank the slave because he did the things which were commanded, does he? So you too, when you do all the things which are commanded you, say, "We are unworthy slaves; we have done *only* that which we ought to have done" (Luke 17:7-10).

Making yourself too big yields a non-faith entitlement mindset; not a receiver and one who needs but, instead, a demander and one who is owed. This type of attitude will keep you from being used by God—from doing things like forgiving and serving—because you insist on getting what you deserve and have earned. When I think I am bigger than I actually am, then I more easily excuse myself from what I am actually called to do. When I walk in faith, seeing Jesus as being so big that I am relatively small, then I more readily do what is consistent with who I am. When we compare ourselves only to Jesus, then we stay in our place and are also raised up. Comparing ourselves to others makes us a big fish in a small pond—out of place (big fish) and not raised up (small pond)—while comparing ourselves (the servant, steward, or slave) to Jesus (the Boss, Owner, or Master) makes us a small fish in a big pond. This keeps us in our place (small fish) and raises us up (big pond).

We have a hard time forgiving others because we compare ourselves to them. We give ourselves the benefit of the doubt and inevitably rationalize why we should not forgive. We mix into the recipe of "excuse validation" our rights, our deserving, our earning, and our being owed relative to the other person. We make ourselves too big—not a mustard seed but a mulberry tree. The huge mulberry tree view of self, which is your own non-servant perception that focuses on self and withholds forgiveness, can be eliminated and "planted in the sea" if you have faith like the small mustard seed that is represented by a proper perspective of yourself that is not full of yourself. In this way, we make ourselves small and can forgive.

When we compare the astronomical level at which Jesus (the Master) is willing to forgive to our (the subordinate) relatively minuscule level at which we are to forgive, then we are freed up to forgive. If He forgives seventy times seven (Matt. 18:22), then we can forgive seven times a day (if we understand Who He is and Who we are relative to Him). To not do that is tantamount to idolatry in the same way that to not serve, even at the lowest level, is an idolatrous act. To not be willing to "wash windows" when the One Who is greater than you "washed feet" is to not understand what He has "done to you."

> You call Me Teacher and Lord; and you are right, for *so* I am. If I then, the Lord and the Teacher, washed your feet, you also ought to wash one another's feet. For I gave you an example that you also should do as I did to you. Truly, truly, I say to you, a slave is not greater than his master, nor *is* one who is sent greater than the one who sent him. If you know these things, you are blessed if you do them (John 13:13-17).

To forgive, there needs to be some give-and-take; but when there is too much take and not much to give, then you are not very up for giving. Deserve is the enemy of serve because it tends to *remove* serve. To say "I *deserve*" is to say "I *don't* serve." To forgive, to serve, and to be a follower of Christ, you have to have faith like a mustard seed. Faith, in this sense, has everything to do with how you see yourself and, therefore, how you see Jesus. When you ask Him, "Lord, increase my faith," you are actually asking, "Lord, help me to see myself as being smaller so I will see you as being bigger." When you decrease, He increases. This is increased faith! Do you want more faith? If you do, then you will have to see yourself rightly and say, "I have done only that which I ought to have done."

NOVEMBER 2

HUMILITY NAILS SELF TO THE CROSS

"With humility of mind regard one another as more important than yourselves."
Philippians 2:3

Bitterness can be deadly. Medical studies have shown a link between bitterness and illness. A root of bitterness can blossom into a tree of problems (Heb. 12:15). This does not have to be. "Let all bitterness and wrath and anger and clamor and slander be put away from you, along with all malice" (Eph. 4:31). How do you put it away? Those who are humble do not judge others. They trust that God is capable of correctly judging the case. This is a remedy for bitterness and turmoil.

Humility is closely related to the concept of "rest" and peace. "'Come to Me, all who are weary and heavy-laden, and I will give you rest. Take My yoke upon you and learn from Me, for I am gentle and humble in heart, and YOU WILL FIND REST FOR YOUR SOULS'" (Matt. 11:28-29).

Humility enables a person to give everything to God instead of holding onto it. Bitterness is anger that refuses to let go. It strangles a person with anxiety and anxiety leads to sickness. Humility is healthy; it lets go of bitterness and casts anxiety on God.

> You younger men, likewise, be subject to *your* elders; and all of you, clothe yourselves with humility toward one another, for GOD IS OPPOSED TO THE PROUD, BUT GIVES GRACE TO THE HUMBLE. Therefore humble yourselves under the mighty hand of God, that He may exalt you at the proper time, casting all your anxiety on Him, because He cares for you (1 Peter 5:5-7).

Humility chooses to be considerate of people instead of being embittered against them. It does this by looking away from itself and looking toward others. Moses pleaded with God on behalf of the people of Israel at the expense of giving up glory for himself (Num. 14:11-19). The humility of Moses (Num. 12:3) allowed him to negate his own benefits for the sake of benefits for others.

> The LORD said to Moses, "I have seen this people, and behold, they are an obstinate people. Now then let Me alone, that My anger may burn against them and that I may destroy them; and I will make of you a great nation." Then Moses entreated the LORD his God, and said, "O LORD, why does Your anger burn against Your people whom You have brought out from the land of Egypt with great power and with a mighty hand? Why should the Egyptians speak, saying, 'With evil *intent* He brought them out to kill them in the mountains and to destroy them from the face of the earth'? Turn from Your burning anger and change Your mind about *doing* harm to Your people" (Exod. 32:9-12).

A lack of humility desires to have all of the blessing. It does not share. Humility produces a sincere desire to share blessings. It is the thing that makes a person want to see others succeed.

> But two men had remained in the camp; the name of one was Eldad and the name of the other Medad. And the Spirit rested upon them (now they were among those who had been registered, but had not gone out to the tent), and they prophesied in the camp. So a young man ran and told Moses and said, "Eldad and Medad are prophesying in the camp." Then Joshua the son of Nun, the attendant of Moses from his youth, said, "Moses, my lord, restrain them." But Moses said to him, "Are you jealous for my sake? Would that all the LORD's people were prophets, that the LORD would put His Spirit upon them!" (Num. 11:26-29).

Pride yields a secret desire to see others fail. It generates jealousy and bitterness with respect to the abilities and talents of others. Humility puts others ahead of itself and desires the best for them. "Do nothing from selfishness or empty conceit, but with humility of mind regard one another as more important than yourselves; do not *merely* look out for your own personal interests, but also for the interests of others" (Phil. 2:3-4).

It is humility that champions the workings of the body of Christ. Without humility, arms would want the whole body to be one big arm. Noses would want a "nose body," and the appendix would envision the body as one huge appendix. Pride wants all the attention, but humility is able to share the spotlight. It is only in humility that the body of Christ can work:

> For through the grace given to me I say to everyone among you not to think more highly of himself than he ought to think; but to think so as to have sound judgment, as God has allotted to each a measure of faith. For just as we have many members in one body and all the members do not have the same function, so we, who are many, are one body in

Christ, and individually members one of another. Since we have gifts that differ according to the grace given to us, *each of us is to exercise them accordingly* (Rom. 12:3-6).

NOVEMBER 3

BESTEST FRIENDS

*"A man of **too many** friends comes to ruin, but there is a friend who sticks closer than a brother."*
Proverbs 18:24

How many really best friends do you have? If you are like most people, then you probably do not have more than a handful of intimately close friends. Best friends are people with whom you have shared your deepest secrets and who know more about you than most others. They are those who have been with you through the highs and lows of your life.

Descriptive words that mark a strong friendship include loyalty, consistency, and unconditional commitment. A strong friendship cannot be something superficial; it has a depth to it. There is "a friend who sticks closer than a brother" (Prov. 18:24) and Who "loves at all times" (Prov. 17:17). Superficial friends may only be your friend for what they can get from you, since "those who love the rich are many" (Prov. 14:20) and "every man is a friend to him who gives gifts" (Prov. 19:6). These "ulterior motive friends" will disappear when what motivates them is no longer available.

What makes a strong friendship? Friends help each other. They are willing counselors. "Oil and perfume make the heart glad, so a man's counsel is sweet to his friend" (Prov. 27:9). A good friend's counsel may take the form of guidance, exhortation, or confirmation. It may also take the form of challenge and rebuke. "Iron sharpens iron, so one man sharpens another" (Prov. 27:17). Friends must help each other to grow, even if it hurts. A true friendship should be able to offer and accept both types of counsel.

Who can you be completely honest with both in terms of what you tell him or her about yourself and what you are willing to tell them about themselves? A good friend is willing to jeopardize the friendship to help his friend. He will be the one who tells his friend what others know but are not willing to say. His concern goes beyond his desire not to be in an uncomfortable situation. "Better is open rebuke than love that is concealed. Faithful are the wounds of a friend" (Prov. 27:5-6). Temporarily, the tolerance of superficial friends may be desired. Ultimately, the sincerity of a close friend will be appreciated. "He who rebukes a man will afterward find *more* favor than he who flatters with the tongue" (Prov. 28:23).

Friends should be careful to avoid certain things. Slander and friendship do not mix. "A perverse man spreads strife, and a slanderer separates intimate friends" (Prov. 16:28). Talking behind the other's back, ridiculing, and "whispering" have destroyed many good friendships. There is a "trust" that strong friendships are built on, and slander breaks that trust. Since friends are not perfect people and friendships are not perfect relationships, forgiving and forgetting are essential actions. "He who conceals a transgression seeks love, but he who repeats a matter separates intimate friends" (Prov. 17:9). The lack of forgiveness can turn into bitterness. Bitterness can turn into anger and hostility. Hostility turns into rebellion. Rebellion turns into apathy. Apathy results in death. The relationship dies. This process has destroyed many good friendships!

Close friends are loyal to each other, consistent in their actions toward one another, and have an unconditional commitment to each other. We all want to have close friends, but we must also remember that we have to *be* a close friend if we are going to have close friends. Be your best to your best friend!

NOVEMBER 4

IF A TREE FALLS IN A FOREST

"He who has ears to hear, let him hear."

Mark 4:9

If a tree falls in a forest and no one is there to hear it, does it make a sound? Of course it does! Sound is the substance, and the hearing of the sound is the reception of that substance. The reception of something does not create that something, just as the something itself is not the reception of it. If no one hears a tree fall in a forest, did anyone hear it? Of course not! So, too, if sound waves are produced by a falling tree, are there sound waves? Of course there are!

Truth is truth. Whatever is truth is truth on its own merits. Something or someone outside of it does not have to make it truth in order for it to be so. It is, in its most fundamental sense, objective, not subjective. The subject is not its determiner, nor its definer. It is what it is! God is God, not because somebody perceives Him to be God but because He *is* God! My perception, or lack thereof, does not put God on the throne or take Him off. God is on the throne regardless of whether I see Him sitting there or not! Whether I proclaim that truth or not, it will be proclaimed because it is true. "But Jesus answered, 'I tell you, if these become silent, the stones will cry out!'" (Luke 19:40). Reality always wins the day because what is real is real. God is real; He is "'I AM WHO I AM'" (Exod. 3:14).

To insist that truth is objective does not negate the subjective dynamic that is associated with it. Truth does not have to be received for it to be truth, but the receiver can receive or reject what already is truth. This leads us to the matter of revelation, the unveiling of truth. God is truth (John 14:6). God reveals truth to us (1 Cor. 2:10). Here is the subjective dynamic. Truth is revealed to the subject. The subject processes that revelation and either receives it or rejects it (1 Cor. 2:12-15), while all throughout that process, truth remains the same. It is not altered by the subject, even though the subject is very much involved.

How is God revealed to His subjects? First, there is what is referred to as general revelation. God is revealed in creation and through experience. To a large degree, man's wicked heart results in him being blind to general revelation (Rom. 1:18-23). Special revelation is necessary for man to come to know God. God's special revelation of Himself is found in the Scriptures. Through the Scriptures, God guides His people into His moral will, which includes His nature, purposes, and designs.

Subordinate revelation is that which is consistent and answerable to Scripture. It is not some sort of "other" revelation, nor is it new or additional revelation. The canon is closed, and what God has revealed of Himself in the Scripture is sufficient and complete. Books will not be added to the Bible. The "closing of the canon" does not mean, however, that God's mouth is now closed. God is still interacting with His people. He is still alive. He still speaks. The Spirit of God guides us into implications and applications of Scripture that remain subordinate to it, that are consistent with and answerable to Scripture.

Our understanding of Divine revelation should neither leave us as postmodern relativists or modern deists. Both stink of existentialism. Christians do not claim to be God, nor do they claim that theirs is a non-relational or non-personal faith. The relativist says that the subject creates the truth. The deist says that the subject is abandoned by the truth-giver and so must fill things in for himself. To say that God no longer speaks is to tout a sort of "insipient deism" in which the Divine absentee Landlord once opened His mouth but now has closed it, once was personally involved with His people but now is not, and once revealed Himself but now has ceased from that very activity that actually forms the bedrock of Who He is and what He does.

Sometimes, the subordinate revelation debate is cultural or denominational; the way you are used to hearing about God's interactions with man. The phrase, "God spoke to me" or "I felt led" or "I heard from God" may be a bit direct and personal for some to swallow. They may be more comfortable with "God illumined me." No matter the terminology, the Christian understands that God is alive and interacts with him or her in a personal and intimate way that is applicable to their lives. God still directs and guides because God is still there; He is Jehovah Shammah (Ezek. 48:35). Nietzsche was wrong. God is not dead!

Trees have fallen in forests and have made sounds, and people have heard them. Trees continue to fall and to make sounds, and people continue to hear those sounds or hold their hands over their ears so as not to hear. Revelation is life, and *that* is the real "circle of life." Maybe the better question is, "When the tree falls in the forest, are you there to hear it?" Does God's revelation circle around to you? "'He who has ears to hear, let him hear'" (Mark 4:9).

NOVEMBER 5

OPEN YOUR MOUTH!

"Open your mouth for the mute, for the rights of all the unfortunate.
Open your mouth, judge righteously, and defend the rights of the afflicted and needy."
Proverbs 31:8-9

Evangelical Christians have had a varied history with respect to the attention they have given to societal ethics and social concerns. In England during the 1700s, John Wesley and the Methodist movement put their focus on both Word and deed. They were successful at applying the biblical mandate to be salt and light in the societies in which they lived (Matt. 5:13-14). Their influence resulted in the correction of extreme social injustices. Meanwhile, in the United States in the 1800s, the converts of Charles Finney gave their whole lives to the work of the anti-slavery cause. Evangelicals were on the move and involving themselves in the social movements of the day.

By the 1900s, however, fundamentalist evangelicals began to withdraw from a focus on social issues, in part, due to an overreaction to the increase of theological liberalism. Evangelicals disassociated themselves from those liberal movements and the social concern activities they were typically involved in. Furthermore, a "what is the use" mentality, driven by the pessimism that came with World War I and the negative view of the future that came with dispensational theology, led to even more of a tendency to ignore social concerns and to be silent when it came to issues of social justice.

In the 1960s, fundamentalist evangelicals began to get involved in social issues once again, albeit with a tendency to get sucked into the liberal theologies that often seemed to be connected with being a "causer." Certainly, Christ calls His people to minister to the needy (Prov. 19:17) and be a voice for social justice (Isa. 1:17). At the same time, of course, He calls the Church to hold on to pure doctrine (2 Tim. 1:13) and to not go after other gospels (Gal. 1:6-9). Where is the balance?

First, it must be understood that Christianity is more than the doing of good works. It is a relationship with God Himself. "Therefore they said to Him, 'What shall we do, so that we may work the works of God?' Jesus answered and said to them, 'This is the work of God, that you believe in

Him whom He has sent'" (John 6:28-29). Christian ethics and social concern must be rooted in a relationship with God. This relationship results in service and action. Here is the balance.

Ultimately, it is salvation that will transform society, not simply service, action, and social involvement. The greatest expression of social concern is evangelism. The Gospel is the solution to all needs. The most primary need is spiritual. Then, out of the resolution of spiritual needs comes sociopolitical concerns. Social service that relieves human needs is a natural outworking of spiritual rebirth. Social action should seek to remove the causes of human need and replace the corrupt systems associated with them. When these things happen, the process comes full circle as there then tends to be in society an increase in spiritual concerns.

The Gospel is naturally and inextricably linked to social concerns and social justice. The Church must be a change agent in society. It is the salt of the earth and the light of the world. It cannot remain silent. Its leader commands, "Open your mouth" (Prov. 31:8-9).

NOVEMBER 6

COMMUNICATING THE GOSPEL

"Now after John had been taken into custody, Jesus came into Galilee,
preaching the gospel of God, and saying,
'The time is fulfilled, and the kingdom of God is at hand; repent and believe in the gospel.'"

Mark 1:14-15

It did not begin when "Jesus came into Galilee, preaching the gospel of God" (Mark 1:14). The Gospel and its proclamation go all the way back to the Garden of Eden when God rebuked Satan and, in so doing, announced the Good News of His substitutionary blood that would be shed on behalf of man, who had just fallen to sin and was in desperate need of redemption (Gen. 3:15). This is the Gospel, the Good News. Man needs, and God provides. The Gospel is "Jesus"; it is "God saves."

Jesus is revealed throughout the Bible and throughout history (John 5:39-40, 20:30-31, 2 Tim. 3:15, Luke 24:25-27). From the time when Abraham confessed his need for God and God promised His provision—"Then he believed in the LORD; and He reckoned it to him as righteousness" (Gen. 15:6)—to the time when the Gentiles did the same and God poured out His Holy Spirit upon them (Acts 10), the Gospel has been proclaimed to mankind. This Good News—people need, and God provides—includes many points of truth. God is the Creator; sin is universal. People are in desperate need. Since they are separated from God and have no way to get themselves back to Him, God provides a way for people to reconnect with Him. Jesus is the Son of God; Jesus is the Lord of all; Jesus is the Savior via His atoning death and resurrection, and whoever believes in Him and trusts that His provision meets His need will be saved.

When communicating the Gospel cross-culturally, there can be barriers that keep people from accepting it because it threatens their culture. At Philippi, rejection of the Gospel came when those listening to Paul and Silas accused them of "proclaiming customs which it is not lawful for us to accept or to observe, being Romans" (Acts 16:21). At Thessalonica, cultural rejection of the Gospel came in the form of not being willing to replace loyalty to the Roman emperor with the Lordship of Jesus (Acts 17:7). In Jerusalem, Paul's presentation of the Gospel was rejected when Jews from Asia cried out, "'Men of Israel, come to our aid! This is the man who preaches to all men everywhere against our people and the Law and this place; and besides he has even brought Greeks into the temple and has defiled this holy place'" (Acts 21:28).

Some of these cultural barriers can be addressed by making sure Jesus is the Stumbling Block and not the culture of the presenter that is being forced upon the listeners. The humility of the missionary can also resolve potential conflict. He must be humble enough to learn and appreciate the culture of the people and communicate with them across cultural bridges.

The Incarnation serves as a powerful model for Christian witness. Jesus said that His coming should be a model for our going; "as the Father has sent Me, I also send you" (John 17:18, 20:21). Incarnational ministry begins with our attitudes and perspectives.

> Do nothing from selfishness or empty conceit, but with humility of mind regard one another as more important than yourselves; do not *merely* look out for your own personal interests, but also for the interests of others. Have this attitude in yourselves which was also in Christ Jesus, who, although He existed in the form of God, did not regard equality with God a thing to be grasped, but emptied Himself, taking the form of a bond-servant, *and* being made in the likeness of men. Being found in appearance as a man, He humbled Himself by becoming obedient to the point of death, even death on a cross (Phil. 2:3-8).

Our attitude must allow us to renounce our status, lest we refuse to relate to others on their level. It must allow us to renounce our independence, lest we never put ourselves in the place of being other-oriented. It must allow us to identify and share life with the people, lest we remain separated and irrelevant.

The Gospel message crosses cultures. Jesus' disciples must cross cultures with it since God so loves the *world* (John 3:16) and wants disciples to be made in all *nations* (Matt. 28:19). It is not a matter of whether or not the Gospel is compatible with various cultures; it is a matter of whether or not we will take the Gospel to all cultures. God is the God of culture!

NOVEMBER 7

GRACE ME, WASH ME, CREATE IN ME, DELIVER ME!

> *"Be gracious to me ... Wash me ... Create in me ... Deliver me."*
> Psalm 51:1-2, 10, 14

What does it mean to truly repent? It means to turn to a Person. It is not simply turning to *a* way but turning to *the* Way, Jesus Christ. He is "the way, and the truth, and the life" (John 14:6). To repent is to turn to the abilities of Jesus Christ. It is not so much the process of declaring your actions as it is the process of asking to be acted upon. We must cry out to God, "Please grace me, wash me, create in me, and deliver me!"

"Be gracious to me . . . Wash me thoroughly from my iniquity and cleanse me from my sin . . . Create in me a clean heart . . . Deliver me from bloodguiltiness, O God, the God of my salvation" (Psalm 51:1-2, 10, 14). The psalmist introduces his repentant discussion with, "Be gracious to me, O God." True repentance includes the understanding that God's grace is necessary. God's actions on my behalf are unmerited. I am unworthy.

Counterfeit repentance does not include the understanding of the desperate need for God's grace. It exhibits an attitude that tries to earn or deserve the right to come to God. It forgets the Good News! Jesus graciously came to us to die in our place and conquer sin on our behalf. He gets it! He sits on the throne of grace so that we can turn to Him (Heb. 4:14-16).

The Psalmist also understands that God's cleansing is desperately necessary. He confesses, "I am unclean. I am dirty." Counterfeit repentance exhibits an attitude that says, "I will wait until I do enough good things that I feel clean enough to approach God." Repentance understands that you cannot wash yourself. It cries out, "God, please wash me!"

The psalmist continues by expressing His need for God to continue creating in him: "Create in me a clean heart, O God, and renew a steadfast spirit within me" (Psalm 51:10). True repentance includes the understanding that God is still at work in you. It says, "I am unfinished. I am imperfect." Counterfeit repentance does not include the understanding of the desperate need for God to continue to be at work in you. It exhibits the attitude that says, "I will wait until I have time to change myself so that I feel changed enough to approach God."

Finally, the psalmist resonates with our need for God to "not lead us into temptation, but deliver us from evil" (Matt. 6:13). True repentance includes the understanding that God is the Deliverer. It says, "I am unable to deliver myself. I am useless by myself." Counterfeit repentance does not include the understanding of the desperate need for God's deliverance. It exhibits an attitude that says, "I will 'go through the motions' so that I feel like I am useful enough to approach God."

The ironic alternative to not admitting that you are useless is to do useless things (Mal. 1:10). God does not want a form without the substance. He is not pleased with the "motions"; He does not delight in your sacrifices and burnt offerings. He desires a broken and humble spirit. He is the only One Who can deliver you and make you useful. You cannot deliver yourself. You do not have to feel useful in order to come to God. Do you need to turn to God, so He can make you useful again, but instead go through the motions in order to feel useful? Do you needlessly carry around the ball and chain of the uselessness of sin, the guilt of sin? Do not carry it. Let it go!

Repentance is the point of coming to the end of yourself and turning to God's ability. It is not so much the process of declaring your actions as it is the process of asking to be acted upon. Change me, O God. Please, grace me, wash me, create in me, and deliver me!

NOVEMBER 8

A FAST WAY TO BENEFITS

*"But you, when you fast, anoint your head and wash your face, so that your fasting will not be noticed by men ... and your Father who sees **what is done** in secret will reward you ... store up for yourselves treasures in heaven."*

Matthew 6:17-20

Does the Bible indicate that there are benefits that come from fasting? If fasting is done sincerely and with correct motives, it can be done with a certain expectation of benefits, since Jesus made that a point of His own teaching. "'But you, when you fast, anoint your head and wash your face so that your fasting will not be noticed by men, but by your Father who is in secret; and your Father who sees *what is done* in secret will reward you'" (Matt. 6:17-18). Fasting is described as being efficacious (Matt. 6:19-20).

Many biblical passages concerning fasting are set in the context of "distress situations," including penitence (Lev. 16:29-31, 1 Kings 21:27, Jonah 3:5-10, Acts 9:9), sorrow (1 Sam. 31:13), the need to make a critical decision (Gen. 24:33, Acts 14:23), the need for God's protection or deliverance (Judges 20:26, 1 Sam. 7:6, 2 Chron. 20:3, Ezra 8:21-23, Matt. 17:21), and the need for God's intervention and direction (Deut. 9:9-21, 2 Sam. 12:15-23).

It is incorrectly argued that Jesus instructed His followers to no longer fast because His coming effectively eliminated distress situations:

> Then the disciples of John came to Him, asking, "Why do we and the Pharisees fast, but Your disciples do not fast?" And Jesus said to them, "The attendants of the bridegroom cannot mourn as long as the bridegroom is with them, can they? But the days will come when the bridegroom is taken away from them, and then they will fast" (Matt. 9:14-15).

Jesus denounced fasting that was done with impure motives while, at the same time, promoting fasting itself, saying, "'When you fast . . .'" (Matt. 6:16-17) and "'then they will fast'" (Matt. 9:15). Jesus assumed His disciples would fast and be benefitted by it.

Fasting can be seen as a practice that mourns the removal of the bridegroom and facilitates a closer relationship between Him and us "who are absent from the Lord" (2 Cor. 5:6). The Holy Spirit brings God's people into relationship with the removed Christ, and fasting can facilitate that operation inasmuch as it facilitates an expression of need for the Spirit and enhances the attitude of emptying self for the purpose of being filled with the Spirit.

Since there is a dual nature to the coming of the kingdom of God—it is "already *and* not yet"—there was no fasting within the parameters of the first coming of Christ (Incarnation), but there is fasting in preparation for the second coming (return of Christ). To the degree to which fasting can express or manifest—and even prompt or establish—inner attitudes of the heart like repentance, humility, and reliance upon God, is the degree to which fasting is appropriate now. Fasting can express our ongoing need to repent, to be humble, and to rely on God. All of these have their benefits. Repentance receives grace and mercy (Joel 2:12-13). Humility leads to grace and exultation (James 4:6-10). Reliance on God results in straight paths (Prov. 3:5-6). Yes, the Bible indicates that there are benefits to fasting. Fasting is described as being efficacious as a means of grace. There is, indeed, a *fast* way to benefits!

NOVEMBER 9

DO YOU HAVE A RELATIONSHIP WITH THE LAW?

"For truly I say to you, until heaven and earth pass away,
not the smallest letter or stroke shall pass from the Law until all is accomplished."
Matthew 5:18

Since we are not saved by the Law, is it simply done away with? As followers of Christ, what is our relationship to the Law? Jesus renounced the superficial and cheapened form of the Law, known as the scribal law, which was created by the hypocritical, and therefore nonethical, attitudes and behaviors of the scribes and the Pharisees. On the other hand, Jesus' relationship to the true Law, and therefore His relationship to ethics, was to reestablish it rightly and to stand up for its validity.

> Do not think that I came to abolish the Law or the Prophets; I did not come to abolish but to fulfill. For truly I say to you, until heaven and earth pass away, not the smallest letter or stroke shall pass from the Law until all is accomplished. Whoever then annuls one of the least of these commandments, and teaches others *to do* the same, shall be called least in

the kingdom of heaven; but whoever keeps and teaches *them*, he shall be called great in the kingdom of heaven. For I say to you that unless your righteousness surpasses *that* of the scribes and Pharisees, you will not enter the kingdom of heaven (Matt. 5:17-20).

Jesus declares His loyalty to the minutest detail of the God-given Law. It is not simply broad and general principles that Jesus is advocating as being characteristic of His ethic, but specific details—"the smallest letter or stroke" or "jots and tittles." Attention to detail is not necessarily indicative of Pharisaical legalism. Legalism is satisfied with emptiness, externalism, humanistic traditionalism, superficiality, and hypocrisy. Why concern yourself with the weightier issues of justice and mercy as long as you are being seen as giving something to the needy? "'Woe to you, scribes and Pharisees, hypocrites! For you tithe mint and dill and cummin, and have neglected the weightier provisions of the law: justice and mercy and faithfulness'" (Matt. 23:23).

Any Pharisaical concern for detail is merely a platform for boasting, "Look at me and blow the trumpets for I am tithing mint and dill!" While demanding this, the Pharisee kicks out of the way a beggar who is seated at the steps of the temple, the very kind of person that the Pharisee's "tithe" is supposedly meant for. Jesus wants nothing to do with this sort of Law and ethics. Jesus' own fulfilling of the Law is a validation of detail. However, it is a validation of the details of the true and full Law. Followers of Christ are not to be advocates of legalistic ethics, but they are to be proponents of Christ ethics.

Jesus could not invalidate the Law—not even a teeny, tiny bit or a miniscule jot or tittle's worth—since it remains binding until the end of the world. Jesus speaks as though the Law can never lose its binding force. Even as sin is the transgression of the Law, righteousness is defined as conformity to the law.

> So then, the Law is holy, and the commandment is holy and righteous and good. Therefore did that which is good become *a cause of* death for me? May it never be! Rather it was sin, in order that it might be shown to be sin by effecting my death through that which is good, so that through the commandment sin would become utterly sinful. For we know that the Law is spiritual, but I am of flesh, sold into bondage to sin . . . I find then the principle that evil is present in me, the one who wants to do good. For I joyfully concur with the law of God in the inner man, but I see a different law in the members of my body . . . So then, on the one hand I myself with my mind am serving the law of God, but on the other, with my flesh the law of sin (Rom. 7:12-25).

There is a direct relationship between the Law and what is holy and good. For the believer, the Law changes from that which is associated with bondage to that which is viewed with delight. Both the Old and New Testaments describe the Law of God and its applied ethics as being the pleasure or joy of the believer. "I delight to do Your will, O my God; Your Law is within my heart" (Psalm 40:8) is reflective of "If you keep My commandments, you will abide in My love; just as I have kept My Father's commandments and abide in His love. These things I have spoken to you so that My joy may be in you, and *that* your joy may be made full" (John 15:10-11).

What is the Christian's relationship to the Law? We should not speak of a *Christian* ethic as if ethics have changed due to Christ's coming. Christian ethics and the moral Law of God are one and the same. They always have been, and they always will be, even "until heaven and earth pass away!" (Matt. 5:18).

NOVEMBER 10

GOD KEEPS GETTING IN THE WAY

"I will not drive them out before you in a single year, that the land may not become desolate and the beasts of the field become too numerous for you. I will drive them out before you little by little."

Exodus 23:29-30

Spirituality begins with our understanding that it is God who draws us to Himself. Jesus said, "'No one can come to Me unless the Father who sent Me draws him'" (John 6:44). It is God Who makes our relationship with Him a possibility. Moreover, God is constantly intervening in our lives. The fact that God keeps "getting in the way" can serve as a profound definition or description of the idea that God is a God of mercy and grace. Our relational response to God is a possibility only because God is constantly involved in our lives. In fact, if God was not directly involved with you this very second, you would instantly evaporate. "If He should gather to Himself His spirit and His breath, all flesh would perish together, and man would return to dust" (Job 34:14-15). God is constantly involved with us for our own benefit. This is good news. Please, God, get in my way!

The constancy of Divine intervention in our lives includes God's constant control. He is Sovereign. God knows and understands everything. This enables His constant intervention.

> I will send My terror ahead of you, and throw into confusion all the people among whom you come, and I will make all your enemies *turn* their backs to you. I will send hornets ahead of you so that they will drive out the Hivites, the Canaanites, and the Hittites before you. I will not drive them out before you in a single year, that the land may not become desolate and the beasts of the field become too numerous for you. I will drive them out before you little by little, until you become fruitful and take possession of the land (Exod. 23:27-30).

God's omniscience results in a Sovereign intervention in our lives. It is constant because His omniscience is constant. He always knows everything and is, therefore, always in control. In the midst of His constant control, He intervenes for our own benefit, even when we might think that the opposite action is beneficial. He may not "drive them out before you" immediately since He knows that if He did, you would be in danger. You might not think of this, but the omniscient God does.

Some years ago, a tragic plane crash took the lives of the players of the Zambian national soccer team. No one knew that would happen. Nevertheless, God knew and was in control. Two players on the team were Christians. One of them did not go on the trip because he was uncharacteristically left off the travel team. The other did not go because he was injured in practice the day before. Both players were distressed to see the plane leave without them. Later, however, they recognized the intervention of God on their behalf.

Perhaps you are looking for a new job. You are praying. There's a great opportunity that you desire, but it fails to materialize. You only see the apparent great opportunity, but God sees the whole picture. There is something better further down the line. Rest in God in the things you cannot control, knowing that He is in control and constantly intervening on your behalf. The great Puzzle-maker knows all of the pieces and understands where they need to go. He can intervene in your puzzle and put it together! "'For I know the plans that I have for you,' declares the LORD, 'plans for welfare and not for calamity to give you a future and a hope'" (Jer. 29:11).

There is no peace in deism. God is not an absentee Landlord. Praise God that He truly is involved with His creation. He intervenes constantly. In His intervention, He becomes our peace, rest, and hope. "Trust in the LORD with all your heart and do not lean on your own understanding. In all your ways acknowledge Him, and He will make your paths straight" (Prov. 3:5-6). Thank God that He keeps getting in the way!

NOVEMBER 11

THE SPIRITUAL GIFTS OF FAITH AND PROPHECY

"For to one is given the word of wisdom through the Spirit . . . and to another faith . . . and to another prophecy."

1 Corinthians 12:8-10

The gifts of the Spirit are wondrous things. Not the least of these wonders is the gift of faith and the gift of prophecy (1 Cor. 12:9-10). We should speak of the gift of faith as that which is a special faith, as opposed to saving faith (Eph. 2:8), or faith that is a fruit that marks one's character (Gal. 5:22). It is a temporary faith that is received for a special occasion or for a specific situation and purpose (Acts 27:24-25, 44). The "situation" might be the need to resolve a problem or "move a mountain" in our lives (Mark 11:22-23). The gift of faith is not simply a condition of the mind. It is not that which is "welled up." It is a manifestation of the Holy Spirit (1 Cor. 12:7) that is given as a gift and is to be opened and used in a particular situation at a particular time.

The Holy Spirit activates this faith. It cannot simply be activated by human will. God is Sovereign in this manifestation as in all manifestations of the Spirit. A member of a small group took part in group prayer for another member who was deaf in one ear. As the group prayed for healing, he experienced a surge of faith for the healing of the woman's ear to the point that "he knew that he knew that he knew" that the woman's hearing would be restored. He prayed for healing with this fresh sense of faith, and the woman's deaf ear was healed. This is the gift of faith working together with the gifts of healing.

The use of the gift of prophecy sometimes promotes controversy in the body of Christ. Perhaps, the main reason for this debate is the idea that prophecy would come to be equal to or even trump the Word of God. After all, it is the prophet's prophecies that are viewed as Old Testament Scripture. While this is true, it is not true that all that was prophesied by the prophets in the Old Testament was put forth as Scripture (1 Sam. 19:20-24). It is not necessary that prophecy be made equal to Scripture. It must be consistent with Scripture and subordinate to it, but it does not have to produce new books of the Bible. Otherwise, when a believer speaks forth the heart of God, we would have to publish a new Bible with sixty-seven books that includes a new book titled, "First Neighborhood Outreach." Inevitably, sometime soon thereafter, someone else would reference God's heart in desiring to equip a neighborhood outreach, and another book would need to be added to the Bible called, of course, "Second Neighborhood Outreach." Within a very short time, there might be a thousand new books of the Bible.

Of course, that is ridiculous, just as it is ridiculous to think that God no longer speaks to and through His people. Prophecy does not automatically equal Scripture. The canon is closed; however, God's mouth is not closed. We are not deists. God is still an immanent God. He still intervenes and is involved with us. He is still, even after the closing of the canon, a personal God Who communicates and has relationship with His people. And He still manifests Himself through the gifts of the Holy Spirit, including the gift of prophecy.

The Spirit-sourced gift of prophecy (1 Cor. 12:10) is not the same as the Christ-sourced gift of prophet (Eph. 4:11). Another way to say this is that all may prophesy (Acts 2:17, 1 Cor. 14:31) but not all are prophets (1 Cor. 12:29). What is the Spirit-sourced gift of prophecy? Prophecy is based on a revelation from God (1 Cor. 14:30-31), not on human reflection or conceptualization. Although it can be predictive, it is mainly the authoritative speaking of God's heart. Prophecy can confront or exhort, but it will usually edify and esteem. It can offer specific direction ("personal prophecy"); however, it should be a confirmation to the person it is directed to (Acts 13:2). Prophecy is mainly for believers (1 Cor. 14:22), but it can have a powerful effect on unbelievers (1 Cor. 14:24-25).

In prophecy, of course, God does not actually speak. He gives the one who prophesies the words to speak. He speaks for God (which is a brief, but accurate, definition of prophecy). A preacher preached a message in his church on Father's Day. As the message went forth, he increasingly sensed the love of God for His people. He began to emphasize and describe the Father's heart for His children. The Spirit of God manifested Himself in the gift of prophecy.

A word of prophecy is not an ecstatic utterance. The one who prophesies is not out of control or in a state in which he lacks his senses; he is not senseless. The Spirit manifests Himself through the vessel, not in spite of the vessel. The one who prophesies uses his own faculties to bring forth the word of prophecy. Thus, there are dangers as the perfect flows through the imperfect. And so, there should be warnings. Be careful to avoid requests for personal prophecy: "Can you give me a word?" This is tantamount to saying, "Can you read my palm?" Avoid self-serving prophecy: "You will come into much money; and if you tithe on that money into my ministry, you will get even more money." That is not prophecy. That is opportunism!

NOVEMBER 12

INSTRUMENTS, THEMSELVES, ARE NOT THE MUSIC!

"It came about when Ahab heard these words, that he tore his clothes and put on sackcloth and fasted... 'Do you see how Ahab has humbled himself before Me? Because he has humbled himself before Me, I will not bring the evil in his days.'"

1 Kings 21:27-29

Spiritual disciplines or "means of grace" like prayer, Bible study, giving, and fasting can be viewed as acts that, when rooted in holy inspiration, place a person in a right position before God that which better prepare them to receive God's grace. Fasting, for example, that is prompted by genuine repentance is an outward expression of an inward attitude that positions us rightly before God. Here it must be remembered that if something is outside the will of God, fasting will never put it inside His will. Fasting is a means, not a cause; it can be an instrument but is in no way the music itself!

And so, fasting can facilitate a proper attitude before God. It does not make one righteous—only the blood of Jesus can do that—but it can be a means to express the reality of righteousness (right standing before God), which would include an attitude of dependence, need, humility, and desire for Him. Simply because the expression of something necessitates its appropriate substance—lest it be an empty container—does not automatically negate the usefulness of such an expression. Tithing mint, dill, and cumin is useless without justice, mercy, and lovingkindness; but when that expression is motivated by that substance, the expression is appropriate. Jesus tells us that "'these are the things you should have done without neglecting the others'" (Matt. 23:23).

God's reprimanding of Israel, at times, regarding the outward expression of the offering of sacrifices is not His way of saying that He changed His mind or that He was wrong to require these sacrifices and, in fact, did not want them anymore. He is saying that He does not want them without the substance or contents that make them legitimate. "For You do not delight in sacrifice, otherwise I would give it; You are not pleased with burnt offering. The sacrifices of God are a broken spirit; a broken and a contrite heart, O God, You will not despise" (Psalm 51:16-17). It is a proper heart attitude that is acceptable to God. External forms that facilitate a sincere expression of those corresponding attitudes can be holy before God. They can be a means of grace by becoming a means of expressing a correct posture before God.

There is nothing wrong with a biblical form, as long as it is sincerely associated with and expressive of a biblical substance. There is nothing wrong with the mold, as long as it holds the filling. There is nothing wrong with something external, as long as it truly facilitates an expression of something internal. There is nothing wrong with a spiritual discipline, as long as it *is* spiritual; and there is nothing wrong with a means of grace, as long as it is not understood to be the grace itself.

For example, Ahab seems to have been truly broken before God (internal). His fasting (external), then, became acceptable to God as it facilitated an expression of his brokenness. In this sense, fasting became a means of grace.

> It came about when Ahab heard these words, that he tore his clothes and put on sackcloth and fasted, and he lay in sackcloth and went about despondently. Then the word of the LORD came to Elijah the Tishbite, saying, "Do you see how Ahab has humbled himself before Me? Because he has humbled himself before Me, I will not bring the evil in his days" (1 Kings 21:27-29).

Spiritual disciplines or "means of grace" like prayer, Bible study, giving, and fasting can be viewed as acts that, when rooted in holy inspiration, place a person in a right position before God, which better prepares them to receive God's grace. Means of grace can be useful instruments, but they can never be the music itself. We may be lamps, but only He is the Light! (John 8:12, Matt. 5:14-16).

NOVEMBER 13

BLAST OFF!

"Thus it is written, that the Christ would suffer and rise again from the dead the third day, and that repentance for forgiveness of sins would be proclaimed in His name to all the nations, beginning from Jerusalem. You are witnesses of these things. And behold, I am sending forth the promise of My Father upon you; but you are to stay in the city until you are clothed with power from on high."

Luke 24:46-49

Just before Jesus ascends into Heaven, He mandates His disciples with the Great Commission and tells them how they will be equipped to achieve it (Matt. 28-18-20, Acts 1:8, Luke 24:46-49). They will take the Gospel to the nations after being empowered by the Holy Spirit. Then an incredible thing happens:

When the day of Pentecost had come, they were all together in one place. And suddenly there came from heaven a noise like a violent rushing wind, and it filled the whole house where they were sitting. And there appeared to them tongues as of fire distributing themselves, and they rested on each one of them. And they were all filled with the Holy Spirit and began to speak with other tongues, as the Spirit was giving them utterance. Now there were Jews living in Jerusalem, devout men from every nation under heaven. And when this sound occurred, the crowd came together, and were bewildered because each one of them was hearing them speak in his own language (Acts 2:1-6).

What an incredible redemption; a sort of missiological redemption. The missionary idea (Gen. 12:1-3) began after "the LORD confused the language of the whole earth; and from there the Lord scattered them abroad over the face of the whole earth" (Gen. 11:9). The existence of scattered nations with a multitude of languages coming out of Genesis 11 leads to a chosen missionary people in Genesis 12. Now, some two thousand years later, God's missionary people are empowered to go to the nations and "language" plays, a highlighted role as "men from every nation under heaven" heard these empowered ones speaking in their own languages. In a sort of symbolic way, the Great Commission was fulfilled on that extraordinary Day of Pentecost.

Blast off! The Spirit is poured out; and immediately, the church begins to grow in Jerusalem (Acts 1-7). Then it continues to grow in Judea and Samaria (Acts 8-12). Finally, its missionaries begin to take the Gospel to the uttermost parts of the earth (Acts 13-28).

As the Church continued to obey Christ's commandment to go, it started to take on its own identity. Missionaries were sent to Antioch, and it was there for the first time that the Church was recognized as something other than a Jewish sect. The disciples of Christ became known as "Christians" (Acts 11:22-26). For the next two thousand years, these Christians would take the Gospel to almost every place and people on earth. The empowered Church must continue to go so that He will return. When the Gospel goes to all nations, "then the end will come" (Matt. 24:14). So, let's go! Blast off!

NOVEMBER 14

LEADERS MUST LEAD FROM THE CROSS

"For whoever wishes to become great among you shall be your servant, and whoever wishes to be first among you shall be your slave."

Matthew 20:26-27

A *Christian* leader, by definition, must be a follower of *Christ*. A follower of Christ Who bore "His own cross" (John 19:17), by definition, must "'deny himself, and take up his cross daily and follow'" Him (Luke 9:23). And so, a Christian leader must pursue selflessness.

A Christian leader is motivated by concern for others, not by concern for self. The leader must be other-oriented, not self-oriented. A leader will put the focus on others' accomplishments more than he will shine the light on himself. Nehemiah exhibited this aspect of selfless leadership when he emphasized the accomplishments of the workers who were rebuilding the walls in Jerusalem (Neh. 3). A selfless leader is willing to put his reputation on the cross taking more of the blame than he deserves. He is also willing to put his sense of accomplishment on the cross taking less of the credit than he deserves.

A Christian leader must be able to take his eyes off himself in order to put his eyes on others. If he is too concerned about himself and his own problems, then he will not be able to help others. He must be free from himself so that he can be a slave of others; for "whoever wishes to become great among you shall be your servant, and whoever wishes to be first among you shall be your slave" (Matt. 20:26-27). A Christian leader must also be free from himself so that he can have compassion on others. Jesus "felt compassion for them" (Mark 6:34) because He was able to look away from Himself and His own needs and look toward others and their needs (Mark 6:31-39). Nehemiah led multitudes of people in a massive project to rebuild the walls in Jerusalem. He was not so full of himself that he could not put himself into the shoes of others. He felt compassion for those he was leading. "When I heard these words, I sat down and wept and mourned for days; and I was fasting and praying before the God of heaven" (Neh. 1:4).

A Christian leader is willing to sacrifice for those he is leading. In a marriage, "the husband is the head of the wife" (Eph. 5:23). His actions as the leader in the marriage are summarized in his realization that he is to give himself up for her (Eph. 5:25). If a leader is not sincere in this way, then he is not able to effectively lead his people. If he is not willing to lay down his life for those he is leading, then he eventually loses motivation because he eventually loses his sense of purpose. Without a strong sense of a well-defined purpose, it is difficult to continue on as a leader; the leader will become a victim of burnout. A leader's purpose must focus on blessing God and those who are being led. Without pure motives, burnout can occur. It can also occur when intake (relationship with God) is less than output (relationship with others). It can occur when a leader works outside of his gifts. All of these causes of burnout are traced back to not having a strong sense of well-defined purpose, which, in turn, is traced back to a lack of selflessness.

Leaders cannot allow themselves to be hindered by a conflict of interest. They cannot allow their own interests and desires to get in the way of the interests and needs of the people they are leading. In order to be an example, leaders may need to lay aside their privileges, so they can relate to their people and exhibit solidarity with them. Nehemiah led in this way: "Now that which was prepared for each day was one ox *and* six choice sheep, also birds were prepared for me; and once in ten days all sorts of wine *were furnished* in abundance. Yet for all this I did not demand the governor's food *allowance*, because the servitude was heavy on this people" (Neh. 5:18).

Jesus exhibited perfect, selfless leadership. All of the aspects of a cross-centered style of leadership are wrapped up in the incarnation:

> Therefore if there is any encouragement in Christ, if there is any consolation of love, if there is any fellowship of the Spirit, if any affection and compassion, make my joy complete by being of the same mind, maintaining the same love, united in spirit, intent on one purpose. Do nothing from selfishness or empty conceit, but with humility of mind regard one another as more important than yourselves; do not *merely* look out for your own personal interests, but also for the interests of others. Have this attitude in yourselves which was also in Christ Jesus, who, although He existed in the form of God, did not regard equality with God a thing to be grasped, but emptied Himself, taking the form of a bond-servant, *and* being made in the likeness of men. Being found in appearance as a man, He humbled Himself by becoming obedient to the point of death, even death on a cross (Phil. 2:1-8).

NOVEMBER 15

WE NEED THE WORD, NOT JUST WORDS!

*"Be diligent to present yourself approved to God as a workman who does not need to be ashamed, accurately handling the word of truth. But avoid worldly **and** empty chatter."*

2 Timothy 2:15-16

Improve your serve. More specifically, improve your service of the Word. We are called to be diligent workmen of the Word (2 Tim. 2:15). Studying the Bible is hard work. It is something that we must work at in order to improve. One way to gain more from the Scriptures comes from this biblical principle: "When you study the Old Testament, look for Jesus." This is a biblical principle because Jesus is the Word of God (John 1:1). Jesus explained it this way: "'You search the Scriptures because you think that in them you have eternal life; it is these that testify about Me . . . For if you believed Moses, you would believe Me, for he wrote about Me'" (John 5:39, 46). The Old Testament can only be fully understood when we read it through the lens of the Person of Christ, just as the Old Covenant is better understood in light of the New Covenant.

You can do a brief review of Old Testament quotes and allusions found in the New Testament as a way to prepare yourself to be better equipped to find Jesus in the Old Testament. Similarly, you might do a brief review of the Messianic prophecies found in the Old Testament. Here, you should be intent on linking the fallen condition of humanity with its Christological solution. Overall study of and preaching from the Old Testament should be done with more of an insistence upon interpreting it in light of the New Testament.

With respect to improving your ministry of the Word, you should consider your prophetic role. Modern Western cultures need a prophetic voice that stands in opposition to "postmodern" tendencies to reject authority and conviction. In response to the relativism produced by such a pluralistic society that has lost all sense of belief in the existence of absolutes, our proclamation of the Word must be authoritative without being condescending or combative. In order to be a light to a non-absolutist society, prophetic voices must speak dogmatically about biblical truth. However, to speak dogmatically without patience, love, and sincere concern for those being spoken to will end up being counterproductive.

Postmodern relativism and pluralism must be countered by firmly offering and standing on the most foundational Christian foundations—the deity of Christ and the uniqueness of salvation in Him. For example, one of the great truths that needs to be shared authoritatively is the fact that God will judge each individual according to their response to the Gospel message. Postmodern thinking dismisses individual responsibility because it believes that society—not individuals—creates truth and the proper response to it. Thus, society is responsible, not individuals. Clearly, a prophetic voice is needed.

Improve your serve, both your service of the study of the Word and your service of the proclamation of the Word. We do not need words. We need the Word!

> Remind *them* of these things, and solemnly charge *them* in the presence of God not to wrangle about words, which is useless *and leads* to the ruin of the hearers. Be diligent to present yourself approved to God as a workman who does not need to be ashamed, accurately handling the word of truth. But avoid worldly *and* empty chatter, for it will lead to further ungodliness, and their talk will spread like gangrene (2 Tim. 2:14-17).

NOVEMBER 16

IT'S LIKE A LEAVEN

"He spoke another parable to them, 'The kingdom of heaven is like leaven, which a woman took and hid in three pecks of flour until it was all leavened.'"

Matthew 13:33

The Gospel is not a new thing. Its proclamation goes all the way back to the Garden of Eden (Gen. 3:15). It has been, currently is, and will continue to be spread throughout the world. It is the very nature of the Gospel; it spreads. It is like a leaven (Matt. 13:33). The kingdom of God has always been growing, albeit, in a largely hidden and unnoticeable way. "The kingdom of heaven is like a mustard seed, which a man took and sowed in his field; and this is smaller than all *other* seeds, but when it is full grown, it is larger than the garden plants and becomes a tree" (Matt. 13:31-32). God has always used a missionary people to achieve this growth. Sometimes, they cooperated voluntarily; and sometimes, they were reduced to cooperating involuntarily. In either case, God's missionary plan went forth, for, as Job said to God, "No purpose of Yours can be thwarted" (Job 42:2).

God called Abraham to be a missionary nation (Gen. 12:1-3). Israel was used by God to "bless all the nations." Sometimes, this blessing was spread via voluntary going (Gen. 12:1), sometimes via involuntary going (Egyptian captivity and Babylonian exile), sometimes via invasion (Sennacherib and the Assyrians), and sometimes via a benign attraction (Queen of Sheba). Finally, after Israel's leaders rejected the king of the kingdom, Jesus took the missionary assignment from her and gave it to a new missionary nation. The Church inherited the same ancient assignment to spread the Gospel (Matt. 21:33-42, 1 Peter 2:9). Jesus established this transition when He said, "'Therefore I say to you, the kingdom of God will be taken away from you and given to a people, producing the fruit of it'" (Matt. 21:43).

Initially, the Church spread the Gospel in the Roman Empire. In 312 A.D., the Roman emperor, Constantine, declared himself to be a Christian. By 380, Christianity became the official religion of Rome. However, Roman Christianity made no special attempt to fulfill the Great Commission.

The Barbarians invaded and inherited a Christian culture. They emphasized mission, but their emphasis did not include reaching out to the Vikings. The Vikings invaded; and again, the conquerors became conquered by the faith of their captives. For the most part, God's missionary plan was going forth involuntarily.

The Reformation brought a fresh sense of faith to the Church. Worldwide Gospel expansion began in very significant ways. Empires such as England and Spain began to send out explorers in order to expand their empires. Christianity went with them. From 1500 to 1900, the Gospel message was spread all over the world. People like William Carey were instrumental in challenging the Church to use biblical missionary practices. The most important method for effective and efficient missionary work was established; a missionary must work himself out of a job by equipping indigenous leaders to lead their own churches.

In the late 1800s, missionary strategists began to focus on unreached inland areas. People like Hudson Taylor went to China, for example. Mission societies were formed; and student movements produced young, zealous bearers of the Gospel message who went all over the world. In the mid-1900s, many mission societies began to realize the need for missionaries to be sent to hidden unreached people groups. People like Cameron Townsend (Central American Indians) and Donald McGavran

(Asian Indians) began to identify and reach hidden tribal peoples. This focus on unreached groups has brought the Church to its current place in its missionary obligation.

The fulfillment of the Great Commission is not far off. There is still work to be done. Perhaps, the maturing of the relatively young churches of Africa, Asia, and Latin America will result in the consummation of all things: "'This gospel of the kingdom shall be preached in the whole world as a testimony to all the nations, and then the end will come'" (Matt. 24:14).

NOVEMBER 17

WON'T YOU BE MY NEIGHBOR

"Do not devise harm against your neighbor."

Proverbs 3:29

According to Scripture, you cannot live out your Christianity alone. We are not only *better* together, but also, we *must* be together. To follow God's commands, you need another person. We are to love each other (John 13:34), be devoted to and honor one another (Rom. 12:10), live in harmony with one another (Rom. 12:16), and build up one another (Rom. 14:19). These are just a few of the many "one another" sorts of commands in the Bible. The "one-anotherness" of these commands requires that we live in relationships.

Relationships are important because it is through relationships with others that we can practice our walk with God. It is fair to say that the quality of our relationships with others is an expression of the quality of our walk with God. Many people would say that they do not have a problem getting along with most people around them. Yet these same people struggle to get along with "the guy next door."

In any case, God calls us to be good neighbors. What does a good neighbor look like? A good neighbor is not a "big mouth." He is trustworthy and can keep certain things confidential. "He who despises his neighbor lacks sense, but a man of understanding keeps silent" (Prov. 11:12). A good neighbor does not plan to hurt his neighbor. "Do not devise harm against your neighbor, while he lives securely beside you" (Prov. 3:29). He does not spread strife. "Do not go out hastily to argue *your case*, otherwise, what will you do in the end, when your neighbor humiliates you? Argue your case with your neighbor, and do not reveal the secret of another" (Prov. 25:8-9).

A good neighbor is a good example and guide. "The righteous is a guide to his neighbor, but the way of the wicked leads them astray" (Prov. 12:26). Part of this role is to simply be available. "Do not forsake your own friend or your father's friend, and do not go to your brother's house in the day of your calamity; better is a neighbor who is near than a brother far away" (Prov. 27:10). A good neighbor is kind, even to those who do not like him. "If your enemy is hungry, give him food to eat; and if he is thirsty, give him water to drink; for you will heap burning coals on his head, and the LORD will reward you" (Prov. 25:21-22). He is generous in his judgments and does not let his "heart be glad" when his neighbor stumbles (Prov. 24:17). A good neighbor uses tact. "Let your foot rarely be in your neighbor's house, or he will become weary of you and hate you" (Prov. 25:17). He respects the feelings of others. He does not force himself upon his neighbor and does not overstay his welcome. He is sensitive. He does not become a nuisance. He does not cross over social boundaries.

To be neighborly is to be loving. Love is the action of a good neighbor. It is what is necessary to fulfill the law. To follow God's commands, you need your neighbor. You need someone to love. "For the whole Law is fulfilled in one word, in the *statement*, 'YOU SHALL LOVE YOUR NEIGHBOR AS YOURSELF'" (Gal. 5:14). Do you want to be loved? Love your neighbor!

NOVEMBER 18

HAVE YOU EVER SEEN A MOUNTAIN MOVE?

"Truly I say to you, if you have faith and do not doubt, you will not only do what was done to the fig tree, but even if you say to this mountain, 'Be taken up and cast into the sea,' it will happen. And all things you ask in prayer, believing, you will receive."

Matthew 21:21-22

Faith is powerful. It can move mountains; it is not intimidated by the impossible (Matt. 17:20). Faith results in salvation, sanctification, and relational status. In the category of "salvation results," faith leads to forgiveness. "Everyone who believes in Him receives forgiveness of sins" (Acts 10:43). Faith results in justification. "Therefore let it be known to you, brethren, that through Him forgiveness of sins is proclaimed to you, and through Him everyone who believes is freed from all things, from which you could not be freed through the Law of Moses" (Acts 13:38-39). Faith can yield freedom from judgment. "He who believes in Him is not judged" (John 3:18).

Jesus challenges us to have faith for freedom from spiritual death. "'I am the resurrection and the life; he who believes in Me will live even if he dies, and everyone who lives and believes in Me will never die. Do you believe this?'" (John 11:25-26). Faith works "'so that whoever believes will in Him have eternal life. For God so loved the world, that He gave His only begotten Son, that whoever believes in Him shall not perish, but have eternal life'" (John 3:15-16).

Faith walks in the land of the impossible; therefore, faith walks in the land of salvation. Salvation is impossible with man; but with God's gift of faith to man (Eph. 2:8), all things are possible. "When the disciples heard *this*, they were very astonished and said, 'Then who can be saved?' And looking at them Jesus said to *them*, 'With people this is impossible, but with God all things are possible'" (Matt. 19:25-26). More specifically, "'All things are possible to him who believes'" (Mark 9:23). Faith results in salvation, while a lack of faith results in condemnation: "'He who has believed and has been baptized shall be saved; but he who has disbelieved shall be condemned'" (Mark 16:16).

In the category of "sanctification results," faith leads to an escape from darkness and an embracing of the Light; it leads to becoming sons of the Light. "'While you have the Light, believe in the Light, so that you may become sons of Light . . . I have come *as* Light into the world, so that everyone who believes in Me will not remain in darkness'" (John 12:36, 46).

Faith results in spiritual life. The Word of God is the source of faith. It has been written "so that you may believe that Jesus is the Christ, the Son of God; and that believing you may have life in His name" (John 20:31). Faith results in sanctification (Acts 26:18). "He made no distinction between us and them, cleansing their hearts by faith" (Acts 15:9).

In the category of "relational status," faith leads to adoption into God's family. "But as many as received Him, to them He gave the right to become children of God, *even* to those who believe in His name" (John 1:12). As adopted children of God, the receiving of an inheritance is linked to faith (Acts 26:18). Faith gives us access to God, since "we have boldness and confident access through faith in Him" (Eph. 3:12). Faith introduces us to justification, peace, and grace. "Therefore, having been justified by faith, we have peace with God through our Lord Jesus Christ, through whom also we have obtained our introduction by faith into this grace in which we stand" (Rom. 5:1-2).

The efficacy of faith in your life is all-inclusive. The degree to which you are successful in life is determined by the degree to which you trust God and have faith in Him. So "put your trust in the LORD your God and you will be established. Put your trust in His prophets and succeed" (2 Chron. 20:20). Faith equals success!

NOVEMBER 19

YOU CAN'T SEE HIM, BUT HE IS THERE

"In the same way the Spirit also helps our weakness."

Romans 8:26

Spirituality begins with the Spirit. God must draw us to Himself. Jesus said, "'No one can come to Me unless the Father who sent Me draws him'" (John 6:44). It is God Who makes our relationship with Him a possibility. Moreover, God is constantly intervening in our lives. In fact, if God was not directly involved with you this very second, you would instantly evaporate. "If He should gather to Himself His spirit and His breath, all flesh would perish together, and man would return to dust" (Job 34:14-15). God is constantly involved with us for our own benefit. The Holy Spirit acts on our behalf. This is good news!

> In the same way the Spirit also helps our weakness; for we do not know how to pray as we should, but the Spirit Himself intercedes for *us* with groanings too deep for words; and He who searches the hearts knows what the mind of the Spirit is, because He intercedes for the saints according to *the will of* God. And we know that God causes all things to work together for good to those who love God, to those who are called according to *His* purpose (Rom. 8:26-28).

The Holy Spirit is intervening in our lives for our benefit. He is causing "all things to work together for good." The constant active presence of the Holy Spirit results in the various pieces of the puzzles of our lives being fitted together. The Father, the Son, and the Holy Spirit all play a role in this constant intervention. The Father constantly knows what is happening in our lives. He is in constant control. That constant control benefits us as it is worked through the grace vehicle of the constant Divine favor of the Son. The One Who is constantly in control also happens to be constantly for us. The constant control of the Father that is worked through the constant Divine favor of the Son is enacted in accordance with the constant active presence of the Holy Spirit. It is not just that He controls everything and is on our side, but it is also that He acts on our behalf. Indeed, the Spirit intervenes, actively working in our midst to put things together for us in the right way. "For it is God who is at work in you, both to will and to work for *His* good pleasure (Phil. 2:13).

How many times this year has God intervened for you? How many times this week has God intervened to save your life in ways that you are not aware? How many times has He intervened to put a right person in a right place at a right time, which may not even be part of your "puzzle" until next week? How many times today has He intervened to remind you of something, or to put a certain desire in your heart, or to set a certain caution in your mind? The most foundational description of the mercy and grace of God is that He gets in our way.

> O LORD, You have searched me and known *me*. You know when I sit down and when I rise up; You understand my thought from afar. You scrutinize my path and my lying down, and are intimately acquainted with all my ways. Even before there is a word on my tongue,

behold, O LORD, You know it all. You have enclosed me behind and before, and laid Your hand upon me. *Such* knowledge is too wonderful for me; it is *too* high, I cannot attain to it. Where can I go from Your Spirit? Or where can I flee from Your presence? If I ascend to heaven, You are there; if I make my bed in Sheol, behold, You are there. If I take the wings of the dawn, if I dwell in the remotest part of the sea, even there Your hand will lead me, and Your right hand will lay hold of me (Psalm 139:1-10).

So we say, "Please God, get in my way!" The constancy of Divine intervention in our lives is determined by the constancy of the Sovereignty of the Father (constant control), which is worked through the constancy of the grace of the Son (constant Divine favor) according to the constancy of the power of the Holy Spirit (constant active presence). Since we are in constant need of God, He is in constant contact with us. He is Jehovah Shammah—"God is there" (Ezek. 48:35).

NOVEMBER 20

LOVE IS THE ANSWER TO KNOWING TOO MUCH

"Love never fails."

1 Corinthians 13:8

The greatest thing about your marriage will also be the worst thing. Marriage, by its nature, emits a unique dynamic when it comes to relationships. No other relationship breeds mutual knowledge as much as the marriage relationship. You know your mate better than you know anyone else, and your mate knows you better than he or she know anyone else. This is amazing! This is marvelous. It is the greatest thing about your marriage. At the same time, it is the worst thing about your marriage.

The most foundational human relationship is the marriage. After each of the first five days of creation, the Divine assessment was that "it was good" (Gen. 1:25). On the sixth day, God made His prized creation; and "it was very good" (Gen. 1:31). "God created man in His own image, in the image of God He created him; male and female He created them" (Gen. 1:27). Then "the LORD God fashioned into a woman the rib which He had taken from the man, and brought her to the man" (Gen. 2:22). The institution of marriage was established when God determined "a man shall leave his father and his mother, and be joined to his wife; and they shall become one flesh" (Gen. 2:24).

This is the very first human relationship. It is unique in that it is first and, therefore, most foundational. It is also unique because it is reflective of the nature of God. God, who is a *singular plurality* (the Trinity), creates mankind as male and female, who become a singular plurality in marriage. Two become one. Marriage is foundational to the nature of God. Marriage is fundamental to the continuance of the human race. Without the two who become "one flesh," humanity becomes extinct. Other humans come from the marriage. It is the Creator's plan to continue creating. Mankind continues in the realization of the two becoming one in the marriage relationship. Propagation is the essence of marriage making the marriage relationship foundational and unique.

The marriage relationship is foundational to evangelism. Inasmuch as it is a unique reflection of God and His nature, it is a fundamental expression of God's revelation of Himself. This shapes the nature of the marriage relationship. It is unique and profound in its intimacy. You cannot get closer to someone than being "one" with that person. This is foundational to all humanity. People, most primarily, are called by God to know Him and make Him known by entering into intimate relationship with Him. The husband and wife also are called to intimately know each other and have "relations with" each other (Gen. 4:1). This is evangelistic in that it reveals God's nature and His plan for redemption.

Marriage is most fundamental to human society and, thus, the most significant human relationship. The greatest thing about marriage is the intimacy that is inherent to its establishment. Marriage produces closeness. This "greatest" thing is also the "worst" thing. The fact that you know so much about each other means that you know too much about each other. Knowing so much about each other would be wonderful, except for the fact that we are fallen sinners. Just as marriage is the closest human relationship to the nature of God (made in His image), it is also the closest human relationship to the fallen nature of man. Adam and Eve—the married couple—fell to sin together—two as one. All people—the idea of inherited original sin—are sinners via the marriage relationship. Sin is passed down.

Moreover, the sin of the parents (they are not perfect and do not raise their children perfectly) exasperates (Col. 3:21) the sinful nature of their children. If marriage is the most foundational relationship of human society and, therefore, reflects the nature of God most constructively, then it is also the relationship that potentially reflects the fallen nature most destructively. Another way to say this is to say that the greatest thing about marriage can be the worst thing about it.

You know more about your mate than anyone else. Herein lies the potential bliss. Herein lies the potential problem. Before the fall of man, there was only bliss; there was no problem. After the Fall, however, Adam knowing Eve and Eve knowing Adam included Adam and Eve intimately knowing each other's sinful tendencies. With someone you do not know so well, there is not so much of a problem. However, with your husband or wife—your best friend who you know things about that nobody else knows—there is a problem. How do you make sure this potentially best thing does not fall into the ditch of the potentially worst thing? The temptation is to think that you can change the other person or that you should demand that the other person change him or herself. The truth is that you must change—not so much to change yourself but to change *your* sinful ways of dealing with *their* sinful ways.

Love is the answer to avoiding the possibility of forfeiting bliss because you know your mate so well, the answer to the unique dilemma of the "knowing too much" dynamic of marriage. More specifically, the answer is unconditional love, *agape* love. The most effective and pragmatic piece of marriage counseling is that your marriage must be defined by 100/100 love and not 50/50 love. It cannot be "you scratch my back, and I will scratch yours" or "you start doing this, and I will stop doing that." It has to be "I will scratch your back regardless of whether you scratch mine or not," and "I will do this even if you do not do that." Love is the answer because no matter who it is that you know better than anyone else, that person is not perfect; and you know it more than you know it with anyone else. Someone once said, "I love people; I just cannot stand my wife!" That is just another way of saying, "I know people; I just know my wife better!" Interestingly, it is because you know your wife better that you need more love—not because there is more sin but because you are more aware of sin. Love is the answer.

> Love is patient, love is kind *and* is not jealous; love does not brag *and* is not arrogant, does not act unbecomingly; it does not seek its own, is not provoked, does not take into account a wrong *suffered*, does not rejoice in unrighteousness, but rejoices with the truth; bears all things, believes all things, hopes all things, endures all things. Love never fails (1 Cor. 13:4-8).

NOVEMBER 21

THREE PLAYERS ON THE GOSPEL TEAM

"For our gospel did not come to you in word only, but also in power and in the Holy Spirit and with full conviction; just as you know what kind of men we proved to be among you for your sake."

1 Thessalonians 1:5

Paul described what might be called "the complete Gospel" as consisting of three equally important elements, all working together: the *proclaimed* Gospel, the *power* of the Gospel, and the *people* of the Gospel.

The proclaimed Gospel—"for our gospel did not come to you in word only"—is the content of the message, the most basic of which is delivered to the Corinthians by Paul. "For I delivered to you as of first importance what I also received, that Christ died for our sins according to the Scriptures, and that He was buried, and that He was raised on the third day according to the Scriptures" (1 Cor. 15:3-4). The Gospel is a message from God to man of His story of redemption that has gone forth in all of history—that is, "according to the Scriptures." Man needs God. God provides for man. Man must confess this need and accept God's provision. This is the essence of the contents of the Gospel; it has been the essence of the contents of the Gospel, and it will forever be the essence of the contents of the Gospel. It is really Good News!

The power of the Gospel—"but also in power and in the Holy Spirit and with full conviction"—is the means by which it is delivered. It does not just come "in word only," but it also comes by the power of the Holy Spirit. "For I am not ashamed of the gospel, for it is the power of God for salvation to everyone who believes" (Rom. 1:16). This power is not just "for show." It is an effectual power. It is the same power that raised Jesus Christ from the dead (Ephesians 1:19-20). The power of the Holy Spirit convicts man of sin. "'And He, when He comes, will convict the world concerning sin and righteousness and judgment'" (John 16:8). The convicting power of the Holy Spirit is what leads people to repentance. It is powerful. It is really powerful!

The people of the Gospel—"just as you know what kind of men we proved to be among you for your sake. You also became imitators of us"—have been transformed by it so that they become a living example of it. "And do not be conformed to this world, but be transformed by the renewing of your mind, so that you may prove what the will of God is, that which is good and acceptable and perfect" (Rom. 12:2). Paul had become so transformed by the Gospel that his life became a living expression and example of the Gospel itself. In this sense, he became a living witness. Of course, the credibility of the witness affects the jury. The people of God become a really important part of the complete Gospel. The Gospel is that which is proclaimed by the power of God through the people of God.

NOVEMBER 22

MAKE ROOM FOR JESUS!

"'MAKE READY THE WAY OF THE LORD.'"

Mark 1:3

The question in the Christian life does not pertain to God's availability to us but to our availability to God. The flow is always available, but the vessel is not always ready for use. "'Keep watching and praying... the spirit is willing, but the flesh is weak'" (Mark 14:38). It is these sorts of "means of grace"—watching and praying, for example—that make us available to God. They make room for Jesus!

It is God Who avails Himself to us, and it is we who make ourselves available to Him. We are called to prepare ourselves for the King of kings to live in and work through us. It is by the means of repentance, for example, that we "'MAKE READY THE WAY OF THE LORD'" (Mark 1:3). Repentance is not a cause of salvation. It is a conduit for it. The source or contents must be received. Turning away from self and turning to God is a means by which to receive His grace. We make ourselves available to God. We must offer ourselves to God to receive what only God can offer.

All means of grace—whether it be prayer, fasting, Bible study, or any other spiritual discipline—have the same dynamic in common. They are designed to empty you of you to make room for Jesus in you. To be filled with grace means to be emptied of self—emptied not to earn or to cause, but to make room for and receive. Means of grace do not create God's presence, activity, and intervention but appropriate that which is already available.

Involving oneself in a means of grace is to agree with what God wants to do, confess that God must do it, and receive what God has done. Prayer, for example, is saying to God, "Yes, I want You and Your works, and I know that I must come to You to get that so that I can receive what You have already done." All prayers, by their nature, are prayers of a conduit. "For we are His workmanship, created in Christ Jesus for good works, which God prepared beforehand so that we would walk in them" (Eph. 2:10).

The end product of any means of grace is the actuality of Galatians 2:20, Christ on earth operating in and through His people. Means of grace are simply ways that facilitate grace—Christ Himself! He is the end. The means are not the end. Christ Himself is the grace that the means are meant to facilitate. The means are not simply meant to facilitate us being like Christ but are meant to facilitate Christ in us (Gal. 2:20). The means do not simply result in Christ helping us to be like Him; rather, they make us available for Christ to live in and work through us.

The fruit of Christian discipleship and spirituality is much more profound and mystical than the more humanistic idea that Christ's followers simply act like Him; it is, rather, the actuality of Christ acting in and through His people. Means of grace do not simply result in, "It is no longer I who live, but I who now lives like Christ." It is much more mysterious and much more humanly impossible. "[I]t is no longer I who live, but Christ lives in me" (Gal. 2:20). I am no longer the actor, but the one who is acted upon. I am a receiver of contents—not the actual Flow, but the channel through which the contents flow. I am the wire, not the Electricity flowing through that wire. I am the pot, not the Potter (Isa. 64:8). I am the branch, not the Vine (John 15:5).

My job is to make myself available to Jesus, to be acted upon by Him by whatever means necessary! Lord, show me how to make room for Jesus—as much room as possible!

NOVEMBER 23

GET SMALLER

"The apostles said to the Lord, 'Increase our faith!' And the Lord said, 'If you had faith like a mustard seed.'"

Luke 17:5-6

Can our faith increase? Jesus' disciples certainly thought so. They requested such an increase from Him. Jesus responded to their request with a simile and a parable.

> He said to His disciples, "It is inevitable that stumbling blocks come, but woe to him through whom they come! It would be better for him if a millstone were hung around his neck and he were thrown into the sea, than that he would cause one of these little ones to stumble. Be on your guard! If your brother sins, rebuke him; and if he repents, forgive him. And if he sins against you seven times a day, and returns to you seven times, saying, 'I repent,' forgive him." The apostles said to the Lord, "Increase our faith!" And the Lord said, "If you had faith like a mustard seed, you would say to this mulberry tree, 'Be uprooted and be planted in the sea'; and it would obey you. Which of you, having a slave plowing or tending sheep, will say to him when he has come in from the field, 'Come immediately and sit down to eat'? But will he not say to him, 'Prepare something for me to eat, and *properly* clothe yourself and serve me while I eat and drink; and afterward you may eat and drink'? He does not thank the slave because he did the things which were commanded, does he? So you too, when you do all the things which are commanded you, say, 'We are unworthy slaves; we have done *only* that which we ought to have done'" (Luke 17:1-10).

A stumbling block is anything that keeps someone from Jesus. We make ourselves bigger at Jesus' expense when we sin. In order to turn back to Jesus—to repent—we have to make ourselves smaller; we have to become those "little ones." When you refuse to forgive one of these little ones, you are, in effect, acting as a stumbling block. Jesus warns His disciples regarding this possibility with alarming words. He then challenges them to be ready to forgive multiple times if necessary, even seven times a day!

It is in this context that the disciples make their request. To be called to forgive the same person over and over again every day stirs within them a desperate sense of inability. They cry out, "'Increase our faith!'" (Luke 17:5). Jesus responds by explaining that faith is like a mustard seed. This is its nature—smallness. If they could get more faith—more smallness—they would even be able to throw the mulberry tree of unforgiveness into the sea.

We often struggle to forgive others because we see ourselves as too big. We may get hurt by others and the associated assault strikes at our pride. We find ourselves saying, "Don't you know who I am? I am important. I am better and bigger than you. You don't do that to me. I am not going to forgive you." Ultimately, if we are going to forgive, we are going to have to get smaller. We need more faith. We need to see ourselves like mustard seeds.

Jesus describes this self-perception in a parable. In the story, Jesus tells about a slave who has an attitude that is consistent with his position, a position that is lower or smaller than the position of his master. He does not think more of himself than he ought (Romans 12:3). He does not see himself as having earned or deserved anything. His master does not owe him, and he is not independent of his master. He does not display the attitude of entitlement but understands that he has only done what he "ought to have done." He depends on the master, submits to him, and comes to him for his provision. His is an attitude of smallness. He resembles a mustard seed. He sees himself as being small and his master as being big. His smallness is his big faith!

Jesus needed His disciples to understand that if they wanted more faith, they would need to follow the road of faith—a road that denies self and embraces Jesus. It gets on a cross so as to follow Him. The more you get rid of yourself, the more room you have to be full of Him. The smaller you get, the bigger He gets. "Then Jesus said to His disciples, 'If anyone wishes to come after Me, he must deny himself, and take up his cross and follow Me'" (Matt. 16:24). To follow Him, you cannot follow yourself or any other agenda (Luke 16:13). This is the whole idea of "Lordship." Faith, in that sense, is Lordship. It is who you make lord. Your faith is determined by how much you see Jesus as your Lord.

If He is Boss, then you are not. By definition, you cannot have two masters (Luke 16:13). The less you are your own master, the more your faith increases.

To increase your faith, you must put Him ahead of everything else, including yourself (Matt. 6:33). To be filled, you have to be emptied (Matt. 5:3). To be first, you have to be last (Matt. 20:16). To see, you have to be blind (John 9:38-41). To get, you have to give (Luke 6:38). To live, you have to die (John 12:24). To forgive, you have to get smaller! To have more faith, you have to have more of the attitude of faith; you have to seek less of yourself, so you seek more of Jesus (Heb. 11:6). Since faith is coming to God—"he who comes to God must believe" (Heb. 11:6)—you must see yourself in such a way as to be less likely to come to self; your smallness leads you to Him. "'He must increase, but I must decrease'" (John 3:30). The smaller you get, the bigger He gets. The smaller you are, the bigger your faith is!

This is faith. When I know I can do nothing without Him (John 15:5), then I trust Him, seek Him, acknowledge Him, and know Him in all my ways (Prov. 3:5-6). When I recognize my need and my "smallness," then I seek His provision and His "bigness." We are moving "from faith to faith" (Rom. 1:17), since we are moving from partially knowing Him to knowing Him fully (1 Cor. 13:12). "This is eternal life, to know God" (John 17:3). Increased faith is increased dependence on and relationship with Him, which is decreased self-sufficiency and less ignoring of Him. So when we say, "Increase our faith," He says, "Okay, get smaller!"

NOVEMBER 24

RIGHT AND WRONG: IS THERE SUCH A THING?

"Out of the ground the LORD God caused to grow every tree that is pleasing to the sight and good for food; the tree of life also in the midst of the garden, and the tree of the knowledge of good and evil."

Genesis 2:9

Postmodern philosophy does not champion morality or immorality. It does not advocate for good or bad, for right or wrong. It believes in none of that. For how can something be right or wrong if there is no absolute final authority, no definer? Ethics assumes definition; and if truth is made truth by the subject, then there is no such thing as objective truth. A singular definition sourced in One definer becomes countless definitions sourced in countless "definers." Of course, that sort of pluralism by necessity produces a relativism that, by definition, *seems* to reject the idea of an objective definer. Goodbye to morality or immorality. Who is to define such things? Hello to amorality. There are no definitions! Goodbye to good and bad (morality) or right and wrong (ethics). Hello to neutrality and the "it depends" ethic and tolerance and its "I'm okay, you're okay" amorality.

Of course, neutrality is a myth. Even if there could be such a thing, it would still be a definition, an ethic. The fact that it takes a definition to claim a non-definition exposes the hypocrisy of the myth of neutrality. A supposed amoral worldview does not free someone from definition; it only stakes a claim as to who is the definer. Ethics cannot go away. It is never a matter of an absence of definition. It is always a matter of whose definition will be adhered to. And so, whether you are a modernist, an existentialist, a postmodernist, or a Christian, you will espouse some sort of ethic. The tree of the knowledge of good and evil exists for all humanity.

Since a moral God made man in His image (Gen. 1:27), man is a moral being. Since man rebelled against his Creator and took on a fallen image, he acquired the potential to be immoral. "Then the LORD God said, 'Behold, the man has become like one of Us, knowing good and evil'" (Gen. 3:22). The ability to do good—acquired at Creation—was corrupted by the Fall of man. Man has been moral and immoral, but he has never been amoral. And so, man is an ethical being.

Ethics is that which concerns itself with the nature of moral obligation and, thus, determines the rule of right conduct that is used to distinguish between that which is right and wrong. It is the study of that which determines the moral relation man has to himself and to others. Ethics is all about what is right and what is wrong. Solomon's proverbs are designed to "know wisdom and instruction, to discern the sayings of understanding, to receive instruction in wise behavior, righteousness, justice and equity" (Prov. 1:2-3). If Solomon's words are heeded, "then you will discern righteousness and justice and equity *and* every good course" (Prov. 2:9). God does not make His definitions a secret. "He has told you, O man, what is good; and what does the LORD require of you but to do justice, to love kindness, and to walk humbly with your God?" (Micah 6:8).

Adherents of the Bible are called to live holy and moral lives (Lev. 19:2, 1 Cor. 6:18), be an example of holiness and righteousness (Matt. 5:13-16), and be an advocate and defender of justice and godliness (Jer. 22:16). Christian ethics and secular ethics are different. Christian ethics are based on God's law, the Bible. Secular ethics are based on self-law and acceptable public policy and popular opinion. Christian ethics claim an internal Empowerment, the Holy Spirit. Secular ethics rely on an external influence—heroes, peer pressure, environment, culture, and genetics. Christian ethics are motivated by gratitude, love, and desire for communion with God. Secular ethics are inspired by philanthropic interests, self-interest, and philosophical adherences—a desire for rewards from men. Christian ethics point toward Christlikeness: God's glory. Secular ethics are directed toward the progress of humanity.

Man is, by nature, an ethical being. He is very aware of the idea of right and wrong. Neutrality is a myth. Even he who proclaims, "There is no right or wrong," is admitting by his statement that something is right and something is not right. What is right is that "there is no right or wrong," and what is not right is that "there is right or wrong." Man cannot avoid ethics. Everyone has a definer! The only difference is who or what your definer is.

NOVEMBER 25

WHAT ARE THE GREATER GIFTS?

"Earnestly desire the greater gifts."

1 Corinthians 12:31

It is not wrong to desire to have something that is good. God delights to "'give what is good to those who ask Him'" (Matt. 7:11). The Christian community should be zealous for all of the gifts so as to edify the Church (1 Cor. 14:12). Are some gifts more desirable, more important, or more edifying than others? Paul encourages the Corinthians to "earnestly desire the greater gifts" (1 Cor. 12:31).

First of all, it cannot simply be stated that the answer to this question has to do with the order in which the gifts are listed in 1 Corinthians 12:8-10. This would make prophecy only the sixth most important gift, yet Paul indicates that prophecy is a greater gift: "Pursue love, yet desire earnestly spiritual gifts, but especially that you may prophesy" (1 Cor. 14:1). It is not that love is the greater gift either. Love is not a gift. It is a fruit (Gal. 5:22). When Paul says that he will show a more excellent way, he is referring to the way (of love) in which all of the gifts will operate most effectively (1 Cor. 13). It is important to note that Paul is not saying that love should be sought as a substitute for the spiritual gifts. He is actually saying that they must exist together. Paul says in 1 Corinthians 14:1, "Pursue love, yet desire earnestly spiritual *gifts*." The gifts are not complete without love. It might also be said that love without the gifts is not complete when we realize that the whole context of this reference to love is the existence and practice of the gifts. The great "love chapter" is sandwiched between two verses that tell us to earnestly desire spiritual gifts (1 Cor. 12:31, 14:1).

One clear answer to our question is that prophecy is a greater gift (1 Cor. 14:1, 39). It is true that "greater is one who prophesies ... so that the church may receive edifying" (1 Cor. 14:5). Prophecy or prophet is the only gift that appears in all three lists of gifts (Rom. 12:6-8, Eph. 4:11, 1 Cor. 12:8-10). The purpose of the gifts is to edify the Church, and it seems that prophecy is especially useful for that (1 Cor. 14:3-5). Prophecy is to speak forth as inspired by God. This is, of course, something that, by its very nature, is very edifying.

Another greater gift seems to be the gift of tongues when it is accompanied by interpretation of tongues. "Now I wish that you all spoke in tongues, but *even* more that you would prophesy; and greater is one who prophesies than one who speaks in tongues, unless he interprets, so that the church may receive edifying" (1 Cor. 14:5). This seems to equate tongues with interpretation to prophecy. This combination edifies the Church more than tongues alone (1 Cor. 14:6, 19). This is not to say that tongues should be discarded. Paul says, "I thank God, I speak in tongues more than you all" (1 Cor. 14:18), and "I wish that you all spoke in tongues" (1 Cor. 14:5). It is just that when tongues is combined with interpretation, it is then more edifying to the Church making it a "greater" gift.

In summary, we can say with some assurance that the answer to our original question is that both prophecy and tongues with interpretation are the "greater gifts" referred to in 1 Corinthians 12:31. None of the other spiritual gifts are mentioned after Paul's reference to this idea of greater gifts. Paul then concluded his discussion by referring specifically to those two gifts: "Therefore, my brethren, desire earnestly to prophesy, and do not forbid to speak in tongues. But all things must be done properly and in an orderly manner" (1 Cor. 14:39-40). Therefore, there do seem to be gifts that are more desirable; nevertheless, it should be remembered that we are to "desire earnestly" all spiritual gifts.

NOVEMBER 26

DO WE HAVE TO DO THE SERMON ON THE MOUNT?

*"Do not think that I came to abolish the Law or the Prophets; I did not come to abolish but to fulfill. For truly I say to you, until heaven and earth pass away, not the smallest letter or stroke shall pass from the Law until all is accomplished ... For I say to you that unless your righteousness surpasses **that** of the scribes and Pharisees, you will not enter the kingdom of heaven."*

Matthew 5:17-20

It is an understatement to say that Jesus' Sermon on the Mount (Matt. 5-7) challenges its hearers. Am I really supposed to think that I can attain to its standards? The desire to answer this question with an emphatic, "Of course not!" leads some to say that the Sermon is only meant to describe what life in Heaven is like. Others might say that the Sermon assumes a sort of "spiritual evolution" in which mankind is progressively moving closer to a self-sourced attainment of salvation by works and that the instructions of the Sermon on the Mount are dependent upon how spiritually evolved man is currently. Both of these views distort Jesus' relationship to the Law and how that relationship affects man.

This distortion is no more blatant than when the term "fulfill" (Matt. 5:17) is understood either as "adding to" the Law or "subtracting from" the Law. Both of these errors fail to recognize that "the law of the LORD is perfect" (Psalm 19:7). God's Law, or His Word, is commensurate with Himself and, therefore, does not change. It needs nothing more, and it warrants nothing less. Jesus did not "fulfill" the Law in the sense that He came up with something new and better, nor did He do away with the Law in the sense that it is no longer applicable. The Law is perfect just as it is, and it is eternal in its perfection (1 Peter 1:25). It will not change, and it will not go away.

Is the Sermon on the Mount for us today? What did Jesus mean when He said He fulfilled the Law? Jesus explains, "For I say to you that unless your righteousness surpasses *that* of the scribes and Pharisees, you will not enter the kingdom of heaven" (Matt. 5:20). There is no addition and no subtraction. Your righteousness does not have to surpass that of the Pharisees in the sense that you need more righteousness with respect to the Law. You just need the actual, full, real, and unadulterated Law. The Pharisees did not keep the Law at all; they just looked like they were keeping the Law. Jesus is saying to His hearers, "You do not need more Law. You need the heart of the Law."

Similarly, your righteousness does not have to surpass that of the Pharisees in the sense that you need less righteousness with respect to the Law. It may be wrongly reasoned that since nobody can outdo the righteousness of the Pharisees, Jesus must mean that He is doing away with the requirements of the Law. This is how Paul responds to that: "May it never be!" (Rom. 6:2). The impossibility for man to do the Law does not mean that God forfeits it; it does mean that God, in Christ, would have to do the Law for man. The Law is perfect; and nothing is added, and nothing is taken away. The Sermon on the Mount is for us today!

It is in this context that we come to understand the "brotherhood" between the Law and the Gospel. The essence of the Gospel is that "we need" so "God provides." We are kidnapped sinners, so He pays our ransom; and we cannot do the Law, so He does the Law for us and through us. We are all Pharisees. Not one of us does the Law (Mark 10:18). This, in no way, means that the Law just gets thrown away as if a "mega exemption" is enacted. There is no mega exemption, just a mega execution! Jesus, the perfect Lamb of God, died and "fulfilled" the Law in you by accomplishing it Himself. You cannot do the Law, but He can do it for you. Still, that does not make it go away. You still do it. In Christ, you are both credited with doing it, and you are enabled to do it (Gal. 2:20). "Do we then nullify the Law through faith? May it never be! On the contrary, we establish the Law" (Rom. 3:31).

> Therefore there is now no condemnation for those who are in Christ Jesus. For the law of the Spirit of life in Christ Jesus has set you free from the law of sin and of death. For what the Law could not do, weak as it was through the flesh, God *did*: sending His own Son in the likeness of sinful flesh and as *an offering* for sin, He condemned sin in the flesh, so that the requirement of the Law might be fulfilled in us, who do not walk according to the flesh but according to the Spirit ... For the mind set on the flesh is death, but the mind set on the Spirit is life and peace, because the mind set on the flesh is hostile toward God; for it does not subject itself to the law of God, for it is not even able *to do so,* and those who are in the flesh cannot please God ... If Christ is in you, though the body is dead because of sin, yet the spirit is alive because of righteousness (Rom. 8:1-10).

Is the Sermon on the Mount for us today? Yes, it is for us because we cannot do it, but Jesus can. Jesus lived the Law because He is the Law. Yes, it is for us because we can do it inasmuch as we allow

Jesus—the only One Who can really do the real Law—to do it in and through us. Jesus continues to live the Law because He is the Law in us. The Sermon on the Mount sounds insurmountable and inapplicable because it is; and at the same time, it is not! The Sermon was for Him yesterday and is still for us today because it is still for Him to do through us today. This is "the hope of glory"—"Christ in [us]" (Col. 1:27).

NOVEMBER 27

GOD IS NEVER WRONG

"God is love ... Love does no wrong."

1 John 4:16, Romans 13:10

For some people, the existence of evil and its consequences are problematic with respect to their view of God. Why do bad things happen? Does God even exist? If He does exist, then what kind of character does He possess? He must be evil or, at the very least, unfair or wrong in the way He goes about His business. If He is a good God, then why does He not do away with sickness, war, natural disasters, and the multitude of atrocities that we often see on our evening news? Something or someone must be blamed for these things! The problem, of course, comes when we try to blame the wrong Person. God is never wrong!

If God is such a good God and Creator, then why does evil exist? First, we must understand that God did not create evil, since evil is not created. Evil is a twisting and corruption of creation. It turns around all that God said was good (Gen. 1). This backward action is a proof of the existence of God, even as evil is a proof of goodness; "evil" backward is "live." It is a proof of the character of God, even as light exposes the darkness. Without good, evil would have nothing to twist and would, therefore, not exist. The fact that evil exists is a proof of a good God's existence. The presence of a counterfeit, by definition, means that the genuine article exists. God is never wrong!

Why does a good God allow evil to continue? He allows it because He is God; He is Sovereign. He uses evil for His purposes. Just like evil is a flip-flopper, God is a bigger and better flip-flopper. He is a Sovereign Redeemer. He is big enough to use the new polluted, corrupted, and twisted "nature of man" (Gen. 3) to turn it around to the original "nature of man" (Gen. 1-2); He redeems (Psalm 119:154) by using evil for His purposes. "And we know that God causes all things to work together for good to those who love God, to those who are called according to *His* purpose" (Rom. 8:28). God uses evil as a tutor (for us), a judge (for justice), and a glorifier (for Himself). God is never wrong!

Why does a good God not destroy evil and just be done with it? The answer is: He is destroying evil now; and one day, He will destroy and banish it completely. There is a "kingdom war" that is being fought between good and evil that is more real than what might be seen on the big screen when a new superhero movie comes out. This kingdom war started in Genesis 3 and has been escalating ever since. Bad things happen because of it. Make no mistake. God has been winning this war; He is winning this war; and He will, ultimately, end this war. There is a Champion. Read the end of the book! God is never wrong!

If man entered into evil and took on a fallen nature by the use of his free will that God gave him, then why does God judge him for expressing that free will? Is that not God's fault? It seems unfair! These are questions and assertions that stem from a misunderstanding of "free will." God created man in "His own image" (Gen. 1:27); and therefore, He created him with a free will. "The Lord God commanded the man, saying, 'From any tree of the garden you may eat freely; but from the tree of the knowledge of good and evil you shall not eat, for in the day that you eat from it you will surely die'" (Gen. 2:16-17). God loves man more than everything else in His creation, so He gives him a free will. He gives him a choice. Justice or "fairness" implies that there is choice, and choice implies that there is free will. Free will makes no sense without choice, and choice makes no sense without justice. Is it really a choice if the choice is not evaluated? God is never wrong!

Free will actually establishes God's fairness; it does not negate it. If man was created as a robot—the opposite of free will is "determinism," which claims there is no free will—then the question of "fairness" would have a different answer. No justice or "evaluation" implies that there is no choice, and no choice implies that there is no free will. If there really is no choice, then can it really be evaluated? God's evaluation or justice is only "unfair" with no free will. Free will does not point to God's unfairness. It establishes His fairness. God is never wrong!

When all is said and done, God will be shown to be right; and those who have used their free will to choose Him will be evaluated or "deemed right" as well God did not create evil. He uses it for His purposes and will soon banish it forever. Our free will choice of sin and its consequences are not God's fault. God is never wrong!

NOVEMBER 28

CAN YOU RELATE?

*"For though I am free from all **men**, I have made myself a slave to all,
so that I may win more."*

1 Corinthians 9:19

Cross-cultural missionaries must find ways of identifying with the people they are trying to reach. This does not mean that they have to deny who they are, nor should they want to. Although Jesus identified with mankind and became like us, He did not try to hide who He was. He showed in many different ways that He was God. In His identification with another culture, He did not deny His own culture. At the same time, missionaries must not allow their own culture to prevent them from finding points of contact with their target culture. A lack of identification with the people must not be a stumbling block for them to receive the Gospel. Jesus must be the only Stumbling Block. The way in which the Gospel is presented must not stand in the way of the Gospel itself.

A missionary must identify with the people because he must be sensitive to present the Gospel in a culturally relevant way. This does not mean that the missionary must try to imitate other people or be transformed into another person. The power of habit makes it difficult for someone to reject their own culture. Much of what we do is done unconsciously. An American cannot walk like a tribal villager whose walk has been formed over many years of carrying heavy loads on his back. For the American missionary to think that he should walk like the tribal villager is not necessary. Furthermore, it would be seen as fake and, therefore, inconsistent with the nature of the Gospel. The goal of identification is not to be a great actor or a master of disguises. It is to create a climate for effective communication and relationship building.

The idea of cultural identification does not have to do with "faking someone out." It has to do with "dying to yourself." You can better relate to others by dying to your preferences with regard to things like food, clothes, transportation, and housing. Paul identified with others for the sake of the Gospel. He accepted the fact that he was Paul, while accepting the challenge to be willing to let go of his "rights." "But we endure all things so that we will cause no hindrance to the gospel of Christ"

(1 Cor. 9:12). The challenge of identification is not based on the ability to deceive others. It is based on the ability to die to yourself.

> For though I am free from all *men*, I have made myself a slave to all, so that I may win more. To the Jews I became as a Jew, so that I might win Jews; to those who are under the Law, as under the Law though not being myself under the Law, so that I might win those who are under the Law; to those who are without law, as without law, though not being without the law of God but under the law of Christ, so that I might win those who are without law. To the weak I became weak, that I might win the weak; I have become all things to all men, so that I may by all means save some (1 Cor. 9:19-22).

Whether you are a cross-cultural missionary or you are crossing the street to build a stronger relationship with your neighbor, it is important to consider how to relate to the one you ultimately want to share the Gospel with. How can you enter into their world and walk with them along their path? How can you find a relevant door through which you can enter their "living space" and share the Gospel in an applicable way? The power is in the message; the content of the Gospel. The release of that power is in the communication of that message—the Gospel messenger's method. The "sent ones" (the meaning of the word "missionary") must find ways of identifying with the people they are trying to reach. Can you relate?

NOVEMBER 29

PARENTS MUST NOT BE HATERS

"He who withholds his rod hates his son, but he who loves him disciplines him diligently."
Proverbs 13:24

The English word *parent* is derived from a Latin word meaning "to bring forth." If you are a parent, how you "bring forth" your children is one of the most important things you will ever do. It is critical for your children because if you do not bring them forth, they will be left behind. Parenting is the societal dynamic that moves things forward. The success of a society can only be as prolific as the quality of its parents.

A "disciple" is one who learns or follows. To "discipline" is to train a disciple, to train someone to follow. Discipline is used by a parent to bring forth a child. This is not an easy job. It can be hard on the parent and the child. In any case, it is worth it. Wisdom is life itself. "Does not wisdom call, and understanding lift up her voice? . . . For he who finds me finds life and obtains favor from the LORD. But he who sins against me injures himself; all those who hate me love death" (Prov. 8:1, 35-36). A hard way to life is better than an easy way to death. "Discipline your son while there is hope, and do not desire his death" (Prov. 19:18).

Parents must, at times, engage in tough love. "Do not hold back discipline from the child, although you strike him with the rod, he will not die. You shall strike him with the rod and rescue his soul from Sheol" (Prov. 23:13-14). In order to show the way to a child, the child cannot always get his *or* her way. "The rod and reproof give wisdom, but a child who gets his own way brings shame to his mother" (Prov. 29:15). Children who are not directed and corrected bring shame to themselves and to their families. Children left to themselves will remain in their folly. Discipline will move them out of it. "Foolishness is bound up in the heart of a child; the rod of discipline will remove it far from him" (Prov. 22:15). Someone may say, "I do not discipline my children because I love them." The truth is that they do not discipline their children because of laziness, weakness, deception, or hatred. "He who withholds his rod hates his son, but he who loves him disciplines him diligently" (Prov. 13:24).

Although instruction and training sometimes necessitate the rod, it is not the only method of discipline. It is "my teaching" (Prov. 3:1) that leads a child to "the way he should go" (Prov. 22:6). Parents must be teachers and instructors. The wisdom put forth in the book of Proverbs is prefaced by the entreaty, "Hear my son, your father's instruction and do not forsake your mother's teaching" (Prov. 1:8). In general, training and instruction should provide direction. Specifically, they should mold and form the character of a child. The goal is to equip the child to walk down the road of life in a successful way (Prov. 3:23). The wisdom of parents' guidance produces fruit in the life of their children:

> The beginning of wisdom *is*: Acquire wisdom; and with all your acquiring, get understanding. Prize her, and she will exalt you; she will honor you if you embrace her. She will place on your head a garland of grace; she will present you with a crown of beauty. Hear, my son, and accept my sayings and the years of your life will be many. I have directed you in the way of wisdom; I have led you in upright paths. When you walk, your steps will not be impeded; and if you run, you will not stumble. Take hold of instruction; do not let go. Guard her, for she is your life (Prov. 4:7-13).

It should be understood that training does not by itself create wisdom. The instruction must be received. The conditional "if" nature of this dynamic is clear in Proverbs 2:1: "My son, if you will receive my sayings . . . " Parental instruction must be received. There is no unconditional recipe for raising children. Though discipline is implemented and training and instruction are offered, children can still reject it and go astray. "A wise son makes a father glad, but a foolish man despises his mother" (Prov. 15:20). The failure of a parent is not necessarily in the lack of response from a child to wisdom. In the end, each individual must choose his own way. The failure of a parent is in the neglect of instructing and enforcing (disciplining). Do not fail. Do not hate!

NOVEMBER 30

EMBRACE JESUS AND LET GO OF YOUR SHAME

"And the man and his wife were both naked and were not ashamed."
Genesis 2:25

Why do we flee from Jesus? There can be many reasons. We might want to get away because we struggle to obey Him. Sometimes, we want to leave Him because we are afraid of situations or other people. Sometimes, we are just ashamed.

> They came to a place named Gethsemane; and He said to His disciples, "Sit here until I have prayed." And He took with Him Peter and James and John, and began to be very distressed and troubled. And He said to them, "My soul is deeply grieved to the point of death; remain here and keep watch." And He went a little beyond *them*, and fell to the ground and began to pray that if it were possible, the hour might pass Him by. And He was saying, "Abba! Father! All things are possible for You; remove this cup from Me; yet not what I will, but what You will." And He came and found them sleeping, and said to Peter, "Simon, are you asleep? Could you not keep watch for one hour? Keep watching and praying that you may not come into temptation; the spirit is willing, but the flesh is weak." Again He went away and prayed, saying the same words. And again He came and found them sleeping, for their

eyes were very heavy; and they did not know what to answer Him . . . And they all left Him and fled (Mark 14:32-41, 50).

Jesus' disciples felt a sense of failure and shame. It was most immediately derived from the fact that they did not obey Him. They did not wait, watch, and pray; but instead, they slept. Their shame, perhaps, resulted in an unwillingness to look at Jesus in the face, even though His would have been a look of forgiveness and reassurance.

We may also feel a sense of failure and shame. We might repeat the same type of sin over and over again. We begin to feel ashamed of ourselves. We may want to flee because we feel too unworthy and embarrassed to look at or go to Jesus. We feel like failures. In fact, we do fail. Nevertheless, we must look to Jesus and not flee from Him; "for we do not have a high priest who cannot sympathize with our weaknesses" (Heb. 4:15). "Let us also lay aside every encumbrance and the sin which so easily entangles us, and let us run with endurance the race that is set before us, fixing our eyes on Jesus" (Heb. 12:1-2).

Sometimes, we flee from Jesus because we are ashamed of Him. It is difficult to accept that the way of God is the way of the cross. In a paradoxical way, the cross is life through death; that which appears to be a defeat is actually the victory. The idea that we cannot save ourselves and that Jesus had to die in our place is hard to swallow. It is a stumbling block (Gal. 5:11). Peter stumbled over it repeatedly. He was ashamed of the cross and did not want to be associated with it.

> From that time Jesus began to show His disciples that He must go to Jerusalem, and suffer many things from the elders and chief priests and scribes, and be killed, and be raised up on the third day. Peter took Him aside and began to rebuke Him, saying, "God forbid *it*, Lord! This shall never happen to You." But He turned and said to Peter, "Get behind Me, Satan! You are a stumbling block to Me; for you are not setting your mind on God's interests, but man's" (Matt. 16:21-23).

> Then He poured water into the basin, and began to wash the disciples' feet and to wipe them with the towel with which He was girded. So He came to Simon Peter. He said to Him, "Lord, do You wash my feet?" Jesus answered and said to him, "What I do you do not realize now, but you will understand hereafter." Peter said to Him, "Never shall You wash my feet!" Jesus answered him, "If I do not wash you, you have no part with Me" (John 13:5-8).

We flee from Jesus because we are ashamed. Whether it is being ashamed of ourselves or being ashamed of the cross, the outcome is the same. We avoid the One Who wants to find us. "They heard the sound of the LORD God walking in the garden in the cool of the day, and the man and his wife hid themselves from the presence of the Lord God among the trees of the garden" (Gen. 3:8). Prior to the Fall of man, there was no shame. "And the man and his wife were both naked and were not ashamed" (Gen. 2:25). Allow Christ to take your shame and defeat it on the cross (Heb. 12:2). Embrace His righteousness. Embrace Him. Let go of your shame. Enter into His presence!

NOTES

December

DECEMBER 1

THE STORMS OF LIFE WILL COME

*"And the rain fell, and the floods came, and the winds blew and slammed against that house; and **yet** it did not fall, for it had been founded on the rock."*

Matthew 7:25

The strength of a building lies in its foundation. The foundation holds up the structure that is built on it. Without a strong foundation, the building might very well fall down. It is the foundation that counts because it is the foundation that you can count on. You can have the most beautiful looking structure; but if it does not have a strong foundation, then it really does not matter because it will fall when the storms of life come. And yes, the storms of life will come!

Therefore everyone who hears these words of Mine and acts on them, may be compared to a wise man who built his house on the rock. And the rain fell, and the floods came, and the winds blew and slammed against that house; and *yet* it did not fall, for it had been founded on the rock. Everyone who hears these words of Mine and does not act on them, will be like a foolish man who built his house on the sand. The rain fell, and the floods came, and the winds blew and slammed against that house; and it fell—and great was its fall (Matt. 7:24-27).

What is this house? "You are God's field, God's building" (1 Cor. 3:9). You are the building, and it is your life that must have a strong foundation. What is your life's foundation? A Christian life must be built on the kingdom of God.

The kingdom of God is God's *basileia*. This is a Greek term that is best translated as "reign" or "rule." To build your life on the kingdom of God is to build it on the rule of God—that is, on submitting to, obeying, and following Him. We look to Him for definition and direction. That should be our default mode of existence. "'But seek first His kingdom and His righteousness, and all these things will be added to you'" (Matt. 6:33). His rule in our lives must be "first of all" both in order and importance. Nothing goes ahead of it, and nothing stands before it. All is built on it, and all is built for it. The degree to which nothing goes ahead of it and nothing goes before it is the degree that everything else will be built on it. Your foundation allows you to build your building, and it also allows you to hold that building up.

The kingdom of God is past, present, and future. It is past in the sense that it overcomes and redeems the Fall. It is the kingdom of God in your life that goes back to the garden and reverses the sin of man. Adam and Eve's sin revolved around the desire to eat from the tree of the knowledge of good and evil, the tree of definition. The root of the sin was that "'in the day you eat from it your eyes will be opened, and you will be like God, knowing good and evil'" (Gen. 3:5). Adam and Eve were tempted to be their own definers. Adam's foundation became himself. He now defined right and wrong, good and bad, what to do and what not to do, what rules to follow and what rules not to follow. He became his own kingdom; the kingdom of God became the kingdom or rule of Adam.

Adam became his own God. This is called humanism. It is still, in one way or the other, the reigning philosophy or worldview practiced by all of humanity. There is one alternative, however, and that is to put first the kingdom or rule of God and to make the kingdom of God and His righteousness your foundation. This alternative foundation redeems man; it brings back that which was lost—God being the only Definer. When we build our lives on the kingdom of God, we find again that precious life that was in the garden before the Fall. We find life, and it is a "'treasure hidden in the field'" and "'one pearl of great value'" (Matt. 13:44-46). It is a life that puts the kingdom of God "first of all" as its foundation.

The kingdom of God is past, but it is also present and future. The kingdom of God is present, since Jesus died on the cross and said, "It is finished" (John 19:30). We are not waiting for the kingdom to come, for it has already come (Matt. 12:28). At the same time, the kingdom of God is future. Its ultimate movement ranges from the garden of Creation (Gen. 2:8-17) to the garden of recreation (John 19:41-20:18) to the garden of re-recreation (Rev. 2:7, 22:1-5).

Our lives stand chronologically in the gap of this "already and not yet" kingdom in the sense that our lives are being lived out between the King's first and second coming. Thus, the purpose of my life must be to move from "the already" to "the not yet," from the present to the future. I can do this by knowing God myself, since it is being in relationship with God that allows me to live in His kingdom now and for all eternity (John 17:3). I can also do it by making God known to others, since the future kingdom of God will come when Jesus returns and Jesus will return when the Gospel of the kingdom is "preached in the whole world as a testimony to all the nations, and then the end will come" (Matt. 24:14). Thus, if I am moving from the "kingdom already" to the "kingdom not yet," then the purpose or foundation of my life should be to bring the Gospel to the nations.

The storms of life will come. Nevertheless, if you build your life on the foundation of the kingdom of God past, present, and future, then when those storms come, your house will stand. The strength of a building lies in its foundation. The strength of a life lies in its God. Build your life on the strong foundation of Jesus Christ!

DECEMBER 2

WHEN SAVING BECOMES HOARDING

*"Your abundance **being a supply** for their need."*

2 Corinthians 8:14

Materialism is a worldview that places material things above all else. Ultimate reality is viewed through the lens of one's money and possessions. Without realizing it, we can get deceived into trusting in the wisdom of the world. It might be said that it is wise to save as much money as possible. As is true with many tenets of worldly wisdom, there is some truth and biblical wisdom to this assertion. "Go to the ant, O sluggard, observe her ways and be wise, which, having no chief, officer or ruler, prepares her food in the summer *and* gathers her provision in the harvest" (Prov. 6:6-8). The ant is wise because it gathers and saves.

However, the main point of the proverb is not that it is wise to save but that it is wise not to be lazy. Moreover, the saving that is done is not done simply for the sake of saving. It is wise saving. There is a purpose to it. The purpose is relatively short-term and represents the wisdom of being proactive with regard to future responsibilities. It is not the worldly wisdom of pointlessly hoarding or selfishly storing up things based on greed.

As is true with most aspects of worldly wisdom, the truth that it contains is corrupted and applied in a wrong way. The world uses this collection of "wisdom" to rationalize two things: the practice of keeping for yourself everything that you receive and the practice of trusting in your savings instead of trusting in God. Much "wise" saving is nothing more than an attempt to find security in money instead of God. This is materialism! We might struggle with this because we misunderstand God's supply as being limited and not boundless. Our "wise" statement might be, "There's only so much where that came from!" God's wisdom says, "Provision for what you need never runs out because you cannot out give God!"

> So that the same would be ready as a bountiful gift and not affected by covetousness. Now this *I say,* he who sows sparingly will also reap sparingly, and he who sows bountifully will also reap bountifully. Each one *must do* just as he has purposed in his heart, not grudgingly or under compulsion, for God loves a cheerful giver. And God is able to make all grace abound to you, so that always having all sufficiency in everything, you may have an abundance for every good deed (2 Cor. 9:5-8).

When saving becomes senseless excess, it is no longer saving; it is waste. Excess is often seen in the Bible as an opportunity to mutually supply needs. This is described as "your abundance *being a supply* for their need, so that their abundance also may become *a supply* for your need" (2 Cor. 8:14). This even meant for some folks that they began selling their property and possessions and were sharing it with others, as anyone might have need (Acts 2:45). Sharing with others is even said to be a motive for work: "performing with his own hands what is good, so that he will have *something* to share with one who has need" (Eph. 4:28).

The point in each of these passages is not that it is wrong to save but that it is right to give. It is all about alternatives. We are free to give more when we do not have to save everything. Storing or saving is often linked to giving.

> Instruct those who are rich in this present world not to be conceited or to fix their hope on the uncertainty of riches, but on God, who richly supplies us with all things to enjoy. *Instruct them* to do good, to be rich in good works, to be generous and ready to share, storing up for themselves the treasure of a good foundation for the future (1 Tim. 6:17-19).

Storing or saving is often redefined in Scripture (James 5:1-5). "'Do not store up for yourselves treasures on earth, where moth and rust destroy, and where thieves break in and steal. But store up for yourselves treasures in heaven, where neither moth nor rust destroys, and where thieves do not break in or steal'" (Matt. 6:19-20). The wisdom of the world inevitably points us away from God. This is the problem. The worldly wisdom that tells us to save everything is not based on a desire to be wise. It is based on a desire to trust in money instead of God. It is based on the fear of man and looking unwise and unprepared before others. However, if we are fully prepared and "without needs" with respect to the future, then we do not need God any longer. We no longer need faith. This is the reality of worldly wisdom. It rejects faith and chooses a false security instead of the real security that is found in trusting in God.

> And He told them a parable, saying, "The land of a rich man was very productive. And he began reasoning to himself, saying, 'What shall I do, since I have no place to store my crops?' Then he said, 'This is what I will do: I will tear down my barns and build larger ones, and there I will store all my grain and my goods. And I will say to my soul, "Soul, you have many goods laid up for many years *to come;* take your ease, eat, drink *and* be merry."' But God said to him, 'You fool! This *very* night your soul is required of you; and *now* who will own what you have prepared?' So is the man who stores up treasure for himself, and is not rich toward God" (Luke 12:16-21).

DO GOOD TO ALL PEOPLE

"And the seed whose fruit is righteousness is sown in peace by those who make peace."
James 3:18

Social justice and its expression are an ongoing aspect of public discourse. It is understood by many to be a critical topic with regard to public policy, both in terms of politics and culture. God calls His people to a high standard of social responsibility. The ethics of social concern is addressed in a variety of ways in Scripture. There is a biblical hierarchy of concern that moves from a responsibility for one's own—for self, natural family, and spiritual family—to a responsibility for all people. Proper conduct toward God, oneself, and others is fundamental in knowing and following God. It is the essence of obedience.

Advocacy for social ethics began right away in the human story. God's very first words to man were, "'Be fruitful and multiply, and fill the earth, and subdue it; and rule over the fish of the sea and over the birds of the sky and over every living thing that moves on the earth'" (Gen. 1:28). With that, God establishes the mandate of responsibility that is upon mankind. He is to be productive as he uses God's resources responsibly. Next, after God's first words to man, comes His first question to him. After Adam and Eve sin, God asks them, "Where are you?" as He rhetorically points to the reality of human self-responsibility (Gen 3:9). Then, the rhetorical questions continue; but this time, it is the man who poses the question to God. After murdering his brother, Abel, Cain asks, "'Am I my brother's keeper?'" (Gen. 4:9). Cain is arguing that he does not have to be socially responsible, but God's implied answer is the very opposite.

The Scripture clearly and repeatedly argues not only for responsibility to one's own but for responsibility to all people. It encourages us "to be ready for every good deed, to malign no one, to be peaceable, gentle, showing every consideration for all men" (Titus 3:1-2) and challenges us that "while we have opportunity, let us do good to all people" (Gal. 6:10). We are called to love all people (1 Thess. 3:12) and to "seek after that which is good" for them (1 Thess. 5:15). Social responsibility especially focuses on meeting physical and material needs (1 Tim. 6:18, Heb. 13:16, Rom. 12:20).

God does not forget the poor. "Now when you reap the harvest of your land, you shall not reap to the very corners of your field, nor shall you gather the gleanings of your harvest. Nor shall you glean your vineyard, nor shall you gather the fallen fruit of your vineyard; you shall leave them for the needy and for the stranger" (Lev. 19:9-10). God blesses those who do not forget the poor. "But when you give a reception, invite *the* poor, *the* crippled, *the* lame, *the* blind, and you will be blessed" (Luke 14:13-14).

Social responsibility focuses on defending the defenseless like orphans and widows. "You shall not afflict any widow or orphan. If you afflict him at all, *and* if he does cry out to Me, I will surely hear his cry" (Exod. 22:22-23). It includes justice for the oppressed.

> But if a man is righteous and practices justice and righteousness, and does not eat at the mountain *shrines* or lift up his eyes to the idols of the house of Israel, or defile his neighbor's wife or approach a woman during her menstrual period—if a man does not oppress anyone, but restores to the debtor his pledge, does not commit robbery, but gives his bread to the hungry and covers the naked with clothing, if he does not lend *money* on interest or take increase, *if* he keeps his hand from iniquity and executes true justice between man and man, if he walks in My statutes and My ordinances so as to deal faithfully—he is righteous *and* will surely live (Ezek. 18:5-9).

Social responsibility also includes concern for rulers and authorities. "First of all, then, I urge that entreaties *and* prayers, petitions *and* thanksgivings, be made on behalf of all men, for kings and all who are in authority, so that we may lead a tranquil and quiet life in all godliness and dignity" (1 Tim. 2:1-2). Rulers are to be obeyed (Rom. 13:7) and honored (Titus 3:1). Civil responsibility even includes paying taxes (Matt. 22:17-21). Christians, most significantly, manifest their civil responsibility by being salt and light in a decaying and dark world (Matt. 5:13-16). They do this when they do what is right. Ethics and goodwill go hand in hand, just as righteousness and peace find themselves coupled together. "Respect what is right in the sight of all men. If possible, so far as it depends on you, be at peace with all men" (Rom. 12:17-18).

The peace that comes to a society through the avenue of social responsibility and social justice should be the work of God's children inasmuch as it is true that "'blessed are the peacemakers, for they shall be called sons of God'" (Matt. 5:9). The banner of social justice reads, "And the seed whose fruit is righteousness is sown in peace by those who make peace" (James 3:18).

DECEMBER 4

WHY YOU SHOULD REFUSE TO BE COMFORTED

"Blessed are those who mourn, for they shall be comforted."

Matthew 5:4

Sin is sad. The proper response to sin is to mourn. When reflecting on the sin of God's people, Jeremiah declares, "My sorrow is beyond healing, My heart is faint *within me!*" (Jer. 8:18). Sin will "grieve the Holy Spirit of God" (Eph. 4:30). When we understand the seriousness of sin, we understand James' words: "Cleanse your hands, you sinners; and purify your hearts, you double-minded. Be miserable and mourn and weep; let your laughter be turned into mourning and your joy to gloom" (James 4:8-9). Why is the Scripture commanding us to be miserable and mourn and weep? It does not seem right that God would tell us to put on sadness and gloom. There must be an explanation. The explanation is that 'blessed are those who mourn, for they shall be comforted'" (Matt. 5:4). Not being comfortable with your sin and, instead, mourning over it leads to its defeat. Those who mourn give of themselves and are comforted via putting self-comfort on the cross and, thus, bearing the fruit of peace.

Blessings are free. Like salvation, you cannot earn them (Eph. 2:8-10). That does not mean, however, that they are not costly. We try to hang onto that which is not our own (1 Cor. 6:19-20). The beatitude includes a challenge or an obligation, a cost. It is quite a challenge to let go of the seemingly soothing effect of sin and, instead, mourn over it. To mourn is to be broken over your sin and the sin of the world. It is the correct response to Jesus' command to repent (Matt. 4:17). There is true emotion in true repentance. "For the sorrow that is according to *the will of* God produces a repentance without regret, *leading* to salvation, but the sorrow of the world produces death" (2 Cor. 7:10). Blessed mourning is not being sad for yourself—that is pride—it is being sad for God. This sadness includes a corporate aspect. Mourning is done for the sin of the world and for humanity. The psalmist mourns, "My eyes shed streams of water, because they do not keep Your law" (Psalm 119:136).

Jesus is our Example of One Whose mourning was associated with sin. He was "a man of sorrows and acquainted with grief . . . Surely our griefs He Himself bore, and our sorrows He carried" (Isa. 53:3-4). Due to the cruel result of sin and the sin of unbelief, "Jesus wept" (John 11:35). Jesus mourned over sin so as to do something about its devastation.

We must die to self by giving away or letting go of self-comfort—being satisfied with yourself and with this life. Contentment in a fallen world and in a fallen body is not a godly attribute. Sin must be hated so much that we become very uncomfortable with our sin and the sin of the world. We must die to the tendency to overlook sin; we must mourn.

The provision or blessing bestowed upon those who mourn is that they will be comforted. Those who repent—turn from their sin instead of being comfortable with it—are forgiven (Luke 24:47). The burden of guilt is lifted. Jesus the Comforter says, "'Come to Me, all who are weary and heavy-laden, and I will give you rest. Take My yoke upon you and learn from Me, for I am gentle and humble in heart, and YOU WILL FIND REST FOR YOUR SOULS. For My yoke is easy and My burden is light'" (Matt. 11:28-30). The fruit of the Spirit that corresponds to this beatitude is "peace" (Gal. 5:22). Those who mourn are at peace with God and with themselves. Jesus says to them, "'Peace I leave with you; My peace I give to you; not as the world gives do I give to you. Do not let your heart be troubled, nor let it be fearful'" (John 14:27).

The nature of the kingdom of God—relative to the kingdoms of this world—is that it is backward; it is "flip flopped." Each beatitude in the Sermon on the Mount, therefore, is cloaked in irony. "Blessed are those who mourn, for they shall be comforted'" (Matt. 5:4) means we must not become comfortable with ourselves; then we will be comforted by Jesus!

DECEMBER 5

GOD IS SALVATION

> *But what does it say?* "**THE WORD IS NEAR YOU, IN YOUR MOUTH AND IN YOUR HEART**"—*that is, the word of faith which we are preaching, that if you confess with your mouth Jesus as Lord, and believe in your heart that God raised Him from the dead, you will be saved; for with the heart a person believes, resulting in righteousness, and with the mouth he confesses, resulting in salvation. For the Scripture says,* "**WHOEVER BELIEVES IN HIM WILL NOT BE DISAPPOINTED.**" *For there is no distinction between Jew and Greek; for the same Lord is Lord of all, abounding in riches for all who call on Him; for* "**WHOEVER CALLS ON THE NAME OF THE LORD WILL BE SAVED.**"
>
> Romans 10:8-13

What does the name "Jesus" mean? It means "God is salvation" or "God saves." No matter if it is written in Hebrew (Yeshua), Croatian (Isus), or Arabic (Isa), it always means "God saves." When we see that name in the Scriptures, it is "God saves" that we are seeing.

So, the woman in desperate need of healing in Mark 5:25-28 who heard "about Jesus," more specifically, heard about "God saves." When Philip "preached Jesus" to the eunuch in Acts 8:35, he preached "God saves." In the same way, "the whole city" came out to meet "God saves" (Matt. 8:34); they believed in "God saves" (John 12:11); they followed "God saves" (John 1:37); they sat down at the feet of "God saves" (Luke 8:35); they gained freedom in "God saves" (Gal. 2:4); they were sanctified in "God saves" (1 Cor. 1:2); and they fixed their eyes on "God saves" (Heb. 12:2). We have the role of the needy ones. We are the branches. God has the role of the Provider. He is the Vine. We depend on God for all things. Jesus says, "'I am the vine, you are the branches; he who abides in Me and I in him, he bears much fruit, for apart from Me you can do nothing'" (John 15:5). This is why it is "God saves me" and not "I save myself."

We are called to confess and repent. We are to confess Jesus. We must confess that it is God Who saves and not we ourselves. Who is Jesus? "Peter answered and said to Him, 'You are the Christ'" (Mark 8:29). He is the Messiah, the anointed One, and the One Who saves.

We are called to repent and believe (Mark 1:15). We repent from trying to save ourselves; trying to be our own savior. We must confess that we are sick. We believe that it is God Who must save us. We must believe that He is the Physician. "*It is* not those who are healthy who need a physician, but those who are sick'" (Matt. 9:12). To understand that you are needy and He is the Provider is to be driven to "call on the name of the Lord," and to call on that name is to be saved (Rom. 10:13).

A long-distance swimmer became exhausted in the middle of the ocean, five hundred miles from the nearest beach. Someone rode by in a boat and threw him a waterproof copy of a book on swimming. That did not solve his problem. Then someone jumped in next to him and began to show him how to swim. That was not the solution. Next, someone pulled him into a boat, fed him, and then threw him back into the water. That did not solve the problem either. Finally, someone pulled him into the boat and carried him five hundred miles to land and, in effect, did the swimming for him. That was the only solution. It is the same way with Jesus. He does not simply give us instructions on how to be saved. Nor does he simply show us the way or merely help us to help ourselves. He replaces us and does it all.

Yes, Jesus means "God saves." He is the "All-inclusive." Everything is held together in "God saves" (Heb. 1:3). Everything is summed up in "God saves." At the end of the day, we cry out, "Come, Lord Jesus" (Rev. 22:20).

DECEMBER 6

GO FOR WHAT COUNTS

"If any man's work which he has built on it remains, he will receive a reward. If any man's work is burned up, he will suffer loss; but he himself will be saved, yet so as through fire."

1 Corinthians 3:14-15

Blessed are the soccer goalies who stop penalty shots in the World Cup, for their names will be in the newspapers for two weeks. Blessed are those who own the fastest cars, for they will arrive at their destination one minute before the others. "'Blessed are the poor in spirit, for theirs is the kingdom of heaven'" (Matt. 5:3). "'Blessed are the pure in heart, for they shall see God'" (Matt. 5:8).

There is nothing necessarily wrong with stopping a penalty shot or driving a fast car. That is not the question. The question is, "What counts?" If you stop a shot but lose the game anyway or if you drive fast and get there sooner only to arrive at the wrong place anyway, then what difference does it make? Alternatively, if you get the "kingdom of heaven" and get to "see God," then what you have done really counts. It counts because it remains, instead of perishing.

> Do you not know that those who run in a race all run, but *only* one receives the prize? Run in such a way that you may win. Everyone who competes in the games exercises self-control in all things. They then *do* it to receive a perishable wreath, but we an imperishable. Therefore I run in such a way, as not without aim; I box in such a way, as not beating the air; but I discipline my body and make it my slave, so that, after I have preached to others, I myself will not be disqualified (1 Cor. 9:24-27).

What are you striving for? What type of wreath will you be receiving? A minister stood by the bed of a dying Christian man. The man was distraught. The minister tried to encourage the man in his salvation. The man responded, "I am not afraid to die. I know that I am saved in Christ. I am not afraid. I am ashamed. I have lived much of my Christian life in selfishness and must now meet my Savior empty-handed."

Many people spend their whole lives involved in activities and pursuits that are insignificant in light of eternity—chasing dreams that have no eternal use, setting goals that have no eternal meaning, and pursuing ambitions that have no eternal purpose. Much time can be wasted on things that will mean nothing in the end. It is like a dog chasing a train. What is he going to do with it even if he were to catch it? Even if he is "successful," his success is useless.

The futility of life will never be so obvious as at the final judgment when many of the goals, activities, and events of our lives that seemed so precious to us are swallowed up in a moment of time as if they had never occurred. What a waste! Even Christians (those who "will be saved") will realize lost opportunity ("suffer loss"). They "will be saved, yet so as through fire" (1 Cor. 3:15).

> According to the grace of God which was given to me, like a wise master builder I laid a foundation, and another is building on it. But each man must be careful how he builds on it. For no man can lay a foundation other than the one which is laid, which is Jesus Christ. Now if any man builds on the foundation with gold, silver, precious stones, wood, hay, straw, each man's work will become evident; for the day will show it because it is *to be* revealed with fire, and the fire itself will test the quality of each man's work. If any man's work which he has built on it remains, he will receive a reward. If any man's work is burned up, he will suffer loss; but he himself will be saved, yet so as through fire (1 Cor. 3:10-15).

Jesus puts forth a radical message and a challenging instruction. "'If anyone wishes to come after Me, he must deny himself, and take up his cross and follow Me'" (Matt. 16:24). Jesus does not say this because He is a "party pooper" and just wants you to suffer. He wants you to have success. He knows what will count in the end, what will be successful. Perhaps this will be the greatest revelation of all when we get to Heaven. We will understand fully, it was all about Jesus! He, Himself, is success!

Whatever is built on Him will last. The degree to which you follow Him—and, thus, die to yourself—will be the degree to which what you do will actually be worth it. Perhaps, some will say when they die, "We should have gone for what counted. Give us another chance, Lord." Of course, your only chance is now! Instead of looking back and regretting, look ahead so as not to regret. When we live today for what we can have tomorrow, we extinguish the power of death, which tries to haunt us with the fear of having no tomorrow. You can go for what counts now and avoid the tragedy of futility. Rewards are waiting for you. Going for what counts is based on how you count!

> But whatever things were gain to me, those things I have counted as loss for the sake of Christ. More than that, I count all things to be loss in view of the surpassing value of knowing Christ Jesus my Lord, for whom I have suffered the loss of all things, and count them but rubbish so that I may gain Christ, and may be found in Him, not having a righteousness of my own derived from *the* Law, but that which is through faith in Christ, the righteousness which *comes* from God on the basis of faith, that I may know Him and the power of His resurrection and the fellowship of His sufferings, being conformed to His death; in order that I may attain to the resurrection from the dead (Phil. 3:7-11).

DECEMBER 7

THE AMBASSADORIAL PRINCIPLE

"Therefore, we are ambassadors for Christ."

2 Corinthians 5:20

A sovereign nation is such because it claims its own authority or rule. It sends its ambassador to another nation as its representative to communicate its desire and will; that is an expression of its sovereignty. The kingdom of God—or rule of God—is led by "the blessed and only Sovereign, the King of kings and Lord of lords" (1 Tim. 6:15). This Sovereign commissions His own ambassadors to represent Him. "He is Lord of lords and King of kings, and those who are with Him *are the* called and chosen and faithful" (Rev. 17:14). Followers of Christ are these "called and chosen and faithful" ones; they are His ambassadors.

There is what might be called "the ambassadorial principle" of Christian ministry. This is similar to the principle of stewardship. The steward does not own; he only takes care of what is owned by another. He is a receiver and a responder, not a source and a sovereign. An ambassador does not send himself to another nation to represent his nation. He is not his own source. He does not have his own authority, nor does he provide his own resources. He does not supply his own calling, nor does he choose or empower himself. He is an ambassador. By definition, he is assigned and empowered by the one he is representing.

An ambassador does not create his own message or walk out his own mission on his own terms. He operates according to the mission given him by the one he is representing; he carries it out according to his terms. An ambassador is not free to do or say whatever he wants, and he does not pay himself. He does what he is told, and he is compensated by whom he represents. An ambassador does not take credit for the work that is accomplished; for that work is, in fact, the work of the one he is representing (Eph. 2:10, Phil. 2:12-13). It is a full representation. So it is the one who is represented who is credited with the launching of the work, the proceeding of the work, and the results of the work. By definition, the official press statement given by an ambassador regarding his work must be, "For from Him and through Him and to Him are all things. To Him be the glory forever. Amen" (Rom. 11:36).

There are certain traits that are most fundamental in the job description of an ambassador. The most critical of these traits is selflessness. As an ambassador, you are not your own (1 Cor. 6:19); for if you were, then by definition, you would not be an ambassador. This is the essence of the "ambassadorial principle" of Christian ministry. It is not about you. In fact, the only way it can be about you at all is that it is about Christ, Whom you are representing. When you no longer live (represent yourself) and He lives in you (you represent Him), then you live. "I have been crucified with Christ; and it is no longer I who live, but Christ lives in me; and the *life* which I now live" (Gal. 2:20).

Duplicity is nowhere to be found in ambassadorial work. Ambassadors are a singular lot. How many entities can an ambassador really represent and not be disqualified by his archenemy, "Mr. Conflict of Interest"? It is especially true for the ambassador that "'you cannot serve God and wealth'" (Luke 16:13). Who are you going to represent, God or yourself? You are going to be an ambassador for somebody. Will it be self-representation or God-representation? Since an ambassador can really only represent one, there has to be a rejection of the other. "If anyone wishes to come after Me, he must deny himself, and take up his cross and follow Me. For whoever wishes to save his life will lose it, but whoever loses his life for My sake and the gospel's will save it" (Mark 8:34-35). The ambassador lives his life for the sake of the sovereign who commissioned him. That singular allegiance requires a singular message. The ambassador does not say what he wants to say; he only says what the sovereign wants to say. He is an ambassador.

The "ambassadorial principle" is even woven into the incarnation of God. God the Son became the perfect Representative of God the Father (Heb. 1:3). If you receive the Representative Who was sent, then you receive the Sender because the Representative only does what the Sender would do (John 5:19). "'Truly, truly, I say to you, he who receives whomever I send receives Me; and he who receives Me receives Him who sent Me'" (John 13:20). The Divine Ambassador, speaking on behalf of the Divine Sender, only speaks what the Sender wants Him to speak. "'For I did not speak on My own initiative, but the Father Himself who sent Me has given Me a commandment *as to* what to say and what to speak. I know that His commandment is eternal life; therefore the things I speak, I speak just as the Father has told Me'" (John 12:49-50).

Christians are now ambassadors of Christ, and so we say, "He has committed to us the word of reconciliation. Therefore, we are ambassadors for Christ, as though God were making an appeal through us; we beg you on behalf of Christ, be reconciled to God" (2 Cor. 5:19-20). Our message is His message, the message of the Gospel. The expectation is "that utterance may be given to me in the opening of my mouth, to make known with boldness the mystery of the gospel, for which I am an ambassador in chains; that in *proclaiming* it I may speak boldly, as I ought to speak" (Eph. 6:19-20).

The ambassadorial principle guides Christianity. It defines Christian calling and identity. The Christian life is only understood within its parameters. Attitude, character, walk, and ministry all flow out of its reality. Final personal outcomes will be dictated by it—by who is seen at the "pearly gates." Only Jesus wins. Jesus has to be seen. Who are you representing? Who represents you? Who is seen? Jesus is the only One Who can enter. Do you have ambassadorial status?

DECEMBER 8

AM I TO BE PERFECT?

"'Therefore you are to be perfect, as your heavenly Father is perfect.'"
Matthew 5:48

After reading Matthew 5—one of the most challenging chapters in the entire Bible—the last thing the reader is thinking is, "I can be perfect!" The Sermon on the Mount makes you feel anything but perfect. Yet that is one of Jesus' concluding thoughts. "'Therefore you are to be perfect, as your heavenly Father is perfect'" (Matt. 5:48). I do not even know if I can do one of those things that He has just talked about—like "turn the other cheek" or "rejoice" when I am persecuted—yet He is telling me that I am to be perfect.

Jesus' most foundational theology of ethical perfection is found in the Sermon on the Mount. His most foundational teaching point on ethical perfection is found in the very first line of His sermon: "'Blessed are the poor in spirit, for theirs is the kingdom of heaven'" (Matt. 5:3). How can we be perfect when that is the furthest thing from what we are? The only way we can be perfect is for the perfect One to act through the imperfect— to live in us (Gal. 2:20). For that to happen, the imperfect must get out of the way. It must empty itself or become "poor in spirit." The most foundational ethical requirement is not to do this or that; it is selflessness. According to the way the kingdom of God works, to be ethical is to be selfless.

God uses our inability to keep the Law to direct us toward having the attitude that will result in the opportunity to be equipped to do the Law. It is the attitude of one who is hopelessly deficient.

For fallen man to have hope, he must first recognize and admit his utter hopelessness. The first and critical step in helping morally depleted man is to get him to admit he is morally depleted. This truth leads Jesus to proclaim such seemingly cryptic statements as, "*It is* not those who are healthy who need a physician, but those who are sick; I did not come to call the righteous, but sinners'" (Mark 2:17), and "'If you were blind, you would have no sin; but since you say, *We see,* your sin remains'" (John 9:41).

Ultimately, ethics is summarized by the words "surrendering," "submitting," and "dying to self." In a fundamental sense, these are the only ethical actions of men. Do you want to know how to be an ethically correct person? Trust in God and not in yourself. Surrender to Him in faith and relationship, and He will make your paths straight (Prov. 3:5-6). Christian ethics are "empty vessel" ethics; for then, and only then, can true ethics be worked through the person who is naturally unethical.

Only in the light of our understanding of Matthew 5:3 can we begin to understand a call to ethical purity and blamelessness. We are ethically perfect in as much as we allow the ethically perfect Christ to work through us. "As for God, His way is blameless; the word of the LORD is tried; He is a shield to all who take refuge in Him. For who is God, but the LORD? And who is a rock, except our God, the God who girds me with strength and makes my way blameless?" (Psalm 18:30-32).

We begin to approach the impossibility of being consistent in this perfection when we remember that it is the Law that leads us to repentance. The Law "has become our tutor *to lead us* to Christ" (Gal. 3:24), pointing us toward the greatest ethical action of all in God's economy: the ethic of repentance. The combination of Law and Gospel is the combination of commandment and enablement or obligation and promise. Christ's fulfilling of the Law implies His accomplishment of it. By the work of the cross, Christ is our Justification (Replacement/Representative). And by the result of the cross (Christ in us via relationship or access to Him), He is our righteousness, our holiness, and our sanctification.

The Christian has ethical responsibility (mandate) because he has ethical privilege (enablement). The Christian is called to be perfect. The ethical and Law-abiding Christ works and lives in an unethical and Law-breaking man. Only in this way does man become perfect. He is both perfectly forgiven in his disability and perfectly enabled in his God-sourced ability. He is perfect as his heavenly Father is perfect! Whenever, and to whatever degree, the imperfect lets in the perfect, the imperfect, for that moment and in that situation, becomes perfect. Although it is understood that our engagement in the perfecting process will not be done perfectly, we are still called to it. I confess that it is "not that I have already obtained *it* or have already become perfect, but I press on so that I may lay hold of that for which also I was laid hold of by Christ Jesus" (Phil. 3:12). So keep letting Him in and be perfect!

DECEMBER 9

TRIBES, TONGUES, PEOPLES, AND NATIONS

> *"'But you will receive power when the Holy Spirit has come upon you; and you shall be My witnesses both in Jerusalem, and in all Judea and Samaria, and even to the remotest part of the earth.'"*
>
> Acts 1:8

God commands His messengers to take His message to all the nations (Matt. 28:18-20, Gen. 12:1-3). What are the "nations"? They are not simply the two hundred geopolitical countries in the world. The Greek word is *ethnos*, which is more precisely translated "ethnicity, tribe, or people group." Just as Africans do not understand themselves as such (Africa is a continent, not an ethnicity), American Indians do not understand themselves that way either. The Cherokee—an ethnicity or tribe—speak of themselves as being of the Cherokee "nation." The Hutu do not understand themselves, most fundamentally, as Rwandan (a geopolitical country); they are of the ethnicity or tribe of the Hutu. There are between fifteen thousand and twenty thousand "nations" in the world. In India alone, there are three thousand ethnic groups. In the Democratic Republic of Congo, there are over two hundred languages spoken. Jesus shed His blood for each and every one of them: "You were slain, and purchased for God with Your blood men from every tribe and tongue and people and nation" (Rev. 5:9).

A "people group" perspective, as opposed to a "country" perspective, will affect our missions strategy. At the very least, it will make for a more culturally sensitive strategy. A people group is a sociological group of people. It is not a political group of people. Ethnic "nations" are not connected by political boundaries—the Yao people, for example, span Zambia, Malawi, and Mozambique—but are connected by sociological factors like language, culture, religion, and ancestry. A more encompassing group might be recognized as a "megasphere" in which are identifiable "macrospheres" and "minispheres." The Muslim megasphere includes the Sunni and Sufi macrospheres. The Sunni macrosphere includes the Yoruba speaking and the Igbo speaking minispheres (Nigeria). To understand these distinctions is to understand and be sensitive to the particular needs of the people you may be trying to reach.

The work of missions or evangelism works its way out from the local church just as those first 120 disciples worked their way out from the upper room (Acts 1:12-15). The "formula" is derived from Jesus' instruction, "'You shall be My witnesses both in Jerusalem, and in all Judea and Samaria, and even to the remotest part of the earth'" (Acts 1:8). The first step is local evangelism to those who live and work around you. It is evangelism to your own people, to your Jerusalem. The next step is evangelism that only needs to cross over one major cultural barrier. This is outreach to your Judea and Samaria. Finally, there is evangelism that crosses over several barriers, including language, culture, climate, and distance. This is when you go to the remotest part of the earth. The book of Acts is the story of this progression played out in the New Testament Church. From Peter's ministry in Jerusalem (Acts 1-7) to Philip and Peter in Samaria and Caesarea (Acts 8-12) to Paul in Philippi and Rome (Acts 13-28), the Gospel went to the nations.

In the last two thousand years, the Church has expanded its worldwide reach. The Gospel has been taken to every continent and every geopolitical country. It has not yet been taken to every *ethnos* (tribe, tongue, nation, people group). Nigeria has certainly been reached with the Gospel. The Doka of Nigeria, however, remain unreached. So it is not over yet, since "this gospel of the kingdom shall be preached in the whole world as a testimony to all the nations, and then the end will come" (Matt. 24:14). Every tribe, tongue, nation, or people group must be reached. This is ultimately what a missionary is: a priest of God. A priest is one who connects people to God, one who connects the nations to God. This is exciting! The end is near; and at the end, those priests—those connectors—will reign upon the earth. "Worthy are You to take the book and to break its seals; for You were slain, and purchased for God with Your blood *men* from every tribe and tongue and people and nation. You have made them *to be* a kingdom and priests to our God; and they will reign upon the earth" (Rev. 5:9-10).

DECEMBER 10

ARE YOU AN ETHICAL PERSON?

"Created in Christ Jesus for good works."

Ephesians 2:10

People's ethics are their moral principles that govern their behavior. Ethics is the discipline of philosophy that is concerned with what is good and bad or right and wrong and the actions or works that stem from those beliefs. If Jesus' most foundational theology of ethics is found in the Sermon on the Mount, then His most foundational teaching point on ethics is the first beatitude that states, "'Blessed are the poor in spirit, for theirs is the kingdom of heaven'" (Matt. 5:3). And His most foundational ethical requirement is poverty of spirit or selflessness. James Boice rightly asserts, "We must recognize as a first principle for understanding the Sermon on the Mount that we cannot fulfill the standards of the Sermon by ourselves. Paradoxically, Jesus teaches that the Sermon is only for those who know that they cannot live by it."[18]

The same paradox existed for those living under the Old Testament. The Law was something that sinful man was unable to keep. Thus, the scribes interpreted and reinterpreted the Law so as to make it conform to their sinful tendencies, all the time polluting it more and more, to the point where one could keep the scribal regulations yet be far from keeping the commandment of God. The Law in both the Old and New Testaments reveals man as a sinner (Rom. 3:20).

God uses our inability to keep the Law to direct us toward having the attitude that will result in the opportunity to be equipped to do the Law. How do we define this attitude? It is the attitude of one who is hopelessly deficient. For fallen man to have hope, he must first recognize and admit his utter hopelessness. Those who work with alcoholics say the critical first step in helping an alcoholic is getting him to admit that he is an alcoholic. So, too, the first and critical step in helping morally depleted man is to get him to admit that he is morally depleted. This truth leads Jesus to proclaim such seemingly cryptic statements as, "*It is* not those who are healthy who need a physician, but those who are sick; I did not come to call the righteous, but sinners'" (Mark 2:17).

F.B. Meyer offers an eloquent explanation: "One must see his own deficiency to be able to receive His sufficiency. Being poor in spirit becomes a prerequisite for seeing the Kingdom, just as being an empty vessel stands as a prerequisite for being filled with the ability of Christ."[19] Boice concludes, "If we are ever to understand the ethical teachings of Jesus, we must recognize as a first principle that we just cannot abide by them. And we must come in faith to the only One who did fulfill them and who alone can fulfill them in those who give their lives to Him."[20]

Ultimately, ethics is summarized by the words "surrendering," "submitting," and "dying to self." In a fundamental sense, these are the only ethical actions of men. Do you want to know how to be an ethically correct person? "Therefore they said to Him, 'What shall we do, so that we may work the works of God?' Jesus answered and said to them, 'This is the work of God, that you believe in Him whom He has sent'" (John 6:28-29). Believe not in yourself but believe in God. Trust in God and not in yourself. Surrender to Him in faith and relationship, and He will make your paths straight (Prov. 3:5-6). Christian ethics are "empty vessel" ethics; for then, and only then, can true ethics be worked through you. "I have been crucified with Christ; and it is no longer I who live, but Christ lives in me; and the *life* which I now live in the flesh I live by faith in the Son of God, who loved me and gave Himself up for me" (Gal. 2:20). As Ephesians 2:10 says, "For we are His workmanship, created in Christ Jesus for good works, which God prepared beforehand so that we would walk in them."

In Jesus' introduction to the course *Ethics 101*, He would simply declare to the class, "'Blessed are the poor in spirit, for theirs is the kingdom of heaven'" (Matt. 5:3). He would then begin His lecture: "He who is ethical is he who is selfless; for he who is selfless is he who can let in the only One Who is ethical."

DECEMBER 11

IT'S JUST IMPOSSIBLE

"'The things that are impossible with people are possible with God.'"
Luke 18:27

Faith protects us. The Christian life is a life of spiritual war. It is a life of spiritual conflict. Each piece of spiritual armor that God gives us is essential. Still, *faith* is especially critical: "in addition to all, taking up the shield of faith" (Eph. 6:16). The importance of faith is seen in the realm of the impossible. Salvation is impossible without faith. "'He who believes in the Son has eternal life; but he who does not obey the Son will not see life, but the wrath of God abides on him'" (John 3:36). You must have faith to be saved. Victory over the world is impossible without faith. "For whatever is born of God overcomes the world; and this is the victory that has overcome the world—our faith" (1 John 5:4). Faith is victorious.

It is impossible to please God without faith. "And without faith it is impossible to please *Him*, for he who comes to God must believe that He is and *that* He is a rewarder of those who seek Him" (Heb. 11:6). Faith pleases God. It is impossible to effectively pray without faith. "But he must ask in faith without any doubting, for the one who doubts is like the surf of the sea, driven and tossed by the wind. For that man ought not to expect that he will receive anything from the Lord, *being* a double-minded man, unstable in all his ways" (James 1:6-8). It takes faith to pray.

It is impossible to have peace with God without faith. "Therefore, having been justified by faith, we have peace with God through our Lord Jesus Christ" (Rom. 5:1). Faith yields peace. It is impossible to have joy without faith. "And though you have not seen Him, you love Him, and though you do not see Him now, but believe in Him, you greatly rejoice with joy inexpressible and full of glory" (1 Peter 1:8). In faith, there is joy.

It is impossible to be justified without faith. "Nevertheless knowing that a man is not justified by the works of the Law but through faith in Christ Jesus, even we have believed in Christ Jesus, so that we may be justified by faith in Christ and not by the works of the Law" (Gal. 2:16). Faith justifies you. It is impossible to truly live without faith. "I have been crucified with Christ; and it is no longer I who live, but Christ lives in me; and the *life* which I now live in the flesh I live by faith in the Son of God, who loved me and gave Himself up for me" (Gal. 2:20). Faith is life!

It is impossible to be righteous without faith. "For not knowing about God's righteousness and seeking to establish their own, they did not subject themselves to the righteousness of God. For Christ is the end of the law for righteousness to everyone who believes" (Rom. 10:3-4). Faith is linked to God's righteousness. It is impossible to have Christ live in you without faith. "Christ may dwell in your hearts through faith" (Eph. 3:17). Faith means Christ in you. It is impossible to receive the Holy Spirit without faith. "This is the only thing I want to find out from you: did you receive the Spirit by the works of the Law, or by hearing with faith?" (Gal. 3:2). The answer is receiving the Holy Spirit by faith.

How important is faith? It is so important that whatever is not of faith is sin (Rom. 14:23). If faith is absent, then the only thing that is present is iniquity. If faith is present, then the following are not absent: salvation, victory, pleasing God, prayer, peace with God, joy, justification, righteousness, Christ in you, the receiving of the Holy Spirit, and life. What do you want? Do you want sin or life? Have faith. Otherwise, life is just impossible!

DECEMBER 12

GOD IS YOUR GUIDANCE COUNSELOR

"Is this not the fast which I choose ... and the LORD will continually guide you, and satisfy your desire in scorched places, and give strength to your bones; and you will be like a watered garden, and like a spring of water whose waters do not fail."
Isaiah 58:6, 11

Is it correct to say that God spoke to us or that we heard from or were led by God? Does God still speak today? Does not the doctrine of the sufficiency of Scripture imply a certain static nature of God's communication with His people? Although God's special revelation (Scripture) is sufficient, His subordinate revelation in which He communicates with His people in terms of implication and application of Scripture is not static. Yes, God still speaks today! The very nature of Scripture itself assumes this since "the word of God is living and active" (Heb. 4:12). Any form of deism is rejected. God continues to guide His people. Prayer is not a "one-way street." God is both a Listener and a Speaker. He speaks, leads, and illumines His people as the Spirit of truth guides them "into all the truth" (John 16:13).

Any desire for guidance from God should be rooted in a primary desire for God Himself. The motivation behind any means of grace or spiritual discipline—like prayer or fasting, for example—should be to draw closer to God. To be guided by God is to be in fellowship with Him and to be in His will. A relationship-oriented instead of task-oriented perception of prayer or fasting as a spiritual discipline must be applied to its practice. Divine guidance that might come from such activity should be viewed in terms of experiencing the mind of the Lord. Any spiritual discipline should be understood as a facilitator of experiencing Christ in us (Gal. 2:20).

Sometimes fasting is used to seek Divine guidance for a big decision. Charles Stanley writes, "Fasting allows us to think clearer and quicker. As a result, there is a new and constant awareness of God's presence during times of fasting ... During times of fasting, our minds are quicker to discern the things of the Spirit. This is especially important when we're seeking guidance for a big decision."[21]

Moses fasted as he sought God's guidance for some very big decisions (Exod. 34:28). The sons of Israel fasted as they "inquired of the LORD" regarding military strategy (Judges 20:26-27). Elijah fasted on his way to Mount Horeb and experienced an incredible revelation of God and guidance from Him (1 Kings 19:8-18). Esther's fast is connected to Divine guidance (Esther 4:16). Daniel's understanding of visions and dreams is associated with fasting (Dan. 9:3, 20-27).

Revelation and guidance from God are often associated with fasting in the New Testament. In the midst of her "serving night and day with fastings and prayers," Anna received Divine revelation concerning the Christ (Luke 2:36-38). Leaders in the church at Antioch fasted and were guided in their choosing and commissioning of Paul and Barnabas to be sent out (Acts 13:1-3). Later, the decisions made in the appointment of elders were of a critical nature, and they were not entered into without having "fasted and prayed" (Acts 14:23).

Fasting, like other spiritual disciplines, may facilitate God's guidance in our lives. God does speak today. Consistent with His Word, He leads us as we are led to Him.

> To You, O LORD, I lift up my soul. O my God, in You I trust, do not let me be ashamed; do not let my enemies exult over me. Indeed, none of those who wait for You will be ashamed; those who deal treacherously without cause will be ashamed. Make me know Your ways, O LORD; teach me Your paths. Lead me in Your truth and teach me (Psalm 25:1-5).

DECEMBER 13

BEING IN THE RIGHT PLACE AT THE RIGHT TIME

"'The harvest is plentiful, but the workers are few. Therefore beseech the Lord of the harvest to send out workers into His harvest.'"

Matthew 9:37-38

A farmer understands what might be called the "vision of the fruit." His goal is not to plant seed. That is only a method to reach his goal. His goal is to produce fruit. A missionary must also understand the "vision of the fruit." His goal is not to simply *go*. That is only a method to reach his goal. His goal is to produce fruit, to "make disciples" (Matt. 28:19). Like the farmer, the missionary must keep before him the vision in sowing, pruning, and reaping.

To maintain the vision of the fruit, a missionary must pay attention to the vision in sowing. In the parable of the sower (see Luke 8:4-15), a farmer sowed seed on four different types of soils. Only one soil produced fruit. The difference was not in the seed or the sower. It was in the soil. It is the same in missions work. Some people are more receptive to the Gospel than others. They represent the "good soil"; they designate the "right place" for the missionary to go. They will be a priority for the missionary who retains the "vision of the fruit."

To maintain the vision of the fruit a missionary must pay attention to the vision in pruning. A farmer does not have a sentimental concern over a certain tree. If it does not bear fruit then it should be cut down. The employees of the farmer do not want to cut the tree down. They are more concerned about their salaries than they are about the "vision of the fruit."

> And He *began* telling this parable: "A man had a fig tree which had been planted in his vineyard; and he came looking for fruit on it and did not find any. And he said to the vineyard-keeper, 'Behold, for three years I have come looking for fruit on this fig tree without finding any. Cut it down! Why does it even use up the ground?' And he answered and said to him, 'Let it alone, sir, for this year too, until I dig around it and put in fertilizer; and if it bears fruit next year, *fine*; but if not, cut it down'" (Luke 13:6-9).

Missions work can suffer from this same misguided perspective. When the program or position becomes more important than the goal or the mission, then missionaries can be in danger of becoming mere hirelings. The vision in pruning assures that the mission remains. This will be a priority for the missionary who retains the "vision of the fruit."

To maintain the vision of the fruit a missionary must pay attention to the vision in reaping. A farmer sends out his workers into the fields that currently have ripe fruit. This is the "right time" aspect of missions work. It is critical that workers go into the fields and reap the harvest. "'The harvest is plentiful, but the workers are few. Therefore beseech the Lord of the harvest to send out workers into His harvest'" (Matt. 9:37-38). The missionary must consider which fields have the ripe fruit that must be picked now. This will be a priority for the missionary who retains the "vision of the fruit."

Missionary work, like the work of the farmer, requires a vision of the fruit that includes a focus on sowing, pruning and reaping. Success is based on being in the right place at the right time.

DECEMBER 14

BROKEN THEN FIXED

"For as in Adam all die, so also in Christ all will be made alive."
1 Corinthians 15:22

You were made "perfectly fixed." When God created mankind on the sixth day, He made him in His own image. Man was not God, but he was not broken. He lived in the Garden of Eden, the land of paradise where everything worked the way it was meant to work. He was "fixed" by God originally in a sinless, unbroken state. Before mankind had original sin, he had original sinlessness, that which was not broken, however, still having the potential to break.

Then the break came. Man broke off from God—sin is separation from God or spiritual death (Rom. 6:23)—when Adam and Eve ate from that broken tree. Now you are born broken in Adam. "Behold, I was brought forth in iniquity, and in sin my mother conceived me" (Psalm 51:5). You no longer live in the land of paradise. You live in a fallen world with other fallen people as you navigate through your own fallen nature. Things do not work any longer like they were supposed to work. You are still made in God's image, but now you carry within yourself a warring inclination. In your brokenness, you fight against yourself. "For the good that I want, I do not do, but I practice the very evil that I do not want" (Rom. 7:19). Your sin nature breaks you because it breaks you away from God. Original sinlessness yielded to original sin. Now you are broken. You and the trees around you need to be fixed.

God originally created you unbroken. Then things began to break, and you were born spiritually broken in Adam. Now you need to be spiritually born again. Just as you were born broken in the first Adam, you now need to be born again spiritually fixed in the last Adam. "The first MAN, Adam, BECAME A LIVING SOUL. The last Adam *became* a life-giving spirit" (1 Cor. 15:45). The first man broke himself and died. The last man fixed what the first man broke. "For as in Adam all die, so also in Christ all will be made alive" (1 Cor. 15:22). Just as it is sin that breaks us (Rom. 3:23), it is also sin that fixes us. Salvation from sin does not come by ignoring sin. It comes by embracing it. This is the paradoxical nature of the work of the cross. Jesus fixes our brokenness by becoming our brokenness on our behalf. In that sense, sin both breaks us and fixes us! "He made Him who knew no sin *to be* sin on our behalf, so that we might become the righteousness of God in Him" (2 Cor. 5:21). Fixing is expensive.

Once you are rebirthed by the cleansing blood of Jesus Christ, you still live in a broken world. Brokenness is inevitable due to the ongoing reality of the sinful self, sinful others, and a sinful world. Fixing is available due to the love and power of Jesus Christ. "In this world you have tribulation, but take courage; I have overcome the world'" (John 16:33). Brokenness is a result of sin; a result of your own sin and/or the sin of others and/or the sin of the world. Being broken is not always or completely your own fault but is always and completely the fault of sin. Whether we are broken in the battle by our own hand or broken as "collateral damage," it is sin that is the enemy and Christ Who is the Medic and Victor (John 11:4). "'Rabbi, who sinned, this man or his parents, that he would be born blind?' Jesus answered, *'It was* neither that this man nor sinned, nor his parents; *it was* so that the works of God might be displayed in him'" (John 9:1-3). The bottom line is that we all break, and Jesus is the only One Who can fix us (John 13:8-10).

Jesus fixes the broken. He is Jehovah Jireh, the One Who sees your brokenness and provides a remedy. He does not fix apart from the broken. Fixing implies brokenness. Noah was not kept *from* the flood. He was brought *through* the flood. There will be floods in our lives. God does not ignore it as if it is not there. He builds an ark that will take us through it. The broken deluge is fixed in the midst of the flood itself. Jesus is Jehovah Shammah, the One Who is there. Brokenness makes us feel all alone. That is a lie. He is there. His presence fixes that which is broken. Shadrach, Meshach, and Abednego were not kept *from* the fire. They were brought *through* the fire by the "fourth man," who was there with them in the fire (Dan. 3:25). There will be fires in our lives. God jumps in the fire with you and pulls you out.

Man was originally without original sin. This was paradise, the Garden of Eden. Then man broke himself. Jesus died on the cross, so man could be fixed. The ongoing presence of sin in the world results in continued brokenness and fixing. The ultimate fix comes at the ultimate return; the return of Christ returns us to the garden paradise, where there is no longer any brokenness to fix. God takes us back to the future when He completely transforms us (1 John 3:2) and rids the world of sin. With no more sin, there is no more brokenness (1 Cor. 15:26).

This is the story: sin and solution, evil and good, Satan and God, broken and fixed. What is our part in this story? It is to hate sin and desire God. To be fixed from being broken is to hate sin with all your heart, your sin, others' sin, and the sin of the world. To be fixed from being broken is to desire God with all your heart; to trust Him, seek Him, and obey Him. The opposite of sin (broken away from God) is desire or faith (connected to God). To know God is to hate evil (Prov. 1:7, 8:13). "Whatever is not from faith is sin" (Rom. 14:23).

To be broken is to be broken off from God. To be fixed is to be connected back to God. Brokenness is an inevitable part of life. Fixing is God's activity. We must hate sin as it is the fount of brokenness. We must desire God as He is the Fount of fixing. We look forward to being made perfectly fixed again and not being broken anymore as we cry out, "Come, Lord Jesus" (Rev. 22:20).

DECEMBER 15

WHAT'S YOUR PURPOSE ANYWAY?

*"And He appointed twelve, so that they would be with Him and that He **could** send them out to preach."*

Mark 3:14

Purpose is a big deal. It is hard to live without purpose, just like it is hard to find the motivation to do something that seems to have no meaning. What is the bottom line with respect to life? I want to know my purpose because there is nothing else more foundational or essential. The Bible clearly directs us to our purpose in life. The same thread runs throughout all of Scripture. It is a twofold purpose: know God and make God known.

This twofold purpose for living—knowing God and making God known—is even Jesus' stated purpose. Reflecting on His life while praying in the Garden of Gethsemane, Jesus declared, "'O righteous Father, although the world has not known You, yet I have known You; and these have known that You sent Me; and I have made Your name known to them, and will make it known, so that the love with which You loved Me may be in them, and I in them'" (John 17:25-26). Jesus affirms two things here. His purpose is to know God and to make God known. Jesus' self-professed purpose to make God known was established early on in His ministry when He responded to the crowds, saying, "'I must preach the kingdom of God to the other cities also, for I was sent for this purpose'" (Luke 4:43).

Why do you do things? Jesus lists some sacrificial things you might do. You should not do them, however, just to do them. They cannot find purpose in and of themselves. For them to have real purpose and meaning, you must do them "'for My sake and for the gospel's sake'" (Mark 10:29). You would have to do them in order to know God and to make God known.

This same sort of continuum comes to life when Jesus invites Peter and Andrew to "'follow Me, and I will make you fishers of men'" (Matt. 4:19). Jesus proposes that they consider two purposes for their lives; first, to follow Him or to know Him and second, to become fishers of men or to be those who would make Him known. Similarly, Jesus inserts these two purposes of life into the context of choosing the twelve. He appoints them "so that they would be with Him and that He *could* send them out to preach" (Mark 3:14). The twofold purpose for the disciples was to know Him and to make Him known.

Sometimes, we are not sure why something happens or why we are called to do something. Sometimes, life just does not seem to make sense. We ask God why? We need to remember that "God causes all things to work together for good to those who love God, to those who are called according to *His* purpose" (Rom. 8:28). What is His purpose for us? "For those whom He foreknew, He also predestined to *become* conformed to the image of His Son" (Rom. 8:29). It is our relationship with Him that conforms us to His image. We are changed through knowing Him (1 John 3:2). Our purpose in life is to know God.

Jesus' last words to His disciples just before He ascended into Heaven should not be surprising to us. After all, it would be expected that someone's last words to his disciples would focus on directing them toward their purpose. Jesus says to them, "'Go therefore and make disciples of all the nations, baptizing them in the name of the Father and the Son and the Holy Spirit, teaching them to observe all that I commanded you'" (Matt. 28:19-20). Purpose in life is rooted in making God known.

If a pot could feel fulfilled in its existence, it would not be able to do so outside of being engaged in activities that are consistent with what its maker created it for. A pot would feel fulfilled if it boiled water because the potter who made the pot made it to boil water. We are creations of God. The purposes of the creation must be consistent with the purposes of the Creator in order for them to be valid purposes. The creation finds meaning for its existence within the purposes that its Creator has for it.

What are the purposes of God? First, His purpose is to redeem man (1 Tim. 1:15); it is to transform fallen man into the image of the risen Christ (Rom. 8:28-29). Thus, man's purpose is to know God. Second, His purpose is to win back the kingdom from Satan (1 John 3:8, Heb. 2:14); it is to use redeemed man to be the salt and light of the world in order to bring the Gospel message to the nations (Matt. 28:18-20). Thus, man's purpose is to make God known. God's purposes for my life are that He would work *in* me that I can know Him and that He would work *through* me that I would make Him known. If the purpose of life is to live a life of purpose, then, live a life that is full of knowing God and making God known.

DECEMBER 16

SAME OLD (AND NEW) GOD

*"Jesus Christ **is** the same yesterday and today and forever."*

Hebrews 13:8

Sometimes, we read the Bible and think we are seeing two different Gods. We might conclude that there seems to be one God in the Old Testament and another God in the New Testament. The Old

Testament God seems harsher and more wrathful, while the New Testament God seems more loving and compassionate. Of course, this is a misunderstanding of Scripture. It can, at best, minimize one's understanding of Who God is and how the Gospel works and, at worst, completely skew the truth of the nature of God and His purposes. It is a dangerous view of the Scriptures.

God does not change (Mal. 3:6). There are not two different Gods found in two different testaments. God has always been fully holy and fully love because that is His nature, not His mood. Moreover, His holiness and love are not mutually exclusive traits but ones that are in perfect harmony and consistency with each other. The "testaments" are not about different Gods working in different eras with different people. They are about the workings of the one and the same God, Who is working in the same creation and redemption era among the same created and redeemed people.

The work of God is the provision of His revelation of Himself. This is progressive through the testaments. It increases. It becomes clearer and clearer. The New Covenant is not a different covenant than the Old Covenant; it is a better covenant. "Jesus has become the guarantee of a better covenant" (Heb. 7:22). In the New Testament, Jesus brings a more complete revelation of the same God and Gospel seen in the Old Testament (Luke 24:25-27). It is Jesus Who is revealed in both the Old Testament and the New Testament, even as it is the sacrificial goat and scapegoat sacrificed for the sins of the people on the Day of Atonement that is seen in the Old Testament (Lev. 16:5-10), and the perfect "'Lamb of God Who takes away the sin of the world'" seen in the New Testament (John 1:29).

It is not a different God or a different gospel. It is a better or more complete revelation of the same God and the same Gospel. In each testament, the focus is Jesus, or "God saves." The focus is the Gospel, or the "Good News" that even though we are not able, God is able. God has always been providing for man's needs. There is no different God and no different mission of God; there is only less or more revelation of the same thing. This explains why there may seem to be more "extremes" in the Old Testament. Less revelation of God's love—not a God Who is less loving but a love that is less clear to man—magnifies sin and its effects. Less revelation of God's holiness magnifies the devastation that a lesser availability of salt and light has on mankind. Although there may seem to be these "extremes," it should be noted that God is both holy *and* loving in both testaments: the Flood (Gen. 7), the Great Tribulation (Matt. 24), the Day of Atonement (Lev. 23), and the cross (Mark 15).

The danger and tragedy of not seeing the consistency between the two testaments is most profound in the era of the New Testament Church. The Pharisees were rebuked by Jesus over this error: "'You search the Scriptures because you think that in them you have eternal life; it is these that testify about Me . . . For if you believed Moses, you would believe Me, for he wrote about Me. But if you do not believe his writings, how will you believe My words?'" (John 5:39, 46-47).

In a very bizarre way, it could rightly be said that a Jew is not a Christian because he is not a Jew. Another way to say this is that Christianity is more Judaism than Judaism is Judaism. Modern or rabbinical Judaism does not accept the God or Gospel of the New Testament because it has rejected the same God and Gospel of the Old Testament. To shed light on this, rabbinical Judaism must be challenged with the question, "If you do not accept Yeshua as the final Lamb of God, then why do you not still offer sacrifices for forgiveness of sins? How are you now forgiven, and why did it change? Is God and His mission in the Old Testament now different?"

It may be that people sometimes perceive God as being harsher in the Old Testament due to a lack of understanding of how the "judgment" of God works. How could a loving God judge people so harshly? Why would He drown everyone who was not on the ark? Why would He send people to Hell? The rhetorical nature of these questions screams out a lie: "It is God's fault. He is to blame!" No, God is *never* wrong! God is not to blame for our judgment. We are to blame. It is our fault. In that sense, God does not drown us or send us to Hell; we drown ourselves and send ourselves to Hell. "'For God did not send the Son into the world to judge the world, but that the world might be saved through Him. He who believes in Him is not judged; he who does not believe has been judged already, because he has not believed in the name of the only begotten Son of God'" (John 3:17-18).

There is only one God (Deut. 6:4). The Bible does not depict two different gods. The God of the Old Testament was not the moody God Who changed and became the God of the New Testament. The Bible depicts the same God. "Jesus Christ *is* the same yesterday and today and forever" (Heb. 13:8).

DECEMBER 17

FAITH? PRAYER? HOW HUMBLE ARE YOU?

"He has told you, O man, what is good; and what does the LORD require of you but to do justice, to love kindness, and to walk humbly with your God?"

Micah 6:8

Humility dictates faith. How much faith you have is determined by how humble you are. You will not have more faith than your humility allows. As you "walk humbly with your God," you die to faith in self (pride) and replace it with faith in God. Moses was a great man of faith. That is not surprising, since "the man Moses was very humble, more than any man who was on the face of the earth" (Num. 12:3). Humility breeds faith.

The action of faith is seeking and abiding. "And without faith it is impossible to please **Him**, for he who comes to God must believe that He is and *that* He is a rewarder of those who seek Him" (Heb. 11:6). Faith pleases God because faith seeks God. It abides in God. "'I am the vine, you are the branches; he who abides in Me and I in him, he bears much fruit, for apart from Me you can do nothing'" (John 15:5). Faith begins with the acceptance of "'apart from Me you can do nothing.'" This is humility. I cannot do it by myself, so I seek God. My humility—my sense of insufficiency—generates my faith and my sense of God's sufficiency. The opposite of humility—my sense of self-sufficiency—rejects faith. Our pride weakens our faith.

How do you have more faith? You must have more humility. Jesus' disciples asked Him to increase their faith. Let's look at how Jesus responded to them:

> The apostles said to the Lord, "Increase our faith!" And the Lord said, "If you had faith like a mustard seed, you would say to this mulberry tree, 'Be uprooted and be planted in the sea'; and it would obey you. Which of you, having a slave plowing or tending sheep, will say to him when he has come in from the field, 'Come immediately and sit down to eat'? But will he not say to him, 'Prepare something for me to eat, and *properly* clothe yourself and serve me while I eat and drink; and afterward you may eat and drink'? He does not thank the slave because he did the things which were commanded, does he? So you too, when you do all the things which are commanded you, say, 'We are unworthy slaves; we have done *only* that which we ought to have done'" (Luke 17:5-10).

Jesus used a simile to describe what "increased faith" would look like. It would be consistent with the way in which you viewed yourself. If you viewed yourself as being "big," then your faith would not increase. You would, instead, have faith in yourself (pride). If you viewed yourself as being small like a mustard seed, then your faith would increase. You would not have faith in yourself.

Jesus then tells a story to illustrate this idea. The story describes slaves who have this "mustard seed" perception of themselves. They diligently do their work but then do not claim that they have earned or have deserved anything. They do not view themselves as being "big," but they view themselves as being small "mustard seeds." They have a humble attitude that says, "We are unworthy slaves; we have done only that which we ought to have done." They requested, "Jesus, increase our faith.'" Jesus answered, "Increase your humility."

Jesus came into his hometown to teach in their synagogue. People who lived there were offended because He was so popular and respected. "'Is not this the carpenter, the son of Mary, and brother of James and Joses and Judas and Simon? Are not His sisters here with us?' And they took offense at Him" (Mark 6:3). They were thinking, *This is that little Jesus Who grew up here. How is He better than us? We were His higher-ups!* The result was that Jesus "wondered at their unbelief" (Mark 6:6). Conversely, a centurion who understood his inability to help his servant who was paralyzed and severely tormented sought out Jesus and said, "'Lord, I am not worthy for You to come under my roof, but just say the word, and my servant will be healed'" (Matt. 8:8). Jesus responded to his humility, saying, "'Truly I say to you, I have not found such great faith with anyone in Israel'" (Matt. 8:10). Pride yields unbelief. Humility yields faith.

The essence of prayer is humility. The underlying motivation to pray is that you do not rely on yourself, but you rely on God. Prideful people do not pray. The very act of prayer is to humble yourself before God. You ask God because you give up on asking yourself. It is no surprise that "the humblest man on the face of the earth" was also a great prayer warrior. Moses spoke to God out of dependence, emptiness, and humility.

Just as humility yields faith, it also yields prayer. Do you want to have more faith? Do you want to pray more? It is a process. It is a process of "humbling yourself before your God" (Dan. 10:12). You decrease, and then He increases (John 3:30).

DECEMBER 18

THE ONLYNESS OF GOD

"The LORD is our God, the LORD is one!"

Deuteronomy 6:4

God is unique. He is One (Deut. 6:4). There is a certain "onlyness" about Him that describes His nature. It is what theologians call His "aseity." In His independence and self-existence, God needs nothing. He is not "only" in the sense that He is *lonely*; He is "one" in the sense that He is *self-sufficient*. God's "onlyness" is most readily expressed in the Person of Jesus Christ and man's required response to His uniqueness. Jesus is God's *only* Son. "'For God so loved the world, that He gave His only begotten Son, that whoever believes in Him shall not perish, but have eternal life'" (John 3:16). Jesus is the only Extension of God to man in visible form.

> In the beginning was the Word, and the Word was with God, and the Word was God ... the Word became flesh, and dwelt among us, and we saw His glory, glory as of the only begotten from the Father, full of grace and truth ... No one has seen God at any time; the only begotten God who is in the bosom of the Father, He has explained *Him* (John 1:1, 14, 18).

When our eyes are opened to seeing Jesus as the "one and only God," we "have life" because we are not blinded into death by seeking after "one another." There is only one God to seek!

You search the Scriptures because you think that in them you have eternal life; it is these that testify about Me; and you are unwilling to come to Me so that you may have life. I do not receive glory from men; but I know you, that you do not have the love of God in yourselves. I have come in My Father's name, and you do not receive Me; if another comes in his own name, you will receive him. How can you believe, when you receive glory from one another and you do not seek the glory that is from the *one and* only God? (John 5:39-44).

Because Jesus is the only Son, He is the only way. He proclaims His Divinity in this context: "'I am the way, and the truth, and the life; no one comes to the Father but through Me. If you had known Me, you would have known My Father also; from now on you know Him, and have seen Him'" (John 14:6-7). There is *only* one way through the forest of death—Jesus! "And there is salvation in no one else; for there is no other name under heaven that has been given among men by which we must be saved" (Acts 4:12). When our eyes are opened to receiving salvation "in no one else" but Jesus, we have "life" because we are not blinded into death by seeking after another "name under heaven given among men by which we must be saved." There is only one salvation because there is only one God to seek!

Because Jesus is the only Son, He is the only Way. Because He is the only Way, He is the only thing necessary (Luke 10:42). He is enough. We cry out, "My soul *waits* in silence for God only; from Him is my salvation. He only is my rock and my salvation, my stronghold; I shall not be greatly shaken" (Psalm 62:1-2). Jesus is to be our only Focus. "One thing I have asked from the LORD, that I shall seek: that I may dwell in the house of the LORD all the days of my life, to behold the beauty of the LORD and to meditate in His temple" (Psalm 27:4). We are to "'seek first His kingdom'" (Matt. 6:33). His "onlyness" leaves no room for anything else. "'No one can serve two masters; for either he will hate the one and love the other, or he will be devoted to one and despise the other. You cannot serve God and wealth'" (Matt. 6:24). When our eyes are opened to the realization that "'only one thing is necessary'" (Luke 10:42), we have "life" because we are not blinded into death by seeking after "two masters." There is only one focus because there is only one salvation, and there is only one salvation because there is only one God to seek!

Jesus' "onlyness" leads to His "allness." He is "all in all" (Eph. 1:23). *All* things are summed up in Him (Eph. 1:10). We are to trust in Him with *all* our heart and acknowledge Him in *all* our ways (Prov. 3:5-6). He has *all* authority, so we are to go to *all* nations, teaching *all* His commandments; and He is with us *always* (Matt. 28:18-20). Jesus' "onlyness" requires our "all," which then results in His "onlyness." Since Jesus is the only Way, then we give all our life to Him; we take up our cross and die to self so as to live to Christ (Gal. 2:19). When "I have been crucified with Christ and it is no longer I who live, but Christ lives in me" (Gal. 2:20), then *all* of me is gone; and *only* He remains.

Jesus is the only Son, the only Way, and the only Thing necessary. Because He is "Only," He is "All." Because He is "All," we give our "all" to Him confirming His "Onlyness." Yes, it is all about and only about Jesus!

DECEMBER 19

IT'S A MIRACLE

"For to one is given the word of wisdom through the Spirit . . .
and to another gifts of healing . . . and to another the effecting of miracles."
1 Corinthians 12:8-10

The gifts of the Spirit are wondrous things. Perhaps most phenomenal are the gifts of healing and the gift of the effecting of miracles (1 Cor. 12:9-10). The gifts of healing are incredible manifestations of the Spirit. Of course, it is God Who heals. We are only vessels through which the gift flows. All believers can be involved in the ministry of healing: "'These signs will accompany those who have believed: in My name . . . they will lay hands on the sick, and they will recover'" (Mark 16:17-18). Jesus healed by the power of the Holy Spirit (Acts 10:38). He continues to heal by the power of the Holy Spirit through believers (Acts 3:6).

A young missionary stood speechless as he watched God's power for healing worked through a Zairian evangelist. A father brought his young, mangled son to the front of the church for prayer. The boy's body was racked by polio, and he literally looked like a pile of sticks bunched up together, bent and pressed to his side. The evangelist prayed, "*Na nkombo na Yesu*"—"in the name of Jesus"—and the boy's legs and arms instantly dropped and unstiffened. The "pretzel boy" began to run around the church as his father just knelt at the altar and wept. This is the gifts of healing!

There is a pluralistic aspect to this gift. Both "gift" and "healing" are in the plural form. The most literal translation would be *gifts* of *healings*. In a sense, within the one gift are multiple gifts in order to heal multiple sicknesses (Matt. 4:23). It must be remembered that gifts of healings do not occur because of human willpower or personal holiness (Acts 3:12). When used in this gift, one must be able to say along with Peter, "'Men of Israel, why are you amazed at this, or why do you gaze at us, as if by our own power or piety we had made him walk?'" (Acts 3:12). Furthermore, since the gifts are for specific occasions and are not permanent, believers should not portray gifts of healings as if they are resident within themselves or others.

Perhaps, the most extraordinary gift of the Spirit is the effecting of miracles. A more specific translation of this is "the workings or operations of powers." These "workings" are often connected with signs and wonders (Acts 2:22) and are certainly used as a sign of the coming of the kingdom of God in its fullness. Miracles are always done for a purpose—not just as a kind of flippant sort of "show-off" stunt—and are seen in a context of compassion, mercy, and concern (John 2:1-11, Luke 8:22-25). They are not done to gain praise or simply to demonstrate power. Their purpose is to point to and glorify God (Luke 19:37).

Miracles do not contradict the laws of nature. They transcend or may even suspend them. Miracles are so much to do away with the natural as they do more than the natural. God did not, for example, change the properties of water when Peter walked on it. He just made Peter walk on or over the water. It was not so much that he did not sink into the water as it was that he did walk over the water. The natural world is completely and always subject to God's sovereignty. What He has done, He may do again for His own purposes. He is not limited by natural norms and expectations.

A leader of an inner-city ministry that had limited funds organized an outreach to neighborhood kids that used sports as a platform for preaching the Gospel. The sports camp ended with a championship flag football game. The leader purchased as many jerseys as he had funds for and hoped they would be sufficient for the number of kids that showed up for the event. On his way to the field, he picked up the twenty jerseys that he purchased. He counted them before he put the bag into the trunk of his car. There were twenty jerseys. The receipt also said twenty jerseys. He had paid for exactly twenty jerseys. When he arrived at the field, he knew there was a problem. He counted the kids; and there were twenty-five kids, not twenty. He prayed. When he brought the kids over to the sideline, he began to give out the jerseys, counting as he went. When he got to twenty, there were, of course, five kids left without a jersey. He stuck his hand back into the bag, and out came five more jerseys. Each kid got his own jersey. This is the gift of the effecting of miracles.

Of course, Jesus is the great Miracle-worker. His followers are to follow in His footsteps. He says to them "'Truly, truly, I say to you, he who believes in Me, the works that I do, he will do also; and greater *works* than these he will do; because I go to the Father'" (John 14:12). Jesus says this within the context of telling His disciples that He will send them the Holy Spirit. Of course, miracles should regularly accompany the preaching of the Gospel. "And they went out and preached everywhere, while the Lord worked with them, and confirmed the word by the signs that followed" (Mark 16:20).

There is an eschatological aspect to the gift of effecting of miracles. We can expect there to be an increase in the workings of miracles, both Divine and demonic, in the end times (Rev. 11:3-6, 2 Thess. 2:9, Matt. 24:24). Remember, all that is miraculous may not be holy in its origin. Perhaps, this is where another gift of the Spirit comes into play; that is, "the distinguishing of spirits" (1 Cor. 12:10).

DECEMBER 20

THE GOSPEL IN SIX WORDS

"'The time is fulfilled, and the kingdom of God is at hand; repent and believe in the gospel.'"
Mark 1:15

The Gospel is Good News because we have a problem that we cannot solve. We have no hope, but God provides hope by providing a solution to the otherwise unsolvable problem. The Gospel calls those who hear this Good News to give a response. Six words describe this progression that flows from our problem to that which is His solution to our problem and then to our response to that solution. Our problem is seen in our necessity for "atonement," "justification," and "redemption." Our solution is found in the word "instead" or the idea of replacement. Our response is found in the words "repent" and "believe."

First, let's look at the word "atonement." Sin separates us from God. This is a huge problem. We are not one with God, so God provides an "at one ment." We who are separated from God come to be "at one" with Him again through the atonement. Jesus closed the gap of our separation when He shed His blood as a perfect sacrifice to reunite us with Himself. "For it is the blood by reason of the life that makes atonement" (Lev. 17:11). The lost sheep was found (Luke 15:4).

The second word is "justification." God is holy. He is just. He cannot just look away from sin as though it never even happened. Penalties cannot simply be ignored, lest they no longer serve their purpose and function as penalties. Without law and parameters, there is only chaos (Judges 21:25). Someone has to pay for the destruction. The penalty must be enforced. Herein lays our problem. We do not have enough money to pay what we owe for justice to be upheld (Matt. 18:23-25). Our sin has put us in a legal bind. Regret alone does not pay the bill. You regret because it is too late; it is a done deal. You have already done it, and there is no turning back the clock. Sometimes, the saying is "sin happens," but it is more painfully applied when it is said "sin happened." Oh, if I could just do things over again, if it could just be as if I'd never done that, then it would be *just* (as) *if* I'd never sinned. Just if I'd . . . ! Jesus paid the full price on the cross (John 19:30), sprung me from jail with a heavenly bail, and made it so that I am justified—just (as) if I'd . . . never sinned.

The third word is "redemption." In the garden, everything was good (Gen. 1:31). Then man ate from the tree, and he had to leave (Gen. 3:24). How can man get back to the garden? This is the problem. The Fall of man caused him to be *deemed* one way (not good). How can man be *re*deemed (deemed to be good again). To be redeemed is to be in Christ. He wins us back (Titus 2:13-14).

The fourth word is "instead." The hope of the Gospel is not in our problem but in the solution to that problem. There are many dynamics that make up the solution, but they all have one thing in common—God is the Provider. He does what you could not do. In Christ, He is your perfect "instead." Instead of you—Him! You were in a stench type of stead (Luke 15:15), but Jesus jumped in that pigpen *in* your *stead*. You should have been on the cross, but Jesus got on it *instead* (Mark 10:45). God's grand solution to our otherwise unsolvable problem is "instead"!

The fifth and sixth words are "repent" and "believe." With such a merciful solution to such a disastrous problem, there should be an honest response. "'The time is fulfilled, and the kingdom of God is at hand; repent and believe in the gospel'" (Mark 1:15). You were pent up in a place of disobedience and rebellion toward God but now you must accept and turn to another place. You must choose to be pent up in a place of obedience and relationship with God. You must *re*pent. You must believe. You wanted to leave God and get far away from Him so you could say He is not there, but now you must believe. You must be a leaver of disbelief. You must be a believer! The problem is that we are in incalculable need. The solution is that Jesus provides a perfect answer. The response is that we must constantly turn to Him and walk in faith with Him. This is the Gospel. This is the Good News!

DECEMBER 21

THE HALL OF FAME OF FAITH

"For by it the men of old gained approval."

Hebrews 11:2

What if there was a Hall of Fame of faith? Who would be in it? Among others, Abraham, Paul, Joshua, the Roman centurion, the woman with the issue of blood, David, Stephen, Jehoshaphat, Job, the Canaanite woman, Shadrach, Meshach, Abednego, and blind Bartimaeus would all be in the Hall of Fame. These, and many more, are all Hall of Famers!

One of the first Hall of Famers in the history of faith was Abraham. Can you imagine being told to sacrifice your own son? Go on, Abraham. Climb up that mountain, build an altar, arrange the wood, bind Isaac, and lay him on the altar on top of the wood. Then take your knife and slay him. What is Abraham going to say to his son when he inevitably asks him, "Dad, what is going on?" This is where Abraham's faith is especially exhibited. "Abraham said, 'God will provide for Himself the lamb for the burnt offering, my son'" (Gen. 22:8). Abraham trusted in God's provision in a time of unparalleled need. This is the stuff of Faith Hall of Fame legend!

How about Paul? Talk about being in a dire situation! After being caught in a hurricane for days that swept them out to sea, the starving men on the ship resigned themselves to their obvious fate. Paul had a different response and told them, "'Keep up your courage, men, for I believe God that it will turn out exactly as I have been told'" (Acts 27:25). Paul believed God when all seemed lost—a Hall of Famer!

Then there is Joshua. Talk about embarrassing! You are supposed to be a great leader and warrior, but you direct your people to walk around a city while blowing trumpets for six days. Then on the seventh day, you walk around seven times, blow the trumpets, and shout (Josh. 6:15-16). Walls are supposed to just tumble down. Those must have been *very* loud trumpets and shouts! Joshua was not embarrassed. He believed God—another Hall of Famer!

Jesus inducted the Roman centurion into the Hall of Fame of faith. "'Truly I say to you, I have not found such great faith with anyone in Israel'" (Matt. 8:10). The centurion exhibited a "matter of fact" kind of faith. He said to Jesus, "'Just say the word, and my servant will be healed'" (Matt. 8:8). This is what Hall of Famers say!

How about David? When you are a boy and you go up against a giant, what weapons do you need? Maybe you will take with you a tank or a cannon or at least a shotgun. David took a stick, five stones, and a sling. Did he really think he could win? "And David said, 'The LORD who delivered me from the paw of the lion and from the paw of the bear, He will deliver me from the hand of this Philistine'" (1 Sam. 17:37). That is a Hall-of-Fame attitude!

There was a woman who had a hemorrhage for twelve years. She could have easily just given up. Her situation seemed hopeless. Nevertheless, "after hearing about Jesus, she came up in the crowd behind *Him* and touched His cloak. For she thought, 'If I just touch His garments, I will get well'" (Mark 5:27-28). Jesus inducted her into the Hall of Fame, saying, "'Daughter, your faith has made you well'" (Mark 5:34).

A Hall-of-Fame statement of faith came from the lips of Jehoshaphat: "'For we are powerless before this great multitude who are coming against us; nor do we know what to do, but our eyes are on You'" (2 Chron. 20:12). Faith stares at God.

Stephen, another Hall of Fame candidate, did this same staring right before he was stoned to death. "But being full of the Holy Spirit, he gazed intently into heaven and saw the glory of God, and Jesus standing at the right hand of God" (Acts 7:55). That is the faith stare!

Hall-of-Fame faith puts its focus on God. Job (Hall of Fame inductee, *circa* 2000 B.C.) said, "'As for me, I know that my Redeemer lives, and at the last He will take His stand on the earth'" (Job 19:25). The Canaanite woman (Hall of Fame inductee, *circa* 30 A.D.) is another example. "But she came and *began* to bow down before Him, saying, 'Lord, help me!' . . . Then Jesus said to her, 'O woman, your faith is great; it shall be done for you as you wish'" (Matt. 15:25, 28). Shadrach, Meshach, and Abed-nego (Hall of Fame inductees, *circa* 550 B.C.) declared, "'If it be *so*, our God whom we serve is able to deliver us from the furnace of blazing fire; and He will deliver us out of your hand, O king'" (Dan. 3:17). Bartimaeus (Hall of Fame inductee, *circa* 30 A.D.) is another one. "And the blind man said to Him, 'Rabboni, I *want* to regain my sight!' And Jesus said to him, 'Go; your faith has made you well'" (Mark 10:51-52).

Oh, to be famous for your faith! "Now faith is the assurance of *things* hoped for, the conviction of things not seen. For by it the men of old gained approval" (Heb. 11:1-2).

DECEMBER 22

THE BLIND ARE NOT A LIGHT

"Where there is no vision, the people are unrestrained, but happy is he who keeps the law."
Proverbs 29:18

God is a good manager of resources (Matt. 25:14-28). His greatest resource is His people, since His greatest resource is Himself. He works through His people (Phil. 2:12-13). God's people are vessels through which He accomplishes His work in this world (2 Tim. 2:21). His work is to reveal Himself to all people (Psalm 119:105). He does this through witnesses (Acts 1:8)—people who cast vision to others.

Vision is critical. Without vision, the people perish (Prov. 29:18). Without the vision-proclaimers—witnesses or vision-bearers—everything breaks down. When the light does not shine, there is only darkness. Jesus explained it this way: "'I am the Light of the world; he who follows Me will not walk in the darkness, but will have the Light of life'" (John 8:12). The light-bearers must shine their lights, or the lights go out for everyone in the house. "'You are the light of the world. A city set on a hill cannot be hidden; nor does *anyone* light a lamp and put it under a basket, but on the lampstand, and it gives light to all who are in the house. Let your light shine before men in such a way that they may see your good works, and glorify your Father who is in heaven'" (Matt. 5:14-16).

What happens in God's economy when the lamp *is* put under a basket? What happens to the light-bearers who do not shine their lights? This was the situation with the disobedient priests in Malachi 1-2. They were despising, dishonoring, and undervaluing God and His work. Their lights—that were to be used to point others to God—were not shining. Remember, God is a good Manager of resources. If you do not use it, then you lose it! "'For to everyone who has, *more* shall be given, and he will have an abundance; but from the one who does not have, even what he does have shall be taken away'" (Matt. 25:29). If you do not shine your light and cast vision to others, then your light is turned off; and you lose your vision. God does not turn off your light. You turn your own light off.

God says to the disobedient priests, "You have turned off your light, so stop acting like you have not." He says, "I know your deeds, that you are neither cold nor hot; I wish that you were cold or hot. So because you are lukewarm, and neither hot nor cold, I will spit you out of My mouth" (Rev. 3:15-16). Why is "cold" better than "lukewarm"? It is because it is both useless *and* deceptive. That is the nature of hypocrisy. So God calls for the shutting down of the charade for the sake of the one who should be receiving the light (lukewarm light only leads to confusion and deception) and for the one who should be casting the light.

"Oh that there were one among you who would shut the gates, that you might not uselessly kindle **fire on** My altar! I am not pleased with you," says the LORD of hosts, "nor will I accept an offering from you. For from the rising of the sun even to its setting, My name *will be* great among the nations, and in every place incense is going to be offered to My name, and a grain offering *that is* pure; for My name will be great among the nations," says the LORD of hosts (Mal. 1:10-11).

The blind can only lead the blind. You have to see in order to lead other people to see. Disobedience is connected to darkness and disaster. Obedience is connected to vision and success. So, do not "fall into a pit"; instead, be happy! As Matthew 15:14 says, "'Let them alone; they are blind guides of the blind. And if a blind man guides a blind man, both will fall into a pit'" (Matt. 15:14). And another passage in Proverbs reminds us, "Where there is no vision, the people are unrestrained, but happy is he who keeps the law" (Prov. 29:18).

DECEMBER 23

WHY ARE WE NOT HEALED?

*"And the power of the Lord was **present** for Him to perform healing."*
Luke 5:17

In order to rightly answer some of the most often asked questions about the ministry of healing, the most important thing is to understand who you are and who you are not. You are God's creation and servant. You are not God! You cannot be blamed for that which you are not blamable. You cannot be credited for that which you are not credible. God must be understood to be God. You must be understood to not be God.

These "basics" help us more easily answer what otherwise might seem to be perplexing questions. In the New Testament, it seems like everyone was healed. Why does it seem like now some people are healed and some are not healed when we pray for them? First, it must be realized that the picture of all-inclusive, instant, and automatic healing is not what was seen in the New Testament. It is not as though people who lived in and around Israel from 30-90 A.D.—the time of Jesus' and His apostles' ministry—were never sick or never died. Healing was not automatic. Until Jesus returns and the Fall of man is eradicated, sickness exists because it is part of the Fall of man and God is Sovereign over the Fall of man. Some are healed, and some are not. Eventually, all die.

The most astounding healing ministry in history was that of Jesus Christ. This is because Jesus most purely embodied the most astounding message in history: the message of salvation. Physical healing is not equivalent to spiritual healing. It is not the same exact thing as salvation. Jesus' end goal was not to provide physical healing for living life in this world now. The Scripture asserts, "'For God so loved the world, that He gave His only begotten Son, that whosoever believes in Him should not perish, but have eternal life'" (John 3:16). It does not claim, "For God so loved the world, that He gave His only begotten Son, that whosoever believes in Him should not be sick, but have constant physical health." Healing was a big part of Jesus' ministry, as it was—and still is—a big part of His disciples' ministry; but it was not the essence of those ministries. Healing is a sign (Acts 4:30) that points to that essence. It is an indicator of the reality and availability of salvation (Matt. 9:2-8).

The Bible seems to indicate that even Jesus did not heal everyone around Him, in all cases, and at all times. "One day He was teaching; and there were *some* Pharisees and teachers of the law sitting *there*, who had come from every village of Galilee and Judea and *from* Jerusalem; and the power of the Lord was *present* for Him to perform healing" (Luke 5:17). The necessity of including this statement seems to imply that sometimes, "the power of the Lord" was not present to perform healing. Jesus could only do what He saw the Father doing (John 5:19). The Father is not always healing. In His Sovereignty, He reserves the option of using non-healing and sickness for His purposes (John 9:3). Healing is subordinate to that which it points to.

Jesus told His followers, "'Truly, truly, I say to you, he who believes in Me, the works that I do, he will do also; and greater *works* than these he will do; because I go to the Father'" (John 14:12). The book of Acts is full of healing signs performed by Jesus' disciples. The healing ministry continued—and still continues—through His followers now. It does not change. People are still healed, and people are still not healed. Paul asked multiple times for healing from a "thorn in the flesh" (2 Cor. 12:7) but was not healed. Physical healing is not primary. God is Sovereign to use it—or the lack of it—for His purpose, which, with regard to Paul, was "to keep me from exalting myself . . . for power is perfected in weakness" (2 Cor. 12:7-9). Everyone is not always healed. Timothy was not healed of his stomach ailments (1 Tim. 5:23). Trophimus was not healed; and so, Paul had to leave his ministry partner in Miletus (2 Tim. 4:20).

Does God heal? Yes, He does! Do we heal? No, we do not! Our lack of faith get in the way of healing (Matt. 13:58) in the same way that it is used in healing. Our faith does not heal. Healing does not happen because it is sourced by our faith. A lack of faith does not discourage healing. Faith is a conduit, or channel, though which healing can be delivered. A lack of faith does not tie God's hands in the sense of preventing God from doing something or making God do something, but it does provide a conduit through which He may or may not do something. In that way, faith may be a channel for healing or the lack of a channel for a lack of healing. God heals or does not heal. Our faith does not heal or does discourage healing.

You cannot be blamed for that which you are not blamable. You cannot be credited for that which you are not credible. A receiver cannot be blamed for not being a source. Just as faith cannot be credited as the source of healing, it cannot be blamed for not sourcing healing. A receiver can be blamed for not being a receiver. Just as faith can be credited with believing God for healing, it can be blamed for not believing God for healing. God is just. You do not get exalted for being God, and you do not get judged for not being God. A lot of questions are answered simply by knowing who you are and who you are not.

Oftentimes, we do not do our part because we do not understand who we are and who we are not. We think we have to save people, so we shy away from witnessing because we do not want to fail. What if the person does not get saved? We think we have to make our children become a certain something, so we shy away from parenting because we do not want to fail. What if my child does not turn out to be good? We think we have to heal people, so we shy away from praying for the sick because we do not want to fail. What if the person does not get healed?

News alert: you do not save. You do not create destinies. You do not heal. So, witness, parent, and pray for healing. Let God be God, and you can just be you. It is always better that way!

DECEMBER 24

PROBLEM SOLVED: THAT'S THE GOSPEL!

"For the wages of sin is death, but the free gift of God is eternal life in Christ Jesus our Lord."
Romans 6:23

All Gospel presentations should revolve around two major points. Man has a problem, and God offers the solution to that problem. Man has a need, and God offers to provide for that need. Man is a sinner who is separated from God; and God pays for man's sin, which reunites him with God. This is the Gospel—sin and salvation, problem and solution, need and provision.

This message is what needs to be presented to unbelievers, and it is believers who need to do the presenting. They may share the message with family members, like Andrew did with his brother Simon Peter (John 1:40-42); with friends, like Philip did with Nathanael (John 1:45-46); with those who show some interest in spiritual truth, like Paul and Silas did with the Philippian jailor (Acts 16:25-31); with religious people who do not know Christ, like Philip did with the Ethiopian eunuch (Acts 8:26-35); or even with strangers, like Jesus did with "the woman at the well" (John 4:7-26).

Perhaps, the most basic and well-known Gospel presentation is what is commonly referred to as "The Roman Road." This presentation uses four Bible verses that all come from the book of Romans in order to explain the "problem and solution" continuum. We have a problem. It is that "all have sinned and fall short of the glory of God" (Rom. 3:23). There are consequences of our sin—"the wages of sin is death" (Rom. 6:23). There is a solution. "God demonstrates His own love toward us, in that while we were yet sinners, Christ died for us" (Rom. 5:8). We have a response: "If you confess with your mouth Jesus as Lord and believe in your heart that God raised him from the dead, you will be saved" (Rom. 10:9). In summary, we sin; we die; love dies for us; and we confess and believe. This is not to oversimplify the Gospel, for it *is* quite costly; nevertheless, it is not complicated. It is not easy (a lot of death involved), but it is not hard to explain or understand.

Another presentation might be called "The Seven Point Presentation." It, again, focuses on the twofold narrative: problem and solution. The problem actually begins with the fact that God loves you and wants to have a relationship with you (John 3:16). That is a problem because you are a sinner; and thus, you are separated from God (Rom. 3:23). You are dead in your sins (Rom. 6:23). The problem, therefore, is that you died. The solution, however, is that Christ died for you (Rom. 5:6-8). You can be saved through faith in Jesus (Acts 16:30-31), and you can know that you are saved (1 John 5:10-13). As a believer, you must follow and obey God (Acts 5:29). In summary, the Gospel is that God loves you, you are a sinner, you are separated from God, you are dead in your sins, Christ died for you, you can be saved through faith, you can know you are saved, and now you can follow and obey God. It is not easy, but it is not hard.

The content of the Gospel never changes. The methods of delivery may change, but the contents are always the same. This is the Gospel—sin and salvation, problem and solution, need and provision. That is the Gospel. Problem solved. That's Good News!

DECEMBER 25

WHEN I GIVE, I WALK IN MY DIVINE PURPOSE

"Now He who supplies seed to the sower and bread for food will supply and multiply your seed for sowing and increase the harvest of your righteousness."

2 Corinthians 9:10

The Bible is consistent. Whenever there is a command, there is a promise. In other words, whenever there is an obligation, there is an opportunity. The opposite is also true. Whenever there is a promise, there is a command. In other words, whenever there is an opportunity, there is an obligation. Another way to understand this is that we "get to give."

In order to embrace this attitude, we have to first realize that we must receive from God in order to give back to God. We have nothing in ourselves. "'I am the vine, you are the branches; he who abides in Me and I in him, he bears much fruit, for apart from Me you can do nothing'" (John 15:5). We do not serve as our own sources. The Scripture challenges us with this fact: "What do you have that you did not receive?" (1 Cor. 4:7). It is like the five-year-old boy who wants to get his father a present for Christmas. He has no money to buy the present, so he asks his father to give him money. He then buys his father a present with his father's own money. We are like that boy. We give to God what is already His.

At the same time, we must realize that the reason we are supplied by God is to be used by Him to supply and equip others (Eph. 4:11-12). We are blessed to be a blessing (Gen. 12:1-3). Although it is a biblical statement to say that when we give, we get (Luke 6:38), it is incomplete to stop at "we get." It is not so much that "we give to get" as it is that "we get to give." It is "more blessed to give than to receive" (Acts 20:35).

You are a created steward under the supervision of a Divine Owner. The Owner's management style and purposes are rooted in the dynamic of multiplication. This creates a flow of blessing that is not limited. It is not a closed system. Proper stewardship yields more abundance. Abundance is the repeated theme in 2 Corinthians 8-9, a lengthy passage focused on giving, in which the idea of "plenty" is reiterated at least ten times (2 Cor. 8:2, 7, 14, 20; 9:8, 12). Cheerful giving (the steward embracing his role) yields sufficiency and abundance for more "steward work" (the Owner's plan for multiplication).

> Each one *must do* just as he has purposed in his heart, not grudgingly or under compulsion, for God loves a cheerful giver. And God is able to make all grace abound to you, so that always having all sufficiency in everything, you may have an abundance for every good deed; as it is written, "HE SCATTERED ABROAD TO THE POOR, HIS RIGHTEOUSNESS ENDURES FOREVER." Now He who supplies seed to the sower and bread for food will supply and multiply your seed for sowing and increase the harvest of your righteousness;

you will be enriched in everything for all liberality, which through us is producing thanksgiving to God (2 Cor. 9:7-11).

The principle of multiplication lends itself to "give, and it will be given to you . . . pressed down, shaken together, *and* running over. For by your standard of measure it will be measured to you in return" (Luke 6:38). There is no question about God's supply. The question is, why do we receive? The answer is clear. We receive more, so we can then give more. We are, in fact, mandated to give more. In the Divine Owner's system, more opportunity means more obligation. "From everyone who has been given much, much will be required; and to whom they entrusted much, of him they will ask all the more" (Luke 12:48).

Why is it "more blessed to give than to receive?" (Acts 20:35). The Greek term *makarion* that is translated "blessed" could also be translated "happy." God loves a "cheerful giver" (2 Cor. 9:7)—one who is "happy" or "blessed"—because the cheerful giver is one who is embracing his purpose. The most fulfilled that a pot can be is when it is being used for the purpose for which the potter made it. I am most blessed when I am a conduit for God to distribute His resources through me so as to meet needs. Giving makes me happy because when I give, I walk in my Divine purpose.

DECEMBER 26

LET SHAME TURN INTO A KISS

"And I will turn their shame into praise."

Zephaniah 3:19

Why do we sometimes want to avoid God? We may not feel worthy to go to Him because we struggle to obey; we may even repeat a sin over and over again. We are ashamed to approach Him. Our sin separates us from God (Rom. 6:23), and our shame can keep us away from Him.

Prior to the Fall, there was no broken relationship, and there was no shame. Adam and Eve walked with God "in the garden in the cool of the day" (Gen. 3:8) as "the man and his wife were both naked and were not ashamed" (Gen. 2:25). The irony of sin is that we try to avoid the One Who wants to find us. "They heard the sound of the LORD God walking in the garden in the cool of the day, and the man and his wife hid themselves from the presence of the LORD God among the trees of the garden" (Gen. 3:8).

Specifically, we try to avoid the method for reconciliation that God offers us; we stumble over the cross (Gal. 5:11). In our flesh, we want to earn the right of be reconciled to God. We want to work our way back to God, so we can feel worthy to approach Him again. We may be ashamed of the cross (1 Cor. 1:23) and, therefore, not accept it easily. It is "scandalous" to our flesh to think that God had to do it all for us. Indeed, the scriptural idea of the cross as a "stumbling block" comes from the Greek word *eskandalon* from which we get our English word "scandal."

> What shall we say then? That Gentiles, who did not pursue righteousness, attained righteousness, even the righteousness which is by faith; but Israel, pursuing a law of righteousness, did not arrive at *that* law. Why? Because *they did* not *pursue it* by faith, but as though *it were* by works. They stumbled over the stumbling stone, just as it is written, "BEHOLD, I LAY IN ZION A STONE OF STUMBLING AND A ROCK OF OFFENSE, AND HE WHO BELIEVES IN HIM WILL NOT BE DISAPPOINTED" (Romans 9:30-33).

Just like Peter's pride, our pride ironically makes us turn away from the very thing that will bring us back. It is the work of the cross that reunites us with God. There is no other way (John 14:6). Yet we want to work our way back to God in our own power. We are ashamed to have Jesus wash our feet.

> Then He poured water into the basin, and began to wash the disciples' feet and to wipe them with the towel with which He was girded. So He came to Simon Peter. He said to Him, "Lord, do You wash my feet?" Jesus answered and said to him, "What I do you do not realize now, but you will understand hereafter." Peter said to Him, "Never shall You wash my feet!" Jesus answered him, "If I do not wash you, you have no part with Me" (John 13:5-8).

At one time or another, we all avoid getting our feet washed by Jesus. Our shame yields separation. I feel that Jesus should not have to wash my feet. I can wash my own feet! I stumble over the stumbling block of the cross; yet without the cross, Jesus says, "'You have no part with Me'" (John 13:8).

We can be ashamed of ourselves, the cross, or Jesus Himself. In either case, the result is the same. We hide, we separate ourselves, and we act like we do not know Him. There is hope because there is redemption. Peter experienced this redemption after acting like he did not know Jesus three times (Luke 22:54-62).

> So when they had finished breakfast, Jesus said to Simon Peter, "Simon, *son* of John, do you love Me more than these?" He said to Him, "Yes, Lord; You know that I love You." He said to him, "Tend My lambs." He said to him again a second time, "Simon, *son* of John, do you love Me?" He said to Him, "Yes, Lord; You know that I love You." He said to him, "Shepherd My sheep." He said to him the third time, "Simon, *son* of John, do you love Me?" Peter was grieved because He said to him the third time, "Do you love Me?" And he said to Him, "Lord, You know all things; You know that I love You." Jesus said to him, "Tend My sheep" (John 21:15-17).

Jesus restored Peter with three redemptive questions to match Peter's three denials. Each time, Jesus asked, "'Do you love Me?'" and Peter replied "'Yes, I love You,'" we see the wiping away of the stains left by each "'I do not know Him'" (Matt. 26:74). Like Peter, we all fail. However, what counts is the final result. One Saul of the Bible—King Saul in the Old Testament—began well but did not end well. Another Saul—Paul of the New Testament—did not begin well but did end well. Peter denied Christ three times. Pilate defended Christ three times (Luke 23:22-24). In the end, however, Peter repented and was redeemed. Pilate put Jesus to death and was condemned.

At times, we may leave and flee from Jesus. Nevertheless, there is hope because there is redemption. Yes, we failed in the past, but what matters is what we will do today—"now is 'THE DAY OF SALVATION'" (2 Cor. 6:2). It is senseless to hide from Jesus, but it is even more senseless to reject His invitation to return. Let shame turn into a kiss!

DECEMBER 27

THE "HEART" OF THE FOLLOW THROUGH

> *"The scribes and the Pharisees have seated themselves in the chair of Moses; therefore all that they tell you, do and observe, but do not do according to their deeds; for they say **things** and do not do **them.**"*
> Matthew 23:2-3

The person leading the planning session looks at everyone and says, "Are you following me?" You nod your head with a promise, saying, "Yes, I am following you, and I plan on doing what you are proposing." There is a long road, however, between "Are you following" and the "Are you following through?" It is one thing to propose and another thing to produce. It is easier to plan than to actually plant, to say something than to actually do something, to develop action steps than to actually engage in action, to be reflective than to actually be effective, and to promise than to actually deliver. It is important to strategize but only to the degree that you execute. Metaphorically speaking, it is important to brainstorm, but then you must hold your feet to the fire. Ideas must be "put on the table"; but then they must be put into action, lest they just "get tabled." You can keep your head in the clouds; but you eventually have to have your feet on the ground, lest you be so heavenly minded that you are no earthly good.

Puns and metaphors may not seem to depict the significance of this dynamic in our lives. How do you turn theory into practice? This necessary process is described in the Bible in a variety of ways. Faith must lead to works (James 2:17). Seeds must produce fruit (Mark 4:8). Those who have ears to hear must hear (Luke 8:8). Wisdom is vindicated by her deeds (Matt. 11:19). Why is it that we often have a hard time bridging the gap between what we say we are going to do and what we actually do? Some of the blame may go to a lack of skill, ability, or experience. We may not be very goal-oriented or know how to prioritize. We may not be skilled in self-motivation or self-accountability. All of these inadequacies can lead to not getting things done. However, the lion's share of the problem—if we are willing to admit it—is pent up in the complexities of the *heart*. When we really do not mean what we say to begin with, there is very little chance that we are actually going to do something about it.

Hypocrisy is the number one reason we do not follow through with what we initially said. If you are only acting, anyway, you will never actualize in any way. How can teachers actually live what they teach? How can anyone successfully "talk the talk and walk the walk." It is a matter of the heart! Teachers cannot simply be borrowers. They must be owners; "for where your treasure is, there your heart will be also" (Luke 12:34). What is said must be in the heart, not just in the mind. One way to describe hypocrisy is that the heart does not line up with the mind, and so the feet do not line up with the lips. Talk is cheap.

You leave that hour-long meeting at work, where not much was accomplished (yet) but much was discussed, planned, and strategized. You go back to your office with a notepad full of tasks that you have promised to fulfill. Why is it that for some of those promises, the notepad is as far as they will get? The answer is simple. You knew you were not going to do it the moment you said that you would do it. Whether you call this lying or hypocrisy, it still results in the same thing: no execution. Why do we sometimes engage in this charade? Often, it is because we place appearance over substance. Satisfaction with a superficial life will get you nowhere. You may look good temporarily, but reality always wins the day; it will all come out in the wash. If you only say that you will do something to look like you will do something, you will never do anything. Hypocritical seeds only produce fake fruit. It may look good, but it cannot be eaten!

What is a potential piece of plastic fruit to do? Honesty with self and others is the answer. The more you say, "I am not going to do this" at the front end when you know you are not going to do it, the more you will be successful at the back end. You will be more efficient in moving from strategizing to executing because you will not fail at executing something that you were not going to execute to begin with. You will be more effective because you will be successful at executing what you meant to execute from the beginning.

The heart of the follow-through is sincerity. You will do what you say when you meant it to begin with. The path to the follow-through is honesty. When you do not mean it, you know it. Will you be honest enough to act on that knowledge, or will you get sucked into the superficial emptiness of the hypocritical Pharisees who "'say *things* and do not do *them*'" (Matt. 23:3). It really is a matter of the heart.

DECEMBER 28

HUMBLE ENOUGH TO NOT BE OFFENDED

"When we are reviled, we bless . . . when we are slandered, we try to conciliate."
1 Corinthians 4:12-13

Humility has a certain look. It looks away from self. A lack of humility takes every opportunity to point to self; it is a selfish opportunist. Moses had many opportunities to take advantage of his popularity, influence, and fame. He probably could have attempted to gain control of the whole country of Egypt. "The LORD gave the people favor in the sight of the Egyptians. Furthermore, the man Moses *himself* was greatly esteemed in the land of Egypt, *both* in the sight of Pharaoh's servants and in the sight of the people" (Exod. 11:3). Anything less than true humility might have caused him to try to take advantage of the situation. Moses, however, chose to obey God's commands and did not fall to such a temptation. Humility insures obedience. It is an effective weapon against temptation.

A lack of humility results in being easily offended by others. Moses' service to his people included many unjust accusations against him. He did not ignore these accusations, but his humility kept him from being offended. He did not seek revenge against his accusers. He did not try to defend himself, but he did try to lift up and point to God.

> Then they said to Moses, "Is it because there were no graves in Egypt that you have taken us away to die in the wilderness? Why have you dealt with us in this way, bringing us out of Egypt? Is this not the word that we spoke to you in Egypt, saying, 'Leave us alone that we may serve the Egyptians'? For it would have been better for us to serve the Egyptians than to die in the wilderness." But Moses said to the people, "Do not fear! Stand by and see the salvation of the LORD which He will accomplish for you today; for the Egyptians whom you have seen today, you will never see them again forever. The LORD will fight for you while you keep silent" (Exod. 14:11-14).

Being humble enough to understand himself as God's representative, Moses did not see himself as the boss but only as God's vessel; thus, he understood accusations to be complaints against God. "The whole congregation of the sons of Israel grumbled against Moses and Aaron in the wilderness . . . Moses said, " . . . for He hears your grumblings against the LORD; and what are we, that you grumble against us? . . . And what are we? Your grumblings are not against us but against the LORD" (Exod. 16:2, 7-8). To be offended is to expose one's pride. Humble people are not easily offended.

Humility is not vengeful; it allows God to be God. It leaves any necessary vindication to Him and focuses itself on blessing instead of cursing. It says, "When we are reviled, we bless . . . when we are slandered, we try to conciliate (1 Cor. 4:12-13). Without humility, Moses could have easily been offended:

> Then Miriam and Aaron spoke against Moses because of the Cushite woman whom he had married (for he had married a Cushite woman); and they said, "Has the LORD indeed spoken only through Moses? Has He not spoken through us as well?" And the LORD heard it. (Now the man Moses was very humble, more than any man who was on the face of the earth) (Num. 12:1-3).

Moses blessed those who reviled him and tried to reconcile with those who slandered him: "Then Aaron said to Moses, 'Oh, my lord, I beg you, do not account *this* sin to us, in which we have acted foolishly and in which we have sinned. Oh, do not let her be like one dead, whose flesh is half eaten away when he comes from his mother's womb!' Moses cried out to the LORD, saying, 'O God, heal her, I pray!'" (Num. 12:11-13).

Bless those who persecute you; bless and do not curse . . . Never pay back evil for evil to anyone. Respect what is right in the sight of all men. If possible, so far as it depends on you, be at peace with all men. Never take your own revenge, beloved, but leave room for the wrath of God, for it is written, "VENGEANCE IS MINE, I WILL REPAY," says the Lord. "BUT IF YOUR ENEMY IS HUNGRY, FEED HIM, AND IF HE IS THIRSTY, GIVE HIM A DRINK; FOR IN SO DOING YOU WILL HEAP BURNING COALS ON HIS HEAD." Do not be overcome by evil, but overcome evil with good (Rom. 12:14, 17-21).

Humility tells you that you are not God. Pride shouts at you, "You are God!" It began shouting it in the Garden of Eden, and it continues to shout it today. The underlying challenge of many of God's commands is the challenge to relinquish Divinity. The essence of sin is to want to be like God, to want to *be* God (Gen. 3:5, Isa. 14:14). Humble yourself. Do not eat from that tree!

DECEMBER 29

FAITH WINS!

"For whatever is born of God overcomes the world;
and this is the victory that has overcome the world—our faith."

1 John 5:4

The essence of faith is relationship. Christian faith is union with Christ. Union with Christ results in newness of life: "Therefore if anyone is in Christ, *he is* a new creature; the old things passed away; behold, new things have come" (2 Cor. 5:17). When I have faith, then "Christ lives in me" (Gal. 2:20). He says, "'Abide in Me, and I in you'" (John 15:4).

The Christian is saved by faith: "'Believe in the Lord Jesus, and you will be saved'" (Acts 16:31). The Christian is "protected by the power of God through faith" (1 Peter 1:5). The Christian lives by faith. "The *life* which I now live in the flesh I live by faith in the Son of God" (Gal. 2:20).

Faith will be tested many times and in many ways. In the challenging seasons of life, be assured that your "reservation" in Heaven is maintained by your faith, since you have "an inheritance *which is* imperishable and undefiled and will not fade away, reserved in heaven for you, who are protected by the power of God through faith for a salvation ready to be revealed in the last time" (1 Peter 1:4-5). Faith is patient; it knows how to wait on God and renew its strength. "Yet those who wait for the LORD will gain new strength; they will mount up *with* wings like eagles, they will run and not get tired, they will walk and not become weary" (Isa. 40:31). Faith is victorious. "For whatever is born of God overcomes the world; and this is the victory that has overcome the world—our faith" (1 John 5:4).

Faith works in the realm of the impossible; so "if you have faith the size of a mustard seed, you will say to this mountain, 'Move from here to there,' and it will move; and nothing will be impossible to you" (Matt. 17:20). Faith never quits.

Women received *back* their dead by resurrection; and others were tortured, not accepting their release, so that they might obtain a better resurrection; and others experienced mockings and scourgings, yes, also chains and imprisonment. They were stoned, they were sawn in two, they were tempted, they were put to death with the sword; they went about in sheepskins, in goatskins, being destitute, afflicted, ill-treated (*men* of whom the world was not worthy), wandering in deserts and mountains and caves and holes in the ground. And all these, having gained approval through their faith, did not receive what was promised, because God had provided something better for us, so that apart from us they would not be made perfect (Heb. 11:35-40).

Faith does not necessarily make things "easy," but it does make things possible. Faith says, "God is completing his perfect will in my life. Therefore, I can wait. I can endure. I can suffer." It can be difficult to live a life of faith, but we must remember that we are called to endure as "tribulation brings about perseverance" (Rom. 5:3). Do not get discouraged and do not allow your past experiences to bring your faith to a standstill.

An enormous bull elephant was tied to a tiny post. He should have been able to escape easily. However, the elephant tried to escape when he was a baby, but he was not successful. Therefore, the elephant thought that he could never escape and so he never tried. Do not be like the enormous bull elephant. You and your faith are bigger than any collection of past experiences or disappointments. Let your enormous faith pull you away from the tiny posts that seem to be holding you back. Christ is in you, and you are in Christ; so you can boldly say, "I can do all things through Him who strengthens me" (Phil. 4:13). Faith wins!

DECEMBER 30

LAW AND GRACE WALK TOGETHER NOT APART

"Do we then nullify the Law through faith? May it never be! On the contrary, we establish the Law."
Romans 3:31

Some theologians feel more comfortable to describe the ethics of the New Testament in terms of love and grace and would prefer to somehow avoid the idea of Law. They seem to promote the perception of a mutually exclusive relationship between God's Law and God's grace and therefore do not recognize the Law as being the hub of "Christian ethics." This faulty theology stems from an even more erroneous and dangerous tendency of dispensational theology that implies that there are somehow two different Gods in the Bible—one in the Old Testament and another in the New Testament. It would highlight the God of love and grace in the New Testament and the God of Law and holiness in the Old Testament as if there are two different Gods. No, "the LORD is our God, the LORD is one!" (Deut. 6:4). Law and grace are wrapped up in one God Who is always the God of both at the same time.

Love, grace, and faith are not separate from ethics and the Law; they do not exempt us from the Law. Rather, they enable us to do the Law. "Do we then nullify the Law through faith? May it never be! On the contrary, we establish the Law" (Rom. 3:31). We are not "under the Law" because, in Christ, we are over it (Rom. 6:1-19). When we separate the Law from grace, we live in one of two extremes. The Law with no grace easily becomes legalism (Gal. 2:16). Grace without the Law easily becomes a license for sin or antinomianism (Jude 4). The writers of the New Testament had to combat both of these human tendencies to separate God and to separate His Law from His love and grace. Law cannot be understood without grace, and grace cannot be understood without the Law. Ethics and the Law point us to love and grace, while love and grace fulfill ethics and the Law in us. "Therefore the Law has become our tutor *to lead us* to Christ, so that we may be justified by faith" (Gal. 3:24).

The Law and the Gospel are not in opposition to each other. The term "fulfill" as it is used in Matthew 5:17 points to Christ as Validator and Confirmer of the Law. A logical and biblical extension of this sees Christ as the Accomplisher of the Law and, therefore, the Accomplisher of the Law in us (Gal. 2:20, Eph. 2:10). The Law—God's commands to His people representing His moral will but not necessarily His ceremonial, judicial, or civil instructions—is seen as the basis for Christian ethics and morality. Grace is seen as the activity of God in our lives that enables us to do the Law rather than that which exempts us from it.

Sinful man is ethically deficient. Only God is good (Mark 10:18). Our ethical ability is found in Christ alone. This is the reason why the "poor in spirit" are blessed and see the "kingdom" or rule of God (Matt. 5:3). Only those who are empty can be filled with Jesus, Who is the only One Who does the Law; the only One Who keeps the "rules." To be emptied of self is God's grace as it makes room for God's Law by making room for the Lawgiver; it makes room for the kingdom by making room for the King.

Inasmuch as we humble ourselves—die to ourselves—and allow Christ to work in us, we can be perfect. "'Therefore you are to be perfect, as your heavenly Father is perfect'" (Matt. 5:48). It is Christ alone Who is perfect. His perfecting us is nothing less than His living His perfection in us. This is the perfect uniting of the Law and grace.

DECEMBER 31

THE END? PLATFORMS, PLATFORMS, PLATFORMS

*"**It will not come** unless . . . the man of lawlessness is revealed."*
2 Thessalonians 2:3

When will the end come? When will Jesus return? One thing is clear. We do not know the day or the hour. "'But of that day and hour no one knows, not even the angels of heaven, nor the Son, but the Father alone'" (Matt. 24:36). Nevertheless, we can know the "signs" that will point to the Second Coming of Christ and the consummation of His Kingdom (Matt. 24:32-35). We might not know the time, but we can know the signs of the times. These signs are platforms on which the biblically revealed events associated with the end times will be ushered in.

Predicting the end times is a sketchy endeavor. Many prognosticators tend to look at singular issues and declare, "This is it. That is the evil one. This is the moment. That must be what is referred to in the Scripture as '666'!" It is this type of specific calculation that may be what is out of place. Remember, you will not know the specifics, but you may know the generalities, the platforms. What are end time platforms? They are "delivery systems" for that which we know to be consistent with biblical prophecy. They are what could be seen as signs of the times. If someone expected thunderstorms—as an analogous example—then a "sign" or a "platform" for those thunderstorms might look something like this: extremely humid and hot air settling around your area with winds blowing in a cold front that intersects with the stagnate air and results in clouds of charged, moist pressure that are formed and begin to move rapidly in the sky. Observing the presence of the hot, humid air as it mixes with the cold air and seeing the volatile clouds form above you would serve as a platform on which thunderstorms might be realized.

It is just a guessing game to say when a thunderstorm will form, but it is more of an informed analysis to say what type of platform will bring in a thunderstorm. It is just an eschatological guessing game (that we are not really sanctioned to engage in) to say that any particular thing means that *the day* is upon us, but it is a very sanctioned (even expected) act of discernment to say what type of platform or sign might point to the coming of that day. "When it is evening, you say, 'It *will be* fair weather, for the sky is red.' And in the morning, '*There will be* a storm today, for the sky is red and threatening.' Do you know how to discern the appearance of the sky, but cannot *discern* the signs of the times?" (Matt. 16:2-3).

So, what do we know? Perhaps more than any other singular thing, we know that the end will not come before the rising up of the antichrist, the "man of lawlessness" (2 Thess. 2:1-3). We know that this individual will be associated with lawlessness, will ride in on a wave of lawlessness, and will increase lawlessness. This increase will paint his platform with apathy and hate as "most people's love will grow cold" (Matt. 24:12). We may not be able to say exactly who this person is, but we know something about what he will look like and, perhaps more importantly, what will be going on when he arises. What will usher him in and what will be the context of his advent and evil activity? What will be the sign? On what kind of platform will he arrive onto the scene?

The answer to all those platform-driven questions is one thing: lawlessness! What, then, might "the sky is red" be for the end times? It is the platform of lawlessness. The sign of the end times is that law is done away with. That might include many expressions of lawlessness that make up the patchwork of such a platform. It might include philosophical lawlessness in which the idolizing of "sameness"—"everything is law, so nothing is law" or "every man did what was right in his own eyes" (Judges 17:6)—that slithers out of humanistic postmodernism covers humanity in a blanket of anarchy. It might include situational lawlessness, in which extreme health, political, and societal events and dynamics come together in a whirlwind of unruliness.

We do not know the exact time, nor do we know the exact details; we do know the signs, and we can expect certain platforms. The number one sign and the most definitive platform is lawlessness. When the world is overrun with anarchy, then "the sky is red."

> Now we request you, brethren, with regard to the coming of our Lord Jesus Christ and our gathering together to Him, that you not be quickly shaken from your composure or be disturbed either by a spirit or a message or a letter as if from us, to the effect that the day of the Lord has come. Let no one in any way deceive you, for *it will not come* unless the apostasy comes first, and the man of lawlessness is revealed . . . For the mystery of lawlessness is already at work; only he who now restrains *will do so* until he is taken out of the way. Then that lawless one will be revealed whom the Lord will slay with the breath of His mouth and bring to an end by the appearance of His coming (2 Thess. 2:1-3, 7-8).

BIBLIOGRAPHY

Boice, James Montgomery. *The Sermon on the Mount*. Grand Rapids: Zondervan Publishing House, 1972.

Chesterton, D.K. *St. Francis of Assisi*. Garden City: Image Books, 1957.

Eisenhower, Dwight D. "Dwight D. Eisenhower Quotes." Brainy Quotes. Accessed March 20, 2023. http://www.brainyquote.com/quotes/authors/d/dwight_d_eisenhower.html.

Fisher, James. *A Few Buttons Missing: The Case Book of a Psychiatrist*. Philadelphia: J.B. Lippincott, 1951.

Green, Michael. *1500 Illustrations for Biblical Preaching*. Grand Rapids: Baker Books, 1989.

Henry, Gary. "Credibility (April 12)." WordPoints. April 12, 2023. https://wordpoints.com/credibility-april-12.

Meyer, F.B. *The Directory of the Devout Life*. Old Tappan: Fleming H. Revell Co., 1904.

Peterson, Eugene. *Working the Angles*. Grand Rapids: Eerdmans Publishing Co., 1989.

Pilgrim, Walter. *Good News to the Poor*. Nashville: Augsburg Publishing House, 1975.

Stanley, Charles. *Handle With Prayer*. Wheaton: Victor Books, 1984.

Stott, John. *Involvement*. Old Tappan: Fleming H. Revell Co., 1973.

Taylor, Jack. *God's Miraculous Plan of Economy*. Nashville: Broadman Press, 1975.

Weakley, Clare, ed. *Happiness Unlimited*. Plainfield: Logos International, 1979.

Wesley, John. "Wesley's Sermon Reprints: The Use of Money." Christian History Museum. Accessed April 12, 2023. https://christianhistoryinstitute.org/magazine/article/wesleys-sermon-use-of-money.

Wright, David. *Wisdom as a Lifestyle*. Grand Rapids: Lamplighter, 1987.

ENDNOTES

1   Michael Green, *1500 Illustrations for Biblical Preaching* (Grand Rapids: Baker Books, 1989).

2   James Fisher, *A Few Buttons Missing: The Case Book of a Psychiatrist* (Philadelphia: J.B. Lippincott, 1951).

3   Walter Pilgrim, *Good News to the Poor* (Nashville: Augsburg Publishing House, 1975).

4   John Stott, *Involvement* (Old Tappan: Fleming H. Revell Co., 1973).

5   D.K. Chesterton, *St. Francis of Assisi* (Garden City: Image Books, 1957).

6   Ibid.

7   Green, ibid.

8   Gary Henry, "Credibility (April 12)," WordPoints, April 12, 2023, https://wordpoints.com/credibility-april-12.

9   Clare Weakley, ed., *Happiness Unlimited* (Plainfield: Logos International, 1979).

10 David Wright, *Wisdom as a Lifestyle* (Grand Rapids: Lamplighter, 1987).

11 Eugene Peterson, *Working the Angles* (Grand Rapids: Eerdmans Publishing Co.,1989).

12 John Wesley, "Wesley's Sermon Reprints: The Use of Money," Christian History Museum, Accessed April 12, 2023, https://christianhistoryinstitute.org/magazine/article/wesleys-sermon-use-of-money.

13 Jack Taylor, *God's Miraculous Plan of Economy* (Nashville: Broadman Press, 1975).

14 Green, ibid.

15 Taylor, ibid.

16 Dwight D. Eisenhower, "Dwight D. Eisenhower Quotes," Brainy Quotes, Accessed March 20, 2023, http://www.brainyquote.com/quotes/authors/d/dwight_d_eisenhower.html.

17 Green, ibid.

18 James Montgomery Boice, *The Sermon on the Mount* (Grand Rapids: Zondervan Publishing House, 1972).

19 F.B. Meyer, *The Directory of the Devout Life* (Old Tappan: Fleming H. Revell Co., 1904).

20 Boice, ibid.

21 Charles Stanley, *Handle With Prayer* (Wheaton: Victor Books, 1984).

BIBLIOGRAPHY

Boice, James Montgomery. *The Sermon on the Mount*. Grand Rapids: Zondervan Publishing House, 1972.

Chesterton, D.K. *St. Francis of Assisi*. Garden City: Image Books, 1957.

Eisenhower, Dwight D. "Dwight D. Eisenhower Quotes." Brainy Quotes. Accessed March 20, 2023. http://www.brainyquote.com/quotes/authors/d/dwight_d_eisenhower.html.

Fisher, James. *A Few Buttons Missing: The Case Book of a Psychiatrist*. Philadelphia: J.B. Lippincott, 1951.

Green, Michael. *1500 Illustrations for Biblical Preaching*. Grand Rapids: Baker Books, 1989.

Henry, Gary. "Credibility (April 12)." WordPoints. April 12, 2023. https://wordpoints.com/credibility-april-12.

Meyer, F.B. *The Directory of the Devout Life*. Old Tappan: Fleming H. Revell Co., 1904.

Peterson, Eugene. *Working the Angles*. Grand Rapids: Eerdmans Publishing Co., 1989.

Pilgrim, Walter. *Good News to the Poor*. Nashville: Augsburg Publishing House, 1975.

Stanley, Charles. *Handle With Prayer*. Wheaton: Victor Books, 1984.

Stott, John. *Involvement*. Old Tappan: Fleming H. Revell Co., 1973.

Taylor, Jack. *God's Miraculous Plan of Economy*. Nashville: Broadman Press, 1975.

Weakley, Clare, ed. *Happiness Unlimited*. Plainfield: Logos International, 1979.

Wesley, John. "Wesley's Sermon Reprints: The Use of Money." Christian History Museum. Accessed April 12, 2023. https://christianhistoryinstitute.org/magazine/article/wesleys-sermon-use-of-money.

Wright, David. *Wisdom as a Lifestyle*. Grand Rapids: Lamplighter, 1987.

ENDNOTES

1   Michael Green, *1500 Illustrations for Biblical Preaching* (Grand Rapids: Baker Books, 1989).

2   James Fisher, *A Few Buttons Missing: The Case Book of a Psychiatrist* (Philadelphia: J.B. Lippincott, 1951).

3   Walter Pilgrim, *Good News to the Poor* (Nashville: Augsburg Publishing House, 1975).

4   John Stott, *Involvement* (Old Tappan: Fleming H. Revell Co., 1973).

5   D.K. Chesterton, *St. Francis of Assisi* (Garden City: Image Books, 1957).

6   Ibid.

7   Green, ibid.

8   Gary Henry, "Credibility (April 12)," WordPoints, April 12, 2023, https://wordpoints.com/credibility-april-12.

9   Clare Weakley, ed., *Happiness Unlimited* (Plainfield: Logos International, 1979).

10 David Wright, *Wisdom as a Lifestyle* (Grand Rapids: Lamplighter, 1987).

11 Eugene Peterson, *Working the Angles* (Grand Rapids: Eerdmans Publishing Co.,1989).

12 John Wesley, "Wesley's Sermon Reprints: The Use of Money," Christian History Museum, Accessed April 12, 2023, https://christianhistoryinstitute.org/magazine/article/wesleys-sermon-use-of-money.

13 Jack Taylor, *God's Miraculous Plan of Economy* (Nashville: Broadman Press, 1975).

14 Green, ibid.

15 Taylor, ibid.

16 Dwight D. Eisenhower, "Dwight D. Eisenhower Quotes," Brainy Quotes, Accessed March 20, 2023, http://www.brainyquote.com/quotes/authors/d/dwight_d_eisenhower.html.

17 Green, ibid.

18 James Montgomery Boice, *The Sermon on the Mount* (Grand Rapids: Zondervan Publishing House, 1972).

19 F.B. Meyer, *The Directory of the Devout Life* (Old Tappan: Fleming H. Revell Co., 1904).

20 Boice, ibid.

21 Charles Stanley, *Handle With Prayer* (Wheaton: Victor Books, 1984).

ABOUT THE AUTHOR

As an international Bible teacher, Dr. John Mannion has ministered on five continents in over twenty countries. He is the author of MOTMOT, a two-thousand page series of teaching curriculum that is available in fourteen languages. He has served on the faculty of multiple colleges and universities and has founded educational and missions organizations. He has also been involved in the planting and pastoring of churches. Dr. Mannion now serves as president of True North College and senior associate pastor of True North Church. He holds the Doctor of Ministry (D.Min.) degree from Reformed Theological Seminary. John's greatest blessing is his wife Audrey and their six children and their families.

ALSO AVAILABLE

For more information about
Dr. John Mannion
and
Gems of Truth
please visit:

www.bibleschoolforthenations.com

To download the indices and reference material please visit
www.ambassador-international.com/books/gems-of-truth

For more information about
AMBASSADOR INTERNATIONAL
please visit:

www.ambassador-international.com
@AmbassadorIntl
www.facebook.com/AmbassadorIntl

If you enjoyed this book, please consider leaving us a review on Amazon, Goodreads, or our website.

www.ingramcontent.com/pod-product-compliance
Lightning Source LLC
Chambersburg PA
CBHW080221170426
43192CB00015B/2711